Callimachus and His Critics

Callimachus and His Critics

ALAN CAMERON

PRINCETON UNIVERSITY PRESS

PRINCETON, NEW JERSEY

Copyright © 1995 by Princeton University Press
Published by Princeton University Press, 41 William Street,
Princeton, New Jersey 08540
In the United Kingdom: Princeton University Press,
Chichester, West Sussex

Library of Congress Cataloging-in-Publication Data

Cameron, Alan.
Callimachus and his critics / Alan Cameron.
p. cm.
Includes bibliographical references and index.
ISBN 0-691-04367-1 (alk. paper)
1. Callimachus—Criticism and interpretation—History. 2. Greek poetry, Hellenistic—
Egypt—Alexandria—History and criticism—Theory, etc. I. Title
PA3945.Z5C28 1995
881'.01—dc20   95-2674

This book has been composed in Times Roman, using Nota Bene 4,
on a Hewlett-Packard LaserJet 4M

The publisher would like to acknowledge Alan Cameron for
providing the camera-ready copy from which this
book was printed

Princeton University Press books are printed on acid-free paper
and meet the guidelines for permanence and durability of the
Committee on Production Guidelines for Book Longevity
of the Council on Library Resources

Printed in the United States of America
by Princeton Academic Press

1 3 5 7 9 10 8 6 4 2

For Geoff and Jean

CONTENTS

Contents

PREFACE

Books (mine anyhow) have a way of growing in unexpected directions. This one started life as a reinterpretation of the *Aetia* prologue, its limited purpose to show that Callimachus's concern was elegy, not epic. But I soon realized this could not be done without a more detailed examination of the curious modern preoccupation with Hellenistic epic and epyllion, held to be so important for the understanding of Roman as well as Hellenistic poetry (Ch. X; XVI-XVIII). For these misconceptions appear at their starkest in modern scholarly writing on Catullus and the Augustans.

The identification of Callimachus's Telchines led me to reconsider the dates, works, interrelationships and ancient biographies of most of the other leading poets of the age; and thence to a wider study of the transmission and interpretation of their works in the later Hellenistic and Roman age (Ch. IV and VIII). Thus the "Critics" of my title, originally just the Telchines of the prologue, ended up with a far wider reference, ancient and modern. No new papyri of Callimachus have appeared since Lloyd-Jones and Parsons published their *Supplementum Hellenisticum* in 1983, but a number of other new texts help to cast welcome (if sometimes unexpected) new light on the picture I have tried to draw.

Callimachus has generally been considered the archetypal ivory tower poet, his work identified as the first appearance of art for art's sake, poetry for the book rather than fellow citizens. He has been damned with faint praise as a scholar writing for libraries, a court sycophant writing to flatter divine kings. Ch. I-III present a very different perspective, based on the abundant evidence instead of twentieth-century rationalisation of nineteenth-century prejudice against the postclassical. Much of the book is in fact more of a prolegomena to the study of Hellenistic (and so also Roman) poetry than a study of Callimachus alone. It is a social as much as a literary history of Greek poetry in the early third century. I have tried to situate Callimachus as firmly as I could in the real world in which he lived as well as in his real literary context, a world of cities as well as courts, a world of private symposia and public festivals, in which poetry and poets continued to play a central rôle.

As a result, the book has turned out much longer than I had planned or hoped. I trust no one will quote F 465 at me; for wherever Callimachus's mind was when he said that a big book was a big bore (p. 52), his tongue was firmly in his cheek. The notion that he was the uncompromising apostle of the short poem dies hard, but anyone who can count can work out for himself that none of his contemporaries wrote more books or longer poems than Callimachus. Even Apollonius's *Argonautica* was little if at all longer than the four books of the *Aetia*.

Many friends answered questions, discussed problems, gave me references, read chapters, argued me out of perverse solutions or helped me in one way or another: Roger Bagnall, Richard Billows, Pamela Bleisch, Mary Depew, Matthew Dickie, Marco Fantuzzi, Kathryn Gutzwiller, Christian Habicht, William Harris, Adrian Hollis, Richard Hunter, Richard Janko, Arnd Kerkhecker, Peter Knox, Nita Krevans, Luigi Lehnus, Jennifer Lynn, Oswyn Murray, Carole Newlands, Dirk Obbink, Daniel Selden, Alexander Sens, David Sider, Wesley Trimpi, Martin West, Stephen White, Gareth Williams, Jim Zetzel and no doubt many others whose contributions I can no longer recall individually. Hugh Lloyd-Jones made salutary criticisms of a very early (not to say premature) draft, and Sarah Mace helped eliminate obscurities at the last moment. Guido Bastianini gave me information on the Milan Posidippus papyrus, at the time of writing still mostly unpublished. Claude Meillier, on behalf of the Institut de Papyrologie et d'Egyptologie de Lille, kindly supplied the photo of the Lille papyrus reproduced on the dust-jacket. The camera-ready copy was prepared on a BUS 286 and Toshiba Satellite T1800 using Nota Bene 4 and printed on a Hewlett-Packard Laserjet 4.

In conclusion, I would like to name three scholars to whom I owe a more general debt of longer standing: W. W. Cruickshank, who at St Paul's School first introduced me to the meaning of scholarship; Eduard Fraenkel, whose unforgettable Oxford seminars exemplified its methods and something of its history; and Arnaldo Momigliano, who always had time for young unknowns with no legitimate claim on it, and who encouraged without attempting to direct or influence my own first contributions to fields he knew better than anyone.

New York
May 1995

FREQUENTLY USED ABBREVIATIONS

Callimachus is cited by fragment number from vol. I of R. Pfeiffer's edition of 1949; references to the extensive prolegomena and addenda in vol. II (1953) usually by page number; more recent discoveries by their number in *SH*. Pfeiffer 1968 refers to his *History of Classical Scholarship from the Beginnings to the End of the Hellenistic Age* (Oxford 1968); P.M. Fraser's *Ptolemaic Alexandria* (Oxford 1972) is cited as Fraser I or II; Herter's contributions (see Bibliography) are cited by name and year; references to *CA* and *FGE* are by page number; Lehnus 1989 is L. Lehnus, *Bibliografia Callimachea 1489-1988* (Genova 1989). Other abbreviations are normally as recommended in *L'Année philologique* or the *Oxford Classical Dictionary*. See too the introduction to the index.

AP	*Anthologia Palatina*
BMCR	*Bryn Mawr Classical Review*
CA	Iohannes U. Powell, *Collectanea Alexandrina* (Oxford 1925)
CEG	*Carmina epigraphica Graeca* ed. P.A. Hansen
CP	*Classical Philology*
CQ	*Classical Quarterly*
CR	*Classical Review*
CSCA	*California Studies in Classical Antiquity*
F	Fragment
FD	*Fouilles de Delphes*
FGrH	F. Jacoby, *Fragmente der griechischen Historiker* (1923-)
FPL	E. Courtney, *Fragmentary Latin Poets* (Oxford 1993)
FGE	D. L. Page, *Further Greek Epigrams* (Cambridge 1981).
GP	A.S.F. Gow and D.L. Page, *The Garland of Philip* I-II (Cambridge 1968).
GRBS	*Greek, Roman and Byzantine Studies*
HE	A.S.F. Gow and D.L. Page, *Hellenistic Epigrams* I-II (Cambridge 1965).
IEG	*Iambi et Elegi Graeci* ed. M. L. West, i^2 and ii^2 (Oxford 1990 and 1992).
IG	*Inscriptiones graecae*
JHS	*Journal of Hellenic Studies*
JRS	*Journal of Roman Studies*
KP	*Der Kleine Pauly*
LIMC	*Lexicon Iconographicum Mythologiae Classicae*
LGPN	P. M. Fraser and E. Matthews, *A Lexicon of Greek Personal Names* (Oxford 1987-)

PEG	*Poetae epici graeci* ed. A. Bernabé (Leipzig 1987)
PMG	*Poetae melici graeci* ed. D. L. Page (Oxford 1962)
RE	Pauly-Wissowa-Kroll, *Real-Encyclopädie der classischen Altertumswissenschaft* (1894-)
REG	*Revue des Études grecques*
SH	H. Lloyd-Jones and P. Parsons, *Supplementum Hellenisticum* (Berlin 1981)
ZPE	*Zeitschrift für Papyrologie und Epigraphik*

CHRONOLOGIA CALLIMACHEA

These dates are collected here for convenience; a few are documented,* but most (inevitably) are conjectural, justified in the following pages:

ca 320	Birth of Callimachus
ca 300	Hermesianax
	Philitas
ca 300/270	Asclepiades
	Lycophron
	Alexander Aetolus
	Leonidas of Tarentum
285	Ptolemy Philadelphus co-ruler with Soter*
285/4	Theocritus 24
285/2	Callimachus: *Hymn to Zeus*
282	Ptolemy Philadelphus sole king*
290/280	Posidippus: *Ep.* XXIV B-G on Berenice I
279/4	Callimachus: *Epithalamium Arsinoës*
279/4	Sotades: *"Epithalamium" Arsinoës*
279/4-68	Theocritus 15, 16
279/4	Theocritus 17
	Callimachus: *Acontius and Cydippe*
275	Callimachus: *Hymn to Delos*
	Theocritus: 13, 18, 22
	Aratus: *Phaenomena*
ca 270	Callimachus: *Aetia* I-II
	Callimachus: *Hymn to Apollo*
	Apollonius: *Argonautica*
July 268	Death of Arsinoë*
ca 268	Callimachus: *Iambi*
267	Chremonidean war
	Death of Sotades
ca 266	Callimachus: *Hymn* v
ca 264	Posidippus: *AP* v. 202
263/2	Posidippus honoured at Thermum*
	Apollonius librarian
254	Nicander I wins at Delphi*
246	Ptolemy Euergetes king, marries Berenice II*
	Eratosthenes librarian

Sept. 245	Callimachus: *Coma Berenices*
243	Callimachus: *Victoria Berenices*
	Callimachus: *Aetia* III-IV
ca 240	Death of Callimachus
	Rhianus
	Euphorion
ca 200	Nicander II

Callimachus and His Critics

Chapter I

Cyrene, Court and Kings

1

Biographical readings of ancient poetry have been generally discredited in recent times. Yet some of the most famous poems of Callimachus seem so personal and vivid that they continue to be read this way. For example, it is still widely assumed that his literary polemic is a genuine response to genuine criticism rather than an artful way of dramatizing his views. And while it is no doubt significant that none of his erotic poetry is addressed to women,[1] we should beware of taking too seriously epigrams that present him in the grip of mercenary boys.

It is the fastidiousness and disdain his verses breathe that modern readers have most consistently identified as the real Callimachus.[2] Is this in fact the man rather than a pose; does it cast any light on his social standing in real life? According to a recent psychological portrait, it was a calculating pose whereby the "poor schoolmaster from Cyrene" could "justify his position as royal client, but also satisfy his high social aspirations, by associating himself with a line of blue-blooded, antipopulist poets and thinkers from Theognis and Heracleitus through Plato to Cleanthes."[3]

Let us take a closer look at the evidence. Rather more can in fact be pieced together about Callimachus's origins than has so far been realized. He was born in Cyrene, but lived most of his long life in Alexandria. If the family tree and dates for his various works proposed below are accepted, he was born ca 320 and still alive in the 240s and perhaps even later.[4] So he lived to be at least seventy-five and perhaps older still. According to his entry in the tenth-century lexicon known as Suda, before being "presented" at court he was a schoolteacher at Eleusis, a village outside Alexandria. According to the twelfth-century Byzantine polymath John Tzetzes, he was a "court youth" (νεανίσκος τῆς αὐλῆς). Some have combined these details and concluded that Callimachus "somehow caught the attention of Ptol-

---

1. I am assuming, with Denys Page (*The Epigrams of Rufinus* [Cambridge 1978], 103-05), that the Palatine ascription of *AP* v. 23 to Callimachus is mistaken.

2. For the poem that best exemplifies this attitude, Ch. XIV.

3. Peter Green, *Alexander to Actium* (Berkeley 1990), 182.

4. Fraser II. 1004 n. 1 on F 384; Pfeiffer on F 438; Lehnus, *ZPE* 105 (1995), 6-12.

emy" while teaching school and only later earned the title given by
Tzetzes. Proof of this lowly beginning to his career is then found in
epigrams in which the poet himself professes poverty.[5]

But it is bad method simply to combine such disparate scraps of evid-
ence. Let us examine them separately. Paradoxically enough, Tzetzes's
information may be the most solid. It comes in a passage that preserves
priceless details about the establishment of the Alexandrian library under
Ptolemy Philadelphus, and must ultimately derive from some authoritative
Ptolemaic account.[6] Furthermore the title itself, though unknown at the
Byzantine court familiar to Tzetzes, was well known at Hellenistic courts.[7]
To be sure, Tzetzes is capable of misunderstanding or misquoting his
sources, but it is most unlikely that while doing so he should have hit on a
genuine Hellenistic court title; and he could have had no motive to invent
such a detail.

These "royal youths" are an institution modelled on the well documented "royal pages" (παῖδες βασιλικοί) of the Macedonian court, sons of
the king's Companions obliged to perform menial functions for their elders
as a form of apprenticeship for their own future careers in the king's service.[8] Under Philip II and Alexander they were recruited from sons of the
Macedonian nobility; at the courts of the Successors, from sons of their
entourage (known as Friends), Greeks from a wide variety of cities, men of
letters as well as military and political advisers.[9]

In another version of Tzetzes's *Prolegomena*, it is not just Callimachus
but Eratosthenes too who is described as a "youth."[10] It is perhaps no coin-

5. E.g. Cahen 1929, 28; Meiller 1979, 165; Green 1990, 179.

6. *Prolegomena de comoedia* II (*Scholia in Aristophanem* I. 1A), ed. W.J.W. Koster
(Leiden 1975), p. 32. 11; Pfeiffer 1968, 101-02; 105-07; 127-28; Fraser 1972, 321-29;
Koster 1975, xxvii-xxxviii; R. Blum *Kallimachos: The Alexandrian Library and the Origins
of Bibliography* (Madison 1991), 104-13.

7. οἱ περὶ τὴν αὐλὴν νεανίσκοι (Polybius 16. 22. 5); βασιλικοὶ νεανίσκοι (Plut. *Mor.*
760B); cf. νεανίσκοι...ἐν τῷ οἴκῳ τοῦ βασιλέως (Daniel i. 3f.); *puer ex aula* (Horace, *carm.*
i. 29. 7); Headlam on Herodas i. 29. It is therefore most unlikely that Green (1990, 179) was
justified in interpreting it as a homosexual smear.

8. *seminarium ducum praefectorumque*, Curtius 8. 6. 6; see now the full discussion of
the Macedonian pages in W. Heckel, *The Marshals of Alexander's Empire* (London 1992),
237-98. Meillier 1979, 165-6 makes the error of confusing royal pages with the ubiquitous
associations of youths centred on the gymnasium (e.g. M. Launey, *Recherches sur les
armées hellénistiques* [Paris 1950], 859-62).

9. C. Habicht, *Vierteljahrschrift für Sozial- und Wirtschaftsgeschichte* 45 (1958), 1-16;
Fraser 1972, 101-02; L. Mooren, *Aulic Titulature in Ptolemaic Egypt* (Brussels 1975), 2-7,
52-80; G. Herman, *Talanta* 12-13 (1980-81), 103-49; R.A. Billows, *Antigonus the One-Eyed*
(Berkeley 1990), 246-50.

10. νεανίαι ἦσαν Καλλίμαχος καὶ Ἐρατοσθένης, p. 23. 1 Koster. Tzetzes himself
apparently interpreted his source to mean that they were contemporaries (Ἐρατοσθένης δέ, ὁ
ἡλικιώτης αὐτοῦ, p. 32. 13 = Anon. Cram. II p. 43. 10), but no informed source can have
said that; Eratosthenes was a generation younger.

cidence that it is precisely Callimachus and Eratosthenes whom Strabo singles out as being "honoured by the kings of the Egyptians." The formula he uses (τετιμημένοι παρά), though not striking in itself, corresponds to one of the styles applied to the king's Friends. According to the pseudonymous *Letter of Aristeas* (well-informed about Ptolemaic terminology: Ch. III. 2), the writer and a colleague were addressed by Philadelphus as "honoured by us" (τιμωμένους παρ' ἡμῖν).[11] It may be that both Callimachus and Eratosthenes were royal pages and subsequently Friends. When Eratosthenes was appointed to the Alexandrian library on the accession of Euergetes, his Suda-entry uses the term normally applied to residence at court.[12] A poem and an anecdote he himself told in his later years reveal him on close terms with both Ptolemy Euergetes and Arsinoe Philopator.[13]

The title of royal page was certainly never conferred on village schoolmasters. If Callimachus was indeed a "court youth," his father must have been a member of Soter's entourage and he himself must have spent his youth at court. Cyrene was the first land outside Egypt to fall under Ptolemaic control in 322, when some aristocratic Cyrenean exiles invited Soter to intervene.[14] As we shall see, Callimachus's father was probably one of those exiles.

The profession of poverty in the epigrams is always linked to the theme of love. It is surely a pose: lovers expect costly gifts, but the poet has only his verse to offer (Ch. V. 2). The story that Callimachus was a schoolteacher (which according to Bulloch "we have no reason to disbelieve")[15] is almost certainly outright fiction. It is sometimes supposed that he enjoyed the modest but respectable status of teacher of literature (γραμματικός), but this was not to emerge as a distinct stage in the educational hierarchy until ca 100 B.C., and the Suda entry specifies elementary instruction (γράμματα ἐδίδασκε).[16] The elementary schoolteacher was at the very bottom of the social scale: "he's either dead or teaching the alphabet," runs a line from comedy.[17] Indeed, as a recent paper by Alan Booth has shown, the accusation of being an elementary teacher (or even

---

11. Strabo 17. 3. 22; Aristeas, *Ad Philocratem* § 40, p. 114 Hadas; for the same formula at the Seleucid court, E. Bikerman, *Institution des Séleucides* (Paris 1938), 40-50.

12. διέτριψε; G. Herman, *Talanta* 12/13 (1980/81), 103-49, with Ch. VIII. 4.

13. Athen. 276 BC; *FGrH* 241 F 16; for the poem, below § 2.

14. A. Laronde, *Cyrène et la Libye Hellénistique* (Paris 1987), Ch. II-VI and XII.

15. Bulloch 1985, 549.

16. Meillier 1979, 165 does not distinguish between the two levels: on γραμματικοί, Booth, *Hermes* 106 (1978), 117-25. There were no schools in Egypt at all when Ptolemy arrived: H. Maehler in *Egypt and the Hellenistic World* (Louvain 1983), 191-203. When third-century writers are so described (Philicus addresses his colleagues as γραμματικοί in *SH* 677), the term means "scholar" (Pfeiffer 1968, 157-58). This may also apply to the statement in his Suda-entry that the former slave Rhianus παιδευθεὶς ἐγένετο γραμματικός.

17. ἤτοι τέθνηκεν ἢ διδάσκει γράμματα, *Com. adesp.* 20 (iii. 401 K).

the son of one) was actually an insult in both Greek and Roman times—and when used as an insult usually untrue as well. The most memorable example is Demosthenes's vivid picture of the young Aeschines preparing the ink and mopping the benches in his father's schoolroom.[18] Epicurus wrote that his former teacher Nausiphanes "abused me and called me a schoolteacher," and there can be no question of the abusive tone in Timon's dismissal of Epicurus in turn as a "schoolteacher's son from Samos, the most uneducated of mortals." To place the school in a village (as in Callimachus's Suda-entry) is a further diminishment of the victim. Epicurus dismissed Protagoras as a "village schoolteacher."[19]

In his fifth *Iamb* Callimachus warns an elementary teacher not to molest his pupils—an early colleague, so it is sometimes inferred.[20] But he begins by superciliously commiserating with the fellow on his lot: "Since fate [has decreed that] you [teach] the alphabet..." It is inconceivable that Callimachus himself ever taught in a village school. But a number of distinguished men of letters are said to have been his disciples: Apollonius, Eratosthenes, Ister, Philostephanus, Hermippus. As Booth put it, "To demote a poet from teacher of men at a lofty level to teacher of boys at the meanest level was of course particularly tempting and galling."[21]

For a contemporary parallel there is an epigram by a poet Callimachus is known to have admired, Aratus:[22]

αἰάζω Διότιμον, ὃς ἐν πέτραισι κάθηται
Γαργαρέων παισὶν βῆτα καὶ ἄλφα λέγων.

Poor Diotimus, who sits on the rocks teaching the kids of Gargara their ABC.

Gargara is a mountainous site (whence the rocks) on the gulf of Adramyttium, refounded in the early Hellenistic period with "half-barbarian" immigrants.[23] The victim is plausibly identified by Stephanus of Byzantium, who quotes the poem, as Diotimus of Adramyttium.[24] Stephanus himself states as a matter of fact that Diotimus taught elementary school in Gargara, but why should a famous poet like Aratus, an intimate of kings,

18. Dem. *de cor.* 129, 258, with H. Wankel, *Demosthenes: Rede für Ktesiphon* II (Heidelberg 1976), 691 (the scholiast on 129 uses the telling term χαμαιδιδάσκαλος); A. D. Booth, "Some Suspect Schoolmasters," *Florilegium* 3 (1981), 1-20.

19. D. L. 10. 8 and 10. 3 (γραμμοδισκαλίδης) = *SH* 825, with M. di Marco, *Timone di Fliunte* (Rome 1989), 230-32; D. L. 10. 8 (Protagoras).

20. γραμματοδιδάσκαλον; e.g. Pfeiffer 1968, 125 n. 2.

21. Booth 1981, 6.5. The incredulity with which Alcibiades is said to have greeted an elementary teacher who could correct a text of Homer (γράμματα διδάσκεις Ὅμηρον ἐπανορθοῦν ἱκανὸς ὤν, Plut. *Alc.* 7) would surely be a characteristic ancient response.

22. *AP* xi. 437, with Gow-Page, *HE* II. 106-7; Booth 1981, 6-7.

23. Demetrius of Scepsis, cited by Strabo xiii. 1. 51 and 58, with W. Leaf, *Strabo on the Troad* (Cambridge 1923), 258-63.

24. Steph. Byz. pp. 198-8 Meineke; Susemihl 1892, 538-39.

bother with a nobody in such a remote outpost? Diotimus is usually identified as the author of an epic *Labours of Heracles*, which survived long enough to be quoted in Roman times (*SH* 392-5). The explanation is surely that Aratus was just making fun of one of his peers, a fellow poet. It was enough that he was born in Gargara. If he (or his father) was ever a teacher in any sense, it was not at the elementary level. It was surely a similar lampoon on Callimachus, or perhaps a joke in a contemporary comedy, that someone in a later age mistook for biography.[25]

If Callimachus's grandfather was, as he proudly states in an epigram, a general in Cyrene (*AP* vii. 525. 3-4; pp. 78-79), he himself was surely born to wealth and standing. A. Laronde has recently pointed out that Cyrenean aristocrats, as befits descendants of a warrior élite, liked names with military associations: compounds with -(h)ippos like Kallippos and Melanippos; with -machos like Kudimachos, Zeuximachos and Kallimachos.[26] The epigram purports to be the epitaph of Callimachus's father, but only names his son (the poet) and his own father (the general). It has sometimes been inferred that the father made no such mark in life, remembered, like Abraham Mendelssohn, as his father's son and his son's father. But that misses the emphasis of the poem. Perfectly catching the understated style of archaic epitaphs, Callimachus characterizes his own and his grandfather's achievements in three words each: the general "commanded the arms of his fatherland" ($\pi\alpha\tau\rho\acute{\iota}\delta o\varsigma\ \ddot{o}\pi\lambda\omega\nu\ \mathring{\eta}\rho\xi\epsilon\nu$) while the poet "sang songs that silenced envy" ($\mathring{\eta}\epsilon\iota\sigma\epsilon\nu\ \kappa\rho\acute{\epsilon}\sigma\sigma o\nu\alpha\ \beta\alpha\sigma\kappa\alpha\nu\acute{\iota}\eta\varsigma$)—an allusion to the literary feuds discussed in later chapters. The balance of the structure suggests that poet routed the enemy no less than general. It would have spoiled this elegant equation to introduce a third achievement.

By great good fortune the decree in which Soter set up a new constitution for Cyrene after his intervention in 321 has survived. The body of the decree describes the new constitution (a moderate oligarchy) in some detail, and then follows a list of the first magistrates appointed.[27] One of two men who is to be both ephor and nomothetes (and so evidently a person of great authority) is Androkles son of Kallimachos. Since the constitution lays down that ephors are to be not less than 50 years old, it follows that Androkles was born no later than ca 370. This same Androkles son of Kallimachos is listed together with his brother Theudorus son of Kallimachos and Kallimachos himself on a military register datable to ca 345.[28] Kal-

---

25. Compare the mistaken inferences from jokes about Philitas in comedy (App. B).

26. Laronde 1987, 129, citing several further examples.

27. *SEG* ix. 1 (lines 84 and 87) with P. M. Fraser, *Berytos* 12 (1958), 120-27; translation in M. M. Austin, *The Hellenistic World from Alexander to the Roman Conquest* (Cambridge 1981), 443-45. The list of names (not in Austin) is reedited with prosopographical commentary in Laronde 1987, 95-124; on the date, Laronde 85-94; R. S. Bagnall, *The Administration of the Ptolemaic Possessions outside Egypt* (Leiden 1976), 25-29.

28. *Dialect. graec. ex. epigraphica* (Leipzig 1923), 234; Laronde 1987, 99, 122 n. 13.

limachos's brother Philon, another military man, rebuilt the great altar of Apollo in Cyrene (we think of the poet's hymn for a festival of Apollo at Cyrene). Kallimachos and Philon were sons of Annikeris, a wealthy Cyrenean said to have ransomed Plato.[29] There is no way of discovering what truth lies behind the curious story of Plato being sold into slavery,[30] but Annikeris of Cyrene was a real person, recorded in Cyrenean inscriptions of the right period. He is said to have been in Greece to compete in the chariot race at Olympia, and another anecdote presents him giving an exhibition of chariot driving at the Academy, to Plato's disapproval.[31] It is hard to see why a character so remote from Plato's world should appear in these stories if there was no basis in fact somewhere.

Kallimachos is the obvious candidate for identification as the poet's military grandfather.[32] In another mock epitaph (*AP* vii. 415) Callimachus calls himself Battiades, "son of Battos," the name of the mythical founder and several early kings of Cyrene. But Battos is not otherwise found at this period,[33] and only later biographers took the patronymic literally (pp. 78-79). Strabo, who knew how to read poetic texts, saw it as no more than a claim to descent from the ancient royal house, as indeed the pompous epic formation suggests.[34] Either of Annikeris's known grandsons might have been the the poet's father, though Androkles was part of the restored government in Cyrene, whereas the poet seems to have grown up at court in Alexandria.

That the family rather than just Callimachus lived in Alexandria is strongly suggested by his sister's marriage. According to another Suda-entry, his nephew (Callimachus the younger) was the daughter of Megatima and Stasenor (= Doric Stasanor). Now Stasanor is an exceptionally rare name, together with its cognate Stasandros localized on Cyprus.[35] The first bearer to achieve wider renown was Stasanor of Soloi, one of Alexander's Companions, satrap of Areia and Drangiane from 328. He was confirmed in his satrapies by Perdikkas, but two years later Antipater appointed another Cypriot, Stasandros (no doubt a kinsman), to Areia and Drangiane and moved Stasanor to Bactria and Sogdia. In 317 we find Stasandros fight-

---

29. Laronde 1987, 110-12; D. L. iii. 20, with Laronde 110-3 (family tree on p. 118).

30. For the various versions, A. S. Riginos, *Platonica* (Leiden 1976), 86-92; K. Gaiser, *Festschrift R. Muth* ed. P. Händel and W. Meid (Innsbruch 1983), 111-28.

31. Aelian, *VH* 2. 27; Lucian, *Dem. Enc.* 23; Riginos 1976, 152; Gaiser 1983, 116; Meillier 1979, 335-37 confuses Annikeris with the third-century Cyrenaic philosopher Annikeris—who may have been related to Callimachus.

32. So in brief F. Chamoux, *RÉG* 73 (1960), xxxiii; Lehnus 1993, 76.

33. Laronde 1987, 99; *LGPN* s.v.

34. πρόγονον δὲ [Βάττον] ἑαυτοῦ φάσκει Καλλίμαχος, Strabo 837: see Ch. III. 2, for the pseudo-patronymics of other poets of the age.

35. *LGPN* 411; 2 examples of Στασάνωρ and 5 of Στάσανδρος, all from V-IV c. Cyprus; one Στασάνδρα from II c. Cyprus.

ing with Antigonus, who in 316 confirmed Stasanor in Bactria and Sogdia.[36] When we find another Stasanor in Alexandria a generation later, it is natural to see him as the son of one of these two earlier ministers of the Successors, and to assume, as we should expect from a Cypriot, that he came to Alexandria in the retinue of Soter. For Cyprus was another early Ptolemaic possession.[37] We may draw two inferences. First, such a man would not have married Callimachus's sister unless she had been perceived as his social equal. Second, she presumably lived at court with her brother.

Recognition of his presence and standing at court may help to explain where and how Callimachus acquired his obviously superior education. Nothing suggests that an advanced literary education of this nature was available in fourth century Cyrene.[38] According to his Suda-entry, he was the pupil of Hermocrates of Iasos, perhaps the grammarian of that name quoted in a late grammatical work as an authority on Greek accents.[39] But Iasos was a Ptolemaic possession,[40] and Alexandria (as the Zenon papyri reveal in detail) the natural goal for ambitious Carians.[41] It may well have been in Alexandria that Callimachus sat at his feet. In addition, at the court of Soter he will have had the opportunity to meet and learn from the most distinguished scholars, poets and thinkers of the age: Zenodotus of Ephesus, Philitas of Cos and Strato of Lampsacus were among the tutors of his near contemporary, the future Philadelphus.

This may also have a bearing on another contentious issue: Callimachus's "Cyrenean" period. There seems little doubt that some of his poems not only refer to, but were actually written in Cyrene: a number of (mainly erotic) epigrams and perhaps the *Hymn to Demeter*, but more importantly the *Hymn to Apollo*. For reasons given more fully in Ch. XV, there are strong reasons for identifying "our kings" in line 68 as the Battiad kings of Cyrene and "my king" in 26 as King Magas of Cyrene. So far it has been the universal assumption that any poem written in Cyrene must date from the poet's youth, before he moved to Alexandria.[42] It is sometimes inferred that he fell on hard times, whence the village school. But it would be strange for the panegyrist of Magas to have fallen on hard times, and a village school is an implausible interlude between the courts of Magas and Philadelphus. It is also to mistake genre for autobiography to assume that erotic epigrams are inevitably products of a passionate youth.

36. E. Honigmann, *RE* IIIA. 2153; Billows 1990, 448-9.
37. Bagnall, *Ptolemaic Possessions* (1976), 34-79.
38. The few texts suggest the standard education of the gymnasium: Laronde 1987, 129.
39. [Serg.], *Expl. Don. (GLK* IV. 530), *Ioseum* MSS, *Iasium* Wasius; Susemihl II. 668.
40. Bagnall, *Ptolemaic Possessions* 104, an inscription from the reign of Philadelphus.
41. C. Préaux, *Les Grecs en Égypte* (Brussels 1947), 12-14; Fraser 1972, 67-68.
42. Meillier 1979, 115-54; Laronde 1987, 336-38 and 362-67.

Furthermore, on this hypothesis Callimachus would have grown up in Cyrene and won favour at the court of Magas before trying his fortune in Alexandria. That implies arrival in Alexandria no earlier than ca 280 and no younger than his mid-thirties. What then of his status as court youth? And what of the *Hymn to Zeus*? Attempts have indeed been made to identify the again unnamed king of this poem as Magas.[43] But that seems out of the question. Zeus's brothers (Callimachus writes, following Hesiod rather than Homer), though older, did not grudge him heaven as his portion; some versions absurdly claim that they drew lots, but it must have been by his strength and achievements that Zeus won the best portion (56-66). It is impossible to doubt the relevance of this curiously pointed development to the fact that Philadelphus won the throne of Egypt despite being likewise the youngest of several brothers. It does not at all fit Magas, some 12 years older than Philadelphus. Since all of these brothers (including Magas) did in due course very aggressively grudge Philadelphus his portion, it seems inevitable to conclude that the poem dates from soon after Philadelphus's accession in 283.[44] This would explain why Callimachus chose to say so much about the subject of accession in the first place; and why he did not exploit the stock Ptolemaic motif of Zeus's marriage to Hera as a mythical paradigm for sister-marriage, writing as he was before Philadelphus married his sister Arsinoë (between 279 and 274).[45] If Callimachus was indeed a court youth, it follows that he was already living at the court of Soter before Magas proclaimed himself king of Cyrene on Soter's death.

What then of the "Cyrenean" poems? There is a simple alternative. The *Hymn to Apollo* and other poems written in Cyrene date, not from the poet's youth, but from some later period. In favour of this hypothesis it might be observed that Callimachus's datable Ptolemaic poems all cluster at either the beginning or the end of his career. The *Hymn to Zeus*, the poems on the wedding and divinisation of Arsinoë and (as argued in Ch. IV-VI) *Aetia* I-II and *Iambi* between ca 283 and 268; the *Coma Berenices* and *Victoria Berenices* in 246/5. Of course, some of the undatable poems may fall in the late 260s and 250s, but there remains a gap during which we might hypothesize a prolonged absence from Alexandria. No specific reason is necessary for a man to visit his native land from time to time, especially if he could return as a famous poet. Every other poet of the age we know of travelled widely, from city to city and court to court, and Callimachus was surely no exception (Ch. VIII. 5). If any weight is to be attached to the fact that Callimachus the younger is given the ethnic Cyrenean in his Suda-entry, it would seem that he too did not reside permanently in Alexandria.

---

43. Meillier 1979, 61-78; Laronde 1987, 366.
44. For a full account of the various views, J. J. Clauss, *Class. Ant.* 5 (1986), 155-70.
45. So Wilamowitz, *Textgeschichte der griechischen Bukoliker* (Berlin 1906), 55.

The period of hostilities between Philadelphus and Magas (unfortunately not closely datable) may also have played a part.[46] Patriotic Cyreneans may have fallen out of favour. Or he may have been sent as Philadelphus's ambassador to Magas, a rôle often played by distinguished men of letters at Hellenistic courts. So for example the Athenian comic poet Philippides under Lysimachus, the architect Sostratus of Cnidos and Callimachus's friend the poet Heracleitus of Halicarnassus under Philadelphus; Gonatas appointed the Stoic philosopher Persaeus governor of Corinth.[47] It is at any rate suggestive that Callimachus's return to Ptolemaic court poetry coincides with the arrival of Euergetes's Cyrenean bride Berenice—and the appointment of the Cyrenean Eratosthenes to the Alexandrian library.

Then there is the question of Callimachus and the Alexandrian library. Now that the Oxyrhynchus list has proved that he was never chief librarian, there has been much speculation as to why he was not appointed, mostly linked to the famous supposed feud with Apollonius (who did become librarian). "That he was in the running is certain," claims Peter Green,[48] but that is an anachronistic assumption. We have little information about the position and none about the circumstances. For all we know the gentleman scholar may have disdained what amounted to a full-time professional position with responsibilities (one of which was tutoring the royal children—not perhaps everyone's idea of bliss).[49] On the other hand he may simply have been living in Cyrene when the post fell vacant.

2

According to Green, "Callimachus's waspishness to his rivals was matched only by his servility to the great," by an "unpleasant groveling streak." Actually there is nothing in Callimachus to match the flattery Augustus elicited from his poets to far less modern disapproval. Embarrassed apologists for the "apparent excess" of Vergil's speculations about the nature of Augustus's future deification (*Georgics* i. 24-42) are right to posit the influence of Hellenistic encomium, but wrong to name Callimachus in particular.[50] This sort of extravagant ingenuity is common enough in the later Hellenistic epigrammatists preserved in Philip's *Gar-*

---

46. For what is known of Magas, F. Chamoux, *Revue historique* 216 (1956), 18-34.

47. *PCG* vii (1989), 332-5; Sext. *Adv. gramm.* 1. 276; W. Swinnen, *Anc. Soc.* 1 (1970), 39-52; Plut. *Arat.* 18.

48. Green 1990, 204; for more details on feud and librarianship, Ch. VIII. 3 and X. 1.

49. Eichgrün 1961, 183-93.

50. Green 1990, 182; R. F. Thomas, *Virgil: Georgics* i (Cambridge 1988), 73, finding none of the usual explanations "totally reassuring."

land,[51] writing for Roman patrons, but not in the court poets of Philadelphus or Antigonus Gonatas.

What does Callimachus actually say about Philadelphus? The implicit comparison of his accession to that of Zeus in the *Hymn to Zeus* opened up unlimited possibilities, yet when the poet finally reaches "our ruler" (unnamed), he says only that "in the evening he accomplishes what he plans in the morning; at evening the big things, the little ones straight away" (86-7). Not a word of Philadelphus's power or the extent of the Ptolemaic empire—and not a word of his divinity. That is mentioned only once, when Apollo in the *Hymn to Delos* refuses (from his mother's womb) to be born on Cos since "that is reserved for another god," θεὸς ἄλλος (165), a tag from Homer (K. 511). Here less than five lines suffice to praise the extent of the Ptolemaic realm, and the only concrete detail cited is the quelling of some Gallic mercenaries, appended to a brief account of the great defeat of the Gauls at Delphi in 279—the achievement not of Philadelphus but of the Aetolians and Antigonus Gonatas. Callimachus assigns the credit to Apollo rather than Philadelphus's rivals, but if his aim had been flattery, it is remarkable that he should even mention much less glorify an exploit in which (as everyone knew) Philadelphus had played no part at all. Elsewhere he repeatedly refers to the various oracles of Apollo (Ch. VI. 7); perhaps after all that was his main concern here.

Indeed he seems to have written an entire poem on the Gallic defeat, not an epic or panegyric, but (after his manner) an aetiological poem on the eponymous nymph Galateia (F 379; Ch. X. 4). As we shall see in detail in the pages that follow (Ch. II. 5; Ch. X. 2-5), panegyrics of the great were a routine phenomenon of the age, by no means restricted to royalty—but they were not to Callimachus's taste. Theocritus wrote a formal panegyric of Philadelphus (dismissed by Green as "the price to be paid for patronage"),[52] but in a lifetime at the court of the Ptolemies, not one from Callimachus. A series of poems on Ptolemaic queens (again, not panegyrics), but not one on the three successive kings he served. Callimachus wrote six hymns, only two of which name Philadelphus while one celebrates (even if it does not name) another king, Magas. We might have expected a Ptolemaic court poet to celebrate the one major Ptolemaic religious innovation (ruler-cult excepted), the introduction of the cult of Sarapis.[53] In Callimachus himself we have no more than one or two casual references to Sarapis in epigrams, and equally casual references to Anubis and Isis,[54] again in epigrams—every one a dedication written for friends. So far as we

---

51. As sensibly observed in the case of Ovid by Hollis's note on *Ars Am.* i. 183ff.

52. Green 1990, 241; contrast F. T. Griffiths, *Theocritus at Court* (Leiden 1979).

53. For the sources, which point to Soter, Fraser I. 246-68.

54. *AP* xiii. 7 (Sarapis); vi. 148 (? Sarapis); F 715 (Anubis; cf. Wilamowitz, *HD* i. 176 n.1); vi. 150, 311 (Isis).

know, neither Callimachus nor any other poet of the age wrote a major poem on an Egyptian theme. We are surely bound to conclude that the Ptolemies did not require that sort of tribute from their poets.[55]

Remarkably enough, a recent book by E.-R. Schwinge has drawn exactly the opposite conclusion: though apparently writing in praise of their royal masters, from whom they needed patronage to survive, in reality Callimachus and Theocritus were subtly attacking them.[56] It was (he argues) to maintain their independence that poets rejected the pressure to write epic in favour of short poems, everyday themes and a playful manner—the latter supposedly concealing bitter hostility.[57]

This is not the place to examine Schwinge's interpretations of individual passages, which have on the whole conspicuously failed to persuade his critics.[58] It would be strange indeed if a modern professor were better able to judge the tone of Callimachus's poetry than the cultivated Philadelphus who knew him all his life. Schwinge's approach presupposes (of course) that poets could not but find it demeaning to praise even the enlightened benefactors of the Museum. In fact, as Frederick Griffiths put it, Greek poets had always "accepted the realities of patronage without embarrassment and would surely be amused by the modern confidence that a network of universities, educational foundations, and cultural ministries shelters art more honorably than might a monarch with taste and flair."[59]

Later chapters will question the widespread but unfounded modern notion that Hellenistic kings expected epics from their poets (Ch. X-XVI). What does call for at any rate brief discussion here is the assumption that Hellenistic monarchies were totalitarian states. The court of Philadelphus was not the court of Domitian—though even under the worst of the Roman tyrants it is too crude to suppose that (for example) a text like Lucan's apostrophe to Nero (i. 33-66) has to be read *either* straight as serious flattery *or* ironically as ridicule. The notion that when deified the corpulent Nero might upset the balance of the celestial sphere is surely playful rather than subversive—and taken as such by the sophisticated Nero.[60]

The factor that has been held to differentiate the courts of the Hellenistic kings from the courts where not only Anacreon and Pindar but also

55. Any more perhaps than Augustus required poems of his poets: P. White, *Promised Verse: Poets in the Society of Augustan Rome* (Cambridge Mass. 1993).

56. *Künstlichkeit von Kunst* (Zetemata 84) Munich 1986, 40-82.

57. This is close to the counter-culture interpretations of Augustan poets (especially Ovid) so fashionable in the 1960s and 70s.

58. J. J. Clauss (*AJP* 109 [1988], 447-9); F. Vian (*RÉG* 101 [1988], 206-8); N. Hopkinson (*CR* 38 [1988], 159).

59. Griffiths 1979, 3.

60. Thus it seems to me a mistake to read it as an "ingenious parody" of Vergil's address to Octavian in *Geo.* i. 24-35 (W. R. Johnson, *Momentary Monsters* [Ithaca 1987], 121); see especially now M. Dewar, *CQ* 44 (1994), 199-211.

Euripides and Thucydides lived without dishonour is ruler cult. It is assumed that divine kings required more extravagant flattery from their poets—an assumption not borne out by what we know of Callimachus and Philadelphus. Ruler cult is not to be interpreted straightforwardly in terms of moral decline and flattery. Recent critics have more plausibly and realistically seen it as a way of accommodating the overwhelming new power of kings within the structure of the Greek cities.[61] Cults were instituted in return for specific benefits conferred, benefits that far exceeded the capacity of the cities. Moreover, all the earliest manifestations of cultic honours for the Successors were offered spontaneously by the cities before any of them had even taken the title of king. It was not till later that individual kings established dynastic cults, and then not all of them (neither Antigonids nor Attalids, it seems). Hostility to ruler cult as sacrilegious in itself ceased with the fourth century. By the third, criticism "takes the form of attacking those who propose to confer cult on a particular king on the grounds that the recipient is unworthy and his supporters scoundrels."[62]

The earliest as well as the most extravagant surviving cult poems on rulers come not from some Hellenistic court, but from democratic Athens, proclaiming Demetrius and Antigonus saviours and benefactors when they restored Athenian liberty in 307.[63] This is natural enough: the honours accorded the kings were an extension and expansion of the long-established system of honouring benefactors within the cities.[64] Cult hymns naturally incorporate flattering identifications with gods, but it should not be thought that either kings or poets took such compliments altogether seriously: "poetry and oratory...have a language of their own; it is of its very essence that it should not be taken literally."[65] For example, when a certain Hermodotus addressed Antigonus the One-eyed as "son of Helios" in a poem, the king remarked that it did not look that way to the boy who emptied his chamberpot.[66] Rather, as Robin Lane Fox put it, "Hellenistic courts were elegant, ironic and not overawed by royalty."[67]

F 1 of Rhianus of Lebena[68] has long been held to be an attack on Hel-

61. S.R.F. Price, *Rituals and Power: The Roman Imperial Cult in Asia Minor* (Cambridge 1984), 23-40; F. W. Walbank, *CAH* VII. 1 (1984), 87-96; H. S. Lund, *Lysimachus: A Study in Early Hellenistic Kingship* (London 1992), 161-74.

62. Walbank 1984, 96; Habicht, *Gottmensch. und gr. Städte*[2] (Munich 1970), 213-21.

63. K. Scott, *AJP* 49 (1928), 137-66 and 217-39; Habicht 1970, 45f; Ch. X. 4.

64. R. A. Billows, *Kings and Colonists: Aspects of Maced. Imperialism* (1995), 73-80.

65. E. Badian, "The Deification of Alexander the Great," *Ancient Macedonian Studies in Honor of Charles F. Edson* (Thessalonica 1981), 32.

66. *SH* 491 (Plut. *Mor.* 182B; 360C); sometimes identified as Antigonus Gonatas.

67. J. Boardman, J. Griffin and O. Murray, *Greece and the Hell. World* (1986), 343.

68. There is no such place as the Bene (Βήνη, ethnic Βηναῖος) given by Steph. Byz. and the Suda and (probably) interpolated in Pausanias (4. 6. 1); on the other hand there is a well-documented village Lebena (Λέβην, Λεβήνα; Λεβηναῖος), the port of Gortyn (Kent Rigsby, *RÉG* 99 [1986], 350-353). That he later lived at Keraiai in N.W. Crete (cf. the alternative

lenistic ruler-cult.[69] It would be remarkable to find such an attack so late in the day. In fact it is simply a moralizing passage (in 21 heavily Hesiodic lines) that contrasts the way poor and rich handle their respective lots:[70]

> The man who lacks the wherewithal of life wanders in sorrow, reproaching the gods. Unmindful of his own virtue and courage, he has not the strength to say a word or do anything, shivering when rich folk pass by, and shame and grief eat up his heart. The man who has an abundance (εὐοχθῆσι), to whom god gives wealth and rule over many (πολυκοιρανίην), forgets that his feet tread the earth and his parents were mortal. In his presumptuousness and wickedness he roars like Zeus and raises his head aloft. Insignificant though he is, he seeks Athena of the fair arms for his wife and aspires to walk the road that leads to Olympus, as though he were about to sit down at table with the immortals.

He concludes with the reflection that Ate punishes rich and poor alike. If Rhianus had wished to attack kings for anything so specific as instituting their own cult, why confuse the issue by attacking their subjects as well? There is in fact no place for kings at all in his antithesis between rich and poor; πολυκοιρανίην is simply one of the attributes that distinguish the rich and powerful from the poor.[71] Pursuing a goddess and reaching for heaven were proverbially hybristic acts (combined in Alcman F 1. 16-17).

If (as Henri Estienne suggested) Rhianus was thinking of Theopompus's account of King Cotys of Thrace, who prepared a wedding banquet for himself and Athena and awaited her arrival in a drunken revel, it would have been because Theopompus had presented him as the classic tyrant.[72] If Rhianus had been writing in Athens at the time, his lines might (as W. Klinger suggested) have been applied to Demetrius's sojourn in the Parthenon in 304/3.[73] Yet over and above the fact that Rhianus actually wrote three quarters of a century later,[74] it was less the fact that Demetrius had set up camp in the temple precincts that shocked people (Diogenes the Cynic used to enjoy its cool spaciousness during the hot Athenian summer) than the riotous orgies he held there.[75] Demetrius's extravagance was not

---

ethnic Κεραΐτης in the Suda) may be attested by a Delphic inscription (Rigsby 353-5).

69. Wilamowitz, *HD* I. 225; Jacoby, *FGrH* 265 (p. 199); Giangrande *CR* 19 (1969), 374; Giangrande, *SMA* i (1980), 35-40, 62-4; Price, *Rituals of Power* (1984), 29 n. 23.

70. *CA* 9-10 = *FGrH* 265 F 60; Hopkinson 1988, 226-29.

71. According to Giangrande, πολυκοιρανίη "always had a political meaning," but not in its original Homeric context (οὐκ ἀγαθὸν πολυκοιρανίη, *Il.* 2. 204) and certainly not (for example) in Arist. *Metaph.* xii. 10. 14; πολυκοίρανε in Aesch. F 238 means no more than "ruling over many."

72. *FGrH* 115 F 31 = Athen. 531 F; Harp. s.v. Κότυς; *FGrH* 115 Komm. p. 361.

73. *Eos* 26 (1923), 79-84 (in Polish); German summary in *Phil. Woch.* 44 (1924), 1304.

74. Wilamowitz and Jacoby, like Klinger, championed an early date: Ch. X. 6.

75. Teles 2, p. 8 Hense² (Diog.); W. S. Ferguson, *Hellenistic Athens* (1911), 118-19.

typical of royal behaviour, and has no bearing on cult practice in Rhianus's day.

One of the few things we know about Rhianus is that he produced editions of both *Iliad* and *Odyssey* based on manuscript study; more than 40 of his readings are discussed in the Homer scholia.[76] It does not follow that he worked at Alexandria (Pergamum is another possibility), but there is certainly no basis for Kaibel's claim that he would not have got on with the scholars "who repaid the royal munificence of Ptolemy with courtly flattery" (Jacoby added the other Hellenistic courts as well).[77]

The truth is that Hellenistic kings were remarkably tolerant of frankness from their associates. Polybius notes the outspokenness with which a deputation from his army addressed Philip V of Macedon, adding that this was characteristic of the freedom of speech Macedonians employed towards their kings.[78] The flamboyant and arrogant Demetrius was less accessible, but this caused offense precisely because his subjects were unused to it.[79] His father Antigonus the One-eyed was well known for his tolerance of insults, even from common soldiers.[80] It is true that he had the caustic sophist Theocritus of Chios executed, but the circumstances are unclear. Certainly Theocritus insulted the king (who was very sensitive about the disfiguring wound that had cost him an eye) by publicly addressing him as Cyclops;[81] but it may have been one of his lieutenants who was really responsible.[82]

Even Alexander, notoriously intolerant and demanding adulation in his later years, could on occasion be surprisingly tolerant. An otherwise unknown Python of Catane mocked his treasurer Harpalus's extravagance towards his mistresses in a satyr-play performed at Alexander's camp in 324, after he had fled from Babylon to Cilicia with 5000 talents but apparently before his departure for Athens.[83] Some have found it hard to

76. M. Van der Valk, *Text. Crit. of the Odyssey* (1949), 107-8; Pfeiffer 1968, 148-9.

77. *Hermes* 28 (1893), 57-59; Jacoby, p. 199.

78. ἰσηγορία, iv. 27. 6; cf. Plut. *Arat.* 48. 4 and Polyb. v. 15. 8.

79. μάλιστα δὴ τὸ δυσόμιλον αὐτοῦ καὶ δυσπρόσοδον [ἐλύπει], Plutarch, *Dem.* 42. Wallace-Hadrill (*JRS* 72 [1982], 33-34) misleadingly implies that Demetrius's behaviour was typical of Hellenistic kings.

80. Seneca, *De ira* iii. 2; Billows, *Antigonus the One-eyed* (1990), 11-12.

81. For the various versions (Plut. *Mor.* 633 C and Ps-Plut. 11A-C; Macr. *Sat.* vii. 3. 12), S. Theodorsson, *Hermes* 118 (1990), 380-2; C. Franco, *Athenaeum* 69 (1991), 445-58; Apelles painted him in three-quarters profile to conceal his disfigurement (*NH* xxxv. 90).

82. On the supposed butcher Eutropion, Billows, *Antigonus* (1990), 386, 437. The details of the execution of Daphidas (*SH* 370-71; Fontenrose, *TAPA* 91 [1960], 83-99; Braund, *CQ* 32 [1982], 354-57) are too fantastic, and it is not only Attalus (? III) but the Delphic oracle he is said to have abused; nor were the Attalids Macedonian.

83. B. Snell's discussion in *Scenes from Greek Drama* (Berkeley 1964), 99-138 has provoked extensive debate on the date and place of this performance: H. Lloyd-Jones, *Gnomon* 38 (1966), 16-17; D. F. Sutton, *The Greek Satyr Play* (Meisenheim 1980), 75-81; R. Lane Fox, *Chios: A Conference at the Homereion in Chios 1984* (Oxford 1986), 118; A. B. Bosworth, *Conquest and Empire* (Cambridge 1988), 149; I. Worthington, *Symb. Osl.* 61

believe that Alexander would allow public criticism of a former trusted friend who had robbed and betrayed him. Yet he had earlier allowed (or encouraged) public criticism of some of his generals at a symposium in front of himself.[84] And among the sayings attributed to Alexander is a witty response to an actor who had abused him.[85]

Many examples of frankness of one sort or another might be cited from the poets. If a couple of suggestions of my own are accepted, Asclepiades wrote an admiring epigram on one of Philadelphus's mistresses while his friend Posidippus wrote a lampoon on the sexual skills of another, the famous Bilistiche (Ch. IX. 2). Then there is the grammarian who insulted Ptolemy Soter to his face (asking who his grandfather was),[86] and Antagoras's cheeky reply to Antigonus Gonatas when the king made fun of his cooking.[87] Theodorus the Cyrenaic is said to have spoken very frankly to Lysimachus.[88]

In addition to the regular kingly qualities listed by Theocritus in his panegyric of Philadelphus we also find the more surprising items: "kindly, cultured, a ladies' man, agreeable as can be."[89] When a modern scholar characterized these words as "witty but inappropriate" because they would have made people laugh,[90] he was assuming laughter of disapproval rather than admiration. To take another example, while many aspects of Demetrius's career met with disapproval, his fame as a lover did not.[91] As for the comparison of Arsinoë to Helen in Theocritus 15. 110, according to one scholar, "it is to be hoped that Arsinoë was at any rate attractive enough to prevent the comparison from sounding absurd"; according to another, it would remind people that she had had several husbands.[92] But in Ch. XVI. 4 we shall see that in an Egyptian context Helen would suggest much more than just beauty—and no one at a Macedonian court would have equated the three royal marriages of the twice widowed Arsinoë with Helen's adultery.

In an epigram addressed to Euergetes, Eratosthenes calls him "my dear fellow" (ὠγαθέ). In the days when the authenticity of this interesting poem

---

(1986), 64; Heckel, *Marshals* (n. 9) 219.

    84. Plut. *V. Alex.* 50. 8.

    85. "You abuse Ajax and Achilles as well"; *Gnom. Vat.* 93, ed. Sternbach (1963), 43.

    86. Plutarch, *de coh. ira* 9 = *Mor.* 458AB; below Ch. III. 5.

    87. Heges. Delph. F 15 in Athen. 340 F; quoted below, Ch. X. 1.

    88. E. Mannebach, *Aristippi et Cyren. Frag.* (1961), T 255-259C; Ch. III n. 162.

    89. εὐγνώμων, φιλόμουσος, ἐρωτικός, εἰς ἄκρον ἁδύς, Theoc. 14. 61, translated by J. Griffin, in *Caesar Augustus: Seven Aspects*, ed. F. Millar and E. Segal (Oxford 1984), 191.

    90. C. W. Vollgraff, *Mnemosyne* 47 (1919), 356.

    91. Plut. *Dem.* 2; *Comp. Dem. et Ant.* 3-4; J. Griffin, *JRS* 67 (1977), 21-2.

    92. K. J. Dover, *Theocritus* (London 1971), 211; Vollgraff 1919, 356; Goldhill, in S. Goldhill and R. Osborne (edd.), *Art and Text in Ancient Greek Culture* (1994), 219.

was doubted, one of the reasons given was the (as it was felt) excessive familiarity of this phrase.[93] On the contrary, this is scarcely the mark of a forger. Archimedes was a Friend of King Hiero of Syracuse, to whose son Gelon he dedicated his *Sandreckoner*, indicated by nothing more fulsome than the curt apostrophe "King Gelon" in the first sentence.[94] In one of the versified anecdotes of Machon, the courtesan Hippe called on King Ptolemy (apparently Philadelphus) one afternoon with the words: "Ptolemy old boy (παππία), I'm dying of thirst." Another makes fun of a central element in royal propaganda, the descent all Macedonian kings claimed from Heracles and the Atreidai (Ch. IX. 2). When Demetrius asked a courtesan if he might enter her from the rear, she named her price and told him to go ahead with a quotation from Sophocles, addressing him as "Son of Agamemnon."[95] When he asked another courtesan's opinion of some gifts sent by his beloved Lamia, who was considerably older than himself, she replied: "my mother will send you more than that if you will sleep with her."[96] It would be rash to rely too much on anecdotes,[97] but they have one common feature which it is hard to believe coincidence, and that is the lack of awe in which the kings were held by those close to them.[98] It is worth noting that there seem to be no similar stories about Roman emperors. As Tacitus noted, Caesar and Augustus put up with abuse and invective, but their successors had to be treated with greater respect.[99]

The most spectactular illustration is the infamous line by Sotades of Maroneia on the marriage of Philadelphus and Arsinoë (279/74):

εἰς οὐχ ὁσίην τρυμαλιὴν τὸ κέντρον ὠθεῖ.[100]

it's an unholy hole he's shoving his prick in.

It was for this insult that he is said to have been executed, dropped into the sea in a leaden jar. Taken by itself, this might seem to prove Schwinge's assumption of a repressive tyranny. Sotades has sometimes been seen as an "opposition" poet. But the truth is he made a point of insulting kings: Lysimachus in front of Philadelphus, Philadelphus in front of Lysimachus

---

93. *CA* 66-7 (*nimis familiare*); Wilamowitz, *Kl. Schr.* ii (1941), 56f.; Pfeiffer 1968, 155.

94. Plut. *Marc.* 14. 7; Arch. ii. 216 Heiberg.

95. Machon 439-49, 226-30 (Gow's note misses the witty allusion to Argive descent).

96. Plut. *Demetr.* 27. On another occasion, when Lamia turned down every perfume Demetrius offered her, he told her to sniff his penis; when she judged this aroma even worse he retorted that it was at any rate royal (Machon 174-87 Gow = Athen. 577F).

97. On the problems of anecdotes, R. Saller, *Greece and Rome* 27 (1980), 69-83; for anecdotes about Hellenistic kings, Billows, *Kings and Colonists* (1995), 63-4.

98. This παρρησία did not (of course) extend beyond this narrow circle.

99. A. Wallace-Hadrill, "Civilis princeps," *JRS* 72 (1982), 32-48; Tac. *Ann.* iv. 34. 5.

100. With Pretagostini, I prefer ὠθεῖ (Athen. and Eustath.), to Plutarch's ὠθεῖς; as we shall see below, he is writing of Zeus in the third person, not apostrophizing Philadelphus.

and (according to his son) "other kings in other cities too."[101] A meeting between Lysimachus and Philadelphus in Alexandria must have fallen between 283 and 281, and Sotades must have been there by invitation, surely (as we shall see in Ch. III. 5) at a symposium. A careful paper by M. Launey has shown that he was not executed until a full decade after the insult to Arsinoë, probably in 267.[102] That is to say, he travelled from court to court abusing the kings of the age for some twenty years with impunity.

It has usually been assumed that Sotades's line was an isolated, embarrassing eccentricity from a maverick, at once visited with terrifying and exemplary punishment. But one of Callimachus's most famous elegies—*Acontius and Cydippe*—alludes to the incident with what can only be described as flippancy. We may begin with Sotades F 16:[103]

Ἥρην ποτέ φασι Δία τὸν τερψικέραυνον,

They say that once upon a time Zeus who delights in thunder and Hera...

It is tempting to infer (with L. Escher) that the poem went on to compare the wedding of Philadelphus and Arsinoë with the union of Zeus and Hera.[104] The parallel was understandably dear to contemporary poets. For example, Theocritus's panegyric on Philadelphus pictures Arsinoë embracing her "brother and husband," a neat variation on Homer's description of Hera in *Iliad* 16. 432 = 18. 356.[105] In his note on this line, the commentator Eustathius writes as follows:[106]

> Some damned sophist justified the Egyptian Ptolemy when he broke the law with his sister, quoting this line [sc. of Homer], as though speaking metaphorically, saying that the king was not going against precedent by having intercourse with his sister, for Zeus did it.

This is a paraphrase of a text (not identified by editors) describing how a contemporary poet justified the marriage on the basis of the "sacred marriage" (ἱερὸς γάμος) between Zeus and Hera. Pretagostini identified Eustathius's "damned sophist" as Theocritus. In fact a closer source (direct

101. Hegesander of Delphi, F 12 (Athen. 620F) = *FHG* iv. 415-16.
102. *RÉA* 47 (1945), 33-45; for more details, Ch. IX. 3 (end).
103. Heph. p. 36. 12 Consbruch; P. Oxy. 220 col. vii. 17 = p. 404. 22 Consbruch; it is quoted anonymously as a specimen of the Sotadean by Hephaestion, but that is no evidence against its authenticity: for example, p. 43. 13 cites Sappho F 1.1 anonymously as a specimen of the Sapphic; cf. R. Pretagostini, *Ricerce sulla poesia Alessandrina* (Rome 1984), 144. As Powell observed in his note on F 16, the ποτέ and φασίν forbid ascribing the line to Sotades's rewriting of the *Iliad* in Sotadeans.
104. *De Sotadis Maronitae Reliquiis* (Diss. Darmstadt 1913), 23-24.
105. κασίγνητόν τε πόσιν τε (17. 130) for Homer's κασιγνήτην ἄλοχόν τε.
106. Eustathius, *Comm. Hom. Iliad.* ed. M. van der Valk, III (Leiden 1979), p. 878. 13-17, on *Iliad* 16. 432; see too Erbse's note on the older Homer scholia, IV (1975), pp. 258.

quotation rather than adaptation) can be found. When discussing the value of apposite quotation, Plutarch cites the case of an unnamed rhapsode (whence Eustathius's inability to supply a name) who *at Ptolemy's marriage*, when "he was thought to be doing something unnatural and unlawful," began his recitation with 18. 356.[107] There can be little doubt that at the court of Philadelphus any reference to the sacred marriage would be construed as an allusion to the marriage of the king and his sister.

But Sotades was no sycophant. His poem must have continued very differently. Indeed, F 16 is surely (as Pretagostini has suggested) the opening of the poem that climaxed in F 1.[108] After beginning as though drawing the same reassuring Homeric analogy, Sotades went on to accuse Zeus himself, and by implication (of course) Philadelphus too of incest. The very surprise of the change of tack would have added to the shock of the final insult. Presumably the poem purported to be an epithalamium (Callimachus wrote a real epithalamium for the occasion, F 392).

Let us turn now to the *Cydippe*. F 75 begins with Cydippe's prenuptial night—an allusion to the Naxian custom that on their wedding eve brides spent the night with a boy whose parents were both alive. Callimachus makes as if to explain the custom as a reenactment of the secret intercourse of Zeus and Hera, and then breaks off, as if embarrassed:[109]

Ἥρην γάρ κοτέ φασι—κύον, κύον, ἴσχεο λαιδρέ
θυμέ· σύ γ᾽ ἀείσῃ καὶ τά περ οὐχ ὁσίη.

They say that once upon a time Hera—dog, dog, hold back, impudent soul! You would sing even what is not lawful.

At one level, this serves (like many another passage in Callimachean narrative) as an indirect characterization of the narrator—a pious but garrulous fellow, unable to keep a secret. But even so, there is something very strange about the exaggerated reluctance to mention this "mystery"—in fact a well-known story told openly by Homer and many later writers. We may contrast Theocritus's irreverent remark that it is something "women know" (15. 64). Indeed Callimachus himself seems to have referred to the union a good deal more casually elsewhere in the *Aetia* (F 48 and perhaps 599). Furthermore, while the analogy of the sacred marriage would explain cases

107. Plutarch, *QC* ix. 1 (736F).
108. Pretagostini 1984, 139-147, basing his argument in part on the fact that Eustathius goes on to quote the story of Sotades, apparently unaware that this passage, a paraphrase of Athen. 621 A, is a later addition from a different source. We have Eustathius's autograph (Laur. 59. 2 and 3), and the many passages enclosed in square brackets in van der Valk's edition (mainly from Athenaeus, whom he did not discover till his work was complete) were supplements added in the top and bottom margins in the bishop's own hand: van der Valk, I (1971), xiii-xvii. What follows reformulates and develops Pretagostini's suggestion.
109. E. g. L.R. Farnell, *Cults of the Greek States* I (1895), 185-6; Pfeiffer ad loc.

where the betrothed couple (as on Samos) actually had intercourse before the wedding night, it is not at all an appropriate aetion for the present situation: Zeus and Hera slept together "unbeknown to their dear parents" and for 300 years,[110] while Cydippe and this boy did so with their parents' approval for just one night. More important, Cydippe and the boy were not brother and sister, nor did they have intercourse.

So why does Callimachus go out of his way *not* to quote a parallel that is not appropriate anyway?[111] Certainly not from a sense of decorum,[112] since he provides quite enough detail for any educated person to identify the allusion.[113] Furthermore, the charade of embarrassment and apology ensures that we pay it far more attention than if he had said nothing in the first place. The actual break-off formula he borrowed from Pindar.[114] The most relevant parallels are *O*. i. 52 (rejecting the traditional version of the Pelops story because he "cannot call any of the gods gluttonous") and ix. 35-41 (refusing to tell the story of Heracles's combat against the gods).[115] In Pindar, this rejection of an unworthy version enhances the hero in question and so the victor to whom he is being compared. Just so Callimachus. The Pindaric way he repudiates the version that Zeus and his brothers drew lots for heaven in the *Hymn to Zeus* redounds to the greater credit of Zeus and so Philadelphus.[116] In Pindar likewise the ostentatious reticence itself "makes the hearer...think of what is not said."[117]

In a rather different way, the Pindaric device in the *Cydippe* directs the hearer's attention first to the mythical parallel and then to the real life situation behind it.[118] The key is provided by Sotades F 16, to which this passage clearly alludes:

Ἥρην ποτέ φασι Δία τὸν τερψικέραυνον.

110. *Il.* 14. 296 and Schol.1. 609, with Pfeiffer's note on Call. F 48.

111. This very inappropriateness has been responsible for much debate about the interpretation of the Naxian rite; D. R. Stuart, *CP* 6 (1911), 302-14; C.Bonner, ib. 402-9; E. Samter, *NJbb.* 35 (1915), 90-98; Herter 1937, 132; Pfeiffer ad loc.; J. H. Oakley and R. H. Sinos, *The Wedding in Ancient Athens* (Madison 1993), 20, 37.

112. So Carole Newlands, *Arethusa* 25 (1992), 42.

113. For a more detailed discussion, see a forthcoming study by Jennifer Lynn.

114. Therese Fuhrer, *AJP* 109 (1988), 53-68; Harder, *HSCP* 93 (1990), 296-97.

115. "One of the ways in which Pindar maintains an oral, impromptu quality in his poetry is by appearing to react to his own statements, as if he were hearing them...for the first time," W. H. Race, *Style and Rhetoric in Pindar's Odes* (Atlanta 1990), 42.

116. Though as Fuhrer remarks (1988, 58), the grounds for Callimachus's rejection of the unworthy version are (characteristically) intellectual rather than moral: it would have been *foolish* to draw lots when heaven was so obviously the most desirable of the three realms.

117. With Callimachus's warning to his θυμός, cf. Pindar's to his στόμα; both confess to childish babble. Further Pindaric examples in *O*. 13 and *N*. 5; other Callimachean examples, *H. Zeus* 60-65 and *H. Dem.* 17-23.

118. Fuhrer's analysis (1988, 63-6) misses this dimension of reference.

The Callimachean context confirms that Sotades was evoking the marriage of Zeus and Hera. It must be Callimachus who alludes to Sotades rather than vice versa. His real purpose was surely to call to mind Sotades's perversion of the Homeric parallel: Sotades really did tell what was not lawful, the dog, the impudent soul. In all probability both Sotades and the *Cydippe* date from soon after the royal wedding, some time between 279 and 274.[119] Since we do not know the occasion of the *Cydippe* and do not have it complete, there is no way of discovering Callimachus's purpose in any detail, but it seems impossible to doubt that it was humorous—and taken in the same spirit. He cannot have intended (or expected) to cause offence, and the fact that he continued to enjoy Arsinoë's patronage proves that he did not.

Nor does this passage of the *Cydippe* stand alone. There is a strangely similar allusion in another famous elegy usually dismissed as nothing more than an elegant trifle, the *Lock of Berenice*. According to Catullus's translation, the new bridegroom Euergetes set off on his Syrian campaign "bearing the sweet scars of the nocturnal struggle he had waged to win the spoils of her virginity (66. 13-14)."[120] The young bride "wept at her sad separation from her dear brother."[121] Since it was only by marrying him that Berenice (in reality his cousin) became Euergetes's "sister," there is clearly a mischievous joke (especially after the earlier sexual allusion) in the suggestion that it was as a brother that the bride missed her new spouse.[122] A more graceful joke than Sotades's, to be sure, but it is nonetheless remarkable to find a court poet making any sort of joke about so delicate a topic as a king's incest.

Another example. Both Philadelphus and Arsinoë were devotees of the mysteries of the Samothracian gods, often identified with the Cabeiroi.[123] This surely is why Apollonius's Argonauts stop off at Samothrace to be initiated;[124] and why Theocritus mentions Iasion, the founder-hero of the mysteries.[125] Callimachus wrote what seems to have been an aetiological elegy on the mysteries of the Cabeiroi, later included in *Aetia* III (Ch. VIII. 5). But he also wrote two decidedly more frivolous pieces. First, an apostrophe to an ithyphallic herm inquiring whether its erection was inspired by the sight of Philetadas, evidently the speaker's boyfriend or at any rate a

119. For a further argument in favour of such a date, Ch. IX. 3.

120. *dulcia nocturnae portans vestigia rixae, quam de virgineis gesserat exuviis.*

121. *fratris cari flebile discidium*, line 22.

122. So J. Griffin, *Caesar Augustus* ed. F. Millar and E. Segal (Oxford 1984), 193-4.

123. Susan G. Cole, *Theoi Megaloi: The Cult of the Great Gods at Samothrace* (Leiden 1984), 22-23, 82.

124. *Arg.* i. 915-21, with Vian's note (pp. 260-61).

125. 3. 49-50; B. Hemberg, *Die Kabiren* (Uppsala 1950), 105f., 313-15; M. Fantuzzi, "Mythological Narrative and Bucolic Poetry," forthcoming.

boy he lusted after. The herm gives a mystic interpretation instead, alluding to twin ithyphallic herms that guarded the entrance to part of the sanctuary complex at Samothrace, aroused by Persephone.[126] Second, an epigram parodying the usual vow of thanks for being rescued from a storm at sea, a dedication of a salt-cellar to the Samothracian gods (the title by which they are known in contemporary inscriptions)—but for being saved from a storm of debt.[127]

Other objections aside, to argue that these poems were covert attacks on either mysteries or monarchs would be to misunderstand the place of religion in ancient Greek life. Provided the relevant rites were properly performed, seriousness was not required in every reference to the divine.

If asked to compare the encomiastic poetry of Callimachus and Pindar, most would probably stress the independence of Pindar, an aristocrat patronized by aristocrats, who (as Gildersleeve put it) "spoke of them and to them as their peer"; "there was a strain of familiar banter in his poems that would not have been tolerated or tolerable in any ordinary man."[128] I would suggest that Callimachus's relations with his patrons were not after all so very different. He was not Green's court sycophant, willing to stoop to any flattery to maintain a royal pension. A man who can joke with successive royal couples about incest knows his royalty. Part of this confidence derived from his longstanding relationship with both kings, as a friend rather than a client; part from his unwavering sense of his own dignity—and no doubt substantial private resources.[129] A well-known fragment scornfully denies "maintaining a hireling Muse" (F 222). Like a later Cyrenean poet, "descended from those whose lineage, from Eurysthenes who settled the Dorians in Sparta down to my own father, has been engraved on the public monuments,"[130] Callimachus too boasted of descent from the royal house of Cyrene. The fastidiousness for which he has become a byword was perhaps after all more than merely a pose; but it was as much social as intellectual.

126. F 199 and 723; Cic. *Nat. Deor.* 3. 56; J. Bousquet, *Rev. arch.* 29-30 (1948), 128; Hemberg 1950, 93; W. Burkert, *Greek Religion* (Cambridge Mass. 1985), 283-84.

127. *AP* vi. 301; Cole 1984, 58, 125; note too *AP* vii. 723.

128. *Pindar: the Olympian and Pythian Odes* (New York 1885), xxvi.

129. It might be noted that, in his account of the rôle played by Alexander, Lycophron, Eratosthenes and Callimachus in building up the Alexandrian library, it is only in connection with the first two that Tzetzes mentions "generous royal gifts" (μεγαλοδωρίαις βασιλικαῖς, *Proleg. de com.* I, p. 22. 1 Koster).

130. Synesius, *Ep.* 41, p. 63. 15 Garzya; see too the Hadrianic inscription discussed by Spawforth and Walker, *JRS* 76 (1986), 97.

Chapter II

The Ivory Tower

1

The greater part of Callimachus's active life was spent at the Alexandrian Museum, a foundation for the promotion of philological and scientific research established by Ptolemy Soter and maintained by his successors.[1] Scholars, poets, philosophers and scientists from all corners of the Greek world were invited to come and work there at royal expense, and a systematic attempt was made to build up the completest possible collection of Greek manuscripts.[2] It was undoubtedly the holdings of this the first serious library of the ancient world that made possible Callimachus's most ambitious scholarly enterprise, the *Pinakes*, a biographical and bibliographical catalogue in 120 rolls of all Greek literature. The wide knowledge of earlier Greek literature of every sort thus acquired has always (and rightly) been seen as an important element in his poetry too. It has become a commonplace that (in Pfeiffer's words) there is "a complete unity of the creative poet and the reflective scholar in Callimachus."

But it is a serious oversimplification to identify the Museum and its library as the sole or even determining influence on his poetry. Callimachus was not the only writer of the age to earn the sobriquet *poeta doctus*. He is but the most celebrated of an entire generation of learned and allusive poets who flourished in the first half of the third century: Alexander of Aetolia, Anyte of Tegea, Apollonius of Rhodes, Aratus of Soloi, Asclepiades of Samos, Hedylus of Samos, Hermesianax of Colophon, Herodas, Leonidas of Tarentum, Lycophron of Chalcis, Mnasalces of Sicyon, Nicander of Colophon, Nossis of Locri, Philitas of Cos, Posidippus of Pella, Rhianus of Lebena, Simias of Rhodes, Theocritus of Syracuse and a variety of lesser lights. Though hailing from many different cities, they are often bracketed together under the label "Alexandrian." But not all lived in or even visited Alexandria, and only a handful ever worked

---

1. Pfeiffer 1968, 96f.; Fraser 1972, 312-19; Astrid Schürmann, *Griechische Mechanik und antike Gesellschaft* (Stuttgart 1991), 13-32; D. Delia, *AHR* 97 (1992), 1449-67; L. Canfora in *Lo Spazio letterario* I. 2 (1993), 11-29; G. Weber, *Dichtung und höfische Gesellschaft* (Stuttgart 1993), 74-101.

2. Pfeiffer 1968, 124; Fraser 1972, 320-35.

in the Museum. The label Alexandrian implies rather a common approach and manner.

I myself prefer (and have usually employed in this book) the more general and neutral term "Hellenistic."[3] The most recent writer systematically to use "Alexandrian," Graham Zanker, defines it narrowly as poetry by Callimachus, his masters and his followers.[4] This seems to me both too subjective and too restrictive, presupposing as it does an explanation in terms of direct personal influence. We might compare the application of the term "Nonnian" to the many early Byzantine poets whose work is characterized by the stylistic and metrical features so conspicuous in the *Dionysiaca* of the early fifth-century Nonnus. In 1972 an unexpected papyrus find showed that Triphiodorus, till then on stylistic and metrical grounds presumed a typical Nonnian poet of the fifth or sixth century, cannot in fact have written later than the third.[5] Influential as Callimachus was, in many respects he was (as we shall see) a child of his age; the Alexandrian, like the Nonnian style evolved gradually, the work of different poets in different places over a number of years.[6]

Zanker attempted to explain Alexandrian poetry as he defined it by the hypothesis that Ptolemaic poets suffered from a "sense of cultural isolation" cut off from their roots in the new foundation of Alexandria, finding it significant that they allegedly "never took up Alexandrian citizenship."[7] But the fact that they continued to be identified by their original ethnics proves nothing in itself. Like most Greek intellectuals in most other periods, poets and philosophers were constantly on the move, rarely settling permanently in any one of the many different cities where they had given recitations or lectures and received citizenship or proxeny.[8] The poets and philosophers of third-century Athens were just as much an expatriate community.[9] Zanker assumes that poets permanently abandoned their native cities for Alexandria. In fact not one can be proved to have done so—not even Callimachus. Alexander and Lycophron divided their time between the courts of Philadelphus and Antigonus Gonatas in Pella.[10] Aratus lived at the courts of Antigonus and Antiochus, but never (it seems) Philadel-

---

3. On the history of the two terms, R. Kassel, *Die Abgrenzung des Hellenismus in der griechischen Literaturgeschichte* (Berlin 1987).

4. *Realism in Alexandrian Poetry: A Literature and its Audience* (London 1987), 1-3.

5. P. Oxy. 2946; Cameron, *Claudian* (1970), 478-82; E. Livrea, *ZPE* 33 (1979), 57-74.

6. We should never forget the all but complete loss of the non-dramatic poetry of the fifth and fourth centuries: Ch. VI. 3.

7. Zanker 1987, 20 and passim.

8. W. W. Tarn and G. T. Griffith, *Hellenistic Civilization*[3] (Cambridge 1952), 84-87.

9. C. Habicht, *Hellenistic Athens and her Philosophers* (David Magie Lecture, Princeton 1988), 3-4; and § 2 below.

10. Tarn's treatment (*Antigonus Gonatas* [Oxford 1913], 223-56), though sometimes fanciful, has not been superseded.

phus; we do not know where he met Callimachus (possibly in Athens: Ch. VIII. 5). Leonidas, Nicander, Posidippus and Asclepiades all travelled widely. Apollonius, the only poet of this remarkable generation to have been born in Alexandria, spent his later years in Rhodes.

Zanker also argued that it was to fill this cultural vacuum that the Ptolemies enlisted the service of poets like Callimachus and Theocritus, to assimilate the recent history of Alexandria and the cult of the Ptolemies to the Hellenic mythical past. Once again, this is to underestimate the universality of the phenomenon. Every new city the length and breadth of the Hellenistic world devised links of one sort or another with the mythical past, declaring some itinerant god or hero (Dionysus, Heracles, Perseus or Orestes) its founder and proclaiming his name on the coinage, in the hope that some day a poet or historian would work out a connected narrative.[11] But this was less a cultural policy than a natural instinct for a Greek community. A famous article by Elias Bickerman brilliantly explained the process. Most Greeks simply assumed that non-Greek peoples were descended, however remotely, from Greek ancestors. They identified non-Greek gods with their closest Greek equivalents, reinterpreted what local informants told them in Greek terms and produced a Greek affiliation that, within its own Hellenocentric terms, was scientifically arrived at.[12]

Apollonius wrote a *Foundation* (Κτίσις) of Alexandria and another of Naucratis (of which, unfortunately, we know nothing), and a *Canobus*, on the catasterism of Menelaus's steersman, killed by a snake-bite when he set foot on Egyptian soil.[13] Theocritus too wrote on Helen and Menelaus, the only documented Egyptian entry into Homeric saga (Ch. XVI. 4). Naturally enough, Posidippus and Callimachus wrote numerous epigrams on new Alexandrian monuments. But surprisingly little of Callimachus's *aetiological* poetry is in fact devoted to constructing a Hellenic past for the Ptolemaic kingdom.[14] As already noted, no attempt to provide a respectable Greek ancestry for Sarapis. If this was an issue that mattered to the Ptolemies, it does not look as if they told their poets. The kings seem to have been more concerned to stress their descent from the Argead royal line of Macedon—more remotely from Heracles and Dionysus. These are themes that run right through Hellenistic poetry (Ch. IX. 2).

In modern times the Alexandrian poets have never been counted among the classics.[15] Indeed, the fact that so little Hellenistic literature of any sort survives has often been presumed a natural consequence of the gradual and inevitable disappearance of the second rate. Even today it is not always suf-

11. For a brief selection, A.H.M. Jones, *The Greek City* (Oxford 1940), 49-50; § 3.
12. "Origines Gentium," *CP* 47 (1952), 65-81.
13. F 1-3 Powell, with D. A. van Krevelen, *Rhein. Mus.* 104 (1961), 128-31.
14. For Egyptian themes in Callimachus, Koenen 1993.
15. Kassel 1987; on modern prejudices, R. Pfeiffer, *JHS* 75 (1955), 69-71.

ficiently appreciated that the process was neither gradual nor inevitable. Rather it was sudden, early and deliberate—as early indeed as the Roman conquest. In a phrase of Pliny well known to art historians, the art of statuary "ceased" in the 121st (296-93) and "revived" in the 156th Olympiad (156-153).[16] This opinion reflects the perspective of a Greek source written not long after the supposed revival, probably the mid first-century neoclassicist Pasiteles. There is a similar gap in Pliny's account of painting.[17] According to Dionysius of Halicarnassus, "from the death of Alexander of Macedon, [rhetoric] began to lose its power and wither away"—a judgment reflecting the rejection of the so-called Asiatic style by the "Atticists" of the late first century.[18] In the same way, ignoring such important writers as Hieronymus of Cardia and Polybius, Quintilian's list of Greek historians leaps "after a long interval" from the age of Alexander to the Augustan Timagenes.[19] Then there is the strange passage in which Menecles of Barca describes an "eclipse" of culture under the Successors, terminated by a "revival" following Euergetes II's expulsion of the scholars of Alexandria in 146.[20] Pfeiffer noted the paradox of this (real enough) Alexandrian diaspora,[21] but did not explain the preceding "eclipse." For despite the "unsettled conditions" cited as explanation by Menecles, the age of the Successors was after all (by modern if not Roman standards) the golden age of Hellenistic literature, scholarship and art.

Modern scholars have often posited a radical discontinuity between Hellenistic and earlier Greek culture—whence (they assume) all that editing, classifying and canonizing of what were now perceived as classics.[22] Yet (in Henrichs's words) there had been a "gradual recognition of old masters and an emerging notion of the classic" for a century and more before the age of Callimachus.[23] Not only is there no evidence that third-century art-

---

16. *cessavit deinde ars, ac rursus olympiade CLVI revixit*, NH 34. 52; cf. 35. 134-35; F. Preisshofen, "Kunsttheorie und Kunstbetrachtung," *Le classicisme à Rome aux 1ers siècles avant et après J.-C.* (Entretiens Fondation Hardt 25, Geneva 1979), 265-73.

17. K. Jex-Blake and E. Sellers, *The Elder Pliny's Chapters on the History of Art* (London 1896), lxxx; J. J. Pollitt, *The Ancient View of Greek Art* (New Haven 1974), 78-79; P. Gros, *RÉL* 56 (1978), 289-313.

18. *Or. vet.* 1, conceding at 4-6 that this style "made itself the key to civic honours and high office"; Bowersock in *Le classicisme à Rome* (1979), 57-75.

19. Quint. x. 1. 73-75; J. Hornblower, *Hieronymus of Cardia* (Oxford 1981), 1-2; O. Kroehnert, *Canonesne poetarum...fuerunt?* (Regim. 1897), 7, 35-37.

20. ἐκλειπούσης...ἀνανέωσις / *cessavit...revixit*, Menecles, *FGrH* 270 F 9 = Andron, *FGrH* 246 (Athen. 184BC).

21. Pfeiffer 1968, 252-53; it is uncertain whether ἐγκύκλιος παιδεία here refers to culture in general or simply education (Marrou, *Histoire de l'éducation dans l'antiquité*[6] [Paris 1965], 568 n. 2).

22. P. Bing, *The Well-Read Muse* (Göttingen 1988), 75 ("sense of rift...."); Zanker 1987, 21; G. Most, *Arion* n.s. 2 (1990), 54-55.

23. Henrich 1993 in Bulloch 1993, 178.

ists and writers thought of themselves as epigones living in a postclassical age. The real break came two centuries later. The end of the first century saw a classicizing revival in most areas of art and literature, accompanied by an often violent repudiation of the achievements (in many areas, notably sculpture, considerable) of the past two centuries. It seems clear that Roman patrons preferred the classics.[24] But the only sort of recent literature not affected was precisely the third-century poets.

The study of Roman Alexandrianism has for thirty years been dominated by a paper of Wendell Clausen. According to Clausen, Callimachus exercised no influence in his own lifetime or for almost two centuries after. His "poetic triumph...took place, long after his death, in Rome," more specifically in the circles of Catullus and Vergil.[25] The truth is very different. Callimachus is imitated by almost every Greek poet of the later third and second centuries, we now have almost 70 papyri, and only Homer is quoted more often by the grammarians. The fact that in addition he was imitated by Roman poets from as early as the second century (not just Ennius but Plautus, Lucilius and Catulus),[26] proves that he had been well known at Rome for a century before Catullus. It is in any case a mistake to consider Callimachus's influence in isolation. There was a regular school of Bucolici Graeci before Vergil, and Aratus was the object of continuous attention throughout the Hellenistic period (Ch. VIII. 2). Vergil knew and imitated Apollonius, Aratus, Nicander and Theocritus as well as Callimachus; Varro of Atax produced an adaptation of Apollonius's *Argonautica*; Aratus was known to Catullus's friend Cinna and translated by Cicero. And the epigrammatists were known in Rome at any rate since ca 100 B.C. through the *Garland* of Meleager.[27] In short, the entire range of Alexandrian poetry was familiar to Roman poets of the late Republic—and by no means only to the so-called New Poets.

A comprehensive explanation is required, and it is simple enough. The domination of fifth- and fourth-century poetry by the theatre meant that there were no non-dramatic classics from the golden age. As the theatre declined in both Greece and Rome, so the Alexandrians came to fill the vacuum in genres other than drama. For the Romans, if not for the moderns, the Alexandrians became classics. By the age of Augustus (if not before) Callimachus and Philitas were the classic elegists;[28] Apollonius,

24. P. Zanker, *The Power of Images in the Age of Augustus* (Ann Arbor 1988), 239f.

25. "Callimachus and Latin Poetry," *GRBS* 5 (1964), 181-96; Ziegler 1966, 30; Otis 1964, 19, with 396-98 (his claim that "all the papyri of Callimachus are relatively late," though repeated by Fantuzzi 1988, xxxiv, has been spectacularly disproved by recent finds).

26. J. Farrell, *Vergil's Georgics and the Traditions of Ancient Epic* (Oxford 1991), 297.

27. On Meleager's influence at Rome, see now my *Greek Anthology* 51-56.

28. See Pfeiffer's testimonia; the Greek canon was Callinus, Mimnermus, Philitas and Callimachus: Proclus in Phot. *Bibl.* 319b; and the tables in Kroehnert 1897, 6, 13, with Wilamowitz, *Textgeschichte der griechischen Lyriker* (Berlin 1900), 63-71. On Philitas, see now P.E. Knox, *PLILS* 7 (1993), 61-83.

Aratus and Nicander were added to the epic canon;[29] Theocritus was recognized as the inventor and master of bucolic; and the Alexandrian epigrammatists were no less the acknowledged masters of the genre they had reinvented.

Their Roman vogue did not last long, but in the Greek world Callimachus remained popular throughout the Roman period, not falling out of favour until the last days of Byzantium.[30] Only six hymns and a selection of epigrams have come down by manuscript tradition. Papyri have restored to us substantial fragments of *Hecale*, *Aetia* and *Iambi*, but the real difficulties of allusive poetry are only compounded by the tattered state of the fragments, and in modern times Callimachus has become a byword for obscurity.

The Victorians were content to condemn what they saw as his artificiality and lack of inspiration. "When I look at this stuff, I cannot decide whether it is the subject matter of his poetry or its language that I find more absurd and inept," claimed the Dutch purist C.G. Cobet in 1861.[31] Modern critics have simply rationalized this prejudice against the postclassical, arguing that Hellenistic poets composed for a different audience and in a different way. The most conspicuous sign of the gulf between classical and Hellenistic times (it is held) is the retreat of literature from public to private space, from the festival to the library. So (for example) the standard modern manual:[32]

> The position of the writer had changed fundamentally by the third century: poetry in particular was no longer written primarily for public performance....[but for] a select few attached to or associated with a royal court.

According to one recent study, the Alexandrian poets were "a marginal and privileged elite writing for their own amusement."[33] "Is the withdrawal of poets from the practical exercise of their art in the community to the solitude of the scholar's study [asks another] ...to be understood as a failure to live up to their responsibility in the new monarchies?"[34] Nor is it just literary scholars who have made such claims. For Claire Préaux too it was only in the royal courts and libraries that "not only the poets but also the readers of their poems" were to be found.[35]

---

29. Quint. x. 1. 54-56; for the Alexandrian canon, Kroehnert 1897, 19-21.

30. For the last known text of *Hecale* and *Aetia* ca 1205, Hollis 1990, 38-40.

31. *Mnem.* 10 (1861), 391. But it would be hard to top the patronizing letter by T. E. Page in Couat 1931, vi-ix: "call this Alexandrian poetry 'artificial,' 'uninspired,' or what you please, none the less in the *history*, at least, of poetry, its place is of the highest interest."

32. A. W. Bulloch, *CHCL* i (1985), 543.

33. Richard Hunter, *MD* 20 (1992), 33.

34. Gelzer 1993 in Bulloch 1993, 146.

35. *Le Monde Hellénistique* ii (Paris 1978), 674-75.

"Written in the library" is a neat enough *metaphor* for learned poetry, but there is not a scrap of evidence that any Hellenistic poet literally wrote in or for a library.[36] "Written for court" is likewise little more than a metaphor for poetry aimed at rulers. There is no direct evidence in Ptolemaic (as opposed to Roman) texts for court as an actual performance location—at any rate in the sense of private performance before a king and his officials and friends. The kings were in fact great promoters of public festivals,[37] and formal poetry in their honour was normally performed publicly in the cities. The Adonis song in Theocritus 15, though performed in the palace (αὐλά, 60), was not a formal presentation before king and court, but a song at the festival of the Adonia held by Arsinoë somewhere within the rambling palace complex but open to the public, who come and go (in large numbers) as they please. Court was wherever a ruler held court,[38] and there is abundant evidence that the most important location for occasional poetry remained the symposium (Ch. III).

There is no direct evidence about the primary, original audiences of the major Hellenistic poets. But (as we shall see) there is abundant evidence that lesser poets continued to perform their work publicly, and many passages in the major poets *imply* that they did the same. Modern critics systematically dismiss such passages without discussion as pretence or convention,[39] preferring their own purely conjectural assumptions about library and court:[40]

> *Since poets now had no function in society*....they treated the relationship to real occasions as part of the convention: so they composed hymns to the gods, without any idea of performing them, or they wrote epitaphs, without any idea of inscribing them on a gravestone, or they wrote symposiastic poetry, without having any real drinking party in mind [emphasis added].

This unargued dogma rests in the last analysis on nothing more solid than a feeling that sophisticated and allusive poetry *cannot* have been publicly performed, that it was "by its very nature, poetry to be read."[41] We might bear in mind that much of Pindar and Aeschylus is also difficult, if in a different way. No one surely would wish to revive the simplistic Victorian assumption of universal Hellenistic decadence, embracing art and philosophy as well as literature, writers and audience alike.[42]

---

36. Actually we know almost nothing about the form or function of libraries at this period. It was certainly not in the library that Callimachus found his wit, his personal style and the original and influential narrative mode of his longer poems.

37. For the dynastic festivals established by the early Ptolemies, Koenen 1993, 74-6; F. Perpillou-Thomas, *Fêtes d'Égypte ptolémaïque et romaine* (Louvain 1993), 151-62.

38. For all that is known about the court of the first three Ptolemies, see now Weber, *Dichtung und höfische Gesellschaft* (Stuttgart 1993).

39. The only exception in recent years is Cairns 1984, 150 and 1992, 14-16.

40. G. Williams, *Tradition and Originality in Roman Poetry* (Oxford 1968), 35.

41. Gelzer 1993, 144; cf. the judgments on Callimachus's hymns cited below, § 8.

42. For example, according to a review in the *Westminster Gazette* preserved in my copy

2

Another common image in modern discussions is that of the ivory tower.[43] This too is pure modern assumption. But there is one well-known text which has often been cited as if it lent some support, from the *Silloi* of Timon of Phlius:[44]

πολλοὶ μὲν βόσκονται ἐν Αἰγύπτῳ πολυφύλῳ
βιβλιακοὶ χαρακῖται ἀπείριτα δηριόωντες
Μουσέων ἐν ταλάρῳ.

This passage is usually interpreted as follows:

Many bookish scribblers are fed in populous Egypt, forever squabbling in the birdcage of the Muses.

The image has always been identified as "rare birds, remote and precious creatures" kept in a zoo, cut off from real life,[45] and it has been assumed that this was the view of Athenaeus, who quotes the fragment. But all Athenaeus actually says is that Timon was satirizing "the philosophers who were kept (τρεφομένους) there, because they were fed (σιτοῦνται) like very costly (πολυτιμότατοι) birds in a hen-coop."[46] Now Philadelphus is known to have bred exotic birds, as several other passages of Athenaeus bear witness; parrots, peacocks, guinea-fowl and pheasants were carried in cages during the great procession of Philadelphus in 275/4 described by Callixenus of Rhodes.[47] But most of these birds were bred to *eat*.[48] βόσκονται in the fragment and τρεφομένους and σιτοῦνται in Athenaeus's commentary

of Ferguson's *Hellenistic Athens* (London 1911), it would have been "better to draw a veil" over the "miserable fall...of a city which had...contributed so much to civilisation."

43. Sainte-Beuve was apparently "the first to use the phrase for the seclusion of an unworldly poet," Pfeiffer 1968, 283, at p. 98 (cf. *JHS* 75 [1955], 73) mildly protesting at its "strangely fashionable" application to Hellenistic poets.

44. *SH* 786 = F 12 in M. Di Marco, *Timone di Fliunte: Silli* (Rome 1989).

45. L. Canfora, *The Vanished Library* (London 1989), 37 (his chapter on the Museum is entitled "In the Cage of the Muses"); Di Marco 1989, 139-43; Lloyd-Jones and Parsons on *SH* 786; a "gilded cage" according to Delia, *AHR* 97 (1992), 1452.

46. ἐπισκώπτων τοὺς ἐν αὐτῷ [sc. ταλάρῳ] τρεφομένους φιλοσόφους, ὅτι ὥσπερ ἐν πανάγρῳ τινὶ σιτοῦνται καθάπερ οἱ πολυτιμότατοι ὄρνιθες (Athen. 22D). πάναγρον (elsewhere = net) could presumably be used for any sort of enclosure for animals.

47. Athen. 201B; 387D; E. E. Rice, *The Grand Procession of Ptolemy Philadelphus* (Oxford 1983), 86-95; date calculated by Victoria Foertmeyer, *Historia* 37 (1988), 90-104.

48. Athen. 654C, 398C-F; Rice 1983, 87; D'Arcy W. Thompson, *Glossary of Greek Birds* (Oxford 1936), s.v. μελεαγρίς, τέταρος, τέτραξ, φασιανός.

strongly suggest that it is a farm, not a zoo that Timon has in mind. The point is not the *seclusion* of these birds as oddities, but their value as delicacies for the table.

W. H. Mineur points out that the word τάλαρος is elsewhere normally used of an *open* basket,[49] and so unlikely to be applied to a closed birdcage.[50] In the context, it is surely a birds*nest*. The hapax χαρακῖται,[51] even if correctly derived from χάραξ = "stake" or "fence," need not bear the monastic associations of its usual translation "cloisterlings." Such a word could suggest the fences of a farm as easily as the cages of a zoo.[52] βιβλιακοί may conceal a double allusion, birds nesting in the papyrus-marshes, but also bookish scribblers.

The final touch rests in the two verbs. First δηριόωντες, an epic term meaning "dispute," sometimes verbally, sometimes physically, with the object of dispute often expressed.[53] Second, βόσκονται. While certainly depreciating at a metaphorical level the salaries of the new Museum professors,[54] at its primary level in the newly established context the word surely evokes a nest full of young birds squawking incessantly in their rivalry for the scraps of food in the parent-bird's beak. Every word now plays its part in building up this vivid picture. There is no suggestion of *caged* birds, of unworldly scholars shut away in a library.[55] The emphasis falls rather on the rivalry and polemic of Alexandrian scholars, amply documented in the *Aetia* prologue and *Iambi* 1 and 13. To be sure a classic case of the pot calling the kettle black, since Timon's *Silloi* are themselves nothing but polemic, a satirical review of almost all ancient philosophers.[56] Polemic was the life blood of third-century intellectuals of every sort (Ch. III. 5).

A recent book by Peter Bing attempts to reinforce current orthodoxy in terms of a different polarity, book culture versus oral culture. There are

49. "From Book-Worms to Reed Warblers," *Mnemosyne* 38 (1985), 383-87; Gow, *Theocritus* II (1952), 107; W. G. Arnott, *CQ* 21 (1971), 156f.

50. He overlooked Athen. 398F, where the company is shown a live pheasant ἐν ταλάρῳ before it is cooked; but this is many centuries later, and Athenaeus may have been echoing his own earlier quotation of Timon.

51. Identified by Mineur as a type of bird, the Great Reed Warbler, known in Dutch as "karekeit," a name "that closely imitates the sound it makes"; it is a quarrelsome bird, notable for "continual aggressive behaviour towards other Great Reed Warblers nesting in the neighbourhood," and builds a nest that "has the form of an open woven basket." But the name is not otherwise known, and such birds were not bred to eat.

52. The alternative interpretation "scribblers" (Pfeiffer, Canfora) seems less likely; as Di Marco 1989, 141 notes, "i sostantivi in -ίτης sono denominativi, e per χάραξ (= "palizzata") non è mai documentato il significata di "calamo.""

53. ἐκπάγλοις ἐπέεσσιν (of Odysseus and Achilles), θ. 76; περὶ νεκροῦ, P. 734; ἀμφ' οὔροισι (of boundaries), M. 421; περὶ Κεβριόναο, M. 756 (with Janko ad loc.).

54. Not to be pressed; it was the quarrelsomeness of the members of the Museum that was Timon's main concern. Kings and tyrants had always supported poets and philosophers.

55. *incolae Musei vallis saepti, libris incumbentes*, Diels, *Po. Phil. Frag.* (1901), 186.

56. See Di Marco 1989, 32f. for this aspect of the *Silloi*.

instructive pages on the penetration of writing terms into the metaphors of poetic inspiration. For example, the Muses learning to write in epigrams of Posidippus and Asclepiades; a passage in the *Aetia* where Callimachus invites the Graces to wipe on his elegies the oil that drips from their hair to their hands.[57] Certainly these poets are picturing their works in the form of a written text, but are we really entitled to infer that they envisaged *only* readers, readers *instead of* (rather than merely as well as) listeners?[58]

Bing also cited acrostichs and figure poems as examples of what he describes as a "sudden efflorescence of purely visual phenomena."[59] To take figure poems first, the shapes that so catch the eye on the modern printed page[60] are obtained by varying the length of successive lines by adding or subtracting metrical units. Thus the ps-Theocritean *Syrinx*, the *Altars* of Besantinos and Dosiadas,[61] and the *Organ* of Optatianus Porfyrius. It has always been assumed that the earliest examples date from the age of Callimachus. Yet it would be surprising if such an enterprise had originated in an age when non-stichic verse texts were copied in continuous lines that took no account of metrical units.[62]

Only three of the traditional corpus of figure poems are certainly ascribed to a third-century poet, Callimachus's contemporary Simias of Rhodes.[63] But they differ in important ways from the *Syrinx* and *Altars*. We may begin with the so-called *Wings of Eros*, six lines of decreasing followed by six of increasing length, the second six metrical pairs to the first six. To me at least its two halves do not in the least look like a pair of

---

57. *SH* 705; *AP* ix. 63; Call. F 7. 11-14; Bing, *The Well-Read Muse* (1988), 15-20.

58. As Bing himself acknowledges (p. 16), "book-rolls appear as attributes of the Muses in vase-painting as early as ca 459 B.C."

59. Bing, 1988, 15 with *HSCP* 93 (1990), 281-82; see too his analysis of Castorion's hymn to Pan (*SH* 310), *AJP* 106 (1985), 502-09. It is characteristic that, while insisting that its playful, learned features are not inconsistent with "genuine religious feeling," Bing takes it for granted that they are inconsistent with performance. More on acrostichs: Ch. XI. 4.

60. "concrete poetry," according to M. M. DeForest, *Apollonius's Argonautica: A Callimachean Epic* (Leiden 1994), 20.

61. Against Theocritean authorship of the *Syrinx*, Gow, *Theocr.* I. 553-54 (with West, *Ancient Greek Music* [1992], 111); Dosiadas is earlier than Lucian (*Lex.* 25), but even if identified with the Cretan historian of that name (*FGrH* 458), otherwise undatable.

62. Turner, *GMAW*[2] 12; the Lille Stesichorus (ca 250, no. 74) is the earliest example of a lyric poem copied out in lines that coincide with its metrical units.

63. *AP* xv. 22, 24 and 27; oldest MS *AP* (my *Greek Anthology* 321), but also in a number of bucolic MSS. In addition to the texts of Legrand, Gallavotti, Gow and Beckby, see H. Fränkel, *De Simia Rhodio* (Göttingen 1915) and G. Wojaczek, *Daphnis* (Meisenheim 1969); on their metres, West, *Greek Metre* 151. Manuscripts offer alternative ascriptions (*Greek Anthology* 306), but Simias is guaranteed by Hephaestion for all three (p. 31. 5 and 8; 62. 5; 68. 12 Consbruch). The form with one μ is put beyond doubt by the material in *LGPN* 406 (common throughout the islands and especially at Rhodes, while double μ appears in only one restored inscription at Cyrene); on his date, *HE* II. 511.

wings on a standing Eros; if anything, disembodied wings seen horizontally:

λεῦσσέ με τὸν Γᾶς τε βαθυστέρνου ἄνακτ', 'Ακμονίδαν ἄλλυδις ἑδράσαντα·
μηδὲ τρέσῃς, εἰ τόσος ὢν δάσκια βέβριθα λάχνᾳ γένεια.
τᾶμος ἐγὼ γὰρ γενόμαν, ἁνίκ' ἔκραιν' 'Ανάγκα.
πάντα δὲ Γᾶς εἶκε φραδαῖσι λυγραῖς
ἑρπετά, πάνθ', ὅσ' ἔρπει
δι' αἴθρας.
Χάους δέ,
οὔτι γε Κύπριδος παῖς
ὠκυπέτας οὐδ' Ἄρεος καλεῦμαι·
οὔτι γὰρ ἔκρανα βίᾳ, πραϋνόῳ δὲ πειθοῖ·
εἶκε δέ μοι Γαῖα Θαλάσσας τε μυχοὶ χάλκεος Οὐρανός τε·
τῶν δ' ἐγὼ ἐκνοσφισάμαν ὠγύγιον σκᾶπτρον, ἔκρινον δὲ θεοῖς θέμιστας.

The content is no less puzzling:

> Look at me, the lord of broad-bosomed earth, who established the son of Akmon [Uranus, the sky] elsewhere, and tremble not if, tiny though I am, my cheeks are heavy with bushy hair. For I was born when Necessity ruled, and all creeping things and those that move through the sky yielded to the dire decrees of earth. But I am called the swift-flying son of Chaos, not of Cypris or Ares, for I did not rule by force, but by gentle-voiced persuasion, and earth and the depths of the sea and the brazen heaven yielded to me. I robbed them of their ancient sceptre and gave laws to the gods (W. R. Paton, Loeb).

The Eros of the old cosmogonies and Plato (*Symp.* 178b), not the Hellenistic putto. But there is not a word to suggest that it is Eros's *wings* the epigram is describing. No more than a passing reference to the fact that he is "swift-flying"; the emphasis falls rather on his unusual beard. The solution, as Wilamowitz saw long ago,[64] is that the poem itself is neither about nor intended to represent the wings of Eros: rather it was inscribed *on* the wings of a statue of Eros.

Reitzenstein raised the banal objection that the inscription to a statue should be on its base.[65] Most are (of course), but certainly not all. Three hexameters are inscribed boustrophedon across the right thigh of an archaic female statue from Naxos; a hexameter runs down the hem of the cloak on four archaic statues of Hera from Samos;[66] a late second-century Tyche from Susa is prominently signed by the artist across her crown.[67] For inscriptions adapted to the shape of the object, we have the circular base of

64. *JDAI* 14 (1899), 51-59; *Textg. gr. Buk.* (1906), 243-45; Fränkel 1915, 57-59, 83.
65. *RE* 6. 1 (1907), 83.
66. *CEG* i. 403 and 422-23, with addenda in ii (pp. 303-04); *CEG* 326.
67. R.R.R. Smith, *Hellenistic Sculpture* (London 1991), fig. 281; the Belvedere Torso of ca 200 is signed on the rock it sits on (ib. fig. 165); cf. the earthenware stele from Metapontum (ca 500), *CEG* 396, with Hansen, *ZPE* 58 (1985), 231-33; and *CEG* 344.

a late fifth-century Attic scyphus inscribed with two lines of verse in three concentric circles, with the final letter in the centre;[68] and a verse inscribed round the perforated base of a late fourth-century pottery lamp from Gela that reads "I belong to Pausanias the best of buggers," where the central hole takes on a new meaning in the light of the inscription that encircles it.[69] Obviously the Eros in question was a special statue, with wings designed for inscription.

Axe, which purports to be a dedication by Epeius of the axe he used to make the wooden horse, consists of six pairs of lines, each pair one metrical unit shorter than its predecessor. It looks like an up-ended triangle—if the lines are centered, an equilateral triangle and so not unlike an axehead. This can hardly be coincidence, and once more, it was surely intended for inscription on a real axehead, a facsimile of Epeius's dedication (said to have been made in a temple of Athena at Metapontum). We do in fact have an exact parallel, a neatly inscribed archaic axehead from Calabria.[70]

Egg consists of ten pairs of lines, each pair one metrical unit longer than the last, a structure spelled out in the poem itself (7-10 and 20). So written, *Egg* too looks like a large (if irregular) triangle. Once again, it could have been written (as Wilamowitz assumed) for inscription around the circumference of an egg-shaped object.[71] We might picture a model egg set in a stand and inscribed only on its top half, with each line of each pair inscribed in the same circle but on opposite sides.[72]

But in Byzantine manuscripts and modern editions each pair in both *Axe* and *Egg* is split up and the lines rearranged. So written, the two longest lines in *Axe* come first and last respectively and the two shortest in the centre. In this form (which of course is unintelligible), it looks like a double axehead. In *Egg* the two shortest come first and last respectively and the two longest in the centre; that is to say, the lines have to be read in the order 1, 3, 5, 7, 9...19, 21, 22, 20...6, 4, 2. Once again, in this form it is unintelligible, nor does it even look much like an egg.[73]

---

68. *CEG* 893, now lost; for Leake's sketch, Vanderpool, *Hesperia* 36 (1967), 187-89.

69. εἰμὶ δὲ Παυσανία τὸ καταπυγοτάτο, *CEG* 896, with Hansen's note; *CEG* 355.

70. Lycophron, *Alex*. 948-50; [Arist.] *Hist. mir*. 108; Justin, *Epit*, 20. 2. 1; Fränkel, *De Simia* 68, arguing that all derive from Timaeus, whom we may suppose known to Simias as he was to Callimachus.

71. "Ich habe in meinem Leben manches Osterei beschrieben," Wilamowitz 1906, 245; *JDAI* 1899, 56; cf. too Gow, *Bucolici graeci* (1952), 179, "Versus ouo solido circumscribendi."

72. The best way to inscribe a long text on an egg-shaped object would be in one continuous line, so that the reader could simply turn the object round as he read and follow the text with his finger. But this would not require any particular metrical form or line length.

73. Rather "une sorte de losange qui ne ressemble à rien," Legrand, *Bucoliques grecs* ii (1927), 223. By contrast, the reverse of anacyclica like *AP* vi. 314 (Πηνελόπη, τόδε σοὶ φᾶρος καὶ χλαῖναν Ὀδυσσεὺς / ἤνεγκεν δολιχὴν ἐξανύσας ἀτραπόν) can easily be constructed in the mind (ἀτραπὸν ἐξανύσας δολιχήν...); my *Greek Anthology* 123.

If Simias had wished to construct a poem that followed the outline of an egg on paper, he could just as easily have engineered ten lines in increasing followed by ten in decreasing length to start with. This is indeed precisely the structure of *Wings*, six split pairs of the same metrical unit as originally written, with no need for rearrangement. If he could do this for *Wings*, why not for *Egg* and *Axe*? Given their identical structure, we are surely bound to read all three poems the same way.[74]

Nothing in the text suggests the need for any such drastic rearrangement.[75] *Egg* describes itself as an egg (the "new warp of a twittering mother, a Dorian nightingale"), but (of course) a metaphorical egg, a poem written by a Dorian poet (Simias). There is no hint in the text that *Egg* (any more than *Axe* or *Wings*) resembled its subject in any way. There are indeed emphatic pointers—but to the metrical complexity of the poem, not its shape.[76] Hermes "took it up from beneath its dear mother's wings and cast it among the tribes of men and bade it increase...from a one-footed measure to a full ten." He beats out the metre with his feet, and his movement is then elaborately compared to newly born fawns galloping through mountain pastures (13-19), recapitulated in the final line, "stamping like them with swift feet the famous god let go the manifold measures of the song." The emphasis on speed and rhythm in fully two thirds of the poem makes it hard to believe that the poet kept (or expected readers to keep) the opening image of an egg in mind.[77]

The *Altar* poems are quite different. Not only does the text explicitly draw attention to its shape; this shape "corresponds not only to the block of the altar itself with its flat upper surface but also to the projecting cornice mouldings and base mouldings."[78] That is to say, whereas *Axe* and *Wings* purport to be inscriptions for (and so on) their respective objects, the *Altars* do not; like *Syrinx* and *Organ*, they are the object itself. Almost all ancient poems that harbour any sort of concealed dimension offer some such pointer in the context, understandably enough given the lack of punctuation and other typographic devices in ancient texts.[79]

---

74. A scholion remarks that *Wings* has to be read differently from *Axe* and *Egg*.

75. Another way of obtaining the shape on paper was suggested by Legrand: an elliptical spiral read from the centre outwards, so that the reader has to turn his text 180 degrees from line to line (*Bucoliques grecs* ii [1927], 225-56; Wojaczek, *Daphnis* [1969], 58, 145). But this is hardly more intelligible than the Byzantine arrangement—as anyone who tries to read Wojaczek's transcription will discover.

76. West, *Greek Metre* 151.

77. According to Wojaczek 1969, 75, the shape was meant to portray the Orphic world-egg! It is no more than coincidence (and hardly surprising) that alphabetical letter-patterns turn up on magical papyri (pp. 61-3), and implausible (not to say absurd) to claim that figure poems "in einen kultischen Zusammenhang gehören" (p. 60).

78. John Onians, *Art and Thought in the Hellenistic Age* (London 1979), 110.

79. For a number of illustrations, Cameron, "Ancient Anagrams," *AJP* 116 (1995).

It was (I suggest) not till the early empire, when figure poems were an established phenomenon, that some ingenious person, having identified *Axe*'s original triangular shape as an axehead, and *Wings*, turned sideways, as a pair of wings, was inspired by a literal interpretation of the metaphor in line 2 to look for ovoid contours in *Egg*. Splitting the metrical pairs into balancing triangles at one stroke improved *Axe* into a double axehead and created (more or less) the desired egg in *Egg*. The idea is no more convincing for being known to the second-century metrical writer Hephaestion (who cites it as a feature of "Simias's *Egg* and other παίγνια").[80]

So Simias's *Wings*, *Axe* and *Egg* are not really figure poems at all. Like many short pieces by Callimachus, Theocritus and other early third-century poets, they were written for inscription and intended to demonstrate metrical virtuosity.[81] Such poetry is certainly experimental, not to say artificial, but the conventional label "book lyric" unnecessarily restricts its medium and function.[82] We may compare an epigram by Callimachus in an otherwise unparalleled seven-syllable metre on an empty quiver, dedicated to Sarapis by a Cretan archer who had fought in a western war.[83] Of all Callimachus's epigrams this is the one most likely to have been a genuine inscribed dedication, and it is tempting to infer from the exceptionally short lines inscription on the quiver itself.[84] The figure poem is perhaps after all an invention of the Roman rather than Hellenistic age.

As for acrostichs,[85] to start with they are certainly pre-Hellenistic, indeed pre-Hellenic (the earliest known are Babylonian). While undeniably a feature of written texts, they are by no means a sign of refinement. On the contrary, in origin they are simply a device for claiming authorship, also common in oracular and magical literature (probably from a much earlier date than the surviving examples).[86] An acrostich requires no great skill from its creator and makes few demands on the reader. The point was not that they should be admired (sometimes indeed they were deliberately concealed),[87] but that they could be produced in proof (or disproof) of authenticity—or even something so banal as evidence for the spelling of a name.[88] They were later to become a central element in Byzantine hymnography.[89] They are particularly common in inscriptional verse, normally

80. Heph. pp. 61. 19f. = 68. 7f.; M. Consbruch, *Bresl. Phil. Abh.* 5. 3 (1890), 80.

81. For a useful list of the metrical experiments of this age (classified under the heading "book lyric"), West, *Greek Metre* 149-52.

82. Note the Palatine scholion to *Egg*: παραινεῖ ὁ ποιητὴς τὸν ἀκροατήν...

83. On the various hypotheses about this campaign, Laronde 1987, 396.

84. So Wilamowitz 1899, 59; *HD* II. 120; Gow was sceptical, *HE* II. 174.

85. For a useful list, E. Courtney, *Philologus* 134 (1990), 3-13.

86. A. Kurfess and Th. Klauser, *RAC* I (1950), 235-38.

87. D. L. 5. 93 for an acrostich concealing a lover's name—as still sometimes happens.

88. Suetonius, *De gramm.* 6 (Opillius rather than Opilius).

89. W. Weyh, *Byz. Zeit.* 17 (1908), 1-68.

to give added prominence to the name of the honorand. The earliest known epigraphic example is a dedication by the orator Aeschines;[90] the earliest literary example an author-acrostich in an early third-century papyrus of the fourth-century tragedian Chaeremon.[91] It is true that Aristotle characterized Chaeremon's plays as better read than acted, but this does not mean they were not written in the first instance for the stage. Indeed there is epigraphic evidence that they were.[92] So it was with Hellenistic poetry. Much of it was no doubt better read, but that does not mean that it was not written in the first instance for performance of one sort or another.

The acrostichs in Nicander are simply traditional author-signatures, and while one of the two in Aratus highlights a literary term (Ch. XI. 4), they are still no more than purely external embellishments added to long poems for publication,[93] telling us nothing about earlier performance contexts. They do not seem to have attracted much attention in antiquity (overlooked, for example, in the full and learned scholia on the two poets). In short, there is nothing characteristically "Alexandrian" about acrostichs; no trace in such poets as Apollonius, Callimachus, Lycophron or Theocritus.

Not only is there no direct, explicit evidence of any kind for this supposed privileging of writing in the Hellenistic poets. In a remarkable fragment of the *Hecale* (F 282 = 109 H) Callimachus himself, diverging (perhaps polemically) from the majority view on a controversial issue, firmly states that ears are more reliable than eyes.[94] At F 43. 16-17, when recalling the food, drink and garlands of a symposium, he remarks that all he has retained is "what I put in my ears"; and at F 178. 30 he talks of "holding his ears ready for any who wish to tell a tale." Three centuries later Strabo renewed the polemic, perhaps indirectly inspired by Callimachus, since he elsewhere quotes the line from F 178.[95] Whatever may lie behind the *Hecale* passage, it does not look as if it was a sheet of papyrus rather than a living audience that Callimachus saw as his primary target.[96]

---

90. *AP* vi. 330 (missed by Courtney), partially preserved as *IG* iv² 255, with C. A. Forbes, *AJP* 88 (1967), 443-48; J. Irigoin, *Recueil Plassart* (Paris 1976), 119-23; *CEG* 776.

91. F 14b Snell (*TrGrF* i), with Snell, *Szenen aus griech. Dramen* (Berlin 1971), 158-68.

92. *Poet.* 1413*b*3; *SIG* 3 ed. 1080 v; Snell 1971, 158-59; O. Zwierlein, *Die Rezitationsdramen Senecas* (Meisenheim 1966), 128-34.

93. Neither at nor anywhere near the beginning or end of the poems. I suggest that when revising for publication both poets selected passages where two or three initial letters already stood in sequence and then rewrote the necessary adjacent lines accordingly (compare Page's account of the mechanics of isopsepha, *FGE* 505-6).

94. Hollis ad loc.; Fraenkel, *Horace* (1957), 393 n. 3; Walbank on Polyb. xii. 27.

95. ii. 5. 11, making the point that, despite his own extensive travels, the greater part of his material nonetheless comes from ἀκοή: M. Laffranque, "La vue et l'ouïe," *Rev. Philos.* 153 (1963), 75-82; F 178. 30, quoted in Strabo ix. 5. 18.

96. As we shall see in § 5 below, in the right context ἀκοή may imply reading, but never reading as distinct from listening.

3

"I loathe everything public," wrote Callimachus in a famous epigram.[97] According to Simon Goldhill, this represents a deliberate, self-conscious "turning away from the public poetry of the fifth century," a "gesture of withdrawal from the persona of the public *sophos*, who speaks out to the citizen body" (it is Aristophanes he has in mind).[98] F. T. Griffiths quotes the same epigram in support of the even more extravagant claim that "both the poets and their detractors agreed that intellectuals were and should be kept at a safe distance from public life."[99] But (as we shall see in more detail in Ch. XIV), though it begins by misdirecting us to literature, this poem is really about love. Even so the only sort of literature it mentions is Cyclic poetry, already condemned by Aristotle.[100] There is no conceivable justification for extending the literary reference to Attic drama—especially when so many other epigrams by both Callimachus and other Alexandrians tell such a different story (§ 7).

It is perhaps understandable that, in his schematic pursuit of the "poet's voice" down the centuries, Goldhill should jump from Aristophanes to Callimachus, but in the real world they are separated by 150 years. Why should Callimachus wish to repudiate the voice of Aristophanes simply because he wrote a different sort of poetry himself—and why so obliquely and so long after it had in any case fallen out of fashion? It was New Comedy that dominated the Hellenistic and (later) Roman stage. Aristophanes was read and interpreted by scholars, but barred by his topicality and extensive use of the now defunct chorus from being re-performed.[101]

Callimachus admired and imitated Aristophanes despite his fall from popular favour (Ch. XI. 5; XVII. 1). Goldhill goes on to claim that "intellectual exclusivity...is as integral to the contextualization of Hellenistic writing as the values and institutions of collectivity and openness are to fifth-century theatre" (p. 224). But there is no point in comparing the sort of Alexandrian poetry that survives (elegy, idyll, epigram) with Attic drama. It is a regrettable fact, but the private poetry of the fifth century and

---

97. ἐχθαίρω τὸ ποίημα τὸ κυκλικὸν....σικχαίνω πάντα τὰ δημόσια, *AP* xii. 43.

98. Goldhill 1991, 223-24; on σοφός of poets, Dover, *Ar. Frogs* (1993), 12-13.

99. Griffiths 1979, 2. For a similar view, Schwinge 1986, passim.

100. Here again see Ch. XIV for more detail.

101. J. Maidment, *CQ* 29 (1935), 13-14; J. Henderson, *Ar. Lysistrata* (1987), lx-lxiii; according to Dover, "one, and only one, copy of *Frogs* (containing major errors) was available to the first generation of scholars at Alexandria; and...all subsequent copies of the play whatsoever were exclusively derived from that copy" (*Ar. Frogs* [1993], 86-87). A revealing statistic (kindly communicated to me by P. Mertens from the forthcoming Pack[3]): of the 75 Menander papyri, 81% are earlier than 300 A.D.; of the 38 Aristophanes papyri, 68% are later than 300.

the drama of the Hellenistic age have alike perished, thus precluding any meaningful comparison.[102] But enough is known of the latter to suggest that any such radical antithesis between openness and exclusivity is a serious oversimplification.

It is pointless to assert (with Préaux) that Aristophanes would have been "unthinkable" in the Hellenistic age. It may be tempting to see the progression from Old to New Comedy in terms of the decline of Athenian democracy in the age of kings.[103] But it would be nearer the truth to see New Comedy as the culmination of a series of changes that arose out of the ever growing popularity of Attic Drama. Theatres sprang up all over the Hellenistic world, and though Athens remained the dramatic capital, many of the poets who flourished there came from other cities and knew their plays would be performed the length and breadth of Hellenistic Greece.[104] This is the main reason New Comedy ceased to concern itself exclusively with the details of Athenian public life. It was less its politics than its intrusive topicality that killed the parabasis (already dropped from the later plays of Aristophanes);[105] it was developments in music and the desire for more realistic plot and characterization that led to the rapid relegation of the chorus to musical interludes.[106]

Not that fourth-century comedy was quite so apolitical as usually supposed. Just as Socrates was mocked by Aristophanes and Eupolis, so we find Zeno, Cleanthes and Epicurus mocked by Philemon, Baton and Posidippus.[107] In 301 Philippides attacked Demetrius for his disgraceful behaviour in the Parthenon and Stratocles for the divine honours he had proposed for Demetrius;[108] Archedicus accused Demochares of fellatio ca 290,[109] and Phoenicides attacked a secret treaty between Antigonus Gonatas and Pyrrhus ca 285.[110] Alexis and Philemon attacked the obsession of Alexander's notorious minister Harpalus with the hetaira Pythionice (Athen. 594D), and Python attacked Harpalus in a satyr-play performed at Alexander's camp.[111] What did disappear for good was the fantasy and

102. So already Hutchinson 1988, 10.

103. "Tragedy and Comedy...were too inextricably interwoven with the political and religious life of the *polis* to be able to survive its dissolution," Giangrande, *SMA* I. 289.

104. A. W. Pickard-Cambridge, *The Dramatic Festivals of Athens*[2] (Oxford 1988), 279f.; G. M. Sifakis, *Studies in the History of Hellenistic Drama* (London 1967); G. Xanthakis-Karamanos, *Studies in fourth-century Tragedy* (Athens 1980), 4-6.

105. Taken by Gelzer 1993, 136 to be "direct evidence for the inner connection between the crisis of poetry and the crisis of the πόλις."

106. M. Silk, *YCS* 27 (1980), 148-49; Dover, *Aristophanic Comedy* (1972), 193-95.

107. T.B.L. Webster, *Studies in Later Greek Comedy*[2] (Manchester 1970), 110-13; I. Gallo, *Vichiana* n.s. 5 (1976), 206-42; Habicht 1988, 9-11.

108. F 25-26 = *PCG* vii (1989), 347; G. Philipp, *Gymnasium* 80 (1973), 492-509.

109. Polyb. xii. 13; C. Habicht, *Hesperia* 62 (1993), 253-56.

110. F 1 = *PCG* VII (1989), 389; Tarn 1913, 115-16.

111. B. Snell, *Scenes from Greek Drama* (Berkeley 1964), 99-138; Ch. I. 2.

obscenity of Old Comedy, features irreconcilable with the Comedy of Manners of New Comedy in a way that political allusions were not.

One of the more versatile of Callimachus's colleagues at the Museum was Lycophron of Chalcis. Best known for the most obscure surviving Greek poem (a 1474-line messenger speech containing 518 words that appear nowhere else in Greek literature), he was one of Philadelphus's tireless cataloguers. Yet he was also a serious tragedian, and wrote at least two plays on contemporary themes, one tragedy and one satyr-play. Among the twenty tragedies listed in his Suda-entry appears the title *Kassandreis*. This would not be an appropriate form to designate children of Cassandra, even if any such had survived.[112] But it is the standard form for the inhabitants of the city of Cassandreia, founded in 315 by Cassander. Now ca 280 a certain Apollodorus seized the city. He is presented as the classic tyrant, said to have tricked his fellow conspirators into eating the flesh of a youth he had butchered. After ruling with monstrous cruelty, he dreamed of being flayed and boiled by Scythians while his daughters danced around him with their bodies glowing like coals.[113] After a long siege Antigonus Gonatas captured the city with the aid of a famous pirate. Since these picturesque details suggest tragic themes, and since Lycophron is known to have lived for a spell at the court of Gonatas, it is hard to resist Niebuhr's suggestion that the *Kassandreis* dramatized the story of the rise and fall of Apollodorus. Given the devotion of the Macedonians to live theatre,[114] there is no reason to doubt that the play was actually staged. We also have fragments from a satyr-play by Lycophron on another contemporary theme, his teacher Menedemus of Eretria.[115] Sositheus wrote a satyr-play poking fun at the famous Stoic Cleanthes.[116]

Philitas, first of the scholar-poets of Alexandria, was enough of a celebrity to be made fun of in a comedy by Strato written for the Athenian stage.[117] He was also honoured by a bronze statue on his native Cos.[118] Philicus of Corcyra provides another good illustration of the complex relationship between a Hellenistic poet and his community. On the one hand his only (partially) surviving work is an obscure hymn in a learned metre

112. Paus. 2. 16. 6 mentions the tomb of twin sons of Cassandra killed by Aegisthus immediately after their parents.

113. Polyaen. iv. 18; vi. 7. 1-2; Plut. *Mor.* 555B, 556D; Diod. 22. 5. 1-2.

114. For a useful collection of texts, Pickard-Cambridge 1988, 279-82; Xanthakis-Karamanos 1980, 13; Philip II's enthusiasm was so notorious that the Athenians used famous actors as envoys in their negotiations with Macedon; Alexander held dramatic contests at Thebes, Tyre and even Ecbatana; Antigonus and Demetrius also held dramatic festivals, and Ptolemy Soter established them on a regular basis in Alexandria.

115. Nauck *TGF²* 817-18; below, § 5.

116. Diog. Laert. 7. 173; D. F. Sutton, *The Greek Satyr Play* (Meisenheim 1980), 82.

117. F 1. 43 = *PCG* VII (1989), 620; App. B below.

118. Hermesianax F 7. 75-78; Bing 1993, 624 n. 17.

(catalectic choriambic hexameters), which opens with the words: "Scholars (γραμματικοί), I bring you a new-fangled composition."[119] Thus far the stereotype of the *poeta doctus*. Yet he was also a popular dramatist, whose picture was painted by the celebrated Protogenes of Caunos, who also painted Alexander.[120] And in the great procession of Philadelphus in 275/4 he led the Alexandrian guild of the Artists of Dionysus as priest of Dionysus.[121]

In § 6 we shall see that a number of other Hellenistic poets—not least Callimachus—took a keen interest in contemporary drama. The fact that this drama has so completely perished is not so much proof of intrinsic inferiority or lack of popular appeal than a consequence of Roman taste and the Attic revival.

4

It is often claimed that Hellenistic poets, living in an age of monarchies, were inspired by a nostalgia for the mythical past of the classical city-state. According to F. Cairns, the antiquarian element in Hellenistic poetry was an attempt by "citizens of now powerless cities" to foster their local identity through scholarship.[122] But it was only the handful of cities that had ever exercised power who lost it under the monarchies. The many small cities that had never enjoyed the luxury of an independent foreign policy were protected from aggression by powerful neighbours, and some actually gained in power and prosperity (Rhodes, for example, and Delos). Furthermore, the antiquarian movement was under way all over the Greek world long before the arrival of the kings. The enthusiasm for aetiology was already prominent in fifth-century tragedy (as early as the *Eumenides*). Certainly the Atthidographers, like the fourth-century orators, revived the past glories of Athens, but many of them wrote before the hegemony of Philip II, let alone the Successors.[123] There was another wave in the third century, when it was visitors like Callimachus, Eratosthenes and Euphorion who wrote aetiological poems on the Athenian past. But it is too simple to explain the popularity of such works straightforwardly in terms of the declining political power of Athens.[124] There is also the more complex

119. *SH* 677-78; K. Latte, *Mus. Helv.* 11 (1954), 1-19; Fraser I. 650-52.

120. Pliny, *NH* 35. 106.

121. Athen. 198C; E. E. Rice, *Grand Procession* (1983), 55.

122. *Tibullus* (Cambridge 1979), 13, cited with approval by Zanker 1987, 16.

123. For their dates, Jacoby, *Atthis* (Oxford 1949), 1.

124. One thinks, for example, of David Cannadine's brilliant correlation between the growth of British royal pageantry and the decline of British political power in E. Hobsbawm and T. Ranger (edd.), *The Invention of Tradition* (Cambridge 1983), 101-64.

phenomenon of oligarchs and democrats in turn mythologizing the historical past—the tyrants and Solon—in the search for "ancestral constitutions" in their own image.[125] Furthermore, the most popular form of poetry in fourth- and early third-century Athens—New Comedy—turned from the mythical past to the bourgeois present.

Curiously enough, the aetiological preoccupation of the Hellenistic poets has been generally judged one of the clearest proofs of their bookishness and remoteness from public life. According to Michael Grant (for example),[126] "They ransacked the most recherché myths and legends, antiquarian histories and obscure points of local topography for whatever titillating details and psychological angles they might be able to provide." The facts are accurate enough, but nothing could be further from the truth than the emphasis.

The interest in local cults and origins for which Callimachus above all became famous was no personal brainwave hit upon in the library of Alexandria. In one form or another it was (as we shall see) the stock-in-trade of the professional poet of the age. The development of aetiological poetry has to be seen in the context of the great outburst of local historical writing all over the fourth- and third-century Greek world.[127] The only contemporary epic poet whose major work has survived in its entirety—Apollonius—can be shown to have positively pillaged both the *Aetia* and other works of Callimachus for just this sort of material (Ch. IX. 3). Our richest single surviving source for the hundreds of lost local histories is the scholia to the *Argonautica*, as a glance at the index of writers in Wendel's edition will show. To take another example, the summaries in Antoninus Liberalis suggest that most of the stories in the lost *Transformations* of Nicander were "set in a particular place and are related at the end to some local landmark or more often a religious rite or object for which they are the aetion."[128]

There can be no question that local traditions of every sort were one of the great passions of the Hellenistic age. It is merely perverse not to recognize the civic significance of aetiological poetry. It was not in a desperate search for obscure themes to entertain each other or their kings that the poets sought out stories that purported to explain some local rite, feature, monument or custom. As we shall see in § 6, these were the themes that pleased the Greek cities, that would win a poet fame and civic honours.

---

125. M. I. Finley, "The Ancestral Constitution," in *The Use and Abuse of History* (New York 1975), 34-59.

126. *From Alexander to Cleopatra* (New York 1982), 261.

127. R. Laqueur, "Lokalchronik," *RE* 13. 1 (1926), 1083-110; Jacoby, *Abhandl. zur griech. Geschichtschreibung* (Leiden 1956), 49-61; C. W. Fornara, *The Nature of History in Ancient Greece and Rome* (Berkeley 1983), 12-23; for details, the massive (and still unfinished) part III of *FGrH*.

128. P.M.C. Forbes Irving, *Metamorphosis in Greek Myth* (1990), 27; Ch. IV. 4.

Royal courts were not after all the only source of patronage in the Hellenistic world.

5

According to Michael Grant, by the third century people "were reading much more than they were sitting and listening."[129] This is no doubt true of Callimachus and his colleagues at the Museum—if we judge by the thousands of manuscripts they catalogued. But of the educated public at large it is much more nearly false. Countless new agonistic festivals were established both by and in honour of the Hellenistic kings, and literary and musical events became much commoner at all sorts of festivals.[130] Furthermore new theatres and odea were erected all over the Hellenistic world.[131] For many sorts of poetry, the first public performance remained the most important not only in the Hellenistic age but right down into the Roman and even Byzantine world.[132] Greek-style symposia were never institutionalized at Rome, but much cultivated by philhellenes (the banquet songs "about the glory of famous men" mentioned by Cato are perhaps an early example).[133] Outside drama there was no tradition of festival performance, but the practice of private recitation became widespread by the early empire.[134] Indeed, one of the commonest complaints against the poetry of the empire is the supposedly harmful influence of declamation and recitation.[135] The second-century Greek medical writer Antyllus recommended declamation as exercise for the chest and larynx; epic was best, followed by iambics and (in third place) elegy.[136]

Surviving texts are often still prefaced by the prologue that addressed the audience on the all important occasion for which they were written.[137]

129. *From Alexander to Cleopatra* (New York 1982), 260.

130. A.H.M. Jones, *The Greek City* (Oxford 1940), 227-35; I. C. Ringwood, *Agonistic Features of Local Greek Festivals* (New York 1927); Sifakis 1967.

131. M. Bieber, *History of the Greek and Roman Theater* (1961), 108-28; Sifakis 1967.

132. A. Hardie, *Statius and the Silvae* (Liverpool 1983); Cameron, *Claudian* (1970); on the continuing importance of public performance, see already E. Rohde, *Der griechische Roman*[3] (Leipzig 1914), 324f.

133. J. Griffin, *Latin Poets and Roman Life* (London 1985), 6f.; the ballads, Momigliano, *Secondo Contributo* (Rome 1960), 69-88; Horsfall, *Riv. di Fil.* 122 (1994), 70-73; Varro's mention of boys and flutes (Non. Marc. p. 107 L) suggests Greek influence.

134. P. White, *Promised Verse* (1993), 60-63; C. Salles, *Lire à Rome* (Paris 1992).

135. G. Williams, *Change and Decline* (Berkeley 1978), 303-06; G. O. Hutchinson, *Latin Literature from Seneca to Juvenal* (Oxford 1992), 146-48.

136. *Oeuvres d'Oribase* ed. U. Bussemaker and C. Daremberg i (Paris 1851), 451.

137. T. Viljamaa, *Studies in Greek Encomiastic Poetry of the Early Byzantine Period* (Helsinki 1968), 71f.; Pliny vividly describes reluctant listeners waiting outside the auditorium till the performer has finished his preface (*Ep.* i. 13. 2).

The only copy of so "bookish" a poem as Paul the Silentiary's ecphrasis of Hagia Sophia (563) is equipped with notes reporting breaks in the recitation during which poet and audience moved.[138] In twelfth-century Byzantium there was a remarkable resurgence of encomiastic literature of every sort, much of it excruciatingly learned—but all of it nonetheless written for oral performance.[139] If oral performance was still the rule in an overwhelmingly bookish culture like that of the Byzantines, it is scarcely plausible to raise the objection of bookishness against the performance of Hellenistic poetry. If many more people were reading books in the third century, at the same time there can be no question that more people than ever before were also "sitting and listening."

Furthermore, obvious and basic though the distinction between reading and listening might seem, we must nonetheless beware of drawing it too sharply. A well-known article by Bernard Knox has refuted the exaggerated notion once current that in antiquity people read everything (including private letters) aloud, but even Knox did not dispute that people normally read poetry aloud—and that it was written to be read aloud and could only properly be so appreciated.[140] Another factor (to be borne in mind when we are considering visual effects) is that many (especially older) people did not actually read in person. Within the dramatic fiction of its frame a slave reads the entire text of Plato's *Theaetetus* aloud to Eucleides and Terpsion.[141] The only detailed description we have of an ancient man of letters at work is that of the elder Pliny by his nephew: slaves both read to him and wrote for him.[142] Many other writers regularly dictated when they wrote, notably Cicero and St Jerome, whose poor eyesight forced him to dictate from about his thirtieth year.[143] We might bear in mind that Callimachus was still writing in his seventies.[144] Terminology is also significant. *Dictare* often in effect means compose;[145] in certain contexts

138. P. Friedländer, *Johannes von Gaza und Paulus Silentiarius* (Leipzig 1912), 227, 229 (τούτων λεχθέντων ἐν τῷ παλατίῳ διῃρέθη ἡ ἀκρόασις, καὶ ἐλέχθη τὰ λοιπὰ ἐν τῷ ἐπισκοπείῳ), 238 (διαιρεθείσης πάλιν τῆς ἀκροάσεως); M. Whitby, *CQ* 35 (1985), 215-28.

139. H. Hunger, *Die hochsprachliche profane Literatur der Byzantiner* i (Munich 1978), 70, 209-11; M. Mullett in R. McKitterick (ed.), *The Uses of Literacy in Early Medieval Europe* (Cambridge 1990), 159-60; P. Magdalino, *The Empire of Manuel I Komnenos, 1143-1180* (Cambridge 1993), 352, on the physical settings for performance, at 345 identifying some 50-60 private sites in addition to the imperial palace and Hagia Sophia.

140. "Silent Reading in Antiquity," *GRBS* 9 (1968), 421-35; cf. P. Saenger, *Viator* 13 (1982), 367-414, who dates the general acceptance of silent reading no earlier than the beginning of the 14th century.

141. ἡμῖν ἅμα ἀναπαυομένοις ὁ παῖς ἀναγνώσεται...παῖ, λαβὲ τὸ βιβλίον καὶ λέγε (*Theaet.* 143BC).

142. *liber legebatur...liber legebatur adnotabatur...audiebat...aut dictabat* (*Ep.* 3. 5).

143. E. Arns, *La technique du livre d'après Saint Jérôme* (Paris 1953), 37-51.

144. Poor eyesight might play a part in his privileging of ears over eyes (F 282).

145. OLD s.v. 2; Saenger 1982, 380.

ἀκούειν means "read."[146] Polybius attacks Timaeus for his excessive
reliance on "hearing" (ἀκοή)—by which (as the context makes clear) he
means *written* sources rather than autopsy.[147] Ἀναγιγνώσκειν was at all
periods the standard term for "read aloud in public."[148] Indeed it sometimes comes close to "publish." The scholarch Lycon († 225) left his
βιβλία ἀνεγνωσμένα to one person and his ἀνέκδοτα to someone else to
polish and publish.[149] The first category must be his own copies of books
he had read publicly.

The Hellenistic world may no longer have enjoyed what John Herington, perhaps with some exaggeration, has called the "song culture" of
Archaic Greece.[150] But it is important to bear in mind that a large part of
even archaic poetry—to be precise, epic, elegy and iambus—was recited
rather than sung. Perhaps the strongest argument for the continued performance of poetry in the Hellenistic age is the fact that it was precisely
song that the more sophisticated Hellenistic poets ceased to write. Many
themes and genres that had earlier been treated in lyric, whether monodic
or choral, were adapted to hexameters, elegiacs and iambics. If Callimachus and his peers had really written for the book, why not go on writing
Sapphics and Alcaics and Pindaric strophes? It is surely no coincidence that
Hellenistic poets more or less confined themselves to the three metres still
available for performance.

Callimachus certainly read, admired and imitated Pindar,[151] and we are
bound to assume that so consummate a metrician had the technical ability to
reproduce the Pindaric forms if he had wished. Pindar must still have been
performed musically from time to time (presumably by professionals) but
Callimachus and his peers will normally have read him as we do—and were
well enough informed to understand the difference. This (I suggest) is
precisely why Callimachus did *not* attempt to recreate Pindaric strophes.
We may compare the rapid decline of choral lyric in Attic Comedy; by the
mid fourth-century dramatic poets wrote only iambic dialogue. Like the
poets of the third century, they confined themselves to what contemporary
audiences were willing to listen to in performance.

146. D. Schenkeveld, "Prose usages of ἀκούειν 'to read'," *CQ* 42 (1992), 129-41.
147. xii. 27 (with Walbank's note); cf. xx. 12. 8; M. Laffranque, *Rev. philos.* 158
(1968), 263-72; contrast Strabo ii. 5. 11 cited above, § 2 end.
148. P. Chantraine, *Mél. Grégoire* ii (Bruxelles 1950), 116-19; LSJ, Bauer, Lampe s.v.
149. D. L. 5. 73; Jerome, *De vir. ill.* 125: *tractatus mihi legit quos necdum edidit.*
150. *Poetry into Drama* (Berkeley 1985).
151. *Hermath.* 18 (1914), 46-72; Fuhrer 1992; Parsons, *Aev. Ant.* 5 (1993), 9; Ch. I. 2.

6

From inscriptions we learn of a large class of poets who travelled from city
to city competing in the mushrooming musical events of the age.[152]
Honorific decrees from Delphi and Delos reveal a series of lyric and (especially) epic poets from the third century on.[153] Two of the lyric poets,
Philodamus of Scarpheia (335/4) and Aristonoos of Corinth (ca 243), have
won a modest renown, owing to the fact that their poems were publicly
inscribed on surviving stones.[154] Similar honours were voted to Cleochares
of Athens at Delphi in 230 for a prosodion, paean and hymn to Apollo (not
preserved) that was performed by a chorus of boys.[155] We have papyrus
fragments of choral poems by Corinna (?250-200 B.C.), one written for a
chorus of girls in Tanagra, another for performance in Thebes. Unlike most
of her peers on the festival circuit, there is no evidence that Corinna ever
left her native Boeotia.[156]

Less attention has been paid to the epic poets: Nicander of Colophon
(254/3); Kleandros of Colophon (254/225); Amphiclos of Chios (246/5);
Eratoxenos of Athens (228/215).[157] When Amphiclos won at Delos in 260,
for once the dedication gives some information about his poem: he
"adorned the temple [of Apollo] and the Delians." At about the same time
we also hear of Demoteles of Andros, who wrote on "the temple and city
and myths" of Delos. The late third-century poetess Aristodama of
Smyrna, the first woman poet known to have publicly performed at a major
festival, "made mention of the ancestors of the city" at both Delphi and
Lamia.[158] An inscription honoring a performance of the second-century
poet Herodes of Priene in Samothrace gives a précis of his subject matter, a
number of Samothracian heroes evidently linked in a poem on the mythical

---

152. J. Frei, *De certaminibus thymelicis* (Diss. Basle 1900), 34-36; M. Guarducci,
"Poeti vaganti e conferenzieri dell' età ellenistica," *Reale Acc. Naz. dei Lincei, Memorie* 323
(1926-29), 629-65; for a more recent list, H. Bouvier, *ZPE* 58 (1985), 119-35; A. Hardie
1983, 15-30; M. R. Pallone, *Orpheus* n.s. 5 (1984), 156-66; on the various games, M.
Wörrle, *Stadt und Fest im kaiserzeitlichen Kleinasien* (Munich 1988), 227-58.
153. Since my purpose is to provide a literary context for Callimachus, I have in general
ignored the abundant epigraphic evidence later than the mid second century B.C.
154. *CA* 162-71; L. Käppel, *Paian: Studien zur Geschichte einer Gattung* (Berlin 1992).
155. *SIG*[3] 450 = *FD* III. 2. 78; Guarducci no. VII.
156. M. L. West, *CQ* 20 (1970), 277-87 and 40 (1990), 553-57; G. Burzacchini,
Eikasmós 2 (1991), 51-52.
157. *SIG*[3] 452; *FD* III. 2. 75; *FD* III. 3. 217 (cf. III. 4. 424); *SIG*[3] 451 = *FD* III. 2.
158; Guarducci nos. II, I, IX, III.
158. *SIG*[3] 382; *FGrH* 400; *SIG*[3] 532; *FGrH* 483; Guarducci XVII; A. Chaniotis, *His-
torie und Historiker in den griechischen Inschriften* (Stuttgart 1988), 334 and 338-40. She
toured with her brother as "business manager" (Tarn, *Hellenistic Civilisation*[3] [1952], 99).

past of the island.[159] Theopompus of Megalopolis was honoured at Delphi ca 200. Amphicles of Delos "hymned the patron gods of the island and the Athenian people" at Delos ca 165/4.[160] The child prodigy Ariston of Phocaea did the same 20 years later.[161] What else did Callimachus do in his *Hymn to Delos*? In Egypt itself, an inscription from Ptolemaïs datable to between 270 and 239 lists three "epic poets" who belonged to the local association of Dionysiac artists: Demarchos (secretary of the association), Theogenes and Artemidoros.[162]

By the first century B.C. we find formal competitions for encomia in both prose and "epic verse" (ἐγκωμίῳ ἐπικῷ). At the Amphiaraa and Romaia at Oropus there were contests for both epic encomium and epic poets (ἐπῶν ποιητής),[163] suggesting that encomiastic poetry had come so to dominate the original category that it was given a new one to itself. It is logical to assume that competitions for epic eulogies were widespread long before they were added to the sacred festivals. Three are recorded: the contest of Antimachus and Niceratus at the Lysandreia on Samos in 401; the "contest in encomia" held by Alexander at the funeral of the Indian philosopher Calanus; and the "traditional contest of the poets" at Mytilene attended by Pompey on his triumphal return from the East in 62, a contest "which took as its sole theme his own exploits."[164]

There were also a great many itinerant poets, who travelled (often uninvited) from city to city giving public recitations.[165] The main elements of such a visit are neatly captured in the following brief decree from Lamia in Thessaly:[166]

> Resolved by the city: since Politas the epic poet the son of Politas of Hypata has visited the city and given recitations in which he made worthy mention of the city, he shall be a public guest and benefactor and given our citizenship for all time.

The best known example is the young Archias, whose triumphal tour from city to city through Asia, Greece, Sicily and Italy is described by Cicero in pages familiar to every student of Latin.[167] Less familiar is Hermocles of Chios, who wrote a hymn to Apollo and gave a public speech on the hero Ion in late third-century Delphi, winning proxeny and various other

159. *I. von Priene* 68-70; L. Robert, *Rev. arch.* 1926, 174-76; Ch. VIII. 2.

160. *FD* III. 4. 145; cf. Habicht, *Chiron* 2 (1972), 114, no. 2; *SIG*^{3} 662 = *IDélos* 1497.

161. *I. Délos* 1506; Guarducci XII.

162. *OGIS* 51 [= *SB* V. 8855] lines 37-40; Fraser II 870 n.1.

163. L. Robert, *Ét. ép. et phil.* (Paris 1938), 21-23; Hardie 1983, 89; *IG* VII. 419. 9f.

164. Plutarch, *Lys.* 18. 6; *SH* 564-65; Chares, *FGrH* 125 F 19; Plutarch, *Pomp.* 42. 7.

165. Hardie 1983, 18-30 (with a useful chart on p. 206).

166. *IG* IX. 2. 63 (s. II); Guarducci XIII; *FGrH* 483 F 2; Chaniotis 1988, 340.

167. *Pro Archia* 4f.; for the relevant passages and poems, *SH* 194-96.

honours in return.[168] In the middle of the next century similar honours were conferred on the historian Aristotheos of Troizen, for giving readings from his history "for several days" at Delphi.[169] Bombos of Alexandria Troas was honoured for public recitations in the gymnasium of Larisa, dwelling on the mythical relations between Larisa and his own part of the world.[170] There are many other examples of local historians receiving such honours. Greek cities everywhere welcomed poets, orators and historians who glorified local traditions.[171] It is clear from the abundant evidence that itinerant visitors, like the competitors at the festivals, invariably gave public recitals.[172]

We now have two fragments of a no doubt second- or first-century hexameter poem on the story of Hero and Leander.[173] The story cannot be traced before the age of Augustus, by when it was familar to Vergil, Horace, Ovid, Strabo and Antipater of Thessalonica, and when it first appears in art on the coinage of both Sestos and Abydos.[174] The author of a story so closely linked to a specific geographical area[175] was surely some itinerant poet writing for the citizens of Sestos or Abydos, perhaps inspired by the local ruins known as Hero's Tower.[176]

If we look among the surviving poetry of the age for "epic" poems praising rulers and "making worthy mention" of local cults and traditions, inevitably some hymns of Callimachus and poems of Theocritus come to mind. Did Callimachus and Theocritus perform on such occasions? Most scholars would answer with an emphatic negative. According to Bruno Gentili, the work of Callimachus and Theocritus[177]

flourished in the narrow world of courts and côteries, exclusively reserved for an intellectual elite. Alongside it, however, there was another type of culture,

168. *SIG*[3] 579; *FD* III. 3. 224; Chaniotis 1988, 304-05.

169. *FD* III. 3. 124; *FGrH* 835 T 1; Chaniotis 1988, 309-10.

170. *BCH* 59 (1935), 55; Robert, *BE* 1936, 367; 1967, 331; Chaniotis 1988, 310.

171. Chaniotis 1988, 290-326 ("Ehrendekrete für Historiker"); Robert, *BE* 1959 n. 330. For the traditions of Apamea in Ps-Oppian, Hollis, *ZPE* 102 (1994), 154-66.

172. ποιουμένους τὰς ἀκροάσεις, *OGIS* 339. 74; δείξεις ἐποιήσατο, *IG* IX. 63; 3 (Politas of Hypata, s. II); ἀκροάσεις καὶ πλείους ἐποήσατο, *SIG*[3] 622, cf. *IG* VII 373 (both Amphicles of Delos, s. II); so too *SIG*[3] 532 (Aristodama, 218/7); *Inschriften von Priene* 69 (Herodes of Priene, s. II); *I. Délos* 1506 (Ariston of Phocaea, 146/5).

173. L. Malten, *Rhein. Mus.* 93 (1949), 65-81; T. Gelzer, *Callimachus and Musaeus* (Loeb ed. 1975), 302-07; *SH* 951 (I A.D.) and 901A (IV/V), with H. Maehler, *Mus. Phil. Lond.* 7 (1986), 109-18.

174. B. V. Head, *Historia Numorum*[2] (London 1911), 261 and 539-40; for other representations in art (pending the entries in *LIMC*), A. and E. Alföldi, *Die Kontorniat-Medaillons* II (Berlin 1990), 132.

175. *Est et Abydo obiacens Sestos, Leandri amore nobilis*, Mela ii. 2 (ca 43 A.D.).

176. Strabo 13. 591; Antipater, *AP* vii. 666. 3, with Gow and Page, *GP* II. 29-30; for a brief history of the two cities, W. Leaf, *Strabo on the Troad* (Cambridge 1923), 116-33.

177. *Poetry and its Public in Ancient Greece* (Baltimore 1988), 174-76; Bing 1988, 38.

not learned or literary in the proper sense of the terms, but what we would now call a *popular* or *mass* culture.... The Hellenistic period presents the spectacle of a culture with two totally different aspects, moving along distinct but parallel lines—learned poetry, libraries and erudition on the one hand; and, on the other, festive performances, popular education, and entertainment, which still operate within the oral institutional framework provided by theaters and public competitions.

The purveyors of this "popular culture" turn out to be the poets listed on the inscriptions from Delphi and Delos and the various other festival sites. Gentili's position is developed in an even more extreme form by Fantuzzi, who writes of the "cultivated poets" of the Museum being separated "as if by a wall" from the poetry "of the people and the public square." This "popular epic" (as he calls it) is said to be "an activity parallel but entirely extraneous to...the official literature."[178] Both terms are inappropriate. The poetry of Callimachus and Theocritus cannot really be described as "official"; nor mythological hexameter poetry performed at traditional festivals as "popular." Indeed, the very idea of "mass culture" in the Hellenistic age is problematic (to say the least). As William Harris put it:[179]

> There is some temptation to juxtapose the written culture of the Hellenistic elite and the oral culture of the masses. But this dichotomy is altogether too sharp. The culture of the elite continued to have a strong oral component, with oratory and performance retaining their important roles.

On the other hand

> Any assumption that the intellectually less demanding genres of Hellenistic literature aimed at, or reached, a truly popular audience of readers should be resisted. The papyri show conclusively that popular literature did not exist in any ordinary sense of that expression.

Gentili's main interest lay in the theatrical performances of the Hellenistic world, where he may be right to stress the "technical abilities of a new type of professional performer, the virtuoso singer of tragic or comic parts." But the hexameter poetry attested by the agonistic inscriptions was newly composed for the occasion. This much at least we may infer from a story told by Vitruvius. When Aristophanes of Byzantium was one of the seven judges in an Alexandrian poetry contest, he rejected the contestants preferred by the crowd and his colleagues on the grounds that "they had recited the work of others, while the judges were supposed to deal with original work." The only true poet, he claimed, was the contestant the crowd liked least: "relying on his memory he produced a large number of rolls from certain bookshelves and, comparing them with the texts recited, he compelled the others to confess their thefts."[180]

---

178. Fantuzzi 1988, xxxiv-xlii (quotations from xxxv and xxxviii).
179. *Ancient Literacy* (Cambridge, Mass. 1989), 125-26.
180. vii, pr. 5-7; the story has been improved in the telling to exemplify Aristophanes's

Since this prize poetry is lost, how can Gentili know that it was, not just inferior to the work of Callimachus and Theocritus, but fundamentally different in both kind and function? Written as it undoubtedly was in hexameters on the traditional themes of epic (myth and the gods), how can it have been significantly different? The distinction he drew between what we might call the festival poets and the Museum poets is not nearly as sharp as he thought. While most of the poets recorded in the Delphian and Delian victor lists are unknown to posterity, one of them achieved a wider renown: Nicander of Colophon. As we shall see (Ch. VIII. 2), it is the earlier of the two Nicanders, the one honoured at Delphi in 254/3, who is to be credited with not only the extant *Alexipharmaca* and *Theriaca*, but also a series of regional epics (Ch. X. 6). Excerpts from these would have made ideal Delphic recitations.

Some famous names also appear among the itinerant poets. Apollonius wrote Ktiseis of Alexandria, Naucratis, Caunos, Cnidos, Lesbos and Rhodes.[181] Naucratis was close to Alexandria and Caunos and Cnidos not far from Rhodes, the two places where Apollonius is known to have lived. The analogy of the many texts cited above strongly suggests that these poems were written for such visits and publicly performed for similar honours. For what they are worth (Ch. VIII. 6), the *Lives* of Apollonius represent him giving a public reading of his *Argonautica* in both Alexandria and Rhodes.

When an audience in Thebes did not applaud a recitation of his *Thebaïs*, Antagoras of Rhodes is said to have lost his temper, rolled up (εἰλήσας) his book and snapped out: "No wonder you are called Boeotians, you have cows' ears" (βοῶν ὦτα). The witticism is characteristic of the sharp-tongued Antagoras (Ch. VIII. 1), the *Thebaïs* is attested elsewhere and it is understandable that a poem on the Theban saga should be publicly performed in Thebes—perhaps indeed specifically written for a visit. The same florilegium preserves two more responses by Antagoras to unappreciative audiences (one set in Aetolia),[182] and two similar anecdotes about another celebrated wit of the age, Theocritus of Chios. First, Anaximenes (evidently the Lampsacene encomiast of Alexander) was giving a long recitation and nearing the end of his roll when Theocritus cried out "cheer up

---

remarkable memory, but there is no reason to doubt the realities of festival competition it presupposes, which had not changed by Vitruvius's day.

181. Sources in *CA* pp. 5-8; Bürchner's articles Caunos and Cnidos (cities on the coast of Caria later incorporated into the Rhodian Peraea) in *RE* XI. 1 (1921), 85-88 and 914-21 give some idea of the rich mythological traditions available for such poems; on Caunos see too now L. Robert, *Documents d'Asie Mineure* (Paris 1987), 487-531.

182. *Gnom. Vat.* 109-11, p. 50 Sternbach.

lads, I see land (γῆν ὁρῶ)." Second, when a bad poet (? Anaximenes again) asked which were the best bits in his recitation (in both cases ἀκρόασιν ποιουμένου, the standard term in third-century festival inscriptions), Theocritus replied "the bits you left out" (παρέλιπες).[183] Ultimately the Theocritus sayings must derive from the biography by his disciple Bryon (Ch. XVI. 2). The value of these anecdotes lies not so much in their truth or falsehood as in the way they focus on public performance.

The first of the Theocritus stories suggests a different interpretation of the most famous saying attributed to Callimachus, "a big book is a big bore" (F 465). Though often assumed to be a crisper formulation of the invective of the *Aetia* prologue against long poems, βιβλίον (a papyrus roll) is not a general purpose term for a literary work, much less a poem.[184] For example, the multi-book *Lyde* of Antimachus that Callimachus attacked in F 1 and 398 (Ch. XI) could have been described as a μέγα γράμμα, but never as a μέγα βιβλίον.[185] On the one hand the *Lyde* (like Callimachus's own *Aetia*) would have filled several βιβλία; on the other, a modest-sized βιβλίον by no means implied a *short* (much less good) poem. While there is an obvious sense in which a large roll was also a large book,[186] "large roll" in itself carried none of the very precise connotations so central to Callimachus's literary polemic. When we bear in mind that Callimachus was in effect the inventor of bibliography,[187] more concerned with books as material objects than any man of his age, a less specifically literary interpretation may suffice. For example (combining the two senses of βιβλίον in a slightly different way), just as Theocritus watched the roll turning in Anaximenes's hands, perhaps what Callimachus had in mind was the *sight* of a large roll in the hands of a poet about to recite—that sinking feeling we all know when we observe the thickness of the manuscript a lecturer takes out of his briefcase at the podium.

F 3 and 4 of Alexander Aetolus are also suggestive. F 3, from a poem called *Musae*, describes how the people of Ephesus ensured, by the prizes they offered, that the best poets of the day should compete at the dedication of a temple to Artemis. F 4 may come from a poem on the oracle of Didyma, near Miletus.[188] Didyma was not far from Ephesus, and a poet welcome at the courts of both Antigonus and Philadelphus might well have felt

183. *Gnom. Vat.* 338 and 348, pp. 132 and 135; for the festival inscriptions, n. 172.

184. "schwerlich ging es die Poesie an," Wilamowitz, *HD* I. 212; "non de nimio poematum ambitu loquitur," Pfeiffer ad loc.

185. Callimachus himself, more offensively, called it a παχὺ γράμμα (F 398). Other common terms were (in verse) πόνος and (in prose) πραγματεία.

186. Though the converse did not hold; the longest poems known to Hellenistic scholars (the *Iliad* and *Odyssey*) were subdivided into exceptionally short individual books.

187. R. Blum, *Callimachus...and the Origins of Bibliography* (Madison 1991).

188. *CA* 122-25, with Ch. VI. 7.

that he could expect similar rewards in the ancient cities of Asia. Stratonike the wife of Seleukos held a poetic contest on the subject of her hair with a talent for prize.[189] Callimachus's Ktiseis are no more than a title,[190] but (as we shall see in Ch. IX. 3) *Acontius and Cydippe* is virtually a Ktisis of Ceos.

A few later examples. Statius's father won crowns at the Pythian, Nemean and Isthmian games and several at the Neapolitan games; his son also won at the Neapolitan games, but thereafter abandoned the Greek festival circuit for the literary life of Rome.[191] Lucan competed in the Neronia of 60 with a panegyric on Nero; Nero himself competed (and of course won) at all the big festivals.[192] In the late empire when the festivals were no more, poets still travelled from city to city writing and performing poems on local dignitaries and antiquities.[193] Claudian wrote on the antiquities (Πάτρια) of Anazarbus, Berytus, Nicaea and Tarsus, and performed a series of panegyrics and epics at the court of Honorius.[194] A century later (476) it happens to be expressly attested that Pamprepigus of Panopolis, a disciple of Nonnus, recited a poem publicly in Constantinople.[195]

7

Though not yet identified as such, we do in fact have a representative specimen of the prize poem virtually intact, Theocritus 24, the *Heracliscus*. According to a scholion in the Antinoë papyrus, the missing final verses of the poem expressed a wish to defeat other poets, evidently in a competition.[196] If one why not others? When listing the king's benefactions in *Idyll* 17, the panegyric *On Ptolemy*, Theocritus gives pride of place to the poetic contests of Dionysus:

οὐδὲ Διωνύσου τις ἀνὴρ ἱεροὺς κατ᾽ ἀγῶνας
ἵκετ᾽ ἐπιστάμενος λιγυρὰν ἀναμέλψαι ἀοιδάν,
ᾧ οὐ δωτίναν ἀντάξιον ὥπασε τέχνας.
Μουσάων δ᾽ ὑποφῆται ἀείδοντι Πτολεμαῖον
ἀντ᾽ εὐεργεσίης (17. 112-116).

189. Lucian, *De imag.* 5.
190. The fourth-century A.D. book list published in *P. Turner* 9, F I. 3 may be a new testimonium: Καλλιμάχου Κ[τίσεις]. On the characteristics of foundation literature, Cairns, *Tibullus* (1979), 68f.
191. Hardie 1983, 6-7, 58-59.
192. M. T. Griffin, *Nero: The End of a Dynasty* (London 1984), 160-63.
193. Cameron, "Wandering Poets," *Historia* 15 (1965), 470-509; *YCS* 27 (1982), 217f.
194. Cameron, *Claudian* 7-10; Christodorus produced another batch a century later.
195. δημοσίᾳ ἀναγνόντα, Malchus F 20 (*FHG* IV. 132 = 23. 12 Blockley).
196. ἐκ διαδοχ(ῆς) νικήσας δικαίως ποιησ( ) κ(αὶ) τὸν ποιητ(ὴν) πάντ(ας) νικῆσαι (Gow II 436); Gow compares *Hom. Hymn.* 6. 19-20, δὸς δ᾽ ἐν ἀγῶνι νίκην τῷδε φέρεσθαι.

> No one who came to the sacred contests of Dionysus skilled to sing his clear-voiced song left without the gift his art deserved. And those mouthpieces of the Muses sing of Ptolemy in return for his benefactions.

We may surely infer that Theocritus himself was one of the "mouthpieces of the Muses" who sang of Ptolemy "in return for his benefactions" (17. 115-6); that is to say, Theocritus won at least one victory in one of the big Alexandrian festivals, the Basileia established in Philadelphus's honour by Soter, or the Ptolemaia established in Soter's honour by Philadelphus.[197]

Let us examine the *Heracliscus* a little more closely. The poem describes (following Pindar's first *Nemean*) how the ten-month-old Heracles strangles two snakes sent by Hera. In the morning his parents summon Tiresias, who prophesies that he will accomplish twelve labours and then become a god. The final section describes his education: he excels not only in boxing, wrestling, chariot-racing and fighting, but in writing and poetry too. This is a rather unusual Heracles—one who bears more than a passing resemblance to the young Philadelphus. Young Heracles is rather puzzlingly said to be "late-born" (ὀψίγονον), an epithet more appropriate for Philadelphus, the late-born son Soter preferred to his older brothers.[198] In praising Heracles's enthusiasm for wrestling,[199] racing and poetry, Theocritus is simply repeating in different terms his account in 17. 112-6 of how Philadelphus patronized the sacred contests.

The emphasis on Heracles's youth suggests that Philadelphus too is young: his achievements, like those of the young Heracles, lie in the future. The emphasis on the future god's human father Amphitruo suggests that Soter is still alive. If so, then it is tempting to accept Koenen's identification of the occasion: Soter's designation of Philadelphus as heir on his birthday in 285/4. For we now know from the agonistic inscription Koenen published that the festival of the Basileia was held on that day.[200] And Theocritus takes great pains to indicate (absurdly enough) the age (and so birthday) of the baby Heracles, when all the dramatic context requires is that "he should indicate some hour which will explain why it is dark and the household in bed."[201]

An additional point (not made by Koenen) is that, while 17 (which evidently dates from after the marriage to Arsinoë II some time between 279

197. L. Koenen, *Eine agonistische Inschrift aus Ägypten und frühptolemäische Königsfeste* (Beitr. z. klass. Phil. 56), 1977; Fraser 231-32, with the new document published by T. L. Shear Jr., *Hesperia* Supppl. 17 (1978), line 53f. with comm. on pp. 33-34; Will I² 202-03.

198. Gow, following LSJ, interprets ὀψίγονον merely "young" applied to Heracles, but obviously it must take on its full sense when applied to Philadelphus.

199. With Hermes, Heracles was the patron of Alexandrian gymnasia: Fraser I. 208.

200. Koenen 1977, esp. 39-63 and 79-86.

201. See Gow's attempt to calculate the time apparently intended (II. 417-19), which must however be revised in the light of the new inscription: Koenen 1977, 85-86.

and 274) explicitly evokes Philadelphus's marriage to his own sister, citing the divine parallel of Zeus and Hera (126-134), 24 says only that young Heracles will become a "son-in-law" of the gods (84). Theocritus does not spell out that Heracles's bride was his half-sister Hebe any more than Homer (*Od.* xi. 603) or Catullus (68. 116). It looks as if 24 is a decade earlier than 17: the marriage it "prophecies" is with Arsinoë I ca 288.[202] More remarkably, Heracles's divine descent is entirely suppressed. In Pindar, Zeus's parentage and Hera's jealousy are mentioned in the first five lines; in Theocritus, though it is Hera who sends the snakes and Zeus who alerts Heracles, nothing is said of their motives. Heracles is described as Amphitruon's son four times (56, 59, 104, 135), at 104 the son of "Argive Amphitruon." Since there is no reference to Thebes, the traditional site of Heracles's birth, the reader is surely being prompted to recall the pretended Argive ancestry of the Ptolemies.[203]

Literary scholars have emphasized, perhaps overemphasized, the ironic reduction of the heroic to the domestic in the *Heracliscus*.[204] That is to say, they find in the poem precisely those features which are felt to be peculiarly Alexandrian. It is undoubtedly a sophisticated and subtle piece. And yet it was recited in a public contest. The very qualities which have been thought to militate in favour of private reading in the library were not after all felt incompatible with public performance.

We do in fact have a useful piece of evidence on audience reaction to poetry in Alexandria in Callimachus's heyday. The bourgeois housewives in Theocritus 15 anticipate a fine song from the "learned" ($\pi o\lambda\dot{\upsilon}\ddot{\iota}\delta\rho\iota\varsigma$) poetess who "won in the dirge last year" (97-8). When she has finished Gorgo praises her cleverness ($\chi\rho\hat{\eta}\mu\alpha\ \sigma o\phi\dot{\omega}\tau\alpha\tau o\nu$) and knowledge ($\ddot{o}\sigma\sigma\alpha\ \ddot{\iota}\sigma\alpha\sigma\iota$) as well as the sweetness of her voice (145-6). The song is clearly being assessed as an original composition by the singer. Dover suspects that the song itself is a "sly parody of the songs characteristic of these occasions and applauded by audiences whose thoughts and tastes, like those of Gorgo and Praxinoa, existed only as strings of clichés."[205] Hardly a

202. Among the traces of the missing end of the poem (170) on P. Ant. are]$\tau\alpha\nu$ $o\mu o\pi\alpha\tau$[, from which Pohlenz reconstructed $\kappa\alpha\sigma\iota\gamma\nu\dot{\eta}\tau\alpha\nu\ \dot{o}\mu o\pi\dot{\alpha}\tau\rho\iota o\nu$. In the light of]$\upsilon\mu\pi o\nu$ (Ὄλυμπον ?) in 168 and $\dot{\epsilon}\rho\iota\hat{\omega}\pi\iota\delta\alpha$ in 170 ("large-eyed, an epithet for a woman), some have inferred that the end of the poem returns to Hebe and makes explicit her relationship to Heracles (Griffiths 1979, 95; Zanker 1987, 179). But a casual reference at the end of the poem need have no contemporary resonance before the marriage with Arsinoë II, nor is this the only possible identification. The woman could be Alcmene and the $\dot{o}\mu o\pi\dot{\alpha}\tau\rho\iota o\nu$ another reference to Heracles's brother Iphicles. There might also be a different contemporary reference; at the time of Philadelphus's designation there must have been some anxiety that his brothers would resent being passed over, a theme evoked in mythical terms by Call. *Hymn to Zeus* 57-9.

203. As noted by Gow II. 415, 418; on the Ptolemies and Argos, Ch. VIII. 2.

204. Griffiths 1979, 91-98; Gutzwiller 1981, 9-18; Zanker 1987, 176-79.

205. *Theocritus: Select Poems* (London 1971), 209; cf. Zanker 1987, 15.

parody; more likely, while trying to catch the flavour of such songs, Theocritus considerably improved on the run-of-the-mill hymn to Adonis. And while there is perhaps something mildly comic in Gorgo's admiration of the fairly routine mythological learning of the singer, she is at least applying the right standards: erudition. If the differences between learned and popular tastes were as deep and obvious as usually assumed, it would be odd for Theocritus to have given his housewives Museum standards when in all other respects he skilfully and consistently gives them attitudes and interests that are so obviously not his own.[206]

It is "inconceivable" (Zanker insists) that Theocritus was writing "for the urban masses of Alexandria." [207] Of course not. No one in pagan antiquity ever wrote (non-dramatic) poetry for such an audience.[208] But that does not leave "small audiences of highly cultivated patrons" as the only alternative. That the allusive idiom of Hellenistic poetry would be unfamiliar to all but the elite of the Museum might seem a natural assumption to a modern reader brought up on the classics. But a cache of second-century papyri from Memphis reveals two young Macedonians of modest circumstances copying epigrams by Posidippus along with passages from Aeschylus, Euripides and Menander.[209] Not the least interesting feature of the Lille papyrus of the *Victoria Berenices* is precisely the fact that the interlinear notes are so elementary, often no more than "simple gloss and paraphrase."[210] And this barely a generation after Callimachus's death, not centuries later when he had become a classic. Here is a concrete illustration of the sort of aids with which people of modest cultural attainments might tackle so difficult a poem—Egyptians who needed to be told that Berenice was not really the daughter of Philadelphus (*SH* 255. 3-6).

The idea that poets wrote exclusively for urban côteries is simply not borne out by the papyri, mostly found in the backwoods. As Parsons put it, "poetry, even difficult poetry, circulated more widely than the age's colossal output of informative and diverting prose."[211] Most Callimachus papyri have been found in small villages, the celebrated Diegeseis, "Cliff Notes" to all his major poems (Ch. IV. 4), in Tebtunis.[212] At a more personal level, as H. C. Youtie acutely spotted, an "érudit manqué" condemned to

206. Systematically treated by Zanker 1987, 9-19.

207. Zanker 1987, 18.

208. And not many Christians either: Arius was criticized by fellow-Christians for trying to court ἀμαθέστεροι through ᾀσμάτια ναυτικὰ καὶ ἐπιμύλια καὶ ὁδοιπορικά (Philostorgius, *HE* ii. 2, p. 13 Bidez); on the metre of Arius's songs, West, *JTS* 33 (1982), 98-105.

209. D. J. Thompson, *Proc. Camb. Phil. Soc.* 213 (1987), 105-21; *Greek Anthology* 7.

210. Parsons, *ZPE* 25 (1977), 4-5; his scepticism whether "this elementary production really had a substantive history in the book trade" perhaps begs the question.

211. Parsons 1993 in Bulloch 1993, 158.

212. On the ownership of the Diegeseis and other papyri found with them, W. Clarysse in *Egypt and the Hellenistic World* (Louvain 1983), 49-50.

spend his days in the tax bureau at Karanis during the reign of Marcus Aurelius amused himself by equipping Egyptian names in his registers with whimsical Greek translations of his own, among them an otherwise unattested poetic term for mousetrap taken from the *Victoria Berenices*.[213]

We should also bear in mind that there were established Greek communities in Egypt long before the foundation of Alexandria. A series of ninety plaster moulds found at Memphis has revealed a local market for high-quality classicizing figures in silver and bronze on a wide range of themes popular in Alexandrian poetry: the royal house; Heracles; Eros and Aphrodite; bucolic scenes. Maehler has drawn attention to what in other respects is a typical Hellenistic Gorgon head, but with cow's ears. He identifies the figure as Io, who fled in bovine form to Egypt to bear Epaphos, the legendary founder of Memphis.[214] No Hellenistic Ktisis of Memphis happens to be recorded, though this may have been the theme of Callimachus's lost *Arrival of Io* (one of his epigrams identifies Io and Isis).[215] We may presume that it was for a similarly cultivated local audience that Apollonius wrote his Ktisis of Naucratis.

"Learned" poetry was not a minority cult but the dominant mode. It is a common frailty of the academic mind to suppose that only those who can identify every last allusion can really enjoy a given work. But it does not require the same erudition to enjoy the mythology of the Adonis song as it did to compose it. The widespread production of mythological handbooks and plot summaries of famous poems (Ch. IV. 4) illustrates an obvious short cut to the understanding of learned texts. To be sure only a minority would appreciate every allusion in Theocritus and Callimachus, but then how many original listeners appreciated every detail in Pindar and Aeschylus? The continuing popularity of Vergil through the Greekless Middle Ages should be warning enough. Similar judgments have been made about learned poetry in other ages where evidence exists to confute them:[216]

> Pope and his contemporaries have been accused of cultivating poetry for a small and exclusive clique. "Poetry was in the hands of a few," we are told, "who kept it within the limits of their narrow interests; it was poetry in a park surrounded by high walls. The people were ignored, not admitted." If this is

213. *Scriptiunculae* ii (Amsterdam 1973), 1039-41 ("what could be more satisfying to a tax clerk with pretensions to learning than a borrowing from Callimachus furtively inserted into a gigantic money register, where no one would ever notice it?"); F 177 = *SH* 259. 33.

214. "Poésie alexandrine et art hellénistique à Memphis," *Chron. d' Égypte* 63 (1988), 113-136; C. Reinsberg, *Studien zur hellenistichen Toreutik* (Hildesheim 1980); N. Icard-Gianolio, *LIMC* v (1992), 663, 670, 676, with the Ptolemaic epigram published by Fraser and Maas, *JEA* 41 (1955), 115-16; J. and L. Robert, *RÉG* 71 (1958), 347.

215. *AP* vi. 150; the story is alluded to in Mosch. *Europ.* 48f.; Forbes Irving, *Metamorphosis in Greek Myth* (1990), 212-16.

216. J. Sutherland, *Preface to Eighteenth Century Poetry* (Oxford 1948), 62; his quotation is from S. Brooke, *Naturalism in English Poetry* (London 1920), 8.

so, the people must have made a habit of climbing the walls: few poets have
been read and admired by so large a proportion of their fellow countrymen as
was Pope in his own day.

As Pickard-Cambridge remarked of Attic drama, "even though some allusions may seem very recondite, an author may at times be aiming at a very
small part of his audience."[217] In the case of Callimachus and Theocritus,
the choice is not between audiences of a dozen or a hundred thousand; at
major festivals there will always have been several hundred and perhaps a
few thousand who understood enough to enjoy themselves.[218]

If a learned and allusive poem like the *Heracliscus*, with its contemporary message coded in a mythical frame, could be written for public
performance, then the case for insisting that other such poems by both
Theocritus and Callimachus cannot have been written for performance is
seriously weakened. From the same period we might think of Callimachus's *Hymn to Zeus*, which (as we have seen) so pointedly manipulates
the tradition about Zeus's ascent to the throne of heaven so that it parallels
Philadelphus's ascent to the throne of Egypt over the heads of his brothers.
J. J. Clauss has argued that the *Hymn to Zeus* was performed on the same
occasion as the *Heracliscus*, the agon at the Basileia commemorating Philadelphus's elevation to co-rule with Soter.[219] Here it is not just the
allusiveness of the poem, but its ironic, not to say flippant handling of
myth that has been held to militate against public performance. But a poetic
competition is not a religious celebration. In fact it was probably written
for a symposium (Ch. III. 4).

Alex Hardie has argued that Theocritus 16, *Charites* or *Graces*, was
also written for a festival. The opening and closing appeal to the Charites,
and the emphatic mention of their affection for Orchomenos (line 105)
point to the Charitesia of Boeotian Orchomenos.[220] This festival in honour
of the Charites drew performers from as far afield as Antioch-on-the-
Orontes.[221] An anonymous first person elegy, the fragmentary *SH* 959 of
the second or third century B.C., mentions Arsinoë, refers to a poet competing with the people (? or a chorus) of Thespiae (ἤρισα Θεσπιάδαις),
and then a couple of lines later we encounter the Charites and Orchomenos.
No connected sense can be extracted, but this could be a poet proclaiming
his victories at the contests in central Greece: among them the Museia of

217. *Dramatic Festivals of Athens*[2] (Oxford 1988), 276; so too Harris 1989, 87.
218. The artificial, atticizing rhetoric of the second sophistic played to packed houses.
219. *Classical Antiquity* 5 (1986), 155-70, with full bibliography of earlier discussions.
220. Hardie 1983, 33-35.
221. See the victor lists (all dating from the early first century B.C.) *IG* VII. 3195-3197
(3195 and 3197 list an ἐπῶν ποιητής; 3196 simply a ποιητής); on the Charitesia see P.
Amandry and T. Spyropoulos, *BCH* 98 (1974), 171-246, esp. 224-8, with J. and L. Robert,
Bull. Épigr. 1946/7 n. 81 (p. 316) and ib. 1974 n. 283 (p. 230).

Thespiae and the Charitesia of Orchomenos.[222] Posidippus's so-called *Seal* refers to triennial contests in honour of Bacchus somewhere in Boeotia, perhaps the Agrionia.[223] More speculatively, Francis Cairns has raised the possibility that Theocritus 26 was performed at the Agrionia.[224]

In so subtle a writer as Theocritus, the claim (17. 115-6) that all contestants got the reward their poetry deserved may have an edge to it. For we know from one of Callimachus's finer epigrams of one poet who failed in the contests:

ἦλθε Θεαίτητος καθαρὴν ὁδόν. εἰ δ᾽ ἐπὶ κισσὸν
τὸν τεὸν οὐχ αὕτη, Βάκχε, κέλευθος ἄγει,
ἄλλων μὲν κήρυκες ἐπὶ βραχὺν οὔνομα καιρὸν
φθέξονται, κείνου δ᾽ Ἑλλὰς ἀεὶ σοφίην (*AP* ix. 565).

Theaetetus has travelled the path of purity. If that path does not lead to Dionysus's ivy wreath, for a while the heralds will proclaim the names of other men, but his talent Hellas will proclaim forever.

There is no reason to doubt that the poet here named is the accomplished author of four epigrams included in Meleager's *Garland* and two more preserved by Diogenes Laertius.[225] The more so since one of them is an epitaph for a Cyrenean (*AP* vii. 499); Theaetetus himself may have been a fellow-countryman of Callimachus. Evidently he had been disappointed in his attempt to win a prize in one of the "sacred contests of Dionysus" (not necessarily drama, since all the Egyptian contests seem to have been under the auspices of Dionysus).[226] Callimachus seeks to reassure him. Whatever the verdict of the judges, Theaetetus has followed the "path of purity"; he has stuck to his poetic principles. These principles (of course) are those followed by Callimachus himself,[227] but here at least they do *not* imply rejection of the public poetry of the past. The metaphors go back to Pindar, who had twice spoken of his poetry as the "path of purity" as well as refusing to "drive along the well-trodden path of Homer."[228] That is to say, Theaetetus ought to continue writing exactly the same sort of "pure" poetry, *despite* his failure with the judges.[229] His art will be proclaimed by

222. Lloyd-Jones, *Gnomon* 29 (1957), 426; M. Feyel, *Contribution à l'épigraphie béotienne* (Le Puy 1942), 88f.; Ch. VI. 1.

223. *SH* 705. 4; cf. L. Robert, *BCH* 69 (1935), 193-98 and *Arch. Ephem.* 1977, 195-216.; Lloyd-Jones, *JHS* 83 (1963), 82 = *Acad. Papers* ii (Oxford 1990), 170.

224. Cairns 1992, 17-21.

225. *HE* 3342-3371 with II. 520-524 and Livrea in *SIFC* 82 (1990), 24-31.

226. Fraser 619, 231; II. 870-71 n. 1-2.

227. οὐδὲ κελεύθῳ / χαίρω τὶς πολλοὺς ὧδε καὶ ὧδε φέρει (*AP* 12. 43); τὰ μὴ πατέουσιν ἄμαξαι / τὰ στείβειν...μηδ᾽ οἷμον ἀνὰ πλατύν, ἀλλὰ κελεύθους / ἀτρίπτους, εἰ καὶ στεινοτέρην ἐλάσεις (F 1. 15-8).

228. καθαρὴ κέλευθος (*O*. 6. 23; *I*. 5. 23); τριπτὸν κατ᾽ ἀμαξιτόν (*Paean 7b*. 11).

229. Gow and Page inferred that Theaetetus "has apparently taken to some other form of literature after failing in a...Dionysiac competition" (*HE* II. 209).

Hellas, if not by the heralds. The use of σοφία for poetry is again Callimachean (F 1. 18), and again, before that, Pindaric:[230] a miniature
encomion of another poet that turns out to be a statement of Callimachus's
own views on poetry.

Callimachus is not depreciating the Dionysiac contests, merely consol-
ing his friend for not winning. Two other epigrams actually suggest that he
himself competed. First the rather enigmatic AP ix. 566, addressed to
Dionysus: poets who win make short speeches, but those who lose complain about injustice.[231] Thomas rather oddly claims this as a "general
attack on drama," but it is clearly nothing of the sort. There is no condemnation of the whole institution: the poem simply concludes with the
wish that its author might fall into the first category. Then there is AP xi.
362, ostensibly about Orestes and Pylades. Orestes may have been crazy,
says the poet, but he wasn't so crazy as to try the one test that really proves
a friend: produce a drama! That way he would have lost Pylades for
sure—just as I have lost many a Pylades myself. The point is evidently that
competing against your friends in the sacred contests is a sure way to lose
them. As always, we cannot straightforwardly identify the speaker with
Callimachus himself, but his Suda-entry does mention "satyr-dramas, tragedies and comedies." For reasons never clearly formulated or justified,
most scholars have refused to believe in them.[232]

Yet the argument that no fragments have survived has little weight
(there are few fragments from any Hellenistic dramatists), nor can we
exclude the possibility that one or two of the otherwise unidentifiable titles
in his Suda-entry (e.g. Semele, Glaucus or Hopes) are titles of dramas.[233]
Weaker still the apriori argument that a hater of bombast cannot have written tragedy.[234] Both Herodas and Theocritus were much influenced by
mime, and some of Callimachus's hymns employ dramatic techniques. Nor
did the Roman "Alexandrians" show any distaste for the stage. Quite the
reverse: Horace's literary epistles repeatedly refer to drama, Ovid wrote a
famous tragedy, and Catullus may have written mimes.[235]

---

230. O. 116; 9. 38; P. 1. 12; 4. 248; 6. 49; N. 7. 23; I. 7. 18; Pa. 7b. 20; see W. J.
Slater, Lexicon to Pindar (Berlin 1969), 468 s.v. B, with G. W. Most, The Measures of
Praise (1985), 144-5.

231. I am simplifying the rather obscurely phrased lines 3-5.

232. "wahrscheinlich irrig," Christ-Schmidt, Gesch. d. Griech. Lit. II. 1[6] (1920), 134;
"non constat," Pfeiffer II. xcv; "I am very sceptical," Fraser II. 841 n. 311; "höchst
unwahrscheinlich," Zwierlein 1966, 137 n.13; "wird heute kaum noch als glaubhaft
angesehen," Schwinge 1986, 32; against such scepticism, Meillier 1979, 258 n. 48.

233. D. Curiazi's identification of a quotation in Etym. Gen. as a fragment of Callimachean satyr-drama (Mus. Crit. 18 [1983], 203-8) is very speculative, but not for that
reason necessarily mistaken.

234. A. Giannini, Dioniso 37 (1963), 48-73; R. F. Thomas, HSCP 83 (1979), 179-206;
Schwinge 1986, 32.

235. P. White, Promised Verse (1993), 53; T. P. Wiseman, Catullus and his World
(Cambridge 1985), 188-98.

It is a fallacy to suppose that, when Callimachus repudiates the beaten track, he repudiates all popular genres simply because they were popular. If we leave dramatic poetry on one side, he achieved his greatest success and fame in the three most popular literary forms of his age: elegy, more particularly catalogue elegy (*Aetia*: Ch. XIII. 3); short epic (*Hecale*: Ch. XVII); and epigram (Ch. III).

It will be worth taking a fresh look at his other references to the stage without presupposing hostility and contempt. Even if the participle λnκυθίζουσα applied to τραγῳδὸς μοῦσα in the one-line F 215 means "booming" (as Horace's imitation would suggest)[236] and mocks tragedy for its bombast, that still falls short of condemning tragedy itself. Aristophanes made fun of tragic bombast, yet awarded Aeschylus the palm over Euripides. For Horace too bombast (in a translation of Callimachus's term) was simply one element in tragedy, which the poet might employ or not as he saw fit.[237] We do not even know which of the *Iambi* the line comes from, and with no context there is no way of knowing just what rôle tragedy played in the poem.

More interesting is the question of Hellenistic satyr-drama. When Dioscorides praised Sositheus for restoring satyr-drama, this did not mean revival of a form neglected in third-century Alexandria, but rejection of the fashionable urbanized satyr-drama of Lycophron, "taking the satyrs out of the city and back into their ancestral wilds."[238] It is tantalizing not to know how Lycophron adapted the conventions of satyr-drama to bring on stage the symposia of his philosophy teacher, but here is intriguing proof that Callimachus was not the only contemporary poet to experiment with the traditional genres.[239] Rather than assume blanket condemnation of all the many different forms of dramatic poetry, we might (for example) expect to find Callimachus supporting Lycophron against the archaizing revival of Sositheus. As for the τραγῳδοί of *Iamb* 2 (F 192. 12) having the "voice of fishes" (that is to say no voice at all), he means (of course) tragic *actors*, not poets,[240] suggesting a reference to modern acting styles rather than the style or subject matter of tragedy itself. Another epigram (*AP* vi. 311)

236. *Ep* I. 3. 14 (*tragica desaevit et ampullatur in arte*), cf. *AP* 97 (*proicit ampullas*); but Cicero and Pliny use the term quite differently (Shackleton Bailey on Cic. *Att.* 14 3n.).

237. See Brink's notes on the passages cited in the last note; Thomas 1979, 189-90.

238. T. P. Wiseman, *JRS* 78 (1988), 8; Sutton 1980, 81-83; R. Seaford, *Euripides: Cyclops* (Oxford 1984), 19-20.

239. Indeed this sort of satyr-play goes back to the age of Alexander at least, with Python's *Agen*: Fantuzzi 1993, 31-36; Ch. I. 2

240. E. Courtney, *ZPE* 74 (1988), 276; for this (the only certainly attested) meaning for τραγῳδός and κωμῳδός, J. and L. Robert, *REG* 71 (1958), 223; C. P. Jones, *CQ* 37 (1987), 208; all the examples alleged = "writer of tragedy" (*LSJ* s.v. III) are uncertain or Byzantine.

celebrates the dedication of a comic mask, perhaps by an actor rather than playwright.

It is in fact striking how many of the Alexandrian epigrammatists wrote on theatrical themes.[241] In addition to a series of epigrams on earlier dramatists, Dioscorides wrote epitaphs for two stars of the Ptolemaic stage, the comic poet Machon and the satyr poet Sositheus just mentioned;[242] Nossis an epitaph on the tragic burlesque writer Rhinthon (*AP* vii. 414); Phalaecus on the crowns of the comic writer Lycon (*AP* xiii. 6). Theocritus commemorates the tripod and statue of Dionysus dedicated by the choregos Damomenes in return for a victory (*AP* vi. 339), and the marble altar dedicated to the Muses "having won renown for his accomplishment" by the musician Xenocles (ib. 337).

Another Callimachean epigram concerns a tragic mask of Dionysus (*AP* vi. 310). Because the mask is represented as yawning with boredom as schoolchildren recite speeches from the *Bacchae*, Thomas claimed it as a condemnation of "the monotony of tragic recitals."[243] But the fact that the mask was dedicated in a schoolroom by a schoolboy excludes so sweeping an interpretation, and its "boredom" is simply a witty explanation of a particular type of mask shown with wide open mouth.[244] Thomas's (certainly mistaken) view that *AP* xii. 43 (ἐχθαίρω τὸ ποίημα τὸ κυκλικόν) is an attack on New Comedy will be discussed in a different context in a later chapter (Ch. XIV. 1). It is hard to believe Callimachus would have written so often and in such a matter-of-fact way about the dramatic contests of his age if he had really despised and shunned them.[245] That live drama was thriving in early third-century Egypt is confirmed by the existence of an active guild of Dionysiac artists, who (led by the scholarly Philicus) participated in the great procession of 275/4.[246]

All in all, we are surely bound to conclude that there is no basis for Gentili's radical distinction between "learned poetry" and "festive performance." The original hexameter poetry written for these festivals was no doubt for the most part poor stuff. But that does not mean that prize poets *composed* differently from Callimachus; that they were in any significant sense oral poets as distinct from than book poets. Those who wrote for the festival competitions were no longer (of course) working within even the

241. T.B.L. Webster, "Alexandrian Epigrams and the Theatre," *Miscellanea di studi Alessandrini...A. Rostagni* (Turin 1963), 531-43, is in fact limited to Dioscorides.

242. Dioscorides XXIII-IV; Webster 1963; Sifakis 1966, 124-26; Sutton, *Riv. di studi class.* 21 (1973), 3-6.

243. *HSCP* 83 (1979), 188.

244. See Gow and Page, *HE* II. 182.

245. As (for example) Schwinge 1986, 32-36 insists. We should bear in mind that he had devoted much labour to compiling a list of Attic playwrights (Blum 1991, 137-42).

246. Rice, *Grand Procession* (1983), 52-58.

vestiges of a genuine oral tradition. Their short poems on cults, myths, origins, rulers and the like were themselves in many cases new genres, a transposition into hexameters of themes that had earlier been treated in choral lyric. They were increasingly composed in accordance with rhetorical patterns that were eventually systematized in the surviving treatises of the Roman Empire and manifested in the surviving epideictic poetry of that age.[247] If they mostly perished without trace, this is simply because they were not good enough to survive, not because they were only written for performance.

8

We come at last to the question of Callimachus's hymns. Reference is usually made to an article of Legrand,[248] which is held to have settled the matter once for all. In fact Legrand suggested a number of possible performance situations (including festival contests), and only claimed to have made it improbable that the so-called "mimetic" hymns (II, V and VI) were performed during cult acts. He pointed out (for example) that the poet could hardly have counted on his dramatic appeals to the snorting of horses and creaking of axles being fulfilled as he spoke. But Legrand was careful not to extend his argument to the other hymns, freely conceding that the *Hymn to Delos* at any rate might well have been publicly performed at a festival on Delos.[249] He then went on to suggest that the *Hymn to Artemis* was performed at a festival to Artemis at Ephesus mentioned in a fragment of the contemporary poet Alexander Aetolus.[250] We have already seen that on the most natural interpretation the *Hymn to Apollo*, recounting as it does the foundation of Cyrene with references to "our city" and "our kings," was written and performed in Cyrene. F. Williams makes much of the "great erudition" Callimachus expected of his readers, specifying "the local traditions of Cyrenean history...and the literary accounts of the city's foundation." To be sure, not everyone could be expected to know such things—but a Cyrenean audience could.[251]

In recent years dogmatism has ruled.[252] Typical is the verdict of the most recent commentator on the *Hymn to Delos*:[253]

---

247. See Hardie 1983, Viljamaa 1968 and E. L. Bowie, "Greek Sophists and Greek Poetry in the Second Sophistic," *ANRW* II. 33. 1 (1989), 209-258.

248. Ph.-E. Legrand, *RÉA* 3 (1901), 281-312; cf. Fraser 652f.; II. 916-17.

249. "c'est sans nul doute à une fête délienne qu'on peut le rattacher avec la plus grande vraisemblance," p. 311.

250. p. 312; F 4 Powell.

251. F. Williams 1978, 4.

252. Cairns 1992, 13-15 has recently protested at this dogmatism.

253. W. H. Mineur, *Callimachus: Hymn to Delos* (Leiden 1984), 10.

> The days are definitely gone, it seems, when Callimachus's hymns were regarded as official pieces of poetry, intended to add lustre to some Delian festival or to compete in some poetical agon on the island.

For Herter, as for Wilamowitz, there could be no question that they were written for recitation in literary circles, primarily at court.[254] For Bing they illustrate the transformation of poetry into "a private act of communication"; their performance is a "literary evocation," an "illusion."[255] F. Bormann in his edition of the *Hymn to Artemis* dismisses the notion of performance as a "misunderstanding" of the nature of the hymns, which he sees as "purely literary creations."[256] Even in the sophisticated recent commentaries of Hopkinson and Bulloch the alternatives have been posed too crudely: if not written to accompany actual ritual acts, then read in the library. If the *Hymn to Athena* can be shown to be no more than an "illusory enactment" of an Argive festival, then it need have no connection of any sort with Argos. But the mention of a *Foundation of Argos* in the Suda-entry (Ἄργους οἰκισμός) surely supports the natural inference of a visit. Hopkinson argues that since "golden ritual objects are unknown in genuine ritual," the festival of the *Hymn to Demeter* must be "a purely literary one."[257] But this is to assume that ritual performance is the only performance possible.[258]

As a subtle recent paper by Mary Depew has illustrated, Callimachus skilfully creates the *fiction* of a ritual performance; the way he handles the conventions of the hymn is mannered and even frivolous.[259] But I cannot for the life of me see why this is supposed to prove that he did not perform at all. Since (as we have seen) Greek poetry and ceremonial literature of every sort from the Dark Ages down to the Crusades was written for performance, why is it that, in the absence of any direct evidence and in defiance of such evidence as there is, we are supposed to make an exception for Callimachus and Theocritus? As we shall see (Ch. III. 2), the very idea of writing poetry solely for reading in book form is an anachronism in the ancient world.

In their anxiety to stress the "otherness" of archaic ritual performance, scholars have exaggerated the similarities between Hellenistic and modern poets: archaic poets worked within an oral tradition, relying on their

254. *HD* I. 182; *RE* Suppbd V. 434.

255. Bing 1988, 17.

256. *Call. Hymnus in Dianam* (Florence 1968), xii-xiii.

257. Bulloch 1985, 3-13; Hopkinson 1984, 35-43.

258. On the other hand, his observation that, unlike *Hymns* 2 and 5, which are explicitly set at Cyrene and Argos respectively, there is no such reference to a setting in the *Hymn to Demeter* might indeed have a bearing on the possibility of actual performance.

259. "Mimesis and Aetiology in Callimachus' *Hymns*," in Harder 1993, 57-77.

memories, while Hellenistic poets worked from books, alluding to passages they had read—just like us. Both sides of the polarity have been overstated. On the one hand, if the text of the archaic poets had not been written down at the time it would not have survived. On the other, we should not (as often implied) picture Callimachus checking his quotations as he wrote like a modern writer. Ancient writers notoriously quote from memory, partly because of the difficulty of locating quotations in unpaginated and unindexed rolls, but more importantly because a central feature of ancient education was learning passages from the poets by heart and performing them aloud; students would compete for prizes in recitation.[260] Writing when they did, inevitably Hellenistic poets had a larger stock of earlier poetry to draw on, no doubt mainly derived from books. Undoubtedly books played an ever more important rôle in Hellenistic culture. But when composing their own work poets may still have relied on their memory more than commonly supposed.

Festival and library are by no means the only alternatives, nor is it necessary to suppose that public performance implies "official" poetry. According to Hopkinson, for instance, "rather than see the *Hymns* as written for reading or declamation...some scholars have clung tenaciously to a poor alternative to actual performance."[261] He was referring to Cahen's suggestion that they were performed at festivals but "outside the formal framework of the festival itself."[262] But is this really so poor or even implausible an alternative? Would not a famous Latin poem provide a close parallel? Until 1890 few informed scholars would ever have believed that Horace's *Carmen saeculare* was performed by a choir of children at the Secular Games of 17 B.C. But in that year a substantial fragment of the Acta of the Games was unearthed, revealing that it had indeed been publicly performed by a chorus of 27 boys and 27 girls. In a famous paper Mommsen at once suggested that Horace's poem was actually sung as a procession song during the ritual.[263] In fact the Acta specify that the poem was performed *sacrificio perfecto*, not till the ritual itself was concluded.[264] Most would now accept Fraenkel's solution, that Horace wrote "a typical Horatian ode, not meant to be part of the religious ceremonies but to be an ideal image of them, and therefore to be performed after the completion of all the sacrifices."

Fraenkel himself insisted that this was a "bold innovation," "in the face of all precedents." Was it really so new? After recapitulating Fraenkel's

---

260. E.g. Marrou 1965, 251-52.
261. *Callimachus: Hymn to Demeter* (Cambridge 1984), 37.
262. Cahen 1929, 281, cf. Fraser II. 916 n. 289.
263. *Reden und Aufsätze* (1905), 351f.; Wilamowitz, *Sappho und Simon.* (1913), 316.
264. *ILS* 5050. 147-49, with Fraenkel, *Horace* 378-382.

analysis, J. K. Newman remarked in passing:[265] "Is there not an obvious model for this kind of poem in the hymns of Callimachus? They too are not part of any religious festival, although sometimes they seek to create the impression that their speaker is in the midst of such a celebration." That the Ptolemies set much store by pomp and ceremonial is amply documented, not least by Callixenus's detailed description of the spectacular procession of 275/4.[266] If Ptolemy wanted, as Augustus did, his most distinguished poets to contribute to the great Alexandrian festivals—the Ptolemaia, Basileia and Arsinoeia—some such compromise was inevitable.[267]

It is no surprise that we do not find the names of Callimachus and Theocritus on the victor lists from Delphi and Delos. To start with the lists are very fragmentary, nor is it likely that such major poets either regularly attended or deigned to compete regularly with such as Amphiclos of Chios and Demoteles of Andros. We only have one Egyptian victor list from Callimachus's lifetime—and from Ptolemaïs, not Alexandria. A poet of Callimachus's stature may not have competed often, but he surely travelled (Ch VIII. 5) and gave the occasional command performance. In this context I will venture two specific conjectures: first, that he wrote his *Galateia*, an aetiological celebration of the defeat of the Gauls at Delphi, for the Soteria established there to commemorate the event (Ch. X. 4); second, that he wrote F 115 on the mysteries of Samothrace for performance on that island (Ch. VIII. 5). The fact that he disliked banality and bombast is entirely irrelevant to the question of performance,[268] and certainly gives no ground for supposing that he repudiated so central an element in the profession of poet.[269]

Callimachus's hymns were no doubt more learned and sophisticated than the poems of Amphiclos of Chios and Demoteles of Andros, but their subject matter was really not so very different. Was the gulf between them so great that, while Amphiclos and Demoteles gave public recitations, Callimachus "address[ed] himself to a small circle of *cognoscenti*" (F. Williams)? As Hutchinson sensibly remarks, "there is demonstrably far more to these works than the conduct of scholarly quizzes and polemics; we cannot reduce them to such a compass by conjuring up readers whose concern with erudition drives out all other interests and responses."[270]

265. *Augustus and the New Poetry* (Coll. Latomus 88), 1967, 350.

266. Rice, *Grand Procession* (1983), with V. Foertmeyer, *Historia* 37 (1988), 90-104.

267. On which see Fraser I. 230-33.

268. ἐχθαίρω πάντα τὰ δημόσια does not either include or imply (e. g.) Horace's *volgo recitare timentis* or *nec recito cuiquam nisi amicis, idque coactus* (*Serm*. i. 4. 23, 73).

269. Which is not to say that he necessarily recited in person; those with a poor voice or insufficient nerve (Isocrates, for example) used stand-ins; cf. Pliny, *Ep*. ix. 34, implying that some authors mimed while their reader read.

270. Hutchinson 1988, 6-7.

The point at issue is whether Callimachus was simply and solely (as usually depicted) the archetype of a new breed, the scholar poet scribbling away in his ivory tower, communicating with a few colleagues in the ancient equivalent of a seminar room. Or whether in many important respects he was actually typical of his age. Furthermore, if some at least of his *Hymns*[271] and Theocritus's *Idylls* were publicly performed on the same sort of occasions as the poems of Amphiclos and Demoteles and the rest of the fraternity, we would have several complete (if superior) specimens of a genre known otherwise only by repute.

9

It was not just the festival hacks who were active in the public arena and received public recognition of one sort or another. Posidippus appears on a proxenos list of 263/62 at Thermum (the religious and political centre of the Aetolian league), explicitly described as "the epigrammatist from Pella."[272] Though not an honour awarded by competition,[273] this clearly represents public recognition of his professional skill. Though hitherto best known to us as the writer of sophisticated erotic and symposiastic poetry, Posidippus did not disdain official commissions. Three of his dedicatory epigrams for Alexandrian monuments have long been known, and the new Milan papyrus has another four dedications by Arsinoë and nineteen epigrams celebrating victors in the equestrian games, all presumably men and women of wealth and position if they could maintain a racing stable.[274] One of them implies a visit to Olympia in the 290s or 280s (p. 145). There is also more than a possibility that the Posidippus who wrote a work *On Cnidos* describing Praxiteles's Cnidian Aphrodite is the epigrammatist. Two epigrams on statues by Lysippus are preserved in the Anthology, and the Milan roll has several more on other statues by famous sculptors.[275] A Delphian proxeny list of 276/75 or 273/72 names Posidippus and Asclepiades together.[276]

271. For example, II, IV and V, with their Cyrenean, Delian and Argive settings.

272. *IG* IX. 1² 17, lines 24-25; Fraser II. 796 n. 44.

273. Contests in epigrams are not attested before the imperial period (L. Robert, *Études épigr. et philol.* [Paris 1938], 22), but it is reasonable to suppose that they existed earlier.

274. Fraser 566-67; II. 810-12; information about the new poems from G. Bastianini.

275. *FGrH* 447; *SH* 706 (perhaps in prose, but that does not exclude ecphrastic epigrams); *APl* 119 (also on the Milan papyrus) and 275.

276. *FD* III. 3. 192; cf. Trypanis, *CR* 66 (1952), 68-69 and Fraser II. 796 n. 45. Neither is identified as a poet, and to that extent the identification must remain speculative, but the two poets had many connections: see my *Greek Anthology*, Appendix 7. An Asclepiades of Samos appears on the same proxeny list at Histiaea as Heracleitus of Halicarnassus (*SIG*³ 492. 1. 17, cf. 1. 26, of ca 266).

A strange passage of Posidippus's *Seal* begs Apollo to command "the Macedonians, islanders and neighbours of the whole Asiatic coast" to honour him, hoping that his statue will stand in the agora of Pella scroll in hand. Lloyd-Jones remarks that the poet is not "likely to have expected to be taken at his word,"[277] but this is no casual wish for immortality. Only the most important civic benefactors were accorded the honour of a statue in the agora (which would be of bronze), after a formal request to the council and people in accordance with strict rules.[278] The request had to come from the would-be honorand himself or (if deceased) his family, which may explain the immodest form of the poem, in effect a poetic version of Posidippus's request.[279] No one would make so precise and public a request for such an honour unless he had a reasonable expectation that it would be granted.

We do in fact have a statue of a poet inscribed with the name Posidippus, represented scroll in hand,[280] hitherto identified as the epigrammatist's homonymous contemporary and fellow Macedonian, the comic poet Posidippus of Cassandreia. According to Richter, the comic poet was "the only bearer of that name sufficiently important to have had a statue erected to him,"[281] and at least one statue was erected to him, by the people of Cassandreia on Delos.[282] But the epigrammatist was just as distinguished in his own field and, as an associate of kings and queens, perhaps a man of wider consequence. We have already seen that a statue of Philitas was erected in his native Cos,[283] specified as bronze and so presumably in the agora. There was also a statue of Aratus in his native Soloi, no doubt the model for the many later representations (coins, a herm, a mosaic and a textile).[284]

Unfortunately nothing but his epigrams now survives to document the life of the prolific and influential Leonidas. His self-epitaph laments a life spent wandering far from his native Italy, despite the compensation of his poetic fame.[285] Few of his extant epigrams suggest commissions, though *APl* 182, on the Aphrodite Anadyomene of Apelles, implies a visit to Cos, where the painting was housed in the temple of Asclepius. Other epigrams

277. *SH* 705. 16-17; Lloyd-Jones, *JHS* 83 (1963), 90 = *Acad. Papers* II (1990), 181.
278. P. Gauthier, *Les cités grecques et leurs bienfaiteurs* (Paris 1985), 31-34, 79-88.
279. The candidate had to be at least 60 (Gauthier 88), which may explain the emphasis on his age. Addressing Pella he tactfully glosses over his Aetolian and Alexandrian honours.
280. A Roman copy, now in the Vatican: G.M.A. Richter, *Portraits of the Greeks*, abridged and revised by R.R.R. Smith (Oxford 1984), 187-89; Smith, *Hellenistic Sculpture* (London 1991), 39, fig. 43; M. Dickie, "Which Posidippus?", forthcoming.
281. Richter, *Portraits of the Greeks* ii (London 1965), 238; 1984 ed. 389.
282. Homolle, *BCH* iii (1879), 369; *Inscr. Délos* 2486; Richter 1965, 238.
283. Hermesianax F 7. 76: Κῷοι χάλκειον θῆκαν, the formal vocabulary of the genre.
284. Pomp. Mela i. 13; Richter 1965, 239-40; 1984, 89-92.
285. *AP* vii. 715; vii. 736 also proclaims the life of the wanderer: *HE* II. 343.

imply visits to Athens and perhaps (Ch. III. 2) to Alexandria as well.[286] The absence of obviously commissioned epigrams (for example, on buildings and local dignitaries) may be a consequence of Meleager's selection.[287] For example, Callimachus (XIV), Posidippus (XII) and Hedylus (IV) all wrote epigrams for various aspects of the dedication of the temple of Aphrodite-Arsinoe on Zephyrium. All are longer than the average literary epigram, and none are preserved in the Anthology tradition. The same applies to Posidippus's other Ptolemaic commissions (XI, XIII and several more in the Milan roll). Indeed the Milan roll contains a much higher proportion of what looks like commissioned work than Meleager.[288] Meleager's tastes were evidently literary rather than historical or encomiastic, and it would not be surprising if he had systematically omitted routine professional work.

Though best remembered by posterity as the inventor of bucolic, Theocritus too seems to have written epigrams for commission: *Ep.* 22, on a bronze statue of the early epic poet Peisander set up by the people of his native Camirus on Rhodes;[289] 18, the bronze statue of Epicharmus set up by his fellow citizens in Syracuse; 17, on a statue of Anacreon on his native Teos (all three, suitably enough, in Doric). 8 celebrates a cedarwood statue of Asclepius made by the craftsman Eetion for a "high reward" from Theocritus's friend Nicias at Miletus.

A poet of the age much admired by Callimachus was Heracleitus of Halicarnassus, whose "Nightingales" he predicted (mistakenly, in the event) would live for ever. Heracleitus was also a man of affairs, known from proxeny lists in Euboea and Chios, and honoured with a statue at Oropus.[290] At about the same time the well-known epigrammatist Mnasalkes of Sicyon was also honoured at Oropus.[291] Mnasalkes may also have composed the epigram for a monument by the famous Siyonian sculptor Thoenias commissioned by the Attalid admiral Dionysodorus and recently discovered at Pergamum.[292] Protogenes's painting of Philicus has already been mentioned (p. 42).

---

286. Gow and Page, *HE* II. 307-8; for Alexandria, Ch. III. 2.

287. For other ways in which Meleager's selection has influenced our perception of Hellenistic epigram, see my *Greek Anthology* (1993), 13-15.

288. To judge from the twenty-five poems published so far (*Posidippo Epigrammi* ed. G. Bastianini and C. Gallazzi, Milan 1993 [in fact 1994]).

289. Since Peisander was best known for an epic on Heracles, the mythical ancestor of the Ptolemies, some Ptolemaic connection might be inferred.

290. W. Swinnen, "Herakleitos of Halikarnassos, an Alexandrian Poet and Diplomat?", *Ancient Society* 1 (1970), 39-52.

291. *IG* vii. 395, with A. Wilhelm, *SB* Wien 179. 6 (1915), 3-6 = *Akademieschriften zur griech. Inschr.* I (1974), 177-80.

292. L. Lehnus, *ZPE* 1996 forthcoming.

No such contemporary honours are recorded for Callimachus, but the author of a recent history of Hellenistic sculpture, unfettered by modern dogma about the ivory tower, took it for granted that there must have been portraits "of the great court poet Kallimachos at Alexandria."[293] Given the almost complete loss of inscriptions and monuments from Alexandria, it is not surprising that nothing of the sort has survived, though it has been suggested that the poet represented on the well known relief by Archelaus of Priene, found in Italy but perhaps originally from the Homereum of Alexandria, should be identified as Callimachus (Ch. X. 3).

All these public honours and civic decrees compel us to question the assumption made explicit in the quotation from Gordon Williams with which this chapter began. His purpose was to contrast serious Roman poets with their frivolous Hellenistic predecessors. By the late Republic, according to Williams, "poetry had achieved a new place and function in Roman society," something Greek poets had been without for many centuries.[294] It is true enough that for a few decades Roman poets cultivated public themes, but that is not quite the same as a place and function in society. The truth is the exact opposite. Unlike their Greek counterparts, who could compete in festivals, give public recitals and win a variety of civic distinctions in cities large and small throughout the Hellenistic world, Roman poets were obliged to remain in Rome and attach themselves to private patrons.[295] Hellenistic poets did not just sit in libraries and entertain each other. Poetry was an honourable and rewarding profession—and not just at the courts of kings.

293. Smith 1991, 39; for various suggested identifications (none to be taken seriously), Richter 1965, 241.
294. See his long chapter "The Poet and the Community," Williams 1968, 31-101.
295. No Roman poet ever "attempted to pursue a literary career from any base but Rome," P. White, *Promised Verse* (1993), 19, 49.

Chapter III

The Symposium

1

In the private sphere, the main context for the performance of poetry was the symposium—a major growth area in the study of early Greek literature and society in recent years. Many scholars now assign almost all early Greek poetry outside epic and drama to the symposium.[1] Once again, however, it is generally assumed that Hellenistic symposia no longer played this rôle. The symposia of sixth- and fifth-century Athens are held to represent an integration of poetry and society which could not persist in an age of kings and courts. To repeat the extreme formulation of Gordon Williams already cited (Ch. II. 1): Hellenistic poets "wrote symposiastic poetry, without having any real drinking-party in mind."[2]

Lesky was prepared to allow that some Hellenistic epigrams were "declaimed at a banquet of friends," but the word "declaim" was carefully chosen to lead up to his next point, held to be symptomatic of the age, that "the spoken epigram took the place of the sung skolion of earlier times."[3] Behind Lesky's remark lies, as so often in judgments on Hellenistic literature, a presupposition of decline, made more explicit in the work of the last decade or so, in which there has been a tendency to privilege song over elegy and even archaic over classical poetry. For example, Gentili's *Poetry and its Public in Ancient Greece* (1988) is almost entirely devoted to archaic lyric, with barely a mention of the Theognidean corpus, the "oldest and richest store of sympotic *Leitmotive*."[4] Even if elegy was sung to the aulos rather than recited,[5] the melody must have been very simple. The disappearance of song proper cannot in any case be explained in terms of Hellenistic "decline."

1. M. Vetta (ed.), *Poesia e simposio nella Grecia antica* (Laterza 1983); Oswyn Murray (ed.), *Sympotica: A Symposium on the Symposion* (Oxford 1990). The classic work remains R. Reitzenstein, *Epigramm und Skolion* (Giessen 1893).
2. Williams, *Tradition and Originality* (1968), 35.
3. A. Lesky, *A History of Greek Literature* (New York 1966), 738.
4. G. Giangrande, "Sympotic Literature and Epigram," *L'Épigramme grecque* (Entretiens Fondation Hardt xiv) Geneva 1968, 103; on sympotic elegy, E. L. Bowie, *JHS* 106 (1986), 13-21 and in *Sympotica* (1990), 221-29.
5. Gentili, *Poetry and its Public* (1988), 35; Bowie in *Sympotica* (1990), 221.

There is abundant evidence that as early as the beginning of the Peloponnesian war Athenian symposiasts preferred speeches from drama to the songs of Alcman, Pindar, Simonides and Stesichorus. When asked to take the lyre and sing a song (μέλος) of Simonides, the young Strepsiades replies that it is old-fashioned to sing to the lyre while drinking and recites a speech (ῥῆσις) from Euripides instead. There are many similar passages in Old and Middle Comedy.[6] Aeschines refers to people reciting speeches at the symposium; Theophrastus's late-learner learns speeches to recite at the symposium and then forgets them.[7] Those inclined to romanticize the otherness of archaic "song culture" talk of a "decline of...creative energy."[8] But if we look at the phenomenon in historical perspective, no such mystical formulas are needed to explain why the dominance of drama and democracy made songs from the age of the tyrants look old-fashioned. The little book of Attic skolia preserved by Athenaeus dates from the same period, "decorous and public-minded" songs whose associations with the tyrants were still remembered a century later.[9] When warned to cap the skolia in polite company, Bdelycleon's father replies: "Of course, no Diacrian will cap them better." The Diacrians were the party that had helped Peisistratus to seize power.[10] It is not surprising that young men who had grown up in the age of the sophists preferred Euripidean speeches in their cups.

So the symposium culture of the late fifth and fourth centuries was already very different from that of the sixth. There is little point (with Lesky) in comparing the symposia of the sixth and third centuries and finding the latter wanting. A more realistic question is, did the third century see a decline from the fourth? I see no reason to believe that it did. As we shall see, the basic form of the symposium remained remarkably constant down the centuries and throughout the Hellenistic world.[11] Tragic speeches (ῥῆσεις) continued to dominate Hellenistic symposia, but much new sympotic poetry was written, particularly in the form of epigram. While it is natural to stress the original features of Hellenistic epigram, it is important not to ignore the strong element of formal continuity with the sympotic elegy of the sixth century (§ 2).

6. Ar. *Nub.* 1354f. (with Dover's note); Eup. F 139, 366; Ephipp. F 16, Antiph. F 85.

7. Aesch. *In Tim.* 168; Theophr. *Char.* 27. 2.

8. Gentili 1988, 30.

9. *PMG* 884-908, with C. M. Bowra, *Greek Lyric Poetry*[2] (Oxford 1961), 373 and 397; W. Rösler, *Sympotica* (1990), 230-36.

10. Ar. *Wasps* 1222-3; Aristotle, *Ath. Pol.* 13. 4, with Rhodes's commentary.

11. By focusing on luxury alone and modishly dismissing Hellenistic royal banquets as "les repas des Autres," Pauline Schmitt Pantel (*La cité au banquet: Histoire des repas publics dans les cités grecques* [Rome 1992], 458) glosses over the important areas of continuity documented in this chapter.

Oswyn Murray suspects that there was a "gradual loss of sympotic culture in the second and first centuries, which resulted in an antiquarian attitude of self-conscious occasional revivalism by the Augustan age."[12] Since the limited purpose of this chapter is to provide a context for Callimachus, that subject can be left to others. But I am delighted to report that such a connoisseur of the field shares my conviction that no such loss had taken place by the age of Callimachus. Indeed the reign of Philadelphus was arguably a new golden age of sympotic poetry.

Since it was at the courts of the Macedonian Successor kings that most Alexandrian poets wrote, it is Macedonian symposia that are most relevant for our purpose. Macedonians took their symposia very seriously.[13] Even on campaign, Alexander is recorded as attending at least twenty-six.[14] The symposium was clearly the key meeting place of king and court. The recently excavated Macedonian royal tombs reveal little but weapons and drinking vessels. There can be no doubt that these gatherings saw some serious drinking. One contest in drinking at Persepolis was said by a contemporary to have led to 41 fatalities, and contemporary gossip-mongers tell stories of the remarkable capacity of the king himself.[15] The Successors had similar tastes: whence the custom of naming types of cup after the kings (antigonis, seleucis and the like).[16]

It was at the symposium that those who could gain an entrée would find the monarch at his ease, where men of wit and intelligence had an opportunity to impress him.[17] It should be borne in mind that most of the first generation or two of Hellenistic kings were men of considerable culture and literary interests. Both Philadelphus and Antigonus Gonatas surrounded themselves with poets and philosophers. Ptolemy Euergetes was so attracted by the charm and wit of a Jew called Joseph that he invited him to dine on a regular basis.[18] The symposia of the kings were presumably

12. "Hellenistic Royal Symposia," to appear in *Hellenistic Kingship: the Royal Parousia*, ed. Per Bilde, Aarhus 1995. I am grateful for an advance text.

13. For the archaeological evidence, R. A. Tomlinson, *Ancient Macedonia* 1 (1970), 308-315; B. Bergquist in *Sympotica* (1990), 37-65.

14. J. M. O'Brien, *Alexander the Great: The Invisible Enemy* (London 1992), 103 (the enemy being drink); E. N. Borza, "The Symposium at Alexander's Court," *Ancient Macedonia* 3 (1983), 45-55; *In the Shadow of Olympus*[2] (Princeton 1990), 241-42.

15. "When Alexander was dining with Medeius the Thessalian he drank toasts with all 20 members of the symposium," Nicobule, *FGrH* 127 F 1 (Athen. 434C; on Medeius, L. Pearson, *Lost Histories of Alexander* [1960], 68-70); Chares, *FGrH* 125 F 19 (Athen. 437A + Plut. *Alex.* 70); Ephippus, *FGrH* 126 F 3 (Athen. 434AB).

16. Athen. 783E.

17. Asked why he had refused a cup of unmixed wine, Callisthenes replied "I have no wish to drink to Alexander and then need Asclepius" (Athen. 434D). There is no basis for the common view that Macedonians always drank their wine unmixed; this was obviously a toast, which was regularly drunk neat (Gow on Theocr. 2. 152; 14. 18).

18. τῇ χάριτι καὶ τῇ εὐτραπελίᾳ, Joseph. *Ant. Jud.* xii. 173.

much larger than private symposia—but surely no larger than the banquets of the tyrants which Anacreon, Simonides and Pindar attended. Pindar's skolion for the banquet given by Xenophon of Corinth mentions the participation of one hundred courtesans.[19] But there is no reason to believe that private symposia of the Hellenistic period were any larger than in classical times: there were twenty guests at the wedding of the Macedonian Caranus (Athen. 129A-C).

For all their hard drinking, there is abundant evidence that even Macedonian soldiers regularly quoted and sang poetry at their symposia, especially Homer and Euripides. The last straw in the fatal fight between Alexander and Cleitus was when Cleitus threw an offensively pointed quotation from Euripides at Alexander: "things have come to a pretty pass in Greece..." (*Andr.* 693). We cannot doubt that both Alexander and Cleitus knew full well how the passage continued: "...when the general takes the credit due his army" (Plut. *Alex.* 51. 8). At one symposium Alexander neatly quoted a line of Euripides to Callisthenes, who had delivered extempore declamations for and against the Macedonians, including apposite quotations from Homer (ib. 53). When pelted with apples by Alexander during a symposium, Anaxarchus retaliated with a line from Euripides: "A god shall be struck by a mortal hand."[20]   One stock Macedonian symposium game was for the guests to compare lines from Homer.[21]

Despite the popularity of dramatic recitation at Hellenistic symposia, singing was not entirely a thing of the past. The clearest proof is one of the most interesting of all extant symposium texts, a papyrus published by Wilamowitz and Schubart in 1907.[22] It is written in a hand that has been dated to 300/280 B.C. (the lifetime of Callimachus) and was found in the tomb of a Greek soldier at Elephantine. First come three skolia in astrophic dactylo-epitrites, each with a title (*Muses, Easy Prey, Mnemosyne*),[23] then a ten line elegy/epigram that lays down the rules of the symposium (laughter, jokes, mutual mockery, some serious talk and obedience to the symposiarch).[24] None of the texts are much older than the date of the writ-

---

19. Or does "hundred-limbed" (ἀγέλαν ἑκατόγγυιον, F 122. 18) imply only fifty (B. A. van Groningen, *Pindare au banquet* (Leiden 1960), 41; Slater, *Lexicon to Pindar* (1969), 161 and s. v. γυῖον)?

20. *Orestes* 271; Plut., *Quaest. conv.* 737A; for other versions, Borza 1981, 78 n. 26.

21. Alexander's favourite was Γ. 179, where Agamemnon is called "a good king and mighty spearman" (Plut. 331C).

22. *BKT* V. 2 (1907), 56-63; *CA* 190-2; see too E. Pellizer and G. Tedeschi, *QFC* 4 (1983), 5-17 and (especially) F. Ferrari, *SCO* 38 (1989), 181-227. On the context of the find, W. Clarysse in *Egypt and the Hellenistic World* (Louvain 1983), 47-8.

23. Page, *GLP* 386-91; *PMG* 917; D. A. Campbell, *Greek Lyric* 5 (Harvard 1993), no. 917; West, *Greek Metre* 139.

24. Page, *GLP* 444-45; *FGE* 443; West, *IEG* ii^2 12-13.

ing. It seems clear that this is a soldier's script for a symposium, the text of
a selection of favourite songs that he took with him to perform at symposia
with fellow Macedonians stationed in Elephantine. Scarcely less significant
than the songs are their conjunction with an epigram.

F. Ferrari has recently identified another such text datable to 120/100
B.C, P. Tebt. 1-2, two copies in the same hand of a sequence of songs and
epigrams in cretics, ionics and iambics: (1) a lament by Helen; (2) a wood-
land scene; (3) and (4) different aspects of love; (5) the power of wine to
excite love. The second copy contains traces of several more poems.[25] It
may be that we can put a name to the owner of these interesting documents:
Menches *alias* Asclepiades, village scribe of Kerkeosiris.[26] Others of the
many papyrus anthologies of tragic and lyric excerpts or epigrams may also
have been intended for the symposium.[27]

Plutarch tells of a guest of Demetrius II of Macedon who was reluctant
to "sing" after dinner until the king sent his small son (the future King
Philip V), at which he responded with a quotation from tragedy, "Bring up
this boy worthy of Heracles and us"—neatly evoking the Heraclid descent
claimed by all Macedonian kings.[28] Since texts referring to later
symposium practice clearly distinguish between the "singing" (ᾄδειν) of
songs and the "speaking" (λέγειν) of speeches (p. 321), it seems that the
quotation was not itself the guest's song. Whether or not the witty response
discharged his obligation, we are entitled to infer that the original request
was specifically for a song. A contemporary description of the wedding of
Caranus the Macedonian by one of the guests quotes Homer twice and a
tragic line and then "a chorus of 100 men singing a wedding hymn"
(ᾀδόντων γαμικὸν ὕμνον).[29] Theocritus 14 describes a symposium in which
a man sang a song called "My Wolf,"[30] and from a little earlier we have
Theophrastus's surly man, who "refuses to sing, recite speeches or
dance."[31] Aristotle's skolion on the death of his friend Hermias in 345/4,
described as a hymn by Diogenes Laertius, is said by Athenaeus to have
been sung daily at banquets.[32]

25. P. Tebt. 1-2; *CA* 185-6; Page, *GLP* 410-13; Ferrari, *SCO* 38 (1989), 185-89.

26. W. Clarysse in *Egypt and the Hellenistic World* (Louvain 1983), 51.

27. See the list of such texts in R. A. Pack, *Greek and Latin Literary Texts from Greco-
Roman Egypt*[2] (Ann Arbor 1965), 1567-1622. There is another sequence of skolia in the I c.
A.D. P. Oxy. 1795 (= *CA* 199-200): G. Tedeschi, in OINHPA TEYXH: *Studi triestini di
poesia conviviale* (1991), 235-53.

28. *TGF* adesp. 399 N[2]; Plut. *QC* 736F; see Ch. IX. 2.

29. Athen. 128A-130D (Hippolochus) at 129F; for the tragic line, *TGF*[2] 576.

30. τὸν ἐμὸν Λύκον ᾆδεν ἀπ' ἀρχᾶς,/ Θεσσαλικόν τι μέλισμα, Theoc. 14. 30-31, with
Gow ad loc. and J. B. Burton, *GRBS* 33 (1992), 227-45.

31. *Char.* 15. 10 (οὔτε ᾆσαι οὔτε ῥῆσιν εἰπεῖν οὔτε ὀρχήσασθαι).

32. Athen. 696 B-7B; D.L. 5. 5; Ch. X. 5 (n. 169).

So whether or not epigrams were simply spoken, it is quite false to suppose that there was no singing at all at Hellenistic symposia. Philodemus's remark that it was the thoughts rather than the melodies of Ibycus, Anacreon and the rest that corrupted the young proves that even in his day their poems were still sung. Indeed the debate between Diogenes of Babylon and Philodemus in the latter's *De musica* only makes sense if both singing and discussing poetry continued to be normal practice at Hellenistic symposia.[33] This debate reflects a long-standing polemic between Stoics and Epicureans. In the preface to a work called *Symposium* dedicated to Ptolemy Soter, Epicurus had advised the king (in keeping with his view that music and poetry had no redeeming moral value) "to put up with recitals of stratagems and vulgar buffooneries at his symposia rather than discussion of problems in music and poetry."[34] An epigram by the Neronian Lucillius invites a friend "under new sympotic rules": no singing of poetry and no literary discussions.[35] Clearly the implication is that both were still common at first-century symposia—all too common for Lucillius's philistine friend.[36] Half a century later Plutarch remarked that "from Homer to the present day the lyre has long been a familiar member of the banquet"—adding that the music should always be accompanied by song.[37]

2

The new sympotic poetry of the age was undoubtedly epigram, which survives in abundance from the age of Callimachus. According to G. Giangrande, most Hellenistic epigrams were pure "book-poetry,"[38] at which the poet merely "pictures himself present at a banquet."[39] But there

33. *De musica* iv cols. 16-18 = A. J. Neubecker, *Philodemus Über die Musik IV Buch* (Naples 1986), pp. 59-62; cf. E. Asmis, *Classical Antiquity* 10 (1991), 1-45 and *Proceedings of the Boston Area Colloquium in Ancient Philosophy* vii, 1991 (1993), 63-93. Manuela Tecusan will be publishing a study of sympotic ἀρετή in Philodemus.

34. Plut. *Mor.* 1095C.

35. οὐ μελοποιὸς ἐρεῖ κατακείμενος· οὔτε παρέξεις / οὔθ᾽ ἕξεις αὐτὸς πράγματα γραμματικά (*AP* xi. 10. 3-4).

36. L. Robert's paper in *L'Épigramme grecque* (1968), 181-291 brilliantly showed how closely many of Lucillius's other epigrams reflect "le milieu grec ou hellénisé de Rome" (p. 286), and there seems no reason to doubt the contemporary reference of this one.

37. Plut. *QC* 7. 8. 4 = *Mor.* 712F-713B.

38. Giangrande, *L'Épigramme grecque* (1968), 93 n. 1. W. Ludwig's contribution (ib. 300) presupposed a sympotic context in passing but did not develop the point.

39. A quotation from G. Pasquali (*Orazio lirico* [Florence 1920], 509), implying that Pasquali had distinguished between earlier sympotic poets actually present at the symposia they described and Hellenistic epigrammatists who were only pretending. In fact Pasquali's point was that Horace (i. 27) "pictures himself" at a symposium *in the same way* as his archaic model Anacreon (F 356*b*).

is no ancient literary form of which it can be said with less plausibility that it was written *for* the book. The average book-roll contains 700 to 1000 lines, whereas some of the finest epigrams consist of only two to six lines. Furthermore, many epigrams imply a context (social, literary or historical) or presuppose a model without which they are barely comprehensible.

Though it soon emerged as an independent genre in its own right, Hellenistic epigram inherited many of the functions and traditions of archaic lyric as well as elegy.[40] Callimachus wrote epigrams in a variety of metres, perhaps as many as ten;[41] Phalaecus in at least four, including the hendecasyllabic line to which he gave his name;[42] Asclepiades gave his name to the complex of metres known after him as Asclepiadean; and Anyte is regularly described in the lemmata to her epigrams as "the lyric poetess" (λυρική, μελοποιός).[43] To judge from the Meleagrian excerpts in the Byzantine tradition, Meleager included only their elegiac poems, but Stephanus of Byzantium cites a hendecasyllable from Callimachus's epigrams (F 395), and Macrobius cites an epigram by Aratus from what he describes as his *liber elegeion*.[44] To be sure, once the precedent had been set others were quick to follow, but we are not entitled to assume that the earliest epigrammatists published books consisting entirely of elegiac epigrams.[45] The first poet known to have done so (on the evidence of the new Milan roll) is Posidippus, also the first poet to be styled "epigrammatist."[46]

The earliest practitioners—notably Anyte and Leonidas—expanded the tradition of authentic funerary and dedicatory epigram. Very different was the work of Asclepiades, who wrote erotic and sympotic epigrams, mainly deriving from the traditions of sympotic elegy.[47] The importance of Callimachus and Posidippus lies in the fact that they united these two traditions. Both applied "that combination of allusiveness, conciseness and wit

40. Cameron, *TAPA* 122 (1992), 305-12.

41. 17, 19, 20, 66, 68, 69, 70 GP; ?F 479, ?F 554, ?F635 Pf.

42. Gow and Page, *HE* II. 459.

43. For Anyte (assuming a book of epigrams) Gutzwiller, *Syll. Classica* 4 (1993), 71-89.

44. Lloyd-Jones and Parsons in their note on *SH* 100 postulate a confusion between epigrams and elegies, but that begs the question.

45. The reason Theocritus's epigrams were not included in Meleager's *Garland* (I suggest) is that there was no separate epigram book of Theocritus; his (relatively few) epigrams in 7 different metres were included inconspicuously along with his other poems. It is not certain that Simonides's epigrams were published in a separate roll either; the two rolls P. Oxy. 2327 and 3965 contained a variety of elegiac poems.

46. *IG* ix² i. 17. 24, perhaps to distinguish him from his homonymous contemporary the comic poet Posidippus, also a Macedonian (from Cassandreia), honoured with a statue in Athens (above, Ch. II. 8).

47. Theognis; Anacreon F2 W; Critias F6 W; Euenus F2; adesp. eleg. 6 W, explicitly described as a skolion. P. Oxy. 3965 has substantially increased our knowledge of Simonides's elegiac sympotica (F 19-33 W²).

that was to become the hallmark of the genre"[48] to epitaphs and dedications no less than to erotic and sympotic themes. It was this expansion and diversification of the genre in the first few decades of the third century that made possible the publication of entire books of epigrams.

What was the social context for this explosion of epigram writing? Literary genres do not spring out of a social vacuum. Bing would no doubt reply that the wider potential audience of the book created its own context. But why epigrams? In any case, as late as the age of Tacitus and Pliny no one wrote poetry direct for distribution in book form. The Roman evidence makes it clear that a formal recitation was an essential preliminary to the launching of a new book,[49] and the primary method of distribution was presentation to friends.[50] A published book was thus an extension of the poet's performance rather than something entirely different. It was aimed at essentially the same audience and arose out of the same social circumstances. In effect poets continued to write for people they knew, not strangers.[51] Since books had been a fixture of intellectual life for centuries and live performance continued unabated, there is little reason to believe that books would in themselves provoke or foster a different sort of poetry.

In the early decades at least of the third century—the creative period—publication of epigrams in book form must have been secondary, a way of preserving the best of the new epigrams rather than the factor that gave birth to them. Callimachus wrote epigrams throughout his life; one at least is no earlier than 246 (*AP* v. 146). Did he publish new books every few years, or just one towards the end of his life? If the latter, then it must have been through informal circulation that he exercised the influence he did on his contemporaries.

When a poet published a collected edition of his epigrams, naturally he exploited every possible link (whether of similarity or contrast) to arrange them as artfully as possible.[52] But it is pure assumption that these links and contrasts were originally composed for this written context. An instance often alleged is Callimachus's mock epitaphs for his father and himself (XXIX and XXX GP), neither actually named. The subject of XXX is styled "Battiades," of XXIX "father and son of Callimachus." It has been claimed that the missing name in each epitaph can (and was meant to) be supplemented from the other:[53] thus Battiades (XXX) is identified as Callimachus from XXIX, while the unnamed father (XXIX) is identified as

48. Cameron, *Greek Anthology* 3.

49. Harris, *Ancient Literacy* (1989), 225-26; White, *Promised Verse* (1993), 60-63.

50. Or loan for copying; still true in Libanius's day (Norman, *JHS* 80 [1960], 122-26).

51. R. Starr, "Circulation of Literary Texts in the Rom. World,"*CQ* 37 (1987), 213.

52. See my *Greek Anthology* Ch. II.

53. Livrea, *Hermes* 120 (1992), 294 (with earlier references); Walsh, *Arethusa* 24 (1991), 93-94; despite Livrea's ingenious argument, I still believe XXIX. 5-6 interpolated.

Battos from Battiades. Whence the assumption that they were written to be read together, on the page of a book, not inscribed or performed.

Yet for all its elegance, the mutual supplementation theory rests on two improbable premises: (a) that the father's name was really Battos (against, p. 8); and (b) that Battiades was intended as a real puzzle rather than a sobriquet well known to contemporaries. For Callimachus was by no means the only poet of the age to be known by such a pretentious style. His rival Asclepiades is called Sikelides without comment or explanation by both Theocritus and Hedylus; and Theocritus himself was early identified with the poet Simichidas who competes with Lycidas (yet another patronymic) in his seventh poem.[54] Since neither Sikelos nor Simichos are names attested in the islands, neither can have been genuine patronymics (Asclepiades's father may actually have been called Herodotus).[55] For whatever reason, poets of the age apparently called each other by *mock* patronymics.[56] The only one that has a still identifiable rationale (in a Cyrenean poet) is Battiades, an allusion to the legendary founder of Cyrene, perhaps first used by rivals in mockery rather than by Callimachus himself in pride. If so, then the two epitaphs do not after all supplement each other and there is no evidence here that they were composed together for the book.[57] Though both purport to be epitaphs, XXIX is in fact literary polemic (p. 181) and XXX sympotic (p. 86). Despite certain formal similarities, they were surely written at different times, in different contexts and for different purposes. Callimachus may eventually have juxtaposed them in a collection of his epigrams, though if he did it should be noted that Meleager separated them again in his *Garland*.[58]

The principal forum for the epigram in the early third century (I suggest) was the symposium. One of the most characteristic features of Hellenistic epigram is variation on a theme.[59] Giangrande insisted that variation in epigram was purely literary and bookish, no different from variation in any other genre, the ultimate yardstick always being Homer.[60] But epigram is not epic, not least because the major themes of so many

54. A playful self-reference need not imply the biographical initiation fantasies often inspired by this poem: see further Ch. XVI. 1.

55. J. P. Barron, *The Silver Coins of Samos* (London 1966), 138-39.

56. There is also Astakides in Call. ep. 36 (*HE* II. 193), and Dosiadas; for the others, Gow, *Theocritus* II. 129-30.

57. The lack of name in XXIX is not in itself remarkable; the name of the deceased is often separately inscribed on the tomb (Meillier 1979, 139), especially when it does not fit the metre (65 examples in *GV* i). One of the new Posidippus epitaphs, apparently for a real person, apostrophises her as just Ἀσιῆτι γύναι (no. XI Bastianini-Gallazzi).

58. They appear as 415 and 525 in the long Meleagrian sequence *AP* vii. 406-529 (unbroken only to 506: my *Greek Anthology* 126).

59. For a detailed study, see Tarán 1979 and in *JHS* 105 (1985), 90-107.

60. *L'Épigramme grecque* 345-46.

Alexandrian epigrammatists are after all the central preoccupations of the symposium itself (wine and love), its preparations (the delightful shopping poems of Asclepiades and Posidippus), and the revels that follow.[61] Let us reconsider the practice of variation in the light of symposium practice.

"Let us hear each speaker in turn; this is the essence of the symposium," says the Elephantine epigram (lines 7/8). From the earliest times, one of the dominating structural elements in the conduct of the symposium was competition. Each guest was expected to make a literary contribution of some sort according to his ability: those who could play the lyre would accompany themselves singing an entire song; others would sing or recite a poem, or at any rate a stanza or two. Each man was expected to cap the contribution of his predecessor.[62] This capping is neatly illustrated by Bdelycleon's instructions to his father quoted above.[63] There are balancing pairs in the sequence of twenty-five Attic skolia preserved by Athenaeus; and some elegiac pieces in the Theognidea "have the character of replies or retorts."[64] The second of the two erotic distichs in P. Tebt. 1-2 responds to the first.

Plato's *Symposium* is in effect a contest in encomia on Eros. E. N. Borza has remarked on the element of competition present in many stories about Alexander's symposia, from who could drink the most to the capping of quotations from Homer and Euripides. Borza has also described the increasingly bitter rivalry between Callisthenes and the philosopher Anaxarchus of Abdera, a rivalry acted out at Alexander's symposia.[65]

Another form this competition took was riddles, propounded to symposium guests in succession; those who solved them would win applause, a crown or kisses; those who failed would have to drink their wine neat, mixed with brine or drain their cups without taking a breath.[66] There are several examples already in Theognis, and two in hexameters are quoted from Simonides.[67] Bk xiv of the Anthology preserves many riddles

61. For the shopping poems, App. C. F. O. Copley (*Exclusus Amator*, Madison 1956) refuses to pronounce on the reality of the κῶμοι presupposed by Alexandrian epigram. Naturally no one would wish to press the details in these poems, but post-symposium κῶμοι certainly still happened in Hellenistic cities. For example, the future king Antigonus Gonatas "often" bullied the philosopher Zeno to go on κῶμοι with him, on one occasion to the house of Aristocles the citharode (D. L. 7. 13); when Antigonus asked his teacher Menedemus whether he should go on κῶμοι, he was reminded that he was the son of a king (ib. 2. 129); a handsome youth called Cleochares told revellers (κωμάσαντας) that he was willing to open the door, but his admirer Arcesilas the Academic would not allow it (ib. 4. 41).

62. The texts (said to derive from Dicaearchus and Aristoxenus) are assembled by Reitzenstein 1893, 3-13; see too F. Wehrli, *Dikaiarchos²* (Basel 1967), F 88-89 with pp. 69-71.

63. τούτοις ξυνὼν τὰ σκόλια ὅπως δέξει καλῶς, Ar. *Wasps* 1222-3.

64. West 1974, 16-17, citing examples.

65. Borza 1983, 51; *Anc. Mac. Studies...C. F. Edson* (Thessalonica 1981), 73-86.

66. Antiphanes F 124; Clearchus in Athen. 457C and 458F.

67. Theognis 257-60, 261-66, 861-64, 1229-30; Athen. 456C = Chamaeleon F 34² Giordano.

and puzzles in the form of epigrams. Many are certainly Roman, but none have reliable ascriptions and there seems no good reason to doubt that some are Hellenistic or at any rate based on Hellenistic models.[68] One example will suffice: "My father-in-law killed my husband and my husband killed my father-in-law; my brother-in-law killed my father-in-law and my father-in-law my father." Answer: Andromache, who had two husbands, Hector and Pyrrhus. Achilles (Pyrrhus's father) killed Hector; Pyrrhus killed Priam; Paris (her brother-in-law) killed Achilles; and Achilles killed her father Eetion. Macedonian symposiasts would have enjoyed this sort of thing. It is also instructive that Archimedes should have cast his famous "cattle problem" in the form of an extended epigram and sent it to his Alexandrian colleagues.[69] While we may doubt whether anyone actually solved it over wine, the form may have been influenced by this symposiastic riddle tradition. Lycophron's *Alexandra* is simply a vastly expanded riddle, surely meant to amuse rather than instruct—and if so, perhaps performed in extracts before a live audience, to test their ingenuity.

Antigonus of Carystus quotes distichs on scorpions and wasps by Archelaus the Egyptian, characterized as "one of those who explained paradoxa to Ptolemy in epigrams."[70] As Fraser has already remarked, this curious phrase suggests "an autoschediastic or symposiac performance." It is understandable that "believe it or not" riddles should have been popular at the symposium. Callimachus wrote paradoxa in prose, mainly preserved in the same book of Antigonus (F 407-11), and his disciple Philostephanus wrote paradoxa in epigrams.[71] Many of the poets included in Philip's *Garland* specialized in paradoxa and anecdotes in epigram form.

More than a third of the so-called *Letter of Aristeas* (§§ 187-292) is devoted to a series of symposia[72] at which Philadelphus asks each of the seventy-two translators of the Septuagint in turn a question about kingship: when asked how the king should conduct himself at symposia, the ninth guest on the seventh day replied "Invite lovers of wisdom" ($\phi\iota\lambda\text{o}\mu\alpha\theta\epsilon\hat{\iota}\varsigma$). To be sure it is an out-and-out forgery, but the writer is familiar with the details and terminology of Ptolemaic court procedure and wrote no later than the end of the second century B.C.[73] Not only was he clearly

68. See F. Buffière's introduction to the Budé *AP* xiv (1970) for a useful survey.

69. *SH* 201 or (with translation and notes), I. Thomas, *Greek Mathematical Works* ii (1941), 202-07; Fraser I. 406-09, with II. 587-91. It was sent, as the heading puts it "to those who study such things in Alexandria" in a letter to Eratosthenes.

70. Ant. Car. *Rerum mirab. coll.* ed. O. Musso (1985), 19. 4; cf. Fraser 1972, 778-9; II. 1086-7; *SH* 125-9; see too M. M. Sassi, in *Lo spazio letterario* I.2 (1993), 457-65.

71. *SH* 691, with Fraser I. 524; Page, *FGE* 21.

72. Modern discussions and translations always refers to "Banquets," but the Greek systematically uses terms like συμπόσιον, συμποσία and κατὰ τὸν πότον.

73. O. Murray in *RAC* Supp. I (1986), 573-87; *Studi Ellenistici* II (Pisa 1987), 15-29.

influenced by real life royal symposia; he has even adapted to his purpose the capping of responses to the king's questions.[74]

Asclepiades wrote an epigram on Ajax,[75] and we know from the Homer scholia that his friend Posidippus wrote another on a non-existent Trojan hero "Berisos" obtained from reading as one word the verb βῆ, the particle ῥ᾿ and the real proper name Ἶσος in *Iliad* xi. 101.[76] It is tempting, with Reitzenstein, to see this as an example of a symposium game described by Athenaeus: a contest in naming Greek and Trojan heroes in alphabetical order.[77] There are many other linked pairs of sympotic epigrams by Asclepiades and Posidippus[78] which might (but of course do not have to) have been originally written for the symposium.

The publication of a handful of epigrams from the new Milan papyrus may provide a concrete example. Here is the second couplet of a hitherto unknown quatrain by Posidippus:[79]

στεῖχε < τέ > μου παρὰ σῆμα· Μενοιτιός εἰμι Φιλάρχω
Κρής, ὀλιγορρήμων ὡς ἂν ἐπὶ ξενίης.

Walk past my tomb; I am Menoitios son of Philarchos, a Cretan, short of speech as you might expect in a foreign land.

And here is a well known distich by Callimachus (*AP* vii. 447):

σύντομος ἦν ὁ ξεῖνος, ὃ καὶ στίχος οὐ μακρὰ λέξων
"Θῆρις Ἀρισταίου Κρής" — ἐπ᾿ ἐμοὶ δολιχός.

The stranger is short—and the inscription is brief as well: Theris, son of Aristaios, Cretan—but it's long for me.

There seems to be a connection,[80] but it is hard to define. Neither straightforwardly imitates the other. It is as if each were an independent response to a theme (perhaps proposed by a symposiarch): an epitaph on a laconic Cretan.[81] Obviously each is more interesting when read in conjunction with the other. But the Callimachean parallel is not quoted in the Milan roll, nor is it likely that Callimachus included the Posidippus poem in any edition of his own epigrams.

74. For the more radical suggestion that the Seder ritual of the Passover itself was influenced by Hellenistic symposium literature, S. Stein, *Jour. Jewish Stud.* 8 (1957), 13-44.

75. Cameron, *Greek Anthology* (1993), 391-93.

76. Athen. 457EF; Reitzenstein 1893, 95; Merkelbach, *Rhein. Mus.* 99 (1956), 124; Cameron, *Greek Anthology* 372-76.

77. For an ingenious alternative explanation, implausibly taking Βήρισον as a serious toponymic variant, G. L. Huxley, *JHS* 102 (1992), 153.

78. E.g. *AP* xii. 135 ~ v. 199; xii. 75 ~ 77; xii. 166 ~ 45; Reitzenstein 1893, 91f.

79. G. Bastianini and C. Gallazzi, "Il poeta ritrovato," *Rivista "Ca' de Sass"* 121 (1993); *Posidippo Epigrammi* (Milan 1993 [? 1994]), no. XXV.

80. Noted also by M. Gronewald, *ZPE* 99 (1993), 28-29.

81. Compare Callimachus's laconic dedication by a Cretan: Τίν με, λεοντάγχ᾿ ὦνα συοκτόνε, φήγινον ὄζον / θῆκε "Τίς;" Ἀρχῖνος. "Ποῖος;" Ὁ Κρής. "Δέχομαι" (*AP* vi. 351).

Three contemporary epigrams on the appearance of Aratus's *Phaen-omena*, by Callimachus, Leonidas and King Ptolemy, might be explained in the same way. They have nothing in common (and so are not variations in the ordinary way) except for the fact that all three, in one way or another, apply the same adjective (λεπτός) to poet or poem (Ch. XI. 4). Given the contribution by the king himself, once more perhaps a contest at a royal symposium. It is not necessary to suppose that they were all com-posed for or performed (still less improvised) at the *same* symposium, any more than those on the laconic Cretan. They may have been, but the gen-eral point is enough for my thesis.

We shall come to another case in Ch. XI, the series of epigrams about the *Lyde* of Antimachus of Colophon. Three poets—Asclepiades, Pos-idippus and Hedylus—wrote epigrams in its praise, while Callimachus attacked it. Callimachus's reply (F 398) makes fun of both the *Lyde* and Asclepiades. No doubt each poet eventually included his own piece in his collected epigrams, but this will have separated a pair more enjoyably read together. Surely Callimachus wrote in the first instance for an audience familiar with Asclepiades's poem and able to savour every detail of his reply. At this point we should bear in mind that these poets not only lived and wrote in early third-century Alexandria. As a "youth of the court," Callimachus must have been a regular participant in royal symposia since his teens;[82] Posidippus was a Macedonian; and Asclepiades wrote on one of the king's mistresses (Ch. IX. 1). The obvious context for them to have compared poems is (of course) the symposium—more specifically the king's symposium.

It was at a Ptolemaic symposium, according to Diogenes Laertius, that the dialectician Diodorus of Iasus was embarrassed by Stilpo of Megara and nicknamed Cronus, "oldfashioned" (a nickname he seems in fact to have inherited from his teacher Apollonius).[83] The same passage quotes an epigram of Callimachus that neatly mocks Diodorus's views.[84] Whether or not Callimachus wrote it on the spot, it is enough in itself that we can link one of his epigrams with an event at one of Philadelphus's symposia. The mock epitaph on Philitas discussed in Appendix B was also surely written for an Alexandrian symposium.

It seems clear that epigrams continued to be performed at symposia in later times. The fact that one of Callimachus's sympotica is written on an

---

82. *praecipuus honor habebatur quod licebat sedentibus vesci cum rege*, Curtius 8. 6. 5. Hammond (*The Macedonian State* [Oxford 1989], 56) mistranslates "allowed to sit with the king at table," but the king and his Friends *reclined*. The point is that pages *sat* while their elders reclined. Only adult males were allowed to recline—originally (it was said) only males who had killed a wild boar (Hegesander Delph. F 33 = Athen. 18A).

83. ii. 111; cf. Strabo 14. 2. 21.

84. Quoted Ch. VIII. 4; there seems no good reason, with Wilamowitz, *HD* I. 59 n. 1, to locate this meeting in Megara (D. Sedley, *PCPS* 203 [1977], 109 n. 37).

outer wall of the so-called auditorium of Maecenas suggests that it was featured at the symposia that took place inside.[85] And a well known passage
of Gellius describes a symposium at which a chorus of Greek boys and
girls "sang" poems of Anacreon and Sappho and "some delightful and
elegant erotic elegies of recent poets as well."[86] Since someone then
"sang" Latin translations of epigrams by Meleager and Asclepiades,[87] it is
likely enough that the Greek "erotic elegies" were actually epigrams by
Callimachus, Meleager and Co.

In his poetic invitation to a symposium (*AP* xi. 44), Philodemus promises that Piso will hear things "sweeter than the land of the Phaeacians."
Surely not (as sometimes thought) praise of Epicurus, but poems, his own
sympotic epigrams. Just so when Catullus promises Fabullus *meros amores*
(*c*. 13), this means love poetry,[88] like ἔρως in Posidippus I (analysed
below, § 4). Cicero's claim that Philodemus described Piso's lust, de-
bauchery and banquets in his verses clearly implies the surviving sympotic
epigrams.[89]

3

The most explicitly sympotic among the third-century epigrams are by
Hedylus of Samos, a younger contemporary of Callimachus and Asclepiades. A recent study has characterized them as "metasymposiastic,"[90]
implying a contrast with genuinely symposiastic (namely archaic) poetry. It
is often assumed that improvisation was an essential feature of early
sympotic poetry,[91] though there is little or no direct evidence. Examples
are alleged from the skolia corpus in Athenaeus and Theognis,[92] but these
are the balancing pairs already quoted. Rather than a written record of
improvisations, in their present form they were clearly written to be performed together in sequence—proof (on the contrary) that even in the
archaic period many symposiasts used written song-books. Updating or
modifying or parodying old songs by altering a line or two or adding or

---

85. O. Murray, "Symposium and Genre in the Poetry of Horace," *JRS* 75 (1985), 43.

86. *ubi eduliis finis et poculis mox sermonibusque tempus fuit...qui canerent voce et psal-
lerent...* Ἀνακρεόντεια *pleraque et Sapphica et poetarum quoque recentium* ἐλεγεῖα
quaedam erotica dulcia et venusta cecinerunt (*NA* 19. 9. 3-4).

87. *resupinus capite convelato voce admodum suavi versus cecinit,* ib. 10.

88. So Marcovich, *Quad. Urbin.* 40 (1982), 131-38, though without quoting Posidippus.

89. *In Pisonem* 70; Murray, *JRS* 75 (1985), 42-43. In what has so far been deciphered
of the Herculaneum papyri, Philodemus makes no reference to his own poems, though he
mentions epigrams at *Poem.* 5. xxxviii. 10 Mangoni: M. Gigante, *Cron. Erc.* 22 (1992), 5-8.

90. L. Landolfi, *Quad. Urbin.* 24 (1986), 78.

91. Gentili 1988, 20; R. Thomas, *Literacy and Orality in Ancient Greece* (1992), 124.

92. E.g. Landolfi 1986, 83.

substituting new stanzas may have been common enough, but improvisation of complete poems, much less complete poems good enough to survive in that form must have been exceptional in any age. Indeed, the only archaic examples explicitly cited as improvisations are hardly poems at all, but versified jokes by Simonides: a parody of a Homeric line at a banquet of Hiero; and a ponderous complaint about warm wine.[93] Homeric parody remained a favourite parlour game at Macedonian symposia.

Improvisation is not in itself a distinctive feature of oral culture. So far from being unique to archaic symposia, improvised poetry was in fact especially characteristic of Roman symposia: Cicero's client Archias and Martial are well known examples.[94] Martial's survive because he was vain enough to publish them, but at all periods the best sympotic verse was surely composed in tranquillity to be performed cup in hand.

Two of Hedylus's poems imply extempore composition over wine:

ἐξ ἠοῦς εἰς νύκτα καὶ ἐκ νυκτὸς πάλι Σωκλῆς
    εἰς ἠοῦν πίνει τετραχόοισι κάδοις,
εἶτ' ἐξαίφνης που τυχὸν οἴχεται· ἀλλὰ παρ' οἶνον
    Σικελίδεω παίζει πουλὺ μελιχρότερον (VI GP).

From dawn to dusk and back to dawn again Socles drinks from four-gallon jars, and in no time he is a wreck. But while he's drinking, he writes more sweetly than Sicelides [Asclepiades].

Perhaps an actual sympotic contest.[95] For Giangrande, these are just motifs. The hyperbolic "four-gallon jars" is said to come from Anacreon, and the poet Socles is "seen as behaving in the same sympotic tradition as Anacreon."[96] Hedylus will (of course) have been familiar with Anacreon, but one does not have to go to literature to hear boasts about consumption of liquor (least of all at a Macedonian court), and as it happens no extant poem of Anacreon claims to have been written either at the symposium or while drunk. Hedylus repeats the latter idea in another epigram (V GP):

πίνωμεν, καὶ γάρ τι νέον, καὶ γάρ τι παρ' οἶνον
    εὕροιμεν λεπτὸν καί τι μελιχρὸν ἔπος.
ἀλλὰ κάδοις Χίου με κατάβρεχε καὶ λέγε "παῖζε
    Ἡδύλε"· μισῶ ζῆν ἐς κενὸν οὐ μεθύων.

Let us drink; for in wine I may find a theme that is new, something subtle and sweet. So soak me with jars of Chian and say "Play away, Hedylus." I hate living for nothing and not being drunk.

***

93. F 26 W² (Athen. 656 CD); F 25 W² (Athen. 125 CD) with *FGE* 301-02; in both cases the same verb ἀπεσχεδίασε.

94. P. White, *JRS* 64 (1974), 42-43; A. Hardie, *Statius and the Silvae* (Liverpool 1983), 76-85; there is much material already in E. Rohde, *Der griechische Roman*³ (1914), 332f.

95. Of course, Asclepiades may simply be a standard of excellence, as in Theocr. 7. 40.

96. *PMG* 373. 2; Giangrande 1968, 159.

Not only is the idea of finding inspiration in wine not directly attested in archaic poetry. More significant, the terms in which Hedylus formulates the idea are overwhelmingly Alexandrian. What he hopes to find in the wine is something "new," "subtle" and "sweet" (νέον, λεπτόν, μελιχρόν). The last two qualities in particular are notoriously the polish and refine ment we associate with the new poetry of Callimachus.[97] Hedylus is not after all simply affecting to recreate the world of Anacreon. Indeed he explicitly presents himself as what he is, an Alexandrian epigrammatist, forever striving to vary traditional motifs in a witty and original way.

What has led some to doubt that Hedylus V and VI are authentic sympotic poems is the fact that VI closes with the exhortation "drink and write"(καὶ γράφε καὶ μέθυε). According to Bing, this reference to writing rather than singing "acts as a punchline, aiming to unsettle"; and Gow and Page remark that "γράφε...does not suggest a symposium."[98] But it is one thing for a poet to use song-terms when describing how his serious poetry glorifies gods, heroes or patrons—as Callimachus does regularly in his hymns or his epithalamium for Arsinoë.[99] But it is quite another if he is simply referring to composition, especially of something so informal as an epigram. Callimachus draws precisely this distinction in a distich that pur ports to be his epitaph (AP vii. 415):

Βαττιάδεω παρὰ σῆμα φέρεις πόδας, εὖ μὲν ἀοιδήν
  εἰδότος, εὖ δ' οἴνῳ καίρια συγγελάσαι.

The "song" (ἀοιδή) is his serious poetry (Aetia, Hymns, Hecale), con trasted with amusing improvisations over wine (οἴνῳ καίρια συγγελάσαι)—evidently sympotic epigrams.

When referring to the composition (rather than performance) of his poems, Callimachus naturally refers to placing a writing tablet on his knees.[100] The unknown author of the parodic mini-epic Battle of Frogs and Mice likewise claims to have written with tablet on knee. Though still sometimes ascribed to the fifth century, this work is now generally assumed Hellenistic.[101] More specifically, the reference to writing with tablet on knee may actually be an imitation of Callimachus.[102] Since every-

97. Timotheus also proclaims the novelty of his poetry: PMG 796, 791. 203.

98. Bing 1988, 21; Gow and Page, HE II. 294; Landolfi 1986, 84.

99. HZ 1, 4 (ἀείδειν); HAp 17 (ἀοιδῇ); HAr 2 (ὑμνέομεν), 269 (ἀοιδῇ); HDel 1 (ἀείσεις); F 392 (ἀείδειν).

100. F 1. 21-2; so too Meleager, AP vii. 417. 7 (ἐχάραξα τάδ' ἐν δέλτοισι).

101. J. Wackernagel, Sprachliche Untersuchungen zu Homer (Göttingen 1916), 188-99; M. L. West, HSCP 73 (1969), 123 n. 35; H. Wölke, Untersuchungen zur Batrachomyomachia (Meisenheim 1978), 46-70; H. S. Schibli, ZPE 53 (1983), 7-11; for the pos sibility that the mice on the Archelaus relief (ca 221/205) refer to the Batr., Ch. X. 3.

102. Wölke 1978, 60, 86-89; line 116 may echo F 117. 16 (the Mousetrap): Wölke 241.

one in antiquity wrote with tablet on knee,[103] caution is in order, but the verbal parallel, though not exact,[104] is close. A recent treatment has inferred from "the bodily stance of the performer" that the poem was recited before a small circle; "before a large audience or in a theatre he would have stood." But the context makes it clear that (as in Callimachus) the reference is to composition rather than performance.[105]

Herington emphasizes that the Aristophanic scenes that portray Euripides and Agathon respectively composing make no mention of writing.[106] But Euripides's wardrobe of ragged costumes and Agathon's effeminacy had comic potential obviously lacking to pens and tablets.[107] In any case, since there can be no doubt that Euripides did produce written texts, what is gained by Herington's compromise conclusion that he "did not take to his pen...until late in the composition?" That is how Gibbon wrote; indeed I write that way myself. Machon tells a story of Lais the courtesan accosting Euripides pen and tablet in hand and asking why he wrote something in one of his tragedies.[108] The text is Ptolemaic, but could as easily have been fifth-century; elsewhere Aristophanes pictures Euripides book in hand (*Frogs* 1409). By ca 400 the Pronomus vase shows a dramatic poet holding one roll while another leans against his stool. Next to him is a lyre. No conflict here between song and book; it is their combination that symbolizes his poetry.

A more speculative case is the *Writing Tablets* (Δέλτοι) of Antimachus of Colophon, so called (as B. Wyss suggested) because "each poem was written on one writing tablet."[109] That is to say, it was a miscellany of short, occasional poems, like the miscellany of elegies by Mimnermus that Antimachus himself may have compiled (Ch. XI. 3). The author of a newly published elegiac fragment that seems to mention Antimachus's beloved Lyde (Ch. XI.1) goes on to address a writing tablet (π[ί]ναξ, πῆ πρῶτον ἐπέλθω;), and Parsons has made the attractive suggestion that it might come from the Δέλτοι.[110] If these conjectures are on the right lines, we would have, from before the end of the fifth century, two features generally assumed Hellenistic: (a) a poetry book edited by the poet; and (b)

103. A. Dain, *Les Manuscrits*[3] (Paris 1975), 24-25; Turner, *GMAW*[2] 5-6.

104. Call. ἐμοῖς ἐπὶ δέλτον ἔθηκα / γούνασι ~ *Batr.* 2-3 ἀοιδῆς, ἣν νέον ἐν δέλτοισιν ἐμοῖς ἐπὶ γούνασι θῆκα (where θῆκα refers to the poem, not, as in Call., to the tablet).

105. "Die...körperliche Haltung des Vortragenden," Wölke 1978, 88; the passage is correctly interpreted by T. C. Skeat, *PBA* 42 (1957), 184.

106. *Ach.* 383-479; *Thesm.* 25-265; Herington 1985, 46-47; cf. Thomas 1992, 124.

107. Whence the modern film cliché that writers compose with tape recorders, allowing us to hear what they are writing, often merging into voice-over narrative.

108. πινακίδα καὶ γραφεῖον...ἔγραψας, 404-06 Gow.

109. Wyss 1936, xxiv-v (*quia singula carmina singulis pugillaribus continebantur*).

110. Cited by its editor, W. Brashear, *Proceedings of the 20th International Congress of Papyrologists*, ed A. Bülow-Jacobsen (Copenhagen 1994), 287.

a poet who quite explicitly looked upon his work in terms of a written text. Nita Krevans has recently drawn attention to a number of ways in which Antimachus anticipates his critic Callimachus; here perhaps are two more.[111]

For a contemporary of Euripides to speak of his poems as writing tablets does not (I suggest) represent a revolutionary attitude to his craft. Antimachus did not *compose* these elegies for the book rather than a live audience. In all probability he wrote them for the symposium: the only line quoted from the Δέλτοι refers to the river Euleus, where especially tasty eels were to be found.[112] He composed on tablets; performed before a live audience; and later published in book form. As Krevans observes (by letter), there is an implied contrast in the new fragment between the song about Lyde (ἀείσας) and the writing tablet, parallel to the contrast drawn above between the elevated songs and sympotic improvisations of Callimachus. Furthermore the reference to "pouring out" (ἐκκέχυσαι) in line 7 would suit wine at least as well as inspiration.[113]

Hedylus VI is simply irrelevant to the question of reading versus live performance. It is not a published book that the γράφε implies, but the tablet on which Socles jots down the lines that come to him as he drinks and listens to his fellows. Once he has finished—presumably nothing more than an epigram—he will recite it to the applause of his companions. Exactly this sequence of events is described in Petronius's banquet: "Trimalchio...called at once for a tablet (*codicillos*) and after a short period of thought recited the following" (*Sat.* 55. 2). The best commentary is Catullus 50, a vivid picture of two poets engaged in a sympotic contest, experimenting and improvising:

> Hesterno, Licini, die otiosi
> multum lusimus *in meis tabellis*,
> ut convenerat esse delicatos:
> *scribens* versiculos uterque nostrum
> ludebat numero modo hoc modo illoc,
> *reddens mutua* per iocum atque *vinum*.

Typically (of course) symposiasts sang others' poetry. But the poets themselves (whether Hellenistic or archaic) will naturally have jotted down ideas while still uncertain about the form or details of a poem taking shape in their minds—and also so as to have a record of their improvisations, in the hope of working them up into something more polished some day.[114] It is

111. In Harder 1993, 149-60.

112. F 74 = Athen. 300C; the linked citation from Demetrius of Skepsis mentions river and eels, Antimachus just the river.

113. As Brashear 1994, 288 suggests; less probably, perhaps the wax of the tablet.

114. There is no evidence of any sort for Nagy's improbable claim that "all attested poetry and song from Homer to Pindar" was composed without the aid of writing (*Pindar's Homer* [Baltimore 1990], 18-19). Contrast the common sense of J. Herington: "Only the

unlikely that any third-century audience would be "unsettled" by the idea that poets composed with pen and tablet.

Two less well known works of the early third century that would have been ideal for the symposium are the *Silloi* of Timon of Phlius and the *Chreiai* of Machon of Sicyon. Timon's *Silloi* are a series of lampoons on philosophers by someone who was a visitor to the courts of both Philadelphus and Gonatas[115]—and a natural symposium animal. His biographer Antigonus described him as "fond of wine," and he wrote a sympotic work, a *Funeral Banquet of Arcesilas*.[116] On one occasion he undertook to outdrink Lacydes of Cyrene, head of the Academy at Athens. On the first night Lacydes left first, at which Timon quoted Achilles's boast on the death of Hector; on the second night Timon threw in the towel, at which Lacydes quoted a boast of Diomedes.[117] The *Silloi* too are full of Homeric allusion and parody, just the sort of thing for Macedonian symposia.

Machon's *Chreiai* are mildly scurrilous anecdotes in iambic verse, some no more than 4-6 lines long, mainly devoted to courtesans, eating and drinking. Gow notes that successive anecdotes about the same person are not connected syntactically, and that the name of the person concerned is always repeated, usually in the first line: "if he had expected or wished to be heard or read continuously he would presumably have put his anecdotes together very differently."[118] Since moreover one of them apostrophizes listeners, it is natural to infer that they were written to be performed before a live audience. The successive anecdotes about the same hetairas recall the balancing items in archaic songbooks, intended for capping.

We might also add Herodas's *Mimiambi* to the dossier. The debate about their intended audience has always tended to lurch between the two extremes of book-poetry and stage production.[119] Given their subject matter and modest length (100 lines or less), why not (as Reitzenstein suggested a century ago) the compromise of symposium performance?[120] The

---

existence of written texts can account for its astounding sophistication, refinement, and variety and also for the transmission and preservation of its songs in reasonably uncorrupt form" (*Poetry into Drama* [Berkeley 1985], 41). Rolls containing or representing epic and lyric poetry are common on Attic vases from the Persian wars on: H. R. Immerwahr, *Class. Med. and Ren. Studies in Honor of B. L. Ullman* i (Rome 1964), 17-48 and *Antike Kunst* 16 (1973), 143-7. Nagy even argues for the oral composition of inscribed epigram (p. 18 n. 7)!

115. Diog.Laert. 9. 110; Di Marco 1989, 3.

116. On the title (περίδειπνον), J. Martin, *Symposion* (Paderborn 1931), 162-66; L. Tarán, *Speusippus of Athens* (Leiden 1981), 230-3; Di Marco 1989, 13.

117. D. L. 9. 110 and Athen. 438 BC, both explicitly citing Antigonus of Carystus.

118. A.S.F. Gow, *Machon* (1965), 23-24; ἴσως δ᾿ ἂν...τις...τῶν νῦν ἀκροατῶν (188).

119. G. Mastromarco, *The Public of Herondas* (Amsterdam 1984), with P. Parsons, *CR* 31 (1981), 110.

120. Reitzenstein 1893, 37 n. 1 (on p. 38); but Plut. *QC* 712 E which he cites in support refers to what Plutarch considers suitable for symposia in his own, not Herodas's day.

different speaking parts could have been divided among the appropriate number of symposiasts.[121]

4

Posidippus I is interesting in a rather different way (*AP* v. 134):

Κεκροπὶ ῥαῖνε λάγυνε πολύδροσον ἰκμάδα Βάκχου,
  ῥαῖνε· δροσιζέσθω συμβολικὴ πρόποσις.
σιγάσθω Ζήνων ὁ σοφὸς κύκνος, ἅ τε Κλεάνθους
  μοῦσα· μέλοι δ᾽ ἡμῖν ὁ γλυκύπικρος ἔρως.

Pour on us, Attic jug, the dewy rain of Bacchus, pour away; let our bring-your-own party be drenched. Let us hear nothing of that learned swan Zeno, or the poetry of Cleanthes. May bitter-sweet love be mine.

The setting is concrete and contemporary. The leading figures in the literary world of early third-century Athens were its philosophers.[122] Most of them attended symposia regularly, and many wrote sympotic dialogues:[123] Zeno for one did both.[124] Cleanthes wrote poetry, though serious poetry; given the context, we might infer that it was written for his own symposia (some of his moralizing iambics are cast in dialogue form).[125] It is a real and recognizable type of symposium that Posidippus repudiates—and an equally recognizable (indeed more traditional) type that he urges in its place.

A striking parallel is provided in the *Sympotic Notes* of Zeno's pupil Persaeus, a work that offered guidance for behaviour at royal symposia—presumably reflecting his own experience at the symposia of his friend and patron Antigonus Gonatas in Pella. Syllogisms were "alien to the present occasion, when even a gentleman is permitted to get drunk"; but "aphrodisia" were entirely appropriate, even praiseworthy if handled in a moderate and decent fashion.[126] We do not need to suppose that Posidippus had read Persaeus's book (as a well-known Macedonian he may actually have been a guest at Gonatas's table as he surely was at Philadelphus's), but his poem makes precisely the same point. The "bittersweet love" of the last line must mean poetry about love (like *amores* in Catullus 13); "bittersweet" could hardly describe the sort of encounter possible at

---

121. The same context and mechanism might be suggested for the Theocritean mimes.

122. C. Habicht, *Hellenistic Athens and her Philosophers* (Princeton 1988).

123. R. Hirzel, *Der Dialog: ein literaturhistorischer Versuch* I (Leipzig 1895), 359-67.

124. A Περὶ συμποσίου; for his attendance at symposia, D.L. 7. 13, 26.

125. Cleanthes F 7 and 9 (*CA* 230-31).

126. ἀλλοτρίως...τοῦ παρόντος καιροῦ, ὅτε καὶ ὁ καλὸς κἀγαθὸς ἀνὴρ μεθυσθείη ἄν, Athen. 607B-F and 162C (*FHG* ii. 623), from the "Memoirs of Stilpo and Zeno" (162C).

the symposium itself. What Posidippus has in mind is the sort of erotic poetry he and his peers wrote in the form of epigram.

More relevant still is another passage in Persaeus's book (Athen. 162C): his discussion of when pretty boys and girls (τοὺς ὡραίους καὶ τὰς ὡραίας) were to be brought in, when they should be allowed to preen themselves (ὡραϊζομένους) and when they should be sent packing for their insolence (ὡς ὑπερορῶντας). So far as I know this remarkable passage has never received the attention it deserves. It is clear that these boys and girls were not brought in to perform sexual services. Elsewhere Persaeus describes with horror how some Arcadian visitors to Antigonus's court lost control at the appearance of some Thessalian topless dancers, getting up from their couches and shouting and committing "many other such vulgarities" (Athen. 607D). He also mentions "auctions" of flutegirls to the highest bidder, presumably for subsequent sexual services in private. Ideally (it seems) these symposiastic "aphrodisia" were conducted in a seemly fashion. Apparently at a certain point boys and girls were paraded around the banqueting room to act out various sexual rôles or types in sequence, beginning with flirtatiousness and ending with insolence, after which they were dismissed.

What did the guests do while these rôles were being played out? Persaeus mentions erotic talk,[127] and since many of the erotic epigrams of Callimachus and Asclepiades and their successors evoke just such sexual stereotypes, ranging from the flirtatious to the insolent, it is tempting to conjecture that any poets present would have recited poems appropriate to the type of the moment. Old favourites (for example) like Theognis 237-54, on the fame Theognis has brought Cyrnus despite his contemptuous behaviour; or perhaps Callimachus LXIII or VII on haughty girls and boys respectively. Asclepiades's brilliant gallery of female types (Appendix C) would have been particularly effective if appropriately mimed while the poet recited.

Perhaps we have the outline at least of a poem written expressly for the occasion, Callimachus *Iamb* 14, equipped in the Diegeseis with a heading that has always caused puzzlement: "for pretty boys" (πρὸς τοὺς ὡραίους). After giving the first line, "Lemnos was the happiest of islands once,"[128] the Diegetes summarizes the plot in two sentences. First "Lemnos, happy of old, became unhappy when the women attacked the men"; and then "So you too should look to the future." The "you" must be the pretty boys of the heading. In the standard version, it is the Lemnian women who initiate the events that lead to the massacre, by dishonouring Aphrodite. It seems

---

127. περὶ ἀφροδισίων...μνείαν ποιεῖσθαι, Athen. 607B.
128. Ἡ Λῆμνος τὸ παλαιόν, εἴ τις ἄλλη, F 226.

clear that, like Apollonius, Callimachus blamed the men.[129] In the light of the Persaeus passage, it is tempting to infer that he wittily adapted the Lemnian story as a cautionary tale for the pretty boys' haughty routine at the symposium.

Persaeus also had sections "concerning sweetmeats, breads and ...especially kisses (περὶ φιλημάτων)." Again, hardly kisses exchanged in casual symposium encounters, but kisses that were part of symposium culture, kisses that could be regulated somehow. Surely the kisses that we hear of from comedy and elsewhere as prizes for the archetypal symposium game, kottabos. "Let us play for kisses" (περὶ φιλημάτων) cries Heracles in a play of Plato.[130] Significantly enough there is also a reference to the practice in Callimachus's *Pannychis* (F 227. 7), claimed for the symposium later in this section.

A number of other epigrams celebrate symposium performers: for example, Dioscorides on a girl who sang "The Horse," evidently the story of the wooden horse, for he goes on to claim that he and the Trojans perished together in the blaze (*AP* v. 138). Two epigrams of Philodemus describe a girl whose songs excite him (*AP* v. 131; ix. 570), another one who excites him though "unable to sing the songs of Sappho" (xi. 41). They do not specify the symposium, but another links such songs with wine and "tipsy courtesans" (xi. 34). An epigram by the Augustan Argentarius neatly links wine, women and song (x. 18). From a later date we have a witty epigram by Strato on guests who ogle pretty wine waiters.[131] All these poems would have gained immeasurably in effect if actually written for symposium performance.

A different sort of illustration of the way in which Alexandrian sympotic poetry reflects its own real world rather than a world peopled entirely by traditional literary motifs is Asclepiades XXV. The poet sends his slave out to do the shopping for a symposium: the last and evidently most expensive item on his list, which he hopes to get on credit, is five silver perfume flasks (presumably it is to be a small gathering). Such extravagance would have been entirely alien to the classical symposium. But we happen to have a first-hand account of a Macedonian symposium of the period that describes how silver and gold perfume flasks were given to each of twenty guests.[132]

---

129. F. Vian, *Apollonios de Rhodes* i² (Paris 1976), 27-29 (source a lost play of Aeschylus); Hypsipyle's account suppresses the murder (she was hoping to persuade the Argonauts to stay on Lemnos). It is unfortunate that we know so little of the many comedies on the theme: Aristophanes F 356-75; Nicochares F 11-14; Antiphanes F 144-5; cf. Alexis F 134; Diphilos F 54; on the interpretation of the myth, W. Burkert, *CQ* 20 (1970), 1-16.

130. Plato F 46; Eubulus F 3 (with Hunter's note); Soph. F 537P; cf. Plato *Rep.* 468BC, Xen. *Mem.* ii. 6. 33.

131. *AP* xii. 175; cf. Martial ix. 25, with my comments in *CQ* 32 (1982), 170-71.

132. Athen. 129A-C; for more details, Appendix C.

Different again is the plea for a rustic symposium by another third-century poet, Nicaenetus of Samos:

οὐκ ἐθέλω, Φιλόθηρε, κατὰ πτόλιν ἀλλὰ παρ' Ἥρῃ
δαίνυσθαι Ζεφύρου πνεύμασι τερπόμενος.
ἀρκεῖ μοι λιτὴ μὲν ὑπὸ πλευροῖσι χάμευνα...
                   ...ἀλλὰ φερέσθω
οἶνος καὶ Μουσέων ἡ χαρίεσσα λύρη,
θυμῆρες πίνοντες ὅπως Διὸς εὐκλέα νύμφην
μέλπωμεν, νήσου δεσπότιν ἡμετέρης.

My wish is not to feast in the city, Philotherus, but by a shrine of Hera, enjoying the breath of the west wind. Sufficient for me is a simple pallet beneath my ribs... But let wine be brought and the lyre dear to the Muses, so that, drinking to our heart's content, we may celebrate the glorious bride of Zeus, the mistress of our island.

Giangrande completely misunderstood this poem, which he described as "anti-sympotic" and so characteristic of the postclassical period.[133] On the contrary, Nicaenetus wants to strip the symposium down to its essence, its two basic ingredients—wine and song. It is just the luxury of the city he wants to leave behind.

We might also consider a quite different sort of example: a poem by Callimachus that is more puzzling than editors have allowed. A bronze cockerel is speaking:[134]

According to Euaenetus, who set me up (I have no idea myself), I, a bronze cock, was dedicated to the Tyndarids in return for his [or my] victory. I believe the son of Phaedrus, grandson of Philoxenus.

What (and whose) is the victory, and why does the cock not know? Who is this unnamed person identified by his father and greatgrandfather, and why is he so pompously identified? Why does the cock trust him rather than Euaenetus? There cannot have been many who knew all the answers on the day the poem was written, and most of them will have forgotten by the time it was included in a published book. It was surely written for those few who knew, and if so where but at a local symposium?

Iamb 12, "written for the seventh-day celebration of the birth of a little girl to Leon, a friend of the poet," must have been originally intended for one or the other of two domestic occasions, the amphidromia (a purification ceremony) or the naming of a newborn child.[135] There must have been many such poems, but we only know of one more; an epigram of Hedylus

133. Nicaen. IV (Athen. 673 BC); Giangrande 1968, 144-46; Hardie 1983, 133-6.
134. Gow and Page, *HE* II. 181; P. Ferrari and G. Zanetto, *Callimaco Epigrammi* (Milan 1992), 85-86.
135. The two occasions and the number of days after birth (5, 7 or 10) have been confused in the various accounts: Dawson 1950, 118; Deubner, *Rhein. Mus.* 95 (1952), 374-77.

mentions a piper called Theon who "sang of the birth" of his son.[136] In Ch. VI. 3 below I have collected some of the evidence for the countless poems written for weddings and funerals. Wedding songs were performed at various stages of the ceremony, but one of them was certainly the wedding banquet. Pindar refers to a bridegroom being toasted at the symposium; the choral hymn at the wedding of Caranus in Macedon ca 300 was performed at a symposium just before dark; and in Catullus 62 the chorus of boys and girls rises to sing as evening falls and the banquet ends. With its amoebean contest and separation of the guests by sex, the setting of this poem is thoroughly Greek.[137] According to Plutarch the evening was the time for "song, dance and the marriage-hymn" (*Mor.* 654F). The probability is that most of these poems for domestic occasions were performed at symposia.

Not all symposium poetry was casual or improvised. Sometimes a famous poet would write something formal for a particular occasion. One elegy of Ion of Chios was written for a royal symposium at Sparta,[138] and we have fragments of several such poems by Pindar.[139] We also have a few lines of a piece by Callimachus in an epodic metre, no. 15 in his *Iambi* (F 227), expressly described in the Diegesis as a "wine-song" (παροίνιον)[140] that appealed to fellow-symposiasts (συμπόταις) to stay awake for an all-night celebration (παννυχίς).[141] The closest parallel is Propertius 4. 6. After finishing his account of the battle of Actium, the poet describes a banquet at which he urges other poets to sing of other Augustan victories while they drink until the break of day.[142] Francis Cairns has compared an account of a festival attributed to Libanius describing a sacrifice after a banquet: poets sing hymns as they drink to the god honoured at the festival.[143] Whether or not (as Cairns argued) Propertius really performed his

---

136. Ep. X. 5 (Athen. 176C) = *HE* 1881.

137. *Ol.* 7. 1-10; Athen. 129F.; Cat. 62. 3, *surgere iam tempus, iam pingues linquere mensas*; E. Fraenkel, *Kleine Beiträge* ii (1964), 97-98.

138. F 27, with F. Jacoby, *CQ* 41 (1947), 8-9; M. L. West, *BICS* 32 (1985), 74.

139. B. A. Van Groningen, *Pindare au Banquet* (Leiden 1960), 84f.

140. Pfeiffer's certain correction for παροίμιον in the papyrus; for the metre, iambic dimeter followed by ithyphallic, see Ch. VI. 7.

141. One of the new Posidippan epitaphs commemorates the death of a girl after a παννυχίς, in Tegea according to Bastianini and Gallazi (καθ' ὑψηλοῦ Τεγέας...ἐξέπεσες, X. 3-4). But it would be odd to "fall from" a city, and why no hint of the cause of death? Surely τέγεος. She fell from a high roof, no doubt a little drunk after the party, like the unfortunate Elpenor, who καταντικρὺ τέγεος πέσεν (κ. 559, λ. 64). The obvious guess is that she had been celebrating the Adonia, a women's festival celebrated on roof-tops (cf. *AP* ix. 158).

142. *sic noctem patera, sic ducam carmina, donec / iniciat radios in mea vina dies*, Prop. 4. 6. 85-86.

143. *Progymn.* 29.7 (VIII. 539 Foerster); hardly later than Libanius, because the festival is obviously pagan.

poem at an all-night banquet after a festival,[144] he must at any rate have had in mind some Hellenistic poem that envisaged such a context. The fact that Callimachus's poem addresses such popular Ptolemaic deities as the Dioscuri and Helen (who is sometimes identified with Arsinoë)[145] strongly suggests that it was written for an Alexandrian symposium after a festival in their honour.

Perhaps the clearest case of all is the *Hymn to Zeus.* "When we are making libations to Zeus, what better subject for our song than the god himself," it begins.[146] It was a well-documented rule of the symposium that a libation had to be poured from the first crater to Zeus.[147] Aware of the tradition but unable to resist modern dogma, the latest commentator writes of Callimachus's "imaginary symposium" as though it were a self-evident fact requiring no comment or explanation. No less dogmatically, though with more justification, Wilamowitz stated bluntly that "we are present at the libation to Zeus Soter, that is to say at a symposium."[148] It is no coincidence that, at 95 lines, this is by far the shortest of Callimachus's hymns, quite short enough for performance before a band of symposiasts. The poet will no doubt have recited his poem at more than one symposium, but given the graceful tribute to Philadelphus with which it closes, it seems natural to infer that the first time was in front of the king himself.

5

W. J. Slater has made the provocative, not to say paradoxical suggestion that Alexandrian scholars actually did much of their work at symposia.[149] He was not able to establish any serious connection, but the literary and antiquarian discussions familiar to us from Plutarch's *Table Talk* and Athenaeus's *Deipnosophists* certainly go back to the age of the Ptolemies. For example, guests at the symposia of Menedemus of Eretria, famous for their poor food, regularly discussed literature and philosophy over wine (ζητήσεις παρὰ πότον).[150] In F 178 Callimachus represents himself at a

144. Cairns 1984, 152-54; occasional symposiastic performance by Roman poets I can accept easily enough, but regular παννυχίδες strain belief.

145. Ch. XVI. 4; the following poem (F 228) commemorates the deification of Arsinoë.

146. Ζηνὸς ἔοι τί κεν ἄλλο παρὰ σπονδῇσιν ἀείδειν / λώιον ἢ θεὸν αὐτόν, lines 1-2.

147. ἐκ Διὸς ἀρχόμενοι / πίνωμεν, παίζωμεν, to quote one example (Ion, F 27. 6-7 W); M. P. Nilsson, *Opusc. Sel.* i (Lund 1951), 428-42; W. Burkert, *Greek Religion* (Harvard 1985), 70-1; F. Lissarrague, *The Aesthetics of the Greek Banquet* (Princeton 1987), 26.

148. Wilamowitz, *HD* II. 1; G. McLennan, *Callimachus: Hymn to Zeus* (Rome 1977).

149. "Aristophanes of Byzantium and problem-solving in the Museum," *CQ* 32 (1982), 346-49; cf. *BMCR* 5 (1994), 451-53.

150. They are known from a satyr play by his pupil Lycophron of Chalchis and the only slightly later biography by Antigonus of Carystus, reconstructed from Diogenes Laertius ii. 17 by Wilamowitz, *Antigonos von Karystos* (Berlin 1881); see now D. Knoepfler, *La vie de Ménédème d' Érétrie de Diogène Laërce* (Basel 1991).

symposium in the house of his Athenian friend Pollis, asking his neighbour just the sort of sympotic question we read of in the later treatises. In F 43 he recalls what he had heard at perhaps the same symposium (Ch. V. 1). There is also the story of how Philadelphus played a trick on Sosibius "the wonderful problem-solver" (ὁ θαυμάσιος λυτικός). The implication is that the king himself was irritated by Sosibius's far-fetched "solutions" to literary problems. The illustration cited—why the elderly Nestor was the only man able to lift his cup when it was full—is of obvious sympotic relevance. Athenaeus quotes from a written version of Sosibius's (indeed preposterous) solution,[151] but the king surely heard an oral version, and if so where but at the symposium?

Slater's main text was a solution ascribed in the Hesiod scholia to a certain Comanus the "chief winepourer" (ἀρχιοινοχόος), presumably the second-century Alexandrian grammarian of that name.[152] Blank and Dyck objected that such titles were purely honorific, and that Comanus was simply a court official.[153] Certainly this was not a suggestion casually thrown out by an ordinary waiter as he refilled the king's cup. But royal wine-waiters were young nobles, like Iolaus the son of Antipater,[154] obliged to perform menial services, including waiting at table.[155] Whether or not the suggestion was actually made at a symposium, Comanus was a person of consequence who regularly attended royal symposia. We may even be able to identify him. Fraser dismissed as "most unconvincing" the suggestion that he was Comanus the "first Friend" (τῶν πρώτων φίλων) of Ptolemy VI Philometor (180-145).[156] Our knowledge of Comanus's rank as "winepourer" in all probability derives from a response to his views published under the title *Against Comanus* by Aristarchus (ca 216-144). That is to say, Comanus wrote before Aristarchus. The name is not uncommon, but a high-ranking friend of the king might well have been a royal wine-pourer in his youth. If so, we would have another Alexandrian scholar who (like Callimachus and Eratosthenes) was less a royal pension-

---

151. Athen. 493E-4B (take γέρων by anastrophe with the preceding line; Nestor was the only old man who could lift the cup).

152. F 16 in A. R. Dyck, ap. F. Montanari (ed.), *I frammenti dei grammatici Agathocles...* (Berlin 1988), 221-65; quoted in West, *Hesiod Works and Days* (1978), 72.

153. D. L. Blank and A. R. Dyck, *ZPE* 56 (1984), 22-24, against Slater 1982, 348.

154. ἀρχιοινοχόος in Plut. *Alex.* 74. 2; οἰνοχόος βασιλικός in Arr. *Anab.* 7. 27. 2; Cf. W. Heckel, *The Marshalls of Alexander's Empire* (London 1992), 293. As Athenaeus noted, citing a series of examples from Homer on, "the boys of the best families acted as wine-pourers (ᾠνοχόουν) among the ancients" (Athen. 424E).

155. *quippe inter epulas hi sunt regis ministri*, Curtius 5. 1. 42; on the pages, Ch. I. 1.

156. *CR* 67 (1953), 43, citing references and bibliography.

ary than a Friend, the sort who might participate in the king's symposia as an equal.

The symposia of Menedemus were particularly important, because among the regular participants "he welcomed Aratus and Lycophron the tragic poet and Antagoras of Rhodes." Poets were surely invited in the expectation that they would contribute poems of their own as much as for their views on the poems of others. There is certainly evidence for poets performing their own works at Macedonian symposia. The songs of a certain Pranichus or Pierio holding some generals "up to shame and ridicule" were performed at a symposium in front of Alexander.

Another poet at any rate offered to recite poems of his own. Hegesianax of Alexandria Troas, when asked to dance in front of Antiochus the Great, replied: "Your Majesty, would you rather watch me dance badly, or listen to me recite my poems well?"[157] An epitaph on the dramatist Philicus, who ended his days in Alexandria, pictures him enjoying the "festive old age of Alcinoos the Phaeacian" and bids him go revelling to the isles of the blest, "rolling forth his melodious songs."[158] The Phaeacians, who listened to Odysseus and Demodocus while they banqueted, were thought of as the archetypal symposiasts.[159] Of course, not even famous poets always made serious contributions to the festivities: Euphorion once got so drunk at a symposium in the house of the philosopher Prytanis that he urinated into an expensive drinking cup.[160]

6

According to lines 5-6 of the Elephantine epigram, symposiasts foregathered "to mock and throw amusing abuse at each other." Here too there is continuity with the archaic age. Abusive banter at the symposium is first attested by a simile in *Hymn to Hermes* 56-7 (ἠύτε κοῦροι ἡβηταὶ θαλίῃσι παραιβόλα κερτομέουσιν),[161] and documented by a number of passages in the Theognidean corpus. A famous example in the form of an epigram is the mock epitaph on Timocreon of Rhodes.[162] But polemic of

157. Plut. *Alex.* 50. 8; Athen. 155AB = *FGrH* 45 T 3; Jacoby, *RE* 7 (1912), 2602-06.

158. *SH* 980; D. L. Page, *Greek Literary Papyri* i (1942), 452-55.

159. T. Dorandi, *Filodemo: Il buon re secondo Omero* (Naples 1982), coll. 18-19, translated by Asmis [n. 34] 1991, 29, cf. p. 36; also Philodemus, *AP* xi. 44 quoted above; E. Kaiser, "Odyssee-Szenen als Topoi," *MH* 21 (1964), 217-20.

160. Hegesander of Delphi, F 38 and 21 (*FHG* IV. 416).

161. G. Nagy's claim that this banter is "associated with the theme of 'philotes befitting hetairoi' (ἑταιρείῃ φιλότητι)" (*Best of the Achaeans* [Baltimore 1979], 245), misunderstands the Greek; in the context the φιλότης has to be that between Zeus and Maia.

162. *AP* vii. 348, with Page, *FGE* 252-53, "first delivered (and no doubt often repeated) as a *skolion* at the symposium."

all sorts was especially characteristic of the Hellenistic age. Poets, philosophers, grammarians, all attacked each other in the most uncompromising terms. Some of this polemic filled the pages of academic treatises, but much was vulgar and personal.

For example, Epicurus is said to have "set a depth of polemic hitherto unplumbed among ancient philosophers."[163] Doubts have recently been expressed as to whether he really said all these things.[164] But one factor has been overlooked. As we have already seen, Epicurus actually recommended "vulgar buffoonery" (φορτικὰς βωμολοχίας) rather than poetry at symposia. Is it coincidence that it is precisely vulgar buffoonery that is the hallmark of his polemic? Perhaps he did say these things, though at a symposium. Prometheus in Lucian's dialogue of that name (§ 8) remarks that it is best to leave resentments provoked by sympotic misunderstandings at the symposium. But when repeated outside this context and committed to writing, such abuse naturally took on a different complexion.

We have already considered the most remarkable example of such abuse, Sotades's line on the marriage between Philadelphus and Arsinoë. How did he get away with it? Perhaps more to the point, *where* did he get away with it? Hardly at a formal performance in open court. The only possible context where he could have recited such a poem in front of the king is at a symposium. It was at a symposium that one of Lysimachus's lieutenants made a crude joke about the king's wife (by a curious coincidence the very same Arsinoë before she married Philadelphus), skilfully adapting a line of tragedy so that he pronounced τήνδε Μοῦσαν, "this Muse," as τήνδ' ἐμοῦσαν, "this vomiting woman" (Arsinoë was apparently given to vomiting). Plutarch cites the story as an example of a joke that is licensed at the symposium but intolerable outside.[165] Then there is the story of Ptolemy Soter mocking a grammarian for his ignorance, asking him who was Peleus's father; "I'll tell you if you tell me first who was Lagus's father," replied the grammarian. When "everyone" was indignant at his impertinence, the king said: "if a king can't take jokes, then he

---

163. J. M. Rist, *Epicurus: An Introduction* (Cambridge 1972), 9.

164. David Sedley, "Epicurus and his professional rivals," *Études sur l'Épicurisme antique*, ed. J. Bollack and A. Laks (Lille 1976), 121-59.

165. I am assuming that Plut. *Mor.* 634E preserves the original version of this anecdote, while the version that he was kept in a cage like a wild beast and mutilated (Athen. 616CD; Plut. 606B; Seneca, *De ira* iii. 17. 2-4) is a later development once Lysimachus had been transformed into a tyrant (H. S. Lund, *Lysimachus: A Study in Early Hellenistic Kingship* [London 1992], 10-12), influenced by the story that Alexander once shut Lysimachus himself up with a lion (Lund 6-8). We may compare the story of Lysimachus and Theodorus the Atheist. Diog. Laert. ii. 102 describes, plausibly enough, how Theodorus spoke frankly to Lysimachus on an embassy from Soter; Cicero and Seneca have Lysimachus threaten him with torture and death (sources in E. Mannebach, *Aristippi et Cyrenaicorum Fragmenta* [Leiden 1961], T 255-259C). The line is *TGF*[2] adesp. 395.

shouldn't make jokes."[166] Where else but over their cups would a mere grammarian dare to speak to a king like this? At least three of the witticisms of Theocritus of Chios were delivered at banquets; his last, fatal joke was in response to a pressing invitation to the table of Antigonus the One-eyed.[167] Theocritus's satirical epigram on Aristotle over the Hermias affair was surely written in the first instance for the symposium.[168] It was at the symposium that abusive poems were sung about Alexander's generals; and at the symposium that enemies of Aratus of Sicyon attacked him in front of Philip V "with great wantonness and scurrility."[169]

We saw in Ch. I. 2 that Callimachus mischievously alluded to Sotades's poem in his *Acontius and Cydippe*. Might not this poem too have been intended in the first instance for a symposium? In addition to the erotic theme of the poem as a whole, there is an explicit allusion to the symposium within the poem (F 69):

πολλοὶ καὶ φιλέοντες Ἀκοντίῳ ἧκαν ἔραζε
οἰνοπόται Σικελὰς ἐκ κυλίκων λάταγας.

Many of his lovers in Sicilian fashion tossed the last drops of wine from their cups to the ground in honour of Acontius.

This is evidently a form of kottabos, a game in which guests tried to hit various objects with the last drops of wine out of their cups. It was common to utter the name of a beloved while flicking the cup to bring luck.[170] Kottabos prizes are mentioned in another Callimachean poem already claimed for the symposium, *Iamb* 15 on the all-night festival (F 227. 6). In keeping with the prevailing attitude towards the Hellenistic age, Ziegler's entry for kottabos in the *Kleine Pauly* (1975) characterizes it as a game popular from the sixth to the fourth century, despite the fact that his source, Schneider's entry in the large *Pauly* (1922), cited a kottabos-stand from Naucratis no earlier than the third century.[171] Schneider reasonably concluded that "Egyptian Greeks continued to amuse themselves with kottabos," and even compared Callimachus F 69. At the very least, this kottabos-stand and the soldier's symposium-text prove the continued existence of traditional symposia in both Elephantine and Naucratis. And if there, why not in Alexandria? Naturally this does not in itself prove that Callimachus performed this particular poem at a symposium, but it would

166. Plutarch, *de coh. ira* 9 = *Mor.* 458AB.

167. See the texts collected by Müller, *FHG* ii (Paris 1860), 86-7; *Gnom. Vat.* 339, 341.

168. *FGE* 93-95; Ch. X. 5 (n. 169).

169. Plut. *Alex.* 50. 8; *Arat.* 48. 4; Polyb. v. 15. 1-3 (with Walbank's note).

170. For details, K. Schneider, *RE* 11.2 (1922), 1528-41; Lissarrague 1990, 80-86. For its Sicilian origin—a characteristic Callimachean aetion in passing—see Schneider 1530.

171. Published by A. Higgins, *Archaeologia* 51 (1888), 384f., pl. XIII (p. 390 on the date); cf. G. Körte, *Abh. Gött.* 12. 1 (1909), 47; Schneider 1541.

be a characteristic Alexandrian touch to introduce a detail of the performance context into the poem being performed.

Callimachus's own celebrated polemic embraces several genres. Not to mention epigrams, short pieces like the *Aetia* prologue and *Iambi* 1 and 13 would have been ideal for the symposium. Also relevant is the single couplet that survives from the so-called *Grapheion* or *Pen* (F 380): "he drew [εἵλκυσε] the keen anger of the dog and the sharp sting of the wasp; his bite has the venom of both." Characteristically enough, scholars have been more interested in speculating about the mysterious lost *Pen*[172] than in examining its only fragment. Whether or not Callimachus himself went on to make the point explicitly, his own polemical technique is obviously very different, witty and erudite rather than crude and biting.[173] In effect F 380 is a comparison of different polemical styles. Modern critics have devoted enormous effort to reconstructing the literary feuds that provoked Callimachus's polemic, taking it as axiomatic that the feuds were what mattered and the polemic merely a regrettable if entertaining character defect. Contemporaries (even when they were its object) may have been much more interested in the polemic itself.

7

It is often assumed that postclassical sympotic poetry was entirely apolitical.[174] Most doubtless was, but perhaps not quite all. The praise of Spartan heroism we find rather suddenly in epigrammatists of the second half of the century (completely absent from poets of the first half) may have been inspired by the short-lived revival of Sparta and the hope of some Greeks that she would lead the resistance to Macedon.[175] And it may be more than coincidence that two at least of these poets (Dioscorides and Damagetus) have connections with Alexandria, the great rival of Macedon.[176]

If the epigram was the poetic form par excellence of the Hellenistic symposium, then it is not surprising that we do not have much political poetry. The later anthologists who preserved most of what we have of Hellenistic epigram were attracted by its timeless rather than its ephemeral qualities. And yet the epigram was ideally suited to political invective, as can be seen (for example) from the savage attacks on Philip V of Macedon

172. M. Gabathuler, *Hellenistische Epigramme auf Dichter* (1937), 64; Pfeiffer's note.

173. W. Bühler, in *Archiloque* (Entretiens Hardt X), Geneva 1964, 225-47.

174. According to Murray 1985, 45, for Alcaeus "public and private are one—the drinking group is a political group. Later sympotic poets ignore the public sphere."

175. Damagetus, Dioscorides, Nicander: E. Degani, in *La cultura ellenistica* (Milan 1977), 290-91.

176. Gow and Page, *HE* II. 223-24 and 235.

by Alcaeus of Messene. The mock epitaph on Philip's defeat at Cynoscephalae (196) circulated widely in the weeks that followed the battle. Lines 3-4 naming the Aetolians before the Romans is said to have offended Flamininus, and it is no coincidence that they are missing in the Anthology tradition. Almost certainly Alcaeus deleted them from the version he ultimately published in book form. This is virtually proved by the fact that he reused one of the offending lines in another epigram praising Flamininus alone (*APl* 5). The six-line version was presumably preserved in a biography of Philip, where Plutarch found it.[177] This is apparently a case where we have a pre-publication copy of an epigram.

It opens as follows:

ἄκλαυστοι καὶ ἄθαπτοι, ὁδοιπόρε, τῷδ' ἐπὶ νώτῳ
Θεσσαλίης τρισσαὶ κείμεθα μυριάδες.

Without tears, without burial, passer-by, upon this hill we lie, thirty thousand men of Thessaly.

Plutarch goes on to quote a brilliant reply by Philip himself:

ἄφλοιος καὶ ἄφυλλος, ὁδοιπόρε, τῷδ' ἐπὶ νώτῳ
'Αλκαίου σταυρὸς πήγνυται ἠλίβατος.

Without bark, without leaves, passer-by, upon this hill stands a lofty stake to impale Alcaeus on.

The ascription is plausible enough: Philip was an educated man who quoted the poets.[178] The Anthology has preserved another, anonymous attack on Alcaeus, as follows:

'Αλκαίου τάφος οὗτος, ὃν ἔκτανεν ἡ πλατύφυλλος
τιμωρὸς μοιχῶν γῆς θυγάτηρ ῥάφανος (*AP* ix. 520).

This is the tomb of Alcaeus, killed by the wide-leafed daughter of the earth, punisher of adulterers, the radish.

Gow and Page describe this piece, envisaging as it does a very different end for the poet, as "irrelevant to his political epigrams," and suggest that it might have been inspired by "quite other circumstances." Yet there are closer links between the two poems than they recognized. The σταυρός in Philip's epigram is not the cross of Roman crucifixion but the stake of oriental impaling.[179] No one at the court of the flagrantly adulterous Philip[180] can have cared whether Alcaeus was an adulterer. The relevance

177. Plut. *Flam.* 9; Gow and Page, *HE* II. 11-12.
178. Polybius 23. 10. 10.
179. LSJ cite only one example (Plut. *Artax.* 17) s.v. σταυρός, but several more s. vv. ἀνασταυρίζω, ἀνασταυρόω, ἀνασκολοπίζω and ἀνασχινδυλεύω. Gow and Page, *HE* II. 591.
180. Supposedly with the daughter-in-law of Aratus of Sicyon before he was 20 (Plut. *Arat.* 49. 1; 50. 1-2).

of the traditional punishment for adulterers[181]—the insertion of a large radish up the rear—is simply that it was another (and particularly demeaning) form of *impalement*. And whereas the stake in the first epigram had (inevitably) been shorn of its leaves in the process of sharpening necessary for successful impalement, an especially leafy radish would naturally increase the victim's discomfort in the other sort of impalement! Obviously Philip's poem came first, and then by a train of thought readily comprehensible in people bent on painful vengeance, one sort of impaling suggested another. This is a case where there can surely be no doubt about priority—even if a priority of no more than a matter of minutes.

Editors have naturally suggested Philip as author of both poems, but a drinking companion is at least as likely. Like Philip II, ever eager for a symposium and always surrounded by "poets of ribald songs,"[182] Philip V loved to carouse with his companions.[183] Indeed, one of Alcaeus's lampoons actually pictures him at the symposium poisoning his companions, and another is devoted to two victims of his poisoned cups.[184] It seems natural to picture the symposium as the context in which Philip and his Friends took their literary revenge on Alcaeus.

                                   8

There can be no question that by Callimachus's day people read a lot more. But that does not mean they did nothing but read. In public, there was more poetry to be heard at festival competitions and from visiting celebrities than ever before. In private there were the symposia, still flourishing at the courts of the Ptolemies and Antigonids. It is a gross oversimplification to think of an age of reading *succeeding* an age of listening. The Roman and Byzantine evidence makes it clear that oral performance retained its centrality in social life for more than a millennium after publication of poetry in book form had become routine.

It is not any difference between the *way* Callimachus and (say) Simonides acquired their knowledge of poetry that matters. It is the gap between them that really made the difference. If Simonides had been brought up on Attic tragedy and comedy, the Sophists, Herodotus, Plato, New Comedy and the Atthidographers, inevitably he would have written

---

181. As Philip's grandfather Gonatas once remarked to a boastful adulterer, "Radish has as good a flavour as cabbage" (D. L. 2. 128).

182. ποιητὰς αἰσχρῶν ᾀσμάτων...περὶ αὐτὸν ἔχει, Demosthenes *Ol.* 3. 19; for Philip II at the symposium, Theopompus as quoted by Athen. 435B-D.

183. Polyb. v. 15. 2; Livy 37. 7. 12.

184. *AP* ix. 519 and xi. 12; Philip was said to have poisoned both Aratus and his son (Plut. *Arat.* 52. 2-3; 54. 1) and many others (for a list, Walbank, *CQ* 37 [1943], 4).

very differently. This is the true source of the "bookish" character, the allusiveness, the "mixing of the genres" in Alexandrian poetry. The poet who has another two centuries of literature in his head cannot write with the innocence of the age of Marathon.

This is not to say that nothing had changed in poetic practice. Anacreon and Simonides wrote their occasional poetry entirely for symposium performance. They will have kept written copies for their own purposes, but almost certainly never thought of publishing it in book form. Callimachus may have used the symposium as a forum to try out new ideas with a view to subsequent publication. Indeed, many of his shorter poems may first have seen the light of day at Alexandrian symposia. Of course, the eventual publication of short poems together with other poems in book form will have brought about important changes of emphasis.[185] The artistic arrangement of epigrams by similarity and contrast of themes will have added to the reader's appreciation of individual poems.[186] In particular, some of the shorter aetiological pieces may have taken on a very different significance when adapted into the narrator's dialogue with the Muses in *Aetia* I-II, a frame that seems to have encroached on individual components more than many such organizing devices.

Even so, their final form is bound to have been influenced by their original form and the symposium context for which they were composed. One last illustration. We have already seen that the best-preserved episode from *Aetia* I-II is set at a symposium. No less significant, given the modern reputation of the *Aetia* as the most bookish work of its age, is the form in which the other stories in books I-II are cast: "why did it please the Parians to sacrifice to [the Graces] without flutes and garlands?"..."why is it that the Anaphaeans sacrifice [to Apollo] with shameful words?"..."why do the Icians worship Peleus?"[187] Sympotic questions and answers. It is no coincidence that the earliest surviving example of a genre with a long future should be in that most traditional sympotic verse form, elegy.

---

185. As Pliny put it, when discussing the revision of his poems for publication in book form, *plerisque mutatis ea quoque mutata videntur quae manent* (*Ep.* viii. 21. 4).

186. *Greek Anthology* 19f.; the case of the *Iambi* will be discussed in detail in Ch. VI. 7.

187. F 178 + 43 (§ 5 above); F 3; 7. 19; 178. 23.

Chapter IV

Prologue and Dream

1

We now know a fair amount about Callimachus's most famous work, the *Aetia*. We still only possess a fraction of the original text intact, but thanks to the so-called Diegeseis (plot-summaries with the first line of each aetion) and a few other fragments from ancient commentaries, we do at least know the sequence of episodes through much of the poem and are better able to order the surviving fragments.

The largest gap in our knowledge of the structure of the poem has been filled by Peter Parsons's reconstruction of the beginning of Bk III on the basis of the recently published Lille fragments. It now seems that the opening poem of III was an aetiological epinician of a Nemean chariot victory of Queen Berenice II, a pendant to the poem on the Lock of the same Berenice that closed Bk IV.[1]

Progress has been slow, and inevitably many ingenious and attractive conjectures have had to be jettisoned along the way. But two that have so far withstood every advance in our knowledge are (A) Pfeiffer's theory that the famous prologue revealed to us in 1927 is not the original preface to the *Aetia* but a polemical addition to either a second edition of the *Aetia* or a collected edition of the poet's work published in his old age;[2] and (B) the assumption that this polemic was directed at contemporary epic poets. So secure a fixture has this collected edition[3] become in modern accounts of Hellenistic, "neoteric" and Augustan poetry that we are in danger of forgetting that it is a conjecture, originally devised to solve problems that can now be solved in simpler ways. To give only one illustration of the wider implications, it has been suggested that "in their constant self-revision, as in other characteristics, the Augustans were the heirs of Cal-

---

1. *ZPE* 25 (1977), 1-50; *SH* 254-269; Livrea, *ZPE* 34 (1979), 37 and *CQ* 39 (1989), 146-47; Turner, *GMAW*[2] no. 75 for a plate; for further bibliography, Lehnus 1989, 81-85; Marcotte-Mertens 1990, 419-20.

2. *Hermes* 63 (1928), 302-41; Wilamowitz, letter to J. Loeb dated 28/4/1931 (W. M. Calder, *Wilamowitz: Selected Correspondence 1869-1931* [Naples 1983], 223-4); Lehnus 1989, 55-62; Livrea, *Hermes* 123 (1995). For the history of the interpretation of the prologue, see now G. Benedetto, *Il sogno e l'invettiva* (Florence 1993).

3. Despite some doubts subsequently expressed by Pfeiffer himself (II. xxxvi-vii).

limachus, who was the first poet to arrange (and revise for the purpose) his own collected works."[4] The only evidence for this "self-revision" is the hypothesis that the *Aetia* prologue is a later addition. As for the alleged polemic against epic poetry, it seems not to have been realized that this too is a conjecture, for which there is no evidence whatever (Ch. X).

The Diegeseis revealed that the *Lock of Berenice*, till then assumed an independent elegy, was actually the final aetion of Bk IV of the *Aetia*. The fact that Catullus's translation (*c.* 66) contains ten lines (79-88) missing from P. Oxy. 2258[5] has often been thought to prove that Callimachus himself revised the poem for the revised edition.[6] Also, since there now seems to be no doubt that Apollonius borrowed extensively from the *Aetia* (Ch. IX. 3), he could be supposed to have used the first edition, ca 270. This would be consistent with the common assumption that Theocritus, none of whose works can be dated later than the 270s, seemed to criticize Apollonius's treatment of certain Argonautic adventures in Idylls 13 and 22.

Callimachus is held to have prepared this new edition ca 245, adding the *Lock* (F 110), a new prologue (F 1) and an epilogue (F 112). Those who have expressed doubts about this revised edition, principally E. Eichgrün, have believed that there was no collected edition at all before 245.[7] It was not till then (according to this minority view) that Callimachus first put together all the aetiological poems he had written over the years in four books.

Parsons's new reconstruction of *Aetia* III-IV has shown that these are not the only possibilities. If III began with a poem on Berenice that cannot be earlier than 246, there is no need to see the poem on her Lock that concludes IV as an addition to a hypothetical second edition. As far as Theocritus is concerned, in Ch. XVI we shall see reason to doubt Theocritus's supposed criticisms of Apollonius. Indeed, in all probability Theocritus wrote first.

As for Catullus, the "additional" lines in *c.* 66 are on any hypothesis a puzzling digression from the main theme of the poem:[8] the lock suddenly interrupts her address to Berenice to urge all newly married couples to offer her libations and avoid "foul adultery." Callimachus was notoriously fond of aetiologies, but why complicate his compliment to Berenice (who was not a newlywed) in so inappropriate a fashion? As E. Lobel tartly

4. J.E.G. Zetzel, "Recreating the Canon: Augustan Poetry and the Alexandrian Past," *Critical Inquiry* 10 (1983), 105 n. 34.

5. Which offers lines 43-55, 65-78 and 89-94. This late (s. VII) papyrus seems to have contained separate elegies rather than a complete *Aetia*; for example, the *Victoria Sosibii*, not so far as we know included in the *Aetia* (Pfeiffer, II. xxiv-v).

6. For bibliography up to 1988, Lehnus 1989, 104-113; add Koenen 1994, 94, 111.

7. Eichgrün 1961, 52-66; Reinsch-Werner 1976, 6, 325; Herter 1973, 206-7.

8. For example, see M.C.J. Putnam, *CP* 55 (1960), 223-28.

remarked:[9] "A poem of which the aetion is the forming of the constellation Berenices plokamos is not improved by the superposition of an aetion concerning a marriage custom." To make so pointed and irrelevant an addition to the original version might be thought to imply that there was some question about Berenice's fidelity! If this had been so, naturally Callimachus would not have republished the poem at all. On the other hand, there are many similar developments about the importance of fidelity in marriage in other poems of Catullus (61. 96-101; 64. 334-6; 68.27-30, 136-40). It is now generally recognized that Catullus's translations from the Greek are freer than once assumed,[10] and there is much to be said for the hypothesis that 79-88 were added by Catullus.[11] The separate appearance of the *Lock* an entire millenium later in P. Oxy. 2258 cannot reasonably be assumed to derive from a hypothetical preliminary publication rather than from the *Aetia* itself or a later selection drawn from the *Aetia*.

Since the *Victoria Berenices* celebrates a Nemean victory, we can make an educated guess about its date. Berenice married Ptolemy Euergetes shortly after his accession on 7/8 January 246. The Nemean games took place in July/August of the second and fourth years in each Olympiad, which gives the following possibilities: 245 (4th year of the 133rd Olympiad), 243 and 241 (2nd and 4th years of the 134th Olympiad). 245 seems unlikely; there was civil unrest in Egypt serious enough to recall Euergetes from his campaign in Syria.[12] νύμφα in *SH* 254. 2 might be thought to support 243 rather than 241, though as Parsons judiciously remarks, "the word may mean 'wife' as well as 'bride'; and...Ptolemy II and Arsinoë II could still qualify as νυμφίος and νύμφα, after six years of marriage."[13] But hardly after 241, though Lehnus has recently argued that Callimachus lived into the reign of Attalus I of Pergamum (241-197), perhaps as late as 235.[14]

9. In his introduction to P. Oxy. 2258 (1952, p. 98): "79-88 are easily separable and to my taste their equivalent is gladly to be dispensed with."

10. Herter 1973, 205; A. Spira, *Dialogos: Festschr. H. Patzer* (Wiesbaden 1975), 153-62; Stephanie West, *CQ* 35 (1985), 61-65.

11. Putnam, l.c.; T. P. Wiseman, *Catullan Questions* (Leicester 1969), 20-25; N. Marinone, *Berenice da Callimaco a Catullo* (Rome 1984), 59-76; Koenen 1994, 94. For an ingenious (to me unconvincing) alternative to both views, Hollis, *ZPE* 91 (1992), 21-28.

12. *in Aegyptum domestica seditione revocatus*, Justin 27. 1; H. Hauben, "L'expédition de Ptolémée III en Orient et la sédition domestique de 245 av. J.C.," *Archiv für Papyrusforschung* 36 (1990), 29-37.

13. Parsons 1977, 8, citing Theoc. 17. 129 and Call. F 228. 5.

14. *ZPE* 105 (1995), 6-12: according to F 438 (Athen. 252C), Lysimachus, called a pupil of Theodorus by Callimachus and of Theophrastus by Hermippus, was the flatterer and teacher of Attalus and author of a work *On the education of Attalus*. But to have had either of these teachers L. will have been fairly old by his connection with Attalus, and Callimachus is only cited for his connection with Theodorus, no doubt many years earlier.

As for the *Lock*, Stephanie West has pointed out that "Conon's ingenious compliment would have worked much better if he could point to a group of stars which had clearly only just risen, and on this hypothesis the relevant period is at or shortly after the heliacal rising of Coma, about 3 September."[15] In all probability the *Coma Berenices* dates from September 245, since we can hardly doubt that court poet and court astronomer collaborated in the proclamation of Conon's "discovery"—in fact a diffuse cluster of 5th-6th magnitude stars barely visible to the naked eye.[16]

It was presumably writing the second Berenice poem that suggested the idea of using them to frame a new collection of *Aetia*, Bks III-IV, no doubt (as Parsons has suggested) incorporating other pre-existing material along with new episodes written specially. In view of Callimachus's advanced age we may presume that the new instalment soon followed the second poem, at any rate not later than ca 240. But we are not obliged to date I-II so late. Indeed if, as the London scholia suggest, they were dedicated to Arsinoë, not later than 268 (Ch. VI).

The hypothesis of a revised edition might be held to explain the mention of royal patrons separated by 30 years; but even if the work as a whole was revised ca 240, why postpone praise of Berenice to III-IV?[17] We shall soon see that there are serious problems with both collected (§ 2) and revised (§ 3) editions. More important, the differences between I-II and III-IV are not limited to the framing of III-IV by Berenice.

It is now clear that the two pairs are quite different in structure. The appearance of Muses at the beginning or end of aetia in the two new fragments *SH* 238. 8 and 253. 13-14 has put it beyond reasonable doubt that I-II were a continuous dialogue between poet and Muses. If I am right in combining F 178 and 43 at the beginning of Bk II (Ch. V. 1), that would make the story of the Sicilian cities (43) the second aetion in II after that of Peleus on Icos (178), and the Muse who takes responsibility for the Sicilian cities is Clio. Κλειὼ δὲ τὸ δεύτερον ἦρχ[ετο μ]ύθου (F 43. 56) surely means more than just "Clio spoke again"; rather this was the second time she had spoken on behalf of her sisters. From F 31*b* ("Thus she spoke, and at once my heart asked them again") it appears that he addressed them collectively,

15. West 1985, 65; so too Marinone 1984, 40.

16. West 1985, 61-66; Koenen 1994, 90 n. 151. Conon of Samos is otherwise known as a mathematician: Fraser II. 581-2; O. Neugebauer, *A History of Ancient Mathematical Astronomy* II (Berlin 1975), 572 n. 4. Even if there was "no such rank" as "court-astronomer" (Neugebauer l.c.), Conon certainly moved in court circles.

17. It is true that Vergil reserved his praise of Augustus till the proem to *Georg.* III, but that is surely because he was following Callimachean precedent (so Thomas 1983, 92f.; Comm. 36-37). Though it is not impossible that *Georg.* III-IV are a later continuation of I-II: so R. Sabbadini, *RFIC* 29 (1901), 16-22 and (adducing the Callimachean parallel as well as the two books of Nicander's *Georgica*) E. Fantham, *CP* 86 (1991), 165-6.

but that just one replied.[18] So at F 7. 22 it is Calliope who ἤρχετο the second aetion.[19] We know from the Schol. Flor. that the poet "said he heard [the first aetion] from Clio,"[20] and at *SH* 238. 8 Erato speaks.[21] It would be logical if each of the nine sisters had spoken in turn,[22] in which case Clio's second utterance should mark the tenth aetion. Since we know that Clio was the first to speak, that would make eight in Bk I.[23]

In III-IV Callimachus dropped this dialogue framework. Thanks to the Diegeseis, we have a synopsis and first line for every aetion in the second half of III and the whole of IV, and neither here nor in the extant fragments is there any reference to interventions by Muses.[24] In I-II successive aetia are cast in the form of questions by the poet followed by answers from the Muses. This is not the format of III-IV; not one of the 17 episodes in IV, to judge from their opening lines, began with a question. Instead the aetia emerge in a variety of ways during the course of the story. The story of Acontius and Cydippe (middle of Bk III) has no main aetion at all; instead a dozen or more allusions to aetia *not* told (Ch. IX. 3), most conspicuously the refusal to explain the prenuptial customs of Naxos (Ch. I. 2).

We are fortunate enough to have both beginning and end of this famous poem (F 67-75), perhaps originally written as an independent elegy (cited by Ovid as *Cydippe, Rem.* 382). It opens with the words "Love himself taught Acontius" (αὐτὸς Ἔρως ἐδίδαξεν Ἀκόντιον) and concludes with the claim that it was from the historian Xenomedes that "the story came to my Muse" (ἐς ἡμετέρην ἔδραμε Καλλιόπην). The narrator of I-II would not have been content with the authority of a mere mortal historian (here praised for his "love of truth"). He would have asked one of the Muses for confirmation; "Muse" here means no more than poem.[25] In the continuous narrative of I and II, the transitional dialogue with the Muses must often have obscured the division between one aetion and the next. Bks III-IV by contrast consisted of a series of separate elegies.[26]

18. Livrea 1994 less plausibly inferred from this line that they sometimes spoke together.

19. The list in *Theog.* 77-79 might have suggested that Clio and Calliope were the two most important of the Muses.

20. π(αρὰ) Κλειοῦς φησιν ἀκη[κο]ένα[ι], line 30 (I. 13 Pf.).

21. Polymnia (?), F 126. 3; Calliope again, F 759; unnamed "youngest daughter of Mnemosyne," F 735.

22. Presumably the sense of ἀμοιβ[in the Oxford scholion 2*a*. 47 (II. 104 Pf.).

23. Six in Pfeiffer, plus another more recent find (n. 75 below); 8 might seem on the short side compared with the 17 attested for IV by the Diegeseis, but prologue and Somnium must have been equivalent to another two.

24. F 86 begins by apostrophizing the Muses in the traditional way to inspire his song.

25. Hutchinson 1988, 45, perhaps rightly, sees this as a conscious "undoing of the fiction in the earlier books."

26. Note how the Diegesis to the first aetion in IV begins "This is the first elegy." (F 86 Pf.). It is doubtful whether this could have been said of the successive aetia in I-II.

It is a natural (and surely correct) assumption that Propertius IV and Ovid's *Fasti* are, in their different ways, attempts to write Roman versions of Callimachus's *Aetia*. Ovid chose to follow the structure of *Aetia* I-II, with each book a continuous narrative in which the narrator constantly cross-questions Muses and a variety of other gods and goddesses. Yet Propertius wrote a series of entirely separate elegies. In the light of the grandiose claims to originality in the opening poem (*Umbria Romani patria Callimachi...sacra diesque canam et cognomina prisca locorum*, 64, 69), it was not inevitable that he should maintain the structure of his own earlier elegy books, despite the presence of a few love poems in IV. The answer is surely that both Roman poets followed Callimachean practice: Ovid, *Aetia* I-II, Propertius, III-IV.

As we shall see in Ch. VI, Bks I-II should be dated some 30 years earlier, to ca 270. If Callimachus saw fit to add a new prologue to his continuation, he would (of course) have placed it before Bk III. Any prologue transmitted before Bk I is surely the original prologue to Bks I-II.

2

We must not be misled by modern parallels. It is now commonplace for a writer to reissue his collected works in an omnibus volume. But it is doubtful if there is any ancient parallel for the sort of collected edition Pfeiffer and his followers seem to have envisaged. And for a very good reason; the length of the papyrus roll. As F. G. Kenyon bluntly put it,[27]

> [one] consequence of the size of the roll is that collected editions of an author's work could not exist, except in the sense that the rolls containing them could be kept in the same bucket.

The length of the "books" into which ancient works were divided was largely determined by the length of the roll. This is why individual books usually contain something between 700 and 2000 lines of text. It has been estimated that the individual books of the *Aetia* were in the neighbourhood of 1000 lines long; each book will have filled one roll. It is significant that what Parsons has convincingly identified as the beginning of Bk III is in fact the beginning of a roll.[28]

Only with the spread of the codex after ca 200 A.D.[29] did it become possible to collect between two covers the contents of as many as 10

27. *Books and Readers in Ancient Greece and Rome* (Oxford 1932), 62-63.
28. P. Oxy. 2173; Parsons 1977, 48.
29. "The codex scarcely counted for Greek literature before about A.D. 200," C. H. Roberts and T. C. Skeat, *The Birth of the Codex* (London 1983), 37; for the more recent literature, W. V. Harris, "Why did the Codex Supplant the Book-Roll?," *Renaissance Society and Culture: Essays in Honor of Eugene F. Rice, Jr* (New York 1991), 77-85.

rolls—or even more. In Callimachus's lifetime we might guess that his poetical works circulated in nine or ten rolls: four for the *Aetia*; one for the *Hymns* (ca 1090 lines), *Iambi* (ca. 1000), *Hecale* (1000/1500 lines) and epigrams (more than 300 lines extant); and one or perhaps two for minor epic and elegiac poems.[30] From late antiquity we do indeed have a number of leaves from two substantial codices that once contained all or most of these works: P.Oxy.1011 (IV s.) and 2258 (VI/VII s.).

It may be helpful to compare the evidence for another "collected" edition thought to have originated in the Ptolemaic age: Pindar. Following the lead of Callimachus's *Pinakes*, Aristophanes of Byzantium collected and classified Pindar's poems, divided them into 17 books, and may even have arranged them in what he considered an appropriate sequence.[31] The list in the so-called *Vita Ambrosiana* of Pindar, moving as it does from poems addressed to gods to poems addressed to men, has generally been thought to reflect Aristophanes's sequence. But the two other Pindar *Lives*, Horace's Pindar ode (4. 2) and above all the second century P. Oxy. 2438 give or imply quite different sequences. Not only is there no justification for the common assumption that the Ambrosian sequence was followed in ancient "collected" editions of Pindar. It is hard to see how there could have been a stable sequence. Yet it is commonly assumed (for example) that it was "by error" that the *Nemeans* were transferred to codex before the *Isthmians* in what was to become the archetype of our manuscript tradition.[32] Since the Nemean games were the least important, Aristophanes may well have placed the *Nemean* book (eked out by a miscellaneous appendix) last in his sequence, but since it is clear from quotations in the grammarians and scholia that Pindar's works were cited by title rather than book number,[33] there cannot really have been any "correct" sequence at the roll stage. To give another example, Bowra suggested that it was because the four books of epinicians came last in the "collected" edition that they alone survive, preserved by some accident.[34] But this is the sort of accident that could only happen with the controlled sequence of a codex. In any case, as Race pointed out, it is only in the Ambrosian list that the epinicians come last; all the others place them in the middle. P. Oxy. 2438

---

30. F 378-392; (F 383 is now identified as the *VB*); on the so-called *Lyrica*, Ch. VI. 7.

31. Pfeiffer 1968, 183-84 (cf. 130 on Callimachus); W. R. Race, "P. Oxy. 2438 and the order of Pindar's works," *Rhein. Mus.* 130 (1987), 407-410.

32. "Par suite d'une erreur," J. Irigoin, *Histoire du texte de Pindare* [Paris 1952], 100; "the order of the last two was mistakenly reversed," F. J. Nisetich, *Pindar's Victory Songs* (Baltimore 1980), 19.

33. E.g. ἐν παιᾶσιν (F 68), ἐν διθυράμβοις (73), ἐν ὑπορχήμασιν (112), ἐν θρήνοις (138), to cite the merest handful of examples.

34. C. M. Bowra, *Pindar* (1964), 159-60, with Race, l.c.

gives the *dithyramboi* in first place and closes with the *threnoi*—as it happens the sequence implied by Horace. During the half millennium before the victory of the codex, the collected works of Pindar amounted to no more than 17 separate rolls in a box labelled Pindar.[35] There was no way anyone could control the order in which the various books were either copied or read, and losses must have been random. The thirteen books that failed to survive no doubt mostly perished before the advent of the codex. Of the fifty Pindar papyri so far published, no more than four or five come from codices.[36] On the other hand, three of these are very early codices (II/III A.D.), suggesting that this form was chosen precisely because it offered the possibility of collecting all of Pindar in one volume.[37]

The same applies to the so-called alphabetical edition of Euripides. As is well known, a single codex preserves a more or less alphabetical sequence of nine plays. Mechanical explanations devised to explain the omission of the four or five known plays missing under theta and iota[38] in this manuscript presuppose not merely, in Zuntz's phrase, "the complete Alexandrian edition,"[39] but a complete copy of that edition in perfect sequence.[40] Now Aristophanes *may* have catalogued the plays in alphabeti-

---

35. P. Ant. I 21 is a parchment slip (σίλλυβος or *index*) of the sort attached to a papyrus roll as title (F. Bilabel, *RE* III.A.1 (1927), 99-100), bearing the words Πίνδαρος ὅλος in "a slanting third-century hand." Since "no roll could have contained the entire works of Pindar," C. H. Roberts suggests either that it "was attached to a series of rolls," or (less probably) to a codex "in the transition period between roll and codex" (P. Ant. I [1950], p. 47). Why not to the box that contained the rolls? Some of the *capsae* illustrated in T. Birt, *Die Buchrolle in der Kunst* (Leipzig 1907) seem to carry external labels (Abb. 162, 163, 169, pp. 252-3, 260); so too pll. 1174-5 in Daremberg and Saglio s.v. *capsa* (I.2. 911), and R. Garucci, *Storia della Arte cristiana* II.1 (1873), pl. 23. 2. It was also standard practice to gather rolls in bundles with a cord to hold them together; Birt Abb. 165 (p. 256) seems to show a label attached to such a bundle.

36. E. G. Turner, *The Typology of the Early Codex* (Phila. 1977), 113. For an up-to-date list of Pindar papyri (unfortunately without dates or descriptions), see the latest Teubner editions by B. Snell/H. Maehler, I (1987), vi, and II ed. Maehler (1989), vi-vii; R. A. Pack, *The Greek and Latin Literary Texts from Greco-Roman Egypt*[2] (Ann Arbor 1965), 1350-85; 1904-7; M. F. Galiano, "Los papiros pindáricos," *Emerita* 16 (1948), 165-200.

37. P.S.I. II.147 (II), P.S.I. II.145 (II/III), P. Ant. II.76 (III, parch.); see Roberts and Skeat 71-2 for the suggestion that some of the very few early non-Christian codices may have been "one-volume editions" of long works (e.g. Plato, *Republic*, Xenophon, *Cyropaedia*, Achilles Tatius). It might be added that these three codices lend little support to the fashionable doctrine, first stated by Wilamowitz (*Einleitung in die griechische Tragödie* [Berlin 1889], 175f.) and developed on no better evidence by Irigoin (pp. 93-105), that the age of the Antonines saw a deliberate selection of the four books of epinicians, which alone made the transition to codex. P.S.I. II. 147 (*Paean* 6) and 145 (F 334 M) preserve poems from other books. For scepticism about his similar views on the tragic selection, see W. S. Barrett, *Euripides Hippolytos* (Oxford 1964), 51-52; G. Zuntz, *An Inquiry into the Transmission of the Plays of Euripides* (Oxford 1965), 254-56.

38. Barrett 1964, 51 n. 2; Zuntz 1965, 277.

39. Zuntz 1965, 277.

40. Until the empire, alphabetization was normally by first letter alone; *Greek Anth.* 39.

cal sequence, and papyri have now revealed a separate book of alphabetically arranged hypotheseis (§ 4 below). But before the codex, a collected *edition* of Euripides can only have meant a pile of rolls grouped in one or more buckets for each letter of the alphabet. Since few private individuals of the third or fourth century A.D. are likely to have owned all 74 plays,[41] any codex not compiled in a major library is likely to have been incomplete. Indeed, a complete alphabetical Euripides in codex may never have existed.

If we turn to the poets of the third century, most of the major figures published separate editions of their epigrams. Since individual epigrams were written for a variety of occasions over the years, these too will have amounted to collected editions.[42] But in view of the tiny compass of the epigram, even two or three hundred would only have made one small roll. It is not with collected editions of this sort that we are concerned, but with the oeuvre of a living poet already published in a number of separate rolls over a period of years. It is difficult to see how the collected edition envisaged by Pfeiffer could have differed from the original editions, separate poems in separate rolls. For example, the so-called epilogue allegedly added to link the *Aetia* to the *Iambi* in this collected edition could not have performed this function in separate rolls. It would have stood at the end of its roll, and the allusion to the *Iambi* was not in itself explicit enough to ensure that the reader would select that roll next (Ch. VI. 2).

On Pfeiffer's hypothesis, prologue and epilogue were both specially written for this collected edition, with the epilogue providing a transition not only between works, but between genres. On the other hand, the prologue does not represent a transition from anything else to the *Aetia*. It clearly is what it has usually been called, a prologue. We should therefore expect it to introduce the first poem in this collected edition. That would give *Aetia* and *Iambi* in first place, followed by *Hecale, Hymns* and epigrams. The second century Diegeseis do indeed give the sequence *Aetia, Iambi, Hecale, Hymns*, and if the Schol. Flor. are part of the same work (see § 4 below), their summary of the *Aetia* prologue does seem to come from the beginning of a roll.[43] Pfeiffer's edition of the fragments follows this sequence,[44] but in view of what has been said, there is no reason to suppose that it reflects the order of an official collected edition. There is

---

41. We are all familiar with the sad sight of "complete" sets of Dickens, Scott, Balzac, Dumas and even encyclopaedias missing the odd volume in second-hand bookshops.

42. We now know a good deal more about such editions than we did a few years ago: my *Greek Anthology*, Ch. I-II.

43. Pfeiffer II. xviii; the Diegeseis begin half way through Bk III (Pfeiffer I p.71) and break off after *Hymn* ii, leaving the rest of the papyrus blank (Pfeiffer II. xii).

44. Which, though no doubt a convenient working hypothesis, "geht nicht ohne einige Schwierigkeiten ab," as Herter 1973, 189-90 put it.

also a first-century book-list (overlooked in *SH*) that gives the sequence
Aetia I-III (with no Bk IV), *Hymns*, *Epigrams* and *Hecale*, to judge from
its date all in roll form.[45] It is difficult to see how there can have been a
stable sequence at the roll stage: for Callimachus's works, like Pindar's,
were cited by book title, not book number.

The only collected edition concerning which we have enough evidence
to discern a sequence of poems, the seven leaves of the fourth century
codex (P.Oxy. 1011) that alone preserve the epilogue, offer a quite different order. On f. i[r], which bears the original page number 152, stands the
conclusion of the tale of Acontius and Cydippe, the central aetion of Bk III
(F 75). On the verso of f. ii, numbered 186,[46] stands the epilogue (F 112)
and the beginning of the *Iambi* (F 191). The 16 folia (32 pages) lost
between ff. i and ii must have contained the second half of *Aetia* III and all
of IV. The 150 pages missing before f. i must have contained some 6000
lines, clearly a good 2000 lines more than we can comfortably allot to
Aetia I-II and the first half of III. As Pfeiffer himself reasonably conceded,[47] in this codex both *Hecale* and *Hymns* must have preceded *Aetia*
and *Iambi*.

The iambic paraphrases of Marianus of Eleutheropolis (ca. 500 A.D.)
seem also to have followed the sequence *Hecale, Hymns, Aetia*, epigrams[48]
(naturally omitting the *Iambi*). And an epigram that stands at the head of
the *Hymns* in medieval manuscripts announces the sequence *Hymns,
Hecale, Aetia*, minor works.[49]

Of course, if there was no official collected edition, this sequence
would have no more authority than that suggested by the Diegeseis. But it
is better attested, albeit in documents of a later date, and has certain
advantages. For it would give a sequence in harmony with the traditional
hierarchy of the genres: epic, hymn, elegy, iambus, epigram. At all events,
there is no good evidence (a) that Callimachus issued his own collected edition; (b) that the *Aetia* opened such an edition; or (c) that the *Aetia*
prologue was designed to introduce the collected works as a whole rather
than just the *Aetia*.

45. Published by Sijpesteijn and Worp, *Chron. Ég.* 1974, 324-7 (cf. Lehnus, *Riv. Fil.*
1990, 26-7). The same list also has Hesiod in the sequence *Catalogue, Works and Days* and
Theogony, and its list of *Odyssey* books closes with χ, ψ, ω, γ, δ.

46. Despite Pfeiffer (II. xxii), the number is no longer to be found on f. ii itself, but is
inferred from the 188 on the immediately following f. iii[r]. For a clearer statement of these
details, see A. S. Hunt, *P. Oxy.* vol. VII (1910), pp. 18-19, 34.

47. II. xxxvii; for more detailed calculations, Hollis 1990, 339-40.

48. Suda s.v. Μαριανός (Pfeiffer, T 24; II. xxxviii).

49. Pfeiffer, T 23, with II. xxxviii.

3

Nowadays an author will often add a new preface to an otherwise unchanged reprint of a work written long ago. But before printing there could be no reprints. Not even the author had much chance of modifying the text of a work long in circulation. For example, the revised edition of Cicero's *Academica* failed to supplant the original edition; one book of each has come down to us. This example is the more striking in that the second edition was published barely a month after the first.[50] If Callimachus had issued a new edition of the *Aetia* with a new preface after 20 years, there was little likelihood of its driving the original edition off the market.

Editors of classical texts have a well-known weakness for postulating second editions to explain certain sorts of problems in the medieval transmission. Very few stand up to critical scrutiny,[51] and the few we know to have existed lend no support to Pfeiffer's hypothesis. Moreover, the term is often applied loosely to what are really continuations rather than revised editions. Continuations are common enough, books added to what (if only retrospectively) can be counted a single work. For example, the successive books of Horace's *Satires* and *Epistles* and Bk IV of the *Odes*; the successive books of Propertius and Tibullus; Bk 3 of Ovid's *Ars Amatoria*; the successive books of Statius's *Silvae* and Martial's *Epigrams*. Examples in prose works are innumerable.

These multi-book continuations share two features: (a) new prefaces (if any) are placed before the new book(s) being added, *not* at the beginning of the work; and (b) the implication of these new prefaces is invariably that the preceding book(s) already in circulation have been left untouched (the prefaces and epilogues to successive books in Polybius, Diodorus Siculus and Vitruvius are particularly clear examples). On the face of it, the addition of two more books to the *Aetia* would be a simple case of continuation, and if Callimachus had thought to add a new preface, it would have stood before Bk III. And we know from P. Oxy. 2173, the beginning of a roll containing the beginning of the *Victoria Berenices*, that Bk III began without a preface.

50. Cic. *Att.* 13. 32. 3 (305 SB) implies that ed. 1 was not yet published by the end of May 45, while ed. 2 was already being copied for publication by the end of June (*Att.* 13. 21a = 327 SB). All the evidence is set out in O. Plasberg, *Cicero: Acad. Rel. cum Lucullo* (Leipzig 1922), i-xv; R. Philippson, *RE* VII. A. 1 (1939), 1128-1135.

51. For a convenient and generally sensible examination of most such "second editions" see H. Emonds, *Zweite Auflage im Altertum* (Leipzig 1941)—unfortunately accepting the second edition of the *Aetia* (and omitting Paul Alex. cited below).

It is only in the much rarer case of revised editions that we find a new preface at the beginning of the entire work, and its function is to alert readers to the circumstances of the revision. A good example is Apollonius of Perga, a generation after Callimachus. In the preface to his *Conic Sections*, Apollonius warns his dedicatee Eudemus that he had "a little too hastily" given an unrevised draft of his work to a departing friend, whence unrevised copies of the first two books passed into general circulation.[52] The definitive edition (he adds) is now being published book by book as he completes the revisions. A later case is Paul of Alexandria's *Introduction to Astrology*, with a preface promising to correct the errors of his first edition.[53]

Ovid's *Amores* is perhaps the only certain case of a revised ancient poetry book. The circumstances are explained in a brief preface at the beginning of the new edition:[54]

> Qui modo Nasonis fueramus quinque libelli
>   tres sumus; hoc illi praetulit auctor opus;
> ut iam nulla tibi nos sit legisse voluptas,
>   at levior demptis poena duobus erit.

> We who were once the five books of Naso are now three; the poet preferred his work this way. Though even now you may not enjoy reading us, the removal of two books will at any rate lessen your pain.

It will be obvious that this is no sort of parallel to the *Aetia* prologue. For all their characteristic wit, the chief function of these lines is to explain that Ovid has pruned the first edition by three fifths of its contents.[55] If in addition he added (as generally assumed) one or two new poems and revised the old, the three-book edition must have differed considerably from its predecessor.[56] There is no such hint in the *Aetia* prologue that it introduces an expanded or revised edition.

It has been alleged that the *Ars Amatoria* too appeared in a second edition. According to Murgia, "the publication of *Ars* 3 must have been

---

52. I (1891), p. 2 Heiberg = *Greek Math. Works* ii. 280-02 Thomas; T. L. Heath, *Apollonius of Perga: Treatise on Conic Sections*, edited in modern notation (Cambridge 1896), lxix, with Fraser II. 603 n. 328 and Cameron, *GRBS* 31 (1990), 116-18.

53. πάνυ καλῶς, ὦ φίλε παῖ Κρονάμων, ἐψευδογραφηκότας ἡμᾶς ἀνευρὼν ἐν τῇ πρὸ ταύτης ἐκδόσει τῶν εἰσαγωγικῶν προετρέψω ἑτέραν συντάξαι, ed. Ae. Boer (Leipzig 1958), p. 1. 5; no trace of the first edition has been found (Boer, p. x n.1).

54. I cannot believe, with G. P. Goold (*HSCP* 74 [1970], 128), that this epigram, with its hallmark Ovidian whimsy, is the work of a later editor.

55. *Multa quidem scripsi, sed quae vitiosa putavi, emendaturis ignibus ipse dedi* (*Tr.* IV. 10. 61-2). Ovid's juvenilia may have been less successful than generally supposed (P. E. Knox, *Ovid's Metamorphoses and the Traditions of Augustan Poetry* [Cambridge 1986], 4), which might explain why no trace of the five-book edition has survived.

56. For modern views, Cameron, *CQ* 18 (1968), 320-33; A. S. Hollis, *Ovid Ars Amatoria Book 1* (Oxford 1977), 150-51; R. Syme, *History in Ovid* (Oxford 1978), 1-8.

accompanied by a second edition of *Ars* 1-2,"[57] on the grounds that the concluding couplet of *Ars* 2,

> ecce, rogant tenerae, sibi dem praecepta, puellae:
> vos eritis chartae proxima cura meae,

Look, the young women are asking for instructions; you will be the next care of my poem,

"could only have been added in a second edition to form a connection to *Ars* 3." Certainly this was the purpose of the new couplet, but that hardly implies a new edition of 1-2 as a whole. If Ovid had really wanted to re-issue his poem as a three-book *Ars* catering for women as well as men, why did he not insert a couplet extending the summary of contents at 1. 35-40 to cover Book 3? Why did he not at any rate drop the link couplet at the end of 1,

> Pars superat coepti, pars est exhausta laboris;
> hic teneat nostras ancora iacta ratis,

Part of my task remains, part is now finished; Here let the anchor be thrown to hold my ship firm,

which continues to imply two books? He even left the elaborate sphragis that brings Book 2 to its close. The couplet that links 2 and 3 may originally have been prefixed to 3 rather than appended to a new edition of 2,[58] and of course there is no new preface. The *Ars* is really just another case of continuation.

It has also been claimed that Martial re-issued books of his epigrams in new editions, perhaps even in a collected edition.[59] Once again, the evidence crumbles to the touch. In vii. 17, the library of his oldest friend Julius Martialis is said to contain "seven books I sent you marked with the author's own pen."[60] This means (of course), *not* that the poet had issued a second, corrected edition of Bks i-vii, but that he had corrected in his own hand what we would call typographical errors in the copies he originally sent Julius. That is why he goes on to say that his corrections increase the

---

57. C. E. Murgia, *CP* 81 (1986), 203; cf. *AJP* 107 (1986), 80, 86; for a different argument, no more compelling, Syme 1978, 13-20; Hollis was sceptical (ed. of Bk 1, 1977, xiii).

58. Compare Hesiod, *Theog.* 1021-22, which can as easily be identified as the beginning of the *Catalogue of Women* as the end of the *Theogony*. Since Ovid is also turning to address women, humorous evocation of Hesiod is a distinct possibility.

59. See the discussions in L. Friedlaender's ed. (1886), 50-67 and M. Citroni's ed. of Bk i (1975), ix-xxi; J. P. Sullivan, *Martial: the Unexpected Classic* (Cambridge 1991), 15. The issue has often been confused by the private editions Martial presented to friends: see the important discussion by P. White, *JRS* 64 (1974), 44-48.

60. *septem quos tibi misimus libellos / auctoris calamo sui notatos*, vii. 17. 6-7; on Julius Martialis (no relative), see *PIR*[2] I. 411.

value of the books (*haec illis pretium facit litura*). This interpretation is put beyond doubt by vii. 11, to another old friend:

cogis me calamo manuque nostra
emendare meos, Pudens, libellos.
o quam me nimium probas amasque
qui vis archetypas habere nugas.

You make me correct my books with my own hand and pen, Pudens. What excess of love and approval that you want my trifles in autograph!

Further evidence for this "collected edition" of i-vii has been found in the opening poem of Bk i:[61]

hic est quem legis ille, quem requiris,
toto notus in orbe Martialis
argutis epigrammaton libellis:
cui, lector studiose, quod dedisti
viventi decus atque sentienti
rari post cineres habent poetae.

It's him! I, the man you're reading, am the man you're looking for, Martial, famous throughout the world for his witty books of epigrams: to whom, enthusiastic reader, you have given, while he is alive and can appreciate it, such glory as few poets have after their deaths.

It is alleged that Martial could not so have characterized himself when publishing Bk i, and that this poem was added as a new preface for the new edition of i-vii, by when he was really famous. But not to mention the possibilities of hyperbole and irony, Martial was already in his mid forties and a well-known figure before the publication of what he rather perversely styled Bk i (preceded by at least three other books, in full or part extant). Furthermore, we should expect such a new preface to make some explicit allusion to its function, to the additions or excisions of this hypothetical revised edition. By contrast, x. 2 is quite explicit about the second edition of Bk x:

festinata prior, decimi mihi cura libelli
    elapsum manibus nunc revocavit opus.

The composition of my tenth book, hastened before, has recalled the work that slipped from my hands.

Not that "haste" was the real reason. Between the first and second editions of Bk x fell the assassination of Domitian: praise of the new regime had to replace praise of the old.[62] But there is nothing in i. 1 to suggest a revised

61. The translation is from Peter Howell's ed. of Bk i (1980), to whose common sense I am much indebted.
62. Sullivan 1991, 44-52.

edition of i, still less a collected edition of i-vii, nor is there anything in the preceding prose epistle to suggest that it is anything other than the original preface to i.[63] Exactly the same can be said of the *Aetia* prologue. The myth of the second edition of Apollonius's *Argonautica* (again no preface) will be discussed in detail later (Ch. VIII. 6).

To sum up: there is no known example of a multi-roll collected edition of the works of a living poet. New prefaces at the beginning of works imply a thoroughgoing revision, not the addition of new installments. Prefaces to new installments are placed before the installment itself, not before books already published. It is not out of the question that, when publishing *Aetia* III-IV, Callimachus saw fit to add a new prologue to a roll containing I-II, whether or not it was part of a new or collected edition. But it would certainly be without parallel. Furthermore, the *Aetia* prologue was undoubtedly the best known and most influential single poem of Callimachus. It was constantly imitated by the poets and quoted by the grammarians and metricians of the following centuries, Greek and Roman alike. When P. Oxy. 2079 was published, much of it was already familiar from quotations or at once recognized from imitations and adaptations. This surely implies that it was the original prologue to the *Aetia*, the opening passage of every copy of the poem. By contrast, the *Somnium* (on Pfeiffer's view the original opening of the poem) is only quoted once in extant literature.[64]

More than just a detail of chronology is involved. If the prologue was a new poem added by Callimachus in his old age to introduce a collected edition of his life's work, then it would become a far more important document. Not just one sally in a continuing pamphlet war, but the poetical credo he had evolved over a lifetime's reflection on his craft—"a major document of the European poetic tradition" as one scholar portentously dubs it.[65]

But while we need not doubt the basic seriousness of the sentiments expressed is the *Aetia* prologue, it is essential not to overlook the humour that is never far from the surface in Callimachus. Unfortunately, this splendid piece of fantasy has been treated with almost unrelieved seriousness by modern Telchines more interested in poetics than poetry. Fortunately, it is not difficult to establish that the prologue is an integral part of the original conception of the *Aetia*.[66]

---

63. Howell's comm. and T. Janson, *Latin Prose Prefaces* (Göteborg 1964), 110-12.

64. A fact to which Wilamowitz long ago drew attention (*HD* I 186), emphasized (against Pfeiffer) by Ida Kapp, *Philologus* 84 (1929), 175.

65. J. K. Newman, *The Classical Epic Tradition* (1986), 515.

66. This approach is not new, though it has never been worked out in detail; those who have expressed it before (e.g. Eichgrün and Reinsch-Werner) have believed that the first and only edition of the *Aetia* was not published till ca 245.

4

We do not as yet have a papyrus on which what Pfeiffer distinguished as fragments 1 and 2 join. So we are not in a position to see whether he drew the line between the prologue and what is generally known as the *Somnium* correctly—or whether such a line exists at all.[67] But we do now have extracts from no fewer than three sets of scholia on F 1-2: the London and Florentine scholia printed facing F 1-2 in Pfeiffer vol. I, and the Oxyrhynchus scholia printed in the addenda to vol. II (pp. 100-106). Anyone who wants to form a true idea of the nature and extent of these three sets of scholia will be well advised to study them in their original publications[68] as well as in Pfeiffer's book, where they are cited piecemeal over a number of pages.

Neither the London nor the Florentine scholia indicate any break between prologue and *Somnium*.[69] Only in P. Oxy. 2262 is a coronis to be found, at the bottom of F 1 col. i, the break in the commentary presumably reflecting a break in the poem at the same place. But this coronis does not divide the prologue from the *Somnium* in any clearcut or straightforward way. The lemmata and notes immediately preceding the coronis are laconic, but suggestive: [ὑπο]κρίσι[ε]ς glossed ἀποκρίσε[ι]ς, and [?ἀμν]-ήσαιτε glossed ἀναμνήυαιτέ μ[ε]. A plural addressee is being asked to "remind" the poet of some "answers." Since the last persons named in the prologue were the Muses, who subsequently reappear throughout Bks I-II answering the poet's questions, it seems natural to identify the addressees as the Muses.

Since these lemmata appear before the coronis, they cannot be assigned to the *Somnium*. Arnd Kerkhecker has raised the possibility that they belong to a transitional passage between prologue and *Somnium*, an "invocation of the Muses." This suggestion has provoked much inconclusive recent discussion about whether this invocation belonged to the original conception of either prologue or *Somnium*, or was added as a link passage when the prologue was prefixed to the second edition.[70]

---

67. E. Livrea's recent proposal (*Hermes* 1995) to insert F 114-5 between F 2 and 3 would have radical repercussions on the interpretation of prologue and Somnium. I myself believe it to be mistaken (*ZPE* 1996 forthcoming).

68. P. Lit. Lond. 181; P.S.I. 1219; P. Oxy. 2262; nos. 5, 24 and 20 in the prolegomena to Pfeiffer II, with subsequent bibliography; L. Torraca'a otherwise useful separate edition of the prologue unaccountably omits P. Oxy. 2262. On the London and Oxyrynchus scholia, see now E. Livrea, *Hermes* 1994.

69. Cf. C. Meillier, *ZPE* 33 (1979), 40 = *RÉG* 92 (1979), 103.

70. *ZPE* 71 (1988), 16-24; see too P. Bing, ib. 74 (1988), 273-75; R. L. Hunter, 76 (1989), 1-2; N. Krevans, 89 (1991), 19-23; A. Harder, 96 (1993), 11-13; Livrea 1994.

I would suggest that the Florentine scholia are a more reliable guide to the structure and divisions of the *Aetia*. As has long been noticed, they are entirely different in nature from the London and Oxyrhynchus scholia. No word-for-word glosses, indeed no philological notes at all, but plot summaries. Not merely plot summaries, since there are also a few nuggets of genuine erudition, but in the main summaries of the story told in each successive aetion. Instead of quoting one word of the text as lemma and then explaining it before moving on to the next word, they quote just one lemma for each section, and it is always a whole line. They begin by quoting the first line of the prologue, and then proceed to identify the Telchines before summarizing Callimachus's argument about Mimnermus and Philitas and finally describing his dream on Helicon and meeting with the Muses (lines 1-20). They then cite a second full line as lemma, before summarizing the first aetion (why people sacrifice to the Graces on Paros without flutes and garlands: lines 22-37). The third lemma is F 7. 19, introducing the second aetion of Bk I (on the Argonauts). As Maas at once pointed out,[71] the Florentine scholia are close kin of the so-called Diegeseis in P.Mil. Vogl. 18, a sequence of summaries of individual aetia which similarly begin by citing the first line in full.[72] A third papyrus was published in 1952, a brief sequence from later in Bk I with obvious links to the Schol. Flor. (P. Oxy. 2263).[73] And a fourth in 1991 from the Michigan collection by L. Koenen, W. Luppe and V. Pagán, the right-hand part of a column which appears to tell the story of King Teuthis and a statue of Athena with bandaged thigh.[74] This story is known to have been treated in the *Aetia*, according to Hollis in Bk I.[75] Badly damaged though the Michigan papyrus is, the summary begins with the remains of a hexameter line (ending with the epic form Ἀθήνης).[76] Oddly enough, despite the formal similarities it did not occur to the editors to connect this scrap with the three other Callimachean summaries.[77]

71. *Gnomon* 10 (1934), 437; P. Mil. Vogl. I [next note] 155-6; cf. Pfeiffer II. xxviii.

72. Originally published by M. Norsa and G. Vitelli; republished with useful introduction, notes, essays and plates by A. Vogliano, with appendixes by L. Castiglioni and P. Maas in P. Mil. Vogl. I [formerly cited as *PRIMI*] (1937), 66-173.

73. Most conveniently now read in Pfeiffer II. 108-112, but for the links with the Schol. Flor. see E. Lobel, *P. Oxy.* XX (1952), 125.

74. "Explanations of Callimachean αἴτια," *ZPE* 88 (1991), 157-64: P. Mich. inv. 6235 F 1. 9-24.

75. *SH* 276 with F 667; cf. Hollis, *CQ* 32 (1982), 117-20, not cited by Koenen, Luppe and Pagán. L. Lehnus now suggests (*ZPE* 91 [1992], 20) that the preceding aetion in P. Mich. concerned the Leucadian Diana: see too Hollis, ib. 92 (1992), 115 n. 2.

76. On the question whether there was enough room for an entire line, Hollis, *ZPE* 92 (1992), 116-17.

77. Whence their suggestions that it is not "a line by line commentary of the *Aetia* but restricts its scope to lines mentioning an αἴτιον" and that "the verse referring to the statue will have stood at the end of the episode" (p. 164).

Pfeiffer rejected Maas's identification,[78] arguing (like Vitelli and Norsa) that the Schol. Flor. were excerpts from a much larger learned commentary, whereas the Diegeseis (he claimed) were simply compiled from the Callimachean text. This is now the standard view.[79] But the similarities between these four texts are much closer than generally recognized.

A) There are clear links between the P. Oxy. sequence and the Florentine scholia. First, both cite the same recondite local history (Agias and Dercylus) as Callimachus's source, using the identical formula (there is no source reference in what survives of the Michigan fragment, but we do not have its conclusion).[80] Second, both begin new sections by stating that the poet (not identified by name) "seeks the reason" (ζητεῖ τὴν αἰτίαν) for the story in question (twice in Schol. Flor., once, partly restored, in P. Oxy.). In the second P. Oxy. summary we find instead the formula δι' αἰτίαν ταύτην, with which we may compare ἀπὸ αἰτί[ας ταύτας...] in the second line of the Michigan fragment.[81]

B) As for the Milan Diegeseis, though lacking any learned references, those to both the first and fifth *Iambi* do at any rate supply information not given in the text of the poem (Ch. VIII. 7). The second of the two summaries on the P. Oxy. fragment (Pfeiffer II. 110) is pure summary, with no learned reference.

C) There is also a telling link between the Milan Diegeseis and the Schol. Flor., of no small importance for any assessment of Callimachus's response to his critics: the Diegesis to *Iamb* 13 refers to criticisms of the *Iambi* in exactly the same words (τοὺς καταμεμφομένους αὐτὸν ἐπὶ τῇ πολυειδείᾳ ὧν γράφει ποιημάτων) as the Florentine criticisms of the *Aetia* ([καταμε]μφομένοις αὐτοῦ τὸ κάτισ[χνον τῶν ποιη]μάτων).[82]

D) It is true that the Milan summaries usually begin by describing how the poet (again unidentified) "says" or "narrates" what he says (φησί, ἱστορεῖ), rather than with the formula ζητεῖ τὴν αἰτίαν, but then they only survive for books III-IV, and this different formula may simply reflect the difference between the manner in which individual aetia are presented in I-II and III-IV. It was only in I-II that the poet *asked* the Muses for the explanation. In III-IV, rather than beginning each section with a query

78. Pfeiffer 1934, 5-6; in 1953 he briefly withdrew his objections (II. xxviii), but since his first thoughts have been more influential (see Torraca 1969, 18-19), and the issue is more important than generally realized, a full discussion is justified.

79. Coppola (e.g. 1935, 170-71) went so far as to cite the Schol. Flor. under the name of the late first century commentator Epaphroditus as though there could be no doubt on the matter. For Epaphroditus, Ch. VIII, n. 47.

80. τὴν δ' ἱστορίαν ἔλαβεν παρὰ Ἀγίου καὶ Δερκύλου (Flor.); ἔλαβε δὲ τὴν ἱστορίαν...παρὰ Ἀγία καὶ Δερκύλου (P. Oxy.)—omitting a few dots and brackets.

81. I restore ταύτας rather than the editors' τοιαύτας on the strength of the second P. Oxy. summary.

82. Again, first pointed out by Maas, P. Mil. Vogl. I. 167.

about the origin of some surprising present-day practice (as in I-II), he seems usually to have simply narrated his stories together with the aetion.

It is also important to situate these plot summaries within what was in effect an established subgenre. As early as the fourth century, Theopompus produced a two-book epitome of Herodotus, and Phayllus an epitome of the epic cycle, cited by Aristotle. Asclepiades of Tragilos, a disciple of Isocrates, produced summaries of the plots of tragedies under the title *Tragodumena* in at least six books.[83] A certain Glaucus wrote *On the Stories* (περὶ μύθων) *of Aeschylus*, if Glaucus of Rhegion then perhaps as early as the end of the fifth century.[84] Heraclides Ponticus, a disciple of Plato, wrote *On the Stories of Euripides and Sophocles*;[85] Dicaearchus of Messene, a disciple of Aristotle, *Hypotheseis of the Stories of Euripides and Sophocles*.[86] Whether the omission of Aeschylus from the last two titles presupposes Glaucus or is simply due to accidental omission is unknown. Philochorus wrote a work *On the Stories of Sophocles* in five books, and a *Letter to Asclepiades* (presumably the Tragilan) cited for the story of Hecuba in the scholia to Euripides.[87] These works will have compared other versions and sources (Glaucus, for example, compared Aeschylus's *Persae* with Phrynichus's *Phoenissae*, of which he quoted the opening line).[88] Philochorus also produced an epitome of a work on sacrifices by an otherwise unknown Dionysius and (according to the Suda) an epitome of his own Atthis.[89] This last may in fact have been the work of the late Republican grammarian Pollio of Tralles, who also compiled other epitomes.[90]

The best surviving parallel is the plot summaries of Greek drama found prefixed to individual plays in our medieval manuscripts and now known from the papyri to have circulated together in book form. They fall into two groups, and though neither type has survived in anything like its original form, as Zuntz in particular has shown their main lines can still be distinguished.[91] The first, once assumed to derive from the *Hypotheseis* of

83. *FGrH* 115 F 1-4; Ar. *Rhet.* iii. 16. 7, with the note of Cope and Sandys; *FGrH* 12.

84. *Hyp. Aesch. Pers.* 1, with E. Hiller, *Rhein. Mus.* 41 (1886), 428-31; Jacoby, *RE* 7. 1 (1910), 1418; G. Lanata, *Poetica preplatonica* (Florence 1963), 278-9.

85. Περὶ τῶν παρ᾽ Εὐριπίδῃ καὶ Σοφοκλεῖ <μύθων>, Diog. Laert. 5. 87; even without the supplement, the sense can hardly be in doubt (F. Wehrli, *Herakleides Pontikos*[2] [Basel 1969], F 180, p. 122).

86. Ὑποθέσεις τῶν Εὐριπίδου καὶ Σοφοκλέους μύθων, Sext. Emp. *Adv. math.* 3.3; F. Wehrli, *Dikaiarchos*[2] (1967), F 78-84, pp. 68-71; Kassel 1985.

87. *FGrH* 328 F 90 nos. 21 and 23, with IIIb Suppl. I (1954), p. 376.

88. So already T. Bergk, *Griechische Literaturgeschichte* III (1884), 179 n. 6.

89. *FGrH* 328 no. 15 with Suppl. I pp. 256 and 374.

90. *FGrH* 193; Susemihl I. 831 n. 8 with 846 n. 66 (Diophanes of Bithynia).

91. There is now a substantial bibliography on the subject: G. Zuntz, *The Political Plays of Euripides* (Manchester 1955), 129-146; E. G. Turner, *Greek Papyri* (Oxford 1968), 101; Pfeiffer 1968, 192-96; M. W. Haslam, *GRBS* 16 (1975), 150-56; J. Rusten, ib. 23 (1982), 357-67; H. M. Cockle, *P. Oxy.* vol. 52 (1984), 27-31; R. Kassel, ΣΧΟΛΙΑ: *Studia...D. Hol-*

Dicaearchus, simply summarize the plot; the second, often attributed in manuscripts to Aristophanes of Byzantium, include (in their fullest form) a number of scholarly details (scene, chorus, actors, date, other plays presented, competitors, result, other treatments of the myth). The "Dicaearchan" hypotheseis open by quoting the first line of the play and then proceed with the summary. As Turner observed when publishing the important Euripidean sequence P. Oxy. 2455, "the method is analogous to that of the Callimachean *Diegeseis* and no doubt goes back to Callimachus' *Pinakes*."[92] The papyri have also revealed an alphabetical sequence of Menander epitomes, perhaps to be identified with (or at least derived from) the *Periochai* of Menander ascribed to the presumably Hellenistic poet and grammarian Sellios or Sillios Homeros.[93]

More relevant to an inquiry into epitomes of Callimachus's *Aetia* is an epitome of the elegy his *Aetia* superseded, the *Lyde* of Antimachus, by the well-known second century scholar Agatharchides of Cnidos, author of a number of other epitomes as well as various historical works. It would be interesting to know whether Agatharchides contented himself with summarizing the many myths in Antimachus's poem, or also discussed sources and alternative versions. Agatharchides was the secretary of Heracleides Lembus, himself author of epitomes of the biographies of Satyrus, Sotion and Hermippus the Callimachean.[94]

Rusten dated the extant Euripides hypotheseis to the first or second century A.D.[95] But they were surely not *composed* in this form: rather the original Dicaearchan and Aristophanic summaries underwent a constant process of abridgment, expansion and fusion, losing much of the erudition but acquiring new details thought relevant by successive readers. Just so, I suggest, the Callimachean Diegeseis. Given Callimachus's early and continuous popularity, it is unlikely that curious readers had to wait till the Roman period for summaries.

By as early as the second century B.C. the epitome had become an established semi-scholarly genre.[96] Some are more concerned with mythography

---

werda (Groningen 1985), 53-59; A. L. Brown, *CQ* 37 (1987), 427-31.

92. *P. Oxy.* vol. 37 (1962), 33, echoed by Pfeiffer 1968, 195.

93. Pfeiffer 1968, 196; Suda s.v. Σέλλιος and Ὅμηρος Σέλλιος; he also wrote a Περὶ τῶν κωμικῶν προσώπων.

94. Photius, *Bibl.* 213, p. 171. 19B.; Jacoby on *FGrH* 86; H. Gams, *KP* I (1964), 115-16; Fraser I. 515-17, 550. Agatharchides's other epitomes were of descriptions of the Red Sea in one book; on the Troglodytes in 5 books; and another on those who wrote about the winds. Much more on the *Lyde* below.

95. *GRBS* 23 [1982], 366-67.

96. While we rightly warn our students off "Cliff Notes" on the classics, a careful summary of a long and complex work with a few scholarly references may be of service even to serious readers (e.g. Nabokov's *Lectures on Don Quixote*, 1983).

than scholarship, and even have modest literary pretensions: for example, the *Diegeseis* (under this very title) of miscellaneous myths by the Augustan Conon;[97] the summaries of erotic tales by the late Republican poet Parthenius of Nicaea;[98] those of transformation tales by the perhaps somewhat later Antoninus Liberalis.[99]

Inasmuch as none of the three is keyed to a specific text, they fall into a rather different category. But the two last named are equipped in the only manuscript to preserve them with marginal notes naming a variety of works, principally poems. It has often been assumed that these are the names of the sources that offered the versions given.[100] But the discovery of a papyrus of Euphorion's *Thrax* has shown that Parthenius 13 and 26 are not after all summaries of that poem, but full accounts of two stories Euphorion himself summarized in five and seven lines respectively.[101] The fact that these source references are written in the margins rather than the body of the text has generally been held to suggest that they were added by a later redactor.[102] But the fact that they are written in the same hand as the body of the text might equally be held to imply the opposite: namely that they are an integral part of the original text. When the compiler's aims were purely mythographic, he did not need to provide sources. But if Parthenius's book, as its preface announces, was intended to provide his patron Cornelius Gallus with themes for his own poems, then it would have been helpful to cite poems in which Gallus could find either more details or a model oblique reference to the myth in question.[103] If Parthenius and Antoninus had given their references in the equivalent of footnotes (perhaps originally as in the extant manuscript in the margins), they were very likely to be dropped at random by successive copyists.[104] The original text

97. Text in F. Jacoby, *FGrH* 26, to which may now be added a recently published papyrus which offers a somewhat fuller text of §§ 46 and 47 (M. A. Harder, P. Oxy. 3648; vol. 52 [1984], pp. 5-12). On Conon see especially now A. Henrichs, *Interpretations of Greek Mythology* ed. J. Bremmer (London 1987), 244-47.

98. See J. Stern's annotated translation *Parthenius: Erotika Pathemata* (New York 1992).

99. F. Celoria, *The Metamorphoses of Antoninus Liberalis* (London 1992).

100. So (e.g.) P.M.C. Forbes Irving, *Metamorphosis in Greek Myth* (1990), 27-29, 34-5, distinguishing the manner of Nicander and Boios on the basis of Antoninus's summaries.

101. *SH* 413. 12-16 and 415. 12-18; P. E. Knox, *PLILS* 7 (1993), 63-65.

102. M. Papathomopoulos, *Antoninus Liberalis: Les Métamorphoses* (Paris 1968), xi-xxii; Stern 1992, 106-07.

103. "with sources cited in a way Callimachus would have approved," T. P. Wiseman, *Cinna the Poet* (Leicester 1974), 55, though without discussing the technical questions.

104. So Stern's counter-argument from the random survival of such references in the Parthenius MS proves nothing. Similarly his observation: "we may wonder why the notations, if they are truly by Parthenius, fail in three cases (11, 14 and 34) to mention sources which Parthenius actually quotes within the body of the text" (p. 106). But why should Parthenius waste space repeating in "footnotes" references already quoted in his text?

scribes of the *Greek Anthology* cite many hundreds of author names in the margins of the unique Palatine manuscript, but they evidently omitted as many again; for the corrector of the Palatine manuscript added several hundred more undoubtedly authentic ascriptions from the more carefully copied exemplar to which he often refers.[105] If this is the true explanation, then in Parthenius we would have a securely dated late-Republican example of an epitome equipped with source references.

Since our four Callimachus papyri do not overlap, there is no way of telling whether or not all four derive from the same work. There seems no problem in seeing the P. Oxy. fragment as part of the same work as the Schol. Flor., but the rather less scholarly Diegeseis may reflect a somewhat abridged and simplified redaction. There is also the possibility that, as with the Euripides hypotheseis, there were two different redactions from the start, one scholarly and the other mere précis, though, as Lobel observed,

> there is no obvious reason why, when once such an account of the contents of the *Aetia* had been written, it should have been thought worth while to do the work over again, particularly if it was to lead to a result of which the general character is so little dissimilar.[106]

The "Dicaearchan" Euripides hypotheseis are entirely different in character from their more scholarly twins, not least precisely in the summary, those in the latter group often being compressed into a single sentence.[107] The simpler Callimachean Diegeseis could easily have been abridged from their more scholarly twin. And there may actually be some evidence. The seventh century P. Oxy. 2258 preserves the remains of a summary of the *Hecale* (christened *argumentum* by its editor) that can be compared with the summary in the Diegeseis.[108] Despite the sorry state of the *argumentum*, there are sufficient verbal parallels to make it fairly clear that the two summaries are related. Yet it is the much later *argumentum* that is fuller, perhaps because it is closer to the original than the abridged Diegeseis. It is also interesting to note how, as with the Euripides hypotheseis, what was originally one of a sequence in a separate book was in time transferred to serve as introduction to the work it summarized in a codex.

The most relevant conclusion for our present purpose is that there is no reason to see the Schol. Flor. as an abridgment of a standard ancient commentary, that is to say, from a series of learned notes on various topics

---

105. See my *Greek Anthology* (1993), Ch. V. Some of the author citations in Parthenius and Antoninus may likewise have been restored at some stage from another, fuller exemplar.

106. Lobel, *P. Oxy.* XX (1952), 125.

107. Zuntz, *Political Plays of Euripides* (1955), 131: "The terse appreciation of *Suppl.*, ἐγκώμιον Ἀθηνῶν, bears the mark of [Aristophanes's] pen."

108. F 230 + add. on p. 506 Pf; better now in Hollis 1990, pp. 65-66, with commentary on pp. 135-36 pointing out all the parallels.

under a series of lemmata. Their most obvious characteristic is undoubtedly
section by section epitome. Apart from summarizing prologue and dream,
the first section boasts only one learned note, the identification of the Telchines (Ch. VIII). The Schol. Flor. to the Paros episode likewise consist of
plot summary plus just one learned note, on its sources (Agias and Der-
cylos and Aristotle's *Parion Politeia*). The first item on the P.Oxy. fragment has exactly the same structure: summary plus source reference. More
important than the differences between the three sets of summaries is surely
the shared feature of summary and single lemma for each section, in each
case a whole line, a practice (though found in the Derveni papyrus) foreign
to the standard commentary form.

We should not oversimplify the history of scholarly literature and
assume that the full-scale philological commentary was the norm.[109] It was
in fact a later development, of the late Hellenistic and Roman rather than
early Hellenistic age (Ch. VIII). The distinction is the more important in
that, since the first full commentary on Callimachus may have been that of
the Augustan Theon (Ch. VIII), the credentials of the Schol. Flor. would
then become correspondingly later and lower. But the scholarly epitome
was established by the second century B.C. The original version of the
Diegeseis may well have been Hellenistic.

The distinction is also important for a just assessment of the compiler's
purpose and success. If he was trying to abridge a traditional learned commentary, then he did a pretty poor job; he dropped most of the learning.
On the other hand he systematically added a feature not found in traditional
commentaries: plot-summary. It is mainly because they saw the writer as an
incompetent *commentator* that so many modern critics have felt able to disregard his interpretation when it does not fit their theories.[110] But the
moment we look on him as primarily an epitomator, there is no call to
depreciate unduly his modest achievement.

Moreover, if his main concern was to summarize Callimachus's poem,
we must at any rate credit him with a grasp of its basic structure. He
divided the *Aetia* into its major natural constituent parts, one section for
each aetion.[111] In the Milan Diegeseis at least, these sections are sharply
set off from each other on the papyrus by a variety of devices.[112] It must

109. Even in his second thoughts, Pfeiffer stuck to his assumption that the Diegetes drew
"e commentario eruditionis pleno" (II. xxviii).

110. For example, on the comparison between long and short poems in F 1 (Ch. XI. 2).

111. The Diegeseis enumerate at least 19 aetia in Bks III-IV, 15 of them in IV. Individual sections vary considerably in length, but we should not be on safe ground in inferring
that the longer ones summarize longer aetia, since, quite apart from the fact that some stories
might be harder to summarize than others, on occasion the Diegetes supplies information
over and above his summary (such as sources).

112. Castiglioni, P. Mil. Vogl. I (1937), 70.

be held significant that he bracketed what we call prologue and *Somnium*
together in one section. This is not to say that the coronis in the Oxyrhynchus scholia is a mistake. If we had the combined prologue/*Somnium* section entire, we too would no doubt see it as falling into two parts, and
might well indicate our analysis with a new paragraph. The question is,
how important a break does the coronis mark? If we had the commentary
entire, we might see at once that the scribe made rather frequent use of
such divisions.[113] We are hardly in a position to assess the significance of
his paragraphing from just one example.

There is in fact another proof that the beginning of the Graces-aetion
marks the first significant division of the *Aetia*. The natural assumption that
the metrician Hephaestion turned to the beginnings of his chosen poems
when selecting his illustrations for the various forms of each metre has
been spectactularly confirmed by the Callimachean discoveries of this
century: thus he cites the opening lines of no fewer than five of the
Iambi.[114] To illustrate three of the possible forms of the pentameter, he
cited the first three available examples from the *Aetia* prologue (2, 6,
20).[115] For the fourth there were at least four examples in the second half
of the prologue (26, 30, 36, 38), but what Hephaestion actually cites is the
first pentameter of the Graces-aetion (F 3. 2). It looks as though, not finding what he was looking for in the first 25 lines of the first main division
of the poem, he turned to the beginning of the next division. It follows that
his text included prologue and Somnium in the same division.

5

M. Pohlenz tried to distinguish prologue from *Somnium* on the ground that
each contained a striking scene of poetic initiation: the warning by Apollo
and the meeting with the Muses. "Is it credible that Callimachus could have

---

113. The coronis may mark the end of a poem, but also subdivisions within a poem. For
example, in the I s. B.C. and II A.D. Pindar papyri P. Oxy. 659 and 841, a coronis marks
each new strophe, while a paragraphus marks antistrophes and epodes. Other examples are
listed in E. G. Turner, *Greek Manuscripts of the Ancient World*[2] ed. P. J. Parsons (BICS
Suppl. 46, London 1987), p. 12; note esp. Turner no. 74, the III B.C. Lille Stesichorus. In
Turner's no. 15 (Alcman, late I B.C./early I A.D.) we find "metrical division into groups of
3 verses by paragraphus, 3 groups of 3 forming a strophe marked by a coronis"; P. Oxy.
1083 and 1174 (both II s. Sophocles; Turner 28 and 34) use the coronis to mark the end of
lyric passages; there is an unexplained coronis in Turner 40, a late III B.C. Menander
papyrus. To turn to a text closer to the *Aetia* in form, the II s. B.C. tattoo poem (Ch. X. 3)
has paragraphi between each section (II. 3, 13; III. 17), as do many papyri of the Hesiodic
Catalogue of Women (F 10, 25, 177; 26 has two coronises instead).

114. Pfeiffer II. xxxii; I am counting F 227, 228 and 229 as *Iambi* (Ch. VI. 7).

115. Heph. p. 52 Consbruch (1906, when the lines were not yet identifiable as such).

devised both conceptions at the same time and placed them so close together?"[116] Kambylis decided that it was, on the ground that Apollo's warning was not really a poetic initiation.[117] But is the *Somnium* either?

So it has usually been assumed. Kambylis's book devotes 55 pages to the subject, arguing that both Callimachus and Hesiod were represented as drinking from the same sacred spring on Helicon. Nonetheless, as Pfeiffer rightly insisted, there is not a scrap of evidence that the *Somnium* showed either Callimachus or Hesiod drinking water at all, let alone from the same fountain.[118] The soundness of his instinct will be demonstrated in detail later (Ch. XIII. 1). It is paradoxical that modern critics should have attributed such significance to an initiation by water for which there is no evidence.[119] For there can be no doubt what ancient readers saw as Callimachus's poetic initiation: the warning from Apollo. Every major Augustan poet includes a clear and detailed variation on the theme.[120]

But the strongest argument against a separate initiation in the *Somnium* lies elsewhere, in the *tone* of Callimachus's dealings with the Muses. Behind the concept of the Muses lies "the poet's feeling of dependence on the external."[121] Hesiod they "taught noble poetry" (*Theog.* 22); the poet is commonly described as their "servant" (θεράπων).[122] Not so Callimachus. Right from the start he behaves as their equal, their "boon companion."[123] No humble requests for aid: instead he bombards them with questions.[124] Who were the parents of the Graces? Before they can answer he tells *them* three versions he knows already (Schol. Flor. 30-35). Why is the founder of Zancle invoked without a name? Once again, no idle query: he knows no other founder of a Sicilian city (and he quotes at least ten examples) who "comes to its customary feast without being named" (F 43. 54-5). Contrast the simple, humble appeal to the Muse that opens the Iliad: "which of the gods brought them together in strife?"

We may be sure that much of the charm of the opening scene of the *Aetia* lay precisely in the fact that, after raising the reader's expectations, Callimachus did *not* go through all the usual rigmarole of initiation. He

---

116. *Hermes* 68 (1933), 320.

117. *Die Dichterweihe und ihre Symbolik* (Heidelberg 1965), 90: "Beide Teile bilden eine Einheit durch die gleiche Thematik des Dichtertums, das in Traumprolog, der die eigentliche Dichterweihe enthält, mehr visionär-symbolisch behandelt wird, während das Telchinengedicht, auf eine andere Ebene, polemisch-programmatisch ist."

118. In his note on schol. Flor. 16.

119. As Kambylis concedes: "stehen wir hier nicht auf festem Boden..." (p. 74), before advancing firmly forward.

120. Handled fully (and often) by W. Wimmel, *Kallimachos in Rom* (1960).

121. Penelope Murray, *JHS* 101 (1981), 89.

122. Hesiod, *Theog.* 100 (with West's note); Choerilus, F 2. 2 = *SH* 317. 2.

123. συνέστιος, as in *AP* vii. 41, with Ch. XIII. 1.

124. Well characterized by Hutchinson 1988, 44.

was much too busy making the most of the unexpected opportunity to quiz scholars as learned as the Muses, to make up for the deficiencies of the library at Alexandria.[125] He had already come as close to initiation by the Muses as he wanted when describing how they smiled on him as a child (prol. 37-8).

The chief merit of Kerkhecker's paper was to recognize the continuity between prologue and *Somnium* that makes it hard to draw a hard and fast line between them. The invocation to the Muses does indeed form a transition,[126] but this is hardly news. For we have the beginning of this transition in prol. 37-8:

Μοῦσαι γὰρ ὅσους ἴδον ὄθματι παῖδας
μὴ λοξῷ, πολιοὺς οὐκ ἀπέθεντο φίλους.

Those whom the Muses looked upon with favour when they were children, they do not abandon in their old age.

What can this refer to but the *Somnium*? Where else within so brief a compass can the Muses have looked on the young with such favour as when they answered the young Callimachus's dream questions on Helicon? Lines 37-8 must begin a section that culminated in the old poet falling asleep and his young counterpart meeting the Muses in a dream. As I read the context behind ὑπο]κρίσι[ε]ς and [?ἀμν]ήσαιτε, he asks the Muses to remind him of the answers they gave him in his dream. The prologue is neither a self-contained poem nor a new preface, still less a preface to Callimachus's collected works. It is simply the introduction to the *Aetia*.

There are a series of close and pervasive thematic and structural links between prologue and *Somnium*.[127] First, there is that recurring characteristic of Callimachus's critics, their malignity, a note hit at once by the very name he gives them: Telchines, spiteful sorcerers with the evil eye. At line 17 he refers to their βασκανίη, "malignity,"[128] and in line 8 he claims that their malignity hurts only themselves. Now the very first thing the Muses tell Callimachus in the *Somnium* (F 2. 5) is not to behave badly to others because he will only hurt himself:

τεύχων ὡς ἑτέρῳ τις ἑῷ κακὸν ἥπατι τεύχει.

---

125. Compare F 178, where he seizes the opportunity of quizzing a dinner companion from Icos about an Ician custom that has been puzzling him.

126. So already Pfeiffer (II. 105): "lemmata F 1*a*, 20 sqq. non iam ad invectivam in Telchinas scriptam pertinere (ut F 1*a*, 1 sqq.) apparet, sed ad poetae somniantis cum Musis dialogum"; cf. Hutchinson 1988, 81 n. 109.

127. This point has often been made in general terms (e.g. Kambylis 1965, 90; Meiller, *ZPE* 1979, 40; Livrea 1995), but without a full analysis—and without drawing the logical conclusion (for example, even Livrea still clings to the notion of a "senile prologo" prefixed to a "giovanile proemio").

128. Cf. φθόνος in *H. Apollo* 105f., perhaps written about the same time: Ch. XV.

the man who causes evil to another causes evil to his own heart.

Appropriately enough after the mention of Hesiod in line 2, the line is adapted from *Works and Days* 265:

οἴ τ᾽ αὐτῷ κακὰ τεύχει ἀνὴρ ἄλλῳ κακὰ τεύχων.

the man who causes evil to another causes evil to himself.

Both passages are quoted together by Eustathius.[129] The preceding and following lines are too fragmentary to allow reconstruction of the context, but the link with prologue 8 is unmistakable:

[...........]τήκ[ειν] ἧπαρ ἐπιστάμενον.

Whichever supplement we accept (Housman's μοῦνον ἐόν or Pfeiffer's σφωίτερον),[130] the sense is much the same: the malice of the Telchines harms only themselves. The Muses are surely warning young Callimachus to avoid the pitfall into which the Telchines have fallen. That is to say, the *Somnium* is still concerned with issues raised in the prologue. *Somnium* presupposes prologue.

Second, the core of the prologue is the hilarious sequence of little-and-refined vs big-and-crude contrasts, but they arise out of and again merge into the framing motif of the favour of the Muses. In line 2 the Telchines are said to be "no friends of the Muses," and in the last couplet we are told that those whom the Muses favour as children they do not reject when old. This is the crucial difference between Callimachus and his critics: they are not dear to the Muses, he has been since childhood. Having said this, Callimachus immediately procedes to explain how and where he won the Muses' favour. The *Somnium* relates how they came to visit him on Helicon one day when he was minding his flocks as a lad. Nor are the two Muse passages in the prologue simply tacked on at the beginning and end, so as to dovetail into the *Somnium*. The series of contrasting pairs culminates in the donkey and the cicada, obviously chosen for this position because the cicada was said to be dear to the Muses (Plato, *Phaedrus* 259c, 262d; *Anacreontea* 34). Prologue builds up to *Somnium*.

Third, though Callimachus's debt to Hesiod has often been exaggerated (Ch. XIII), there can be no doubt that the *Somnium* is explicitly modelled on the proem to the *Theogony*. Now prol. 37-8 (just quoted), in which the Muses "look not askance on children" (ἴδον ὄθματι παῖδας μὴ λοξῷ), are clearly modelled on a later passage from that same proem (81-3):

129. *Comm. Hom.* p. 522. 15; cf. M. van der Walk, *GRBS* 24 (1983), 370-71, who argues that Eustathius knew the beginning of the *Aetia* at first hand.

130. Both said to be a little too long for the space; C. Meillier suggests the shorter but otherwise not particularly appealing αὐτῶλες (*ZPE* 33 [1979], 40).

ὅντινα τιμήσουσι Διὸς κοῦραι μεγάλοιο
γεινόμενόν τε ἴδωσι διοτρεφέων βασιλήων,
τῷ μὲν ἐπὶ γλώσσῃ γλυκερὴν χείουσιν ἐέρσην...

Whomsoever of heaven-nourished kings the daughters of great Zeus honour and look on favourably at birth, they pour sweet dew upon his tongue...

Here we have not only the motif of the Muses looking with favour (ἴδωσι)[131] at birth (γεινόμενον) on those they plan to honour, but also the association of dew with literary inspiration that, differently developed (as the food of the cicada), plays a key role in the last section of the prologue. This identification of Callimachus's source is not new. Prol. 37-8 were already cited in the Scholia to *Theog.* 82, whence Pfeiffer was able to restore the missing words in line 38. The same passage of Hesiod was in Callimachus's mind when he wrote both prologue and *Somnium.*

No less striking is the threefold recurring childhood motif. It appears first at prol. 5-6, where the Telchines accuse him (in a puzzling phrase) of writing παῖς ἅτε, "like a child." Then (2) there is the boast at 37-8 of winning the Muses' favor as a child, immediately picked up (3) by his meeting them on Helicon ἀρτιγένειος, "sprouting his first beard" (F 2. 18). This obviously poetic adjective is otherwise first found in an epigram by Diodorus of Sardis on the future emperor Tiberius (κοῦρος ἔτ᾽ ἀρτιγένειον ἔχων χνόον).[132] It would not be surprising if Diodorus had borrowed the adjective (if not the entire phrase) from so famous and widely quoted a passage as the beginning of the *Aetia.*

This last detail provides the final and most explicit link. At prol. 34-7 Callimachus expresses the wish that he might shed his old age. Most readers have been too preoccupied with the bizarre imagery and tortuous syntax of these lines to notice that the wish is in fact fulfilled. Not indeed in the fanciful terms in which it is developed at prol. 32-4 (transformation into a cicada feeding on dew), but in a more straightforward if nonetheless unexpected way. For a few lines later the old poet appears as a young man.

The main reason this crucial point has been overlooked is the fact that we have only scholia here, not original text. So no one has tried to determine at what age Callimachus represented himself having his dream: was he recalling a dream he had long ago as a young man; or did the old poet dream he was young again?[133]

Surely the latter. If the former, we would have two epiphanies to youths by gods of poetry (Apollo and the Muses) within the space of a few lines, whether or not both are treated as poetic initiations. If it is the old poet

131. See W. Headlam on Herodas 4. 73.

132. *AP* ix. 219. 5 = Gow and Page 2103, with *GP* II. 266.

133. The importance of the distinction was first brought home to me in discussion with Jennifer Lynn.

dreaming he is young again, there is no such unwelcome duplication. For it is only Apollo who is a true epiphany. As we have seen, the encounter with the Muses is treated more as an opportunity to quiz senior colleagues. If it is the old poet dreaming he is young again, then his wish for rejuvenation is no sooner made than fulfilled, and it is hard to believe this a coincidence neither noticed nor intended by the poet. On the other hand, if he was recalling a dream he had when young, there would be no connection with the wish for rejuvenation, which would remain unfulfilled and unexplained. Old age presupposes youth.

All now fits into place. This is the climax for which the earlier emphasis on the ills of old age has been preparing us. The old poet falls asleep, his head full of the Muses and fantasies of recapturing his youth, and appropriately enough he has a dream in which he meets the Muses on Helicon as a lad. As happens in dreams, he is not in fact his young self again, but possessed of the erudition and curiosities of his mature years with a battery of questions to ask.

So *Somnium* and prologue are linked (1) by a common allusion to the same passage of Hesiod, by the recurring motifs of (2) childhood and (3) friendship of the Muses, and (4) by the fulfillment of the wish for rejuvenation.[134] If so, then *Somnium* presupposes prologue.

It could (of course) be argued that Callimachus deliberately and skilfully composed the (later) prologue so that it would run seamlessly into the *Somnium*.[135] But what would have been the point? If the prologue was intended to be a retrospective polemic against criticisms that had dogged Callimachus all his life, why take such pains to dovetail it into just one specific early poem? If prologue and *Somnium* "represent two distinct stages in Callimachus's literary development,"[136] why confuse the issue by so carefully blurring the division between them?

The simplest and most natural explanation is that both passages are part of the same poetic conception, written one after another. The reply to the Telchines is the prologue to the original edition of the *Aetia*. It is prologue and *Somnium* combined that set up the frame of dialogue with the Muses for the rest of the poem (*Aetia* I-II). Together they constitute what is in effect the aetion of the *Aetia*.

---

134. C. Meillier (*ZPE* 33 [1979], 40) suggests that the "swarm" (ἑσμός) of Muses in F 2.2 picks up the "buzzing" of the Telchines (ἐπιτρύζουσιν) in prol. 1, but it is not clear that the verb means "buzzing" rather than (e.g.) the more contemptuous "squeaking" (see Ch. XII, n. 4), and in any case this seems both a less obvious link in itself and of no clear thematic significance.

135. See Kerkhecker 1988; Livrea 1994.

136. As claimed by T. M. Klein, *Ziva Antika* 26 [1976], 357-61), with *Somnium* devoted to the Homer vs Hesiod debate and prologue "attacking poets writing within the elegiac tradition itself." My own view on these issues will become clear as the book progresses.

Chapter V

The Ician Guest

1

To the links already listed between prologue and *Somnium* may be added a link between the prologue and *Aetia* II. One of the better preserved individual episodes in the *Aetia* is Callimachus's conversation with the Ician guest at a symposium (F 178).[1] Pfeiffer listed it among the "fragmenta incertae sedis," but now that Parsons has filled up all but one of the gaps left in our knowledge of Bks III-IV, that leaves I-II. Another argument is that 178 (as we shall see) joins F 43, which features the Muses in dialogue with the narrator, a motif now known to be restricted to I-II.

Developing an idea of L. Malten and Wilamowitz,[2] J.E.G. Zetzel has recently made the attractive suggestion that 178 actually began Bk II.[3] Some years ago, when there was no way of excluding III, A. Swiderek made a similar proposal.[4] I would like to offer more detailed reasons for accepting this suggestion.

1) The first 30 lines of the fragment do no more than set the scene for the telling of an aetion. Callimachus's pace is not usually so leisurely, and it would be surprising if he had so interrupted the flow of his narrative with so static a passage at any later point than the beginning of a book.

2) The fragment begins as follows:

> Nor did the dawn of the Opening of the Jars [Pithoigia] pass unheeded, nor the day on which the Pitchers of Orestes bring a white day for slaves. And when he kept the yearly ceremony of Icarius's child, your day, Erigone, lady most lamented by Attic women, he invited his friends to a banquet, among them a stranger who had recently arrived in Egypt on some private business. He was an Ician by birth, and I shared a couch with him—not by design, but it is a true saying of Homer that god brings like to like (Trypanis, adapted).

1. For literature on this intriguing fragment, Fraser II. 1027 n. 118; R. Scodel, *ZPE* 39 (1980), 37-40; Lehnus 1989, 117-19; R. Hamilton, *Choes and Anthesteria: Athenian Iconography and Ritual* (Ann Arbor 1992), 48-49, 119-21; K. Fabian, in OINHPA ΤΕΥΧΗ: *Studi triestini di poesia conviviale* (Alessandria 1991), 131-66, with new text and full bibliography.
2. *Hermes* 53 (1918), 173-74; see Pfeiffer on F 185.
3. *ZPE* 42 (1981), 31-33.
4. *J. Jur. Pap.* 5 (1951), 234 n. 18.

The name of the man who threw this party must have been given in a couplet or two preceding the present line 1. This missing passage presumably also named at least one other Attic festival that he kept up in Alexandria (to explain the "nor"). We do in fact know his name from a quotation in Athenaeus (477C): Pollis.

These festivals are introduced in allusive terms that (in an aetiological poem) suggest that Callimachus is going to explain their origin. Yet he says not another word about them. Why then mention them at all? Apparently because they form part of his characterization of Pollis, an Athenian who migrated to Alexandria where he continued to observe all the Attic festivals. Why this elaborate characterization of a figure who does not play any further part in the poem? For it is the Ician guest, not Pollis, who becomes Callimachus's only human informant before the Muses resume this rôle.

If Pollis was not an interlocutor, Callimachus must have had another reason for introducing him so prominently. The most likely, as Wilamowitz saw, is that Pollis was, in effect if not formally, the dedicatee of the book—though he was not able to say which book.[5] Pollis was surely a real person, a friend or patron of Callimachus. Pollis is a good if rare Athenian name.[6]

3) We have already seen that Callimachus seems to have dropped the framework of a dialogue with the Muses in Bks III-IV. But he certainly kept it up till the end of II. Muses appear at the beginning or end of aetia at F 43. 56 from Bk II, and in the two new fragments *SH* 238. 4 and 8 and 253. 13-14, the first probably and the second certainly from Bk II. Yet in F 178 he gives us, not Muses on Helicon, but human beings in a carefully described human setting.[7] Where but at the beginning of a book could he have accommodated such an episode within his supernatural framework? Apart from the desire to honour Pollis, we may be sure that Callimachus was anxious to avoid the monotony of beginning two consecutive books with an appeal to Muses.

F 43. 12-17 give a glimpse of how he engineered the transition back to the Muses:

> All the soft amber ointments and sweet-smelling garlands I put on my head on that occasion soon lost their fragrance, and nothing that passed my teeth and

5. On multiple dedicatees in ancient poems, see now D. Obbink, "The Addressees of Empedocles," *MD* 31 (1993), 51-98.

6. Malten, p.150; a dozen examples are listed in the unpublished files of Attic prosopography (vol. 21) compiled by B. D. Merritt and kept in the epigraphy library of the Institute for Advanced Study at Princeton. It is also the name of a well-known Spartan general and diplomat of the early fourth century: Schaefer, *RE* 21. 2 (1952), 1415-7.

7. It was for this reason that Fraser (l.c.) rejected Swiderek's proposal, as being incompatible with the mise-en-scène of F 43: so too Pfeiffer on F 185, and cf. Hutchinson 44 n. 36. I hope that the suggestion put forward below will take care of this objection.

plunged into my ungrateful belly lasted till the following day. The only things that remain with me are what I put in my ears.

A coronis in the papyrus here indicates that this is the end of an episode. The garlands and food of some symposium previously mentioned are no more, but Callimachus still remembers what he heard there. We can hardly doubt that this is the same symposium. He would not have been so uninventive as to repeat so obvious a theme within the same book; and if we read the proper name Θέτις at 43. 6, that would nicely link 43 to 178, concerned with the worship of Peleus (178. 24). Then at F 43. 56-7, after nearly 40 lines mostly too worn to make anything of, comes the following:[8]

ὡς ἐφάμην· Κλειὼ δὲ τὸ δεύτερον ἦρχ[ετο μ]ύθου
χεῖρ' ἐπ' ἀδελφειῆς ὦμον ἐρεισαμένη.

I suggest that F 178 + 43. 1-55 are not narrative, but a speech by young Callimachus. It is at 43. 56-7 that we discover the Muses have been present all the time and Callimachus has simply been telling them what he learned at the symposium.[9] In 43. 18-55 he lists 10 Sicilian cities where the founder is invited to the sacrifice by name. After that, since he has never abandoned the framework of conversation with the Muses, all he has to do is turn to Clio and wait for her to answer his question, why the people of Zancle invoke their founder anonymously. Fortunately we have her answer in full (58-83).

If F 178 is indeed the first episode in Bk II, while not perhaps a formal preface, it is certainly the one place in the book where anyone would look for personal or programmatic statements. And there is one couplet that stands out for its similarity of theme and tone to the central section of the prologue.

Callimachus describes how he is sharing a couch with the Ician, not by design but according to the Homeric saying that "god brings like to like":

καὶ γὰρ ὁ Θρηικίην μὲν ἀπέστυγε χανδὸν ἄμυστιν
οἰνοποτεῖν, δ' ἥδετο κισσυβίῳ.

For he too hated the greedy Thracian draught of wine, and delighted in a small rustic cup (F 178. 11-12).

ἄμυστις is the supposedly Thracian custom of draining the cup without pausing for a breath; the κισσύβιον was a rustic cup made of wood.

It was not (of course) Callimachus's purpose to give an account of the drinking habits of early third century Icos. In their context, the function of

---

8. F 43. 56-7, omitting one or two dots and brackets.
9. The Muses may have given their approval to the Ician's solution to his query about Peleus in the gap between 178 and 43.

these lines is simply to lead up to his inquiry about the worship of Peleus on Icos. No motive is needed for two men sharing a couch to strike up a conversation; what could be more natural? And yet Callimachus supplies a motive, and in the hyperbolical, antithetical style of the prologue.[10] His real purpose was surely to recapitulate the critical principles of the prologue.

He does not just say that the Ician shared his own inclination to moderation in drinking. There are in fact a number of quite different possible preferences a moderate drinker might entertain: he might prefer diluted to neat wine; discreet sips to the Thracian draught; small cups to large; or a simple wooden cup to an ornate gold one. Either explicitly or implicitly, Callimachus combines all these possibilities into one preposterous super-antithesis—and then adds that the Ician "hates" the one and "delights" in the other. Even this contrast is forced, for while a moderate drinker might well hate the Thracian draught, why should he take such active pleasure in a small wooden cup? And how did Callimachus discover the complex oenophile preferences of his neighbour before speaking to him? For while it is conceivable that some of the guests had been practising the Thracian draught, there are not likely to have been any kissybia at this refined Alexandrian party (according to Asclepiades of Myrlea, they were restricted to "swineherds, shepherds and country people").[11]

It is the way Callimachus handles the kissybion that would have alerted well-informed contemporaries to the wider implications of the passage. For its two main characteristics were "size and rusticity."[12] The kissybion that Odysseus handed the Cyclops (*Od.* ix. 346) must have been fairly large, as Athenaeus observed (481E), and so too the βαθὺ κισσύβιον of Theocritus 1. 27, whether we place its elaborate carvings inside (Gow) or outside (Dale). And yet Callimachus describes it as ὀλίγῳ, "tiny". In the ordinary way we should not expect so scholarly a poet to slip up on a point of Homeric usage like this.[13] The "slip" was deliberate, its purpose to draw attention to the subtle conflict between the rhetoric of his antithesis and the actual meaning of the word. For the epithet that so misdescribes the kissybion is one of those Callimachean code-words for little-and-pure. There is ὀλιγόστιχος in the prologue (F 1. 9); and *Hymn to Apollo* 112, πίδακος ἐξ ἱερῆς ὀλίγη λιβάς, the "tiny drop from the sacred spring" that is contrasted with the muddy torrent of the Euphrates. For those who missed this

---

10. As briefly noted already by Halperin 1983, 170.

11. Athenaeus 477BC; on Asclepiades's book, below, Ch. VIII.

12. H. Ebeling, *Lex. Homericum* (Leipzig 1885), s.v. (pp. 801-2); A. M. Dale, *CR* 2 (1952), 129-32 = *Coll. Papers* (Cambridge 1962), 98-102; C. Gallavotti, *Par. del Pass.* 21 (1966), 421-36; Halperin 1983, 167-74; Gutzwiller 1991, 90.

13. Ancient critics criticized Callimachus for equating the κισσύβιον with the ἄλεισον mentioned in the following line, but he does not do this (see Pfeiffer's note; Dale, l.c.).

there was one further hint, the exaggerated antithesis, so unexpected in the ostensible symposiastic context, between "hating" and "delighting," ἀπέστυγε and ἥδετο.

Finally, it is not till he has identified the Ician as a kindred spirit through his drinking preferences that Callimachus poses his aetiological question. The Ician performs the function of the Muses at the beginning of Bk I; both prefer little-and-pure to big-and-crude, and both supply Callimachus with aetiological information. These two lines are meant to stand out from their context, a momentary flashback to the prologue. The opening of Bk II, like the *Somnium*, presupposes the prologue.

2

In a recent paper Annette Harder has detected signs of polemic and programme in two recently published *Aetia* fragments, *SH* 239 and 253.[14] Both fragments are so badly damaged that no coherent context can be discerned. The argument is based on individual words without a context, and to that extent must be classified as speculation rather than hypothesis.

SH 239 is from a third or fourth century codex, and the other side carries the words: "and Erato replied thus" (238.8). So it must be from *Aetia* I or II. Putting together various hints, Harder came up with the following general interpretation:

> The speaker, i.e. Callimachus, is involved in some kind of unpleasantness; he
> first attempts a dignified and restrained attitude; then hunger reduces him to
> unwonted fierceness. A hint of the "subtle" poet being forced by circumstances
> to display anger "in the grand style" may be detected (p. 27).

As Harder herself freely admits, this is all very fragile. Even if the reconstruction itself is on the right lines, there is nothing to show that the speaker is Callimachus rather than the protagonist of some unidentifed aetion. Nor does any of it bear any clear relationship to any literary polemic with which Callimachus is known to have been associated.

No more compelling is the link she draws with the reference to poverty in 253. 11. Without a context in either fragment we cannot tell whether there is any real parallel at all, nor is it easy to see why Callimachus's poverty should be the fault of his literary enemies. A different explanation will be suggested below.

Better to forget about 239 and concentrate on 253. Taken by itself, 253 is decidedly more promising. 253 is in the same hand as 252, evidently a fragment from the same first century A.D. roll; indeed they may even have

14. "Some Thoughts about Callimachus SH 239 and 253," *ZPE* 67 (1987), 21-30.

formed top and bottom of the same column. 252 is concerned with the story of Phalaris's bull, which is known to have appeared in Bk II. It follows that 253 too comes from Bk II. Once again, no connected sense can be made out, but there is clear mention of a dream (τὸν ὄνειρον, 12; ἐνύπν[ιον], 10) and the Muses (Μουσέων, 13). In such close conjunction, Muses and dream clearly evoke the opening scene of *Aetia* I. Accepting Zetzel's argument for placing the meeting with the Ician guest at the beginning of Bk II, Harder suggests that 253 came from near the end of the same book.[15]

This is an attractive notion, and it is odd that Harder herself missed the strongest argument in its favour. No one seems to have put into words the obvious guess as to how Bk II ended. Since it now seems clear that Callimachus made no use of the convenient device of conversation with the Muses throughout III-IV, it is tempting to infer that this was because he had himself cut off this possibility. Bk I opened with the young shepherd falling asleep and meeting the Muses. Surely Bk II closed with him waking up, now a poet. If so, then unless Callimachus was willing to recreate the circumstances of the dream in the continuation of his poem, he was bound to turn to other devices in III-IV.

The words [? ὄν]αρ ὁππότ᾽ ἔληξε θεῆς in *SH* 253. 14 suggest that something to do with the gods is ceasing. What? Either a dream, or perhaps a Muse's voice (suggest the editors), "ut aetii finem habeamus." If the dream, perhaps rather "*Aetiorum* finem." For a few lines earlier they tentatively supplement 253. 7 οὐχ εὕδων. If Callimachus was "not sleeping," he was awake. Alternatively, perhaps a promise of what he would retain of his conversations with the Muses when he awoke. Either way, these two hints combined surely lend support to the suggestion that 253 fits shortly before the termination of those conversations and so of Bk II.

Taking Pfeiffer's second edition for granted, Harder concluded that, if she was right,

> literary controversy of some kind formed part even of the supposed early edition of *Aetia* I-II, long before the prologue was added (p. 30).

But once we subtract *SH* 239, little remains that, on Harder's own analysis, can really be so described. What we have in 253 is the two principal ingredients of the *Somnium*. The only line in the fragment that can be fully read, thanks to a line quoted by Artemidorus and Stobaeus,[16] is 253. 9:

---

15. So too Zetzel, *CP* 82 (1987), 354, rejecting the view of Lloyd-Jones and Parsons that it came from the beginning of Bk II. Quite apart from the superior claim of F 178 to this place, it is highly unlikely, as Zetzel observes, that Callimachus would have begun both I and II with his dream.

16. All relevant texts cited by Pfeiffer on F 475.

αἰεὶ τοῖς μικκοῖς μικκὰ διδοῦσι θεοί.

The quotations make it clear that the subject is poverty, and Artemidorus confirms that the context is dreaming:

> Dreams both good and bad portend things good and bad on a large scale for important men and women...but for the humble, good and bad things on a very small scale—especially good dreams... True then is the saying of Callimachus: "Small are the gifts the gods bestow on the small."[17]

The implication is that it was in a dream that the humble gifts Callimachus mentions were promised to him by the gods. This has to be *the* dream, and the gift in question the gift of poetry. And we can perhaps go further still. For in that dream Callimachus presents himself as both a boy and (since a shepherd) a poor boy; that is to say, doubly μικκός. The themes of poetry and poverty are often elsewhere linked in Callimachus.[18]

Here too there may have been a double meaning, for did not Apollo command him to practice the slender style? It is surely more than coincidence that the opposite of "slender"/λεπτός in Callimachus's poetic lexicon was "fat"/παχύς, a word whose primary non-literary metaphorical meaning was wealthy. The preceding line had perhaps evoked others who dreamed of τὸ παχύ, whether fat purses or fat poems. Callimachus naturally pronounced himself satisfied with smallness in every department of life. The θύος...πάχιστον of prol. 25 likewise implies extravagance and ostentation, contrasted with the modest offering Callimachus would make to his gods—or the small rustic cup that he and his like-minded Ician friend preferred to drink from. I venture to believe that, if this quotation had been identified among the fragmentary traces at the end of F 1 or 2, it would have been interpreted along these lines long ago. And yet, thanks to its link to *SH* 252, this clear evocation of both prologue and *Somnium* in 253 can be assigned with something approaching certainty to Bk II.

We may also compare *SH* 253 to the so-called epilogue (F 112). This passage, while almost as fragmentary and incoherent as *SII* 253, once more

17. Artemidorus, *Onir.* iv. 84, p. 300.11 Pack.

18. A well-known epigram of Callimachus (*AP* xii. 150) claims that the Muses (= poetry) and poverty are the two sovereign remedies against love; the poet congratulates himself on having both. Although the text of *Iamb* 3 (F 193) is incomplete and uncertain, the poem seems to close with the speaker ruefully but proudly stating that he chose poetry and poverty. And in *AP* xii. 148 a mercenary lover complains that the poet is poor, to which he replies μὴ λέγε, πρὸς Χαρίτων, τοὺμὸν ὄνειρον ἐμοί. To tell someone his own dream is a proverbial expression for telling him something he already knows (*HE* II. 162, 183), in the context implying that other lovers have made the same complaint. But might there not be another layer of meaning as well? For Callimachus, dream inevitably implies *the* dream, the most famous (if fictionalised) statement of his poverty. See too F 549 and 695. For wider discussions of the motif of poverty and love, Giangrande, *L'Épigramme grecque* (1968), 135-9; Cairns, *Tibullus* (1979), 37-8; Gutzwiller, *Rhein. Mus.* 126 (1983), 215-6.

mentions Muses and quite explicitly refers back to the *Somnium*. The next chapter will argue that F 112 was originally appended to Bk II. I suggest that we place them together. Bk II ended with *SH* 253 + F 112.

If the two principal suggestions put forward in this chapter are on the right lines, then Bk II both began and ended with echoes of the same polemic as the *Aetia* prologue. The prologue was composed at the same time as and forms a unity with the original two-book edition of the *Aetia*.

Chapter VI

Epilogue and Iambi

1

There is no good reason to doubt that the prologue is anything but what it appears to be, the opening of the original edition of *Aetia* I-II. The onus probandi rests with those who would believe otherwise. *Aetia* III-IV were added ca 245. How long before this were I-II published? Three texts converge to support a date around 270 B.C.: the London scholion to F 2; the so-called epilogue, F 112; and *Iamb* 16.

According to the London scholiast, it was not nine but ten Muses that Callimachus encountered on Helicon. He implies that the tenth was Arsinoë. Then came the publication of another fragmentary commentary on the passage,[1] from which it emerged that this identification was no more than a commentator's guess, one of three guesses in fact. Evidently Callimachus himself did not explain the allusion. Pfeiffer at once asked readers to delete his original note "de Arsinoë in Aetiorum initio commemorata." Certainly she was not named. But that still leaves the question of the identification of this tenth Muse. One of the new commentator's guesses, nine Muses plus Apollo μουσηγέτης, we may surely exclude at once. The male Apollo is not likely to have been counted along with the Muses as number ten (contrast F 203. 1, 228. 1, where he is listed together with, but separately from them). It must have been a female that Callimachus had in mind. And what more obvious or graceful compliment to pay a cultivated queen? In a later epigram (XV) he numbered Berenice as the fourth Grace.[2] In view of her relatively advanced age, tenth Muse was perhaps a more tactful style for Arsinoë. In his poem on her death Callimachus announces that he cannot begin without the aid of the Muses (F 228. 1).

The London scholiast may have been guessing (inevitably so in the circumstances) but he was not merely guessing. As we shall see in Ch.VIII, the prosopographical notes in these early commentators on the *Aetia* are often well informed. The interesting question is, why should a late scholiast have guessed Arsinoë rather than Berenice? A commentator who was merely guessing might have been expected to guess Berenice, who

1. F 2a (II. 102 Pf.).
2. Note too F 587 (ironically) for the eighth wise man.

plays so prominent a rôle in the last two books of the *Aetia*, not to mention epigram XV. The fact that he makes the much less obvious identification with Arsinoë suggests informed conjecture rather than shot in the dark.

There is also external evidence. Arsinoë on Helicon may have been more than a poetic fiction. According to the standard reconstruction by M. Feyel, it was Arsinoë III Philopator (wife of Ptolemy IV Philopator) who was instrumental in providing the funds to reorganize the Mouseia of Thespiae, held on Helicon, some time between 215 and 208.[3] Certainly Arsinoë Philopator was honoured on Helicon. But according to Pausanias, there was also a statue of Arsinoë Philadelphus on Helicon.[4] Of course, he may have confused Arsinoës, but the inscription on the base must have indicated which was meant, and Pausanias (who was generally well-informed about Hellenistic Greece) usually read inscriptions on statues rather carefully.[5]

Pausanias's Arsinoë was borne by a bronze ostrich. This ostrich has worried critics, some of whom think he wrongly identified a phoenix.[6] But according to Callixenus, yoked pairs of ostriches drew chariots at the grand procession of Philadelphus. Philadelphus is known to have bred exotic birds, and there is ample evidence for ostriches as beasts of burden in both ancient and modern times.[7] Furthermore, in the light of Pausanias and Callixenus, we should perhaps reconsider the possibility that the mysterious "winged horse of Arsinoë" in Callimachus's *Lock of Berenice* is to be identified as an ostrich.[8] There may have been some connection between Arsinoë Philadelphus and ostriches now lost to us.

In the light of the evidence of Pausanias and Callimachus's tenth Muse, we are perhaps entitled to infer that Arsinoë Philadelphus played a rôle in the reestablishment of the Mouseia some sixty years before the contribution of her namesake. She may quite literally have been associated with the cult of the Muses on Helicon. Callimachus's allusion would then be more than a courtly compliment.

3. M. Feyel, *Contribution à l'épigraphie béotienne* (Le Puy 1942), 88-117; A. Schachter, *The Cults of Boiotia 2* (*BICS Suppl.* 38. 2, London 1986), 158-79.

4. ix.31.1: καὶ Ἀρσινόης ἐστὶν ἐν Ἑλικῶνι εἰκών, ἣν Πτολεμαῖος ἔγημεν ἀδελφὸς ὤν.

5. C. Habicht, *Pausanias' Guide to Ancient Greece* [Berkeley 1985], 64-94 and 103; *Class. Ant.* 3 [1984], 40-56. Note his similarly precise reference to Arsinoë II at i.7.1: οὗτος ὁ Πτολεμαῖος Ἀρσινόης ἀδελφῆς ἀμφοτέρωθεν ἐρασθεὶς ἔγημεν αὐτήν.

6. D. B. Thompson, *AJA* 59 (1955), 200-01; Griffiths 1979, 59.

7. Athen. 200F; E. E. Rice, *Grand Procession of Ptol. Phil.* (1983), 90; Ch. II. 1.

8. See Ellis and Kroll on Cat. 66. 54; N. Marinone, *Berenice da Callimaco a Catullo* (Rome 1984), 196; no ostriches in the elaborate and learned recent discussion by Koenen 1993, 100-105. Ostriches do not fly (of course), but then Berenice's lock did not make a real flight; "winged horse" is a fair enough description of the ostrich (taller and faster than the horse, according to Pliny, *NH* 10. 1).

2

Now for the so-called epilogue. In the fourth-century codex P. Oxy. 1011 the following damaged elegiac couplets (F 112) apparently separated *Aetia* and *Iambi*:

> [..........]ιν ὅτ᾽ ἐμὴ μοῦσα τ[........]ᾷσεται
> [....]του καὶ Χαρίτων[.........]ριᾳ μοιαδ᾽ ἀνάσσης
>   ....]τερης οὔ σε ψευδομ[ένῳ στό]ματι
> πάντ᾽ ἀγαθὴν καὶ πάντα τ[ελ]εσφόρον εἶπεν[......]
>   κειν...τῷ Μοῦσαι πελλὰ νέμοντι βοτά⁹
> σὺν μύθους ἐβάλοντο παρ᾽ ἴχνιον ὀξέος ἵππου·
>   χαῖρε, σὺν εὐεστοῖ δ᾽ ἔρχεο λωϊτέρῃ.
> χαῖρε, Ζεῦ, μέγα καὶ σύ, σάω δ᾽ [ὅλο]ν οἶκον ἀνάκτων·
>   αὐτὰρ ἐγὼ Μουσέων πεζὸν [ἔ]πειμι νομόν.

....when my Muse....and of the Graces....of our queen...you not with false speech....said you were good and fruitful in all things....to whom the Muses told stories as he tended his tawny sheep by the footprint of the fiery horse. Fare well, and go with even greater prosperity. Hail greatly you too, Zeus, and save the entire royal house. But I will pass onto the prose pasture of the Muses.

These lines are followed by the subscription "Callimachus, *Aetia* IV" (ΚΑΛΛΙΜΑΧΟΤ [ΑΙΤΙ]ΩΝ Δ), and, on the next line, by the title "Callimachus, *Iambi*" (ΚΑΛΛΙΜΑΧΟΤ ΙΑΜ[ΒΟΙ]), followed by the beginning of what we know from the Diegeseis to be Callimachus's *Iambi*. They are generally known as the "epilogue" to the *Aetia*.

Many eminent scholars have thought that the "prosaic pasture of the Muses" mentioned in the last line alludes to Callimachus's prose works. Even the usually judicious Herter felt that, given (what he presumed to be) the late date of the epilogue, this was the more natural interpretation: the old poet will devote his few remaining years to scholarship.[10] But there is no hint that Callimachus is (in effect) retiring from poetry. Quite the contrary. The claim that he is about to "move on" or "attack" (ἐπέρχεσθαι often implies hostile intent) suggests a new venture. Why should he describe returning to his scholarly routine in such grandiose terms? By 245 he had been writing these prose works on and off for the past 50 years.[11]

9. πελλά Maas (*Hermes* 60 [1923], 239) for the weak πολλά; applied to sheep by Theocr. 5. 99 and according to Gow "used exclusively of wool, hides, feathers."

10. Herter 1931, 394 and 425; 1937, 144-45 and again 1973, 207-08, listing adherents of both views; see too D. L. Clayman, *ZPE* 74 (1988), 277-79. There is also the question whether to read πεζός (of the poet) or (as I would prefer) πεζὸν with νομόν (or even νόμον; see Herter here too).

11. In fact this interpretation *requires* a late date for the epilogue. If it were early, the

Wilamowitz "could not believe that a Greek would call iambics prose,"[12] but this is not quite what Callimachus says. πεζός is not the Greek for prose. It is an adjective, "walking," and when applied metaphorically to a word like λέξις, naturally designates prose, speech that walks rather than dances. But applied to poetry it would just as naturally imply less elevated poetry, poetry that walks rather than dances.[13] There is in fact evidence from Attic tragedy and comedy that it could be applied to verse not performed to music.[14] Since the only sort of dramatic verse not performed to music was iambics,[15] by implication iambics are indeed a πεζός νόμος, a "walking mode" (Callimachus is, of course, playing on νόμος = melody and νομός = pasture). Horace surely had Callimachus in mind when he referred to his own satires as *Musa pedestris*, for the immediately preceding lines contain a clear echo of the *Aetia* prologue.[16] There are in addition several passages in the Homer scholia recording the athetesis of lines as "too prosaic."[17] Similar examples can be found in later Greek writers.[18] It is hard to believe that so obvious an extension of πεζός was not already to be found in Hellenistic literary criticism. Already in the fourth century we find Aristotle remarking that iambic trimeters are close to the rhythms of everyday speech.[19] If we make the assumption that πεζός can denote iambics, it can scarcely be coincidence that the poem that follows the epilogue in the only manuscript that carries it is indeed in iambics.

---

future tense (ἔπειμι) would imply that Callimachus's poetical masterpiece, the *Aetia*, preceded *all* his scholarly works in prose.

12. *HD* I 210. So too Herter 1937, 144: "bezeichnet πεζός sonst im Griechischen immer die Prosa."

13. Horace describes his *Satires* as "creeping," *repentes*, so close are they to the ground (*Epist.* ii. 1. 251).

14. καὶ πεζὰ καὶ φορμικτά, Sophocles, F 16; cf. *Com. adesp.* 601 (III 516 Koch): παῦσαι μελῳδοῦσ᾽, ἀλλὰ πεζῇ μοι φράσον; see too Plato, *Soph.* 237A, and Photius, *Lex.* ii. 70 N, πεζῷ γόῳ· ἄνευ αὐλοῦ ἢ λύρας, with A. C. Pearson's note on Soph. F 16 (*The Fragments of Sophocles* I [1917], 14); Dawson 1950, 148.

15. A. M. Dale, *CQ* 13 (1963), 310; A. Pickard-Cambridge, *The Dramatic Festivals of Athens*[2] (1968), 156.

16. *Serm.* II. 6. 17 (see p. 460). At *AP* 95 the language of comedy is *sermo pedestris* (see Brink ad loc.).

17. πεζότεραί εἰσι καὶ τοῖς νοήμασι ψυχραί: Γ. 432; cf. Β. 252a, I. 688-92a.

18. Leo the mathematician claims of a poem of his (published by L. G. Westerink, *ICS* xi [1986], 205) that σαφηνείας ἕνεκα καὶ γλυκύτητος τὰς τραχυτέρας ὁ λόγος ἀποστρέφεται λέξεις, χρῆται δὲ πεζοτέραις καὶ μᾶλλον Ὁμηρικαῖς—i.e he will avoid the flowery Nonnian style for something "plainer and more Homeric." Cf. πέζευέ μοι τὴν λέξιν, ἀγροικοστόμει in that keen Callimachean Greg. Naz., *carm.* II.1.12.295.

19. *Poetics* 1449a21f.; *Rhet.* iii.8, 1408b33f. So too Cicero: *senarios...vix effugere possumus*, *Orator* 189; cf. 196, *iambus...humili sermone*.

Lines 5-6 clearly refer back to the *Somnium* (F 2. 1), and line 9 forward to the *Iambi*. The lines undoubtedly mark a link or transition between the two works. But what sort of link? Parsons's modification of Pfeiffer's solution was what he called a "bipartite *Aetia*" (i.e., I-II, followed years later by III-IV) "to which a new prologue (F 1) and a new epilogue (F 112) gave external unity." But quite apart from the doubts already cast on the "newness" of the prologue (where there is no hint of a new or collected edition), bringing back the Muses at the end of IV would serve only to underline their absence in the very differently structured III-IV. It is the themes of the *Somnium*, not the supposedly new prologue that the epilogue recapitulates; and so far from simply tying the *Aetia* together, it culminates in the *Iambi*.

If scholars had not been so hypnotized by the notion of a collected edition, they would long ago have seen that there are a number of alternative possibilities. In what follows I discuss three, suggestions by Dee Clayman, myself and (most attractive of the three) Peter Knox.

3

D. L. Clayman has recently proposed an explanation in generic terms.[20] According to Clayman, it was through the epilogue that Callimachus "wilfully connected two poems of distinctly different genres" in order to "invite us to read the *Iambi* as a specific development of the *Aetia*" (p. 278-9). "Where evidence is available (she claims), the *Iambi* appear to be comic developments of the *Aetia* originals, reflecting the previous poem back on itself through a distorted lens, like a satyr play on a tragedy" (p. 285).

Two illustrations. Since *Iamb* 1 is set outside a temple of Sarapis, and temples of Sarapis "were the sites of healing cults that specialized in incubation therapy," she claims that the scholars who assemble there "have come for a dream cure, and their prayers are answered by a vision of Hipponax (p.280)." This is then held to be a parody of the *Somnium*. But there is no suggestion of a dream appearance in *Iamb* 1, and it is more natural to compare the *Aetia* prologue. Both deal with jealous critics. But in *Iamb* 1 the critics are jealous of each other, not (as in the prologue) of Callimachus, and the poet (in this case Hipponax) does not flail them with picturesque abuse. Instead he administers a gentle and indirect rebuke, telling them how each of the seven wise men rejected the cup of Bathycles in turn. We are obviously being invited to compare these two opening poems, but

20. *ZPE* 74 (1988), 277-86, following up ideas more briefly stated in her 1980 monograph.

the crude term "parody" comes nowhere near pinning down this subtle complex of similarities and differences. In particular, there is no sign that the level of seriousness is in any straightforward way related to metre or dialect.

Iamb 9 (F 199), a conversation between a passerby and an ithyphallic herm, is alleged to be a parody of the conversation between the poet and Delian Apollo in an unplaced *Aetia* fragment (F 114). In form, both are expansions of a familiar type of funerary epigram in which the tomb tells a passerby the name, family and manner of its occupant's death.[21] In F 114 Apollo explains the iconography of his statue. The Graces in his right hand and bow in his left symbolize favours and punishment respectively, with the right hand more ready to reward than punish.[22] As for F 199, despite the initial suggestion that the herm was aroused by a handsome boy, the poem then offers a serious explanation of its erection in religious terms (Ch. I. 2).[23] The elegiac poem may have been more elevated in tone, and the iambic metre and Doric dialect may better have suited the sexual over-tones of F 199,[24] but once again, "parody" and "comic development" do not seem at all the right terms. Indeed, the very idea of a poet parodying his own work is paradoxical, nor is the difficulty disposed of by praising him as "unafraid to turn his wit against himself" (p. 285).

Parody of high genres like epic and tragedy is understandable and well documented,[25] but it is not easy to conceive what would count as parody of Callimachean elegy, itself ostentatiously hostile to the high style. Certainly poets of the age experimented with the genres, combining dialect, metre, theme and treatment in original and unexpected ways (the so-called "crossing of the genres").[26] But it is a grave misunderstanding of this phenomenon to interpret it in terms of parody—or even to assume that the various genres had ever existed in rigid isolation.

Clayman is developing a familiar view, most forcibly stated by L. E. Rossi, that Callimachus exemplifies a "new and revolutionary" attitude towards the traditional literary genres.[27] According to one scholar, he

---

21. W. Rasche, *De Anthol. graecae epigr. quae colloquii formam habent* (Diss. Münster 1910); R. Kassel, "Dialoge mit Statuen," *ZPE* 51 (1983), 1-12; Cameron, ib. 1996.

22. Pfeiffer, *JWCI* 15 (1952), 21-32 = *Ausgewählte Schriften* (Munich 1960), 55-71.

23. Furthermore, since the framework of F 114 is an address by the poet rather than query to the Muses, it surely comes from the first part of Bk III, before the list provided by the Diegeseis begins (Cameron 1996). It is the thesis of this chapter that the *Iambi* were published before *Aetia* III-IV.

24. On a continuum of poetic elevation running from epic to (say) mime, iambic would certainly fall lower than elegy, but not dramatically lower. On the appropriateness of iambics for sexual themes, West, *Studies* 25.

25. Much evidence is collected in brief compass by Denniston and Dover, *OCD*[2] 783-4.

26. W. Kroll, *Studien zum Verständnis der römischen Literatur* (1924), 202-24; "confusion des genres" in Ph.-E. Legrand, *Étude sur Théocrite* (Paris 1898), 418-29.

27. *BICS* 18 (1971), 83.

deliberately "flouted" them;[28] according to another, "it is almost as if the Alexandrians undertook to analyze and define the rules of the classic genres in order to be able to violate them all the more vigorously."[29] Clayman goes a step further: "By mixing up the form of one genre with the content of another, Callimachus demonstrates the emptiness of both."[30] I myself doubt whether even the older approach in terms of a striving for novelty at all costs does justice to the facts of social and literary history.

The most startling innovation (it is usually held) is Callimachus's epinicia in elegiacs and iambics. But this was more than a perverse decision made in an ivory tower. Callimachus and his generation were not so much repudiating choral lyric as responding in their own way to changes beyond their control and already complete before they wrote. Choral lyric flourished at a particular stage of Greek society. It was not just poetry, but an "indissoluble complex of poetry, melody and dance."[31] By the fourth century this complex was no more, and not merely for the lack of a new Aeschylus or Pindar. As we have seen (Ch. III. 1), the songs of Alcman and Stesichorus and Simonides seemed old fashioned already to the generation of the Peloponnesian war.

According to G. Nagy, the increasing dominance of Attic drama "played a major role in the obsolescence of lyric poetry in other media and by extension in other genres."[32] Certainly drama was absorbing the best efforts of the best poets in fifth-century Athens, but not elsewhere till the fourth, and it was less a case of one genre gobbling up the others than inevitable social and musical changes. The patrons of Simonides and Pindar had been aristocrats and tyrants, and it is no coincidence that the last identifiable choral epinicion by a prominent poet was one by Euripides on the wealthy and flamboyant Alcibiades.[33] It is not surprising that the less egalitarian Hellenistic age saw the revival of private patronage. Already by the end of the fifth century poets (including Euripides) were flocking to the court of Archelaus of Macedon.[34]

28. Hutchinson 1988, 55 (though note too the more cautious remarks at pp. 14-16).

29. D. M. Halperin, *Before Pastoral* (Yale 1983), 204.

30. Clayman 1980, 51.

31. Winnington-Ingram, *OCD*[2] 711; West, *Ancient Greek Music* (Oxford 1992), 344-48.

32. *Cambridge History of Literary Criticism* i, ed. G.A Kennedy (Cambridge 1989), 66 (repeated in *Pindar's Homer* [Baltimore 1990], 108). His claim that according to Plato, *Laws* 700d-01a "the poetry of theater" leads to transgressions of genre, is based on a misunderstanding of the passage; in the context, θεατροκρατία (contrasted with ἀριστοκρατία) does not (of course) mean "the dominance of the theatre," but uninformed audiences rather than qualified critics judging performers (cf. 659B), and its only link with the breakdown of genres is that both are said to be products of excessive liberty.

33. On the poem, C. M. Bowra, *On Greek Margins* (Oxford 1970), 134-48. Alcibiades also commissioned paintings of his victories by Aristophon the brother of Polygnotus: L. Moretti, *Olympionikai* (Accad. dei Lincei, Memorie Ser. viii. 8. 2, 1957), 109.

34. R. M. Errington, *A History of Macedonia* (Berkeley 1990), 26.

It was not just the patrons and politics of Simonides and Pindar that had dated but the music too. In choral lyric music had been subservient to the poetry.[35] Developments associated particularly with the names of Phrynis and Timotheus brought it about that "ultimately music was to have unchallenged supremacy over poetry, with the text becoming a libretto for the music."[36]

Yet the athletic festivals themselves went from strength to strength (Ch. II. 5). How was a thoughtful poet of the third century, aware of the two centuries of social, literary and musical change that separated him from the age of Pindar, going to face up to the problem of praising the victor in the games? Pindar had been poet, composer and choreographer in one. To revive the complexities of strophic composition without the music and dance would have been mere archaizing. It was suggested above (Ch. II. 3) that this is precisely why Callimachus did *not* attempt to recreate Pindaric song. Like most of his contemporaries he restricted his composition to the three metres available for non-musical performance: hexameters, elegiacs and iambics.

Pindaric themes and even techniques could be imitated, but a different metrical form was inevitable. The only question was which one. For the encomion, by common consent (for reasons given in Ch. X. 2), the mantle fell on the hexameter. We have a couple of hexameter encomia by Theocritus and a fragment of another by Nicander. To demonstrate his expertise, Callimachus did write the odd poem in metres other than the standard three, though normally in stichic or epodic form. Of these, the most famous was his poem on the death and apotheosis of Arsinoë Philadelphus in 268, in Archebuleans.[37] Modern scholars sometimes classify these poems as "lyric," and even postulate an entire book of lyric poems (Μέλη). Inasmuch as a poem in a stichic metre (however complex or unusual) must have been recited rather than sung, it is unlikely that Callimachus himself would have called such poems μέλη, and we shall see reason to doubt whether this hypothesized lyric book ever existed (§ 7).

Surprise has often been expressed that no Hellenistic poet wrote in such relatively simple lyric forms as the Sapphic (revived by Catullus) and Alcaic, both Horatian favourites. The answer is again the same. There was

35. In recent years there has been some dispute as to whether epinician (and some other) lyric poetry was in fact performed by a chorus: against, M. Davies, *CQ* 38 (1988), 52-64; M. Heath, *AJP* 109 (1988), 180-95; M. Heath and M. Lefkowitz, *CP* 86 (1991), 173-91; for, A. P. Burnett, *CP* 84 (1989), 283-93; C. Carey, *AJP* 110 (1989), 545-65 and *CP* 86 (1991), 192-200. As extant the evidence of the scholia may not compel belief, but it would be surprising if Callimachus got it wrong (F 384. 37-9).

36. B. Gentili, *Poetry and its Public in Ancient Greece* (Baltimore 1988), 24-31; West, *Greek Metre* 138-52. What survives is far less complex than early lyric and never strophic.

37. F 228; Wilamowitz's original publication (*SB Berlin* 1912, 524-37) is still worth consulting; for the date, § 6.

no living tradition of festival or symposium performance at Rome (apart from drama at the Ludi Scaenici).[38] Catullus and Horace saw no problem in reproducing archaic song in book form; for Roman readers Sapphics and Alcaics were hardly more artificial than iambics or hexameters. It was quite otherwise for Callimachus and his peers, writing within a living but changing tradition of performance. Having not only read but also heard Sappho and Alcaeus sung to music, Hellenistic poets were well aware of the problems of reproducing them for contemporary performance. It is surely significant that the only archaic form Callimachus actually revived was the one that still lent itself to non-musical performance: iambus.

Many of the themes (especially erotic and sympotic) of the Lesbians and Anacreon tended to be subsumed into what we now call epigram, which in the early Hellenistic age were often quite long and not invariably written in elegiacs.[39] The epigram was arguably the most lasting contribution made by the Hellenistic age to Greek literature. There was no dispute among contemporaries or successors about the rôle Callimachus played in this process. Together with Asclepiades and Leonidas, he was an acknowledged master (Ch. III. 2). To give only one example, Rhianus, otherwise known as the author of a series of long epics, was in his epigrams very much a disciple of Callimachus (Ch. X. 6).

The other dominant poetic form of the early Hellenistic age was undoubtedly elegy. Callimachus was no innovator here either. His immediate predecessors and contemporaries all wrote elegies; Philitas, Hermesianax, Alexander Aetolus. It was then that the long elegiac *Lyde* of the late fifth-century Antimachus came into its own. It is most unlikely that contemporaries saw Callimachus's choice of the elegy for an epinicion or a hymn as a "flouting" of tradition. The mere fact that he wrote *three* elegiac epinicia hardly suggests the "revolutionary" experiment that Rossi (for example) supposed.[40]

Indeed it is by no means clear that elegiac epinicia were a Hellenistic innovation at all. We have two fragments from an elegy on Alcibiades by Critias opening "And now I shall crown Alcibiades the Athenian, son of Kleinias."[41] Since Alcibiades bred race-horses and won chariot victories at the Nemean, Olympic, Pythian and Panathenaic games,[42] this may have

---

38. Which is not to deny private performance for patrons or even occasional public performance before the growth of *recitationes*; but there was no institutional framework, no traditions or conventions.

39. See my *Greek Anthology*, Ch. I; above, Ch. III. 1.

40. Rossi *BICS* 18 (1971), 83, "nuovi e rivoluzionari precetti."

41. καὶ νῦν Κλεινίου υἱὸν ᾿Αθηναῖον στεφανώσω, F 4-5 West. For more generally encomiastic elegies from the fourth century, Ch. X. 5.

42. Moretti, *Olympionikai* (1957), 109; J. K. Davies, *Athenian Propertied Families* (Oxford 1971), 20-21.

been an informal epinicion, intended for the symposium rather than a public gathering. Furthermore, as Therese Fuhrer has pointed out, even in the heyday of Pindar and Simonides athletic victories always had been celebrated in elegiacs, in the form of agonistic epigrams inscribed on victory monuments.[43] By the late fourth and (especially) third century such epigrams had become longer and more elaborate, more literary, characterized by mythological allusion and motifs from classical epinicion.[44] While archaic and classical victor epigrams do little more than enumerate festivals and victories, the twelve fluent lines on a chariot victory by the father of Attalus I of Pergamum (268/4) are almost pure narrative.[45] Posidippus wrote almost 20 epigrams on equestrian victories (Ch. IX. 2), most of them functional pieces of 4-6 lines, but one of 14 lines, badly damaged but mainly narrative as far as it can be read.[46]

A distinguished epigrammatist himself, Callimachus will certainly have been familiar with this development. Callimachean epinicion is not so much a repudiation of the choral tradition as a fusion between choral epinicion and agonistic epigram. An elegiac epinicion must in any case seem less of an innovation now that we know Simonides wrote elegies on Artemisium and Plataea and perhaps Marathon and Salamis too.[47] Though narrative rather than encomiastic in form (Ch. XI. 3), poems on such spectacular Athenian victories must have had an epinician flavour. It is suggestive that Theocritus 16 addressed to Hiero of Syracuse can be shown to have drawn on at least two passages of Simonides's elegy on Plataea.[48] Elegiac epinicia may actually have been more traditional in form than the hexameter encomia of his contemporaries. The difference lay in content and treatment rather than form.

An iambic epinicion (*Iamb* 8) might seem more surprising, but so might an iambic hymn to a god, and yet we have Castorion's on Pan.[49] Rather than assume sheer perversity as Callimachus's motive, we should be asking rather what aspect of the iambic tradition he was hoping to harness here. In general (of course), it was to the old Ionic iambus that he was looking, but what of its adaptation by the tragedians of fifth-century Athens? Since the only line assignable with certainty to *Iamb* 8 is straightforward narrative ("The Argo once, the south wind gently blowing..."),[50] it is tempting to posit the prologue or messenger's speech in tragedy as his classical model.

43. Fuhrer 1992, 100-04; Fuhrer 1993, 90-94.
44. W. Peek, *Hermes* 77 (1942), 209-11; Ebert 1972, 19-22, 191-92, 205-08.
45. Ebert 1972, no. 59 (pp. 176-81), touched on further in Ch. VIII. 2.
46. Unpublished at the time of writing; information from G. Bastianini.
47. P. Parsons, P. Oxy. LIX (1992), 3965, pp. 4-50; M. L. West, *IEG* ii^2 pp. 114-22.
48. Parsons 1992, 31; *Aevum Antiquum* 5 (1993), 12.
49. *SH* 310, with P. Bing, *AJP* 106 (1985), 502-09.
50. F 198, quoted and discussed below, Ch. IX. 3.

There is in fact a notorious parallel for the independent messenger speech, by a contemporary and colleague of Callimachus: Lycophron's *Alexandra*. And while this is certainly a reductio ad absurdum of the form, there is no reason why a serious poet should not use it for a narrative that, like so many tragedies, culminated in a local aetion. Callimachus would not be breaking the rules of the epinicion so much as combining it with the messenger speech. But one other obvious possibility is an epode, trimeter alternating with dimeter or ithyphallic (like *Iambs* 5-7). If F 222 or 223 come from 8, that would establish stichic iambics, but 222 is not narrative. On the other hand the evocation of Simonides in 222 ("I do not keep a hireling Muse, like Simonides") would be apposite enough in a personal coda to an epinicion.

Rossi also found Callimachus's one elegiac hymn (v, to Athena) surprising, but short hymnal invocations in elegiacs are found as early as the archaic age, and we now have the long hymnal proem to Simonides's elegy on the battle of Plataea (F 11. 1-20 W²). From the fourth century we have the parodic hymn on simplicity in elegiacs by Crates the Cynic.[51] As Hutchinson sensibly observed, "the effect of parody would have been spoiled had the metre seemed a startling novelty."[52] Bulloch has already drawn attention to the short elegiac hymn to Demeter quoted by Aelian from an otherwise unknown Aristocles.[53] The date is unknown, but it is not obviously later than Callimachus and shares with the *Hymn to Athena* both Doric dialect and a fictionalized narrative aetiology of the festival (Argive, as in Callimachus) it purports to celebrate.[54] At a much lower level of quality, there are the four hymns by a certain Isidorus inscribed at an early first-century B.C. temple of Isis near the village of Medinet Madi in the Fayum, two in hexameters, two in elegiacs.[55] They are undoubtedly genuine cult hymns, and while it is easy to assume direct imitation of Callimachus's fifth hymn,[56] why pick that as a model if it were an eccentric experiment unconnected to "real" hymns?

We have just one line from Callimachus's epithalamium on Arsinoë (F 392), apparently the first: Ἀρσινόης ὦ ξεῖνε γάμον καταβάλλομ᾽ ἀείδειν. Pfeiffer was reluctant to admit the possibility that the poem might have been in elegiacs, on the grounds that this would be without parallel before Paulinus of Nola (*carm.* 25). He disallowed an elegiac fragment of at least

51. Bulloch 1985, 35; *SH* 361; H. Diels, *Poet. Philos. Fragm.* (1901), F 12, p. 221.
52. Hutchinson 1988, 16.
53. Bulloch 1985, 36-37; Page, *FGE* 30-31 (treating it as an epigram); *SH* 206.
54. A more plausible origin is given by Paus. ii. 35. 5; Page, *FGE* 30 for a comparison of the two versions.
55. V. F. Vanderlip, *Four Greek Hymns of Isidorus and the Cult of Isis* (Toronto 1972); Fantuzzi 1993, 58.
56. Isidorus certainly knew Call.: *H* 4. 18, γράμμ᾽ ἀναλεξάμενοι ~ *AP* vii. 471. 4.

24 lines on (again) the wedding of Arsinoë on the grounds that the papyrus classifies it among the "epigrams of Posidippus" (*SH* 961). But even though, given its metre and modest length, such a poem might eventually be (re)published in a book of epigrams along with other occasional poems, taken by itself theme and occasion must surely be held to make it a wedding poem. We cannot be certain that Callimachus's poem was substantially longer. There may also be another Hellenistic example, four lines from an elegiac epithalamium on Thetis ascribed to an otherwise unknown Agamestor of Pharsalus on the uncertain authority of Ptolemy the Quail.[57]

Hexameters were certainly the norm for Hellenistic epithalamia: Theocritus 18; a fragment on Achilles and Deidamia ascribed to Bion; Catullus 62 and 64 and Calvus F 6 Morel. Several celebrate mythical weddings, a tradition that goes back to Hesiod, whose *Wedding of Ceyx* may have established the hexameter as one of the main media for wedding poetry.[58] Most of the fragments from Sappho's epithalamia are also in hexameters.[59] There were different sorts of wedding poem for different stages of the wedding, and we do not know the precise occasion for which Callimachus wrote. That it was not a poem of the highest formality, nor even apparently addressed to the royal couple is suggested by the rather surprising apostrophe to a stranger (ὦ ξεῖνε). If this is a pointer to inclusion within a frame, that would imply the *Aetia* and so elegiacs. On the other hand, καταβάλλομ᾽ ἀείδειν suggests the rhapsodic formula ἄρχομ᾽ ἀείδειν, which would imply hexameters.

The ritual lament is another interesting case.[60] Simonides and Pindar wrote lyric threnoi, but there was also an elegiac lament tradition.[61] Parthenius used elegiacs for the lament on his wife Arete (*SH* 608-14); Calvus for his wife[62] and Catullus for his brother (101), both surely following Hellenistic models. But Erinna's *Distaff* (perhaps as early as the fourth century) was in hexameters, as was Bion's *Lament for Adonis*. In *Iamb* 13. 18 Callimachus implies that he has been accused of mixing dialects, whence Rossi inferred that such mixing of dialects was also a bold innovation. But a generation before Callimachus Erinna's lament was in a mixture of Doric and Aeolic (*SH* 400-401).

Another axiom of modern criticism that stands in need of reassessment or at any rate more subtle formulation is the assumption that the scholar-

---

57. *SH* 14, taking the rather dubious figure of Ptolemy Chennos more seriously than most; in any given case, who can tell?

58. F 263-9 M-W, with West and Merkelbach, *Rhein. Mus.* 108 (1965), 300-17.

59. Cf. too the dactylic F 44: D. Page, *Sappho and Alcaeus* (1955), 71-74, 121-23; A. P. Burnett, *Three Archaic Poets* (Harvard 1983), 219-23; dactylic wedding songs also in Ar. *Birds* 1732f.; Eur. *Phaethon* 109-16 Diggle.

60. M. Alexiou, *The Ritual Lament in Greek Tradition* (Cambridge 1974), 102f., 131f.

61. West, *Studies* 4-9.

62. F 15-16 Morel, with E. Fraenkel, *Kleine Beiträge* (Rome 1964), 109-10.

poets of the third century, now accustomed to write for the book and unfamiliar with the original performance context of classical and archaic poetry, adopted and modified their poetic forms "with little regard for the function for which they were originally composed."[63] It was Callimachus and his peers (it is held) who in effect invented the genres, by turning occasion into genre. Ch. II-III have already questioned the assumption that these occasions "were no longer a part of the lives of the new poets."[64] And the fact that (for example) Pindar's epinicians were classified by festival and Sappho's poems by metre proves only that these were convenient ways of organizing a large number of poems in managable units, units of a size to fit the average papyrus roll. Bibliographical convenience is hardly a secure guide to literary intention.

Did Callimachus really misread Pindar and Simonides? Did he really treat the old genres cavalierly? Ch. XVII will demonstrate how very carefully he *distinguished* the traditions of elegy and epic. Did contemporaries really object? Alexandrian poetry (as we have seen) is traditionally held to represent a sharp break with the past, book poetry by scholars writing under kings as opposed to "oral" poetry arising spontaneously out of civic occasions. Too little account has been taken of the fact that we have virtually no occasional poetry, indeed precious little non-dramatic poetry of any sort between the age of Pindar and the age of Callimachus. In effect, we are obliged to compare Alexandrian poetry with Attic drama, and in consequence perhaps to exaggerate its originality—and perhaps also its connection with the new monarchies.

Kenneth Dover once remarked that if we had more late fifth- and fourth-century poetry we might decide "that Hellenistic poetry began not with the great Alexandrians but with the deaths of Euripides and Sophokles."[65] But even earlier texts can spring surprises. As Parsons has remarked of Simonides's elegy on Plataea,[66]

> Essentially, it represents the rhapsodic form: hymn, transition, heroic narrative. But here the old heroes move into the hymn, new heroes occupy the narrative; the whole structure is transposed into elegiacs,[67] and compassed in (at a guess) two hundred lines. Miniaturisation, crossing of genres—wouldn't we be tempted to call that Hellenistic?

Another relevant factor is the highly polemical way Callimachus chose to characterize the reaction of his critics. The extravagant hyperbole should

63. Carol Dougherty, "Archaic Greek Foundation Poetry: Questions of Genre and Occasion," *JHS* 114 (1994), 45.

64. Dougherty 1994, 45; see also Ch. X passim.

65. *Theocritus: Select Poems* (London 1971), lxxi.

66. *Proc. of the 20th International Congress of Papyrologists* (Copenhagen 1994), 122.

67. Perhaps rather a continuing tradition of elegiac narrative: Ch. XI. 3.

caution us against taking this polemic as proof that his work was quite as controversial as it implies. No doubt he experimented more overall with genre, metre and dialect than his contemporaries, but in individual cases he may have had better precedent than we can now document.

Certainly Callimachus wanted to link *Aetia* and *Iambi* in a way that emphasized the generic difference between them. But that does not make *Aetia* and *Iambi* an example of what Clayman called "supra-generic composition." On the other hand, the movement implied by his terminology (ἔπειμι) clearly suggests a passage from one work to the other, and so a connection of some sort between the *publication* of the two books. Which brings us back to the relationship of the poems *as books*.

4

One possibility is that F 112 is not an epilogue to the *Aetia* but a prologue to the *Iambi*. In the fourth-century codex P. Oxy. 1011 the epilogue does indeed immediately precede the *explicit* "*Aetia* Bk IV" and the first of the *Iambi*. But in what is usually and rightly considered our most reliable guide to *Aetia* IV and the *Iambi*, the much earlier Diegeseis, they do not. After meticulously summarizing 17 separate aetia (from the Delphic Daphnephoria to the Lock) in *Aetia* IV, the Diegeseis pass directly to the first of the *Iambi*. No epilogue. In view of their concern with the structure and content of the poem and the obvious care with which they were compiled we should not be quick to postulate accidental omission (whether by the Diegetes himself or from the text he used). Such an omission would be the more surprising in that the Diegeseis go straight on to the first of the *Iambi*, to which the epilogue seems to provide a transition.

Could it be that the subscription was simply misplaced in error? If the words ΑΙΤΙΩΝ Δ were placed before instead of after the epilogue, it would at once become preface instead of epilogue.[68] It is worth noting that, since titles were normally written at the end rather than the beginning of the roll,[69] the title here was presumably added when the original rolls were transferred to codex. For example, P. Oxy. 2173 preserves the beginning of *Aetia* III on the first column of its roll, and there is neither title nor author's name. The same is true of the British Museum Herodas papyrus. Inevitably this practice changed once it became necessary to distinguish

---

68. Since the Diegeseis do not record a preface to the *Iambi*, it has to be conceded at once that they do not support this hypothesis any more than Pfeiffer's. Indeed this is one of the reasons I myself prefer Knox's explanation.

69. G. Cavallo, *Libri scritture scribi a Ercolano* (Suppl. Cron. Ercol. 13) 1983, 22 (all 70 cases where a title is preserved); E. G. Turner, *Greek Manuscripts of the Ancient World*[2] (1987), 13-14 (emphasizing that very few roll beginnings have been preserved).

consecutive works in a codex.[70] So the context in which the epilogue stands does not in any case exactly reflect the layout of any edition produced within several centuries of Callimachus's lifetime.

It would be natural enough for a court poet to have prefaced his newest poetry book with an address to the Royal House. And what seemed so anomalous in an epilogue to the *Aetia*, the reference to the ensuing *Iambi*, would now become the raison d'être of the poem. A preface would also be a suitable place to find a comparison between the work there announced and the rest of the poet's oeuvre, especially if it marked a new departure for him. We might compare the beginning of what was apparently intended to be the original preface to Ovid's *Fasti*:[71]

> nunc primum velis, elegi, maioribus itis:
>   exiguum, memini, nuper eratis opus.

Now for the first time you sail with ampler spread, my elegies; as I recall, till now your theme was but slender.

Not this time a different metre, but a more ambitious theme.

If Callimachus equipped his *Aetia* with a prologue, why should he not have done the same for his *Iambi*? There is also another factor which might be held to point in the same direction: the hymnic clausula. There are three features that these lines share with the traditional rhapsodic clausula: 1) χαῖρε followed by an apostrophe of the relevant god; 2) a wish for blessings of one sort or another; and 3) an announcement that the poet is about to embark on another song, almost always introduced by αὐτὰρ ἐγώ and ending καὶ ἄλλης μνήσομ' ἀοιδῆς.[72] Archaic hymns were originally written as preludes to further epic recitations.[73] There is a clear example of a transitional αὐτὰρ ἐγών in the *Hymn to Apollo*, between the two divisions of the poem (177-8); and perhaps another at Empedocles B 35.[74]

The first and second elements are often found towards the end of the sphragis of Greek and Roman poetry books.[75] The closest parallel is perhaps Posidippus's *Seal*, where the poet's closing prayer (for himself) is introduced by αὐτὰρ ἐγώ.[76] But virtually without exception later poets drop the promise of another poem. It is absent from all six of Cal-

---

70. At the roll stage it was rare for more than one work to be copied on the same roll: not a single example from Herculaneum (Cavallo 1983, 14).

71. *Fasti* ii. 3-8; moved to Bk II on Augustus's death and replaced by a new preface addressed to Germanicus.

72. See N. J. Richardson's note on *Hy. Dem.* 495.

73. Richardson, l.c.; W. G. Thalman, *Conventions of Form and Thought in Early Greek Epic Poetry* (Baltimore 1984), 120.

74. As argued by Dirk Obbink, *MD* 31 (1993), 68-9.

75. W. Kranz, *Rhein. Mus.* 104 (1961), 3-46 and 97-124 = *Studien zur antiken Literatur und ihrem Fortwirken* (Heidelberg 1967), 27-78 (here 102 = 62).

76. *SH* 705. 21, with Lloyd-Jones, *JHS* 83 (1963), 92 = *Acad. Papers* ii (1990), 185.

limachus's hymns (though interestingly enough two of Theocritus's poems end this way).[77] Callimachus's hymns were clearly not designed for this function. But he may nonetheless have revivified this fossilized element in the hymnic clausula to give it a real function, adapting the short hymn to a new literary purpose, the preface, where it could serve as a genuine prelude to another and longer work. There is in fact an earlier example, in the newly found elegy on Plataea by Simonides: at the end of a long proem, the poet turns to invoke the Muse and embark on his narrative with the words αὐτὰρ ἐγώ.[78]

It is true that F 112 would be the first elegiac preface to a non-elegiac work,[79] but this would not surprise in Callimachus, given his evident delight in experimenting with form and metre. The fact that the work preluded was in this case of a lower rather than higher genre would be a piquant inversion the alert reader was intended to savour.

5

In a codex where *Iambi* followed *Aetia*, it is easy to see how an elegiac preface to the *Iambi* might have come to be associated with the elegiac *Aetia* instead. But before postulating an error in our only witness, we should first explore all the possibilities of taking these lines as an epilogue. For there are in fact several other examples of what we might call transitional epilogues.

The most famous is the two lines at the end of Hesiod's *Theogony* that prelude the *Catalogue of Women* (νῦν δὲ γυναικῶν φῦλον ἀείσατε...). Then there is the rewriting of the last line of the *Iliad* to link it to the *Aethiopis* (...Ἕκτορος, ἦλθε δ᾽ Ἀμαζών), and some have thought that ὄρνιθας κρίνων in the last line of the *Works and Days* preludes the *Ornithomanteia*. But these works are related in a very different way from *Aetia* and *Iambi*. Though differing among themselves, all are attempts to organize *pre-existing* epics into a continuous corpus.[80] Few will wish to trace Callimachus's inspiration to Cyclic epic![81]

There are also many examples in Hellenistic prose literature of a writer closing one book of a multi-book work with a reference forward to the con-

---

77. Theocr. 17. 135-37 (the encomion of Philadelphus); cf. 1. 145.

78. F 11. 20 West[2]; Parsons, *P. Oxy.* LIX (1992), p. 32; Obbink, *MD* 31 (1993), 68-9.

79. Under the empire the reverse was to become standard: an iambic preface to a hexameter poem (Cameron, *CQ* 20 [1970], 119-29). Claudian regularly gave his hexameter poems elegiac prefaces.

80. M.L. West, *Hesiod Theogony* (Oxford 1966), 49-50, 437; *Hesiod Works and Days* (Oxford 1978), 364; *The Hesiodic Catalogue of Women* (Oxford 1985), 2, 126.

81. Though apparently so F. Cairns, *Tibullus* (1979), 223 and Koenen 1993, 92.

tents of the next book.[82] For example, the closing sections to books 15, 16 and 17 of Diodorus Siculus promise the stories of Philip II, Alexander and the Diadochi respectively. The end of Dionysius of Halicarnassus's *Lysias* preludes his *Isocrates*, the end of his *Isaeus* promises his future treatment of Demosthenes, Hyperides and Aeschines. Here the author's intention is not to link items in a sequence, but to make sure readers keep an eye open for books planned but not yet published. Bk 1 of Ovid's *Ars Amatoria* closes with a couplet warning the reader that he still has half the work to read (*pars superat coepti, pars est exhausta laboris*): didactic poems did not normally run to more than one book.[83]

But in all these cases the point is *continuation*, whether a new installment of the epic cycle or a new book of a multi-book work, whether prose or verse. So far from promising a continuation of the *Aetia*, Callimachus was explicitly announcing something *different*: not just a different theme, but a different genre. Nonetheless, in the light of the later texts it should be clear that, even as an epilogue, F 112 does not need to be seen as a later addition. The promises of Diodorus and Dionysius are obviously original, made before they had finished, much less published the books promised.

Peter Knox has recently drawn attention to one other category of transitional epilogue. While there is no exact Greek analogue to F 112, there is a highly suggestive parallel in an Augustan poet: the epilogue to Bk iii of Ovid's *Amores*, which bids farewell to Elegy as the poet passes on to bigger things (namely tragedy):[84]

corniger increpuit thyrso graviore Lyaeus
    pulsanda est magnis area maior equis.
inbelles elegi, genialis Musa, valete,
    post mea mansurum fata superstes opus.

The hornèd Lyaeus [Dionysus] has struck me with his *heavier* thyrsus; I must pound the earth with mighty steeds on a *mightier* course. *Farewell*, elegies, congenial Muse, work that will live on after I am gone.

That is to say, Ovid's next book will be in a higher genre.[85] We might also compare, though not this time an epilogue, the vague promise of an

---

82. See the close of Polybius 3, 4, 5; Diodorus 1, 15, 16, 17, 18, 19, 20; Dion. Hal., *Opusc.* pp. 53, 124 Usener-Radermacher; all 10 books of Vitruvius; Herodian 2; cf. L. Canfora, *Conservazione e perdita dei classici* (Padua 1974), 9. I exclude the quite different practice of giving cross references to works already published: e.g. Xenophon, περὶ ἱππ. xii. 14 and often in the historians and Plutarch's *Lives*. G.B. Conte's interesting paper "Proems in the Middle," (*YCS* 29 [1992], 147-59) does not touch on any of these questions.

83. But *AA* i and ii were presumably published together; and the link couplet to Bk iii was likewise presumably added together with Bk iii, not in advance of it.

84. iii. 15. 17-20 (Showerman's transl. adapted).

85. The first poem in the book presents a more elaborate scene in which Tragoedia begs Elegeia to release Ovid for *maius opus* (iii. 1. 24).

Augustan epic in the proem to *Georgic* iii. Since it is unlikely that anyone
before Callimachus had so self-consciously proclaimed a plan of progres-
sing through the hierarchy of the genres, these passages must surely be seen
as at any rate indirect imitations.[86]

When Ovid wrote *Amores* iii. 15, he had begun work on his one tragedy, *Medea*. When Vergil wrote the proem to *Georgic* iii, he had already
begun work on the *Aeneid*. By analogy, we may surely conclude that when
Callimachus wrote the epilogue to the *Aetia*, he was writing but had not yet
published the *Iambi*.

At first sight, this might seem to imply that the publication of the *Iambi*
has to be placed after *Aetia* IV, that is to say, after ca 245. But (as Knox
pointed out) there is an alternative.[87] Not an epilogue added for a (non-
existent) collected edition or even a second edition ca 245, but the original
epilogue to *Aetia* I-II published ca 270. The final line would not then be a
segue into the poem that followed it on another roll. It would be a promise
of a poem not yet published, a statement of literary intent. Callimachus was
proud of his versatility (cf. *Iamb* 13), and announces that, having labored
on the heights of Helicon (the *Aetia*), his next work will be a product of its
lower slopes.

In his original article, Knox supposed that it was Callimachus himself
who, after adding III-IV, moved the epilogue from the end of II to the end
of IV. But what was the advantage in moving it to the end of IV, where the
announcement of the (now long published) *Iambi* made no better sense and
the evocation of the Muses would come as a surprise after their two book
absence? And if it was Callimachus who moved it, why is it missing from
the Diegeseis at this point? On the assumption that the four books of the
Aetia remained on four separate rolls in Callimachus's lifetime, what was
the harm in leaving the epilogue where it belonged, at the end of II?[88] If
this is where the Diegetes found it, that would explain his failure to mention it at the end of *Aetia* IV. It was surely a later copyist who found it
anomalous to have an epilogue between the two halves of a work now written continuously in a codex. Though originally written for another purpose, once *Iambi* followed directly after *Aetia* in a codex, the epilogue
made a neat transition between them.[89]

Two further considerations lend support to this hypothesis. First, it was
pointed out in Ch. V. 2 that *SH* 253, with its reference to the Muses and
three or four references to a dream or dreaming, would dovetail very nicely

---

86. R.F. Thomas has already shown that the proem to *Georgic* iii is influenced in other
ways by the proem to *Aetia* III (*CQ* 33 [1983], 92f.), so another level of Callimachean imitation would not be surprising.

87. "The Epilogue to the *Aetia*," *GRBS* 26 (1985), 59-65.

88. We do not have the Diegeseis for this portion of the *Aetia* to check.

89. Knox later accepted my modification, adding a new argument of his own (n. 91).

into the epilogue. *SH* 252, from the same papyrus and in all probability the same column as 253, is certified as coming from Bk II. If the argument is accepted, there is no more to be said.

Second, after describing the young shepherd's meeting with the Muses, a regrettably lacunose and abbreviated passage of the Schol. Flor. goes on to describe (it seems) the *extent* of his conversations with the Muses. Here is the text of the scholia on F 2 with part of Coppola's restoration:[90]

ἀ]π᾽ αὐτ(ῶν) ἀρχὴ[ν] λαβὼν ἐ(πὶ) ὅσ(α) ἀ[........μέχρι τοῦ ἐπ]ιλόγου.

taking his beginning from them [the Muses] ......up to the epilogue.

As Knox acutely pointed out in a second article,[91] the writer was apparently saying something about the organizing framework of conversation with the Muses. Now the most obvious fact about this framework is its limitation to *Aetia* I-II. Any commentator who said anything about it at all must have said this. After saying where it began (ἀρχὴ[ν] λαβὼν), the Diegetes must have gone on to say where it ended, namely with the end of Bk II. Whatever the details of the restoration, so long as we read ἐπ]ιλόγου (the almost inescapable supplement in any case),[92] it follows that he knew of an epilogue at the end of Bk II.

An epilogue in the middle announcing a different poem will certainly have looked anomalous when all four books were copied into a codex. But there was no reason why Callimachus himself should have deleted the original epilogue when he first added III-IV, nor would it have made any sense to transfer these references to earlier plans and patrons to the end of IV. More generally, we have seen in Ch. IV that it was not normal practice to revise earlier installments when adding new ones. Ovid's *Ars Amatoria* provides a nice parallel.[93] When adding Bk 3, Ovid too left the closure of the original edition untouched; he did not delete or move the epilogue to 2; or update the original table of contents (1. 35-40) or the lines announcing 2 as the second half of the work.[94] All he did was add a couplet *after* the

90. G. Coppola, *Cirene e il nuovo Callimaco* (Bologna 1935), 171 (with a different interpretation); for a more cautious text, Pfeiffer vol. I, p. 11.

91. "The Epilogue to the *Aetia*: An Epilogue," *ZPE* 96 (1993), 175-8.

92. Following the editio princeps of Vitelli and Norsa (*Bulletin de la société royale d'archéologie d'Alexandrie* 28 (1933), 126, Pfeiffer prints simply].λόγου, as though the trace before λ was not distinguishable as any particular letter. In fact (as pointed out by Knox and confirmed by Roger Bagnall and Dirk Obbink) the upper two thirds of a nearly vertical stroke are clearly visible in Vitelli and Norsa's plate (not repeated in *PSI* 1219). The papyrus itself is now in Cairo, but Manfredo Manfredi has shown me a photograph he took 20 years ago which shows the same traces.

93. The *Ars* was heavily influenced by the *Aetia* (Hollis on 1. 25, 27-8, 457 and 647-56), and Knox 1993, 177-78 has suggested that Ovid may have imitated the format of the four-book edition.

94. 1. 771-72, modelled, as Hollis points out, on the similar lines marking the half-way point in the *Georgics* (ii. 541-2). For examples of individual components in Augustan poetry books not brought up to the date of publication, Fraenkel, *Horace* (1957), 287-8.

original epilogue to announce the new book and a perfunctory new epilogue at the close of 3, repeating verbatim the original sphragis from the end of 2: *inscribant spoliis NASO MAGISTER ERAT*.

6

If the purpose of the epilogue was indeed to prelude the *Iambi*, it would follow that when Callimachus published the *Aetia*, he had not yet published the *Iambi* but was on the point of doing so: in other words, that *Aetia* and *Iambi* were published in fairly quick succession. So long as F 112 was supposed to be the epilogue to a new edition of the *Aetia* completed no earlier than 245, it seemed to have no independent chronological interest. But if it is the epilogue to a work published ca 270, the chronological consequences are far-reaching.

First, there is the identification of "our queen" in lines 2-3. Since Ptolemy Philadelphus already had an heir by Arsinoë I, and was unwilling to complicate his love life by marrying again after the death of Arsinoë II, there was no queen of Egypt between then and Euergetes's marriage to Berenice II in 246. It used to be thought that the death of Arsinoë II was "one of the most secure dates in all Hellenistic history": 9 July 270.[95] It is placed in year 15 of Philadelphus by the Mendes stele, and the day date was inferred by Pfeiffer from Callimachus, whose poem on the apotheosis of Arsinoë associates her death with a new moon.[96] But the Pithom stele has her still alive in year 16 of Philadelphus, and places her death in year 17. As Hazzard and Grzybek have shown, these are not alternative dates, but products of alternative chronologies. To start with Philadelphus computed the start of his reign from the death of his father Soter in January 282, but later from his co-regency with Soter in 285.[97]

His motive was political, to forestall rival claims to Soter's throne from his older half-brothers Keraunos and Magas. As we have already seen, this situation is obliquely but nonetheless emphatically reflected in Callimachus's *Hymn to Zeus* 57-9. The change was made almost at once in the Macedonian calendar, but not till much later in the Egyptian dating system. Thus many demotic documents long continued to bear dates two years out

95. E. Grzybek, *Du calendrier macédonien au calendrier Ptolémaïque* (Basel 1990), 103.

96. F 228. 6, with note; *Kallimachosstudien* (Munich 1922), 1f.; Grzybek 1990, 109-12.

97. This reform of the Ptolemaic calendar and the confusion it generated is discussed by R. Hazzard, *Phoenix* 41 (1987), 140-58; Grzybek 1990, 115-134 (on the Pythom stele, ib. 69-101); H. Hauben, *Chron. d'Égypte* 62 (1992), 143-71.

of harmony with the revised Macedonian calendar. The Mendes stele reflects this older reckoning. Arsinoë died in the month of Pachon 269/8, that is to say between 26 June and 25 July 268. The evidence of Callimachus enables us to pin the day down to 1, 2 or perhaps 3 July.[98]

So the reference to "our queen" must have been written either after 246 (Berenice) or before 268 (Arsinoë).[99] Current orthodoxy is Berenice.[100] But while it might seem natural and appropriate enough to add an epilogue in honour of the new queen, nothing could have been less necessary—indeed positively anticlimactic. Did not *Aetia* III-IV already both begin and end with spectacular poems in her honour? Nonetheless the most conspicuous feature of the epilogue remains that abrupt announcement of the *Iambi*. It would be a rather curious way for a septuagenarian poet to end what he must have known was his most famous work.[101] Why were future plans so important to him so late in his career?

There is also another problem with attaching the epilogue to *Aetia* IV. The only lines that can be read with any confidence are the last four, where (in the usual manner of a sphragis) we might have expected the poet either to name himself or to anticipate his immortality. Instead he recapitulates virtually verbatim the *Somnium* from *Aetia* I. And the reference to the Graces (Χαρίτων) in line 2 also recalls the first aetion after the *Somnium* (F 3-7), the beginning of the dialogue with the Muses. This recapitulation is more problematic than has been acknowledged. For the organizing device of the Muses had been dropped in *Aetia* III-IV, which must have consisted of separate elegies. Why then evoke their first appearance so prominently in an epilogue to Bk IV? If with Parsons we answer, to give "external unity," that is precisely what it does not do. As the epilogue to IV it would underline the discontinuity of the device of the Muses in the *Aetia* as a whole.

98. Grzybek 1990, 107-12; Hauben 1992, 160-2; Koenen 1993, 51 n. 61.

99. It is of course theoretically possible that Callimachus continued to refer to Arsinoë as "our queen" after her death, but on balance this seems less likely. If we had the text of the epilogue complete, all would no doubt be clear.

100. Pfeiffer II. xl; Eichgrün 52f.; other references in Herter 1973, 205; add Fraser II. 1029 n. 128 ("now evident"). A. Platt read the traces in line 2 as μαῖα δ᾽ ἀνάσσης [ἡμε]τέρης, "nurse of our queen," which he himself interpreted as Aphrodite. But Coppola saw a reference to Cyrene, Berenice's birth-place, a suggestion developed in a different way by A. Barigazzi, *Prometheus* 7 (1981), 97-107. Mention of Cyrene would fulfil one of the standard elements of the sphragis (Wilamowitz, *Sappho und Simonides* [1913], 296-300; Lloyd-Jones, *JHS* 83 [1963], 96), since it was Callimachus's birth-place as well as Berenice's.

101. The last nine lines of Ovid's *Metamorphoses* provide a parallel of sorts for a personal sphragis capping a long narrative poem that otherwise culminates in praise of his sovereign. To be sure, Ovid was not contemplating another major work at the time, but he was looking forward to a new stage in his reputation: his posthumous fame.

On the other hand, if F 112 is the original epilogue to *Aetia* I-II, every-thing falls into place. As we have already seen, the original edition of I-II must have ended with some such episode in any case. Callimachus must at any rate have described how he woke up. But in view of the polemical note on which he had begun, it is likely that he closed with some brief remarks on the significance of his dream, picking up and rounding off the issues raised in the prologue. This is precisely what we find in the epilogue: recapitulation of both the *Somnium* and the first aetion. And while "my muse" (ἐμὴ μοῦσα) in line 1 could just be a reference to the poet's own inspiration, in the context of the *Somnium* she is surely Arsinoë, the queen of line 2.[102] Having earlier identified her as the tenth Muse, and so doubly the inspirer of his *Aetia*, he can now re-use the conceit to associate her with his further literary plans. This would also give further resonance to the hymnic clausula; for it was a common motif of archaic hymns to close with a fresh apostrophe to the god or goddess apostrophized at the beginning of the poem (σεῦ δ᾽ ἐγὼ ἀρξάμενος μεταβήσομαι ἄλλον ἐς ὕμνον).[103]

Nor would the announcement of the *Iambi* any longer be so abrupt. Our thoughts are once more on the slopes of Helicon and the styles appropriate to the various genres. Callimachus has merely extended the central motif of the *Somnium*, so that the slope of Helicon comes to represent the hierarchy of the genres. The literary/topographical descent down Helicon to the *Iambi* now comes as no surprise. Most poets graze their flocks on only one part of this slope, but Callimachus pays no more attention to these rules than to those he had rejected in the *Aetia* prologue. This is what the critics of his *Iambi* complain about (F 203. 31-3). Now that Callimachus has con-jured up again the atmosphere of the prologue and *Somnium*, we are quite prepared for metaphors of style.

If the queen of the epilogue is indeed Arsinoë, then she was surely still alive when Callimachus wrote. It is theoretically possible that she had recently died and that it was as a new god that Callimachus identified her as the tenth Muse. But this can hardly be true of the oblique allusion in the *Somnium*. And while shrines to the Muses were often erected *in memoriam*, there seems to be no example of the deceased being identified as a Muse. And if [ὅλο]ν is the correct restoration in the penultimate line, the prayer that Zeus "save the entire royal house" guarantees a plurality of sovereigns. The implication is that Callimachus began by addressing Arsinoë alone and then associated Philadelphus with her for the final prayer.

---

102. It is unlikely that Callimachus would have been so tactless as well as uninventive as to repeat for Berenice his compliment to Arsinoë.

103. *H.* 5. 293; 9. 9; 18. 1; cf. 31. 18 (ἐκ σέο᾽ δ᾽ ἀρξάμενος); 32. 18 (σέο δ᾽ ἀρχόμενος).

7

If Arsinoë was alive when Callimachus published *Aetia* I-II plus epilogue, they must have appeared before her death in July 268. If the interpretation just advanced is on the right lines, then the *Iambi* will soon have followed. Herter insisted that we could not hope to pin down a date of composition for the book as a whole, since the individual pieces could have been written at various times throughout the poet's long life.[104] While observing that several individual iambs "seem to refer to the background of Callimachus's earlier life in Alexandria," Fraser too was prepared to allow that their collection in book form might be as late as the famous collected edition of Callimachus's old age.[105] In fact it seems to be generally agreed that Callimachus did not collect the *Iambi* into book form till late in his life. There is no serious basis for this view beyond the late date assumed for the epilogue on the basis of the presumed lateness of the prologue. Yet the closing line of the epilogue suggests more than the republication of *iuvenilia*. The novelty and boldness of which the poet was evidently so proud surely consisted in the *writing* of these *Iambi*, not in having 17 of them copied on to one roll 20 or 30 years later.

A number of papyri contributed to the rediscovery of the *Iambi* in the first half of this century, but our best witness to the sequence of poems within the book is the Diegeseis. They list and summarize 17 poems between the end of the *Aetia* and the beginning of the *Hecale*. But in recent times only the first 13 have been counted as *Iambi*, with the last four classified as *Mele*.[106]

These four poems in "lyric" metres have been associated with the mention of "Mele" (μέλη, "songs") in the list of Callimachus's works in his Suda-entry. But that one word in a suspect part of the list[107] is hardly secure evidence that Callimachus published a complete book of lyric poems. Nothing is ever quoted from such a book. Moreover there are problems in identifying these four poems with such a book.[108] In the first place, there is no hint in the Diegeseis that the *Iambi* end with 13 or that the next four poems form a new book. There is no new title between 13 and 14.

---

104. Herter 1973, 216.

105. Fraser I. 734; the "early" poems turn out to be those that refer to his supposed schoolteaching days.

106. Clayman 1980, 4-7; against, C. Gallavotti, *Antiquitas* i (1946), 11-22 and A. Ardizzoni, *Miscellanea di Studi Alessandrini...A. Rostagni* (Turin 1963), 257-62.

107. Pfeiffer judged the nine preceding items dubious ("De carminibus Ἰοῦς ἄφιξις-κωμῳδίαι adhuc non constat," p. xcv).

108. Koerte 1938, 87-89; Gallavotti 1948, 11-21.

Second, to judge from the length of their summaries and what else we know about them, these four poems are not nearly long enough to make up a book. Nor is there any evidence for other lyric poems by Callimachus that might have filled out such a book.[109]

To draw a line after 13 would give us a neat iambic book, opening and closing with programmatic poems—just the way scholars like to envisage Hellenistic poetry books. But it leaves an insoluble mess between *Iambi* and *Hecale*. In effect, we should be forced to postulate *three* omissions by the Diegetes: (a) the closing colophon to the *Iambi*; (b) the new title introducing the *Mele*; and (c) the other dozen or so lyric poems that would have filled out a reasonably sized book. It is obviously *possible* either that he was this careless or that his source was defective in this way, but we should not be quick to make so drastic an assumption. Nowhere else can the Diegetes be shown to have made (or reproduced) any substantial errors or omissions, let alone anything on this scale.

It is true that there are also problems in counting the four poems as *Iambi*. Unlike 1-13 (according to Pfeiffer), three of the four have separate titles; they are not written in what we now recognize as iambic metres; and their subject matter seems different.[110]

First the argument from separate titles. Even if true, it would prove no more than that some poems were better known or circulated separately. Some episodes in the *Iliad* were known by separate titles (Teichoscopia, Catalogue of Ships); perhaps too some episodes from the *Aetia* (Acontius and Cydippe, Lock of Berenice). But the truth is that only 17 (F 229) has an unmistakable title, cited by Hephaestion as *Branchus*. But no title when the same Hephaestion cites 15 and 16. So it can hardly be held significant that he cites 1 (anonymously) and 7 without a title. Athenaeus cites 15 as ἐν παννυχίδι (668C), but this could be as much a description as a title; the poem is about a night-festival, as is the context (the phrase ἐν ταῖς παννυχίσιν, referring to festivals not poems, appears both before and after the quotation). ἐκθέωσις Ἀρσινόης and πρὸς τοὺς ὡραίους, given by Pfeiffer as the titles of F 226 and 228 from the Diegeseis, may likewise be descriptions rather than titles. If they are titles, then why not the headings ἐπίνικος Πολυκλεῖ, εἰς ἕβδομα θυγατρίου γεννηθέντος Λέοντι γνωρίμῳ τοῦ ποιητοῦ and πρὸς τοὺς καταμεμφομένους αὐτὸν ἐπὶ τῇ πολυειδείᾳ to 8, 9 and 13 in the same Diegeseis? There is really nothing here to separate 1-13 from 14-17.

Next the supposed metrical difficulties. We must bear in mind that in its original usage iambus implies a type of poetry rather than a metre.[111] To

109. The extant fragments in unusual metres (F 399-401) are probably from epigrams.
110. Clayman 1980, 52-54.
111. West, *Studies* 22f.

be sure Callimachus broadened the original conception, but the metrical variety of his own collection is proof enough that he did not substitute a metrical for a thematic link. When the Diegeseis were first published, Pfeiffer argued that the trochaic 12 (F 202) had been misplaced, and really belonged with the so-called "Mele."[112] This is a view now universally abandoned. There can be little doubt that Archilochus and Hipponax would have counted trochees as iambus. How different are 14-17? If 14 and 15 had been transmitted earlier in the sequence, it is doubtful whether their presence would have caused any misgivings. 15 (though not so treated by Pfeiffer) should be analysed as an epode, iambic dimeter followed by ithyphallic.[113] It is indeed so set out in the Berlin papyrus and by Hephaestion, and the Diegetes likewise quotes only the opening dimeter. This scarcely sets it apart from 6 and 7, in iambic trimeters plus ithyphallic. The one surviving line of 14 is a phalaecean hendecasyllable, perhaps used stichically, as by its "inventor" Phalaecus (Ep. 3) and Theocritus (Ep. 16). But an epode is also possible, perhaps combined with an iambic line. For we have an epodic epigram by Callimachus in phalaeceans alternating with iambic dimeters catalectic.[114] No one (I think) would have queried the iambic credentials of this combination if it had appeared among the *Iambi.*

As for stichic phalaeceans, here we may compare the practice of Catullus. In four separate poems (36.5; 40.2; 54.6; F 3) Catullus applies the term *iambi* to his own verses, in every case in the sense "lampoons" (that is to say using it as a generic rather than metrical term). As it happens, all four of these poems are in phalaeceans. In one or two cases the *iambi* he mentions could be identified as other poems not yet written. For example, 54.6-7 (addressed to Caesar): *irascere iterum meis iambis / immerentibus, unice imperator.* But if we take all four together, it seems impossible to doubt that Catullus counted phalaeceans as *iambi.*[115] Where did he get this idea? If we believe the Latin metrical writers, Sappho wrote them stichically,[116] but if so why were they known as phalaeceans? More important, of the Hellenistic poets only Callimachus used them in an influential book entitled *Iambi.* Catullan practice might be held to suggest that Callimachus used the line stichically.

The metrical case against including 14-17 (F 226-9) among the *Iambi* has to be that *none* of them can plausibly be classified as iambic. If two out of four can reasonably be so classified, the case against the remaining two is substantially weakened. The case for assigning them to a book of lyric poems has to be that all four can be more plausibly classified as lyric than

---

112. *SB München* 1934, 42-43; cf. Clayman 1980, 5.
113. See Pfeiffer on F 227; I owe this point to Arnd Kerkhecker.
114. *AP* xiii. 24 = 20 Gow-Page, with *HE* II. 177.
115. So most comm. and (e.g.) J. K. Newman, *Roman Catullus* (Hildesheim 1990), 49f.
116. Caesius Bassus (*GLK* vi. 258. 15) and Victorinus (*GLK* vi. 148. 13); F 230 V.

iambic. To the best of my knowledge no one has attempted to show this, and for a good reason. As pointed out above (§ 3), none of Callimachus's poetry is lyric in the strict sense, as he must have been well aware. If there is a single feature that differentiates the Ionian tradition of iambus from the Aeolic and Dorian lyric traditions, it is that the Ionians used relatively few metrical units in stichic or epodic forms while the lyric poets composed in increasingly elaborate and complex strophic patterns.[117] So far as we know Callimachus never attempted strophic composition, even as an experiment.

F 228 (16) is in Archebuleans (in effect five anapaests); F 229 (17) in choriambic pentameters catalectic. Since both lines are used stichically, neither is in any real sense a lyric poem. The Archebulean occurs here and there in the lyric poets and the lyric parts of tragedy, but always as one element in a larger structure. It is characteristic of Hellenistic poets to take such elements and use them stichically for entire poems. It was for this reason (not because they "invented" the lines in question) that the metrical writers christened them Asclepiadean, Phalaecean, Sotadean—and Archebulean.[118] Nothing is known of Archebulus of Thera save that he was the "teacher" of Euphorion;[119] but to have earned his modest immortality, he must have appropriated the line for entire poems before Callimachus —which in this case means before July 268. Choriambic pentameters, by contrast, are an artificial creation, presumably by Callimachus himself.[120] But choriambs were often associated with (or substituted for) iambs in earlier poetry of many kinds,[121] as (of course) the name implies. If challenged, Callimachus could easily have justified the inclusion of choriambs in a book of *Iambi*.

More generally, however, and perhaps more important, even if he used metrical units derived from lyric rather than iambus, Callimachus did not use them as building blocks in the construction of a lyric strophe, but stichically or in alternation as epodes in the manner of the iambographers—which is really just another way of saying that he wrote for recitation rather than musical performance. Even though not built up from traditional iambic units, 14-17 nonetheless represent an extension of the method of the iambographers.

We must also bear in mind that there were no authorized texts of Archilochus and Hipponax. Collections of archaic *Iambi* available to Hellenistic readers "may have included a minority of poems that would not

---

117. For a brief account, West, *Greek Metre* 146f.

118. Maas, *Greek Metre* (Oxford 1962), 11.

119. Lloyd-Jones, *ZPE* 13 (1974), 210 = *Academic Papers* II (1990), 220.

120. Philicus went one better, with choriambic hexameters catalectic: *SH* 676-80.

121. West, *Greek Metre* 57-58, 82, 100, 105, 166; T. Cole, *Epiploke* (Cambridge 1988), 30-39; cf. Ardizzoni 1963, 262.

individually have been so classified."[122] We might compare Callimachus's epigrams, which included poems in perhaps as many as ten metres other than the elegiac couplet.[123] Gow doubted whether lines in trochaic pentameters and greater Asclepiads "really come from an epigram" (*HE* II. 217), and taken by themselves it is doubtful whether anyone would have so identified them. But if included in a book entitled *Epigrams*, epigrams they were and so they were cited. And while (as we have seen) Callimachus was not the first to write a hymn in elegiacs, the anomaly is underlined by inclusion in a book of hymns alongside its all-hexameter fellows. It seems clear that he felt no obligation to impose metrical uniformity on books consisting of separate poems. If he had one or two poems that otherwise seemed to fit his new book well enough, who was going to complain?[124] And would he have cared? *Iamb* 13 replies contemptuously to critics who fault him for not following the rules—as though warning of worse to come! It is perhaps significant that the four poems moderns have sought to banish from the *Iambi* all follow this provocative piece.

Seeing how little we know about the content of so many of the *Iambi* (3, 5, 6-11), it is rash to insist that 14-17 "have no themes in common" with 1-13.[125] For that is to focus on plot at the simplest level, what the Diegetes could summarize in a couple of sentences to the exclusion of less obvious but perhaps more important themes. Thus if we forget about Hipponax for a moment, we shall discover that 1 and 17 share a preoccupation with the oracle and temple of Apollo at Didyma. 17 was an account of the founding of the oracle at Didyma by Branchus, a beautiful boy to whom Apollo had given the gift of prophecy. As H. W. Parke acutely noticed, Callimachus's interest in the subject is obviously connected with Ptolemaic interest in Miletus at the time. After a century and a half of disuse following the sack by the Persians, the oracle was refounded in the late fourth century on the model of Delphi.[126] A new charter legend was invented, bringing the eponymous hero Branchus from Delphi.[127] As usual, Callimachus will have dug out the relevant local histories and produced a suitably modified version.

The story of the seven sages that is the core of *Iamb* 1 exists in many versions, conveniently collected by Diogenes Laertius (i. 28-33). Cal-

---

122. West, *Studies* 22.

123. 17, 19, 20, 66, 68, 69, 70 GP; ?F 479, ?F 554, ?F635 Pf.

124. It is not as if classification by metre was the standard organising principle in Hellenistic editions of the lyric poets: Sappho, but not Pindar.

125. Clayman 1980, 53.

126. "The Temple of Apollo at Didyma," *JHS* 106 (1986), 124, 129-30.

127. For the scanty evidence on the story of Branchus, the Branchidae and Didyma see H. W. Parke, *The Oracles of Apollo in Asia Minor* (London 1985), 2-6, 55-6; J. Fontenrose, *Didyma: Apollo's Oracle, Cult and Companions* (Berkeley 1988).

limachus gave it a contemporary twist. In earlier versions, the object passed round from one sage to the next was a silver tripod found by fishermen. It was apparently from Maeandrius of Miletus that Callimachus got the story that it was a golden cup donated by Bathycles the Arcadian. And the poem itself provides a specific illustration of the way he used local historians. For according to Maeandrius, when the cup came back to Thales the second time, he dedicated it to Apollo Delphinius, that is to say, he placed it in the chief shrine of Miletus *before* the building of the new temple of Didyma, the Didymaeum.[128] But Callimachus has Thales both originally receive and subsequently dedicate it in the Didymaeum.[129] Modern students of *Iamb* 1 are almost exclusively concerned with Callimachus's satiric persona and debt to Hipponax. Well-informed contemporaries would also have noticed how neatly he had updated the story of Bathycles's cup. And when they reached 17 they would have recalled how neatly (if unexpectedly) the book was tied together by Didyma.

Nor is this the only other poem in the book that shows the benefits of Callimachus's Milesian researches. When singing its own praises in *Iamb* 4, the laurel tree briefly describes how Branchus struck the Ionians with laurel branches to heal them when they had aroused Apollo's wrath. The allusion is not entirely casual: the laurel makes much of its services to Apollo's oracle in Delphi. A prophetic laurel also makes an appearance in *Iamb* 5 (F 195. 32), and according to the Diegesis, an oracle of Apollo played a major part in 7 too (F 197).

It is striking how much both Didyma and Delphi were on Callimachus's mind during the writing of the *Iambi*. There may also have been a related episode in the *Aetia*. Pfeiffer pointed out that πολυγώνιε in F 114. 2 points to the block of stone (γυλλός) worshipped as Apollo at Miletus, and Livrea has now made the attractive suggestion that the interlocutor who addresses the god in this fragmentary dialogue is in fact the boy Branchus. Livrea further suggests that F 114 should be placed between F 2 and 3, that is to say in Bk I, which (as we have seen) was published shortly before the *Iambi*. More probably it belongs in Bk III, but that need not mean that the poem in question was written as late as 245.[130] F 108 from *Aetia* IV may also have featured an oracle of Didymean Apollo (p. 253).

Since most of these allusions in the *Iambi* are subsidiary to the main concerns of the various poems, it is natural to infer that they are an incidental result of recent research on Apollo and his oracles—which suggests in turn that the book as a whole was written within a relatively short space of time.

---

128. *FGrH* 492 F 18; Parke 1986, 130.
129. Dieg. 1. 18; F 191. 57.
130. *Hermes* 123 (1995), with my reply in *ZPE* 1996.

Apollo and the Muses form another link between several poems towards the end of the book. 13, the reply to critics of the poet's polyeideia, opens by addressing Apollo and the Muses. Modern readers of Callimachus will at once think of the opening scene of the *Aetia*. More immediately relevant, however, is 15 (headed *Pannychis*), a drinking song in honour of Helen and the Dioscuri, which likewise opens with Apollo and his choir (Ch. III. 3). Helen was sometimes identified with Arsinoë in Ptolemaic cult and literature (Ch. XVI. 3). The next poem (16) commemorates the deification of Arsinoë, again opening with an evocation of Apollo and his choir of Muses before going on to describe how Arsinoë was snatched away by the Dioscuri. Apollo also provides a link with 12, a poem for the seventh day celebration of the birth of a friend's daughter. The seventh day of the month was sacred to Apollo,[131] and most of what remains of the poem is devoted to describing how Apollo celebrated the birth of Hera's daughter with a hymn. So 12 and 13 are linked to 15 and 16 by Apollo in his capacity as god of poetry.

There are also significant papyrological links. 15 and 16 are preserved in fragments on (probably) adjacent leaves of a third-century codex in Berlin.[132] 17 is preserved on the last column of a second-century roll from Oxyrhynchus which also contained *Iambi* 4, 5, 6, 7 and a few unplacable iambic fragments.[133] As Gallavotti saw, the presumption is that 17 was the last poem in a roll that otherwise consisted of the *Iambi*.[134] Thus the Oxyrhynchus roll supports the evidence of the Diegeseis that 17 was the final poem in the *Iambi*,[135] while the Berlin codex at any rate confirms the juxtaposition of 15 and 16 in the Diegeseis.

There is also even earlier evidence. Horace's *Iambi*[136] likewise consist of 17 poems. Recent research has tended to focus on Horace's debt to the archaic iambographers—justifiably enough (it might seem), given his own express reference to "Parian iambics" (*Sat.* i. 19. 24-5).[137] Yet when Horace claims to be Archilochus without Lycambes, we are surely meant to

131. See West on Hesiod, *Theog.* 770 (p. 352).

132. First published by Wilamowitz, *SB Berlin* 1912, 524-44 (several more fragments of this same codex subsequently turned up: Pfeiffer II. xx). Given the location of the two poems in the Dieg., the fact that the pieces of P. Berol. 13417 containing them were sold together creates a presumption that they were found together—and so consecutive in the codex.

133. P.S.I. 1216 + P. Oxy. 2171 + 2172: Pfeiffer II. xi.

134. *Antiquitas* i (1946), 11; *Parola del Passato* 8 (1953), 464.

135. The clinching argument in Parsons's demonstration that the Victoria Berenices opened *Aetia* III was his observation that in P. Oxy. 2173 its first line "is the first line of the column in the first column of the roll" (*ZPE* 25 [1977], 48).

136. Horace himself refers to *Iambi* (*Epod.* 14.7; *Ep.* i.19.23; ii.2.59; *carm.* i.16.2-30), but that need not imply that the title *epodon liber* is not his: see the recent discussion by A. Cavarzere, *Orazio: il libro degli epodi* (Venezia 1992), 9-14.

137. Notably Fraenkel's *Horace* (1957), 24-75.

think of Callimachus proclaiming himself Hipponax without Bupalos (F 191. 1-4).[138] At the very least, archaic forms are being mediated through Alexandrian sensibility. Under the circumstances, at a time when (following Vergil's *Bucolics*) multiples of 10 were all the vogue for triumviral poetry books, it is hard to believe it coincidence that Horace settled on the same unusual number[139] of *Iambi* as Callimachus.

Accepting the general validity of the Horatian parallel, Clayman attempts a compromise, suggesting that "the four poems which follow the original *Iambi*...were added to a manuscript of the *Iambi* in antiquity in order to fill out the "book," and that the total of 17 poems was known at Rome."[140] Such a hypothesis conflicts with everything we know about the make-up of Hellenistic books: not one of 70 rolls from Herculaneum of which enough survives to judge contains more than a single book.[141] No professional copyist would have taken it on himself to add alien material to "fill out" blank space at the end of a roll. Moreover, Hellenistic books *invariably* close with an *explicit* naming author and book (again, all 70 from Herculaneum); even if there had been such an addition to a roll containing the *Iambi*, it would have been clearly marked off from the principal contents of the roll. So it is a defective as well as an anomalous roll we are being asked to hypothesize, a roll whose lack of *explicit* misled Horace into ascribing 17 poems to Callimachus's book and Catullus into believing that Callimachus counted hendecasyllables as iambics. It is not as if *Iambi* 1-13 were so small a collection as to suggest a make-weight to fill out an average length roll. The best estimate of the length of 1-13 is ca 1000 lines.[142]

Clement of Alexandria describes the purification of the Milesians by Branchus on the authority of one Apollodorus of Corcyra, and then adds that "Callimachus also tells the story in his *Iambi*."[143] It has been claimed that the reference may be to the brief mention of Branchus in *Iamb* 4,[144] as indeed it may. But if Clement remembered Callimachus at all on the subject, is it not more likely that he remembered the more detailed treatment? If so, then 17 is quoted from the *Iambi*—and without separate title.

Callimachus may have written most of the *Iambi* specially for his projected new book. But it is in the nature of things that a prolific, experimental poet will have had a few other poems to hand not originally so

---

138. J. K. Newman, *Roman Catullus* (Hildesheim 1990), 47-48; Cavarzere 1992, 22.

139. Unusual—but not (of course) unparalleled. No one seems to have remembered in this connection that the final book of the *Aetia* also contained 17 poems.

140. Clayman 1980, 7.

141. Cavallo 1983, 14, 22-3; the Herculaneum rolls are the closest parallels we have (in place as well as time) for the sort of Greek texts available to Catullus and Horace.

142. Dawson 1950, 133-36.

143. Clem. Alex. *Strom.* 5. 8. 48; cf. F 194. 28-31 Pf. with F 75 Schneider.

144. F 194. 28-31; Clayman 1980, 6.

designed that he finally decided to include. In at least one case it is easy to divine reasons for inclusion that far outweighed metrical considerations.

We have seen that such indications as there are converge to suggest that *Aetia* I-II were published before Arsinoë's death in 268 and the *Iambi* soon after. 1-13 carry no explicit indication of date, but if we include 14-17, we at once gain a very explicit indication. Arsinoë died on 1 or 2 July 268. Callimachus's poem on her apotheosis must have been written soon after, very likely before the month was out. If his principal patron died just when he was putting together a book of occasional poems, what more natural than that he should have included in that book the poem he wrote for the occasion? Indeed, how could he have left it out?

The early 260s would also suit 17. Ptolemaic influence over Miletus seems to have lasted from ca 279 to 259.[145] Philadelphus presented the city with a large gift of land in 279/8, and it is reasonable to assume that at some point he also contributed something more specifically to the slowly rising temple of Didyma (work was begun by Seleucus ca 300—and continued for another half millenium).[146] If the oracle greeted Seleucus as son of Apollo,[147] it can hardly have done less for Philadelphus.

The sheer number of references to Didyma and Delphi in the *Iambi* might be thought to suggest some special preoccupation. Nor was Callimachus the only poet of the age to be so interested in the revival of Didyma. Parthenius preserves a long elegiac fragment from the *Apollo* of Alexander Aetolus, telling of the unhappy love of Antheus and the wife of King Phobius of Miletus, a version of the tale of Joseph and Potiphar's wife.[148] The narrative is couched throughout in the future tense, and F. Jacobs long ago realized that it is meant to be a prophecy by Apollo.[149] Modern scholars have assumed that the poem was a "collection of love stories with unhappy endings."[150] But (a) this is to generalize from the only surviving fragment, and (b) if this was all Alexander wanted to do, why cast all his stories in so cumbersome a framework as prophecies by Apollo? Since Phobius was king of Miletus, it is surely Apollo of Didyma who is speaking. I suggest that the organizing framework of the poem was oracles of Didyma, Apollo's varied clientele down the centuries, kings and pharaohs as well as mythical lovers. That would include such historical figures as Croesus, Alexander, Seleucus[151]—and perhaps Philadelphus.

---

145. C. B. Welles, *Royal Correspondence in the Hellenistic Period* (New Haven 1934), 73; Bagnall, *Ptolemaic Possessions* (1976), 173.

146. Welles 1934, 74; Parke 1986, 125-6.

147. C. Habicht, *Gottmenschentum und griechische Städte*[2] (Zetemata 14) 1970, 86.

148. *CA* 122-24; J. Stern, *Eranos* 85 (1987), 35-39.

149. *Animadv. in Epp. Anthologiae Graecae* I.2 (Leipzig 1798), 239.

150. Barber, *OCD*[2] 42; Knaack, *RE* I. 2 (1894), 1447; Couat 1931 (1882), 111.

151. It was Seleucus who returned the bronze statue of the god that Xerxes removed in 493, but Alexander may have left him out if he was writing under Philadelphus.

According to Parthenius, after the death of his wife and her beloved, Phobius decided that he was cursed and yielded his throne to Phrygius. Did he perhaps (at least in Alexander's version) consult Apollo about his plight? Or did Phrygius receive an oracle about his future elevation?[152]

Elsewhere Parthenius tells a story which the marginal notes in the only manuscript derive from Apollonius's *Foundation of Caunus* and the *Lyrcus* of the perhaps slightly later Nicaenetus of Samos.[153] The childless Lyrcus of Caunus was told by the oracle at Didyma that he would beget a child by the first woman he slept with after leaving the oracle—which turned out to be a certain Hemithea. Diodorus preserves a more detailed account of Hemithea which says nothing about the oracle (v. 62-3). This seems to be another case of an early story updated by third-century poets to give prominence to the refurbished oracle of Didyma.[154] Once again, this updating took the form of a transparent duplication of a well-known Delphic oracle: the one to the childless Aegeus, future father of Theseus. Callimachus, Alexander and Apollonius were all pensionaries of Philadelphus. It is tempting to conjecture that they were all responding to some specific act of patronage to Didyma by Philadelphus. Such patronage would have to have fallen before 259. So in all probability *Branchus* was written before then.

It is a natural assumption that the benefactions, glory and destiny of Philadelphus played a prominent rôle in *Iamb* 17. Here we may compare the slightly earlier *Hymn to Delos* (ca 275: Ch. IX. 3). From his mother's womb the unborn Apollo warns his mother not to stop at Cos, because that is reserved for the birth of Philadelphus (iv. 162-70). If so, the *Iambi*, like *Aetia* II and IV, will have ended with compliments to the ruling house. This would explain why the *Apotheosis of Arsinoë* was not given the place of honour at the end of the *Iambi*. There was only one person who could have dislodged the dead queen from this position: Philadelphus himself.

One minor consequence may be less welcome in some quarters. Over the past decade or two a disproportionate amount of research has been invested in the analysis of Greek and Roman poetry books, revealing complex principles of arrangement held to add immeasurably to the significance of individual poems.[155] Some scepticism is in order, but it need not be total. No one will deny that juxtaposition may sometimes add something to separate poems on linked or contrasted themes; or that emphasis may be added by (say) a prominent location within the book. One of the main

---

152. So little is known about these shadowy figures that such details could have been invented with impunity. On Phrygius, Höfer in Roscher's Lexicon III.2 (1902-9), 2470.

153. Little is known about these works, *CA* 4-5 and 1; for Nicaenetus's date, *HE* II. 417.

154. So Parke 1985, 56; Fontenrose 1988, 228.

155. See the various contributions in *Augustan Poetry Books* (*Arethusa* 13. 1, 1980); M. S. Santirocco, *Unity and Design in Horace's Odes* (Chapel Hill 1986); for what is known about the *Garlands* of Meleager and Philip of Thessalonica, my *Greek Anthology*, Ch. I-II.

reasons for closing the *Iambi* with 13 has always been the assumed appropriateness of this poem for that function. The book would then both begin and close with answers to critics, 1 implicit and 13 explicit. It seemed inevitable that 13 was a closing epilogue balancing the *Aetia* prologue.

That 13 fulfills some such function seems clear enough. But it does not have to close the book to do so. Its "programmatic" nature is so obvious that it would have been superfluous to give it this additional emphasis, better reserved for something less obvious. Nor does the book lose all structure if we include 14-17. Quite the contrary. While 1 has one sort of link with 13 (iambic poetry) it has an entirely different sort of link with 17: Apollo of Didyma. Indeed, in one capacity or another Apollo ties together a number of other poems too. Given Callimachus's well-known concern with poetics, it is interesting that the link between 1 and 17 should *not* for once be Apollo in his capacity as god of poetry. If we had the book entire we should no doubt discover a number of other links and contrasts. But we should not expect them all to concern literary theory. Modern critics are in danger of forgetting Callimachus's poetry for his poetics.

To recapitulate the chronological results: the *Aetia* were published during the brief reign of Arsinoë (279/4-268), presumably not long before her death, since they advertise the *Iambi*, which appeared soon after her death. Let us suggest ca 270 for the *Aetia*, ca 268 for the *Iambi*.

Postscript: The early date here suggested for the *Iambi* reopens the question of the relationship between Callimachus and Phoenix of Colophon. With the exception of Pfeiffer (on F 191. 1), most have dated Phoenix first and concluded that Hipponactean iambics were "taken up by poets before Callimachus" (Hutchinson 1988, 49). There are three parallels between *Iamb* 1 (F 191) and F 4 of Phoenix. (1) Phoenix not only told the story of Bathycles and the seven sages, but the same version as Callimachus, with the gold cup (p. 168); (2) both describe Thales as "most beneficial," using the same rare word ὀνήϊστος (Call. F 191. 67); (3) both seem to have illustrated these "benefits" by the example of his astronomical observations (Phoenix 4. 1 ~ Call. F 191. 54-5). Then in Phoenix F 1 a speech by the Assyrian Ninos opens with the words ἄκουσον...οὐ γὰρ ἀλλὰ κηρύσσω (F 1. 13-15) and *Iamb* 1 of Callimachus opens ἀκούσαθ'...οὐ γὰρ ἀλλ' ἥκω (the particle combination is Comic: see Headlam on Herodas vi. 101 rather than Denniston, *GP* 31, who took the Callimachean line for genuine Hipponax). The echoes are more than verbal; the later clearly took from the earlier both the theme of Bathycles's cup and the frame of a warning voice from the grave. It is hardly likely that a poet of Callimachus's originality and stature cobbled together the entire conception of his first *Iamb* from two of Phoenix's moralizing iambics. Far more likely that Phoenix, more concerned with content than form, borrowed the frame for two of his homilies from the same poem of Callimachus. For κηρύσσω of a first-person warning from the grave, note Callimachus again, *AP* vii. 272. 5. Since Phoenix wrote a lament on the destruction of Colophon by Lysimachus ca 294 (Fraser II. 883 n. 61; 1030 n. 136), he must have been somewhat older than Callimachus. So if he is the imitator, then the *Iambi* must at any rate be placed in the first rather than the second half of Callimachus's career. Ca 268 would then become a terminus post quem for Phoenix. The Posidippus addressed in F 6 could be the dramatist or (more probably) the epigrammatist of that name, but "may of course be neither" (Gow, *HE* II. 483).

Chapter VII

Callimachus Senex

1

But there is a problem with this conclusion. The *Aetia* prologue refers repeatedly to the poet's old age (F 1. 6; 33-6; 38). It has therefore been assumed, on the well known axiom that writers die soon after their latest datable reference, that his old age fell on or close to the date of his latest known poems, namely 245. Whence the hypothesis of a new prologue added many years later to the collected edition. But if (as on my hypothesis) the prologue formed an integral part of the original edition of *Aetia* I-II ca 270, Callimachus would be complaining of old age twenty-five years before his last datable work.

There is certainly a temporal displacement. Whereas in the prologue the poet is an old man, in the *Somnium* he is a boy "sprouting his first beard." But it does not follow that the prologue was *written* later than the *Somnium*. For already in the prologue the old poet twice looks back to his youth (21-22, 37-38). Indeed, the emphasis on the youth of the boy in the dream itself implies an older dreaming poet.

The temporal displacement is simply an aspect of the mise-en-scène of the poem. Nowadays we are used to a work of fiction opening on a retrospective note: the author, now an older and wiser man, tells how it all began.[1] The *Aetia* is not straightforwardly retrospective: the poet does not recall an actual experience of his youth, but dreams himself young again. The poem is presented as knowledge obtained from the Muses by his younger dreaming self, thus illustrating the claim of the prologue that "those the Muses look on with favour as boys, they do not abandon when grey" (37-8). On the narrative level the references to old age in the prologue build up to the poet's dream rejuvenation.

It is not as if the prologue were simply an autobiographical addition to a work of fiction. Though still recognisably the elderly scholar answering his critics, the speaker of the prologue is hardly less a fictional construct than the young shepherd who cross-questions the Muses on the slopes of

---

1. By implication, this is already true of his model Hesiod: *Theog.* 22f. describe how the Muses "*once* taught Hesiod glorious song," evidently written *after* he had become a poet. Parts 1 and 3 have benefited from last-minute first aid by Sarah Mace.

Helicon. It is this speaker, not the shepherd, who claims that the god Apollo appeared to him when he first put a writing tablet on his knees (F 1. 21-2) and contemplates turning into a cicada (32). And it is not human beings he addresses, but spiteful goblins (1-2). In its tone as well as in its themes and models (pp. 129-32), prologue merges seamlessly with *Somnium*.

If born ca 320, Callimachus would have been between forty-five and fifty in 270 when he published *Aetia* I-II complete with prologue. Two questions present themselves. First, could a man in his late forties have described himself in the terms of the *Aetia* prologue? Second, whatever his age, why refer to it so often and so emphatically?

2

Pfeiffer solemnly laid down that a man had to be at least 60 before he could say that old age pressed down on him like Sicily on Enceladus.[2] Not only is this to misread fantasy as biography; it is to apply inappropriate modern criteria to the misreading.

Though much work has been done in the last few decades on the age to which people might live in the ancient world, little attention has been paid to the age at which they began to think of themselves as old. The two are by no means the same. Many an individual lived to seventy or eighty, but the median life expectancy in the ancient world was perhaps less than thirty.[3] Obviously a man who in fact lived to eighty might well have had intimations of mortality much earlier. Since we so seldom have a precise and reliable birthdate for anyone in antiquity, it is not easy to judge at what age people were first described as, or thought of themselves as old.

An important study by Creighton Gilbert has shown that in the Renaissance men were widely perceived as being old by their forties.[4] According to Dante, old age began at forty-five; according to Thomas Elyot at forty, to be succeeded at fifty by "age decrepite." Erasmus's poem "On the Discomforts of Old Age" was written when he was only thirty-nine:[5]

2. F 1. 35-36; Pfeiffer 1929, 333, endorsed by Herter 1937, 107: "in Wahrheit muß der Mann, auf dem das Alter lastet wie Sizilien auf Enkelados, ein Sechziger gewesen sein."

3. That is to say, as "in other pre-industrial societies unaffected by modern advances in medicine and hygiene," P. A. Brunt, *Italian Manpower*[2] [1987], 133 with 719; R. Duncan-Jones, *Structure and Scale in the Roman Economy* (Cambridge 1990), 93-104; T. G. Parkin, *Demography and Roman Society* (Baltimore 1992), 105-11.

4. "When did a man in the Renaissance grow old?," *Studies in the Renaissance* 14 (1967), 7-32.

5. Dante, *Convivio* IV. 24; Elyot, *The Castel of Helthe* (1534), First Book, sigs. 10b-11a (Gilbert, p.13); C. Reedijk, *The Poems of Desiderius Erasmus* (Leiden 1956), 280-90.

...How lately did you see this
fresh Erasmus blooming in mid-youth?
Now, quickly turning about, he
begins to notice the hurts of pressing old age,
and move towards a change...

Like both Dante and Elyot, Erasmus's poem makes it clear that old age was thought of as following directly on youth. Michelangelo started claiming that he could not work so hard "because he was old" at the age of forty-two. If this letter had not been precisely dated (2 May 1517) it would certainly have been referred to a much later stage in the life of a man who after all lived to be almost ninety. Gilbert quotes countless other well documented examples, concluding with a series of cases of what he calls the Castagno pattern: "biographers assign a birth date far too early, and later correct it upon the discovery of better data":

> Andrea del Castagno, the classic instance, was cited in all literature before 1920 as born either in 1390 or 1410, but is now understood on rather full evidence to have been born in or near 1421.

In most cases, these original false dates were inferred from "references to forty-five-year-old artists as 'old' taken to mean sixty-five." In Callimachus we have a classic case of a reference to old age "taken to mean sixty-five." Unfortunately, classical scholars almost never discover "better data" enabling them to refine such guesses. Nonetheless, there is no reason to believe that either life expectancy or attitudes to old age in the Renaissance were any different from those that prevailed in antiquity.

If the onset of old age could be placed as early as the forties, it follows that those who lived into their eighties or nineties (as not a few undoubtedly did in antiquity)[6] spent more than half their lives classified as old. The implication of the epigram of Sophocles cited in Plut. *Mor.* 785b (= T 163 Radt) is that a man who lived to be ninety already considered himself old when fifty-five. It is therefore relevant to note that the Greeks did indeed recognize successive stages of old age. The most comprehensive list is to be found in the Lexicon of Julius Pollux: starting with terms that simply classify a man as above military age (namely fifty),[7] moving on to "greying" (προπόλιος, ὑποπόλιος, μεσαιπόλιος), prematurely or freshly old (ὠμογέρων),[8] to "old" (γέρων, γηραιός) and finally extreme old age (ἐσχατογήρως, βαθυγήρως). An interesting passage of Galen distinguishes three stages of old age, the first of which he characterizes as "the newly

---

6. Parkin 1992, 105-11.

7. ἐκ τῆς ἀπομάχου ἡλικίας, ἐκ τῆς ἀπομάχου, ἐκ τῆς ἀπολέμου, ἐκ τῆς ἀστρατεύτου, ὑπὲρ τὸν κατάλογον, ὑπὲρ τὰ ἐξήκοντα ἔτη γεγονώς, i. 83. 20f. Bethe; cf. Aristoph. Byz. *Frag.* ed. W. J. Slater (Berlin 1986), 35-6.

8. ὠμός properly = "unripe," "raw", an epic metaphor (West on Hesiod, *Theog.* 705).

old, still able to perform civic duties,"[9] presumably meaning men below fifty.

The figure of sixty given in most modern discussions for the onset of old age in antiquity refers to the age at which men were normally released from a variety of civic obligations, in both Greece and Rome.[10] There are also a great many Greek and Latin texts, beginning with a famous and influential poem of Solon (F 27 West), that divide man's life into ten multiples of seven, the last two (from 56 and 63) representing decline. We also find other combinations and multiples, and in later times such ideas were further influenced by astrology.[11] It was for other reasons again—eugenics—that Plato and Aristotle laid down that men should not beget children after fifty-four or fifty-five.[12] But (of course), the neat results thus obtained bore no relation to the genuine life expectancy of real people, still less to personal perceptions of old age. And it is with perceptions rather than arbitrary norms that we are here concerned.

At Rome old age was traditionally held to begin at forty-six, as Cicero remarks in *de senectute* 61. According to the latest commentator on this work, this was "an old idea that no longer obtained; in Cicero's own time *senectus* was reckoned to begin around sixty."[13]

But a careful analysis by P. Venini of the numerous old men listed in *de senectute* shows that at least eight died before reaching the age of sixty, and there are many more we have no way of checking.[14] For example, L. Aemilius Paullus, cos. 219 and cos. II 216 (§ 75): assuming that the Lex Villia Annalis reflects normal career patterns at this time, he is unlikely to have been much more than forty-two at his first consulate, and so probably well under fifty when killed at Cannae in 216. The great orator Crassus is made to refer to himself as *senex* in Cicero's *de Oratore* (ii. 15). The dialogue is set in September 91 B.C., a few days before Crassus died at the

---

9. τῶν ὡμογερόντων...δυναμένων ἔτι πράττειν τὰ πολιτικά, VI. 379 K; for the third category he uses the rare term πέμπελος, otherwise found in Lycophron, *Alex.* 682, 826.

10. W. Suder, *Actes du 110ᵉ Congrès national des sociétés savantes, Montpellier 1985, Histoire médiévale* I (1987), 65-79; C. Gnilka, "Greisenalter," *RAC* xii (1983), 996-99. For some obligations (e.g. military) the cut-off point falls earlier (46/50), for others (e.g. *tutela*) later (70). Unfortunately nothing relevant in G. Minois, *History of Old Age from Antiquity to the Renaissance* (Chicago 1989); he does not raise the question here considered or cite the texts here assembled—not even the fundamental article by Gilbert.

11. The classic study is F. Boll, "Die Lebensalter," *Neue Jahrbücher* 31 (1913), 93f. = *Kleine Schriften zur Sternkunde* (1950), 156-224; E. Lamirande, *Cahiers des études anciennes* 14 (1982), 227-33; Gnilka, *RAC* xii. 997.

12. *Rep.* 460E; *Pol.* 1335b35; Aristotle alludes to Solon, but his vaguer "four or five years after 50" shows that he did not take Solon's calculations too seriously. W. L. Newman's commentary (III [Oxford 1902], 476) indignantly lists great men sired by fathers over 50 (William Pitt the Younger, for example).

13. J.G.F. Powell, *Cicero: Cato Maior de Senectute* (1988), 173; Gell. 10. 28. 1.

14. "La vecchiaia nel *de senectute* di Cicerone," *Athenaeum* 38 (1960), 98-117.

age of forty-eight. As usual, Cicero knew exactly how old Crassus was,[15] and chose his dramatic date with great care.[16] Then there is the complaint about the worries of old age that Sallust puts into the mouth of C. Aurelius Cotta during his consular year of 75 B.C.[17] If Cicero knew Cotta's exact dates we may be sure Sallust did too: born in 124,[18] he died the year after the speech in question, in 74. Once again, a forty-nine-year-old *senex*. Livy twice describes Hannibal as *senex* (once yet again in a speech put in his own mouth) just before giving his exact age as forty-five.[19] Cicero provides another example. Having claimed that the poet Archias was no more than sixteen when he arrived in Rome in 102, he goes on to refer to him as old in a speech delivered in 62. A century ago Reinach disputed Archias's age in 102 simply and solely on the grounds that Cicero could not plausibly have called a fifty-six-year-old man old.[20] Of course, Cicero might well have exaggerated Archias's youth to enhance his precosity, but no one would have been surprised at a fifty-six-year-old *senex*. There is an amusing scene in Plautus's *Miles Gloriosus* where Pleusicles regrets asking the elderly Periplectomenus to do something so childish, so unbecoming his years and character.[21] "Do I really seem to you on the brink of Acheron, ready for a coffin?," replies Periplectomenus, indignantly protesting that he is barely fifty-four and fit as a fiddle.[22]

According to Cassius Dio, Macrinus was an old man (γέρων) when he made his bid for the purple, "for he was three to five months short of being fifty-four."[23] It may be instructive to reproduce in full Philostratus's comment on the death of the second-century sophist Polemo of Smyrna:[24]

> When he died he was about fifty-six years old, but this age, in other professions the beginning of old age, for a sophist still counts as youth, since in this profession a man's knowledge grows more adaptable with advancing years.

15. Cf. *Brutus* 161, with G. V. Sumner, *The Orators in Cicero's Brutus* (1973), 94; for the care Cicero took with his chronology, A. E. Douglas, *Cicero: Brutus* (1966), lii-liv; E. Badian, *Hommages...M. Renard* I (1969), 54-65; (on his knowledge of orators' birth dates and methods of research), Sumner 1973, 155-76; Powell 1988, 273-9.

16. For the well-documented practice of setting a dialogue shortly before the death of the principal interlocutor, see the examples collected in *JRS* lvi (1966), 28-29.

17. *Hist. Rell.* F 47. 2 (p. 77 Maurenbrecher): *in his miseriis cuncta me cum fortuna deseruere; praeterea senectus per se gravis curam duplicat....*

18. G. V. Sumner, *The Orators in Cicero's Brutus* (1973), 109-10.

19. XXX. 28. 5; ib. 30. 10; XXX. 37. 9; F. Münzer, *Römische Adelsparteien und Adelsfamilien* (Stuttgart 1920), 106.

20. *pro Archia* 5 (*praetextatus...senectuti*); T. Reinach, *De Archia Poeta* (Paris 1890), 2.

21. *me tibi istuc aetatis homini facinora puerilia / obicere neque te decora neque tuis virtutibus.../ eam pudet me tibi in senecta obicere sollicitudinem* (618-23).

22. *itane tibi ego videor oppido Acheronticus? / tam capularis?..../ nam equidem hau sum annos natus praeter quinquaginta et quattuor, / clare oculis video, pernix sum pedibus, manibus mobilis* (627-30). I owe this reference to Otto Zwierlein.

23. Dio 78. 40. 3 (III. 449. 14 Boissevain).

24. *Vit. Soph.* 543, trans. W. C. Wright (Loeb ed.), adapted.

Clearly Philostratus was struck by the discrepancy between societal expectation and performance in his own profession.[25]

In his *Life of Malchus*, written in 386/7 A.D., Jerome refers to himself as a *senex*: "What old (*senex*) Malchus told me as a young man (*adulescentulus*), I have told you as an old man (*senex*)." Jerome's long life and many works are well documented, and though there have been several attempts to take his birth date back a decade or more on the basis of this very passage, a careful study by A. D. Booth has confirmed that Jerome was indeed born "in the second half of 347 or early in 348."[26] We are left with a secure example of a forty-year-old *senex*. An early Byzantine work of the seventh century lists 18 patients healed by Saint Artemius (a specialist in ailments of the testicles), of whom three are designated old. Their ages are fifty, sixty and sixty-two.[27] A later poet from Cyrene, Synesius, wrote to an old friend that he was not only the older of the two, but now an old man (οὐ σοῦ πρεσβύτερος μόνον, ἀλλὰ καὶ ἤδη πρεσβύτης). Synesius's dates cannot be pinned down closely,[28] but since he was born not more than a year or two before 370 and dead by 413, he cannot have been more than forty-five at the time. Since all three of his young sons died within a space of a year or so in 412/3, it is easy to see why he might have felt old so early. We may compare the case of Basil of Caesarea, who died, after a long and painful illness, at the (by modern standards) early age of forty-nine. In a letter written when he was only forty-three or -four to a younger man he speaks feelingly of "us old men" (ἡμεῖς οἱ γέροντες).[29] Two years later he refers ruefully to a correspondent's wish that he enjoy a "robust old age" (γῆρας ἰσχυρόν): no chance, Basil replies, unable even to enjoy the pleasures of eating now that he has lost all his teeth![30] It is in the nature of self-predications of old age to be subjective reactions, prompted by personal circumstances rather than arbitrary social categories.

This subjectivity is particularly evident in poetry. Philodemus's farewell to love (*AP* xi. 41), lamenting his grey hairs, was written when he was

25. It is remarkable how many sophists he lists lived to an active old age in their 70s.

26. "The Date of Jerome's birth," *Phoenix* 33 (1979), 346-53, with full bibliography; P. Hamblenne's attempt (*Latomus* 28 (1969), 1081-1119) to take Jerome's birth back to 386/7, while misguided, cites much material in Jerome bearing on old age.

27. *Miracula S. Artemii* ed. A. Papodopoulos-Kerameus, *Varia Graeca Sacra* (St Petersburg 1909), 13, 16, 22.

28. *Ep.* 117. D. Roques, *Études sur la Correspondance de Synésios* (1989), 26-35, presses texts outrageously to reach over-precise results: Cameron *JRA* 5 (1992), 419-30.

29. Epp. 176 of 374 (Basil was born between 329 and 331): "Basile n'avait pas beaucoup plus de quarante ans quand il écrivit cette lettre, et il se met au nombre des vieillards!," comments Basil's latest editor Y. Courtonne with evident surprise (*S. Basile: Lettres* II [Paris 1961], 113 n. 1). Similar comments might be cited on other texts assembled here.

30. *Ep.* 232 (of 376); cf. too *Ep.* 162 (of 374).

thirty-seven; Horace's *(Odes* iii. 26) when he was forty-two. *Odes* ii. 4
reassures the poet's friend that he can now admire a girl's beauty with
detachment *(integer)*, since he is past forty.[31] Another retrospective poem
(Odes iv. 3) that both recalls Callimachus's claim that the Muses blessed
his birth *(Quem tu, Melpomene, semel nascentem placido lumine videris)*
and claims to have survived the envy of his critics *(et iam dente minus mor-
deor invido)*, was published when Horace was fifty-two. Boethius draws a a
pathetic picture of his dotage:

> intempestivi funduntur vertice cani
> et tremit effeto corpore laxa cutis.

This is reminiscent of a well known exile poem by Ovid *(Tristia* iv. 8):

> iam mea cycneas imitantur tempora plumas,
> inficit et nigras alba senecta comas.
> iam subeunt anni fragiles et inertior aetas...

Ovid was fifty-five when he wrote this poem, depressed by his continuing
exile. Boethius was only forty-five, but awaiting execution in jail.[32]

When we are reduced to inferring a man's age from such vague and
often hyperbolical terminology, Renaissance attitudes are surely a better
guide than the guesses of an age with a life expectancy in the seventies. For
example, in *Brutus* 60 Cicero says that Plautus died in 184, and in *de sen.*
50 that as an old man the poet took great pleasure in his *Truculentus* and
Pseudolus. The birth date of 254 given in all the handbooks is simply a
combination from these two passages: if Plautus died a *senex*, he must have
been at least seventy in 184.[33] In the light of the passages here assembled,
it should by now be clear that he *might* have been much younger than seventy when he died. After all, Shakespeare retired when he was forty-nine.

We have seen that the epitaph on Callimachus's father (XXIX)
represents him proudly telling passers-by that he is the father and son of a
Callimachus; the one "commanded the arms of his fatherland," the other
"sang songs that silenced envy" (pp. 7; 78-79). Commentators on the
epitaphs preserved in the Anthology like to debate which are "real" and
which "literary," as though such a distinction could be made on the basis
of their form or tone alone.[34] Yet who could have guessed that John Gay's
cynical lines

> Life is a Jest, and all Things shew it,
> I thought so once, but now I know it

31. Nisbet and Hubbard, *Commentary on Horace's Odes* II (Oxford 1978), 76-77.
32. R. Syme, *History in Ovid* (1978), 38-39; Boethius, *Cons. Phil.* i. 1 m. 11-12.
33. E.g. G. Duckworth, *The Nature of Roman Comedy* (Princeton 1952). 49.
34. Gow and Page passim; Peek included in *GV* i those he considered "real" epitaphs.

would be inscribed (as they are) on his tomb?[35] Not that it matters whether the epitaph for Callimachus's father was actually inscribed. Grandfather Callimachus was certainly a real Cyrenean general of the mid-fourth century, and there seems no good reason to doubt that it was indeed the occasion of his father's death that prompted Callimachus to write the poem. A man might compose mock epitaphs on himself at any age and in any mood,[36] but it would be odd to write one for a father long after his death.

Few men are likely to be more than fifty at the death of their father. Yet (even if we exclude the third couplet of the epitaph as an interpolation), the description of Callimachus's songs as κρέσσονα βασκανίης unmistakably evokes the *Aetia* prologue, where the Telchines are described as βασκανίης ὀλοὸν γένος.[37] The epitaph for his father and the *Aetia* prologue were surely written at more or less the same time. If Callimachus lost his father around the time he was working on the *Aetia* prologue, he is unlikely to have been more than fifty at the time.

3

So the references to old age in the prologue are perfectly consistent with a date of composition ca 270. Yet whatever Callimachus's actual age when he wrote, why refer to it as many as three times in less than forty lines, and why in such harrowing terms?

At 35-6 he compares the weight of old age to the weight of Sicily pressing down on the giant Enceladus. As Pfeiffer saw, he took not only the image of Sicily but much of the context from Euripides *Heracles* 637f.[38] After protesting that old age is so burdensome (τὸ δὲ γῆρας ἄχθος βαρύτερον Αἴτνας σκοπέλων) that they would not trade youth for a palace full of gold, the chorus goes on to suggest that the virtuous be rewarded with a second youth. To this image Callimachus added a prayer adapted from a famous poem on old age by Alcman: "if only, if only I were a halcyon, flying over the flower of the wave."[39] This is where he found the conceit of escaping old age by taking to the air, though for Alcman's hal-

---

35. Alexander Pope, *Minor Poems* ed. N. Ault (London 1954), 349-52.

36. E.g. Callimachus's own symposiastic self-epitaph *AP* vii. 415, with Ch. III. 3.

37. Indeed, there can be little doubt that the *Aetia* prologue is the source of the interpolation. On its publication in late 1927, scholars at once saw its relevance to κρέσσονα βασκανίης in XXIX. 4, and this is surely why some ancient reader jotted a couple of lines from the prologue in his margin.

38. The phrase was to become proverbial (e.g. *onus se Aetna gravius dicant sustinere*, Cicero, *De senectute* 4, with J.G.F. Powell's note), but there can be no doubt that Callimachus had the passage of Euripides in mind.

39. οὔ μ' ἔτι...γυῖα φέρην δύναται· βάλε δὴ βάλε κηρύλος εἴην (*PMG* 26); ἱαρὸς ὄρνις in l. 4 is also echoed in the ἱερὸς ὄρνις of Callimachus F inc. 803.

cyon he substituted Plato's transformation of poet into cicada.[40] There may have been other influences too. P. Oxy. 3965 has given us an elegy in which Simonides expresses a wish to journey to the Isle of the Blest, where he hopes to shed old age, don a garland and enjoy the pleasures of an idealized symposium. Like Callimachus, Simonides's rejuvenated alter ego will continue singing.[41]

As these parallels illustrate, the references to old age prepare us for the poet's wish for rejuvenation, which is then actualized in the *Somnium*. Indeed the chorus in the *Heracles* conclude in the first person as an "aged poet...who will never abandon the Muses" (678-86), thus paralleling (and surely suggesting) Callimachus's closing claim that the Muses do not reject his grey hairs (37-8).

The three passages in the prologue are linked in a curious way. Not one of them alludes to old age by itself, but to old age juxtaposed with childhood. Modern critics have unhesitatingly taken the references to old age literally and ignored the other half of the antithesis. Yet it is the childhood motif that plays the key structural role in the transition from prologue to *Somnium*: the boy who wins the favour of the Muses and the privilege of tapping their aetiological expertise.[42]

The most puzzling of the three passages is F 1. 5-6:

ἔπος δ' ἐπὶ τυτθὸν ἐλ[αύνω]
παῖς ἅτε, τῶν δ' ἐτέων ἡ δεκὰς οὐκ ὀλίγη.

Since this accusation of writing "like a child" is put in the mouth of the Telchines, it looks as if the reference to his "years not a few" likewise formed part of their criticism. As Rostagni saw in a brilliant (if misguided) paper written within months of the publication of the prologue, in the mouth of his critics this reproach must have been intended to appear absurd, unfair or untrue. He therefore took the emphasis on old age to be ironical,[43] and ingeniously alleged a reference to the challenge to Cal-

---

40. *Phaedrus* 259BC; the dew it feeds on (cf. Theocr. 4. 16; Leon. *AP* vi. 120) may come from Hes. *Shield* 395: E. K. Borthwick, "A Grasshopper's Diet," *CQ* 66 (1966), 103-12; D. Boedeker, *Descent from Heaven* (Chico 1984), 43, 81-99; M. Davies and J. Kathirithamby, *Greek Insects* (Oxford 1986), 117-24.

41. West, F 22[2], with Parsons, P. Oxy. LIX (1992), 45-49; West, ZPE 98 (1993), 12-14. But the singing, central for Callimachus, is incidental to the other pleasures of the symposium for Simonides; see a forthcoming study by Sarah Mace.

42. It is tantalizing that the incomplete F 471 lacks a context: Μοῦσαί νιν ἑοῖς ἐπὶ τυννὸν ἔθεντο <γούνασι>, where τυννός is Doric for μικρός ("the Muses laid him on their <laps> when he was tiny").

43. "esagerazione ironica," *Riv. di Fil.* 57 (1928), 39; ib. 11 (1933), 207-08 he adds that, coming from the Telchines, the reproach of old age "ha, per sua natura, un valore interessato e sospetto." Herter 1937, 107 simply denied the irony: "unmöglich kann die wunderbare Art, wie sich K. zum Schluß mit seinem Alter abfindet, ironisch gemeint sein."

limachus recently issued by the youthful Apollonius.[44] Explanations in terms of a quarrel with Apollonius have now been rightly abandoned, but Rostagni's instinct was sound. Another hint that we are not meant to take the poet's complaints about old age altogether seriously is the bizarre juxtaposition of the braying of the donkey with the image of the cicada blithely singing as it feeds on dew and sloughs off its skin.[45] The mosaic of picturesque details drawn from famous earlier treatments of old age surely suggests that he is playing with the idea.

The old/young contrast surely formed some part of the criticism to which he purports to be replying, perhaps something on the lines of "old enough to know better." Many a love poet wrote a "farewell to love," a poem protesting that he was now too old for the pastimes of youth: Ibycus F 287, Anacreon F 358, Philodemus, *AP* xi. 41, or Horace, *Odes* iii. 26. It would have been tempting for a critic to retort that he was too old for poetry too.

If the old/young contrast did indeed feature somewhere in a criticism of Callimachus, then ironically (or suitably) enough that criticism may have played a part in suggesting the structure of the *Aetia*.

4

Two other texts relating to old age merit brief consideration. First, the so-called *Seal* of Posidippus, a 28-line elegy closing with a self-identification by the poet, lamenting a hateful old age and claiming to have been loved by Apollo and the Muses (*SH* 705). In view of Posidippus's identification as one of the Telchines (Ch. VIII), it is natural to wonder whether there is any significant connection between two such highly personal poems.

The epithet Cynthius Posidippus gives Apollo (line 9) is otherwise only found in Callimachus; indeed according to Clausen it was his invention.[46] Elsewhere it is always Posidippus who is the borrower (Ch. IX. 2), and if, as seems likely in view of his talk of the afterlife,[47] Posidippus (still alive

---

44. "Apollonio da giovane faceva quel che Callimaco alla sua età non era capace di fare," *Riv. di Fil.* 7 (1928), 5. Other objections aside, the explanation does not really work even on Rostagni's own terms, because at line 6 it is Callimachus who is said to write like a child, whereas his hypothesis would seem to require that Apollonius play this rôle.

45. γῆρας in l. 33 is the technical term for an insect's dead skin (Pfeiffer, *Hermes* 1928, 325-26). The conjunction of singing cicada and fearsome giant is incongruous enough in itself. But on top of that, Enceladus is not just the luckless giant pinioned beneath Sicily, but also the name of a stridulating insect like the cicada: Σ Ar. *Nub.* 158 (I.iii.1, p. 45 Holwerda); Davies and Kathirithamby 1986, 130.

46. *AJP* 97 (1976), 245-7; ib. 98 (1977), 362.

47. New light has been cast on the poet's claim μυστικὸν οἶμον ἐπὶ 'Ραδάμανθυν ἱκοίμην (*SH* 705. 22-23) by the discovery of a gold lamella from a cist-grave in Pella inscribed Φερσεφόνῃ Ποσείδιππος μύστης εὐσεβής (M. Lilimbake-Akamate, 'Αρχ. 'Εργ. Μακ. Θρακ. 3 (1989) [1992], 91-101). Even if the excavator is correct to date the grave to the second half

in 262) really was near death when he wrote, in all probability this is another case. Yet it is difficult to see any trace of polemic. Posidippus simply invites the Muses to leave Helicon, go to Thebes, and help him sing of old age; Apollo he apparently asks to continue favours enjoyed in the past. This can hardly be a response to Callimachus's polemic—nor is it easy to believe that Callimachus could have been provoked by Posidippus, for all the "faded imagery and stilted technique of the lesser writer."[48] Their quarrel (such as it was) may well have been restricted to the dispute about Antimachus's *Lyde* (Ch. XI).

I conclude, unsatisfactorily enough, that insofar as Posidippus is using Callimachean motifs, the imitation is inert and cannot help us interpret the prologue.

Second, F 41, quoted by Stobaeus from *Aetia* I:

γηράσκει δ' ὁ γέρων κεῖνος ἐλαφρότερον,
κοῦροι τὸν φιλέουσιν, ἑὸν δέ μιν οἷα γονῆα
χειρὸς ἐπ' οἰκείην ἄχρις ἄγουσι θύρην.

The old man whom young boys love ages with a lighter heart, the man they lead to his door by the hand as they would their own father.

Who is the speaker? Hardly Callimachus, whether speaking in his own person or as narrator. Presumably a character in some aetion. But after the enormous emphasis on the poet's old age in the prologue and the constant intrusion of the narrator into his stories, the reader is bound to be reminded of the poet—a poet, moreover, renowned for his pederastic epigrams. The fact that these boys treat the old man like their father excludes an explicitly erotic context, but the imitation in Tibullus i. 4. 79-80 does have erotic overtones. Here the poet envisages himself as an old man escorted home by boys he is instructing in the arts of love (*deducat iuvenum sedula turba senem*). Callimachus would not be the only writer to ascribe to one of his characters sentiments that, however appropriate within the context of his fiction, he nonetheless knew would make readers think of himself as well. If so, then on top of the other links discussed in Ch. IV-V, the old age motif too serves to link the prologue to the body of the poem.

---

of the 4th century, it is hard to doubt some connection between these two initiates from Pella called Posidippus: see M. Dickie, "The Dionysiac Mysteries in Pella," forthcoming in *ZPE*.

48. H. Lloyd-Jones, *JHS* 83 (1963), 98 = *Acad. Papers* ii (Oxford 1990), 194.

Chapter VIII

The Telchines

1

It is time to consider the identity of the Telchines. The starting point has to be the detailed though fragmentary list supplied by the Florentine scholia on F 1. Omitting the traces of three names that cannot be deciphered and the unidentifiable "two Dionysii," we are left with "Asclepiades also called Sicelides, and Posidippus...and Praxiphanes of Mytilene." In itself the list looks impressive. All are identifiable contemporaries of Callimachus: Praxiphanes did come from Mytilene; and, though from Samos, Asclepiades was also known as Sicelides (Ch. III. 2).

Nonetheless, since Callimachus himself neither named nor even hinted (as, for example, Pope did in his *Dunciad*) at the names of his enemies, this list cannot be based on first hand information. It must be guesswork. The point at issue is whether the guesswork is late and worthless or early and informed. Late and worthless, according to Mary Lefkowitz.

Building on her work on biographies of the classical poets, Lefkowitz not only dismissed the list as guesswork (Praxiphanes from Callimachus's book *Against Praxiphanes*; Asclepiades and Posidippus from epigrams praising a poem Callimachus disparaged), but even doubted whether the Telchines represented identifiable individuals at all:[1]

> Poets' statements about their own poetry, like the end of the *Hymn to Apollo* or the *Aetia* prologue, are particularly susceptible to misunderstanding. Anyone who has read the Pindar scholia will recognize the process: when the poet makes combative references to himself in opposition to others, the others are identified as specific individuals, Bacchylides or Simonides, no matter how generically they are described, whether as athletes, jackdaws, or as "shrill-voiced birds" or as a "pair of crows." But such statements are conventional; all archaic poets use them. Their function is to show the essential superiority of the present author.

This may well be true of Pindar. But there is a basic difference between Pindar and Callimachus. By the time commentaries came to be written on Pindar, there was no longer any possibility of discovering whether or not fellow poets lay behind those polemical allusions to jackdaws and crows.

---

1. Lefkowitz, *Lives of the Greek Poets* (Baltimore 1981), 120-121.

There were simply no sources from which genuine biographical details could be recovered. It may have been Hellenistic scholars who first identified Pindar's unspecified "envious" enemies as rival poets,[2] but they did so in part at least because they were used to seeing poets behave that way in third-century Alexandria, "ceaselessly wrangling in the bird-nest of the Muses." Indeed, there can be little doubt that Callimachus himself read Pindar this way. "I do not maintain a hireling Muse" (ἐργάτιν...Μοῦσαν), he wrote of Simonides, clearly echoing (as the scholiast noted) Pindar, *I.* ii. 6-7 (ἁ Μοῖσα γὰρ οὐ φιλοκερδής...οὐδ᾽ ἐργάτις). This is more than a verbal echo; Callimachus read into Pindar's text a reference to the greed for which Simonides was to become notorious.[3]

One possibility Lefkowitz does not allow for is that it was the practice of Callimachus himself that influenced Hellenistic interpretation of Pindar. It may be that Pindar did not attack rival poets, nor, two or three centuries later, could Hellenistic scholars have identified them if he had. But Callimachus did engage in controversy both with and about fellow poets, who cannot have been hard to identify. And recent papyrus finds reveal that annotated texts of Callimachus were being produced within a generation of his death (§ 9). Ancient identifications of Callimachus's enemies are not to be treated with the same disdain as those of Pindar. More generally, we should not view the *Lives* of the Hellenistic poets with the same scepticism as the *Lives* of the archaic and classical poets. Lefkowitz took too little account of the very different nature of the sources available for the lives of Hellenistic writers. To be sure, these sources have seldom survived in their original form, but much of what they said has been preserved in varying degrees of detail and accuracy in later compilations, chief among them Diogenes Laertius and Athenaeus.

Furthermore, it is the *Lives* of the Greek poets that Lefkowitz studied, not the lives of the Greek poets. Since the surviving versions of these *Lives* are mostly products of late antiquity, the end result of centuries of abridgment prefixed to Byzantine copies of their works, it is not surprising that they preserve little of value. But that does not mean that better information based on reliable sources never existed. Ion of Chios recorded anecdotes about Aeschylus and Sophocles in his *Visits*, and there is no reason to believe (as Lefkowitz has suggested) that these too were intended to link the dramatists to their dramas.[4] The Atthidographer Philochorus expressly repudiated the inference from comedy that Euripides's mother was a cabbage-seller, and pointed out that a much quoted line in his *Palamedes*

2. Though it is not impossible that the tradition may go back to Timaeus, who is cited a number of times in the Pindar scholia (*FGrH* 566 F 92-93, 96-97).

3. F 222; so too Theocritus (16. 22-57); Lefkowitz 1981, 50-51; *First-Person Fictions* (Oxford 1991), 158.

4. Lefkowitz 1981, 67-69, 75, 80-82; see now West, *BICS* 32 (1985), 75-76.

could not refer to the death of Socrates because Euripides died before Socrates. Theophrastus cited temple records to prove that Euripides was well-born.[5]

Popular biographies (like those of Satyrus in the third century) continued to reconstruct Euripides out of his own plays and old comedy, not because they knew no better, but because poets were supposed to resemble their creations. The public did not want to hear about a Euripides who was *not* a lower-class, misogynist misanthrope. But it may be a mistake to pay too much attention to biographies. The Attic dramatists aside, there is little evidence that anyone of note wrote formal biographies of poets before the Roman period. Philosophers were another matter, partly because in the popular imagination they seemed to typify the merging of private and professional life, partly because they really were important members of the community.[6] Philosophers had always been an object of fascination to the public, held up to (often good-natured) ridicule throughout the long history of Attic comedy, and honoured with statues that have been described as "among the most striking and enduring creations of Hellenistic sculpture."[7] A great many biographies of philosophers were written between ca 350 and 200 B.C.[8]

It may be that there never were any formal biographies of (say) Callimachus, Theocritus, Aratus and Apollonius in Hellenistic times. But this is not to say that the late antique *Lives* we find in the Suda lexicon or prefixed to their poems in Byzantine manuscripts contain nothing more than late antique guesswork based on their writings. Much prosopographical information about such poets was recorded in scholarly monographs and commentaries on earlier poets, biographies of philosophers and also more general histories and memoirs of the Hellenistic age. Another related genre that seems to have developed in this period is collections of sayings of famous philosophers, rhetors and poets. Though liable to misattribution, especially to more famous names, many of those attributed to lesser names inspire confidence.[9]

It was F. Leo who first drew attention to the fact that Peripatetic and Hellenistic scholars often discussed biographical and historical questions in monographs with titles like *Concerning Archilochus, Hipponax* and the like (Περὶ τοῦ Ἀρχιλόχου, Ἱππώνακτος, κτλ), since then known as περί-

5. *FGrH* 328 F 218 and 221, with IIIb Supp. (1954), 585-87 (citing Theophrastus).

6. C. Habicht, *Hellenistic Athens and her Philosophers* (Princeton 1988).

7. R.R.R. Smith, *Hellenistic Sculpture* (London 1991), 33-40, with plates; Ch. II. 3.

8. J. Mejer, *Diogenes Laertius and his Hellenistic Background* (Hermes Einzelschr. 40) Wiesbaden 1978, 60-95; F. Decleva Caizzi in Bulloch 1993, 303-29.

9. For example, sayings attributed to Theocritus of Chios (Ch. II. 5). The fullest such collection is the so-called *Gnomologium Vaticanum*, ed. L. Sternbach (Berlin 1963); no satisfactory modern study that I know of.

literature.[10] Most of this literature was naturally devoted to the archaic and classical writers, but by no means all. A certain Timarchus wrote at least four books *On* (περί) *the Hermes of Eratosthenes*, perhaps the contemporary of that name mentioned in the Suda *Life* of Apollonius.[11] Athenaeus cites a work *On the Theriaca of Nicander* by Diphilus of Laodicea.[12] And studies of earlier writers often discussed passages of Hellenistic poets in illustration. A good example is the long extract from the first-century B.C. Asclepiades of Myrlea's treatise *On Nestor's Cup*, whose rambling erudition seems to underlie much of Bk xi of Athenaeus—in particular, the source for the interesting discussion of the drinking vessels used in the Pollis episode in *Aetia* II (Ch. V. 1).

Despite the triviality of much that has been handed down about Menander, that is no reason (with Lefkowitz) to dismiss as guesswork stories that link him with Demetrius of Phaleron, Epicurus and Theophrastus.[13] The contemporary Lynceus of Samos, brother of the tyrant Duris and himself a disciple of Theophrastus, wrote a treatise *On Menander* (Περὶ Μενάνδρου) in at least two books. To judge from his other works (known from a number of quotations in Athenaeus), Lynceus was fascinated by the trivial and anecdotal, but it would be absurd to suppose that a contemporary who lived in Athens and even wrote comedies himself preserved nothing of value. Though mainly concerned with Menander's plays, Lynceus is bound to have touched on numerous biographical and prosopographical details, details on which he undoubtedly had first-hand information.

Apollonius the son of Sotades wrote a book *On the poems of his father*, which evidently discussed in detail Sotades's various abusive poems on Ptolemy Philadelphus and other kings of his day. A certain Carystius of Pergamum wrote another work *On Sotades*, and *Historical Notes* in at least three books in which he reported a variety of anecdotes about Hellenistic Kings and dynasts, hetairas, philosophers and poets (including Nicander).[14] Carystius is cited much later in the Theocritus scholia (13. 22). A detailed account of the final arrest and execution of Sotades was included in the *Historical Notes* of Hegesander of Delphi, another collection of stories

10. "Didymos περὶ Δημοσθένους," *NGG* 1904, 254-61 = *Ausgew. Kleine Schriften* II (1960), 387-94.

11. Athen. 501E; cf. Wilamowitz, *Glaube der Hellenen* ii[2] (1956), 314 n. 3.

12. Athen. 314D; M. Wellmann, *RE* V. 1 (1903), 1155-56.

13. Lefkowitz 1981, 113-14, 116; R. L. Hunter, *The New Comedy of Greece and Rome* (Cambridge 1985), 152 n. 7, rightly deprecates her "blanket scepticism...[that] ignores the channels of information open to ancient scholarship." On the links between Menander's plays and Theophrastus, Hunter pp. 147-151.

14. Athen. 620F; Nic. F 127 Schneider; on Carystius, F. Jacoby, *RE* X.2 (1919), 2254-55; *FHG* IV. 356-59. His date depends in part on which Nicander is meant (below).

about Kings and courtiers, hetairas, philosophers and poets.[15] He tells a
nice story about the early third-century poet Antagoras of Rhodes and
Antigonus (presumably Gonatas):[16]

> [Antagoras] was once cooking a dish of conger-eels[17] in the camp with his
> apron on,[18] when King Antigonus, who was standing by, asked him: "Do you
> think, Antagoras, that Homer could have written up the deeds of Agamemnon
> if he had cooked conger-eels?" To which Antagoras made the excellent reply:
> "Do *you* think that Agamemnon could have done those deeds if he had fussed
> about who in his army cooked conger-eels?"

He also comments on evidence of Syracusan usage in the epigrams of
Theodoridas of Syracuse, and describes how Euphorion once urinated into
a drinking cup at a symposium of the philosopher Prytanis.[19] To be sure,
such tales contribute little to the history of literature, but they do at least
confirm the later traditions that Antagoras lived for a while at the court of
Gonatas in Pella and that Euphorion was a pupil of Prytanis of Carystus.[20]

Diogenes Laertius's sources provided him with a number of epigrams
by the poets of the early third century on various philosophers of the age.
For example, he cites one on Crantor by Callimachus's friend and fellow-
Cyrenean Theaetetus (iv. 25);[21] another by Antagoras on Crates and
Polemo, and seven hexameters attributed to Antagoras but described as
spoken by Crantor.[22]

Aratus is quoted three times in Diogenes Laertius: vii. 166 links him
with Dionysius of Heraclea; ix. 113 with Alexander Aetolus and Timon of
Phlius; and ii. 133 with Lycophron and Antagoras at the symposia of the
philosopher Menedemus in Eretria.[23] Another disciple of Menedemus was
the future King of Macedon Antigonus Gonatas (ii. 141). As we shall see,
all eight of these names reappear in the later *Lives* of Aratus. In two cases
at least the ultimate source of both Diogenes and the *Lives* is not in doubt:

15. F. Jacoby, *RE* VII.2 (1912), 2600-02; cf. M. Launey, *REA* 47 (1945), 33-45.

16. Athen. 340 F = F 15 in *FHG* IV 416; Plut. *Mor.* 182F, 668D.

17. γόγγροι, a "mighty dish," D'Arcy Thompson, *Glossary of Greek Fishes* (1947), 50.

18. περιεζωσμένῳ: cf. Alexis F 174. 11; Anaxandr. 41. 2; Arist. *Birds* 1148.

19. F 38 and 21 = Athen. 229A and 477E.

20. Suda E. 3801; on Prytanis, see the Athenian inscription published by B. D. Meritt,
Hesperia 4 (1935), 525f.; L. Moretti, *Iscriz. storiche ellenistiche* no. 28.

21. On Callimachus and Theaetetus, see E. Livrea, *SIFC* 82 (1989), 24-31.

22. Diog. iv. 21, whence *AP* vii. 103; Diog. iv. 26; Wilamowitz, *Antigonos von
Karystos* (Berlin 1881), 69-70; Livrea 1989. Perhaps the hexameters come from a longer
poem in which Crantor was an interlocutor. *AP* ix. 147 celebrates a bridge built ca 320 by a
rich Athenian, Xenocles son of Xeinis (C. Habicht, *Hesperia* 57 [1988], 325); if by
Antagoras, hardly contemporary. See too *HE* II. 29; von der Mühll, *Mus. Helv.* 19 (1962),
28-32.

23. On Menedemus, in addition to Wilamowitz 1881, see now D. Knoepfler, *La vie de
Ménédème d'Érétrie de Diogène Laërce* (Schweiz. Beitr. 21, Basel 1991), 170-203.

the well-informed Antigonus of Carystus. Antigonus is known to have
written biographies of both Menedemus and Timon; he is cited twice by
name on the same page that names both Aratus and Alexander Aetolus (ix.
112-3). He gave a vivid account of Menedemus's rather frugal dinner
parties, of which Athenaeus quotes a detailed excerpt, including a dozen
lines from what was evidently Antigonus's source, the first-hand account of
dinner with Menedemus in a satyr-play by none other than Lycophron.[24]

There are also other pointers to early sources. *Vita III* cites a most
authoritative source for the presence of Persaeus, Antagoras and Alexander
at the court of Antigonus Gonatas: Gonatas himself, in a work either about
or addressed to Hieronymus, evidently that loyal Antigonid servant and
later historian Hieronymus of Cardia.[25] Not surprisingly, no such work is
otherwise attested (it may have been no more than a letter), but a personal
relationship between Gonatas and Hieronymus is implied by Pausanias's
remark that the historian wrote "to please Antigonus."[26] It may, as Jacoby
suggested, have been an invitation to Hieronymus to join the literary and
philosophical circle of Gonatas's court (which would explain the list of its
leading lights). A biographer of the Roman age is not likely to have come
across such a document at first hand. He will surely have found it already
quoted in his source, evidently an early source, perhaps (but not necessarily) Antigonus of Carystus.

Unfortunately, Callimachus did not frequent the philosophical circles of
Eretria. Antigonus of Carystus may also have shared Timon's lack of
enthusiasm for the poets of Alexandria,[27] since in his collection of wonders
he refers slightingly to Egyptian poets in general (19. 3) and Callimachus
in particular (45. 2).[28] But Hermippus was a pupil of Callimachus, and is
bound to have mentioned his master from time to time in his biographies.
That on Hipponax certainly quoted Philitas[29] and surely also Callimachus,
who had posed as Hipponax *redivivus* in his *Iambi*.

---

24. Wilamowitz 1881, 31-43 (Timon), 86-102 (Menedemus); 124-5 (Dionysius). For a
more recent sketch, A. Dihle, *Studien zur griechischen Biographie* (Göttingen 1956); 107-
115; A. A. Long, *Proc. Camb. Phil. Soc.* 24 (1978), 68-69. On the circle of Menedemus,
W. W. Tarn, *Antigonus Gonatas* (Oxford 1913), 22-26.

25. *FGrH* 154 T9: περί MSS, πρός Ruhnken; J. Hornblower, *Hieronymus of Cardia*
(Oxford 1981), 15.

26. i.13.9; cf. 1.9.7; F 15 and 9 Jacoby.

27. Wilamowitz 1881, 163-68; Timon, *SH* 786.

28. Edited by A. Giannini, *Paradox. Graec. Rel.* (Milan 1966) and O. Musso, *[Antig.
Car.] Rerum mir. Coll.* (Naples 1985). I am assuming that Wilamowitz was right to attribute
this work to the biographer (1881, 16-26; Fraser II. 657 n. 62). Musso insists that the extant
text consists of Byzantine extracts (ed. p. 9; *Prometheus* 2 [1976], 1-10), but since they cite
no source later than Callimachus and Myrsilus of Lesbos (*FGrH* 477), we need not doubt that
they are extracts of Antigonus.

29. F. Wehrli, *Hermippos der Kallimacheer* (Basel 1974), F 93 = Athen. 327b.

The earliest known commentary on Callimachus's *Aetia* is that of the Augustan scholar Theon, son of Artemidorus, who also commented on Pindar, Sophocles, Theocritus, Nicander, Lycophron and Apollonius.[30] That is to say, he was something of a specialist on the Alexandrian poets. But we should not make the mistake of supposing that this was either the first commentary on Callimachus or that it was a work of original research. We may compare the rôle he played in the history of the Pindar scholia. Thanks to the unusually informative and well preserved ancient scholia, we know that more than twenty different commentators contributed to the elucidation of the *Olympian, Pythian, Nemean,* and *Isthmian Odes* in the 250 years between Zenodotus and Didymus.[31] Didymus seems to have digested what he could of this embarrassment of scholarly riches, and produced a comprehensive commentary on at any rate these four books of Pindar. The publication of P. Oxy. 2536,[32] the last two columns of what is described in the colophon as a "commentary (ὑπόμνημα) on the *Pythians* of Pindar by Theon, son of Artemidorus" has confirmed (against Irigoin) Deas's thesis that Theon did the job again a generation later.[33]

E. G. Turner, who published this find, postulated a process of excerpting to "mitigate a little of the disappointment that will be felt during an

---

30. C. Wendel, Theon 9, *RE* V A (1934), 2054-59.

31. H. T. Deas, "The Scholia Vetera to Pindar," *HSCP* 42 (1931), 1-78; J. Irigoin, *Histoire du Texte de Pindare* (Paris 1952).

32. E. G. Turner, *Greek Manuscripts of the Ancient World*[2] (1987), no. 61.

33. Irigoin placed Theon before Didymus (1952, 65; cf. Gow, *Theocr.* I. lxxxii). But according to his Suda-entry, Didymus flourished ἐπὶ Ἀντωνίου καὶ Κικέρωνος. The Antony is surely not Cicero's colleague in the consulate for 63, but the triumvir: "in the days of Antony and Cicero [ca 43] and up to Augustus" (no later than ca 20 B.C.). Theon has no entry of his own, but the grammarian Apion attacked by Josephus is said (a) to have been the θρεπτός, house-slave, of Didymus; (b) to have succeeded Theon; (c) to have taught in Rome under Tiberius and Claudius; and (d) to have been the contemporary of Dionysius of Halicarnassus. These four indications do not quite tally. Dionysius came to Rome in 30 and published his *Roman Antiquities* in 7 B.C., implying a maximum lifespan of ca 60 B.C.-10 A.D. But Apion was still teaching at Rome in the reign of Claudius (41-54), confirmed by the fact that the elder Pliny, born in 23 A.D., saw him as a young man (the 40s A.D.), and in the last book of his *NH* (published in 77) refers to a work Apion published *paulo ante* (30.18 and 37.75; L. Wickert, *PIR*[2] A. 918; E. Schürer, *History of the Jewish People* rev. G. Vermes, F. Millar, M. Goodman III. 1 [Edinburgh 1986], 604-5). If he was really a slave of Didymus (Suda A. 3215), it must have been near the end of his life; it would be natural for Didymus to have trained his more promising slaves to assist him (P. Foucart, *Étude sur Didymos* [Paris 1906], 10-11). For θρεπτοί playing this rôle, see Vett. Valens, iii. 13. 16 (perhaps it was in this sense that Agatharchides was the θρεπτός of Cineas, cf. Fraser II. 744 n. 183; Ister was the δοῦλος καὶ γνώριμος of Callimachus). If Apion succeeded Theon, that will have been at Alexandria, and the only time Apion is known to have lived in Alexandria is under Gaius (Josephus, *AJ* 18. 257f.). Theon's professional life must have fallen under Augustus and Tiberius. The following round maximum termini would accommodate all the data we have on the relations between the three scholars: Didymus: 80-1 B.C.; Theon: 50 B.C.-20 A.D.; Apion: 20 B.C.-60 A.D.

examination of the present work."[34] As Turner himself was well aware, this was the same expedient H. Diels had used to mitigate the shortcomings of the Berlin Didymus commentary on Demosthenes published in 1904. More recently Stephanie West took a cooler and sterner look at the Didymus papyrus, claiming that its many defects "cast grave doubt on his reliability and general competence."[35] She pointed out that its most serious shortcomings could not be explained by careless selection or compression. Much of what we have is positively verbose. West instances one section that "could be condensed to a quarter of its present length...without losing anything of substance"; and another where "Didymus has combined two authorities...without adequately digesting them." It is clear that Didymus did little in the way of original research. That had all been done in the preceding two centuries: treatises by a variety of scholars on such questions as authenticity (with a substantial contribution by Callimachus), dating, historical interpretation, language and rhetoric.[36] Didymus did for Demosthenes what he did for Pindar and a host of other classical texts, simply combining his many authorities (not a few at second hand) into comprehensive commentaries. Theon did the same for the Alexandrians.[37]

Much less is known about Hellenistic exegesis of the Hellenistic poets,[38] but there can be little doubt that here too Theon was mainly a compiler of the work of his predecessors. In the case of Nicander, he had at least two predecessors: Demetrius the Pale (ὁ χλωρός) and Antigonus of Alexandria.[39] Demetrius must be the earlier, since Antigonus is twice quoted as rebutting him in the extant scholia (585, 748).[40] Then there is the monograph by Diphilus already mentioned. That the autobiographical opening and closing sections of the *Theriaca* provoked scholarly discussion and controversy we know from the *On Poets* of Dionysius of Phaselis, dis-

---

34. P. Oxy. xxxi (1966), p. 17.

35. "Chalcenteric Negligence," *CQ* 20 (1970), 288-96; E. M. Harris, *CP* 84 (1989), 36-44 ("hasty and slipshod"); briefly, W. S. Barrett, *Euripides Hippolytus* (Oxford 1964), 48.

36. M. J. Lossau, *Untersuchungen zur antiken Demosthenesexegese* (Wiesbaden 1964), 66-128 (pp. 81-5 on Callimachus). For some shortcomings in Callimachus's work on the orators, K. J. Dover, *Lysias and the Corpus Lysiacum* (Berkeley 1968), 20-26.

37. It is tempting to link Theon's activity with the enthusiasm for Alexandrian poetry manifest in the generation of Catullus—or later of the Emperor Tiberius. But there is nothing to link Theon with Rome; he seems to have worked in Alexandria, and the papyri document continuous Egyptian interest in Callimachus during the first and second centuries A.D.

38. The brief sketch in Wilamowitz, *Einleitung in die griechische Tragödie* (Berlin 1889), 186-93 is mainly concerned with the post-Theonic period.

39. It is not perhaps quite so certain as Wilamowitz (1889, 189) and Gow (1953, 16 n. 2) believed that either wrote full commentaries rather than (like Diphilus) a monograph (περὶ τῶν Νικάνδρου Θηριακῶν). The fragment of a commentary on *Ther.* 377-95 published as P. Oxy. 2221 (= *SH* 563) casts no fresh light.

40. The citation of Demetrius of Phalerum as a commentator on Nicander in Steph. Byz. s.v. Κορώπη (F 208 Wehrli) must be a slip for Demetrius the Pale (as Wehrli saw).

cussed below. There is no reason to date any of these critics later than the first century B.C.[41]

The only case we can follow in any detail, that of Aratus, is perhaps not typical, not least because (as we shall see) Aratus is the only major Hellenistic poet on whom Theon did not work. Monographs and commentaries began to appear within a century of Aratus's death. The first known, in at least four books, was by Boethus of Sidon, a Stoic philosopher of the early to mid-second century.[42] Then came another by Attalus of Rhodes, soon followed by yet another (still extant), from the greatest astronomer of the age, Hipparchus of Rhodes,[43] mainly concerned to attack Attalus and expose Aratus's astronomical incompetence. Several more appeared in quick succession, all (it seems) on Rhodes, by Dionysius Thrax, Posidonius, the latter's pupil Diodorus and an otherwise unknown Eudorus, all before the age of Augustus.[44]

A valuable study by Robin Schlunk showed that the *Aeneid* was influenced by interpretations we now read in the Homer scholia,[45] though of course he was not able to identify the form in which Vergil read them. E. Courtney has recently pointed out that *Buc.* vi. 61-3 may derive from the scholia to Theocritus 3. 40-42.[46] Since the *Bucolics* predate Theon, it is less certain than Courtney thought that Vergil got his information from a formal commentary on Theocritus. But even if no full-scale commentary on Callimachus and Theocritus appeared before Theon, this does not exclude a variety of scholarly monographs—or annotated diegeseis. For in general the early Hellenistic age produced monographs and treatises, leaving it to the grammarians of the Roman age to condense their results into commentaries.

It is important to rehearse these facts in this context, because it is customary, when a modern critic is faced with erudite comments on a Callimachus papyrus or a text of the early empire, to assume derivation from Theon or even his successor Epaphroditus.[47] In the case of late antique

41. The commentary by Pamphilus (Suda II. 142) must be later than Theon: Wendel, *RE* XVIII.3 (1949), 336-349.

42. Susemihl I. 62-63; J. Martin, *Histoire du Texte des Phénomènes d'Aratos* (Paris 1956), 20; the four books are attested in Geminus 27. 48. Probably a continuous exposition rather than a commentary, since Geminus uses the term ἐξήγησις, and *Vita II* of Aratus the phrase ἐν τῷ πρώτῳ περὶ αὐτοῦ (p. 12.15 Martin).

43. Datable observations cited in his Aratus commentary range from 161-26 B.C.: O. Neugebauer, *History of Ancient Mathematical Astronomy* I (Berlin 1975), 275-6.

44. Martin 1956, 31; Neugebauer 1975, 840; cf. H. Diels, *Doxogr. Graeci* 19-20. Geminus's Introduction to Aratus was dated as early as 70/50 B.C. by its editor, G. Aujac (*Géminos* [Paris 1975], 19-24), but not before ca 50 A.D. by Neugebauer 1975, 579-81.

45. R. R. Schlunk, *The Homeric Scholia and the Aeneid* (Ann Arbor 1974).

46. *Quad. Urb.* 34 (1990), 103; *Schol. Theoc.* p. 127-8 Wendel.

47. An assumption that vitiates A. Rengakos's discussion in *WS* 105 (1992), 39-67. G. Coppola cited the Schol. Flor. as "Epaphroditus" without qualification (*Cirene e il nuovo Callimaco* [1935], 170-73). For the little that is known about Epaphroditus, see now L.

grammarians or Byzantine scholia, these commentaries may indeed have been the intermediaries. But there is no reason to believe the information itself no earlier than the age of Augustus. And earlier and better sources may often still have been available in the first and second centuries.

The concluding chapter of Lefkowitz's book bears the title "Hellenistic Poets," but it is in fact almost entirely· devoted to the *Lives* of Apollonius and the modern fable of his quarrel with Callimachus. This is understandable, given the importance of this quarrel in modern works on Hellenistic poetry. But it is also highly misleading. The *Lives* of Apollonius are an easy target. In their lack of any genuine ancient erudition they contrast strongly with the *Lives* of some other Hellenistic poets. So before turning to the *Lives* of Apollonius and Callimachus, let us first examine the *Lives* of Aratus and Nicander, poets who were contemporaries of Callimachus, linked both to him and to each other.

2

The most interesting feature of the *Lives* of Aratus and Nicander[48] is the traces they preserve of a dispute about the date of Nicander. *Vita I* of Aratus states roundly that "those" who make Nicander a contemporary of Aratus are mistaken (ψεύδονται): "for Antigonus [Gonatas], at whose court Aratus lived, was a contemporary of the first and second Ptolemies, while Nicander lived in the days of the fifth Ptolemy" (p. 8. 25f. Martin). *Vita IV* makes the same point in even more explicit terms. After synchronizing Aratus, Antigonus and Philadelphus, the writer continues: "so that the common view (τὸ διαθρυλλούμενον) of some that Aratus was a contemporary of the Nicander who wrote the *Theriaca* is patently false (καταφανῶς ψεῦδος); for Nicander lived twelve full Olympiads later" (p. 20. 10 f.). According to the *Life* of Nicander, the poet lived "in the days of the last (τελευταῖον) Attalus, who was deposed by the Romans, whom he addresses as follows" (quoting five hexameters addressed to an Attalus). As we shall see, these lines are probably in fact addressed to Attalus I, whose reign overlapped with that of Ptolemy V. The *Lives* of Aratus and Nicander as we have them have no doubt passed through a variety of redactions, but it seems natural to infer that this view on the date of Nicander was originally formulated by the same commentator. Let us call him the Critic.

Lehnus, *Sileno* 20 (1994).

48. For the five *Lives* of Aratus, Martin 1956, 151-95 and his *Scholia in Aratum Vetera* (Stuttgart 1974), 6-22; for Nicander, A. Crugnola, *Scholia in Nicandri Theriaka* (Milan 1971), 33-34.

The "common view" the Critic attacks is well documented. *Life B* of Theocritus synchronizes Theocritus, Aratus and Nicander, without even suggesting that there was an alternative possibility. And *Vita IV* of Aratus begins by synchronizing Alexander Aetolus, Callimachus, Menander and Philitas. Martin's edition should have mentioned Ritschl's conjecture Νικάνδρῳ for Μενάνδρῳ;[49] an Attic comedian of an earlier generation would be entirely out of place here.

What annoyed the Critic particularly in *Vita I* of Aratus was the story that, though Aratus was in reality a doctor and Nicander an astronomer, King Antigonus told Aratus to write on astronomy and Nicander on medicine. The story has rightly been dismissed ("plainly fictitious," Gow), but it is more than bad biography; it is, of course, a *joke*—a joke made up to explain why both poets wrote on subjects they knew nothing about. It is also a joke that would lose its point unless the two poets were thought to have been *contemporaries*. That does not (of course) prove the story contemporary. It has been argued that it should be later in origin than Hipparchus's attack on Aratus's astronomical competence,[50] but that does not follow either. Despite Hipparchus's attack, Aratus's reputation continued to grow rather than decline. The inventor of the story was well enough informed to know that Aratus spent time at the court of Antigonus. Since it is a story that the Critic is anxious to refute, it was evidently well established in the biographical tradition before his day.[51] For example, it was clearly known, if in a slightly different form, to Cicero, writing in 55 B.C.: compare the following passage of *De Oratore* (i. 69):

> scholars agree that Aratus, a man completely ignorant of astrology, wrote a most polished and excellent poem about the heaven and stars, and Nicander of Colophon, a man who knew nothing about the country, wrote admirably about country affairs in a poetic, not rustic style.

As a translator of Aratus, Cicero is bound to have had a copy of his own, no doubt equipped with whatever commentary was then available. We do not need to assume, with Knaack, that Cicero read a version of the story in a *Life* of Aratus prefixed to his text of the poem.[52] We do not know whether this was the format of Hellenistic editions, nor does it much matter. It is enough that Cicero knew the story, several decades before the earliest possible date for Theon. Already in the Greek tradition, there are

---

49. Quoted by Schneider, *Nicandrea* (Leipzig 1856), 11; cf. the heading Μενάνδρου Ναννοῦς in Stob. 3. 11. 2, where obviously we must correct to Μιμνέρμου. For another (less likely) possibility, Jacoby, *FGrH* IIIb (1955) p. 404.

50. B. Effe, *Hermes* 100 (1972), 501.

51. It seems to have given rise to the idea that Aratus wrote medical poetry himself: *SH* 92-98; F. Kudlien, *Rhein. Mus.* 113 (1970), 297-304; B. Effe, *Hermes* 100 (1972), 500-03.

52. *Hermes* 23 (1888), 312-14.

variations on the original version. In *Vita II* Aratus is a doctor by profession whose best friend was Nicander the mathematician, and (for no stated reason) they simply exchanged poems.

In the Nicander *Life* as we have it, the earlier chronology is not mentioned, but since the later chronology is justified by a quotation that takes up a quarter of the *Life*, we are perhaps entitled to assume that the biographer is implicitly rejecting it. The extant versions of all these *Lives* are reduced and simplified versions of longer and more elaborate texts; in this case the polemic of the Aratus *Lives* may simply have been omitted.

Can we identify, or at any rate assign an approximate date to this Critic? As we have seen, Theon wrote commentaries on Callimachus, Lycophron, Theocritus, Nicander and Apollonius. Furthermore, the extant *Lives* of these poets are all characterized by synchronisations (σύγχρονος, ἰσόχρονος, συνήκμαζε) with most of the others. It will not have been a contemporary who drew up such a list.[53]

The earliest synchronized list of contemporary writers in a biography seems to be a passage in Marcellinus's *Life of Thucydides* (late antique in its present form but based on much earlier sources).[54] It cites the *On History* of Callimachus's contemporary Praxiphanes (of whom more below) for the synchronisation of Thucydides with Plato the comic poet, Agathon the tragedian, Niceratus the epic poet, Choerilus and Melanippides.[55] It is unlikely that these men were exact contemporaries; Agathon indeed may have been as much as twenty years younger than Thucydides. As Wilamowitz pointed out long ago, the context suggests that they met at the court of Archelaus of Macedon (ca 403-399) where three of them are known to have died,[56] and Hirzel added the conjecture that they were all interlocutors in a dialogue by Praxiphanes, like his *On Poets* in which Plato was represented conversing with Isocrates.[57]

Some of the poets synchronized in the *Lives* of Aratus, Nicander and Theocritus lived at the court of Gonatas, but hardly all, and *Vita IV* at least draws a distinction between Aratus "living with" Gonatas and "living at the same time as" various fellow poets.[58] Whether or not these syn-

---

53. These synchronisms are quite different from the synchronisms based on birth, acme and death in the late second century *Chronicle* of Apollodorus: A. A. Mosshammer, *The Chronicle of Eusebius and Greek Chronographic Tradition* (Lewisburg 1979), 113-27.

54. See the detailed anaylsis by Bux in *RE* 14. 2 (1930), 1450-87; for Hellenistic scholarship on Thucydides, O. Luschnat, *Philol.* 98 (1954), 22f.

55. συνεχρόνισε δ', ὡς φησι Πραξιφάνης, ἐν τῷ περὶ ἱστορίας (F 18 W) Πλάτωνι τῷ κωμικῷ, Ἀγάθωνι τραγικῷ, Νικηράτῳ ἐποποιῷ καὶ Χοιρίλῳ καὶ Μελανιππίδῃ, *V. Thuc.* 29.

56. "Die Thukydideslegende," *Hermes* 12 (1877), at pp. 353-61.

57. Diog. Laert. 3. 8; R. Hirzel, *Hermes* 13 (1878), 46-49; F. Wehrli, *Phainias von Eresos, Chamaileon, Praxiphanes* (Basel 1957), 112; A. Momigliano, *The Development of Greek Biography* (1971), 66-67.

58. συνῆν δὲ Ἀντιγόνῳ...συνήκμασε δὲ Ἀλεξάνδρῳ τῷ Αἰτωλῷ...p. 19. 5-7 Martin.

chronisations were introduced into the biographical tradition by the same scholar, it seems unlikely that all derive from one source.

Was it Theon who made these synchronisations? Or was Theon rather the Critic who disputed them? What matters is not so much the identity of the Critic as his place in the tradition: Hellenistic, Roman or Byzantine? Some details in the *Lives* are certainly no earlier than the first century, and so might be ascribed to Theon. For example, the well-founded rejection of Asclepiades of Myrlea's claim (*On grammarians* Bk 11) that Aratus came from Tarsus on the basis of the mention of Soloi in the "knowledgable and reliable Callimachus";[59] followed by the remark that Soloi is "now" known as Pompeiopolis (in fact since 65 B.C.).[60] If Theon is the synchronizer, then the synchronisations are no earlier than the age of Augustus, and the Critic who disputed them later still.

Against the identification with Theon, it must be noted that Aratus, whose name appears in all these synchronisations, is the one major first generation Hellenistic poet Theon seems *not* to have worked on. The Theon of Alexandria to whom *Vita III* of Aratus is attributed in a fifteenth-century Ambrosian manuscript[61] is undoubtedly the well-known Theodosian astronomer[62] rather than the Augustan philologist. For this same manuscript carries Theon the astronomer's commentary on Ptolemy's *Handy Tables*. Martin insists nonetheless, not only that it was the Augustan Theon who wrote this biography, but also that he was responsible for what Martin calls the "Alexandrian edition" of Aratus.[63] This is most improbable.

The extant scholia on Aratus are substantially different in character from the extant scholia on Callimachus, Theocritus, Lycophron and Nicander. The many parallels between the scholia on the latter strongly support the assumption that the extant scholia derive ultimately from a series of commentaries written by the same man—presumably Theon.[64] They are the sort of scholia we might expect a philologist to compile. The Aratus scholia, in contrast, are largely astronomical—the sort of commentary we might expect an astronomer to compile. This is not to say that the extant Aratus scholia owe much or indeed anything to Theon the astronomer. We

59. Καλλιμάχου πολυΐστορος ἀνδρὸς καὶ ἀξιοπίστου Σολέα λέγοντος, *Vita I*.

60. A.H.M. Jones, *Cities of the Eastern Roman Provinces*[2] (Oxford 1971), 202.

61. C 263 inf. (A): Martin 1956, 51; id. *Scholia in Aratum vetera* (Stuttgart 1974), xii.

62. Alan Cameron and Jacqueline Long, *Barbarians and Politics at the Court of Arcadius* (Berkeley 1993), 44-47.

63. Martin 1956, 196-204; accepted by W. Ludwig in *RE* Supp. X (1965), 27; but against see R. Keydell, *Gnomon* 30 (1958), 579-80; Pfeiffer 1968, 121 n. 4. In his edition of the scholia, Martin restated his theory without comment (1974, p. iv).

64. C. Wendel, *Die Überlieferung der Scholien zu Apollonios von Rhodos* (Abh. Göttingen 1932), 108; E. Scheer, *Lycophronis Alexandra* II (1908), liv-lviii; H. T. Deas, *HSCP* 42 (1931), 31-42 (collecting parallels between the Pindar and Theocritus scholia); Theon's work on Pindar has been confirmed by P. Oxy. 841. ii. 37 and 2536.

have seen that a whole series of commentaries on Aratus appeared before Theon, and the emphasis of their work (most notably Hipparchus) was decidedly astronomical rather than philological. The modern critic sees Aratus as just another Alexandrian poet, and pays as little attention to the astronomy as he can get away with. Not so ancient readers. In the eyes of contemporaries, Theon's familiarity with Theocritus, Nicander and the other Alexandrians would not have equipped him to take Aratus in hand. He lacked the requisite technical competence.

So if (the Augustan) Theon did not work on Aratus, there is no case for identifying him as the author of the synchronisations. They were surely made much earlier. On chronological grounds alone there would be a better case for identifying Theon as the Critic—were it not for the fact that it is precisely in the *Lives* of Aratus that the Critic's hand is most apparent. To be able to dispute whether Nicander lived in the first half of the third or second half of the second century, and to refer (however inaccurately) to the cession of Pergamum to Rome, the Critic cannot have lived earlier than the first century B.C.—and might be much later.

Is the Critic's attack on the earlier chronology of Nicander justified? There are two quite separate issues here. First, however valid or invalid the inferences he drew from the five lines addressed to Attalus, the Critic shows no awareness of the crucial fact that there were *two* poets called Nicander of Colophon. About this there can be no doubt whatever. The first is attested by an inscription at Delphi datable to 254/3; the second by the lines on Attalus.[65] The earlier is clearly stated on his proxeny inscript ion to have been the son of Anaxagoras; the later calls himself the son of Damaios (υἱῆα πολυμνήστοιο Δαμαίου, quoted by the same commentator).[66] That they were related is strongly suggested by the fact that, on the available evidence, the name Damaios is exclusively Delphian.[67] In recollection of his long and successful stay at Delphi (we might conjecture), the elder Nicander named his son after a prominent Delphian connection. The two poets may have been grandfather and grandson. So whenever we date the later Nicander, the earlier clearly flourished during the reign of Philadelphus (283-246). The earlier Nicander was indeed a contemporary of Callimachus, Theocritus, Aratus and Lycophron.

65. *SIG*[3] 452; G. Pasquali, "I due Nicandri," *SIFC* 20 (1913), 55-111; J. Beloch, *Gr. Gesch.* IV. 2[2] (1927), 574-9; W. Kroll, *RE* 17. 1 (1936), 250; A. S. F. Gow and A. F. Scholfield, *Nicander* (Cambridge 1953), 3-8; F. Jacoby, *FGrH* 271-2 (IIIa [1954], 229-248); E. V. Hansen, *The Attalids of Pergamon*[2] (Ithaca 1971), 423-431.

66. His Suda *Life* names Xenophanes as father, which must be an error; in the light of Anaxagoras, it looks as if a philosophically-minded copyist confused his philosophers (cf. Gow, p. 8 n. 1). At all events, as Pasquali happily put it, "Nicandro ha troppi padri per poter essere una persona sola" (*SIFC* 20 [1913], 64).

67. *nomen illud rarissimum alibi, si quid video, omnino non exstat*: so Dittenberger in his valuable note on *SIG*[3] no. 452 on p. 452, citing the evidence.

It seems clear that later commentators did not know this. For two of the Aratus *Lives* (*II* and *IV*) claim that Aratus was a contemporary of a *mathematician* called Nicander of Colophon. This figure was evidently created out of the anecdote that Aratus and Nicander wrote on each other's subjects, an alternative way of dealing with the imagined chronological blunder of making the poet Nicander· his contemporary. To have been reduced to such lengths these commentators simply cannot have known that there really was a poet Nicander active before the mid third century.

Before we go any further with the biographical tradition, it will be useful to establish when the younger Nicander lived and which of the two wrote the extant poems. Here again there are two issues: what did the Critic think, and what is the true date? *Vita I* of Aratus dates its only Nicander to the reign of Ptolemy V (204-181), which would harmonize nicely with the statement in *Vita IV* that he lived "twelve full Olympiads later." Later than when? If later than the end of the reign of Philadelphus (283-246), that takes us to 198. So far so good. The problem is that the *Life* of Nicander places him under "the last Attalus to rule Pergamum, who was deposed by the Romans." The last Attalus should be Attalus III (138-3), though he was not "deposed" (κατελύθη) by the Romans, but bequeathed the kingdom to them in his will. The Suda *Life* of Nicander says that he lived under the "new" Attalus (τὸν νέον Ἄτταλον), which should mean Attalus II (159/8-138), repeating in the same words that he was the "last" (implying Attalus III) and was "deposed" by the Romans. Thus far the indications agree, but the Suda *Life* also calls him "victor of the Gauls" (Γαλατονίκην), which unmistakably points to Attalus I (241-197). This is a much more attractive possibility, since the reign of Attalus I overlaps with that of Ptolemy V (204-181) by nearly ten years. On a strict computation we could then assign the younger Nicander to the period 204-197; we have already seen that twelve Olympiads after Philadelphus is 198. One of the younger Nicander's poems may have been datable to ca 200.

Amid such contradictory indications, which do we follow? Γαλατονίκην could be an interpolation. Since our commentator seems to have thought that the five lines of Nicander he quoted support his chronology, it may be worth looking at them a little more closely (F 104):

Τευθρανίδης, ὦ κλῆρον ἀεὶ πατρώϊον ἴσχων,
κέκλυθι μηδ' ἄμνηστον ἀπ' οὔατος ὕμνον ἐρύξῃς,
Ἄτταλ', ἐπεί σεο ῥίζαν ἐπέκλυον Ἡρακλῆος
ἐξέτι Λυσιδίκης τε περίφρονος, ἣν Πελοπηΐς
Ἱπποδάμη ἐφύτευσεν ὅτ' Ἀπίδος ἤρατο τιμήν.

Scion of Teuthras, who continues to maintain the heritage of your fathers, listen and thrust not away from your ear, out of mind, my hymn. For I have heard, Attalus, that your stock dates back to Heracles and sage Lysidice,

whom Hippodameia the wife of Pelops bore when he won the lordship of the
Apian land.

Pelops won Hippodameia for his wife and the "Apian land" by defeating
Oenomaus in a chariot race. Their daughter Lysidice was the mother of
Alcmene and so grandmother of Heracles. Apis, son of Phoroneus and
Teledice, was once master of the Peloponnese,[68] but there was also an
Apian plain in Pergamene territory,[69] so a double allusion may have been
intended. Teuthras was a legendary king of Mysia, adoptive father of his
son and successor Telephus, natural son of Heracles and Auge. According
to Gow and Scholfield, these "genealogical pretensions of the Attalids seem
otherwise unrecorded." Perhaps not in extant literature, but abundantly (for
Heracles at any rate) in coins and inscriptions, and the Telephus saga is
prominently depicted on the reliefs of the great altar of Pergamum.[70] In
fact they are not so much the pretensions of the Attalids as the traditional
claims of Pergamum. As we shall see in the following chapter, the other
Diadochi also claimed descent from Heracles, but by a different route, in
virtue of a dubious claim to kinship with the Argead royal house of
Macedon. That is to say, the claim rested on their original Macedonian
descent, while the claims of the Attalids rested from the beginning on the
local traditions of Pergamum.[71]

Some early commentator may have thought that these lines of Nicander
pointed to Attalus III rather than Attalus I; for example, that the reference
to Attalus "continuing to maintain the heritage of his fathers" (κλῆρον ἀεὶ
πατρῷον ἴσχων) implied a late member of the dynasty. It would certainly
suit Attalus II or III, but it should be noted that the poet goes on to explain
his reference in mythological terms: in the context, this heritage is surely
the heritage of Teuthras and Telephus, Heracles and Pelops. This would
suit Attalus I at least as well as any of his successors.

Moreover there is a detail in these lines that would suit Attalus I better
than his successors. The mention of both Pelops and Hippodameia, by no
means the most conspicuous among the mythological forbears of the
Attalids, inescapably calls to mind the chariot race in which Pelops
defeated Hippodameia's father Oenomaus and won her hand, the earliest
and best known legend of Olympia and in a sense the charter legend of the
Olympic games. Now Attalus I's own father, also called Attalus, won the
chariot race at Olympia—apparently more than once. A monument was

---

68. Roscher I. 421-22, Apis 2. The hero himself was Ἄπις, the Peloponnese Ἀπίς or
Ἀπία: Rhianus, F 13 (*CA* p. 12); Eratosthenes F 5 (p. 59); McLennan on Call. *HZ* 14.

69. Hansen, *The Attalids* 208; R. E. Allen, *The Attalid Kingdom* (Oxford 1983), 40.

70. L. Robert, "Héraclès à Pergame," *Rev. de Phil.* 58 (1984), 7-18.

71. Heracles appears already on the coinage of Philetairus the first dynast, who always
proudly styled himself Περγαμεύς (Robert 1984, 15); for local traditions about Pelops,
Habicht, *Pausanias' Guide to Ancient Greece* (Berkeley 1985), 14.

erected in commemoration at Pergamum, the work of the celebrated Pergamene sculptor Epigonus, prominently sited in the precinct of the temple of Athena[72] and inscribed with a long and particularly fine epigram, badly worn but fortunately still legible.[73]

Another document reveals that this victory continued to be a political asset to the future Attalus I long after the event. Diogenes Laertius has preserved an epigram by the philosopher Arcesilaus of Pitane, who ended his career as head of the Academy. The epigram is addressed to an Attalus:[74]

Πέργαμος οὐχ ὅπλοις κλεινὴ μόνον, ἀλλὰ καὶ ἵπποις
πολλάκις αὐδᾶται Πῖσαν ἀνὰ ζαθέην.
εἰ δὲ τὸν ἐκ Διόθεν θεμιτὸν θνατῷ νόον εἰπεῖν,
ἔσσεται εἰσαῦτις πολλὸν ἀοιδοτέρη.

Pergamum is not famed for arms alone, but often hears its praises resound at holy Pisa for its horses. If it is permitted for a mortal to express the mind of Zeus, she will be more famous still in the future.

Arcesilaus was an intimate of Eumenes I (263-241), and it seems likely that "arms" refers to Eumenes's greatest feat of arms, his defeat of Antiochus I near Sardis ca 262,[75] freeing Pergamum from Seleucid suzerainty. This victory was commemorated by another monument erected in the precinct of the temple of Athena.[76] The possible years for the older Attalus's Olympic victories are 272, 268 and 264. Since the monument is the signed work of Epigonus, still active in 226, we should probably conclude that Arcesilaus's "often" in fact means twice, in 268 and 264. Attalus's second Olympic victory fell only two years before Eumenes's victory in battle. It would be natural for a contemporary poet to have linked these successive, complementary demonstrations of the arrival of Pergamum in the front rank of Greek states.

Which Attalus is Arcesilaus addressing, and what exactly is the point of the poem? According to Page, he is addressing the father of the future king and brother of Eumenes I, predicting the future greatness of his (Attalus's) son. This is possible. It may have been common knowledge that Eumenes was planning to make the younger Attalus, his grandnephew, his successor. But Eumenes can hardly have adopted the young man (which he did at a

72. A. Schober, *JDAI* 53 (1938), 126-49; *Die Kunst von Pergamon* (Vienna 1951), 51. On the temple of Athena, H.-J. Schalles, *Untersuchungen zur Kulturpolitik der Pergamenischen Herrscher im dritten Jhdt.* (Tübingen 1985), 5-22 (pp. 76-77 on Epigonus).

73. L. Moretti, *Iscrizioni agonistiche greche* (Rome 1953), no. 37, pp. 93-99; J. Ebert, *Griechische Epigramme auf Sieger* (Berlin 1972), 176-81; Schalles 1985, 44-45.

74. D. L. 4. 38; Page, *FGE* 18-19.

75. On the date, R. E. Allen, *The Attalid Kingdom* 20-21.

76. *Inschr. von Pergamon* I. 15; Schober 1951, 51; Allen 1983, 20 n. 40.

date unknown) before his natural father's death. And, given the normal vicissitudes of longevity and remarriage, the succession will not have been assured until after the adoption.[77] So it is perhaps more likely that it is the younger Attalus Arcesilaus is addressing, after the adoption but before the succession. Arcesilaus did not die till 241, the very year of Attalus's succession. The twin victories of the first couplet would then be those of both his natural and his adoptive father, and the greater glory prophecied for the future would be his own—an impeccably tactful compliment.

All the more precise indications in the *Lives* of Aratus and Nicander converge on a date ca 200. The Attalus addressed in F 104 looks like Attalus I, and only Attalus I could properly have been styled "victor of the Gauls." We may surely conclude, not only that Attalus I was the younger Nicander's addressee, but also that this was the opinion of our commentator. The rather vaguer references to a "new" or "last" Attalus we might assign to still another scholiast (there are obviously numerous strata in all these *Lives*). Someone may have misunderstood an explanation of F 104 that distinguished Attalus the addressee from Attalus the Olympic victor as ὁ νέος Ἄτταλος. νέος is regularly used to distinguish the younger of two homonyms in contexts where they might be confused, normally for a limited period and without reference to earlier or later bearers of the name.[78] In the case of texts that carried no clear chronological pointers (like poems), this usage was peculiarly liable to lead to mistaken identifications in later times. It was almost inevitable that a reference to "Attalus the younger" with no clear context would later be identified as King Attalus II or III.

3

So the two Nicanders were active from ca 280-250 and ca 200 respectively. Which wrote the extant *Theriaca* and *Alexipharmaca*? The younger, according to almost all modern critics. It is difficult to see why. First and most obvious, the synchronisation with Aratus, especially the joke about the doctor and the astronomer trading subjects, unmistakably identifies the earlier poet as the author of the most famous of the "medical" poems attributed to Nicander. Second, the only evidence adduced is literary. Gow

---

77. The most comprehensive treatment of Attalid genealogy is now Allen 1983, 181-94.

78. Thus Σέλευκος ὁ νέος = Seleucus III in Polybius 4.48.7; ὁ νεώτερος Ἀντίοχος = Antiochus IV (Polyb. 16. 8. 8); ὁ ν. Πτολεμαῖος = Ptolemy VII, thus distinguished from his brother and co-ruler ὁ πρεσβύτερος, Ptolemy VI (Polyb. 29-23.4 and often). For examples from contemporary inscriptions, S. V. Tracy and C. Habicht, *Hesperia* 60 (1991), 232-3; for a full list of other examples in Polybius, A. Mauersberger, *Polybios-Lexikon* I.4 (1975), col. 1650. In the later empire νέος is used as a synonym for Latin *iunior* in the same way: Cameron, *ZPE* 56 (1984), 159-72.

and Scholfield drew attention to some parallels between Nicander, Euphorion and Numenius of Heraclea, assuming in each case that Nicander was the imitator.[79]

In at least one passage one of the two clearly imitates the other,[80] but since Numenius wrote much earlier than hitherto realized, there are no useful chronological consequences. Numenius[81] can only be dated by the doctor Dieuches who is said to have been his teacher. Earlier scholars agreed in placing Dieuches at the beginning of the third century,[82] in which case Numenius "cannot well have written before the middle of the third century" (Gow). The evidence is a passage of Galen listing Dieuches along with ten other names as "ancient doctors" (Diocles, Praxagoras, Erasistratus, Pleistonicus, Phylotimus, Mnesitheus, Dieuches, Chrysippus, Antigenes, Medius, Euryphon), contrasted with more recent figures (τοὺς μετ' αὐτούς) such as Herophilus and Eudemus.[83] But Herophilus flourished in the first half of the third century,[84] and only one of the names on the first list is later than the fourth century.[85] Dieuches is usually bracketed with Mnesitheus, and their sons, doctors again, are mentioned together on an ex-voto from Athens that on well-documented epigraphic grounds cannot be later than the first half of the fourth century. Dieuches himself must have flourished well before the middle of the fourth century, and his pupil Numenius is unlikely to have been active much later than ca 300.[86]

79. Gow and Scholfield 1953, 7 n. 1.

80. See Gow on *Ther.* 237 and 256; and *SH* 589-92.

81. *SH* 568-82, referring only to Diller's unsatisfactory entry in *RE* Supp. VII. 663.

82. Susemihl I. 812; Wellmann, *RE* 5 (1903), 480, no. 3.

83. XV. 136. 1f.Kühn = *CMG* V. 9. 1. 69-70 = test. 69 in H. von Staden, *Herophilus: The Art of Medicine in Early Alexandria* (Cambridge 1988), 191-92.

84. 330/20-260/50: von Staden 1988, p. 50; Eudemus, often bracketed with Herophilus, seems undatable: ib. 62-63.

85. Erasistratus, who is said to have diagnosed the illness that was destroying the future Antiochus I—love for his father's wife (Plutarch, *Demetr.* 38). The story is hardly credible in its developed form, but there seems no call to doubt that Erasistratus was at the court of Seleucus I ca 293: see von Staden 1989, 47 (arguing that he was Herophilus's contemporary, not junior as earlier assumed).

86. *IG* II^2 4359, with J. Kirchner, *Pros. Attica* (1901), 3748, 3765, 10182 (dated to 400-350); in every case OY is written O, and "private texts contain no convincing examples of O for OY later than ca 330" (L. Threatte, *Grammar of Attic Inscriptions* I [Berlin 1990], 258). W. Jaeger (*Diokles von Karystos* [Berlin 1938], 226 n. 2), followed by S. Dow (*Bull. Hist. Med.* 12 [1942], 18-26, argued that this ex-voto commemorated not the famous Dieuches and Mnesitheus, but their grandfathers. Medicine may have been a hereditary profession, and it is true that one list in Ps. Galen (xiv. 683 Kühn) implies a later date for Mnesitheus. But while the ex-voto gives two Mnesithei, the two sons of Dieuches it gives bear different names. J. Bertier, *Mnésithée et Dieuchès* (Leiden 1972), 9, brings Dieuches down to the end of the fourth century on the grounds that "on situe" Numenius in the third, apparently under the impression that there is evidence for the date of Numenius independent of the date of Dieuches.

So the older Nicander, whose only known date is 254/3, must in any case have written long after Numenius. As for the parallels with Euphorion, they are simply not close enough to offer any clear pointer to priority. Since Euphorion was not active before the second half of the third century,[87] he could easily have borrowed from the older Nicander, a contemporary of Aratus and Callimachus.

Hollis lists 14 parallels between Nicander and Callimachus's *Hecale*,[88] of which I would accept at least five. In this case, no one could be in much doubt that Nicander is the borrower. But the *Hecale* seems to have been an early work, written before the *Aetia* (Ch. XVII. 1). The older Nicander could easily have read and imitated a poem written in the 270s.

The same applies to the handful of rather dubious echoes of Aratus, Theocritus and Apollonius alleged in Nicander.[89] Aratus and Theocritus are not usually dated later than ca 270, and it will be argued in the next chapter that there is no compelling reason to date the *Argonautica* later than the 260s. Even if it were allowed that these parallels are in every case imitations by Nicander, they could still have been written by a poet active in 254/3.

If it was the older Nicander who wrote the *Theriaca* and *Alexipharmaca*, we shall have to think again about the distribution of the fragments between the two poets. Beloch assigned most of the numerous titles and works handed down under the name of Nicander to the older, Jacoby to the younger.[90] The older competed at the sacred festivals. Recitations on snake bites and poisons might be hard to swallow, but some of the lost works reveal a wide interest in local history and legend; suitable excerpts from these would have made ideal public performances. According to the *Life*, Nicander "lived mostly in Aetolia, as is clear from his writings about Aetolia and from the rest of his poetry, accounts of the rivers and places of Aetolia." It is clearly to this Nicander that we should assign a *Thebaïca*, *Aetolica*, *Oetaïca* and perhaps a *Boeotica*.[91] Since the Aetolian League had lost all its political power and cultural attractions by 189 B.C., it seems most natural to identify the author of these poems with the older poet, the one honoured at the cultural centre of the League at Delphi.[92] If so, then it should be pointed out that the longer fragments of the *Oetaïca* are as full of obscure fish names as the *Theriaca* are of obscure snake names. Indeed all

---

87. On the chronology of Euphorion, Fraser, *Gnomon* 28 (1956), 578-82.

88. Hollis 1990, 30 and 389.

89. Gow and Scholfield, p. 7 n. 1.

90. See the lists in *FGrH* 271-72; M. Drury, *CHCL* I (1985), 822; R. Keydell, *KP* IV (1972), 96-97; for the new fragments, *SH* 562-563A.

91. ἐν Βοιωτιακῶν, Athen. 329A (= Jacoby F 13): ἐν β΄ Οἰταϊκῶν Dindorf (cf. Athen. 410F, ἐν β΄ Οἰταϊκῶν).

92. G. Nachtergael, *Les Galates en Grèce et les Sôtéria de Delphes* (1975), 329f.

the fragments are so homogeneous in style and diction that most should surely be assigned to the author of the extant didactic poems, namely the older poet—unless we are willing to assume (as Gow acidly remarked) that "the combination of a repulsive style with considerable metrical accomplishment which links [the fragments] to the *Theriaca* and *Alexipharmaca* was hereditary in the family."[93]

4

We may now return to the biographical tradition. There is a passage in the scholia on Nicander that reveals the same polemic against the same earlier chronology. According to what must be an early scholion, the kinsman Hermesianax addressed in line 3 of the *Theriaca* (φίλ᾽ Ἑρμησιάναξ, πολέων κυδίστατε παῶν), was "the friend and pupil of Philitas; he wrote a *Persica* and a poem on his mistress Leontion." This is answered by what must be a later scholion as follows: "Nicander cannot mention this person in his apostrophe, because Philitas is older than Nicander. Indeed Nicander himself mentions Hermesianax as being older in his book *On the poets of Colophon*" (apparently a scholarly monograph in prose). Once again, the later commentator (the Critic again) is evidently unaware that there were two Nicanders.

Moderns, overly impressed by the Critic's alertness to chronology and "a confidence which suggests some positive and adverse information,"[94] have been too ready to assume that he knew what he was talking about. But how well informed was he? He refers to *On the poets of Colophon*, but did he really consult it at first hand? This book must have been the work of the younger Nicander. But what would someone writing ca 200 have meant by referring to the poet Hermesianax "as an older man"? Hermesianax lived a full century earlier than the younger Nicander. If it was the younger poet who wrote the *Theriaca*, he cannot have foreseen that the contemporary Hermesianax to whom he had recently dedicated his poem would be confused by posterity with the poet Hermesianax the disciple of Philitas. In any case, a book on the poets of Colophon written ca 200 must have included the earlier Nicander, securely attested by a Delphian public decree of 254/3 as "Nicander of Colophon." If the Critic had actually read this book, he could not have formulated his argument as he did. He would have known that there were two Nicanders, one of whom was indeed the contemporary of Aratus, Callimachus, Theocritus and Lycophron he was mistakenly trying to excise from the biographical tradition.

---

93. Gow and Scholfield—drawing, however, the opposite inference, that "all seem likely to belong to the younger man" (p. 8).

94. Gow and Scholfield 1953, 7.

If he had known this, he would have realized that he was faced with a quite different set of questions. Which Nicander wrote the *Theriaca*? If the younger, that was the answer to give. If the older, that still left open the question of his relationship to Philitas and Hermesianax. Philitas and Hermesianax undoubtedly belonged to the generation before Callimachus, but there is no good evidence that they died before ca 280/70,[95] and since Hermesianax is said to have been the pupil of Philitas, he at least might well have known the older Nicander (who might have been his pupil; both were Colophonians). Since the only date we have for Nicander is 254/3, the probability is against, but it was a matter that could only be settled by someone with a precise knowledge of the relative dates of all three poets. Indeed, it is just the sort of point the younger Nicander would have been in a privileged position to settle when discussing his grandfather in *On the poets of Colophon*.

The form of his argument proves that the Critic only knew this work at second hand, through a citation in some earlier commentary or monograph. There is at least one other second-hand citation in the *Life* of Nicander. It begins with two citations, one after another, from Dionysius of Phaselis. According to the first, in a book *On the poetry of Antimachus*, Dionysius maintained that Nicander was "Aetolian by birth" (γένος), a claim reflected in the statement in his Suda-entry that "according to some he was an Aetolian." Dionysius can hardly have said that Nicander was *born* Aetolian, since the Delphian decree formally styles the older poet a Colophonian, and Dionysius himself is represented in the second citation, from his *On poets*, as claiming that the younger poet was a hereditary priest of Clarian Apollo, a shrine just outside Colophon. This latter claim is borne out by *Ther*. 958, quoted by the scholiast. If the younger Nicander was a hereditary priest of Colophon, the family must have been Colophonian for several generations. What Dionysius must have said is that Nicander was rewarded for his services to the Aetolian League with Aetolian citizenship, and that he lived in that part of the world for some time. We have seen that the older Nicander seems to have married a Delphian wife and wrote a number of poems on Aetolian subjects.

Fortunately, the date of Dionysius Phaselites can be fixed within fairly narrow limits, on the basis of three mentions in the Pindar scholia. On *Pyth*. ii (II. 31. 4 Dr.) he is quoted among a group of third- and second-century Pindar commentators, the latest in date being Ammonius the successor of Aristarchus. Then on *Nem*. xi inscr. he is cited in a context that itself clearly derives from Didymus. Lastly, on *Ol*. x. 55 he is cited as if later than Aristodemus the pupil of Aristarchus. Aristarchus's death is usually placed ca 144, and Didymus flourished in the second half of the

95. Fraser II. 883 n. 61.

first century B.C. Taken together, these various hints conspire to put Dionysius in the first half of the first century. So he wrote perhaps a century after the younger Nicander. The passage cited must refer to the older, but it is likely that in his *On Poets* Dionysius discussed both Nicanders. It might easily have been through a citation in Dionysius that the Critic derived his knowledge of the younger Nicander's *On the Poets of Colophon*. And given the link between Nicander and Aratus in the biographical tradition, it is tempting (with C. Müller) to identify as the Phaselitan the Dionysius cited in *Vita III* of Aratus (p. 17. 12 Martin) for a work entitled *On the comparison of Aratus and Homer*. All these Dionysius citations are probably at second hand. Did he really discuss the biography of Nicander in two separate works, or is *On the poetry of Antimachus* simply one part of a larger work *On Poets?*[96] A good parallel would be provided by Dionysius of Halicarnassus's *On the Ancient Orators*, which consists of a series of separate books entitled *Lysias, Isocrates, Isaeus* and so on. It may be that the two Dionysius citations derive from different sources, combined by a later biographer unable (or too lazy) to check his references. The work on Aratus and Homer might also be a part of this larger work. Books by Dionysius of Phaselis cannot have remained long in circulation outside the libraries of Alexandria and Pergamum.

Of course, the information included in these biographies in their extant form is trivial enough. But in their extant form they are no earlier than late antiquity, perhaps even Byzantine. We know that the extant *Life* of Lycophron was written by Tzetzes, last in a long line of redactors, combining, rearranging and confusing the data of his predecessors. The Critic, hitherto singled out as a voice of sanity and shrewdness among these scholiasts, falls late in the tradition and on a closer inspection cuts a much less impressive figure.

The reassessment of the Critic has serious consequences for the assessment of the biographical tradition in general. Hitherto it has been assumed that all these biographies were vitiated by a glaring chronological error. Knaack referred to the Nicander synchronisation as a "foolish invention"; Martin (repeatedly) as a "mistaken tradition" or even "legend."[97] If such an error could infect all these biographies, then what else in them could be trusted?

But if the argument advanced here is accepted, at one stroke we have eliminated not only the glaring error, but also the more general cloud of suspicion it engendered. Whatever their shortcomings, the basic chronological framework of the biographies of Aratus and Nicander is sound. In

---

96. So L. Cohn, *RE* V. 1 (1903), 984, no. 136.

97. G. Knaack, *Hermes* 23 (1888), 313 ("thörichte Erfindung"); Martin 1956, 163, 167, 173, 175; Effe, *Hermes* 1972, 501 ("eine wuchernde, legendäre Ausgestaltung.").

particular, we have seen that the synchronisation of Aratus, Alexander
Aetolus, Antagoras, Lycophron, Menedemus and Timon goes back (no
doubt through a long chain of intermediaries) to the biographies of their
younger contemporary Antigonus of Carystus. The shortcomings are
generally of a sort to be expected in the long process of transmission and
abridgment by ever less qualified scholars and copyists. For example, the
substitution of the more familiar name Menander for Nicander in *Vita IV* of
Aratus; or the omission of even less familiar names like Antagoras from all
but *Vita III* (and the Suda); and the mention of Persaeus the Stoic in *Vita
III* and *IV* alone. *Vita I* describes Gonatas as the son of Demetrius Poliorcetes and says he married Phila the daughter of Seleucus and Stratonike.
Every name and every relationship is correct. The Suda *Life* describes Phila
as "daughter of Antipater and wife of Antigonus." Here the first detail is
not correct, but neither is it nonsense. For the elder Phila, Antigonus's
mother, was indeed the daughter of Antipater. We have only to assume that
a reference to (or distinction between) the two Philas was telescoped in the
process of abridgment.

Only the Suda *Life* preserves the names of his teachers Timon,
Menedemus and Menecrates of Ephesus, where again, for the first two at
least, we seem to have a tradition deriving from Antigonus of Carystus.
According to *Vita IV*, Aratus studied with Persaeus in Athens, and followed him to Antigonus Gonatas's court (p. 20. 3 Martin). Both details
seem to be well founded. Diogenes Laertius places Aratus together with
Antagoras and Lycophron in the circle of Menedemus in Eretria (ii. 133);
and Persaeus at the court of Gonatas (ii. 143-4; vii. 6; 36); vii. 12-3 suggests that Persaeus too was mentioned by Antigonus of Carystus. Pausanias
mentions Aratus and Antagoras together at the court of Gonatas (i. 2. 3).[98]
Vita IV says that Aratus was summoned by Gonatas for his wedding to
Phila, and then (with *Vita I*) dates his accession to the throne of Macedon
to the 125th Olympiad, that is to say 277/6 at the latest. This date is
nowhere else directly attested, but agrees with all other indications.[99] *Vita
III* also gives a succinct but accurate account of every stage in the transactions that preceded Gonatas's accession: Seleucus's claim to the throne, his
murder by Ptolemy Keraunos (correctly described as son of Soter and
Eurydice), Keraunos's defeat by the Celts and finally the generalship of
Sosthenes (correctly *not* described as king) before Gonatas took charge.[100]

There is also a small but telling detail of vocabulary. In *Vita III* and *IV*,
the term used to describe Aratus's residence at the courts of both Gonatas

98. H. Usener, *Kl. Schr.* III (1914), 405-06.

99. Tarn, *Antigonus Gonatas* (1913), 112 n. 2 and 166 n. 104; N.G.L. Hammond and
F.W. Walbank, *History of Macedonia* III (Oxford 1988), 1988, 582-83.

100. For the sources, Hammond and Walbank 1988, 243-58—omitting *Vita III*.

and Antiochus I is διατρίβειν (παρά). This was (of course) standard Greek for staying at someone's house, but in the third century, though seldom found in literary sources,[101] it became the commonest formula in the honorific inscriptions of the Greek cities for living at a court. As G. Herman has shown, the Greek cities were ambivalent towards those who enjoyed royal favour, despising them as flatterers and parasites while court-ing them for favours in turn.[102] Whence the neutral formulas and avoidance of court titles in early Hellenistic city decrees. Here at least we find traces of early terminology as well as good information in the *Vitae*. The same term is used in Eratosthenes's Suda-life for his residence at the court of the Ptolemies.

According to *Vita II*, Aratus taught astronomy (μαθήματα) to Dio-nysius of Heraclea,[103] known as "the Renegade" because he deserted the Stoics for the Cyrenaics; according to *Vita I* and *IV*, it was Aratus who studied with Dionysius. Neither Aratus nor Dionysius makes a plausible teacher of astronomy, and the truth (or at any rate something closer to it) is probably to be found in Diogenes Laertius (vii. 167): early in his career Dionysius dabbled in poetry and took Aratus as his model (Ἄρατον ἀπεδέχετο, ζηλῶν αὐτόν). There is no reason to doubt that some more or less accurate information about the relations of Aratus with all these poets and philosophers was available in one or more second- or first-century B.C. commentaries or monographs on Aratus, and was drawn upon by the ear-liest biographers. As the centuries passed, details were dropped, misunder-stood or corrupted, resulting in the five extant redactions.

In the book or books of Dionysius Phaselites we have identified one of the many specialized pre-Theonian monographs that supplied later biog-raphers with information on Nicander and Aratus. If Dionysius himself had nothing on Callimachus, there must have been a number of such works that did. Callimachus is mentioned three times in the Aratus *Lives*. First, his famous epigram on the *Phaenomena* (*Ep.* 27) is quoted, in full or part, in three of the five *Lives*. Second, according to *Vita I* (p. 9. 6 Martin), "Callimachus refers to Aratus as an older man not only in his epigrams but in his *Against Praxiphanes*." This has often been dismissed as a guess, on the grounds that since Callimachus did not mention Aratus's age in *Ep.* 27 there is no reason to believe that he did so in the *Against Praxiphanes* either.[104] But there may once have been other epigrams in which he men-

101. Note however Polyb. 3. 11. 1 (Hannibal παρ᾽ Ἀντιόχῳ διέτριβε); cf. 3. 19. 8; this phrase appears 24 times in inscriptions from Athens, Samos, Delos and Ephesus.

102. "The "Friends" of the Early Hellenistic Rulers: Servants or Officials?," *Talanta* 12/13 (1980/81), 103-49.

103. See von Arnim, *RE* 5. 1 (1903), 973-74, no. 119.

104. Wilamowitz, *HD* I 212 n. 1 ("wer lobt, jünger sein soll"); Hutchinson 214 n. 1.

tioned Aratus, and why should a scholiast have foisted his guesses on a lost refutation of the (by then) obscure Praxiphanes?

It is true that this statement appears to be contradicted by another in *Vita IV* (p. 21. 4) that Aratus "overlapped[105] the Cyrenean as an old man" (γηραιῷ δὲ τῷ Κυρηναίῳ ἐπεβάλετο), but it is a simple matter to correct "old" here from dative to nominative (γηραιὸς δέ) and apply it to Aratus, not Callimachus. Since both go on to cite Callimachus's epigram, there is a clear pointer to the agreed common source of these biographies.[106] It is therefore proper to see whether they can be reconciled and suggestive that it can be done so easily. Third, these same two points are linked in slightly different terms in a Latin translation of *Vita III* from the seventh century (and so despite its inadequacies reflecting an earlier text than the surviving Greek versions):[107] "[Aratus] was very learned, as Callimachus attests, who met him as a boy because of Praxiphanes of Mytilene."[108] Once again, not the contradiction it might appear: when the meeting took place, Aratus was old and Callimachus young. There is no mention in this *Life* of the *Against Praxiphanes*, but since we know that Callimachus had dealings of some sort with both Praxiphanes and Aratus, it seems natural to see all three texts as differing abridgments of an originally fuller citation from this book, describing how the two poets met "because of" the man after whom it was named, Praxiphanes.

5

How and where did they meet? Rohde argued that any such meeting could only have taken place in Athens.[109] Until the publication of what is now F 178 in 1918, Athenaeus's reference to the symposium of the Athenian Pollis (477C) seemed solid evidence for residence in Athens. Since its publication, the Ician guest's remark, "thrice blessed...*if* you have a life ignorant of sea-faring" (line 33), has been widely treated as evidence no less solid that Callimachus never left Alexandria.[110] But quite apart from

105. So LSJ s.v. ἐπιβάλλω II. 9, citing parallels for this rare meaning.

106. Martin 1956, 151-195.

107. E. Maass, *Comm. in Aratum reliquiae* (Berlin 1898), xxxvi-xliv.

108. *factus est autem nimis multum litteratus vir, sicut testatur Callimachus adsistens ei ab infantia propter Praxiphanem Mytilenum*; ἐγένετο δὲ σφόδρα πολυγράμματος ἀνήρ, ὡς μαρτυρεῖ ὁ Καλλίμαχος is all that survives of the original Greek (p. 16. 12f. Martin). *adsistens* appears again on the preceding page of *Vita III* (p. 15. 24), where the Greek original is ἐπιστα θεὶς δὲ τῷ βασιλεῖ, apparently "meeting the king" (Bauer-Arndt-Gingrich, *New Test. Lex.* s.v. ἐφίστημι). For earlier discussions, K.O. Brink, *CQ* 40 (1946), 12-14.

109. *Der griechische Roman*³ (Leipzig 1914), 106-07 n. 3; cf. Susemihl I. 287 n. 10; Cahen 1929, 27.

110. *se numquam mare periculosum transiisse expressis verbis dicit*, Pfeiffer II. xxxix; Trypanis 1958, viii n. c; Fraser II. 1028 n. 122; "certo non amò viaggiare," Lehnus 1993, 90 (citing F 178. 4-9).

the impropriety of identifying the implied life of the narrator and the real life of the author so completely, the Hesiodic colouring casts further doubt on the autobiographical reference of the passage. Not only does the Ician evoke Hesiod's distaste for sea-faring; the line even echoes the formulation of its model (εἰ δέ σε ναυτιλίης δυσπεμφέλου ἵμερος αἱρεῖ, *Theog.* 618). It is hardly conceivable that Callimachus never travelled by sea. No one took the land route from Cyrene to Alexandria, and, like his fellow countryman Synesius many centuries later, Callimachus must have made the trip by sea. It is also relevant to add that, with F 178 assigned to *Aetia* II (Ch. V), the autobiographical reference would in any case be limited to his early years. He may well have travelled more widely in his years of fame. I have already suggested (Ch. II. 8) that he performed at Delphi, and almost certainly we can place him elsewhere too—in Thrace, for example.

AP ix. 336 is a humorous description of a small figure called Heros (Ἥρως) standing guard outside the house of a man called Eëtion from Amphipolis, armed with nothing but a sword. The point (unfortunately obscured by a corruption at the end of line 3) is apparently that a fully-armed horseman might have been expected. There can be little doubt that what the poet has in mind is the so-called Thracian Rider-god, familiar from hundreds of reliefs in that part of the world, normally on horseback brandishing a spear but occasionally shown leading his horse on foot.[111] But commentators all assume that Eëtion's relief stood outside a house in Egypt.[112] It is true that Greek mercenaries in the Fayyum a century or so later worshipped a god called Heron represented in much the same way. But whatever the relationship between the two gods,[113] there is certainly no explicit mention or even hint of Thrace in the Egyptian texts and reliefs. Yet Callimachus clearly associated the Rider with Thrace—indeed he found a footsoldier positively funny for a man from Amphipolis. Where did he get this idea? Whether or not he wrote the epigram in Egypt, he must have acquired the knowledge in Thrace.[114] Only there would the ubiquity of horseman reliefs have made a footsoldier stand out. Only there would he have learned the local name Heros, as in Thracian inscriptions, not the invariable Heron of Egyptian texts.[115] It is in any case unlikely that Callimachus moved in the circles that worshipped Heron in Egypt, mercenaries in the Arsinoite nome.[116]

---

111. Abundantly illustrated in *Corpus Cultus Equitis Thracii* I-V (Leiden 1979-82).
112. Gow and Page, *HE* II. 212; Fraser I. 583.
113. M. Launey, *Recherches sur les armées hellénistiques* ii (Paris 1950), 959-74.
114. So J. Bousquet, *Mélanges C. Picard* i = *Rev. archéol.* 29/30 (1949), 110-11.
115. Heron is found in a small minority of texts in Thessaly and Macedonia (N. Hampartumian, *CCET* IV. 16), but Heros is never found in Egyptian texts.
116. V. Velkov and A. Fol, *Les Thraces en Égypte gréco-romain* (Sofia 1977), 97-99. For the same reason I am not attracted to P. Roussel's ingenious suggestion that Eëtion had quarreled with a billetted cavalryman (*RÉG* 34 [1921], 270-74; Fraser I. 583).

Iamb 7 describes a battered old wooden statue of Hermes at the Thracian city of Ainos, supposedly made by Epeios, best known for the Trojan horse.[117] Of course, Callimachus may have drawn on a written source (the cult of Hermes at Ainos is known from its coinage), and the fact that he mentions a gash on its shoulder does not prove that he saw it in person. But he also wrote an epitaph on a friend called Menecrates from Ainos, who died there from drinking too much strong Thracian wine.[118] Menecrates is addressed as "Ainian xenos," just as Heracleitus is addressed as "Halicarnassan xenos" (*AP* vii. 80). In such a context xenos, guest-friend, suggests mutual visits. Travels in this area might explain his interest in the mysteries of Samothrace, manifested in at least three poems (Ch. I. 2). One is the earliest identifiable reference to the gods by the title—Theoi Samothrakes—under which they are addressed in contemporary dedications.[119] Another, the fragmentary F 115, may have been an aetiology of the mysteries.[120] As it happens, the only other such poems we know of were performed at Samothrace itself, winning their authors crowns in the city Dionysia: a tragedy by Dymas of Iasos on the "deeds of Dardanus";[121] and an epic on "the deeds of Dardanus and Eëtion...and Cadmos and Harmonia" by Herodes of Priene, both second-century poets.[122] Furthermore, as Bousquet has suggested, it might have while she was the wife of Lysimachus in Thrace that Callimachus got to know Arsinoë, perhaps first met at the court of Soter. Her benefactions to Samothrace are commemorated by the so-called Arsinoeion that forms part of the sanctuary, dedicated while she was still queen of Thrace.[123] It might have been at her invitation that he visited the island.

Whether or not he competed himself, it is hard to believe that one so interested in the festivals and oracles of the Greek world never wanted to see the legendary sites in person. A poem so devoted to Attic cult, vocabulary and localities as the *Hecale* was surely written for a visit to Athens. Praxiphanes taught mainly on Rhodes, but was evidently known elsewhere, to judge from a proxeny decree on Delos.[124] Aratus studied

---

117. F 197 with Dawson 1951, 81-3 and C. A. Faraone, *Talismans and Trojan Horses* (Oxford 1992), 105.

118. *AP* vii. 725; on the text, M. Gronewald, *ZPE* 100 (1994), 22-24.

119. *AP* vi. 301; S. G. Cole, *Theoi Megaloi* (Leiden 1984), 58.

120. F 115 (cf. F 583); G. Massimilla, *ZPE* 95 (1993), 33-44; Livrea, ib. 101 (1994), 33-37; Borgonovo and Capelletto, ib. 103 (1995), 13; Cameron, ib. 1996.

121. Guarducci 1929, no. XV; L. Robert, *Rev. arch.* 24 (1926), 173-74.

122. *Inschr. von Priene* 69; cf. 68, 70 (Guarducci XIV); Robert 1926, 174-76; B. Hemberg, *Die Kabiren* (Uppsala 1950), 106 (for the various Samothracian heroes, 312-5).

123. P. M. Fraser, *Samothrace* II. 1 (New York 1960), 50; Cole 1984, 22.

124. Brink 1946; Wehrli, *Phainias von Eresos, Chamaileon, Praxiphanes*[2] (Basle 1969).

with Menedemus in Eretria in the late 290s, but also with Persaeus in Athens (*Vita IV*) and no doubt elsewhere as well. Athens is a possibility for the meeting with Callimachus, but there are obviously others.

In their present form the references to Callimachus in the Aratus *Vitae* are no doubt at second or third hand, but we are surely bound to infer that at some point someone consulted *Against Praxiphanes* directly and found information linking Aratus with Callimachus and Praxiphanes. The floruit in the 124th Olympiad (284-1) given by his Suda-entry supports the implication of these passages that he was indeed somewhat older than Callimachus.

Lefkowitz was rightly sceptical about modern explanations of the hostility between Callimachus and Praxiphanes: namely that Callimachus attacked Praxiphanes for defending Plato or Aristotle against his attacks.[125] There is no need to postulate anything so precise. The few facts we have are suggestive enough. The *Vitae* preserve three details from Callimachus's book that could not have been inferred from the well-known epigram: that Aratus was the older of the two, that Callimachus praised Aratus's learning (πολυμαθῆ), and that they met at Praxiphanes's school.

There is one other point to be won from this complex of biographies of Hellenistic poets. We have seen that the less familiar names tend to be dropped from one redaction or another. But there is one very familiar name that does not appear in a single one of the Aratus *Lives* or the *Lives* of Nicander or Theocritus: Apollonius of Rhodes.[126] By the same token, a name missing from the *Lives* of Aratus, Nicander and Theocritus is Euphorion, nor do we find any mention of Aratus, Nicander or Theocritus in the *Life* of Euphorion. In this case the explanation is beyond doubt. As we have already seen, Euphorion was not active before the second half of the century. If the prosopography of the *Lives* of Aratus, Nicander and Theocritus is as accurate as here argued, we should not expect to find Euphorion in their circle.

The fact that Apollonius is no less systematically absent from their *Lives* and they from his suggests an explanation in similar terms. His Suda *Life* makes him a contemporary of Euphorion and Eratosthenes (ca 275-194), and while he may have been their older contemporary, it is perhaps more relevant to note that his career seems to have been confined to the southern mediterranean: no visits to Athens or Pella. In all probability Apollonius never met Aratus, Nicander or Theocritus, and their *Lives* were right not to mention him. The other poet of the age they never mention is

125. Lefkowitz 1981, 125-27.
126. The list of the Alexandrian tragic Pleiad in Tzetzes's *Life* of Lycophron (II. 4 Scheer) has no ancient authority, including as it does no fewer than four poets (Theocritus, Aratus, Nicander and Apollonius) who are not even tragedians (Fraser II. 871-2)!

Rhianus, who is likewise stated in his Suda-entry, surely correctly, to have been a contemporary of Eratosthenes (Ch. X. 5). What these *Lives* do not say is as accurate as what they do say.

6

Scholarly attention has always focussed on the so-called "ancient" *Lives* of Apollonius rather than his Suda *Life*; they alone tell the famous tale of the initial failure of the *Argonautica*, his retreat to Rhodes and eventual triumphant return.[127] There is no need to go into all the details, much less discuss all the modern hypotheses, since major discrepancies and omissions in both the "ancient" *Lives* cast doubt on the entire story—more serious doubt, indeed, than even Lefkowitz recognized.

Vita I in consecutive sentences claims both that Apollonius turned to poetry late in life and that he first recited the *Argonautica* "as an ephebe." Both *Vitae* imply that, having gone to Rhodes, he stayed there. Depending on which of these versions we choose to accept, the *Lives* can be reconciled with both early and late chronologies for the life of Apollonius and the date of his poem.

But over and above these contradictions loom two other no less disturbing factors. First, the credit of both *Lives* is gravely undermined by a confusion between the author of the *Argonautica* and a later Apollonius of Rhodes, a colorful sophist from Alabanda who set up a famous school of rhetoric at Rhodes ca 120 B.C. (presumably someone ran together consecutive entries in Demetrius's *On Poets and Writers of the Same Name*).[128] It is this that explains the claim in *Vita II*, absurd for the poet, that Apollonius "engaged in public affairs and taught rhetoric" in Rhodes.[129] Strabo uses the identical terminology of the later Apollonius.[130] Almost certainly the same confusion underlies the statement in *Vita I* that the poet "taught with great distinction (λαμπρῶς) there, and was found worthy of Rhodian citizenship and honour among them."[131] The adverb suggests the display

127. I can accept very little of A. Rengakos's recent treatment in *WS* 105 (1992), 39-67.

128. W. Schmid, *RE* II (1895) 140. 64f.; G. D. Kellog, *AJP* 28 (1907), 301-10; Pfeiffer 1968, 143 n. 5; 266. He was also known as "Apollonius the Pansy" (ὁ μαλακός). For Demetrius's book, Ch. XVII. 2.

129. παρεγένετο ἐν τῇ Ῥόδῳ κἀκεῖ ἐπολιτεύσατο καὶ σοφιστεύει ῥητορικοὺς λόγους, p. 2. 7-8. That these words derive from a confusion with the sophist was seen long ago (E. Maass, *Aratea* [1892], 335), but has seldom been noted in connection with the poet.

130. Ποσειδώνιος δ᾽ ἐπολιτεύσατο μὲν ἐν Ῥόδῳ καὶ ἐσοφίστευσεν, ἦν δ᾽ Ἀπαμεὺς ἐκ τῆς Συρίας, καθάπερ καὶ Ἀπολλώνιος ὁ Μαλακὸς καὶ Μόλων· ἦσαν γὰρ Ἀλαβανδεῖς, Strabo 14, 655. The two verbs are clearly meant to apply to Apollonius and Molon as well as Posidonius.

131. p. 2. 1-2; the latter phrase is repeated in *Vita II*, p. 2, l. 10-11.

oratory of the sophist rather than the classroom of the grammarian. Since the sophist was a witty fellow with a taste for polemic, we cannot help but wonder how much else of his biography has helped to shape the *Lives* of the poet.

Second, there are three serious omissions in both *Lives*. First, neither of them so much as mentions the librarianship, which was after all the high point of Apollonius's professional career. Meineke, Wendel and others were mistaken to interpret the claim in *Vita II*, ὡς καὶ τῶν βιβλιοθηκῶν τοῦ Μουσείου ἀξιωθῆναι (p. 2. 13 W), as meaning "he was deemed worthy of the librarianship." As Pfeiffer showed from a number of other passages in later writers,[132] βιβλιοθήκης ἀξιωθῆναι means "be deemed worthy of *inclusion in* the library"—referring (of course) to his poem. Not only would this be an entirely trivial point (works did not have to reach a certain standard to merit inclusion in the library). It would further underline the unhistorical identification of Apollonius with his *Argonautica* to the exclusion of any other aspect of his life and works. Contrary to what is often inferred from this passage, the *Lives* do *not* bring Apollonius back to Alexandria (though *Vita II* does have him buried beside Callimachus):[133] he leaves Alexandria as a youth and spends the rest of his life in Rhodes. As far as the *Lives* are concerned, the question of his librarianship simply does not arise, and it is a fundamental error of method to try to fit it into their accounts.

Second, neither mentions that Apollonius wrote numerous other poems, doubtless spread out over a period of years. The *Lives* clearly imply that his entire career revolved round the early failure and ultimate success of the *Argonautica*. The truth is that fragments from works on the origins (κτίσεις) of Alexandria and Naucratis and an aetiological poem entitled *Canobus* show that he wrote a number of poems in Egypt, just as fragments from similar works on Caunos and Cnidos as well as Rhodes itself illustrate a similarly varied poetic career during the Rhodian period.[134] In his own day, Apollonius's fame did *not* rest on his *Argonautica* alone, and the series of Egyptian poems lends no support to the claim of an early departure from Alexandria. These were mistakes only possible in a later age that knew only the *Argonautica*.

Third, the absence of any fixed points, whether names or dates, in either *Life*: there is no date of birth or death, no list of works; no Ptolemy

132. Pfeiffer 1968, 284-85, citing Eusebius *HE* 3. 9. 2 and *PE* 8. 1. 8, with *HE* 2. 18. 8 and Aristeas *Ep*. 9. Fraser rightly accepted this interpretation in his volume of notes (II. 478 n. 131) but unfortunately followed Wendel in his text (I. 331).

133. If there is any fact behind this claim, it may (as Wilamowitz suggested, *Kl. Schr*. i. 412) have been the other Apollonius who was buried near Callimachus.

134. For the fragments, Powell *CA* pp. 5-7; Maass, *Aratea* (1892), 359-69; D. A. van Krevelen, *Rhein. Museum* 104 (1961), 128-31 : Ch. II. 6.

is identified, whether as patron or pupil. *Vita I* mentions no kings at all, *Vita II* says only that "he lived in the days of the Ptolemies." Wendel emended ἐπὶ τῶν Πτολεμαίων to ἐπὶ τοῦ <τρίτου> Πτολεμαίου, "under the third Ptolemy." This would make good historical sense, and it is true, as Hunter remarks, that the reading of the manuscripts "is too obvious to need saying." Nonetheless this vagueness is of a piece with the rest of the *Life*.[135] By contrast, even the Suda biography, however inaccurately, names Euergetes, synchronizes Apollonius with three writers other than Callimachus and dates (wrongly, in the event) his librarianship. As its format shows, the Suda-entry recognizably derives, like most of its entries for men of letters, from the sixth-century biographical dictionary *(Onomatologos)* of Hesychius of Miletus.[136] The so-called "ancient" *Lives* do not. Unlike the Suda they lack even the standard classification of his works (in this case ἐπῶν ποιητής). Their main purpose is to embellish a single anecdote unknown to the genuine biographical tradition (there is no hint in the Suda-entry of the failure-exile-success story).

The *Lives* were put together, presumably in late antiquity, by someone without access to any reliable information.[137] Unconcerned or unable to give a comprehensive account of Apollonius's multi-faceted life and works, his modest purpose was to explain two things that puzzled him: why, though born in Alexandria, was Apollonius known as the Rhodian; and why were there (as he thought) two editions of the *Argonautica*? The first of his problems (of course) was no problem at all: it was not uncommon for a man who moved to another city to become known by his adoptive ethnic. To give only one example, Posidonius, though born in Apamea, is likewise generally known as Rhodian from his adopted home ('Απαμ- εὺς...ἢ 'Ρόδιος in his Suda-entry). Lefkowitz mistakenly argued that Apollonius "came from Rhodes to begin with." But it is documented that he was born an Alexandrian by earlier and better sources than the *Lives* and the Suda: Strabo and the Oxyrhynchus list of librarians.[138] The statement that he belonged to the Ptolemaic tribe (p. 1. 6) is perhaps the only persuasive circumstantial detail in *Vita I*: Ptolemais is one of the only three tribe names known for Ptolemaic Alexandria, otherwise attested by none other

135. Hunter 1989, 1 n. 3. Note the similar phrase "before the days of the Ptolemies" (πρὸ τῶν χρόνων τῶν Πτολεμαίων) in Tzetzes's account of the Alexandrian library: *Proleg. de com.* I (ed. W.J.W. Koster (Leiden 1975), p. 23. 14.

136. Christ-Schmid-Stählin II. 2⁶ (1924), 1039-40; W. Spoerri, *KP* II (1967), 1122.

137. Precisely because of their lack of serious content, I am reluctant to attribute the *Lives* to either of Apollonius's early imperial commentators, Theon and Lucillus Tarrhaeus (so Wendel 1932, 113 and, without discussion, Rengakos 1992).

138. Lefkowitz 1981, 130; P. Oxy. 1241, II. 1: 'Αλεξανδρεὺς ὁ καλούμενος 'Ρόδιος, and Strabo, 14. 13, 655: Διονύσιος δὲ ὁ Θρᾷξ καὶ 'Απολλώνιος ὁ τοὺς 'Αργοναύτας ποιήσας, 'Αλεξανδρεῖς μέν, ἐκαλοῦντο δὲ 'Ρόδιοι). Rengakos 1992, 50-55 implausibly argues that all these sources were misled by an error in Theon.

than Callimachus.[139] Apollonius is perhaps the earliest known Alexandrian scholar born in Alexandria, itself implying that he was younger than immigrants like Callimachus.

The two editions must have been inferred from the so-called "proecdosis" several times quoted in those very scholia to which the *Life* served as introduction. The failure-exile-success story provided a neat and colorful explanation of both puzzles.

Since the failure-exile-success story was invented without reference to Apollonius's real career, it is not surprising that it cannot easily be fitted into it. The evidence of the minor poems suggests a longish spell in both Alexandria and Rhodes. Since he was born in Alexandria, a disciple of Callimachus (so the Oxyrhynchus librarian list as well as Apollonius's *Suda Life*), and (as we shall see) head of the Alexandrian library before Eratosthenes (ca 245-200), it seems most natural to place the Alexandrian period first. The *Lives* are agreed that it was in Alexandria that Apollonius wrote the *Argonautica*, and slight though their authority is, it finds support in the literary evidence discussed in the following chapter, suggesting publication in the 260s.

The "proecdosis" which is surely the basis for the entire story cannot possibly have been the text of that unsuccessful first recitation.[140] Apollonius would never have *published* a first draft that had met with the disastrous reception described in the *Lives*. Yet the "proecdosis" from which the scholia cite a number of passages was evidently a copy still available for scholars to collate several centuries later.[141] Furthermore, on the evidence of these quotations, the "proecdosis" offered a text that differed only in minor details from the vulgate.[142] Who can believe that these readings derive from a copy of Apollonius's unpublished, rejected first draft? There is no sign that they affected the vulgate, and the now abundant Apollonius papyri lend no support to the hypothesis that a substantially different text ever existed.[143] There is thus no basis for the hypothesis of a youthful

---

139. *AP* vii. 520; Fraser I. 40; II. 113 n. 8. The tradition that he was from Naucratis is only mentioned in connection with his poem on the Origins of that city (Powell F 7 = Athen. 283 E; Herter 1944/55, 222).

140. As rightly emphasized by Herter 1973, 22.

141. It was presumably Theon or the late-first-century Lucillus of Tarrha to whom this stratum of the extant scholia is to be attributed: C. Wendel 1932, 105f.; Vian I xli-ii.

142. The six passages at issue are quoted and discussed as potential author variants by Emonds, *Zweite Auflage* 296-305 and (with full recent bibliography) by M. Fantuzzi, *Ricerche su Apollonio Rodio* [Rome 1988], 87-120. H. Fränkel appeals to the supposed parallel of Ovid's *Metamorphoses* (*Einleitung zur kritischen Ausgabe der Argonautica des Apollonios* [Göttingen 1964], 8), but there is little agreement that this is indeed a case of author variants. For a recent list of other alleged cases, G. Luck, *AJP* 102 (1981), 176-7.

143. "I see the proecdosis as existing in fossilized isolation, and not impinging in the slightest on the vicissitudes of the vulgate," M. Haslam, *ICS* 3 (1978), 67. The fact that its variants are quoted only for Bk I might mean that the collator only read that far; but it might also mean that the proecdosis (whatever this was) only existed for Bk I.

work drastically rewritten.[144]

Third, some scholars have been prepared to follow the Suda-entry in making Apollonius librarian of Alexandria in succession to Eratosthenes, entailing appointment ca 200, more than 40 years after Callimachus's death.[145] But since the Oxyrhynchus list gives *two* men called Apollonius of Alexandria as librarians, one after ("Apollonius of Alexandria, named the eidographos") and one before Eratosthenes ("Apollonius of Alexandria, named the Rhodian"), the Suda-date can be explained as a very simple and natural confusion. Alternatively, it may be (as Blum has suggested) that the Suda-entry is in fact a fusion of the entries for the two different Apollonii. As he rightly points out, it would be odd for a writer who had just called Apollonius a contemporary of Eratosthenes to go on to call him Eratosthenes's successor.[146] Since Eratosthenes was appointed by Euergetes (perhaps under the influence of his new queen, anxious to honour a fellow Cyrenean), that suggests a date ca 245. Following Eichgrün, I would assign tentative outside limits of ca 275-245 to Apollonius's tenure of the librarianship.[147] If he was dismissed to make room for Eratosthenes, that would provide explanation enough for his departure for Rhodes.[148]

It is futile to attempt to fit the librarianship into the failure-exile-success story: to inquire (that is) whether the first recital or the Rhodian retreat happened before or after he became librarian. For example, E.-R. Schwinge dismissed the possibility of an early date for the poem on the grounds that Apollonius could not have been appointed librarian after such a literary failure.[149] But the late date would entail no less of an improbability: that so important a figure in the Alexandrian literary world as its librarian could be driven out of town by one unsuccessful poem. The story of the failure must be stricken from the historical record.

In the case of Apollonius, it is the Suda-entry that preserves the vestiges of ancient tradition. In the case of Theocritus it is the other way around.

144. On the other hand I am not attracted by Fränkel's view (*Einleitung* 8-10) that both versions derive from unpublished drafts of the poet; see too Fantuzzi 1988.

145. "après la mort d'Ératosthène (195)," Vian 1974, x.

146. Blum 1991, 131.

147. I have nothing to add to Eichgrün's meticulous discussion (1961, 15-35) of the evidence or to his conclusions about the sequence of Alexandrian librarians; see too Blum 1991, 127-133, though I am not persuaded by his attempt to insert Callimachus into the list.

148. It is unfortunate that we have no precise information on the dates of Apollonius's Rhodian period, since at some time between ca 262 and 246 Rhodes was at war with Philadelphus. For all that is known of this mysterious episode, R. M. Berthold, *Rhodes in the Hellenistic Age* (Ithaca 1984), 89-92.

149. "Vor allem aber wäre Übertragung und Ausübung von Bibliothekariat und Erzieheramt nach öffentlichem Durchfall mit den Argonautika nicht denkbar," Schwinge 1986, 84.

His Suda-entry, like the first of his "ancient" *Lives*, not only contains nothing not inferred from either the *Idylls* or the anonymous epigram *AP* ix. 434.[150] Like the "ancient" *Lives* of Apollonius it does not follow even the form of the standard literary biography: ethnic, type of writing, teachers, date. *Vita A* · (p. 1 W) gives Philitas and Asclepiades as his teachers, evidently from *Idyll* 7, and dates him to "Ptolemy called Lagous." Once again, modern editors have "corrected" to "Ptolemy called < Philadelphus son of Ptolemy called > son of Lagus." But the only Ptolemy actually identified in the text of Theocritus is precisely the son of Lagus (Λαγείδας Πτολεμαῖος, 17. 14). To be sure the scholia correctly distinguish Lagus, Soter and Philadelphus, but the fact that they also criticize (the probably second-century A.D.) Munatius for bringing Philopator into the picture[151] suggests that not everyone was so well-informed. It is only *Vita B* (p. 2 W) that offers anything both true and independent of the text: a single sentence synchronism with Aratus, Callimachus and Nicander, and a date "in the days of Ptolemy Philadelphus." Hardly a borrowing from a *Life* of Aratus, for none of the extant *Lives* mentions Theocritus. And the fact that *Vita* B names Nicander without querying the synchronism points to a pre-Critic version of the common source that evidently lies behind all these Lives, a version that (rightly) included the name of Theocritus among the synchronisms.

It is too simple to brush aside the entire biographical tradition. The "ancient" *Lives* of Apollonius are largely worthless, but his Suda *Life* is a little better, and the Oxyrhynchus librarian list better still. Theocritus's Suda *Life* is worthless, but one of the other *Lives* preserves a few scraps. And the *Lives* of Aratus and Nicander clearly derive from early Hellenistic tradition. Their prosopography is especially well founded. Good information was available, and there is no reason in principle why the life and connections of Callimachus should have been less well documented than those of his contemporaries.

7

We come at last to Callimachus. Largely no doubt because his major works have not come down to us by manuscript transmission, no *Life* has been preserved by that route. Instead all we have is his Suda-entry, which reads as follows:[152]

---

150. Quoted and discussed further below (Ch. XIII. 2).

151. Schol. p. 318 Wendel, with Gow I. xxix n. 5 and lxxxii-iii.

152. Adapted from the translation in Blum 1991, 124-5. The phrases in square brackets are later insertions, as justified in § 8.

Callimachus, son of Battus and Mesatma, from Cyrene, grammarian, pupil of the grammarian Hermocrates of Iasos, married the daughter of Euphrates [? Euphraios] of Syracuse. His sister's son was the younger (νέος) Callimachus, who wrote about islands in hexameters. He was so zealous that he wrote poems in every metre and many books in prose. He wrote more than 800 books. He lived in the time of Ptolemy Philadelphus, [before he was introduced to the king, he was a teacher in an elementary school in Eleusis, a village outside Alexandria] and lived until the time of Ptolemy Euergetes, the 127th [?133rd] Olympiad, in the second year of which Ptolemy Euergetes began his reign [245].

Among his books are the following: *The Arrival of Io; Semele; The Foundation of Argos;*[153] *Arcadia; Glaucus; Hopes;* satyr plays; tragedies; comedies; songs; *Ibis* [a poem designed to be obscure and abusive against a certain Ibis, an enemy of Callimachus; this was Apollonius who wrote the *Argonautica*]; *Museion; Catalogues [Pinakes] of those who distinguished themselves in all branches of learning, and their writings, in 120 books; Catalogue and record of playwrights, arranged chronologically from the beginning; A list of glosses and writings by Democrates [?Democritus]; The names of months according to peoples and cities; Foundation of islands and cities, and changes of their names; On the rivers of Europe; On marvels and natural curiosities in the Peloponnese and in Italy; On changes in the names of fishes; On winds; On birds; On the rivers of the world; Collection of the marvels of the world according to localities.*

This is dry stuff. With one exception (which we shall soon see is an interpolation) not a hint of all those colourful feuds. Not a word on Callimachus's relations with his fellow scholars and poets. No prosopographical details beyond the basics: the name of his teacher and surprisingly full documentation on his family. But no wild inferences from his more scurrilous poems. Indeed it is a curious fact that the list of his works does not include *Aetia, Iambi, Hecale* or epigrams. We should not expect more than a selection from a bibliography of 800 rolls, but it is certainly surprising that it should be his most famous and controversial works that are omitted.[154]

But if it is dry, it is also sober. There is no call to doubt the names of any of Callimachus's kin, nor those of his sister Megatima and brother-in-law Stasenor given in the entry for Callimachus the younger. We have seen that ὁ νέος is the standard contemporary formula for differentiating between homonyms; and Stasenor and his teacher Hermocrates fit the his-

---

153. Ἄργους οἰκισμός, after Hecker translated "The colony[?] of the Argonauts" by Blum. Earlier views (Schneider, *Callimachèa* II. 141-2) were based on the incorrect assumption that MSS gave the plural οἰκισμοί; "The Building of the Argo" is also perhaps possible.

154. The title ἐκλογαὶ ῥητ[όρων] in the first-century book-list omitted from *SH* (Sijpesteijn and Worp, *Chron. d'Égypte* 49 [1974], 327) may be a corruption of the ῥητορικῶν ἀναγραφή attested by F 430 (Lehnus, *Riv. di Fil.* 118 [1990], 26); ἐκλογαί suggests *Purple passages*, hardly what we expect from Callimachus.

torical context (Ch. I. 1). It is worth noting that no one thought to add his grandfather's name from the mock epitaph *AP* vii. 525. If we accept an easy correction by Kaibel (Εὐφραίου for Εὐφράτου) for his father-in-law, we would have a name common in Sicily, where he is said to have come from.[155] It is also true that, though his *floruit* fell under Philadelphus, Callimachus lived into the reign of Euergetes.

Unlike Apollonius's, Callimachus's Suda *Life* is as detailed and accurate an entry as could reasonably be expected in so late and incompetent a lexicon. A few titles have dropped out of the bibliography, but it is unlikely that the original was ever much fuller. It has the appearance of a classic entry from his own *Pinakes*—in fact no doubt the work of one of his own disciples: the bare minimum of biographical information and a detailed list of writings. No anecdotes, no personal details. It is an austere compilation designed for a limited function. Above all, perhaps against our expectations, it has *not* been filled out with inferences from the poems or biographical stereotypes.

We have already seen that more detailed information, both personal and literary, was available: for example, stories of his relationship with Aratus, reported with quotations from both a poem and a prose work in the *Lives* of Aratus. But we have also seen that in the early period this sort of material is more likely to have been found in scholarly monographs (the περί-literature) or biographies of other writers, especially philosophers. One anecdote, trivial enough in itself, is perhaps worth quoting in this connection if only because I have never seen it quoted before. According to a late florilegium, someone once reported to Callimachus a slander spoken in his presence; "if you hadn't enjoyed listening he wouldn't have said it," replied the poet.[156] Given the centrality of polemic in Callimachus's world, the story is at least ben trovato. The ultimate source was surely a biography—not necessarily a biography of Callimachus. It may also have been in a biography rather than (as Pfeiffer thought) a scholarly work that Athenaeus found the most famous of all Callimachean quotations: "a big book is a big bore" (F 465: p 52).

Predictably enough several interesting items are preserved by Diogenes Laertius. For example, in his *Life* of Pittacus Diogenes quotes *AP* vii. 89, Pittacus's advice on marriage. The fact that he gives his source as "Callimachus in epigrams (ἐν ἐπιγράμμασι)" does not necessarily mean he took it from a book of epigrams (rather than an earlier *Life* of Pittacus). The formula is commonly used to mean no more than "in the form of an epigram." He cites the famous epitaph on Callimachus's Carian friend Heraclitus (*AP* vii. 80) in his *Life* of Heraclitus as one of the other bearers

---

155. G. Kaibel, *Hermes* 22 (1887), 501 ("nusquam crebrius...quam in titulis Siculis").
156. *Flor. Mon.* 209, in Meineke's Stobaeus, iv (1857), 284.

of the name.[157] He also quotes extensively in his *Life* of Thales from the
first of Callimachus's *Iambi*, which tells the story of the cup of Bathycles,
left to the wisest of the seven sages and accordingly given twice to Thales
(i. 23, 25, 28-9). Here Diogenes supplies a detail apparently not mentioned
in the text of the poem: that Callimachus's source was Maeandrius of
Miletus.[158] This is in itself entirely plausible (Maeandrius is twice elsewhere cited as a source for Callimachus in later scholia),[159] and, once
more, surely in the biographical tradition about Thales long before the publication of Theon's commentary. For example, it is bound to have been
cited by Hermippus in his work *On the Seven Sages* in at least four books,
cited six times by Diogenes, once precisely for Thales.[160]

Diogenes Laertius and Sextus Empiricus each quote part of an epigram
on the dialectician Diodorus Cronus. According to Diogenes, Diodorus
earned his nickname when Stilpo of Megara posed him problems he could
not solve at a symposium in front of Ptolemy Soter, after which he went
into a decline (54 GP = F 393):

> Momus himself used to write on the walls: "Cronus is wise.".. Look, even the
> ravens on the rooftops are cawing: "what follows (συνῆπται) [from what]?"
> and "How shall we get to that place (κῶς αὖθι γενήσομεθα)"?

A difficult poem (misunderstood by both Diogenes and Sextus), requiring
some knowledge of contemporary logical controversies. The first of the
ravens' cries (according to M. J. White), alludes to "the truth conditions of
conditional propositions (συνειμμένα)." In the second (again with White)
we should interpret αὖθι not (as Sextus) eschatologically, but as αὐτόθι, an
adverb of place.[161] The ravens are making fun of Diodorus's denial of the
possibility of motion. A similar joke is credited to the celebrated physician
Herophilus, who also lived in Alexandria. Herophilus used Diodorus's
argument against the possibility of motion to prove that he could not really
have dislocated his shoulder![162]

Callimachus also had ties with the Alexandrian medical community. For
example, when describing how Leto gave birth to Apollo, he wittily adapts
her posture as given in the Homeric *Hymn to Apollo* to that recommended
in Herophilus's *On Midwifery*.[163] He was also on personal terms with the

---

157. i. 80 and ix. 17; in both cases Diogenes may have been, here as often elsewhere,
the source of the Anthology tradition: see my *Greek Anthology* 88, 135, 391.

158. *FGrH* 492 F 18; I follow Jacoby in believing that Leandrius of Miletus (*FGrH* 492)
is to be identified with Maeandrius of Miletus (491).

159. *FGrH* 492 F 14 (Schol. Apoll. ii. 705 = F 88 Pf.) and F 15 (Schol. Ar. Pac. 363).

160. Wehrli, *Hermippos der Kallimacheer* (Basle 1974), F 5-16, with pp. 48-54.

161. D. Sedley, "Diodorus Cronus and Hellenistic Philosophy," *Proc. Camb. Phil. Soc.*
23 (1971), 79; M. J. White, "What worried the crows?," *CQ* 36 (1986), 534-37; *HE* II.215.

162. Sext. Emp. *PH* 2. 245; Sedley 1977, 79.

163. Fraser I. 356; Most, *Hermes* 109 (1981), 188-86; Zanker 1987, 124-5.

court physician Philip of Cos, to whom he addressed, as if for his approval, a delightful epigram reviewing possible cures for love.[164]

It should be no surprise to find Callimachus in tune with current developments in medicine and philosophy. We have already seen how poets and philosophers met in the symposia of Athens and Eretria (Ch. III. 4-5). Nor was he the only poet of the age to write on contemporary philosophers. There is also Antagoras on Crates and Polemo; Theaetetus on Crantor; Posidippus on Zeno and Cleanthes; Sositheus on Cleanthes again and Lycophron's entire play on his teacher Menedemus. In circles where such as Diodorus were to be met, the apophthegm "Cretans are always liars" in *Hymn to Zeus* 8 would have evoked not only Epimenides of old but its recent reinvention (when placed in the mouth of a Cretan) as a logical paradox.[165] *Iamb* 1 refers contemptuously to Euhemerus, another controversial figure of the age.[166] And whatever its theme, the *Against Praxiphanes* shows Callimachus unafraid to cross swords with one of the most important living philosophers. This was no bookish recluse, but a prominent figure in the wider intellectual life of third-century Alexandria, likely to be mentioned or quoted by many writers of or on his age.

For example, there is the epigram on Cleombrotus (*AP* vi. 471), the disciple of Plato who supposedly committed suicide after reading the *Phaedo*, a poem that was to be quoted and debated in the philosophical literature on suicide till the end of antiquity.[167] The first extant citation is in Cicero (who wrote long before Theon), both preceded and followed by a reference to Hegesias of Cyrene, known as "Peisithanatos" because of his advocacy of suicide. That is to say, the presumption is that Cicero found the epigram cited in a philosophical discussion of suicide. The tradition that Ptolemy (whether Soter or Philadelphus) forbade Hegesias to lecture on the subject because so many of his pupils were killing themselves,[168] while hardly to be taken seriously, does at any rate date and localize Hegesias's teaching, providing a perfect context for Callimachus's epigram. We may surely presume that it was quoted in Hellenistic suicide literature from the beginning. It is also suggestive that, in a discussion of untimely death a page later, Cicero cites an epigrammatic line of Callimachus ("Troilus wept less than Priam") also quoted by Plutarch in a similar context.[169] The Diodorus epigram is likewise bound to have circu-

164. *AP* xii. 150; *HE* II. 157-58; Fraser I. 369-70.

165. Stephen A. White, *TAPA* 124 (1994), 144.

166. F 191. 9-11; perhaps too in *Hymn to Zeus* 8-9 and F 202. 15-17; White 1994, 144.

167. See the contrasting treatments of Stephen White and Gareth Williams in *TAPA* 124 (1994), 135-61 and *CQ* 45 (1995) respectively, with a full account of earlier discussions.

168. Cic. *Tusc.* i. 83-84; Fraser II. 694 n. 12; White 1994, 142.

169. μεῖον ἐδάκρυσεν Τρωῖλος ἢ Πρίαμος (F 491); Cic. *Tusc.* i. 93; Plut. *Cons. Apoll.* 24 (*Mor.* 113E).

lated in philosophical circles independently of its eventual publication in a collected edition of his epigrams. It was surely in a biography of Diodorus rather than Theon's commentary that Diogenes and Sextus came across it.

The Diegeseis on *Iamb* 1 supply information not given in the text: that Hipponax summons the scholars of Alexandria to "the so-called Sarapideum of Parmenio." The text refers only to "the shrine outside the wall." But there was a shrine of Sarapis dedicated by a certain Parmenio outside the city walls.[170] And as we have already seen, the Florentine scholia to F 7 and the Diegeseis to F 26 provide another example, both naming the same source (the *Argive History* of Agias and Dercylus) in the same words—again named as Callimachus's source in the Milan commentary on Antimachus, where some text to justify the claim is also quoted.[171] Callimachus cannot have named Agias and Dercylus himself, or there would have been no point in identifying them. In the case of the Diegeseis, the usual assumption that such passages derive from Theon or Epaphroditus is certainly possible,[172] but we have already seen that the Diegeseis may be Hellenistic. Diogenes's citation of Maeandrius suggests that Theon was not the first person to unmask Callimachus's sources. I suggest that this sort of scholarly detective work goes back to soon after Callimachus's day, when these early local histories were still familiar.

A certain Hedylus is cited by a late lexicon for an observation made "on the epigrams of Callimachus."[173] Perhaps the contemporary epigrammatist Hedylus of Samos (the name is not common). A commentary by a contemporary has been judged improbable in the past, but it may have been a monograph rather than a commentary, and a second-century B.C. papyrus has now revealed to us a detailed commentary "rich in discursive learning" (new fragments of Diphilus, Sophocles and Theodoridas) on an epigram which cannot be later than the early second century.[174] We saw earlier that it may have been a contemporary Timarchus who wrote a four-book study on the *Hermes* of Eratosthenes. Hedylus was an admirer, imitator and apparently personal friend of Asclepiades and Posidippus.[175] This man will have been well placed to write illuminating commentaries on Callimachus's more polemical epigrams. At the very least, he will have known the names of Callimachus's victims. Another text of the age that must have been equipped very early with explanatory glosses is Lycophron's *Alexandra*,

---

170. Sources in Fraser I. 270-71, 735; II. 426-27; so already A. Koerte 1935, 237.

171. Ch. IV n. 80; P. Mil. Vogl. I (1937), no. 18 = F 65 Pf.; for what is known of the *Argolica* (Dercyllus perhaps revising, completing or continuing the work of Agias), Jacoby, *FGrH* 305, with Komm. in IIIb (1955), 17-24; A. C. Cassio, *RIFC* 117 (1989), 257-75.

172. Norsa and Vitelli, *PSI* xi (1935), 140-41.

173. Et. Magn. 72. 13; cf. *SH* 458.

174. P. J. Parsons, "The Oyster," *ZPE* 24 (1977), 1-12; *SH* 983-4.

175. See Appendix V of my *Greek Anthology*.

perhaps, like *The Waste Land,* by the author himself. Who else would have
known all the answers?[176] P. Oxy. 2528 seems to show Euphorion interpreting his own poems, and the form of the text suggests a commentary
rather than a monograph.[177]

There may also be·a late Republican parallel. L. Crassicius Pasicles
from Tarentum wrote a commentary on the *Smyrna* of Catullus's friend
Helvius Cinna.[178] Since this commentary was Pasicles's main claim to
fame,[179] we may presume it to have been written before he was appointed
tutor of Iullus Antonius, son of the triumvir, namely by ca 30 B.C. Perhaps
then actually before the death of Cinna himself (44 B.C.). If Eratosthenes
and Cinna were elucidated during their lifetime, why not Callimachus?

8

Before we return to the identification of the Telchines, there remains one
last problem of Callimachean biography, the identification of Ibis. Pfeiffer
made the remarkable claim that the identification of Ibis as Apollonius has
no less and no more authority than the Florentine scholiast's identification
of the Telchines.[180] He began with what he characterized as the authority
of Hesychius of Miletus, by which he meant the Suda-entry. But can we be
sure that this detail goes back to Hesychius, much less to Ptolemaic
Alexandria? It occurs near the end of a long list of otherwise unattested
works, all bare titles. Only in the case of *Ibis* is there a descriptive
parenthesis:[181]

...τραγῳδίαι, κωμῳδίαι, μέλη, Ἶβις [ἔστι δὲ ποίημα ἐπιτετηδευμένον εἰς
ἀσάφειαν καὶ λοιδορίαν, εἴς τινα Ἶβιν, γενόμενον ἐχθρὸν τοῦ Καλλιμάχου·
ἦν δὲ οὗτος Ἀπολλώνιος, ὁ γράψας τὰ Ἀργοναυτικά], Μουσεῖον, Πίνακες...

176. On the other hand I am not attracted by Wilamowitz's suggestion (*HD* II. 400) that
Ovid or someone he commissioned was responsible for the small nucleus of genuine information in the scholia to his *Ibis.*

177. Now *SH* 432; Pfeiffer 1968, 150 n. 5.

178. Suet. *De gramm.* 18; a Greek and a freedman: T. P. Wiseman, "Who was Crassicius Pansa?," *TAPA* 115 (1985), 187-96. It was presumably to cover up his Greek origin
that he later took the old Roman cognomen Pansa (for which see I. Kajanto, *The Latin Cognomina* [Helsinki 1965], 241).

179. See the anonymous epigram quoted by Suetonius: *uni Crassicio se credere Zmyrna
probavit...* (Cinna F 11 Morel). He also wrote on grammar and metre: J. Tolkiehn, *Berl.
Phil. Woch.* 31 [1911], 412-416; Schanz-Hosius II, 4. ed. [1935], 379; A. Hillscher,
Hominum Litt. Graecorum ante Tiberii mortem in urbe Roma commoratorum Historia Critica
(Fleckeis. Jahrb. Suppl. 18 (1892), 382-3; Wiseman passim.

180. *neque minus neque plus auctoritatis hoc nomen habet quam nomina Telchinum,
opinor, in Schol. Flor. ad Aet. fr. 1; non est coniectura Byzantina, sed antiqua doctrina
grammatica* (F 382 fin.); so too Webster, *Wien. Stud.* 66 (1963), 68.

181. The passage is already translated above.

The parenthesis clearly falls into two parts. The first (ἔστι...Καλλιμάχου) explains what *Ibis* is: an elaborate invective, aimed at "some" enemy of Callimachus. The formulation is vague, and the implication that the enemy's name was not known.[182] If the writer of this clause had intended from the start to identify the enemy as Apollonius, he would surely have drafted the entire parenthesis quite differently: "an invective *against Apollonius*, Callimachus's enemy." The first clause *may* go back to Hesychius —though scarcely to the original version of Callimachus's bibliography. Why explain this title alone? It is no more baffling as a title than (say) "Hopes" (Ἐλπίδες). But the second clause at any rate (ἦν...Ἀργοναυτικά) *must* be a later addition, by someone who thought he could identify this unnamed enemy.

The only authority any item in this Suda-entry has depends on the assumption that the entry as a whole descends uninterpolated from a Hellenistic bibliography of Callimachus. Any item that looks like an integral part of the list deserves to be considered a genuine Callimachean title unless there is some other objection. For example, there is no real basis for the suspicions often entertained about the tragedies and comedies listed here. On the other hand, it was suggested in Ch. I that the story of Callimachus's schoolteaching days should be regarded as an insult later mistaken for biography. It is true that there was a village called Eleusis outside Alexandria in Ptolemaic times,[183] but since to have any bite the insult must have been contemporary, it is likely to have been circumstantial: the school in *Iamb* 5 may have been in Eleusis, or someone in his family may have lived or even taught there. This sentence too is surely an interpolation. As soon as the text is reread in this light, it should be clear that the bracketed words interrupt a single sentence about the duration of the poet's life:

ἐπὶ δὲ τῶν χρόνων ἦν Πτολεμαίου τοῦ Φιλαδέλφου [πρὶν δὲ συσταθῆναι τῷ βασιλεῖ, γράμματα ἐδίδασκεν ἐν Ἐλευσῖνι, κωμυδρίῳ τῆς Ἀλεξανδρείας] καὶ παρέτεινε μέχρι τοῦ Εὐεργέτου κληθέντος Πτολεμαίου.

What other basis is there for the identification of Ibis? Even without the analogy of the Telchines, there can be little doubt that the poem itself did not name its victim. If it had, there would have been no need for guesswork. In modern times there has been a large and unusually far-fetched literature on the subject. The latest and most comprehensive treatment, sensibly sceptical, concludes that it is "just a plausible inference...from the notorious alleged rivalry of Callimachus and Apollonius."[184] But it was

---

182. This is presumably what Wilamowitz meant when he rather oddly wrote that "Nach den Worten der Suidasvita war A. in der [Ibis] nicht genannt" (*HD* II. 96).

183. A. Calderini, *Dizionario dei nomi geografici e topografici dell' Egitto greco-romano* (Cairo 1935), 110; Fraser I. 46, 200-01, 263; Hopkinson 1984, 32-33.

184. Watson 1991, 121-30 (quoting earlier discussions).

not till the nineteenth century that this rivalry became notorious. There is no genuinely ancient evidence at all. There is no suggestion even in the "ancient" *Lives* that Callimachus played any part in the failure of the supposed first recital. There are just three texts of the Byzantine era, none (in all probability) earlier than the tenth century. First the Suda-entry; second an iambic (or rather dodecasyllabic) epigram prefixed to manuscripts of Callimachus's hymns;[185] and last a marginal scholion in the Palatine Anthology that attributes to Apollonius the Rhodian the following well-known attack on Callimachus:[186]

Καλλίμαχος τὸ κάθαρμα, τὸ παίγνιον, ὁ ξύλινος νοῦς·
αἴτιος ὁ γράψας Αἴτια Καλλίμαχος.

Callimachus—refuse, triviality, woodenhead!
The cause is Callimachus, who wrote the *Causes*.

In a later book of the Anthology (*AP* xi. 275) this epigram stands in the text, attributed to "Apollonius the grammaticus."

There are several objections to crediting the Rhodian with this crude and feeble piece. First, "grammaticus" is the primary attribution, copied from the earlier Anthology of Cephalas, in fact from a section that derives from the second-century Anthology of Diogenianus.[187] Second, on the face of it Apollonius the grammarian is being distinguished from other Apollonii. Third, before we pay too much attention to the attribution to the Rhodian, we should bear in mind that the author of the scholion was himself a Rhodian, given to underlining the ethnics of Anthology poets who hailed from Rhodes.[188] It would not be surprising if this of all scholiasts had jumped to the conclusion that this critic of Callimachus was his famous fellow Rhodian rather than some obscure grammarian.

Wilamowitz had the strange idea that, though not written by the Rhodian, the epigram purported nonetheless to answer the question "What would Apollonius say when driven out of Alexandria?"[189] By late antiquity this was a well-established rhetorical exercise (though never, it seems, of historical figures).[190] But quite apart from the fact that this hypothesis presupposes the rivalry and exile it is supposed (in default of other evidence) to be proving, the simple abuse of the epigram is a far cry from the

185. σκώπτω δ' ἐπαραῖς Ἴβιν Ἀπολλώνιον (line 8), Pfeiffer II. lv and xcviii; not earlier than VI or VII s. and perhaps as late as XII (Bulloch 1985, 80-81).

186. τὸν ποιητὴν ὃν ἔσκωψεν Ἀπολλώνιος ὁ Ῥόδιος ὁ γράψας τὰ Ἀργοναυτικά, on *AP* vii. 41 by Callimachus.

187. See my *Greek Anthology*, Ch. IV.

188. Timocreon, Besantinus, Dosiadas, Simmias; see my *Greek Anthology* 306, and for the identification of the scholiast as Constantine the Rhodian, ib. 300-328.

189. *HD* II. 96-7; A. La Penna, *Ovidii Ibis* (Florence 1957), xxxiii; Page, *FGE* 18.

190. E.g. *AP* ix. 454-80, with Cameron, *BICS* xiv (1967), 58-61.

ingenious rhetoric we normally find in such exercises. It does not fit the situation at all.

Indeed, the most important objection to connecting the poem with Apollonius in any way is simply that there is no coherent literary thrust to the polemic. Line 1 contains mere abuse, and though line 2 attacks the *Aetia*, the attack turns on nothing more profound than a pun (writing the *Aetia* makes Callimachus *aetios*, "guilty").[191] Furthermore, while there are all sorts of reasons, personal, professional and artistic, why Callimachus and Apollonius *might* have quarrelled, it is most unlikely that they quarrelled about the *Aetia*. It is clear from his own preoccupation with aetiology and numerous borrowings from the *Aetia* that Apollonius much admired the poem.

The epigram is surely the product of a much later age. There are several epigrams from the early empire abusing Callimachus as a pedant,[192] and the tradition may go back to Pergamum. There is an interesting epigram by Herodicus the disciple of Crates attacking the pedantry of Aristarchus and his disciples in much the same terms.[193]

Over and above the poor credentials of these late texts, there is one positive reason for doubting that Apollonius was the subject of the *Ibis*. Given the complete loss of Callimachus's poem, all we have to go on is Ovid's *Ibis*, and despite recent denials it is hard to dispute Housman's conclusion about its object:[194]

> Who was Ibis? Nobody. He is much too good to be true. If one's enemies are of flesh and blood, they do not carry complaisance so far as to choose the dies Alliensis for their birthday and the most ineligible spot in Africa for their birthplace. Such order and harmony exist only in worlds of our own creation, not in the jerry-built edifice of the demiurge.

Watson's recent survey of all the Hellenistic curse poems of which we have any knowledge led him to the same conclusion: that their true raison d'être "was the curses themselves, and not the persons or actions which instigated them."[195] They are simply exercises in erudition and ingenuity. This is why there is no early evidence about the identity of Callimachus's Ibis. Contemporaries, familiar with such jeux d'esprit, knew that Ibis was nobody.

---

191. Page, *FGE* 18 ("criminal"); Lloyd-Jones, *Acad. Papers* II. 224 ("guilty").

192. Listed by Gow and Page, *GP* II. 114, and see Düring, next note.

193. I. Düring, *Herodicus the Cratetan: A Study in Anti-Platonic Tradition* (Stockholm 1941), 6-11; Page, *FGE* 62-5 (unaware of Düring).

194. Housman goes on to list curses "too awful to be probable and too improbable to be awful" (*JPh* 35 [1920], 316 = *Classical Papers* III [1972], 1040). Unlike Watson 1991, 131 n. 354, I do not find the counter-arguments of André and La Penna convincing.

195. Watson 1991, 133.

9

Very different is the evidence for the identification of the Telchines. The Scholia Florentina/Diegeseis are a work of modest scholarly pretensions in an established tradition (Ch. IV. 4). It is a genre represented by some quite respectable names. The original work of which our Roman papyri no doubt represent a somewhat abridged and debased version should not be unduly depreciated. For the most part they simply summarize Callimachus's poems. But when they do supply information not given in the text, it is usually good.

The only questionable detail supplied by the Diegeseis is the identification of the schoolmaster who seduces his pupils[196] in *Iamb* 5 as "Apollonius, or Cleon according to some."[197] It is often assumed that both names are guesses, but the point may be that the Apollonius named in the poem was thought to conceal a real-life schoolmaster called Cleon. It is easy to dismiss both names out of hand, but Callimachus mentions many contemporaries by name in his poems, especially his epigrams, and an early commentator might have had some other basis for identifying a schoolmaster in Callimachus's circle. That is to say, if a guess, it may nonetheless have been an informed early guess.

Even if there was no full-scale commentary before Theon, we now know that annotated texts existed from a very early date. The new Lille papyrus of *Aetia* III, written in the late third or early second century B.C., is already equipped with notes (interspersed among the lines of the text) in the hand of the text scribe. Most of them go no further than gloss and paraphrase, but that is immaterial. It is the existence rather than the nature of the commentary that matters. Many Byzantine scholia are no more substantial. We might in any case expect the notes on a contemporary text to be rather different from those on a classic.

In the present context the most significant feature of the Lille scholia is a detailed prosopographical note, an accurate explanation of the dynastic fiction whereby Berenice II, daughter of Magas and Apama, was officially styled the daughter of Philadelphus and Arsinoe.[198] An abbreviated version is to be found in the commentary to F 110. 45 in the sixth- or seventh-century P. Oxy. 2258 (again in the hand of the text scribe). So this particular note in a late antique manuscript goes back 700 years to a text of the

196. ὡς τοὺς ἰδίους μαθητὰς καταισχύνοντα; according to Dawson (1950, 63), the Greek is ambiguous and the reference might be to Callimachus's pupils. But lines 3 and 22 surely exclude the possibility that Callimachus was a teacher too.

197. γραμματοδιδάσκαλον ὄνομα Ἀπολλώνιον, οἱ δὲ Κλέωνα, ἰαμβίξει (Pfeiffer I.185).

198. *SH* 255; for a photo, Turner, *GMAW*² 75.

Aetia written barely a generation from Callimachus's death. For another prosopographical note, we have already considered the first-century London scholiast's identification of the "tenth Muse" as Arsinoe (Ch. VI. 1), which, if correct, must also be early.

The *Aetia* prologue is one of the most entertaining of all ancient invectives. Ancient readers must have been as anxious as their modern counterparts to know the identity of the tasteless, foolish pedants Callimachus so brilliantly pilloried. The earliest, local readers will not have needed to be told. They knew what sort of people he had in mind. But there must have been others less *au courant* who did need to be told. The moment the *Aetia* began to circulate outside Alexandria this need will have become pressing. The work as a whole is highly allusive, and it is not hard to imagine very early copies being equipped with at least a skeleton of explanatory notes.

The names of Asclepiades and Posidippus could not have been inferred from *Callimachus*'s works. If they are inferences, they are inferences by someone who had read the epigrams of both Asclepiades and Posidippus *as well*. The other names on the list are instructive in a different way. No "rhetor" by the name of [Arg]yrippus or [P]yrippus is known,[199] and no one at all by the name Iliones or Idiones.[200] Dionysius, by contrast, is one of the commonest of all Greek names: Susemihl lists more than 40 literary Dionysii from the Hellenistic period alone. Lehnus has recently argued that one of the Florentine "two Dionysii" was the mythographical writer Dionysius "Leather-arm" (Scytobrachion).[201] This may be so (a new papyrus has shown that he lived perhaps a century earlier than formerly thought). More significant is the fact that the scholiast apparently expected his readers to know which "two Dionysii" he had in mind. As Fraser sensibly remarked, "it seems most improbable that such specific learning should be inaccurate."[202] These are plainly not guesses, and it is difficult to believe that anyone compiling such a list in the Roman age would pick such obscure names rather than (say) Apollonius or Rhianus.

The Telchines were not (of course) a fixed body, who could be ticked off one by one on a list. It was a collective title applied in fun to all who did not share Callimachus's views. I would certainly agree with Lefkowitz that the *Aetia* prologue is not to be read seriously as an open letter to a battery of unrelenting critics. But there is one factor that she (like many

---

199. The only names suggested by F. Dornseiff and B. Hansen, *Rückläufiges Wörterbuch der griechischen Eigennamen* (Berlin 1957), 277-78.

200. ἴλειονι or ἴδειονι (reading confirmed by G. Bastianini, *ZPE* 97 [1993], 26 n. 7); for various possibilities, Herter 1937, 109.

201. *FGrH* 32; J. S. Rusten, *Dionysius Scytobrachion* (Opladen 1982); L. Lehnus, *ZPE* 97 (1993), 25-28.

202. Fraser I. 749.

others) underestimates. Whatever the issues involved, the prologue itself clearly addresses a very specific situation.

This is why Pfeiffer and his followers were (I suggest) wrong to see it as a reply to all the critics Callimachus had accumulated in a lifetime of controversy. We actually possess another reply to his critics (*Iamb* 13), no less colourful in style (at lines 19-21 the critics are represented as urging Callimachus's friends to put him in a straitjacket!). But it is a reply to quite different criticisms,[203] entirely concerned with his iambic poetry. It may well be that Callimachus's temperament kept him in constant controversy with his peers, but given his versatility and the variety of his literary interests, it was only to be expected that the controversies would be constantly changing. The preoccupations of the *Aetia* prologue do not reappear in the only slightly later *Iamb* 13; and the issues of *Iamb* 13 are not to be found in the *Aetia* prologue. The obvious solution is that the *Aetia* prologue reflects the issues with which Callimachus was concerned at the time he was writing the *Aetia*. If it was a specific controversy engaged in at a specific moment, then it is likely that certain specific individuals were involved. Assuming that the time was ca 270, there are two aspects of the Florentine list that support this solution.

First, the biggest initial surprise of the Florentine list was the absence of Apollonius of Rhodes. Few will be surprised anymore. Yet if the evidence for the feud is late, that is precisely why we might have expected to find Apollonius's name on any late list of Callimachus's enemies based on guesswork. It is therefore significant that he does not appear. Apollonius was not a person of any consequence at the time Callimachus wrote the *Aetia*, and so is quite properly not mentioned in a list of Callimachus's critics at that moment.

Secondly, there is Fraser's argument that "the presence of Asclepiades raises an immediate query, for Asclepiades can hardly have been alive and active when, in later life, Callimachus published the prologue."[204] Fraser placed Asclepiades's birth ca 340, which is perhaps on the early side (Ch. IX. 1); but he was certainly older than Callimachus, and spoken of with respect by Theocritus (7. 40). Posidippus was active between ca 280 and 263/2, possibly earlier if he is the Posidippus addressed by Phoenix of Colophon (p. 173). Praxiphanes was a pupil of Theophrastus, who was head of the Peripatos between 322 and ca 287; he is not likely to have been born later than 320, perhaps a good deal earlier. Callimachus is known to have written a work with the title *Against Praxiphanes* (F 460), and while

---

203. According to the generally sensible and sceptical discussion of Callimachus's literary polemic by Hutchinson (1988, 79), "It is unnatural not to connect the debates in the two poems." Connect, certainly, but we should not minimise the differences.

204. Fraser I. 749; so too Hutchinson 1988, 82 n.110.

it would be idle to guess at its contents, it is enough that they engaged in some sort of literary dialogue. We know that Callimachus lived to an active seventy, and Asclepiades, Posidippus and Praxiphanes may have done the same. But the chances are obviously against their being exact contemporaries, all still alive in 245.

It may be objected that the Telchines do not need to have been alive and in one place when Callimachus wrote his reply. But if there *was* one time and place where they were all alive together; and if that was the time to which we have on other grounds assigned a prologue which does seem to envisage a specific controversy—surely so much the better. The more so since I hope to show that the *Aetia* and its prologue were inspired by an independently documented controversy between Callimachus, Asclepiades and Posidippus. The evidence is a series of epigrams on an elegy of Antimachus of Colophon called *Lyde*—epigrams it seems reasonable to suppose written by living contemporaries in contact with one another (Ch. XI).

Fraser, of course, was assuming that the *Aetia* prologue dated from ca 245. Once we put it back where it belongs ca 270, all falls into place. Asclepiades and Posidippus travelled widely, but Posidippus was certainly active in Alexandria in the 270s,[205] and the following chapter will attempt to show that Asclepiades was too. Alexandria in the 270s is the one place where Callimachus, Asclepiades and Posidippus at any rate might have met—in fact are sure to have met, at the court of Philadelphus.

205. The Milan roll has four more epigrams linking Posidippus with Arsinoë.

Chapter IX

Mistresses and Dates

1

Since Asclepiades and Posidippus play an important if indirect rôle in the chapters that follow, it may be helpful to reconsider the evidence on their dates, movements and links to the world of Callimachus. Two epigrams, hitherto inadequately interpreted, show them active in Alexandria during the reign of Philadelphus (§§ 1 and 2). One of them will also help to circumscribe more closely the relative chronology of Callimachus's *Aetia*, some idylls of Theocritus, a famous poem of Sotades and Apollonius's *Argonautica* (§ 3):[1]

> τὠφθαλμῷ[2] Διδύμη με συνήρπασεν· ὤμοι, ἐγὼ δὲ
>   τήκομαι ὡς κηρὸς πὰρ πυρί, κάλλος ὁρῶν.
> εἰ δὲ μέλαινα, τί τοῦτο; καὶ ἄνθρακες· ἀλλ' ὅτε κείνους
>   θάλψωμεν, λάμπουσ' ὡς ῥόδεαι κάλυκες.

Didyme has swept me off my feet with her eye. Alas! When I gaze upon her beauty I melt away like wax before the fire. If she is black, so what? So are coals. But when we burn them, they glow like rosebuds.

Didyme is not just a run-of-the-mill charmer who has led Asclepiades on and let him down. Unlike most of his erotic poems, there is no situation, just description. And the essence of the description is that she is black.

In the ordinary way skin black as coal might be thought to suggest a negro: a Nubian, say, or Ethiopian. But (as our own use of the word illustrates) when applied to skin colouring, black is a very relative term, normally implying no more than skin significantly darker than the speaker's. Can the name help?

Didyme is not an uncommon name, but it is above all an *Egyptian* name.[3] Preisigke's *Namenbuch* (1922) cites well over one hundred un-

---

1. *AP* v. 210; an earlier version of §§ 1-2 appeared in *GRBS* 31 (1990), 287-311.

2. Despite a recent defence of P's τῷ θαλλῷ by B. Baldwin (*Emerita* 50 [1982], 145-49), I print Wilamowitz's τὠφθαλμῷ (in Pindar F 123 a boy's flashing eyes make the poet melt κῆρος ὡς). For the singular, found "unwelcome" by Gow and Page (*HE* II. 120; cf. W. Ludwig, *Gnomon* 1966, 23), there are two other examples in Asclepiades: *AP* v. 162. 2 (εἰς ὄνυχα) and xii. 161. 3 (κατ' ὄμματος); cf. too Agathias, *AP* v. 282. 3, ὄμμα δὲ θέλγειν / οὐ λάθε.

3. "charactéristique de l'Égypte," L. Robert, *Hellenica* ii (1946), 8.

differentiated examples of Didymos/Didyme;[4] Foraboschi's supplement at least another two hundred.[5] The Ptolemaic Prosopography lists 32 examples as far as it goes, and of the thirteen learned Didymi listed in Pauly-Wissowa six at least are Alexandrian.[6]

The Egyptians carefully distinguished themselves from their darker Nubian and Ethiopian neighbours in their art.[7] But to the Greeks the Egyptians themselves had always seemed dark-skinned.[8] A number of texts spell out the difference fairly precisely. For example, Achilles Tatius describes Nilotic pirates as "dark-skinned, though not absolutely black like an Indian, but more like a half-caste Ethiopian" (μέλανες...τὴν χροίαν, οὐ κατὰ τὴν ἄκρατον, ἀλλ' οἷος ἂν γένοιτο νόθος Αἰθίοψ).[9] According to Philostratus, those who inhabited the border regions between Egypt and Ethiopia were "less black than the Ethiopians but more black than the Egyptians."[10] Particularly explicit is the description in the probably second-century *Acts of Peter* of a demonic female as "a pure Ethiopian, not Egyptian but completely black."[11] Ammianus's characterization of Egyptians as *subfusculi* implies a contrast with others even darker.[12]

Inside Egypt skin colour was naturally an important identifying characteristic, and personal descriptions in official documents regularly specify whether an individual is dark- or light-skinned, in a series of graded terms.[13] But most Greek texts simply call Egyptians "black" or "dark":

4. No exact count possible, since he simply cites one hundred separate volumes in which the names are to be found (65 for Δίδυμος, 35 for Διδύμη).

5. D. Foraboschi, *Onomasticum alterum papyrologicum* II. 2 (Milan ca 1970), 93-94.

6. *Prosopographia Ptolemaica* VII, ed. L. de Meulemeester-Swinnen and H. Hauben (Louvain 1975), 96-97. It has been suggested that the frequency of the name (together with its Egyptian equivalent Hatre) reflects the frequency of twins in Egypt (P. Perdrizet, *Les Terre cuites grecques d'Égypte* [Nancy 1921], xix, 100 for terra cotta representations of twins; on Hatre, K.F.W. Schmidt, *GGA* 1918, 108, no. 2). The frequency of twin births does vary considerably in different parts of the world (M. Bulmer, *The Biology of Twinning in Man*, Oxford 1970), but it is difficult to believe that all Didymi were one of twins (what was the other called?). There is in fact some evidence that twins were felt to be ill-omened in Egypt: J. Baines, "Egyptian Twins," *Orientalia* 54 (1985), 461-482.

7. J. Vercoutter, *L'Image du Noir dans l'Art occidental* (Fribourg 1976), 33-88; F. M. Snowden Jr, *Before Color Prejudice* (Harvard 1983), 11-13; *GRBS* 32 (1991), 239-53.

8. There is a very full collection of texts relating to ancient perceptions of difference in skin colour, intelligently interpreted, in Lloyd A. Thompson, *Romans and Blacks* (London 1989). Curiously enough (if I am not mistaken), he missed Asclepiades on Didyme.

9. *Leuc. et Clit.* 3. 9. 2; the Nile pirates in Heliodorus (1. 3. 1) are simply μέλανες.

10. *V. Apoll.* 6. 2; the Ethiopians are κατακόρως μέλανες in Ptol. *Geog.* 1. 9. 10.

11. *in aspectu Ethiopissimam, neque Aegyptiam sed totam nigram*, *Actus Petri* 22, in R. A. Lipsius and M. Bonnet, *Acta Apostolorum Apocrypha* I (Leipzig 1891), 70. On the blackness of demons and the like, J. J. Winkler, *JHS* 100 (1980), 160-2; Thompson 110-113.

12. Amm. Marc. xxii. 16. 23.

13. J. Hasebroek, *Das Signalelement in den Papyrusurkunden* (Papyrusinstitut Heidelberg Schr. 3, Berlin 1921), 30 for a list of the terms found: λευκόχρως, μελίχρως, μελάγχρως, ἐπίπυρρος, ὑπόπυρρος, πυρρακής, ἐρυθρίας. According to Hasebroek, the first, "honey-skinned," is the most common, "die typische Hauptfarbe der Ägypter." See too

μελάγχροες (for example) in Herodotus (ii. 104). The ps-Aristotelian *Physiognomonica* classifies the Egyptians together with the Ethiopians as ἀγὰν μέλανες, a sign (the writer alleges) of cowardice.[14] In Aeschylus, the Danaïds refer to themselves as μελανθὲς / ἡλιόκτυπον γένος.[15] In an anonymous fragment χρόαν δὲ τὴν σὴν ἥλιος λάμπων φλογὶ / αἰγυπτιώσει,[16] "make Egyptian" means "make dark." To judge by the titles of numerous lost plays, Athenian audiences were fascinated by stories of Egypt, and it is likely that Egyptians were distinguished from Greeks on stage by appropriately painted masks, just as black and white complexions are clearly differentiated in Greek vase painting.[17]

Snowden insisted that the comparison with coal proves Didyme to have been an Ethiopian—perhaps, like Verdi's Aida, a captive princess.[18] He may be right, but the comparison was surely prompted by the poet's own use of the word "black" rather than the actual hue of Didyme's skin. Plato used the same word of dark-skinned Athenian eromenoi (*Rep.* 474d), who must have looked white compared with even Egyptians. Common though the name is, a plausible candidate can in fact be found. No less a personage than Philadelphus himself had a mistress called Didyme, "one of the native women" (μίαν τῶν ἐπιχωρίων γυναικῶν). The source is the *Memoirs* of the king's great-great-grandson, Ptolemy Euergetes II.[19] In the mouth of a Ptolemaic king, very conscious of his Macedonian blood, "native" clearly means non-Greek, that is to say, Egyptian or (perhaps) Ethiopian. A native mistress is bound to have appeared dark-skinned to Greek observers. Some may have been critical of such a liason. Intermarriage between Greeks and Egyptians was still frowned upon,[20] and though a mistress is not a wife, Euergetes clearly thought the point worth mentioning. A graceful defence such as Asclepiades's poem might have been appreciated by the royal lover.

Asclepiades's epigram has a link to Theocritus 10 that deserves further scrutiny in this context. The reaper Bucaeus is in love with the skinny, sun-

Gow on Theocr. 10. 28.

    14. § 67 = *Scriptores physiognomonici* ed. R. Foerster, I (1893), 72; the claim is repeated by Polemo, ib. p. 244, § 36, and by anon. II p. 107 Foerster. Ps-Aristotle weakens his case somewhat by adding that "excessively pale" people were also cowardly!

    15. *Suppl.* 154-55; 719-20, 745-47; J. Diggle, *Euripides Phaethon* (1970), 79.

    16. *Trag. Adesp.* F 161 = *TrGF* II (1981), 60.

    17. Edith Hall, *Inventing the Barbarian* (Oxford 1989), 139-43.

    18. *GRBS* 32 (1991), 247.

    19. Athenaeus 576 EF (= Jacoby, *FGrH* 234 F4). On Ptolemy's mistresses see too Polybius xiv. 11. 2 and (for Glauce the Citharode) D. B. Thompson, *Essays...K. Lehmann* (1964), 314-22; Fraser II. 818 n. 165. Lady friends of the Ptolemies are collected in a section discreetly entitled "Dames de la Cour" in *Pros. Ptol.* VI (1968), nos. 14713-37; see too S. B. Pomeroy, *Women in Hellenistic Egypt* (New York 1984), 53-4.

    20. Fraser II. 71; N. Lewis, *Greeks in Ptolemaic Egypt* (Oxford 1986), 27-29.

burned Bombyca. To make the best of the second of these defects he claims
that "the violet and the lettered hyacinth are also dark": καὶ τὸ ἴον μέλαν
ἐστί, καὶ ἁ γραπτὰ ὑάκινθος.[21] That is to say, both poets make the best of
a dark skin with a floral comparison introduced by καί. Since they were
contemporaries, both active in Alexandria, there can be little doubt that one
imitated the other. And the imitator was surely Asclepiades. For Theocritus
was clearly inspired by Plato's famous account of how lovers make the best
of the defects of their beloveds, where one of Plato's illustrations had been
calling the dark-skinned (μέλανας again) manly.[22] Theocritus handled dark
skin in a quite different way, as befitted the transference of the motif from
boy to girl. It is from Theocritus that Asclepiades (who shows no knowledge of Plato) has taken both the flower comparison and the formulation.

At 7. 40 Theocritus names Asclepiades (together with Philitas) as a
master in a way that suggests he was the older man (Ch. XVI. 1). So if
Asclepiades is the borrower here, it is likely that the poem dates from
nearer the end than the beginning of his career. There is no reason to doubt
that Asclepiades lived into the early part of Philadelphus's reign. If so,
then so celebrated a poet, spoken of with awe by Theocritus and paid the
compliment of imitation by Callimachus, is sure to have received an invitation to court. Didyme is the first on Euergetes's list,[23] which (since it is
not alphabetical) may mean that she was the earliest. And where but at a
Ptolemaic court is a Greek poet of the age likely to have come across a
young black woman who was his social equal?

The only other detail supplied by Euergetes is that Didyme was μάλ'
εὐπρεπεστάτην τὴν ὄψιν. Now this would most naturally be taken to mean,
quite simply, that she was very beautiful in appearance. But the phrase
could also mean that she had beautiful eyes, no doubt more conspicuous in
a dark-skinned woman.[24] We might compare Damascius's description of
the fifth-century A.D. Egyptian poet Pamprepius of Panopolis as μέλας τὴν
χροίαν, εἰδεχθὴς τὰς ὄψεις, where the plural perhaps suggests "with
hideous eyes" rather than just "with a hideous face."[25] If so, the coin-

---

21. 10. 28, with Gow's note on the identification of the flowers.

22. *Rep.* 474d-475a, with the full account of the history of this motif in R. D. Brown,
Lucretius on Love and Sex (Leiden 1987), 128-32, and the stemma in E. Courtney, *LCM* 15
(1990), 117-18. The incipit ἡ σιμὴ τὸ πρόσω(πον) in P. Oxy. 3724, col. ii. 27 (? Philodemus)
may be a new example.

23. The complete list (in alphabetical order) is: Agathocleia (*Pros. Ptol.* VI no. 14713);
Bilistiche (14717); Glauce (14718); Didyme (14719, not citing Asclepiades); Kleino (14726);
Mnesis (14728); Myrtion (14729); Stratonice (14733).

24. The physical descriptions in Egyptian documents have a surprisingly rich vocabulary
to characterize eyes: γλαυκός, χαροπός, ἐπιχάροπος, εὐόφθαλμος, κάκοψις, κοιλόφθαλμος,
ὑπόσκνιφος, ὑπόστραβος, ὑποστραβαινίξων, not to mention several more mundane terms
(Hasebroek, *Das Signalelement* 33-5).

25. Suda s.v. Παμπρέπιος (IV. 14. 37 Adler, misinterpreted by C. Zintzen, *Damascii
Vitae Isidori Reliquiae* [Hildesheim 1967], 151. But Heliodorus's Nile bandits are
μέλανας...τὴν χροίαν καὶ τὴν ὄψιν αὐχμηρούς, where τὴν ὄψιν presumably refers to facial

cidence with Asclepiades's description (τῷφθαλμῷ Διδύμη με συνήρπασεν) would be complete. Indeed, if Asclepiades's poem really does refer to the royal mistress, then it may well have been known to Euergetes, in part at least the source of his own description.

It should be observed that the poem need not be read as implying that Didyme is Asclepiades's own mistress or even the object of his active attentions. There is nothing to mark her out as the flirt, the reluctant virgin, the betrayer or any other of the female types so memorably depicted in the rest of his erotic verse.[26] And nothing to suggest that his feelings were reciprocated either. He simply states that she has bewitched him with her gaze. The poem is a tribute to her beauty—and a defence of her dark skin. It would be a perfectly acceptable compliment to the mistress of another man—even a king. Furthermore, there is always the possibility that the poem was written before or after Didyme's period as royal mistress. A famous parallel from another age is Thomas Wyatt's sonnet on Anne Boleyn.[27] In the small society of a court it cannot have been easy to steer clear of past and (especially) future mistresses of an amorous monarch.

If the identification is accepted, there are two gains for the biography of Asclepiades. First, though it is clear that Asclepiades exerted a determining influence on the course of the first generation of Alexandrian epigrammatists and had a personal as well as literary relationship with Posidippus and Hedylus, who undoubtedly worked in Alexandria, so far no solid evidence has been produced to locate Asclepiades himself there.[28] If the Didyme poem really does celebrate a mistress of Philadelphus, we would at last have proof.

Second, Asclepiades's dates. According to Fraser, he was born not later than ca 340. That is to say, he would have been ca 60 at the accession of Philadelphus (283/2)—and perhaps a septuagenarian by the time he met Didyme. This early chronology rests entirely on the assumption that he wrote a rhetorical poem on a signet ring (*AP* ix. 752) with a double ascription, to Asclepiades or Antipater of Thessalonica. Style, metrical practice and content alike suit Antipater better than Asclepiades.[29] Gow and Page repeated the ascription to Asclepiades when editing Antipater in their *Garland of Philip* (II. 21), but Page wisely (if silently) dropped the poem from his re-edition of Asclepiades in *Epigrammata Graeca*. It can safely be eliminated from future discussions of Asclepiades's biography.

---

appearance in general, as (e.g.) with εὐπρεπὴς τὴν ὄψιν in Demosthenes 40. 27.

26. For this interpretation of "female types" in Asclepiades, see Appendix C.

27. G. G. Hiller, *Poems of the Elizabethan Age*[2] (London 1990), 29; A. Fraser, *The Six Wives of Henry VIII* (London 1992), 127-28.

28. Fraser I. 557f.; see too Appendix C and my *Greek Anthology* 369-76.

29. I have argued the case more fully in *GRBS* 31 (1990), 291-94.

More relevant is XXXIX G-P = *APl* 68:

Κύπριδος ἄδ' εἰκών· φέρ' ἰδώμεθα μὴ Βερενίκας·
διστάζω ποτέρᾳ φῇ τις ὁμοιοτέραν.

This is a statue of Cypris. But look, is it not perhaps Berenice? I am at a loss.
Whom does it resemble most?

The problem here is a double ascription to "Asclepiades or Posidippus."
Whichever the poet, the subject must be Berenice I, wife of Ptolemy I Soter
rather than Berenice II, wife of Euergetes. Gow eventually decided for
Berenice I, but implied that the question is more open than it is by misdat-
ing Berenice II's marriage with Euergetes to 258 instead of 246.[30] Neither
poet is likely to have been alive that late.

It is particularly hard to decide between Asclepiades and Posidippus,
because the latter so frequently imitates the former. Gow thought the style
and Ptolemaic subject in favor of Posidippus, the Doric dialect in favor of
Asclepiades. A more substantial consideration is that Posidippus never
employs the distich—a statement that can be made the more confidently
now that we have almost a hundred new epigrams by Posidippus, with not
a single distich among them. Indeed his contemporary epigrams are often
quite long: three of 10 and one of 12 lines among the known epigrams; one
(perhaps two) of 14 lines on the new papyrus.[31] But a closely similar distich is securely attributed to Asclepiades (XXI G-P = *AP* xii. 75):

εἰ πτερά σοι προσέκειτο καὶ ἐν χερὶ τόξα καὶ ἰοί,
    οὐκ ἂν Ἔρως ἐγράφη Κύπριδος ἀλλὰ σὺ παῖς.

If you had wings on your back and a bow and arrows in your hand, it is you,
boy, not Eros who would be reckoned the son of Cypris.

A comparison (apparently a painting rather than a statue) to the god, as
XXXIX is to the goddess of love. Compare now XXXVIII (= *AP* xii. 77),
ascribed once more to Asclepiades or Posidippus:

εἰ καθύπερθε λάβοις χρύσεα πτερὰ καί σευ ἀπ' ὤμων
    τείνοιτ' ἀργυρέων ἰοδόκος φαρέτρη

30. So too does Galli Calderini in her useful but inconclusive discussion in *Atti dell'Acc.
Pont.* 1983 (n. 15), 273-77, "probabilmente nel 258." There may have been a betrothal this
early, but it was broken off by Berenice's mother Apama on Magas's death in 250 (E. Will,
Histoire politique du monde hellénistique I² (Nancy 1979), 243-46), and the marriage did not
finally take place till after the death of Philadelphus in 246. As we know from Callimachus F
110 (the *Coma Berenices*), Berenice was still a recent bride when Euergetes left on his Syrian
expedition later the same year, 246.

31. Information from G. Bastianini.

καὶ σταίης παρ' Ἔρωτα φιλάγλαον οὐ μὰ τὸν Ἑρμῆν
οὐδ' αὐτὴ Κύπρις γνώσεται ὃν τέτοκε.

If you were to grow golden wings above and if on your silvery shoulders were
hung a quiver full of arrows, and if you were to stand beside Eros in all his
splendour, never (by Hermes) would even Cypris know which was her son.

This time there can be little doubt. This labored and over-ornate variation
on Asclepiades's elegant and concise poem must be the work of Posidippus.[32] By the same token it is surely preferable to conclude that the
Berenice poem too is by Asclepiades.

Was Berenice alive when the poem was written? It is obviously relevant
that Berenice was the first of a long line of Ptolemaic royal ladies to be
identified with and worshipped as Aphrodite. Theocritus 17. 34-50 seems
to imply that this did not happen till after Berenice's death, by ca 280.
Now Asclepiades *may* have coincidentally compared a statue of the living
Berenice to Aphrodite without any reference to her subsequent divinization
as Aphrodite. But the probability is surely against this. If so, then the poem
should have been written after Berenice's death, and if it is by Asclepiades,
then we would have further evidence for his presence in Alexandria in the
270s.

Asclepiades may (like Callimachus) have lived to a ripe and active old
age. But even so it might be more prudent to conclude that he was born a
decade or so later than ca 340 and did not live much beyond ca 260.

2

Philadelphus's "inclination to amours" (as his great-great-grandson put it)
was common knowledge. Theocritus included ἐρωτικός in a list of his
virtues (14. 61). Bearing this in mind, let us take a fresh look at *AP* v. 202,
another of those epigrams so irritatingly ascribed to "Asclepiades or
Posidippus":

Πορφυρέην μάστιγα καὶ ἡνία σιγαλόεντα
    Πλαγγὼν εὐίππων θῆκεν ἐπὶ προθύρων,
νικήσασα κέλητι Φιλαινίδα τὴν πολύχαρμον
    ἑσπερινῶν πώλων ἄρτι φρυασσομένων.
Κύπρι φίλη, σὺ δὲ τῇδε πόροις νημερτέα νίκης
    δόξαν, ἀείμνηστον τήνδε τιθεῖσα χάριν.

32. So Gow and Page (*HE* II. 142) and Galli Calderini (n. 31), 271-3.

> On the portico of the god who delights in horses [lit. "well-horsed porticos"], Plango has dedicated her purple whip and glittering reins, having defeated with her courser the seasoned campaigner Philaenis, when the colts of the evening have just begun to neigh. Dear Cypris, grant her the true glory of her victory, establishing for her this favour never to be forgotten.

This is said to be no more than a variation on *AP* v. 203 by Asclepiades (quoted and discussed below, Appendix C. 7), a more subtle double entendre likewise turning on what Gow primly described as "the equation between amatory and equestrian exercises." Fraser described v. 202 as a "tasteless" and "immensely crudified" adaptation of Asclepiades's poem.[33] Yet it is not really a question of taste that is involved. The curious thing about the poem is that, despite being more crudely sexual, it is at the erotic rather than the aesthetic level that the metaphor fails.

In Asclepiades, Lysidice dedicates her spur to Aphrodite, a parody of the usual dedication of domestic or professional tools no longer of use. But Lysidice is disposing of her spur because she is such a good "horsewoman" that she does not need it; she can reach the "end of the course" without applying the spur. The metaphor is skilfully maintained throughout. An innocent reader could take it for a poem about a real horsewoman.

Let us now look at *AP* v. 202. First there are the whip and reins Plango dedicates, which do not work so well at the sexual level as Lysidice's spur in Asclepiades. They suggest some leather-clad Mistress rather than a skilful hetaira astride her lover. Worse still, her proficiency is illustrated, not (as we might have expected) by reference to some eager or satisfied man, but by her "unforgettable victory" over another woman, strangely described as a "seasoned campaigner." This woman she "defeated *with* her horse" (νικήσασα κέλητι, l. 3). If this is the man, there is no suggestion that she is servicing him; on the contrary, he is merely the means whereby she defeats her female rival. And what part do the "colts of the evening" play in this race? Obviously one woman may be better in bed than another, but the image of a victorious contest cannot help but suggest a race in which fastest is best. At the erotic level this is hardly satisfactory, since most men would surely prefer the slower woman, the one able to defer rather than hasten the moment of climax. We may contrast here Dioscorides's description of the accomplished Doris, riding her lover all the way to the finish of the "marathon" of love (τὸν Κύπριδος δόλιχον, *AP* v. 55. 4).[34]

The last four words of line 1 are a Homeric formula:[35] as Gow remarks, "the reader is led to expect a heroic theme, or at least one con-

---

33. Fraser I. 570; II. 812.
34. See *HE* II. 239-40; Appendix C. 7.
35. E. 226, 328; Θ. 116, 137; Λ. 128; P. 479.

nected with athletic meetings." But the ensuing parody is hard to make erotic sense of. ἡνία in Homer are always the reins of horses yoked to chariots.[36] When we add in the borrowing of line 4 (of which more below) from Callimachus's fifth hymn, where again the reference is to horses that draw a chariot, the alert reader will have in mind the picture, not of a skilful horsewoman, but of a victorious charioteer.

This incongruous note entirely destroys the image of a woman astride a man that has so far been assumed to be the raison d'être of the poem. It is difficult to believe that even the less subtle Posidippus would have so badly botched the task of writing a coherent variation on this simple theme—much less Asclepiades himself. Is it possible that this was not even the poet's purpose? Was there in fact ever an occasion at the court of Philadelphus when a real hetaira won a real chariot race?

There was. None other than his celebrated Macedonian mistress Bilistiche won two chariot victories at the Olympic games, no less; in the quadriga in 268, and in the pair in 264.[37] Other victories are also possible, but these must have been the most famous. Of our two candidates for author, Asclepiades may not have survived this long, but Posidippus was certainly alive in 263/2 (Ch. II. 9). That the poem not only might but must in any case have been written as late as Bilistiche's triumphs can be established with something approaching certainty.

It has long been noticed that line 4 is a clever adaptation of line 2 of Callimachus's *Hymn* v, to Athena:[38]

ὅσσαι λωτροχόοι τᾶς Παλλάδος ἔξιτε πᾶσαι,
   ἔξιτε· τᾶν ἵππων ἄρτι φρυασσομενᾶν
τᾶν ἱερᾶν ἐσάκουσα....

You bathpourers of Pallas, come out everyone, come out. The mares just now began to neigh, I heard the sacred mares...

It must be the author of v. 202 who is the borrower. In Callimachus the ἄρτι serves a precise and important function; it is because he has just that moment heard the snorting of the horses who draw Athena's chariot that the poet bids the λωτροχόοι come forth and be about their business. But the ἄρτι in v. 202. 4 is entirely otiose; the line refers in the most general terms

36. *habenae equorum iunctorum*, H. Ebeling, *Lexicon Homericum* I (1885), col. 544.

37. *P. Oxy* 2082; Pausanias v. 8. 11; L. Moretti, *Olympionikai: i vincitori negli antichi agoni olimpici* (Accad. Lincei, Memorie, viii. 8. 2) 1957, 136-37; Jacoby, *FGrH* 257a F6 (Komm. p. 852). Fraser II. 210 n. 206, by oversight writes "264 and 260." Bilistiche will not (of course) have driven the chariot herself. In later times women are often listed as victors in chariot events, "femmes fortunées qui entretenaient une écurie de course et non viragos qui s'exhibaient dans l'arène" (L. Robert, *BCH* 1934, 520-1, with examples; cf. my *Circus Factions* [1976], 204). For sources on Bilistiche, *Pros. Ptol.* VI no. 14717.

38. Trans. A. W. Bulloch, *Callimachus: the Fifth Hymn* (Cambridge 1985), 93.

to the "colts" of both Plango and Philaenis, not even to the moment of
Plango's victory, since the poem is supposed to be commemorating her
subsequent dedication to Aphrodite. The effect of the line derives entirely
from its transference *as a whole* from a solemn, hymnic context to a crude,
erotic context.

In fact, since the poet so obviously expected his impudent borrowing to
be recognized, we might wonder why he bothered to change Callimachus's
ἵππων to πώλων. Its connotations of youth—"prancing young colts of the
night" suits the sexual metaphor nicely enough, but are not essential. All
the examples of the "horsewoman" motif collected by Jeffrey Henderson[39]
happen to use ἵππος (as did Asclepiades) or words formed from it, not
πῶλος. Could it be relevant that it was precisely in the category of πῶλοι
that Bilistiche won both her Olympic victories?[40]

Three final details. Commentators have a tendency to classify any pretty
female name found in an erotic context as "suitable for a hetaira." Many of
these names are equally common among respectable women.[41] But both the
names in this poem were borne by notorious hetairas, Plango of Miletus
and Philaenis of Samos.[42] That is to say, the poet is making sure that we
think of his competitors as regular hetairas rather than talented amateurs.

Secondly, Plango's purple whip. πορφυρέην is the only non-Homeric
word in an otherwise formulaic line, and while the adjective is common
enough, it is nonetheless tempting to wonder whether the first word of the
poem has some special significance. From the age of Alexander purple
became (as it had been with the Persians) the colour and prerogative par
excellence of royalty. In particular, Hellenistic kings regularly presented
their ministers and favorites with purple robes, to symbolize their status.
Livy regularly refers to courtiers of Hellenistic monarchs as *purpurati*, evidently reflecting widespread Hellenistic practice.[43] Thus for a contemporary familiar with the practice, to style a hetaira who "rode" the king
as possessing a purple *whip* would be a particularly delicate touch, a nice
blend of compliment and insult.

Third, for all the world as though v. 202 were a genuine dedication,
Hecker and Waltz identified the temple of Cypris with "well-horsed
porticoes" in which Plango is said to have hung her whip and reins as the

---

39. *The Maculate Muse* (Yale 1975), 174; for πῶλος in a different erotic context, see
Eubulus, F 84. 2 (Koch, *CAF* II 193, with R. L. Hunter, *Eubulus: The Fragments* (Cambridge 1983), 176 (note the quaint index entry, p. 259, "of ladies").

40. In 268 with the πωλικ[ὸ]ν [τέθριππον] (*P. Oxy.* 2082); in 264 with the newly introduced πωλικὴ συνωρίς (Pausanias v. 8. 11).

41. As L. Robert has often warned, e.g. *L'Epigramme grecque* (1968), 340-41.

42. Gow and Page, *HE* II. 140-41; on Philaenis, D. W. Vessey, *Revue belge de philol.*
54 (1976), 78-83. The distich quoted by Athen. 594CD from Archilochus (F 331 W) is
assigned to Asclepiades by West (*Studies* 139-40).

43. M. Reinhold, *History of Purple as a Status Symbol in Antiquity* (1970), 29-36.

new temple of Arsinoë-Aphrodite at Canopus. Posidippus did in fact write at least three epigrams on this foundation (XII and XIII GP and a further one on the Milan roll). Nevertheless Gow and Page rightly rejected so literal-minded an approach to what is so clearly a fictitious dedication. Furthermore, Arsinoë's temple was built on a headland at Zephyrium looking out to sea, and (as Posidippus's epigrams and another by Callimachus make clear) Arsinoë-Aphrodite was conceived as a marine deity.[44] It is thus improbable that her temple would have been conspicuously adorned with representations of horses. Indeed, why should any temple of Aphrodite have been decorated in this way? No known cult of Aphrodite associates her with horses. But that still leaves the question, why should the poet specify so unusual a feature for even an imaginary temple of Aphrodite? One possible explanation is that εὔιππων is simply a heavy-handed foreshadowing of the equestrian imagery to come. But there is another possibility. A year or two later Philadelphus dedicated another temple to Aphrodite—to Bilistiche-Aphrodite.[45] No information survives about the appearance of this temple, but given Bilistiches's interests and achievements, some equestrian emphasis is at least a possibility. However this may be, Bilistiche was certainly an Aphrodite εὔιππος, in the literal if in no other sense.

At first sight it might be thought improbable that anyone would dare to write anything so crude and insulting about a king's mistress. Yet we have seen that crude insults about kings' mistresses and even wives were indeed found perfectly acceptable at Macedonian courts—from the right people in the right context, namely his Friends at the symposium (Ch. III. 6). Sotades's immortal line on Philadelphus and Arsinoë is merely the best known of his attacks on most of the kings of the age (Ch. I. 2). From his Suda biography we learn that he also wrote a poem *On Bilistiche*. Coming from Sotades, it is not likely to have been respectful or flattering.

What more tempting occasion to write a poem on Bilistiche than one of her Olympic chariot victories? Callimachus wrote at least two epinician elegies on chariot victories: for Berenice at the Nemean and for Sosibius at the Isthmian and Nemean games. 268/4 may be a little late for Asclepiades, but the real specialist in epinician epigram was Posidippus. The new Milan roll contains no fewer than nineteen epigrams celebrating equestrian victories at all four of the major festivals by a variety of persons. One of the most interesting celebrates an Olympic victory by a Berenice:[46]

ἁγναὶ ἔθ' ἁμὲς ἐοῦσαι 'Ολυμπιακὸν Βερενίκας
παιδίσκαι Μακέτας ἀγάγομεν στέφανον,

44. Fraser I. 239-41.
45. Plutarch, *Amatorius* 9. 9 (*Moralia* 753 EF).
46. G. Bastianini and C. Gallazzi, *Posidippo Epigrammi* (Milan 1993), no. XXIV. XXII and XXIII are also agonistic; information on the others from Bastianini.

ὃς τὸ πολυθρύλητον ἔχει κλέος, ᾧ τὸ Κυνίσκας
ἐν Σπάρτᾳ χρόνιον κῦδος ἀφειλόμεθα.

According to the editors, the chaste παιδίσκαι are a chorus of children, and Berenice is the shortlived daughter of Berenice II (245-238). But this would be very late for Posidippus, and since it is these "girls" who win the crown and take long-standing glory from Cynisca, they must be Berenice's victorious horses. The emphasis on their youth, gender and marital status is merely a poetic way of indicating that she won in the category of πῶλοι with an all female team.[47] The claim to have robbed Cynisca of her glory is illustrated by the inscription to her statue at Olympia, which proudly styles her daughter and sister of Spartan kings and boasts that she was the first woman in Greece to win an equestrian crown—in (probably) 396 and again in 392.[48] His knowledge of Cynisca's boast and use of the simple style "Macedonian" suggests that Posidippus wrote for a statue of Berenice and her team at Olympia. On any hypothesis he overlooked the victory of Euryleonis (another Spartan princess), in (probably) 368,[49] but if he had been celebrating Berenice II or her daughter, how could he have overlooked the two recent victories of Bilistiche, mistress of Berenice's own dynastic father?[50] The victor must be Soter's wife Berenice I (ca 317-277), in which case the poem would be one of Posidippus's earliest, not latest.

No one familiar with Posidippus's work would have been surprised if, despite initial misdirection, *AP* v. 202 should turn out to celebrate (albeit ironically) a chariot victory rather than a simple dedication by a whore. Given the popularity of the genre, it is very likely that contemporaries wrote genuine epinicia for one or both of Bilistiche's victories. Her relationship with the king was not kept discreetly in the background. The anonymous Oxyrhynchus chronicle that records the quadriga victory of 268 styles her bluntly "Bilistiche the Macedonian...hetaira of Ptolemy Philadelphus."[51] This is the more striking in that (as we now know) Philadelphus's wife Arsinoë had been dead for only a week or two at the time, not two years as used to be thought.[52] And what could be more conspicuous than a temple of Bilistiche-Aphrodite?

47. Miltiades won at three successive Olympics with the same team of mares (Herod. vi. 103), and racehorses are often female in Pindar (*O*. i. 41; vi. 14; *N*. ix. 52; *P*. iv. 17; F 31. 2, 89a. 3). With ἀγναί cf. the epitaph of a s. II racehorse at Rome proclaiming her a *virgo* (*CLE* 218. 4). The πωλικὸν τέθριππον was instituted in 384 (Paus. v. 8. 10).

48. μόναν δ᾽ ἐμέ φαμι γυναικῶν Ἑλλάδος ἐκ πάσας τόνδε λαβεῖν στέφανον, Ebert 33.

49. L. Moretti, *Olympionikai* [1957], nos. 373 and 381 (Cynisca) and 418 (Euryleonis).

50. As L. Robert has often pointed out (e.g. Ἀρχ. Ἐφημ..1966, 109), precise claims of this nature in agonistic inscriptions are not normally lightly made (see too my *Porphyrius the Charioteer* [1973], 206-11).

51. *P. Oxy.* 2082 (*FGrH* 257a F6). The traces of ἑταίρα are faint, but no plausible alternative suggests itself.

52. Arsinoë died on 1/3 July 268 (Ch. VI. 6), and the Olympic games were held in July or August (no further precision possible: A. E. Samuel, *Greek and Roman Chronology*

From a curious passage of Athenaeus we learn that her ancestry was discussed by "historians of Argos."[53] For although her Macedonian origin seems impeccably documented (Bilistiche, like Berenike, is a pure Macedonian name),[54] she is said to have claimed descent from the Atreidai. Jacoby was worried by the ethnic "Argive" in this passage, and doubted the identification with Philadelphus's undoubtedly Macedonian mistress.[55] But she is styled ἑταίρα, and the Ἀργεία may be no more than an inference from the claim to descent from the Atreidai. This claim may be less startling than it seems, in view of the well-known pretensions to Argive descent by the Argead house of Macedon.[56] Though certainly attested as early as the fifth century, this theme seems to have been comprehensively promoted by King Archelaus of Macedon (ca 413-399). It was at Archelaus's court that Euripides wrote his *Archelaus*, in which he may actually have invented the mythical character of that name, son of the Heraclid Temenos, who was exiled from Argos and founded the original Macedonian capital city of Aegae (modern Vergina).[57] Archelaus's coinage also advertised this supposed Argive connection.[58]

To enhance the legitimacy of his rule, Ptolemy Soter claimed a connection to the Argead royal house through his mother Arsinoë.[59] Theocritus 17 emphasizes the descent of Philadelphus and Alexander from Heracles, and (as we saw in Ch. II. 7) his *Heracliscus* (24) is a veiled panegyric of Philadelphus. The Antigonids and Seleucids also claimed to be Heraclids, and (if by a different route) the Attalids too.[60] A recently published decree

---

[Munich 1972], 191-94).

53. Athenaeus 596 E = *FGrH* 311 F1, with Komm. p. 54.

54. See O. Masson, "Sur le nom de Bilistiché," *Studia in honorem I. Kajanto* (Arctos Suppl. 2), Helsinki 1985, 109-12 for other examples of names with Macedonian initial non-aspirated B for Φ: e.g. Βίλος for Φίλος, Βίλιππος for Φίλιππος (Plut. *Mor.* 292E) and (most obviously) Βερενίκη for Φερενίκη; ib. 112 for Macedonian names ending -ιχος/ίχα, M. Masson refers me in addition to Μελιννίχη on an inscription from Pella in D. Papakonstantinou-Diamantourou, *Pella* I (Athens 1971), 76, no. 59.

55. ἐκ Μακεδονίας τῆς ἐπὶ θαλάσσῃ, Paus. v. 8. 11; [M]ακετίς, *P. Oxy.* 2062, F 6.

56. Herodotus v. 22. 2; viii. 137. 1; Thucydides ii. 99. 3; v. 80. 2; Isocrates, *Philip* 32; cf. N.G.L. Hammond and G. T. Griffith, *A History of Macedonia* II (1979), 3-4; Harder (next note), 133-37; and see especially now the inscription published by J. Bousquet, *REG* 101 (1988), 39-41.

57. A. Harder, *Euripides' Kresphontes and Archelaos* (Mnemos. Supp. 87), Leiden 1985, 129-37. Archelaus also appears in Euripides's *Temenos* or *Temenidae* (Harder, 289).

58. E. N. Borza, *In the Shadow of Olympus* (Princeton 1990), 172-73.

59. The genealogy from Heracles to Soter through Amyntas I and Arsinoë is recorded by Satyrus, *FGrH* 631, line 11; for the (?later) story that Soter was actually fathered by Philip II, see R. M. Errington, *Alexandre le Grand*, Entretiens Hardt 22 (Geneva 1975), 155.

60. Errington 1975, 155-58; for the Antigonids, C. F. Edson, *HSCP* 45 (1934), 213-46; the Attalids, Ch. VIII. 2; the addition of Perseus to the Antigonid tree, Ch. X. 4.

from Xanthos in Lycia has fascinatingly illustrated the importance of this and other mythological relationships in diplomatic relations between the Diadochi.[61]

This may explain the enigmatic and fragmentary words καὶ πάρος Ἀργει[... in Callimachus's *Victoria Berenices*.[62] In a poem on a victory in the Nemean games, it would be natural and appropriate to allude to the Argive ancestry to which, as a granddaughter of Soter, Berenice could lay claim even before her marriage to Euergetes. We need only assume that Bilistiche too claimed a connection with Macedonian royalty, and the rest follows automatically. We have seen that the only women to win Olympic crowns before Bilistiche had both been royalty, as was the next after her, Berenice II. Her double Olympic victory and her own royal connection had elevated Bilistiche to a station in life where a court poet might deem it prudent to suggest a more flattering origin. It would not be hard to point to other such fictions in Ptolemaic court poetry. For example, in the same *Victoria Berenices* Berenice II is described as the daughter of Philadelphus and Arsinoë II, the "sibling gods."[63] She was in fact the daughter of Magas and Apama, as everyone knew (including the copyist of the Lille papyrus).

The art of polemical poetry has seldom flourished as it did in Ptolemaic Alexandria. A poet who disliked the pretensions of the royal mistress might well have been sorely tempted to write an anti-epinicion for the occasion.

If he did have Bilistiche's Olympic victories in mind, then the introduction of the motif of the racing hetaira would not have been a lapse of taste, but rather the raison d'être of the poem. Whereas v. 203 is an obscene double entendre disguised as a dedication by a horsewoman, v. 202 would be a lampoon on the king's mistress disguised as an obscene double entendre. The horsewoman motif would be literal and primary rather than a metaphorical subtext. But the execution is undeniably crude, and on balance Bilistiche's fellow Macedonian, the less subtle Posidippus, is the more likely author. He might even have known her in the days before chance brought them together at the court of Philadelphus.

61. J. Bousquet, *RÉG* 101 (1988), 12-53, esp. 39-41 on the Heracles connection.

62. No satisfactory explanation has so far been proposed. According to Parsons, "Callimachus may intend a simple parallel: formerly an Egyptian king (Danaus) ruled in Argos; now an Egyptian queen triumphs in the Argive games" (*ZPE* 25 [1977], 10). For a different suggestion, R. F. Thomas, *CQ* 33 (1983), 106-78.

63. *SH* 254. 2, with Parsons, *ZPE* 25 (1977), 6-9. The difference here (of course) is that this fiction also appears on official inscriptions: Fraser II. 384 n. 356.

3

Hitherto the chronological implications of the link between Callimachus and the epigram have seemed minimal. Fraser, for example (after many others), took it for granted that Callimachus's fifth hymn "is to be dated fairly early in the career of the poet, for a line of it was filched by his elder contemporary Posidippus."[64] We shall see that it cannot have been a very early work.

Another link long recognized is that between *Hymn* v. 103-4:

> δῖα γύναι, τὸ μὲν οὐ παλινάγρετον αὖθι γένοιτο
> ἔργον, ἐπεὶ Μοιρᾶν ὦδ᾽ ἐπένησε λίνα.

Noble lady, what has happened is irrevocable hereafter, for so spun the threads of the Fates.

and Apollonius ii. 444-5:

> Αἰσονίδη, τὸ μὲν οὐ παλινάγρετον οὐδέ τι μῆχος
> ἔστ᾽ ὀπίσω, κενεαὶ γὰρ ὑποσμύχονται ὀπωπαί.

Son of Aeson, that is irrevocable, nor is there any remedy hereafter, for my sightless eyes are blasted away.

There is more than a verbal parallel between the two texts. In Callimachus, Athena is addressing Chariclo, having just blinded her son, the future seer Tiresias. In Apollonius, the old seer Phineus addresses Jason, who has just suggested that some god might cure his blindness; the tormented Phineus begs for death instead. Thus while perfectly appropriate in Callimachus, the idea of irrevocability arises more naturally out of the context in Apollonius. As for the verbal parallel, not only do we have the same rare adjective in the same phrase and metrical position, and identical articulation throughout. The decisive point, as A. W. Bulloch pointed out, is that "both have the most unusual feature of the normally proclitic οὐ separated from its adjective by the main caesura."[65] There is no other example of this in Callimachus, notoriously the most fastidious and innovative of metricians, whereas it was apparently a refinement that did not trouble Apollonius. So if it appears this once in Callimachus, it is because it is "excused" (so to speak) by being a conscious borrowing. Here at least, it seems to be Callimachus who is the borrower. Those who recalled the Apollonian context would read Callimachus with the horrific picture of the blind old seer begging for death in their minds.

---

64. Fraser I. 256.
65. *AJP* 98 (1977), 121-23; Bulloch 1985, 41, 214-15.

The chronological implications now become serious. For if (as we shall shortly see) Apollonius drew on *Aetia* I-II, then the date assigned above for the Plango/Philaenis epigram (if my argument is accepted) entails the following sequence: (1) *Aetia* I-II; (2) *Argonautica*; (3) Callimachus *Hymn* v, all written before an epigram dating from (at latest) 264. This squares well enough with the sequence already established in Ch. VI: (1) *Aetia* I-II, (2) *Iambi*, with *Aetia* I-II before and *Iambi* probably soon after July 268. It should be added that Bulloch has also made out a very convincing case for the dependance of *Hymn* v on Theocritus 18.[66] But are there any problems with dating the *Argonautica* this early?

It is generally agreed that Apollonius drew on Nymphis of Heraclea for his own account of that region in Bk ii.[67] The scholia cite Nymphis often,[68] and on ii. 729 directly claim that Apollonius took a detail from Bk 1 of his *On Heraclea*.[69] According to his Suda-entry, this work "went down to the third Ptolemy." Accordingly Vian infers that Apollonius wrote after 246.[70] Matters are not quite so simple. Nymphis wrote two books, a history in 24 books of the Diadochi and Epigoni, that is to say, the first and second generation Successor kings; and *On Heraclea* in 13 books, which went down to the "deposition of the tyrants [ca 364-337], the Epigoni and the third Ptolemy." The likelihood is that the history also went down to 246 (new kings in both Syria and Egypt), by when Nymphis must have been in his seventies. Himself a leading citizen of Heraclea and an exile under the various tyrants who had ruled the city for many years, in 281 he was responsible for the return of the exiles on Seleucus's defeat of Lysimachus. To have played such a rôle he can hardly have been less than 30 at the time and so born no later than ca 310.[71] Such long works must have taken him many years and are likely to have been published in installments. It seems that only the first book of the work on Heraclea was devoted to its mythical past, and it was naturally only the mythical past that concerned Apollonius.[72] Bk 1 might easily have been written as early as the 270s. Jacoby explicitly remarks that it could have been in Apollonius's hands even if he wrote as early as ca 270.

66. Bulloch 1985, 41, 127, 138; A. Taliercio, *Boll. Class. Lincei* 10 (1989), 122-36.

67. See the full analysis of this section in Vian 1974, 156-63.

68. C. Wendel, *Scholia in Apollonium Rhodium Vetera* (Berlin 1935), index, p. 337; the passages are all collected in *FGrH* 432.

69. Νύμφις ἐν τῷ Περὶ Ἡρακλείας α΄ φησί· παρ᾽ οὗ Ἀπολλώνιος ἔοικε ταῦτα μεταφέρειν, p. 184. 13 Wendel.

70. Vian 1974, 156 n. 3; cf. xiii.

71. Jacoby, in *FGrH* 432; P. Desideri, *Studi classici e orientali* 16 (1967), 395-97; Fraser II. 887 n. 83; S. M. Burstein, *Outpost of Hellenism: The Emergence of Heraclea on the Black Sea* (Berkeley 1976), 2-3, 87-89.

72. Five citations specify Bk 1 (F 1-5), six more give no number (F 11-16), and though F 8 appears to specify 6 (ἐν τῷ ς΄), it is surely (as Jacoby saw) an error (the other citation from Bk 6 dates from after the battle of Plataea).

The situation is more complex now that *Aetia* I-II have been separated from III-IV by some 25 years. Those who believed that I-IV were all published together ca 245 naturally dated the *Argonautica* after then. So (for example) F. Vian,[73] who also believed that Callimachus's *Hymn to Apollo* attacked the *Argonautica*.[74] Since he assumed a date of ca 245 for the *Hymn to Apollo*, that seemed to point to a similar date for the *Argonautica*. But the only serious grounds for dating the *Hymn* are its thematic similarities to the *Aetia* prologue; it too can be brought back to ca 270 (Ch. XV).

If *Aetia* I-II can be dated as early as ca 270, then the *Argonautica* can be dated correspondingly earlier. It is possible (of course) that the *Argonautica* too was published in installments. But there is no actual evidence in favour of such an assumption. Then there is the further complication of the alleged second, successful edition. But (as already argued) that is best forgotten (the proecdosis mentioned in the scholia, if it means anything, should mean pre-edition or preliminary draft rather than first published edition).[75] In default of any indications to the contrary, we have to proceed on the assumption that all four books were published together.

Few firm conclusions can be drawn from purely verbal parallels,[76] (a) because of the intrinsic difficulty of deciding priority in such cases; (b) because there is so seldom a secure context in the fragmentary Callimachean text; and (c) because the careers of Callimachus and Apollonius overlapped by some 20 years. Each must on occasion have been influenced by the other. It will be safer to confine the inquiry to cases where the two poets share an Argonautic aetiology, where there can be no doubt that one must have been drawing on the other.

Callimachus had no special interest in the Argonautic saga. In fact only one of the 20 odd episodes in each of the two installments of the *Aetia* seems to have been devoted to the Argonauts, with one more in the *Iambi*. For the purposes of his *Argonautica*, on the other hand, Apollonius was exclusively concerned with stories about the Argonauts. So while we should naturally expect Apollonius to include every Argonautic adventure rescued from obscurity by Callimachus, we should not expect Callimachus to retell Argonautic stories already told by Apollonius—not unless he had come across some fresh angle or new version.

---

73. Vian 1974, xiii.

74. It should be added that even on that assumption, the conclusion did not follow. As we shall see, Apollonius must have known much of this material before so late a collected edition.

75. As rightly emphasized by Herter 1973, 22.

76. For example, Call. F 19, Μελαντείους δ᾽ ἐπὶ πέτρας ~ *Argon.* iv. 1706-7, πέτρας / ῥίμφα Μελαντείους.

In what appears to have been the second aetion of Bk I (F 7-21), Callimachus describes why the people of the tiny island of Anaphe near Crete sacrifice to Apollo Aegletes amid mutual abuse. The story also explains why Apollo received this epithet, because of the ray of light (αἴγλη) he had sent to guide them during a storm.[77] Both these aetia are told by both Callimachus and Apollonius, and there are close verbal parallels as well. For example, according to Apollonius (iv. 1701-6), Jason

χεῖρας ἀνασχόμενος μεγάλῃ ὀπὶ Φοῖβον ἀΰτει,
ῥύσασθαι καλέων...
...πολλὰ δὲ Πυθοῖ ὑπέσχετο, πολλὰ δ' Ἀμύκλαις,
πολλὰ δ' ἐς Ὀρτυγίην ἀπερείσια δῶρα κομίσσειν.

Raising his hands cried to Phoebus with mighty voice, calling on him to save them.... Many, beyond number, were the offerings he promised to bring to Pytho and Amyclae and Ortygia.

Almost word for word what Callimachus said of Jason (addressing Apollo himself):

σοὶ χέρας ἠέ]ρταζεν, Ἰήιε, πολλὰ δ' ἀπείλει·
ἐς Πυθὼ πέ]μψειν, πολλὰ δ' ἐς Ὀρτυγίην... (F 18.6-7).

He lifted up his hands to you, Apollo, and promised to send many gifts to Pytho and Ortygia.

In addition there is a clear echo of this same passage elsewhere in Apollonius, once more singling out the same two sanctuaries of Apollo (Delphi and Delos) under the same two poetic names: cf. i. 418-9, ἄλλα δὲ Πυθοῖ, ἄλλα δ' ἐς Ὀρτυγίην ἀπερείσια δῶρα κομίσσω.[78] The grateful Argonauts set up an altar to "Apollo the Embarker" at Pagasae in Thessaly. All that is left of the penultimate line in the Callimachus papyrus is]ἐπώνυμον Ἐμβασίοιο (F 18. 2), paralleled by Ἐμβασίοιό τ' ἐπώνυμον (βωμόν) in *Argon.* i. 404. There can be no serious doubt who imitated whom here.[79]

Apollonius also drew on a later episode from *Aetia* I. When introducing Hylas at i. 1207f., he digresses on the time Heracles killed the boy's father Theiodamas. There are one or two obscurities in what the poet explicitly represents as an abridgment of a more detailed version that would take him too far afield.[80] That it was Callimachus's version (*Aetia* F 24-5) is put beyond reasonable doubt by a verbal echo in the same passage of Apollonius from the preceding episode in the *Aetia*.[81] Apollonius could not

---

77. The original cult title was actually Asgelatas, subsequently Hellenized and aetiologized as Aiglatas: W. Burkert, *The Orientalizing Revolution* (Harvard 1992), 78-79.

78. See Pfeiffer ad loc. (p. 25); Vian on Apoll. iv. 1705 (1981, 207).

79. Eichgrün 1961, 128-31; Fraser I. 638; Vian 1981, 66-67, 207-08.

80. Note the closing line (1220): ἀλλὰ τὰ μὲν τηλοῦ κεν ἀποπλάγξειεν ἀοιδῆς.

81. *Arg.* i. 1214-5 (γεωμόρου...γύας τέμνεσκεν) ~ F 22 (τέμνοντα...αὔλακα γειομόρον); see too Eichgrün 1961, 133-37; Giangrande, *CQ* 17 (1967), 14-16 (exaggerating the differences between the Apollonian and Callimachean versions); Hunter 1993, 37-8. It may

resist a Callimachean discovery that touched however tangentially on his theme.

Argon. i and iv (and so presumably the whole poem) were undoubtedly written after *Aetia* I. Bk iv was also written after the slightly later *Iambi*. Both *Iamb* 8 (F 198) and *Argon.* iv. 1765-72 tell the aetion of a festival at Aegina called the Hydrophoria.[82] Earlier scholars assumed the priority of Callimachus,[83] but Dawson refused to pronounce[84] and according to Clayman, "There is no way of knowing which version was written first or whether one was meant as a comment on the other."[85] An unduly pessimistic verdict. Callimachus's poem was an epinicion on a certain Polycles of Aegina who had won at the Hydrophoria. It is clear from the Diegesis that he described the festival itself in as much detail as its aetiology:

> An epinicion poem for Polycles of Aegina who won the *diaulos amphorites* in his native land. For this contest there is placed at the end of the stadium an amphora full of water; the contestant runs up to this empty-handed, picks up the amphora, and retraces his steps, and, if he arrives first, wins. The reason is this: before returning home from Aegina the Argonauts landed here and strove to outdo one another while procuring water. The contest is called the Hydrophoria (Dawson's translation).

There seems no reason to doubt that Polycles of Aegina was a real person known to Callimachus who really won the race here described. It was a long established convention of the epinicion that the praise of the victor should embody some relevant and preferably original piece of mythological lore. It was surely when doing his research for this aspect of the poem that Callimachus discovered this tale so congenial to his taste and appropriate for his purpose. If we may for the moment exclude the possibility of Apollonius, where did he find it? The only two known histories of Aegina seem to be later than Callimachus.[86] Jacoby suggested some treatise περὶ ἀγώνων (Callimachus himself wrote a περὶ ἀγώνων in prose, F 403), though of course there may have been an earlier local history we happen not to know of. Whatever the source, the point is that Callimachus had a compel-

---

have been to eliminate the implausibility of a boy following his father's killer that Nicander made Hylas the son of Ceyx instead: Anton. Lib. 26. 1 (with Papathomopoulos's note); Schol. Theocr. p. 259. 10 Wendel; Vian 1974, 47-8.

82. Fuhrer 1992, 205-16.

83. So too Vian, *Apollonios de Rhodes* III (1981), 67; Fraser I. 738 ("once again"), both without further comment; more cautiously, Livrea's notes on the passage (1973, 482f.).

84. Largely on chronological grounds, having concluded from epil. 9 that the *Iambi* were still unpublished by 245 (Dawson 1950, 87, 147).

85. Clayman 1980, 39; Fuhrer 1992, 206, also refuses to express an opinion.

86. *FGrH* 299-300.

ling professional reason Apollonius did not have to dig up this obscure Aeginetan tradition (known only from Callimachus and Apollonius).

If Callimachus were the borrower, we should expect some edge, a different version or at least a different emphasis. Yet there is none. The first line of Callimachus's poem (the only fragment that can be placed with certainty),

'Αργώ κοτ' ἐμπνέοντος ἤκαλον νότου,

The Argo once, the south wind gently blowing,

suggests that Callimachus even gave the same motive as Apollonius for the Argonauts' eagerness to lay in their water as soon as possible, a favouring wind they did not want to lose (in Callimachus gentle, in Apollonius strong):

κεῖθεν δ' ἀπτερέως διὰ μυρίον οἶδμα ταμόντες
Αἰγίνης ἀκτῆσιν ἐπέσχεθον· αἶψα δὲ τοίγε
ὑδρείης πέρι δῆριν ἀμεμφέα δηρίσαντο,
ὅς κεν ἀφυσσάμενος φθαίη μετὰ νῆα δ' ἱκέσθαι·
ἄμφω γὰρ χρειώ τε καὶ ἄσπετος οὖρος ἔπειγεν.
ἔνθ' ἔτι νῦν, πλήθοντας ἐπωμαδὸν ἀμφιφορῆας
ἀνθέμενοι, κούφοισιν ἄφαρ κατ' ἀγῶνα πόδεσσι
κοῦροι Μυρμιδόνων νίκης πέρι δηριόωνται.

From there, cutting rapidly through the boundless sea, they put in on the shore of Aegina. At once they competed in harmless strife about who should fetch water, who should draw it and reach the ship first. For both their need and the unbroken breeze urged them on. There to this very day do the youths of the Myrmidons lift onto their shoulders brimful jars and strive for victory in the footrace.

On the other hand, it is easy to see why Apollonius felt that he could hardly omit from his comprehensive account of the Argonauts' wanderings an adventure which, however unmemorable in itself, had been made famous in a poem of Callimachus. It is hardly necessary to add that, on any hypothesis, Callimachus could not have been wholly dependent on Apollonius, since he so obviously said far more than Apollonius about the festival itself and the race (both of which, unlike Apollonius, he apparently named).

There are also two other factors, which turn the assumption of Callimachus's priority into something approaching certainty. First, the Anaphe story is the second episode in *Aetia* I and the second from last episode in *Argon.* iv. Second, the Hydrophoria story is the final episode in Apollonius's poem. That is to say, these two Callimachean stories appear consecutively in Apollonius. This must be deliberate structuring by Apollonius. It would be a very strange coincidence indeed if Apollonius had got the Anaphe story from Callimachus while Callimachus got the Aegina story from Apollonius.

Most striking of all is the fact that these are the two final episodes of Apollonius's poem. It is true that Anaphe and Aegina were bound to be among the Argonauts' last stops on their way back to Iolcos.[87] But even so there was the adventure with Talos on Crete (iv. 1638-88), which could as easily have been placed after as before the Anaphe episode. Beginnings and ends of poetry books have always been places for special emphasis of one sort or another. In this case the explanation is surely obvious. Apollonius was acknowledging his debt to Callimachus by assigning him the place of honour at the close of his final book.

It can hardly be coincidence that another such structural symmetry signals Apollonius's debt to another leading poet of the age. The last episode in *Argon.* i is the story of Heracles and Hylas, while the following book opens with the boxing match between Pollux and Amycus. Notoriously, both stories are also told, somewhat differently, in two separate idylls of Theocritus (13 and 22 respectively). There are sufficient verbal parallels to make it clear that one poet was imitating the other, but no can agree which (Ch. XVI for more details). The strongest argument in favour of the priority of Theocritus (I would submit) is precisely the fact that the two stories are told consecutively in Apollonius. It would be remarkable if, from all the many Argonautic adventures in Apollonius's poem, Theocritus had chanced to take two in a row—and then treat them in separate poems. On the other hand, there would be nothing surprising in Apollonius juxtaposing the only two Argonautic stories he found in Theocritus. His motive would be the same as in the case of his two Callimachean stories: to underline his debt to poets he admired.[88]

So the only edition of the *Argonautica* we have any good reason to believe ever existed was written after both *Aetia* I-II and the *Iambi*: that is to say, after July 268. What then of *Aetia* III-IV? The third aetion the two poets share, about the anchor of Cyzicus, comes in *Aetia* IV. Unfortunately, we have only the first line and a two-sentence summary:

Ἀργὼ καὶ σὲ, Πάνορμε, κατέδραμε καὶ τέον ὕδωρ (F 108).

To you too, and to your water, Panormus, came the Argo.

According to the Diegetes,

---

87. See fold-out map I "Le retour des Argonautes" in Vian vol. III.

88. Of Theocritus's other poems, 15 and 16 were both written while Arsinoë II was queen, that is to say some time between 279/4 and July 268; and 17 soon after the accession of Hiero, ca 275/4; and as we saw in Ch. II, 24 is probably somewhat earlier, perhaps 285/4. The scholia date his "flourishing" to the 124th Olympiad (284-280); we saw in Ch. VIII that, like much in the *Lives* of Aratus and Nicander, this may be based on genuine information rather than inference from the poems.

[The poet] says that when the Argonauts went ashore at Cyzicus to fetch drinking water, they left behind the stone they had been using as anchor, because it was too light, and took on a heavier one. The first stone was later dedicated to Athena (F 109).

We find the same story in *Argon.* i. 953-60:

ἔνθ' Ἀργὼ προὔτυψεν ἐπειγομένη ἀνέμοισιν
Θρηικίοις, Καλὸς δὲ Λιμὴν ὑπέδεκτο θέουσαν.
κεῖσε καὶ εὐναίης ὀλίγον λίθον ἐκλύσαντες
Τίφυος ἐννεσίῃσιν ὑπὸ κρήνῃ ἐλίποντο,
κρήνῃ ὑπ' Ἀρτακίῃ· ἕτερον δ' ἕλον, ὅστις ἀρήρει,
βριθύν· ἀτὰρ κεῖνόν γε θεοπροπίαις Ἑκάτοιο
Νηλεΐδαι μετόπισθεν Ἰάονες ἱδρύσαντο
ἱερόν, ᾗ θέμις ἦεν, Ἰησονίης ἐν Ἀθήνης.

It was there that the Argo forged its way, driven by the winds of Thrace, and the Fair Haven received her as she sped. There at the bidding of Tiphys they cast off their small anchor-stone and left it by a fountain, the fountain of Artacia. And they took another that suited them, a heavy one. But the first, according to an oracle of the Far-Shooter, the Ionians, the sons of Neleus, in later days (as was right) consecrated in the temple of Jasonian Athena.

There was more than one version of this story. The elder Pliny tells of an anchor the Argonauts left at Cyzicus known as "the runaway stone" (*lapis fugitivus*), because it often ran away and had to be fixed down in lead in the Prytaneum (*NH* 36. 99). In both Callimachus and Apollonius the stone is dedicated to Athena, according to the latter following an oracle of Apollo, presumably (in view of the mention of the Neleids, legendary founders of Miletus) his oracle at Didyma.[89] The epithet Iasonian suggests a healing cult, later referred to Jason and a visit from the Argonauts. The Diegeseis do not mention the oracle, but in view of the interest in Didyma shown in the *Iambi* (Ch. VI. 7), we may reasonably assume compression rather than a different version. Indeed Callimachus's Didymean researches are surely an additional argument in favour of his priority. Furthermore, Apollonius's "Fair Harbour" looks like a gloss on Callimachus's Panormus, "Always-fit-for-mooring." The scholiast on Apollonius glosses "Panormus, the harbour of Cyzicus" (ὁ Πάνορμος λιμὴν τῆς Κυζίκου). They also both give its lightness as the reason the anchor was left behind, when there are obviously other possibilities.

Once again, it is hard to see why Callimachus should devote a whole section of his *Aetia* to the same version of a story already told by Apollonius. It must be Apollonius who drew on Callimachus's poem. But where did he read it? While *Aetia* IV might seem to be the obvious answer, there

---

89. J. Fontenrose, *Didyma: Apollo's Oracle, Cult and Companions* (Berkeley 1988), 209.

are alternatives. The two installments of the *Aetia* were separated by a quarter of a century. We can hardly believe that Callimachus wrote no aetiological elegies during all this time. I quote Parsons's account of the genesis of III-IV:[90]

> The old Callimachus put together two more books, partly at least from poems already composed...[framed by] two stately poems of aetiological content, recently written to the glory of his patroness Queen Berenice.

The obvious parallel is Callimachus's hymns. The corpus of six hymns that has come down to us is arranged with a many-sided symmetry that it is hard not to attribute to the poet.[91] And yet all the indications are that the individual hymns were written at widely separate intervals, with the *Hymn to Zeus* perhaps as early as 285/4, the *Hymn to Delos* 275-4 (below) and one or two generally assigned to the 260s.[92] There is no need (with Bulloch) to connect the edition of the hymns with the supposed collected edition of all the poet's works at the end of his life,[93] but it was certainly not an early book. And yet the hymns were clearly available *before* being collected (we have just seen how 5 was parodied by Posidippus, presumably soon after it was written). Whether they circulated separately, together with one or two other hymns or with other "uncollected" shorter works of Callimachus, there is no way of telling. The chances of survival were obviously much higher for short works incorporated into full-size books. It would be interesting to know in what company short poems apparently not included in the *Aetia* like the epithalamium on Arsinoë or the elegy on Sosibius circulated (the Sosibius poem appears in different company on the two papyri that carry it).

Some of the 25 odd elegies included in *Aetia* III-IV *must* have been composed at intervals between 270 and 245. They will have circulated around the literary circles of Alexandria, which for a decade or two included Apollonius. There is no evidence of any kind or date for the modern assumption of a feud between the two poets (not even in the disreputable "ancient" *Lives*), and, knowing his interest in the subject, Callimachus will surely have shown his younger colleague any new discoveries or poems about the Argonauts. For many years Apollonius had privileged access to uncollected (which is not to say unpublished) poems of Callimachus. The eventual (re)publication of the Cyzicus elegy in *Aetia* IV is not strong enough evidence by itself to date the *Argonautica* after the final publication of *Aetia* IV ca 245.

90. Parsons 1977, 50.

91. Hopkinson 1984, 13; Ch. XVII. 1. It is also significant that there is no variation of sequence in the MS tradition—unlike (for example) the case of Theocritus.

92. Clauss 1986, 155-70; Mineur 1984, 16-18; for earlier bibliography on the dates of all the hymns, Herter 1973, 232-43; on the *Hymn to Apollo*, Ch. XV.

93. Bulloch 1985, 77.

Eichgrün tried to prove that Apollonius knew and imitated the Acontius story in *Aetia* III.[94] Having mentioned the Etesian winds (*Argon.* ii. 498-99), Apollonius goes on to give their aetiology in a long digression (ib. 500-527): the birth to the nymph Cyrene of Aristaeus, who was asked to protect the Minoan isles against a pestilence sent by Sirius; he went to Ceos, built an altar to Zeus Icmaeus and in due course Zeus sent the Etesian winds. In Callimachus, Apollo describes Acontius as "sprung from the priests of Zeus Aristaeus the Icmian, priests whose business it is upon the mountain tops to placate stern Maira [Sirius] when she rises, and to entreat from Zeus the winds whereby many a quail is entangled in the linen nets" (F 75. 33-7). It will be seen that Callimachus does not share Apollonius's interest in the story of Aristaeus himself. He does not mention Aristaeus's rôle in the story of the winds (which he does not even name):[95] in fact he does not directly mention the aetiology at all.[96] He simply purports to be describing the behaviour of the priests in his own day. As G. Huxley rightly remarked, "The seeming omission of Aristaios from the Kallimachean précis as we have it is remarkable in view of the prominent part he had in Keian myth and cult."[97]

The case for Callimachus's priority is weak. It is clear from the much greater detail he gives that Apollonius must in any case have drawn on sources other than Callimachus,[98] and there are no striking verbal similarities.[99] The only detail the two versions share is that the priests prayed on the mountains. On the other hand, this is not a case to presume independence and leave it at that. One of the two did write first, and we may be sure the latter knew the work of the earlier and wrote accordingly. The Acontius story gave Callimachus the perfect opening to tell this exploit of his hero's ancestor. On the face of it, the fact that he refrained from telling a story told in detail by Apollonius might be thought to suggest that this time it was Apollonius who wrote first: Callimachus wrote as he did because he was deliberately avoiding ground already covered by Apollonius. Yet one of the most conspicuous features of the poem as a whole is the numerous passing allusions to local rites and customs and foundation stories which the narrator does not stop to explain.[100]

94. Eichgrün 1961, 119-24.
95. Though see Hollis, *ZPE* 86 (1991), 11-13.
96. Except through the punning etymology αἰτεῖσθαι = Ἐτησίαι (Ch, XIV. 1).
97. "Xenomedes of Keos," *GRBS* 6 (1965), 237.
98. And there were many: see Vian's notes ad loc. (1974, 271-73).
99. Vian 1974, 273 lists "analogies...nombreuses," but they are such as could hardly be avoided by two writers treating the same subject: Apoll. 522 Διὸς Ἰκμαίου ~ Call. 33 Ζηνὸς...Ἰκμαίου; Apoll. 523 ἐν οὔρεσσι ~ Call. 34, ἐπ' οὔρεος ἀμβώνεσσι; Apoll. 525 ἐκ Διὸς αὖραι ~ Call. 36 αἰτεῖσθαι...ἄημα παραὶ Διός; Apoll. 526 ἱερῆες ~ Call. 33 ἱερέων; Apoll. 527 ἀντολέων...Κυνός ~ Call. 35 Μαῖραν ἀνερχομένην.
100. Many of these allusions are explained by Huxley 1965, 235-45.

The Acontius story may in fact have been written before the publication of both *Argonautica* and *Aetia* I-II. First, there is the allusion to Sotades's poem on the marriage of Philadelphus and Arsinoë (Ch. I. 2). Why so pointed an allusion so long after the event as the 240s, when he was composing the Berenice poems? There would seem to be two possible occasions for such an allusion: soon after the marriage itself (some date unknown between 279 and 274); or soon after Sotades's eventual execution, probably in 267. It may have simply been assumed that it was for the insult to Arsinoë (the only example remembered when his poems had perished) that he was executed. It might have been the "epinicion" on Bilistiche that was the final straw. According to the account of Hegesander,[101] Sotades was fleeing from Alexandria when he was captured by Philadelphus's admiral Patroclos on the island of Caudos (just off Crete) and executed. As Launey pointed out, this was surely Patroclos's voyage to the new Ptolemaic base on Ceos at the beginning of the Chremonidean war in spring 267, or at any rate a voyage between Alexandria and Ceos during the war (in any case not earlier than 267).[102] Bilistiche's two known victories fell in 268 and 264. 264 would be too late, but 268 fits perfectly. Sotades recited his poem at an Alexandrian symposium in late summer 268, then beat a hasty retreat once he learned that Philadelphus was less tolerant of insults to his mistress than his wife, little thinking that a Ptolemaic fleet would shortly be following the same route. Yet if Callimachus had been writing in 267, why not allude to the latest Sotades outrage rather than one nearly a decade old? On balance we should probably date the *Cydippe* soon after Sotades's poem on Arsinoë, which in turn immediately followed the royal wedding in 279/4.

Second, Callimachus's poem continues for nearly thirty lines after the wedding of Acontius and Cydippe, an epilogue summarizing the mythical origins of Ceos and the foundation of its four cities (Karthaia, Iulis, Poiessa and Koresia). Since many other local traditions are touched on in the course of the poem, it amounts to a Foundation of Ceos. The statement that Acontius's descendants "still dwell numerous and honoured in Iulis" perhaps suggests that Callimachus wrote at the request of some Cean worthies who claimed him as ancestor. It is striking that the city of Iulis is named no fewer than three times in what survives (F 67. 5; 75. 52, 72).

---

101. Athen. 621A = *FHG* IV. 415-6.

102. "L'execution de Sotadès et l'expedition de Patroklos dans la mer Égée (266 av. J.C.)," *RÉA* 47 (1945), 33-45, accepting Launey's certain correction of Καύνῳ (not an island and in the wrong place) to Καύδῳ (an island on Patroclos's route); see too L. Robert, *Hellenica* xi/xii (1960), 146 n. 5; H. Heinen, *Untersuchungen zur Hellenistischen Geschichte* (Wiesbaden 1972), 143. Launey's own date was 266, assuming a date of autumn 267 for the decree of Chremonides; but the archonship of Peithidemos is now more convincingly assigned to 268-7: Heinen 1972, 102-10, 115-7; C. Habicht, *Untersuchungen zur politischen Geschichte Athens im 3. Jhdt v. Chr.* (Munich 1979), 116 n. 11.

Though the birthplace of two famous poets (Simonides and Bacchylides) and the historian Xenomedes (whom Callimachus names with respect),[103] Ceos had played little part in the wider story of Greece over the centuries. But this changed dramatically in 267. Philadelphus's admiral Patroclos selected the harbour of Koresia as a base for the Ptolemaic fleet in the Chremonidean war, renaming it in honour of the late Queen Arsinoë.[104] The decree of Chremonides notoriously speaks of Ptolemy acting "in accordance with his sister's plan."[105] With the new later date for her death this phrase makes much better sense: Arsinoë must still have been alive during the diplomatic preliminaries and preparations for the war.[106] It is also the more understandable that the new Ptolemaic base for the war that had been her last wish should be named after her. To this end, according to Robert, the tiny town must have been substantially rebuilt, in effect refounded: "il y a nécessairement fait construire des installations, telles que môles, magasins, agora du port, murailles, sans doute aussi des sanctuaires qui ont dû profiter largement à la ville, la transformer."

A thorough surface exploration of the area in 1983-4 has revealed little trace of the expansion Robert so eloquently described, but that may be a consequence of the rapid decline that followed the Ptolemaic evacuation.[107] For a few years at least the base must have been bustling with its new importance.

Callimachus mentions Aphrastus, the mythical founder of Koresia, but not a hint of this second foundation and new dynastic future. Nobody likes arguments from silence, but if Callimachus had been writing after 267, it is hard to believe he could have failed to mention so unexpected a change in the status of Ceos, under the auspices of the principal patron of his own early poetry. Given the loose structure of the epilogue, it would not have been hard to slip in a reference to the future dynastic refounding of Koresia, most simply and neatly in the form of a prophecy in mythical times (a device he was to use for the "future" birth of Philadelphus in *Hymn to Delos* 188).

One of his best known epigrams concerns a shell dedicated by Selenaia the daughter of Kleinias to Aphrodite-Arsinoë in her temple on Cape

---

103. Xenomedes has usually been dated, following Dionys. Hal. *De Thuc.* 5, ca 450, but the other local historians in his list are all too early (C. W. Fornara, *The Nature of History in Ancient Greece and Rome* [Berkeley 1983], 16-20), and X. too may belong in the early 4th c. The fact that Call. calls him πρέσβυς and γέρων may refer to his age at the time of writing rather than, as Jacoby thought (*FGrH* 442, Komm. 288), to his date.

104. As established by L. Robert, *Hellenica* xi/xii (Paris 1960), 146-60 (155 for the date); R.S Bagnall, *Ptolemaic Possessions* (1976), 141-45.

105. ἀκολούθως τεῖ τῶν προγόνων καὶ τεῖ τῆς ἀδελφῆς προ[α]ιρέσει, *IG* ii² 687. 16-18.

106. C. Habicht, *CSCA* 11 (1992), 72; H. Hauben, *Chron. d'Égypte* 67 (1992), 162.

107. Robert 1960, 155-56; J. F. Cherry and J. L. Davis, "The Ptolemaic Base at Koressos on Keos," *ABSA* 86 (1991), 9-28.

Zephyrium.[108] The shell tells of its wanderings over the Aegean "until I fell on the shores of Iulis, so that I might become your admired plaything, Arsinoë" (lines 7-8):

ἔστ᾽ ἔπεσον παρὰ θῖνας Ἰουλίδας, ὄφρα γένωμαι
σοὶ τὸ περίσκεπτον παίγνιον, Ἀρσινόη.

The "shores of Iulis" are in fact the port of Koresia. According to the final line of the dedication, Selenaia was born in Smyrna, presumably the native city of her father Kleinias. To turn up in Alexandria with Callimachus as poet, this must have been a family of consequence. What then were these important Smyrnaeans doing in Ceos? How did Selenaia come by a shell found at Koresia? In the circumstances, the natural explanation is that Selenaia lived there while her father was stationed with the Ptolemaic navy.[109] If so, then this must have been after the renaming as Arsinoë. But even so why mention such a detail? It was standard practice for a dedication to name the dedicant's native city, but there was no call to identify the source of the object dedicated. The key is provided by the final clause that directly links the shell's death at Iulis with Arsinoë. The reference could be simply to the eventual dedication at Zephyrium. But given the renaming of the "shores of Iulis" as Arsinoë, the primary reference of the Arsinoë in line 8 is surely to the former Koresia, underlining the peculiar appropriateness of dedicating to Queen Arsinoë a shell found in the city of Arsinoë. When writing after 267 Callimachus naturally exploited the new name to enhance the standing of Iulis, but when writing the *Cydippe* he was not yet able to do so.

Third, when rummaging through his well-stocked mind for a suitably colourful and original collective denigration of his literary enemies, for whatever reason Callimachus hit on the Rhodian metallurgist-magicians known as Telchines. They are mentioned twice elsewhere in his oeuvre. First in *Hymn to Delos* 31, where Poseidon strikes the mountains with his trident to make the Aegean islands, the trident "which the Telchines had fashioned for him." It is hard to believe that so neutral a reference to their professional expertise was written after the *Aetia* prologue. Second the *Cydippe*, where in his summary of the contents of Xenomedes's history he includes the "insolence and death by lightning" of Demonax and "the wizard Telchines who disregarded the blessed gods"; only old Makelo and her daughter Dexithea were spared (F 75. 64-9).

As in the version of the Cean Bacchylides (with which he must have been familiar),[110] the emphasis quite naturally falls on the sparing of

108. XIV Gow-Page; *HE* II. 168-71; K. Gutzwiller, *CSCA* 11 (1992), 194-209.

109. So Robert 1960, 154-55; Bagnall 1976, 143; she seems to have been unmarried: Gutzwiller 1992, 198-203.

110. Bacch. i, with the detailed discussion in Jebb's edition (1905), 435-49; Snell-Maehler (1970), xxxix-xl; for a full account of ancient sources and modern views, Herter,

Dexithea, for she was to sleep with Minos and bear Euxanthios, the founder of Acontius's native Iulis, mentioned earlier in the poem (F 67. 7). The singling out of the good Telchines who were saved serves to put the crimes of the rest in the background, nor is there any hint of the quality that dominates the characterization of the Telchines of the *Aetia* prologue, their malignity. In prol. 17 the Telchines are βασκανίης ὀλοὸν γένος; in the epitaph on his father, without naming the Telchines Callimachus writes of the βασκανίη of his critics; and in *Hymn to Apollo* 105-13 he mentions Φθόνος no fewer than three times. This is the more striking in that later sources regularly connect the Telchines with precisely this vice.[111] In their present form all these sources are later than and may have been influenced by the *Aetia* prologue. Nowhere do we find any clear explanation or even illustration of this malignity; Strabo offers the rationalisation that they themselves were bewitched by rivals jealous of their craftsmanship (βασκανθῆναι, 14. 2. 7). Their one documented crime is destroying crops by spraying them with the waters of the Styx, which hardly suggests the evil eye. With a couple of easy emendations a late lexicographical fragment can be made to attribute this very crime to them on the authority of Xenomedes, using the very word βασκαίνοντες.[112] But even if we accept this dubious reconstruction, the fact remains that in the *Cydippe* Callimachus chose to employ such vague concepts as insolence and impiety, nowhere even hinting at the evil eye, much less any connection with the Muses or literature. It would have been hard to relate the foundation of Iulis without mentioning Dexithea and the Telchines, and nothing Callimachus says here goes beyond the basic data of the myth as told by Pindar (*Paean* 4) and Bacchylides.

How could he have written like this after elevating the Telchines to the new and idiosyncratic eminence of the *Aetia* prologue? Of course, so long as the prologue was considered Callimachus's last poem, nothing would be gained by proving the priority of the *Hymn to Delos* and *Cydippe*. But if we bring the prologue back to ca 270, the consequences are considerable. If this were the only argument for so early a date, caution might be in order. But this is not true of either the *Hymn to Delos* or the *Cydippe*. The terminus post quem for the *Hymn* is 275, the likely date of the suppression of the Gallic mercenary revolt described at lines 185-87.[113] And as Mineur rightly remarks, this "was only a small success, nothing to be very proud of, and not something to be remembered for a long time."[114] The *Hymn to*

"Telchines," *RE* 5A. 1 (1931), 197-224.

111. Herter 1931, 207-10.

112. *FGrH* 442 F 4, with Herter 1931, 208; Jacoby (Komm. 290) was sceptical.

113. G. Nachtergael, *Les Galates en Grèce et les Sôtéria de Delphes* (1975), 170-71.

114. W. H. Mineur, *Callimachus: Hymn to Delos* (Leiden 1984), 17-18.

Delos cannot have been written more than a year or so after 275, perhaps that very year. It was because the Telchines were in his mind from reading Xenomedes that they sprang so readily to his pen while writing the *Hymn*.

If the *Cydippe* was indeed written soon after the royal wedding (279/4), we might have expected to find it in *Aetia* I-II rather than III-IV. Yet as it stands it could not have been accommodated within the framework of the dialogue with the Muses. All individual aetia in I-II are cast in the form of puzzles, whose solutions the youthful narrator either seeks from the Muses or propounds for their approval. The Diegeseis introduce each story with the formula "He seeks the reason why..." The structure of the *Cydippe* is entirely different. To start with it was much longer than the stories in I-II,[115] and (as we have seen) its many aetia are hinted at rather than told. Callimachus writes throughout as though his listeners know them already—a compliment that would make even better sense if, as suggested, it was originally composed for a Cean audience. There is no central aetion at all (unless it be the claim that Acontius's descendants still live in Iulis). As we saw in Ch. I. 2, after finally making as if to give an aetiology in full (the prenuptial rites of Naxos), the narrator affects to be shocked at his sacrilege and breaks off. Though admirably suited for inclusion in a book entitled *Aetia*, the *Cydippe* could not without radical recasting have been adapted to the framework of I-II.

In an excellent recent essay on Callimachus, L. Lehnus has rightly emphasized the difficulty of tracing any clear lines of development in an oeuvre that extends over more than 40 years.[116] The narrative technique of the *Cydippe* is so bold and innovative (Ch. I. 2; XII. 2) that it might seem tempting to identify it as the poet's maturest style. But on the dating here suggested, it would actually be one of his earlier works.

If these and other suggestions made in earlier chapters are put together in tabular form, we get the following combination of relative and (approximate) absolute dates. Naturally some are conjectural, but nonetheless (I believe) more solidly based and carefully argued than those that have held the field hitherto:

285/4	Theocritus 24†
285/2	Callimachus: *Hymn to Zeus*
290/280	Posidippus: *Ep.* XXIV B-G
279/4	Callimachus: *Epithalamium Arsinoës*
279/4	Sotades: *"Epithalamium" Arsinoës*

---

115. Not only 110 surviving lines with much evidently still missing, but a longer summary in the Diegeseis than usual: I p. 71 Pf.

116. "La poesia di Callimaco nasce adulta come Atena in armi dalla testa di Zeus," Lehnus 1993, 75.

279/4-68	Theocritus 15, 16
279/4	Theocritus 17
	Callimachus: *Cydippe*
275	Callimachus: *Hymn to Delos*
	Theocritus: 13, 18, 22*
ca 270	Callimachus: *Aetia* I-II
	Callimachus: *Hymn to Apollo*
	Apollonius: *Argonautica*
July 268	Death of Arsinoë
ca 268	Callimachus: *Iambi*
267	Death of Sotades
ca 266	Callimachus: *Hymn* v
ca 264	Posidippus: *AP* v. 202

† See Ch. II. 7.

* Earlier than *Hymn* v and the *Argonautica*, but not necessarily this position in the sequence

Chapter X

Hellenistic Epic

1

The modern conviction that Callimachus fought a life-long battle against epic poetry rests primarily on the *Aetia* prologue. But the prologue was not discovered till 1927 (P. Oxy. 2079). The preoccupation with epic goes back to K. Dilthey (1863),[1] building on references in later poets and the pioneer work of Hecker (1842) and Naeke (1845) on the fragments then known.[2] Not only did most of these fragments turn up on P. Oxy. 2079; it was at once seen that Vergil's rejection of epic in *Buc.* vi was adapted from Callimachus's invective, which seemed to provide striking confirmation.

For centuries (it was assumed) poets wrestled with Callimachus's ban on epic, until finally Vergil came up with a formula that enabled him to write a "civilized" epic.[3] Inevitably, this ban was linked to the famous feud with Apollonius (much discussed by nineteenth-century critics).[4] Rostagni made a heroic attempt to insert Apollonius's name into a recalcitrant gap in the Florentine list of the Telchines of the prologue. In 1980 Mary Lefkowitz tried to dispatch the feud "where they sell an ox for a penny" (F 191. 2), but her scepticism was too indiscriminate to compel conviction.[5] Ten years later Peter Green produced perhaps the most extravagant embellishment of the traditional story yet published. He even knew why Apollonius picked Rhodes for his retreat, "the last bastion of genuine freedom...left in the Aegean world";[6] and, like many other believers, seemed to think that the "famous quarrel" rests on ancient tradition:

> It is interesting, and significant, that, insults apart, *what tradition remembered* as the core of the quarrel was a matter not of content but of form, of style. Cal-

---

1. Carolus Dilthey, *De Callimachi Cydippa* (Leipzig 1863), 1-25.
2. Notably μηδ' ἀπ' ἐμεῦ διφᾶτε μέγα ψοφέουσαν ἀοιδήν and εἵνεκεν οὐχ ἓν ἄεισμα διηνεκές, assigned by Naeke to a polemical prologue to the *Hecale* (*Opusc. phil.* ii, Bonn 1845); and by Hecker to a prologue to the *Aetia* (*Comm. Callim.* (Groningen 1842). For a history of the debate, G. Benedetto, *Il sogno e l'invettiva* (Florence 1993).
3. The subtitle of Brooks Otis's *Vergil* (1964).
4. See the full account in Benedetto 1993, 27-91.
5. *ZPE* 40 (1980), 1-19; *Lives of the Greek Poets* (Baltimore 1981), 117-35.
6. Green 1990, 202-04: "Its atmosphere must have offered a welcome contrast to that of the Ptolemaic court, while its culture cannot have helped but be more sympathetic to the epic mode, above all to a poem that in its final form laid such stress on maritime exploration."

limachus was the apostle of concision, of erudite miniaturism, of pungent
irony. Apollonius, on the other hand, wanted to revive the epic... [my empha-
sis].

Fraser too writes of "the controversies which ranged round [the *Argonautica*] when it appeared," as though the issues involved were well documented.[7]

The truth is that both quarrel and controversy are entirely modern
inventions. The ancient Lives say only that Apollonius was forced to leave
Alexandria by the hostile reaction that greeted his poem. Not even these
dubious documents say that Callimachus was among the critics. When
Green (after many others) infers that this criticism was "orchestrated by
Callimachus," this is to rush in where even Byzantine scholiasts feared to
tread. Above all, there is not the slightest hint in the Lives that it was specifically for writing an epic that Apollonius was criticized. If we may take
anything they say seriously, the claim of *Vita I* that he recited the first version "while still an ephebe" implies shortcomings due to inexperience
rather than deliberate choice of the wrong genre. And the fact that he is
said to have gone away to rework and polish his poem suggests that he
acknowledged the justice of the criticisms and that the successful second
version was an improvement on the first.

Even those who reject or minimize the feud and read the *Argonautica* as
a poem in the Callimachean tradition have nonetheless seen epic as the
main object of Callimachus's polemic.[8] Indeed, far more is involved than
the interpretation of the *Aetia* prologue. A thriving school of epic poets
writing on the grand scale has become a central postulate in many areas of
Hellenistic and Roman literature.[9] Such a school was reconstructed in
detail in an influential monograph by K. Ziegler.[10] And it was on the basis
of Ziegler's hypothesis that Lloyd-Jones and Parsons classified much
material in their indispensable *Supplementum Hellenisticum* which can and
should be classified differently.

In a more general survey of Hellenistic poetry Lloyd-Jones wrote of the
"great mass of poets who celebrated kings and battles" in what he describes
as "very uncallimachean" epics.[11] According to Peter Bing, although these

7. Fraser I. 625 ("raged?"); there would be no point in simply multiplying such
opinions.

8. For general scepticism (not going so far as mine), Hutchinson 1988, 79 n. 103.

9. "For most writers of this period 'serious' poetry (outside drama) meant primarily
epic" (A. W. Bulloch, *CHCL* I [1985], 559).

10. Ziegler 1934; [2]1966; closely followed by K. Kost, *Kl. Wörterbuch* (1988), 188-92.
Against Ziegler's estimate of the quality and importance of these poets, see the sensible
criticisms (not, however, questioning their existence) of Otis, *Virgil* 396-8. The basic collection of evidence (apart from the inscriptions: Ch. II. 6) remains Susemihl I Ch. XIV; see too
the valuable list in Fantuzzi 1988, lv-lxxxviii.

11. *Academic Papers* II (1990), 236-37.

epics "by an odd chance, have disappeared almost completely from our tradition....[y]et their works are the backdrop against which we must assess the artistic developments of the Hellenistic élite."[12] Much of G. Zanker's recent attempt to characterize the "realism" of Alexandrian poetry presupposes that "Callimachus was consciously subverting traditional expectations of epic *subject-matter*" (my emphasis). For Zanker, the *Aetia* prologue "is valuable to us because it explicitly shows that readers of Callimachus's poetry missed in it the 'kings and heroes' of traditional epic."[13] To justify the unwavering concentration of his own and his students' research on alleged Homeric word-games in the Hellenistic poets, Giangrande took it as axiomatic that "the epic genre had made a come-back" in the early Hellenistic age. Indeed, he went on to claim that the Hellenistic poets "tried to outdo Homer by writing gigantic works, even longer than the Homeric poems."[14] E.-R. Schwinge writes of "an immense number of epics" written throughout the Hellenistic world, in "affirmation" of the new monarchies.[15]

For Brooks Otis, studying the *Aeneid*,

> The specific problem that confronted [Callimachus and Theocritus] was the validity of post-Homeric epic as this had been 'revived' by the later fifth-century poet Antimachus of Colophon, and exemplified in their own literary circle by Apollonius of Rhodes....We can, I think, see quite plainly why Callimachus and Theocritus rejected Antimachean epic....It is quite clear that by one continuous poem [Callimachus] meant, mainly, Cyclic or Antimachean epic.

Otis was mainly concerned with mythological epic.[16] Ziegler himself was more interested in the historical epic he thought he had discovered. Indeed, he argued that our best witness to this lost historical epic is the *Annales* of Ennius. Others too have connected the emergence of Roman historical epic with this supposed Hellenistic tradition.[17]

To begin with a specific illustration, according to Feeney[18] it was from Hellenistic epic that Latin historical epic derived its conception of divine participation in historical events. He cites some inscriptions that refer to epiphanies of Zeus and Athena in Pergamene battles, arguing that the epics

---

12. Bing 1988, 50.

13. Zanker 1987, 155-56.

14. *PLLS* 2 (1976), 271 = *Scr. Min. Alex.* I (1980), 289; *Cor. Lond.* 2 (1982), 63.

15. Schwinge 1986, passim.

16. Otis 1964, 9-10; for his erroneous belief that it was Antimachus's epic *Thebaïs* that was controversial rather than his elegy *Lyde*, see below, Ch. XI-XII.

17. S. Mariotti, *Il Bellum Poenicum e l'arte di Nevio* (Rome 1955), 11f.; R. Häußler, *Das historische Epos der Griechen und Römer bis Vergil* I (Heidelberg 1976), passim; J. B. Hainsworth, *The Idea of Epic* (Berkeley 1991), 77; G. B. Conte, *Latin Literature: A History* (Baltimore 1994), 78.

18. D. C. Feeney, *The Gods in Epic* (Oxford 1991), 265-68.

that celebrated these battles "must have" included this "divine dimension."[19] But Pritchett gives a list of 49 such battle epiphanies from the sixth to the first centuries, with a particular concentration during the Persian wars.[20] They are commemorated in art, inscriptions and every sort of literature. They are certainly not an innovation of the Hellenistic age, still less confined to epic. Indeed we now know that the gods appear in Simonides's elegy on the battle of Plataea.[21]

Given the importance Hellenistic epic has come to assume in so many areas, it may be worth reconsidering the evidence outside Callimachus. I hope to show that relatively little large scale epic was in fact written during the Hellenistic age; more particularly, little or none in the century or so before Callimachus published *Aetia* I-II.

First historical epic, which has played a major rôle in modern scholarship and for no obvious reason has generally been thought to be the main butt of the *Aetia* prologue. But it is not (as often carelessly stated) poems on "kings and *battles*," but poems on "the deeds of kings and *heroes*" that Callimachus did not write. It was Vergil who, for his own reasons, introduced the idea of war into his famous imitation of the *Aetia* prologue (*cum canerem reges et proelia*).[22] Modern scholars do not always clearly distinguish model from imitation.[23] Just what sort of poems did Callimachus have in mind? Unfortunately there are two short gaps that deprive us of two key words. If we accept Lobel's restoration in line 3 and Wilamowitz's in 4, it looks as if he is talking about mythical themes (F 1. 2-4):

> εἵνεκεν οὐχ ἓν ἄεισμα διηνεκὲς ἢ βασιλ[ήων
>   πρήξι]ας ἐν πολλαῖς ἤνυσα χιλιάσιν
> ἢ προτέ]ρους ἥρωας.

προτέρους clearly implies heroes of old, and "deeds of kings" suits a mythical poem well enough. The leading characters in heroic saga were all βασιλῆες. It should be noted that "deeds of kings and heroes" need not be restricted (as many have assumed) to warfare, the theme par excellence of what German critics call "Großepos." When Horace describes Pollio as writing of *regum facta*, it was the subject matter of tragedy he had in mind, the non-military activities of those same figures from heroic saga (*Sat.* 1.

---

19. *Inschr. von Pergamon* 165, 247, 248 of 167, 144 and 135 B.C.; Feeney 1991, 266-67 ("must have" appears three times on these two pages).

20. W. K. Pritchett, *The Greek State at War* iii (Berkeley 1976), 11-46.

21. The new Simonides (P. Oxy. 3965 F 20 = F 3. 5f.W) confirms Herod. vii. 189 (cf. Pritchett 24) on the invocation of Boreas before Artemision; Castor and Pollux accompany the Spartan kings at F 11. 29f.

22. *E.* 6. 3; for more detail, Ch. XVIII.

23. "heroes and battles," Clausen 1964, 184; "kings and battles," Zetzel, *Ancient Writers* ii, ed. T. J. Luce (New York 1982), 646 and Lloyd-Jones, *Acad. Papers* II (190), 237, all purporting to paraphrase Callimachus.

10. 42-3). He goes on at once to contrast epic (*forte epos*), in which Varius was pre-eminent. The *Aetia* itself is almost entirely devoted to stories about kings and heroes.[24] For example, F 7-9 on the return of the Argonauts; F 3 on Minos; F 22-25 on Heracles: F 26-28 on the royal house of Argos in the heroic age: F 44-6· + *SH* 252-3 on Busiris and Phalaris; *SH* 276 on Teuthis/Ornytus, king of Arcadia; F 66 on the daughters of Io, called ἡρῶσσαι; F 178, why Peleus was worshipped as a hero on Icos. The opening and closing aetia of Bks III-IV deal with living kings and queens; and the first aetion of IV (F 86) the story of some king unnamed. It was not without justification that a well-known anonymous epigram on the *Aetia* describes the Muses as answering Callimachus's queries ἀμφ' ὠγυγίων ἡρώων, "about the ancient heroes."[25]

Pfeiffer objected to the syntax of two nouns (πρήξιας and ἥρωας) in apposition to ἄεισμα: "because I have not written one continuous poem... or the deeds of kings or heroes of old." His ἐς σέβ]ας gives a welcome preposition: "one continuous poem *in honour of* kings or heroes of old" (taking the ἐς with ἥρωας as well as σέβας).[26] Gallavotti (less plausibly) proposed ἐς γέρ]ας and ἢ 'ς ἀγα]θοὺς ἥρωας, thereby making room for a second preposition as well.[27] This certainly makes for easier syntax, but it also involves a change in the reference of the lines. For βασιλήων ἐς σέβας (or γέρας) implies (though it does not require) living kings. Since this is what most scholars have hitherto assumed, it is important to be clear that only one of many possible restorations[28] lends any support.

With or without προτέρους, ἥρωας implies figures of myth. The standard assumption is that Callimachus's words imply *both* sorts of epic, historical and mythical.[29] This is possible, but other restorations are also possible and it would be rash to feel that we can restore missing words in so unpredictable a poet with any confidence. There is thus no real justification for seeing a reference here to long poems on living kings.

24. As noted (reacting to Pfeiffer 1928) by I. Kapp, *Philologus* 84 (1929), 176.

25. *AP* vii. 42.7.

26. For similar examples of one preposition doing double duty, Pfeiffer cites *H.* II. 8 and F 714. 3.

27. *Riv. di Fil.* 93 (1965), 442f.; he was forced to the weaker ἀγαθούς because Wilamowitz's προτέρους plus both ἢ and 'ς would have been too long for the space.

28. See the list in Herter 1937, 98; Pfeiffer and Torraca ad loc.

29. So Wimmel 1960, 79: "Der Zusatz προτέρους schiebt die Heroen betont in zeitliche Entfernung, die Bestimmung ἐς σέβας hebt ein besonderes Moment der Einstellung zu Gegenwärtigen Potentaten hervor."

2

There is certainly some evidence for hexameter poems on rulers in the Hellenistic age. What remains to be shown is (a) whether they were "epics" in the sense under discussion, multi-book "Großepos"; and (b) whether any of them can be securely dated to the century before Callimachus.

There is in fact no solid or explicit evidence for long historical epics at any time in the Hellenistic world. Their existence has frequently been *inferred* from references to "epic poets" in later sources. But without further definition, the terms ἐποποιός and ἐπῶν ποιητής imply no more than poets who wrote in hexameters. As Aristotle put it, "people connect poetry with metre and speak of ἐλεγειοποιοί and ἐποποιοί...in terms of their metre" (*Poet.* 1447*b*14).[30] This usage is amply and consistently documented. Instead of just saying "poet," brief identifications often specify the type of poetry by metre. In Athenaeus, for example, just as Hipponax, Phoenix and Aeschrion are regularly cited as ἰαμβοποιοί, and Alcaeus, Anacreon and Pindar as μελοποιοί,[31] so we find a wide range of poets cited as ἐποποιοί simply because they wrote in hexameters, regardless of their subject matter.

All the following seven have in common is that in all probability not one of them wrote a multi-book Großepos. Nicaenetus of Samos, author of a *Lyrcus* (surely what would now be classified as an "epyllion") and a *Catalogue of Women*,[32] styled "Nicaenetus the ἐποποιός" (Athen. 673B) even when the text actually cited is an epigram; Euphorion, usually assumed to have written a series of "epyllia" and curse poems, but regularly cited as ὁ ἐποποιός (Athen. 182E, 184A, 263D, 436F); Theopompus of Colophon, author of a *Harmation*, "Little Chariot" (183A);[33] Euanthes, author of a *Hymn to Glaucus* (Athen. 296C); and Capito of Alexandria, so styled even when cited for his (presumably prose) *Memoirs* (350C).[34] Pherenicus of Heraclea seems to have written genealogical poetry. He is cited for an otherwise unattested genealogy of the fig-tree Syke, and her

30. Hephaestion begins his introduction to metre with lines written κατὰ στίχον, "such as the verses of Homer and the ἐποποιοί" (p. 58. 17 Consbruch).

31. Athen. 698B; 359E; 335C; 311A, 429A, 429F; 446A; 3B, 24B.

32. *CA* 1-4; *HE* II. 417, and for the *Lyrcus*, above Ch. VI. 7.

33. *SH* 765; perhaps Theopompus the ἐποποιός cited in schol. Ap. Rhod. iv. 57.

34. He is again described as ἐποποιός when cited for a work called *Erotica* (425C). The Philopappus to whom the *Memoirs* (ὑπομνήματα) were dedicated may be the Commagene grandee cos.109 (so *PIR* I² 151) and the poet Q. Pompeius Capito: *RE* 21. 2 (1952), 2268-9 (no. 71) with *RE* 20. 1 (1941), 75. Nonetheless perhaps wrongly omitted from *SH*. Another poet honoured at Athens who might have found a place in *SH* is C. Julius Nicanor the "new Homer" (*PIR* I² 440).

sisters Walnut, Oaknut, Cornel, Mulberry, Poplar, Elm and Vine the Hamadryads (78B); another fragment quoted in the Pindar scholia deals with the descent of the Hyperboreans from the Titans.[35] Finally, a didactic parody by Archestratus of Gela variously known as *Hedypatheia, Deipnologia, Opsopoia, Gastronomia* or *Gastrologia*; being in hexameters it is classified as ἐπικόν (Athen. 4E), just as Archestratus himself is ἐποποιός (335F).[36] Doubt has often been expressed about the statement in his Suda-entry that the famous critic Zenodotus was an ἐποποιός,[37] but once again the term merely implies that such poems as he wrote were in hexameters.

It is also significant that the adjective ἐπικός carries none of the connotations of its modern equivalent. For example, such phrases as "epic simile," "epic colouring," "epic technique," "epic grandeur" could not be rendered in Greek by means of ἐπικός. It is in fact a very rare word, only used to mean "in hexameters," as in Hephaestion (παροιμίαι ἐπικαὶ καὶ ἰαμβικαί, p. 26. 24C).[38] Marinus's Suda-entry tells us that he wrote his *Life of Proclus* in both prose (καταλογάδην) and ἐπικῶς; and Nicander's entry states that most of his poems were written ἐπικῶς. There is also the category ἐπικὸν ἐγκώμιον in the festivals, already discussed in Ch. II. 6.

Full-scale epics have often been inferred from titles like εἰς Κλεοπάτραν δι᾽ ἐπῶν, by Theodorus the tutor of M. Antony's son Antyllus,[39] which actually means no more than "on Cleopatra in hexameters." Indeed, "on Cleopatra" is the characteristic title, not of an epic, but of a formal encomion. The same applies to the "on (εἰς) Antigonus," "on Pausanias" and "on Phila" ascribed to Aratus (*SH* 99, 112, 116), and the "on (εἰς) Eumenes and Attalus" of Musaeus (below). Inscriptions listing victors in the festivals in the category of encomion (whether in prose or verse), regularly use εἰς plus the name of the honorand in the accusative for works that can never have been more than a few hundred lines long.[40]

We do in fact have one complete extant specimen of the εἰς τὸν δεῖνα hexameter eulogy, and it runs to a mere 137 lines: Theocritus 17. The title εἰς Πτολεμαῖον is attested by the Antinoë papyrus[41] as well as medieval

35. *SH* 671-72; F. Stoessl, *RE* 19. 2 (1938), 2035 (no. 3). Perhaps Roman rather than Hellenistic: Christ-Schmid-Staehlin II. 1⁶ (1920), 332.

36. *SH* 132-93; characterization by O. Skutsch, *The Annals of Ennius* (Oxford 1985), 4.

37. K. Nickau, *RE* X A (1972), 43; *SH* 853 (with a query and the comment "dubitant viri docti").

38. Apart from "epic cycle," a formula of very limited reference: Ch. XIV.

39. *SH* 752 (*carmen epicum de Cleopatra*); G. W. Bowersock, *Augustus and the Greek World* (Oxford 1965), 35 n. 5.

40. E.g. εἰς Καίσαρα...λογικῷ ἐγκωμίῳ: L. Robert, *Études épigr. et philol.* (Paris 1938), 21.

41. The MSS offer ἐγκώμιον εἰς Πτολεμαῖον, and Hunt and Johnson restore [ἐγκώμιον] εἰ[ϲ] Πτολεμαῖο[ν] in the papyrus (*Two Theocritus Papyri* [London 1930], 55); but this should probably be rejected, not least because ἐγκώμιον would be flush with the left-hand margin, whereas all other titles in the papyrus are centred.

manuscripts. We also have the opening of what must have been a similar poem by Nicander (F 104), a eulogy of Attalus I through his mythical forbears.

Then there are the "epic poets" Ziegler overlooked:[42] those known from the inscriptions who travelled from city to city competing in the category of ἐπῶν ποιηταί at the various festivals (Ch. II. 6). The earliest documented example is at the Lysandreia established on Samos ca 404, when (with Lysander himself as both theme and judge) Niceratus of Heraclea defeated none other than Antimachus of Colophon.[43] Ziegler attributed epic *Lysandreia* to both Antimachus and Niceratus, but since the only thing we know about the poems is that they were recited in a competition, we should in any case have to postulate prize poems by both in addition to these supposed epics. Why suppose anything more than regular encomia "on Lysander"?

Since there were many different contests at each festival and several competitors for each contest, individual recitations are bound to have been relatively brief. Naturally, poets may often have recited extracts from longer works. The anecdote that Theocritus of Chios sarcastically praised the bits a performer "had left out" (ἃ παρέλιπες) is one illustration, and the younger Pliny deprecated the practice of reading extracts.[44] But it would be illogical to suppose that the primary goal of competitors was other than the competition. Poems on the scale of Cyclic epic were written for a different sort of occasion.[45] Indeed, given the requirement to celebrate the myths, gods and early history of the city hosting the festival, it seems natural to assume that most entries were specially written for the occasion, in which case they will hardly have exceeded two or three hundred lines.

As for the numerous anonymous "epic" fragments found on papyrus over the past few decades,[46] in no case is there any *evidence* (such as a title or book number) for supposing that we are dealing with fragments from epics proper, much less multi-book epics. Some may be. There is no proof

---

42. Also unfortunately omitted from *SH* ("praeteriimus prorsus et scientes...epigraphica omnia"). It is hard to complain when Parsons and Lloyd-Jones have given us so much, but the fact is that there is a substantial body of evidence about Hellenistic poetry that is not to be found in either *CA* or *SH*. Fantuzzi 1988 corrects Ziegler's limitation to literary sources.

43. Antimachus tore up his manuscript in disgust: Plutarch, *Lys.* 18. 8, with G. L. Huxley, *GRBS* 10 (1969), 13; V. J. Matthews, *Eranos* 77 (1979), 43-48.

44. *Gnom. Vat.* 348; Pliny, *Ep.* 8. 21. 4 (*ego nihil praetereo*).

45. Pallone nonetheless takes it for granted that the works of these ἐπῶν ποιηταί were "epos tradizionale" rather than the "nuova poesia Callimachea" (*Orpheus* 1984, 159, 166).

46. In effect the entire section "Epica Adespota" in *CA* (pp. 71-90) and *SH* (pp. 399-458); especially *CA* 78-9 and 82-9 and *SH* 922, 923, 928-35, 937, 947 and 950.

the other way either. But in themselves these fragments lend no support to Ziegler's hypothesis that *long* epics were more characteristic of the Hellenistic age than short hexameter poems, whether or not of the "Callimachean" school. The longest single find, the eleven columns and three loose fragments of P. Chicago, seems to contain parts of several separate poems, "hymns" as they are characterized by Powell. The papyrus itself is of the second century A.D., but one of the poems looks like an epithalamium on Arsinoë.[47]

Here we may compare the numerous similar "epic" papyrus fragments from late antiquity. Four are classified in Heitsch's edition as historical epics, but though they all contain accounts of battles, they also go on to praise the hero who routed the foe.[48] Each one could as easily come, like most of the other such fragments, from an encomion or panegyric. Here we are fortunate enough to have a check in the fully preserved oeuvre of Claudian: thirteen hexameter poems on contemporary themes, of which only two might be described as historical epics (*de bello Gildonico*,[49] *de bello Getico*), the remaining eleven all being panegyrics or invectives. In truth, the epics are so full of panegyric that there is not much difference between them. Length is certainly not the criterion: three of the panegyrics are longer than both the epics. This was the age that saw Nonnus's 48-book *Dionysiaca*, but though parts were no doubt performed, in its entirety so long a work must have been written to be read. Panegyrists (not surprisingly) were careful not to overtax the patience of their patrons. Menander rhetor set very modest maximum lengths for the various encomiastic categories, to which, for all their apparent verbosity, the many surviving imperial panegyrics closely conform. Even those of such a celebrity as Themistius, welcome at the courts of five consecutive emperors, seldom exceed twenty pages.[50] Claudian's earliest panegyrics run to just over 200 lines, and even after he was firmly established at court they never exceed 700 lines. Even if there were no other evidence, this alone makes it clear that such texts were written for public performance.

47. *CA* 82-89, with Goodspeed, *JHS* 23 (1903), 237-47 (ed. pr.); J. U. Powell (and A. S. Hunt), *JP* 34 (1918), 106-28; Fraser II. 935-36, notes 399-402. This mysterious text would surely repay further study.

48. E. Heitsch, *Griechischen Dichterfragmente der röm. Kaiserzeit* i[2] (1963), XXXII, XXXIV, XXXVI and ii (1964), S 10; see the discussion in T. Viljamaa, *Studies in Greek Encomiastic Poetry of the Early Byzantine Period* (Helsinki 1968), 45-60.

49. I cannot understand why J. B. Hall (Teubner 1985) prefers the less well attested title *In Gildonem* (for the evidence, P. L. Schmidt, *ICS* 14 [1989], 405-06); Gildo is attacked here and there, but the poem is certainly not structured as an invective.

50. D. A. Russell and N. G. Wilson, *Menander Rhetor* (Oxford 1981), 437.1 (150), 414.27 (200) and 434.8 (300 lines). At more than 80 pages, Pliny's panegyric on Trajan far exceeds these limits, but the published version was endlessly polished and expanded, according to M. Durry's edition (Paris 1938, 5f.) to three or four times its original length.

Though Theocritus 17 is the only complete poetic encomion to survive from the Hellenistic world, we can fill out our knowledge of the motifs and conventions of the genre from honorific epigrams and a variety of other texts, illustrating a remarkable continuity with the encomiastic poetry of the early Byzantine world.[51] There is a similar continuity in prose encomion: Isocrates's *Evagoras* (itself much influenced by Pindaric encomion), Xenophon's *Agesilaus* and (more surprisingly) Plato were influential models throughout the Hellenistic and Roman world, and Menander rhetor frequently cites all three in the handbook that was to become canonical for late antiquity and the Byzantine world.[52]

The distinguishing feature of the encomia of Claudian and his successors (it used to be thought) was their fidelity to Menander's precepts.[53] We now know that Theocritus 17 is already constructed on essentially the same pattern.[54] For what is genre but the literary expression of social needs, and given both the similarity of the occasion and the conservative nature of Greek literary culture, we should not expect encomiastic poetry in hexameters to change much between the Ptolemaic and Theodosian ages.

Praising the great had always been a serious business. Pindaric epinicion was written in a high style and possessed of a dignity all its own. When choral epinicion fell out of fashion, something as dignified had to take its place, and it was not by chance that the hexameter became, till the end of antiquity, the metre par excellence of panegyric. The heroic metre and style were felt to be the most appropriate medium for praise, whether of a person or city. When Theocritus made those who refused to hire him as panegyrist reply "Homer is enough for all" (ἅλις πάντεσσιν Ὅμηρος, 16. 20), he did not (of course) mean Homer the writer of multi-book narrative, but Homer the great immortalizer, the "celebrator of heroes" (ἡρώων κοσμήτορα) as he is characterized on his own supposed epitaph, obviously not authentic but certainly pre-Hellenistic, indeed discussed by Callimachus in his *Pinakes*.[55] This is put beyond doubt by the way the poem continues: who would have heard of the sons of Priam, Odysseus and so on but for Homer? We can now add that the Theocritean motif is already present in

---

51. For some illustrations, G. Giangrande, *GGA* 223 (1971), 211-16 (reviewing Viljamaa), and below. It might be worth carrying out a more detailed study.

52. D. A. Russell and N. G. Wilson, *Menander Rhetor* (Oxford 1981), xiii-xviii; on Isocrates and Pindar, W. H. Race, *TAPA* 117 (1987), 131-55.

53. For Claudian, L. B. Struthers, *HSCP* 30 (1919), 49-87; Cameron 1970, 253f.; and the forthcoming study of the *In Eutropium* by J. F. Long; for the others, Viljamaa passim.

54. F. Cairns, *Generic Composition in Greek and Latin Poetry* (Edinburgh 1972), 100-20; Alex Hardie, *Statius and the Silvae: Poets, Patrons and Epideixis in the Graeco-Roman World* (Liverpool 1983), 87-89; for other traces of encomiastic rhetorical patterns in Theocritus, Giangrande, *Quad. Urbin.* 12 (1971), 87-93; for their influence in the early empire, Hardie 1983, passim.

55. F 453; T. W. Allen, *Homeri opera* v (1912), 259.

the proem to Simonides's newly recovered elegy on the Battle of Plataea: "Homer secured the immortality of the heroes of Troy; it is now for Simonides to immortalize the Persian War."[56] It is a device that elevates both poet and subject. In embryo it can be found already in Pindar and the Eion epigram of 475.[57]

The divine participation in historical events that Feeney traced to Hellenistic epic was no doubt one of the many Homeric features of Hellenistic as it certainly is of imperial Greek encomion. Menander advises the panegyrist to begin by emphasizing the magnitude of his theme and the grandeur of style required to do justice to it: "only the grandiloquence (μεγαλοφωνία) of Homer would suffice" is one line he suggests.[58] Thus did Homer become the first panegyrist. Indeed, Menander quotes him nearly twice as often as any other model.

To sum up, (a) an ἐποποιός is simply a poet best known for writing in hexameters; and (b) the normal form for a hexameter poem on a ruler to take, in the Hellenistic as in the early Byzantine world, was an encomion of a few hundred lines.

3

Not the least interesting commentary on the standing of Homer in the Hellenistic world is the famous relief by Archelaus of Priene, sometimes known as the Apotheosis of Homer.[59] On the lowest of four registers Homer sits on a throne, the Iliad and Odyssey kneeling on each side of him while Chronos and Oikoumene crown him. Figures identified as Myth, History, Poetry, Tragedy and Comedy make offerings on an altar in front of Homer, followed by Physis, Arete, Mneme, Pistis and Sophia. The upper registers show Apollo with lyre and all nine Muses in a mountain setting (evidently Helicon, as in Hesiod and the *Aetia* prologue) with Zeus and Mnemosyne (their parents). The heavy-handed message is all too clear: Homer, whose fame is everlasting and worldwide, is the source of all literature, prose and verse alike.[60] We may compare the common literary motif (surely Hellenistic in origin) of Homer as the Ocean from which all other

56. Parsons's summary of the fragmentary text (*P. Oxy.* vol. LIX [1992], 32); F 11 W[2].
57. *Nem.* 7. 20; *Isthm.* 3. 53-57; § 5 below.
58. § 369, p. 78 Russell-Wilson; for other texts on Homer the panegyrist, Ch. XVIII. 1. This deliberate cultivation of the high style in encomion explains why it is difficult to categorize a brief papyrus fragment.
59. J. J. Pollitt, *Art in the Hellenistic Age* (Cambridge 1986), 15-16 (with fig. 4); R.R.R. Smith, *Hellenistic Sculpture* (London 1991), 186-87 (with fig. 216); D. Pinkwart, *Das Relief des Archelaos von Priene* (Kallmünz 1965).
60. C. O. Brink, "Hellenistic Worship of Homer," *AJP* 93 (1972), 547-67.

poetic streams flow. Indeed the Homeric phrase "whence every river, every sea and every spring" was applied to Homer himself.[61] The motif was sufficiently hackneyed to be the object of satire. Aelian describes how "the painter Galaton drew Homer vomiting and the other poets collecting the vomit." It is easy to picture the inspiration for such a painting: a trite pictorial representation of Homer as river-god, water gushing from his mouth while the other poets gather it up in jugs.[62]

Aelian also reports that Ptolemy IV Philopator (221-205) set up a temple in Homer's honour, with Homer seated in the centre surrounded by all the cities that claimed him. By good fortune we have what seems to be a contemporary epigram on this Homereum.[63] That Archelaus's relief was found in Italy proves nothing about its original provenance. It was at one time dated on epigraphic grounds to ca 125, but current opinion favours the end of the third century and accepts the old identification of the facial features of Chronos and Oikoumene (clearly intended for portraits) as Arsinoë III and Ptolemy Philopator, thus connecting it with Philopator's Homereum.[64] If so, then the nine Muses on Helicon would take on another level of meaning. For Arsinoë Philopator sponsored a reorganisation of the cult and festival of the Muses on the actual site of Helicon, the Mouseia of Thespiae (Ch. VI. 1).

According to Brink, this heroisation of Homer is anti-Callimachean, representing "the creed of Homeric classicism," a conviction that "is at the root of homerizing in the 3rd and 2nd centuries B.C." The conclusion does not follow. Once more, the Homer who is the object of this veneration is not the author of multi-book narrative, but simply the first and greatest of poets. One of the earliest and least sophisticated illustrations of this attitude is an epitaph on the late fourth-century piper Telephanes of Samos, ascribed in the Anthology tradition to a Nicarchus (*AP* vii. 159):[65]

> Ὀρφεὺς μὲν κιθάρᾳ πλεῖστον γέρας εἵλετο θνητῶν,
> Νέστωρ δὲ γλώσσης ἡδυλόγου σοφίῃ,
> τεκτοσύνη δ' ἐπέων πολυΐστωρ θεῖος Ὅμηρος,
> Τηλεφάνης δ' αὐλοῖς, οὗ τάφος ἐστὶν ὅδε.

---

61. ἐξ οὗ περ πάντες ποταμοὶ καὶ πᾶσα θάλασσα / καὶ πᾶσαι κρῆναι, *Il.* 21. 196-7; Dion. Hal. *Comp.* 24; Quint. 10. 1. 46; cf. Ovid *Amor.* 111. 9. 25-6; Manilius ii. 8-11; Anon. *AP* ix. 183. 3-4; *de subl.* 32. 3.

62. *VH* 13. 22; T.B.L. Webster, *Hellenistic Poetry and Art* (London 1964), 144-45.

63. *SH* 979; Fraser II. 872; Brink 1972, 549.

64. Pollitt 1986, 16; Smith 1991, 186 (for other portraits of the royal pair, Smith's *Hellenistic Royal Portraits* [Oxford 1988], 91-92, 165).

65. Clearly not the early imperial epigrammatist of that name (*HE* II. 427); possibly (as Stadtmueller suggested) a corruption of the Samian Nicaenetus; in any case, surely a genuine epitaph (Peek, *GV* 1727).

Orpheus won the highest prize among mortals with his harp; Nestor by the skill of his sweet-speaking tongue; much-knowing Homer by the craftsmanship of his verses, and Telephanes (whose tomb this is) with his pipes.

It was craftsmanship, not genre that made Homer the supreme poet, and it is by no means only epic poets who were said to inherit his talent or fame. Not to mention Herodotus and Stesichorus, who at least wrote mythical narrative,[66] Euripides[67] and Plato are also characterized as Homer's heirs. We should bear in mind that Aristotle emphasized the tragic element in Homer, and Plato's debt to Homer was the subject of a scholarly treatise by Aristarchus's disciple Ammonius.[68] It is illuminating to find Thucydides described as an imitator of Homer:[69] given the obvious dissimilarity in style and vocabulary, the reference has to be to the general elevation and dignity of Thucydides's narrative. Sappho and perhaps Anyte too are called the female Homer.[70] At least two Hellenistic scholars, Boethus and Dionysius, wrote on the Homeric debts of Aratus, nowadays considered the epitome of the un- or anti-Homeric style (Ch. XIII. 3). Even such a model of Hellenistic miniaturism as the 300 lines of Erinna'a *Distaff* are said to equal Homer (*AP* ix. 190); and the bucolic poet Bion is also compared to Homer (*Epit. Bionis* 70-84). Not even poets styled "New Homer" necessarily wrote epic, since one of them (the Hadrianic Paion) is elsewhere described as a lyric poet (μελοποιός). The Augustan Nicanor is styled "New Themistocles" as well as "New Homer." Since the former title was earned by purchasing the island of Salamis for Athens, we need not take the latter too seriously.[71] Indeed, an early imperial epigrammatist ridicules the indiscriminate Athenian award of such titles.[72]

The most comprehensive visual representations are the semi-circle of poets and sages outside the Ptolemaic Sarapieion of Memphis, where Plato, Protagoras and perhaps Heracleitus join Pindar and others now unidentifiable in flanking a central figure of Homer. And an unpublished late antique mosaic from Seleucia in Pamphylia: a central panel featuring Homer with figures of the *Iliad* and *Odyssey,* surrounded by inscribed panel busts of Anaxagoras, Pythagoras, Pherecydes, Demosthenes, Heraclitus, Hesiod, Lycurgus, Solon, Thucydides, Herodotus, [?Xeno]phon, and at least eight

---

66. *De sublim.* 13. 3; *AP* vii. 75.
67. *AP* vii. 43, with A. D. Skiadas, *Homer im griech. Epigramm* (Athens 1965), 125-26.
68. See the texts collected in D. A. Russell's note on *De sublim.* (1964), 116-17.
69. Marcellinus, *Vita Thuc.* 35 and 37.
70. *AP* vii. 15; ix. 26. 3; Skiadas 1965, 130-33; J. Werner, *Philol.* 138 (1994), 256-9.
71. L. Robert, ΣΤΗΛΗ...εἰς μνήμην Ν. Κοντολέοντος (Athens 1980), 10-20. According to Dio of Prusa, Nicanor's fame brought disgrace on Athens, and on three of the inscriptions both his grandiose titles were erased: A. E. Raubitschek, *Hesperia* 23 (1954), 317-19; C. P. Jones, *The Roman World of Dio Chrysostom* (Cambridge 1978), 31-32.
72. Automedon, *AP* xi. 319, with L. Robert, *RÉG* 94 (1981), 338-61.

others now lost.[73] Herodotus and Thucydides we have already met and Demosthenes, the supreme orator, is no surprise. But the philosophers and lawgivers reflect a yet broader conception: Homer as the fount and measure of every sort of intellectual and artistic achievement.

The erection of the Homereum need not mean that Philopator admired or patronized contemporary epic poets. On the contrary, the iconography of the Archelaus relief and all these Homeric comparisons highlight the universality of Homer's genius and the variety of his influence. Over and above the very different nature of the *Iliad* and *Odyssey*, by the Hellenistic age it was generally believed (by Callimachus for one) that Homer also wrote the comic *Margites* (F 397). Some Hellenistic poetaster produced a parodic *Battle of Frogs and Mice* that later generations were to ascribe to Homer. A new second- or first-century B.C. papyrus has revealed another such poem, a battle between weasels and mice.[74] The two mice by the side of Homer's throne on the Archelaus relief may allude to one or other of these works.[75] We have already seen how he came to be treated by rhetoricians as the supreme orator. In short, Homer became the yardstick for every form of literature. Homeric comparison became a way of saying that *any* writer was supreme in his chosen field. It was moreover during the Hellenistic age that the practice developed of referring to Homer as simply "the poet."[76]

On a pedestal to the right of Apollo's cave in the register above Homer stands a figure holding a scroll, apparently a victorious poet. According to Pinkwart, this figure (who is isolated from the rest of the action) is a standard portrait type. When fourteen figures and the sculptor himself are all identified by inscriptions,[77] it might seem strange that the poet is not. The explanation is surely that he and his achievements were named in full on a separate inscription now lost. If the relief derives from the Homereum of Alexandria, the poet must surely have been an Alexandrian (if not born there, at any rate active in the service of the Ptolemies). What sort of victory does the relief commemorate? The iconography seems too varied and comprehensive to suggest epic—or for that matter any single victory in any one of the many poetic contests. Indeed, as Bieber remarked, it may be

73. J.-P. Lauer and C. Picard, *Les statues ptolémaïques du Sarapieion de Memphis* (Paris 1955); for the mosaic (Antalya museum), R.R.R. Smith, *JRS* 80 (1990), 151.

74. H. S. Schibli, *ZPE* 53 (1983), 1-25; ib. 54 (1984), 14.

75. Not, as once thought, a frog and a mouse: West, *HSCP* 73 (1969), 123 n. 35; Wölke, *Untersuchungen zur Batrachomyomachia* (Meisenheim 1978), 65-68—nor (we might add) a weasel. Since most of the other figures are allegorical and the mice appear to be gnawing at a roll, they may simply represent the forces of decay (cf. Juv. 3. 207, *et divina opici rodebant carmina mures*; Ariston, *AP* vi. 303; Lucian, *adv indoctum* 17). But Homer should be invulnerable to decay, and another layer of allusion is also possible.

76. As shown by A. M. Harmon, "The Poet κατ' ἐξοχήν," *CP* 18 (1923), 35-47.

77. Apollo, Zeus and the Muses did not need to be identified.

"that the presence of all the Muses indicates the victories of some many-sided poet."[78] If the bottom register is meant to illustrate the versatility of a poet honoured as Homer's heir as much as Homer's own versatility, then no Ptolemaic poet fits the bill better than Callimachus.[79] Callimachus alone of the poets of the age could be said to exemplify Myth, History (in the sense of inquiry), Poetry, Tragedy and Comedy.[80] If a living poet be preferred, then no less versatile if less gifted there is Eratosthenes.

Of course, this is pure speculation. If the relief commemorates a single victory, then the honorand might have been some obscure living panegyrist of Philopator or Arsinoë. Alternatively the tripod beside the poet might be held to suggest a tragedian or choregos (Philopator himself wrote tragedies).[81] Callimachus is merely one possibility among many. But the point is that he is at least a possibility. There is no basis for the prevailing assumption that this widespread Hellenistic veneration of Homer has anything to do with the alleged popularity of large-scale epic, nor does it imply a general rejection of the sort of poetry Callimachus wrote.

4

The first to write an epic on a historical theme was Choerilus of Samos, who died ca 400 B.C.[82] His poem on the Persian wars was in more than one book, but how many more is unknown.[83] Indeed, for a work that, on the traditional view, was so influential, very little is known. We also hear that Lysander kept Choerilus in his retinue "to adorn his deeds with his poetry,"[84] which (according to Feeney) shows "how closely linked historical epic and panegyric were from the beginning." But the fact that Choerilus wrote both need not imply the slightest similarity in structure or treatment. Antimachus too wrote on Lysander, but no one has ever sug-

---

78. M. Bieber, *The Sculpture of the Hellenistic Age*[2] (New York 1961), 128.

79. Since the poet's head is broken off, we would not in any case have a portrait of Callimachus. The names of Callimachus and Apollonius have been suggested before, but without any supporting argument. Since Apollonius left Alexandria for Rhodes (Ch. VIII. 3), it is perhaps unlikely that he would have been honoured in Alexandria after his death.

80. For Callimachus's tragedies and comedies, Ch. II. 7.

81. A. W. Pickard-Cambridge, *The Dramatic Festivals of Athens*[2] (Oxford 1988), 78-79; Pinkwart 1965, 84-85.

82. *FGrH* 696 F 33; *SH* 314-32; *PEG* 187-207; G. L. Huxley, *GRBS* 10 (1969), 12-29 (claiming that the *Aetia* prologue had Choerilus in mind); R. Häußler, *Das historische Epos* I (1976), 70-78, 302; F. Michelazzo, *Prometheus* 8 (1982), 31-42 and 9 (1983), 11-28; J. B. Hainsworth, *The Idea of Epic* (Berkeley 1991), 60-64; D. C. Feeney, *The Gods in Epic* (1991), 265-66.

83. *SH* 318; apparently called Περσικά; it is difficult to know what to make of the *titulus* Χοιρίλου ποιήματα βαρβαρικά μηδικά περσ[ικά] in P. Oxy. 1399.

84. Plutarch, *Lys*. 18. 7.

gested that his *Thebaid* was influenced by panegyric. It should also be
borne in mind that Choerilus was not celebrating the deeds of contemporary rulers, but a war fought by a democracy before he was born; his
poem was no doubt strongly partisan, but hardly a fusion of epic and
panegyric.

Also in Lysander's retinue was an otherwise unknown poet called
Antilochus, given his cap filled with silver in return for "a few middling
verses."[85] That hardly suggests a long epic. Hegemon of Alexandria in the
Troad wrote on the "war of Leuctra" (371 B.C.); if that was the title, it
must have been more than an encomion of Epaminondas. Since all we
know of his *Dardanica* is that it described a love affair between Aleuas the
Red of Thessaly and a snake, perhaps an ethnographical rather than a historical epic.[86] We also now have fragments of what has been identified as a
poem on Philip II of Macedon, though Philip V is perhaps more likely.[87]
The exploits of Alexander were celebrated by at least five poets—Agis of
Argos, Anaximenes of Lampsacus, Choerilus of Iasus,[88] Pyrrho of Elis[89]
and Cleo of Sicily.[90]

Their badness early passed into legend,[91] yet it should be pointed out
that none of these criticisms specify *length*. Indeed, only one of them,
Agis, is even said to have been an ἐποποιός. The title *Lamiaca* ascribed to
Choerilus of Samos in his Suda-entry is often assumed to be an epic by the
younger Choerilus on the Lamian war of 323/2. But that would be an
unlikely war for epic treatment and an unusual use of this form of title, and
there is much to be said for Daub's *Samiaca*, an ethnographical poem by
the elder Choerilus on his native Samos.

Not a line of the Alexander poets has survived, but we do have two
suggestive pieces of evidence. Curtius Rufus describes Agis and Cleo as the
worst kind of flatterers, men who told Alexander that he was the new god

85. μετρίους τινὰς εἰς αὐτὸν στίχους, Plutarch, l.c.; *SH* 51. A certain Ion of Samos is
also sometimes cited as a poet of Lysander, but the inscription in question is perhaps a
century later: see my *Greek Anthology* p. 1 n. 3.

86. Steph. Byz. p. 71. 5; Aelian, *NA* 8. 11; *SH* 461-63; possibly the author of a solitary
epigram included in Meleager's *Garland*, *AP* vii. 436; *HE* II. 298-9; Fantuzzi 1988, lxviii.

87. *SH* 913-21. All the proper names suit Philip II well enough, but could also be argued
to fit Philip V, with the Hieronymus of 913. 8 becoming his ally Hieronymus of Syracuse.

88. *SH* 17; *FGrH* 72 T 26-27; *SH* 45 (add *Gnom. Vat.* 348; Ch. II. 5); *FGrH* 153 F 10;
SH 333.

89. Not in *SH*; paid 10,000 gold pieces for his poem (Sextus, *adv. gramm.* I. 282).

90. No entry in *SH*, on the grounds that he may not have been a poet (p. 7, top; *FHG*
IV. 365). In the debate about whether Alexander should be worshipped as a god, Cleo plays
in Curtius (viii. 5) the part played by Anaxarchus in Arrian (iv. 10. 5; cf E. Badian, *Ancient
Maced. Studies...C. F. Edson* [Thessalonica 1981], 28).

91. *FGrH* 153 F VII. 10-12; Brink, *Horace on Poetry* II (1971), 365-66; Philodemus
and Horace imply an early consensus, and Porph. on Horace, *AP* 357 claims that Alexander
himself despised Choerilus.

to whom Heracles and Dionysus, Castor and Pollux would yield. According to Feeney, this proves that there was a "powerful mythological colour" to what he describes as an "explosion" of historical epics about Alexander and the Hellenistic kings.[92] But if these poems really were full of flattery and divine comparisons, they were surely formal encomia rather than historical epics. Comparisons had always been "one of the most characteristic features of the encomion,"[93] and Heracles and Dionysus, Castor and Pollux are of course the stock comparisons for the deified ruler.[94] Feeney himself cites Theocritus 17 as a parallel (Ptolemy Soter dining among the gods with Alexander and Heracles). But that is an encomion. So too in all probability the fragment of what Feeney describes as "a Greek historical epic in which Diocletian and Galerius are compared to Zeus and Apollo." If the emperors are correctly identified, there is a good chance that the poem too can be identified, as the encomion on Diocletian ascribed in his Suda-entry to Soterichus of Oasis.[95]

Second, it was at a symposium that the poems of "Pranichus, or as some say Pierio" ridiculing some of Alexander's generals were performed.[96] These cannot possibly have been epics; perhaps short elegies, or even iambic invectives. The poems that Hegesianax of Alexandria Troas offered to recite to Antiochus III at a symposium (instead of dancing), though characteristically cited in *SH* 464 as a possible epic, were surely sympotic rather than martial.

Even if there were the slightest evidence that they wrote epics in the first place, it is most unlikely that the Alexander poets were Callimachus's target. It is to their subject as much as to the quality of their verses that they owe their reputation. They were the first poets to flatter a king who fancied himself a god and went down in history as a tyrant. Tarn attributed the more extravagant details about Alexander in Diodorus and Curtius to the influence of the Alexander poets, but Pearson rightly assigned a larger rôle in the invention of even the most fantastic details to the much more widely quoted prose historians and memoirists.[97] The poets are nothing but

92. *Herculemque et Patrem Liberum et cum Polluce Castorem novo numini cessuros*, 8. 5. 8; Feeney 1991, 266-67, following W. Kroll, *Sokrates* 4 (1916), 3-4.

93. Viljamaa 1968, 114-16; cf. P. Fargues, *Claudien* (Paris 1933), 210-13.

94. *hac arte Pollux et vagus Hercules / enisus artes attigit igneas, / quos inter Augustus recumbens / purpureo bibet ore nectar...* (Horace, *carm.* iii. 3. 9-12).

95. Heitsch XXII verso 10-11; J. Bidez, *Rev. de Phil.* 27 (1903), 81-85; though see too R. Keydell, *Hermes* 71 (1936), 465-67; Viljamaa 1968, 66-67.

96. Plut. *V. Alex.* 50.8; not in *SH* or even Susemihl, though registered in H. Berve, *Das Alexanderreich auf prosopographischer Grundlage* ii (1926), nos. 639 and 657. There has been much debate about the identification of both defeat and generals: E. Carney, *GRBS* 22 (1981), 155-57; F. L. Holt, *Alexander ther Great and Bactria* (Leiden 1988), 78-79 n. 118; W. Heckel, *The Marshals of Alexander's Empire* (London 1992), 35-37.

97. W. W. Tarn, *Alexander the Great* ii (Cambridge 1948), 55-62; L. Pearson, *The Lost Histories of Alexander* (Oxford 1960), 78.

names: not a single quotation in the entire Alexander tradition. We may be sure that Callimachus despised such mercenary poetasters, but more important, we have to bear in mind that his critics are supposed to have admired the poets attacked in the *Aetia* prologue. No one will believe that they admired the Alexander poets.

It has long been axiomatic that "the Macedonian Diadochi and the Hellenistic monarchs had also their epic eulogists."[98] It is true that victory was important to the Hellenistic kings (most of the Diadochi waited for some significant victory before assuming the royal title),[99] but (as F. W. Walbank has remarked), "Hellenistic kings do not boast of the number of the enemy they have slaughtered in the way familiar from Egyptian and Assyrian temple reliefs, Sassanian rock carvings and the records of Roman triumphs."[100] Walbank made no reference to Callimachus and Theocritus, but they certainly bear out his generalisation. Of course, many would reply that this is only what might be expected of poets who rejected epic, but that does not explain enough. Even on the traditional interpretation of the *Aetia* prologue, epic was not the only way to celebrate a king's military triumphs. We now know from the new Simonides fragments that elegy rather than epic was the medium for recent battles, and elegiac epinicia were Callimachus's speciality. Nor does the analogy of the Augustan poets fit. For while refusing themselves to celebrate the wars of Augustus and Agrippa, Vergil, Horace and Propertius nonetheless repeatedly praise them in their *recusationes* and constantly refer to military epics as an ideal of which they are incapable (Ch. XVIII).

It is not always appreciated that Callimachus's *Lock of Berenice* is an (albeit oblique) epinicion on Ptolemy Euergetes's Syrian war of 246. Barely three lines are devoted to the campaign: the king "went forth to harry the Assyrian borders," fought a "savage battle," and "soon added Asia to the borders of Egypt."[101] It is no answer that Callimachus and Theocritus wrote the sort of poetry in which military affairs simply had no place. For Theocritus at least (like Aratus) wrote a full-scale royal panegyric: Philadelphus is twice styled a warrior with "horsemen and shielded warriors in hosts, harnessed in flashing bronze" about him, but the main emphasis of the poem falls on his divine origin, his promotion of the arts, his generosity and the prosperity he brings. The brief panegyric in 14 again praises his pacific virtues: kindness, love of culture, and generosity "as befits a king."[102] Callimachus's hymns also lent themselves to con-

---

98. Otis 1964, 16; "we know that Musaeus wrote epics on...Attalus," Feeney 1991, 267.

99. S. Sherwin-White and A. Kuhrt, *From Samarkand to Sardis* (Berkeley 1993), 129.

100. *CAH* VII. 1 (1984), 81.

101. Catullus 66. 12, 20, 35-6: on the Syrian war, Heinen, *CAH* VII. 1 (1984), 420-21.

102. 17. 56-57, 92-93, 103; 14. 61-64; for Aratus's panegyrics, *SH* 99, 116.

temporary reference. The *Hymn to Delos* evokes Philadelpus's crushing of a revolt of Gallic mercenaries ca 275, but obliquely, linked to the major Gallic defeat at Apollo's shrine in Delphi, all in the form of a prophecy by Apollo to an as yet unborn Philadelphus.[103] The *Hymn to Zeus* closes with a miniature panegyric of Philadelphus, praising his kingship in very general terms. We do not know how long Theocritus was at the Ptolemaic court, but Callimachus spent much of his life there. It is hard to believe they did not know what their royal patrons wanted.

There is not a single indisputable example of a full-scale epic poem on the deeds of a Hellenistic king. A certain Hermodotus wrote a poem on Antigonus the One-eyed, but he is not said to have been an epic poet and the words cited do not suggest an epic and would not fit a hexameter.[104] In all probability they come from the lyric paean on Antigonus discussed in § 4 below.

The scholia to Dionysius Periegetes, when discussing the Celtic invaders we call Gauls and the Greeks called Galatai, cite the following brief extract from a hexameter poem (F 379):

οὓς Βρέννος ὑφ'ἑσπερίοιο θαλάσσης
ἤγαγεν Ἑλλήνων ἐς ἀνάστασιν.

whom Brennus led from the western sea to destroy the Hellenes.

It was the Aetolians who were mainly responsible for repelling the Gallic attack on Delphi in 279 and harrying their retreat with guerrilla tactics, but the man who decisively defeated them in battle soon after was Antigonus Gonatas. It was precisely this victory that enabled Gonatas to seize the throne of Macedon. If the lines had been quoted anonymously, they would almost certainly have been assigned to an epic on the deeds of Gonatas. Yet here they are quoted under the name of Callimachus. No one wants to attribute a historical epic to Callimachus, and Pfeiffer was surely right to suggest that they come from his otherwise mysterious *Galateia* attested by Athenacus (F 378). For according to a genealogy that seems to derive from the contemporary historian Timaeus, the sons born to the Cyclops and the nymph Galateia were called Galates, Celtos and Illyrios.[105] Callimachus knew Timaeus, and it would be in character for him to have avoided the obvious, a straightforward celebration of the Gallic defeat, and instead to have worked it into an aetiological poem on their mythical ancestress—no doubt prophecied by Apollo's oracle at Delphi.[106] When and for what

103. *H* iv. 171-87, with Mineur 1984, 16-18, 168-80; Ch. IX. 3.
104. Ἑρμοδότου τινὸς ἐν ποιήμασιν αὐτὸν Ἡλίου παῖδα καὶ θεὸν ἀναγορεύσαντος); *SH* 491-2 (Plut. *Mor.* 182C and *Mor.* 360C).
105. *FGrH* 566 F 69, with the other texts quoted in Jacoby's note.
106. F 592 and 621 might come from the same poem: G. Nachtergael, *Les Galates en Grèce et les Sôtéria de Delphes* (Brussels 1975), 184-85.

occasion might he have written such a poem? Surely soon after the Gallic defeat (279). And the obvious occasion is the festival founded to commemorate it, the Soteria at Delphi. There are two other lines that might be attributed to this poem: F 592 and 621.

Servius quotes an interesting line that somehow escaped the editors of *SH*: "a Macedonian spear whistled through the air" (συρίζουσα Μακηδονὶς ἵπτατο λόγχη).[107] According to Hollis, "one cannot doubt that this is a piece of Hellenistic military epic," "most likely" from one of the many poems on Alexander. But it is hardly likely that Vergil would have paid them the compliment of imitation. To have been not merely imitated but identified by critics as a "source" of Vergil, the poem in question must have survived till at any rate the first century A.D. and perhaps as late as the fifth if (as Hollis argues) it was imitated by Nonnus too.[108] Evidently a poem of some distinction that continued to find both readers and copyists. All the major Hellenistic kings were of Macedonian descent. At *Hymn to Delos* 167 Callimachus styles Philadelphus simple "a Macedonian." If it is thought that the Macedonian spear implies Macedonian troops rather than just commander, that narrows the focus to an Antigonid victory. One poem of some distinction we know of that meets all these requirements is Callimachus's *Galateia*.

Modern critics have paid disproportionate attention to the poets of the Pergamene court. On the analogy of the great altar of Pergamum, Ziegler argued that Pergamene epics were also on a large scale and used the same Gigantomachy allegory, thus answering the criticisms of length and theme in the *Aetia* prologue.[109] But quite apart from the inadequacy of the analogy between art and literature, the altar dates from a full century after Callimachus. By no means all Pergamene sculpture was on the colossal scale: the figures in the famous dedication by Attalus I or II on the Athenian Acropolis were barely three feet high. Furthermore, not one of the Attalids was worshipped as a god in his lifetime; a recent study has referred to the "basically civilian model of their publicized style of rule."[110]

All that is known of the Pergamene poets is contained in three Suda-entries.[111] First Leschides:

107. Serv. *Aen.* xii. 691, corr. West, *CR* n.s. 14 (1964), 242; on Servius's attribution of the line to Homer, O. Skutsch, *The Annals of Ennius* (Oxford 1985), 631.

108. Presumably quoted in the collections of Vergilian "thefts" compiled by Perellius Faustus or Octavius Avitus (H. Funaioli, *Gramm. Rom. Frag.* [1907], 544); Nonn. xxx. 307-8; A. S. Hollis, *HSCP* 94 (1992), 281-82.

109. Ziegler 1966, 48, developed by P. R. Hardie, *Virgil's Aeneid: Cosmos and Imperium* (1986), 128-143; Ziegler was criticized on this point by Fantuzzi 1988, l-liii.

110. R. E. Allen, *Attalid Kingdom* (1983), 145-58; Sherwin-White and Kuhrt 1993, 114.

111. Reproduced in *SH* 503, 561 and 723.

Λεσχίδης, ἐπῶν ποιητής· ὃς συνεστράτευσεν Εὐμένει τῷ βασιλεῖ· ὃς ἦν
ἐπιφανέστατος τῶν ποιητῶν. συνῆν δὲ τούτῳ καὶ Πυθέας ὁ ζωγράφος καὶ
Μένανδρος ἰατρός.

Leschides, epic poet; campaigned with Eumenes the king; the most distinguished of poets. Also with him [i.e. at Eumenes's court] were Pytheas the
painter and Menander the doctor.

Since Leschides campaigned with "Eumenes the king," evidently Eumenes
II (197-159/8)[112] rather than Eumenes I (263-241), who never bore the title
king. Furthermore, Menandros was the court doctor of Eumenes II, honoured at Athens in the spring of 189.[113] Pytheas was famous for his
elephant mural at Pergamum.[114] It should be noted that no titles are supplied for Leschides's poems; and while it is reasonable to assume that he
wrote about Eumenes, there is no warrant for postulating a long epic rather
than the standard encomia.[115]

As for Musaeus,[116] since he wrote "on Eumenes and Attalus," presumably again Eumenes II and Attalus II (159/8-138). It has hitherto been
taken for granted that his ten-book *Perseïs* (the only multi-book poem of
the age with the characteristic *title* of an epic)[117] retold the mythological
saga of Perseus son of Danaë. But Musaeus flourished during the reign of
King Perseus of Macedon (179-168), and since the king liked to exploit his
mythical homonym (for example, on his coinage),[118] it is unlikely that a
contemporary *Perseïs* was written without any reference to Macedon. Perhaps then an epic on Perseus. But there is another possibility. In 183 Philip
V of Macedon founded a new city, called Perseïs in honour of his heir
apparent.[119] Might it not have been for this occasion that Musaeus produced his poem? It was about then that Philip first included the hero Perseus on his coinage.[120] There is no need to believe (as sometimes

112. For the date of his death, C. Habicht, *CAH* VII² 334 n. 34.

113. *IG* II² 946 = *SIG*³ 655; the archon was redated to 190/189 by S. V. Tracy, *AJAH*
9, 1984 [1988], 43-7; see too C. Habicht, *Hesperia* 59 (1990), 564-5.

114. Steph. Byz. s.v. Βοῦρα, whence Hecker's Πυθέας ὁ ζωγράφος for the MSS Πυθίας
ὁ συγγραφεύς (*Philol*. 5 [1850], 418, not mentioned by Adler or *SH*, but adopted by Jacoby,
FGrH 172); A. Reinach, *Monuments Piot* 21 (1913), 196 n. 1; A. Rumpf, *RE* 24. 1 (1963),
370, Pytheas 11 or 12. No historian of this name is otherwise recorded.

115. And certainly none for R. E. Allen's assumption that Leschides wrote a
"biography" of Eumenes (*The Attalid Kingdom* [1983], 3).

116. I have no opinion on the puzzling phrase τῶν εἰς τοὺς Περγαμηνοὺς καὶ αὐτὸς
κύκλους in his Suda-entry (*SH* 561): Fantuzzi 1988, lxxiii-iv.

117. Compare the following: *Achilleïs, Aeneïs, Aethiopis, Alcmaeonis, Alexandrias,
Amazonis, Athis, Bochoreïs, Danaïs, Dionysias, Ephesis, Erichthonias, Gaïnias, Gigantias,
Ilias, Meropis, Phocaïs, Phoronis, Thebaïs, Theseïs, Thesprotis* (cf. E. Rohde, *Der griechis-
che Roman*³ [1914], 617).

118. N.G.L. Hammond and F. W. Walbank, *Hist. of Macedonia* III (Oxford 1988), 504.

119. Livy 39. 53. 14; cf. P. Meloni, *Perseo e la fine della monarchia macedone* (Rome
1953), 34-38; Hammond and Walbank 1988, 459.

120. Hammond and Walbank 1988, 462-63.

suspected) that he was experimenting with an alternative mythical descent.[121] For his gold staters bear the hero's head on the obverse and Heracles's club on the reverse, and King Perseus's coinage also shows both heroes. Moreover, Heracles himself was descended from the son of Danaë, twice over: both Amphitryo and Alcmene were born to sons of Perseus.[122] The foundation of Perseïs would have provided a rich theme for a skilful poet able to weave the sagas of Heracles and Perseus together with local traditions.[123] If so, Musaeus's epic would date from before Perseus became king, and, length aside, fall into the Callimachean category of foundation poetry.

Another multi-book Pergamene epic poet has been constructed from the Suda-entry for an otherwise unknown Arrianus (no ethnic), credited with an *Alexandrias* in 24 books, "poems on (εἰς) Attalus of Pergamum" and a translation of Vergil's *Georgics*.[124] For the editors of *SH*, following Meineke, it was "obvious" that the translator of Vergil was a separate, later figure. But a careful recent article by Simon Swain allows us to dispense with this drastic solution. The Attalus on whom Arrian wrote was a Pergamene of a much later age, probably C. Claudius Attalus Paterculianus who flourished ca 210/20 A.D., when the vogue for Alexander and multi-book epics were alike at a new height.[125] After all, it was around this time that a better-known Arrianus wrote the best surviving history of Alexander. Even so, there is no reason to believe that the poems on Attalus were also epics rather than standard encomia.

In fact there is only one of these Asiatic epic poets who might be dated as early as the age of Callimachus. All we know of him is contained in the following Suda-entry:[126]

Σιμωνίδης Μάγνης <ἀπὸ> Σιπύλου, ἐποποιός, γέγονεν ἐπὶ Ἀντιόχου τοῦ Μεγάλου κληθέντος, καὶ γέγραφε τὰς Ἀντιόχου [τοῦ Μεγάλου add. M] πράξεις καὶ τὴν πρὸς Γαλάτας μάχην, ὅτε μετὰ τῶν ἐλεφάντων τὴν ἵππον αὐτῶν ἔφθειρε.

---

121. Meloni 1953, 14; it was perhaps in honour of his Argive wife that Philip gave his son this name (Meloni 13).

122. Alkaios and Electryon: see their entries in Roscher and esp. Hesiod, *Cat.* F 190, with M. L. West, *The Hesiodic Catalogue of Women* (Oxford 1985), 110, 147. This is in fact the same descent from Heracles and Pelops claimed by the Attalids, since Alkaios and Electryon both married daughters of Pelops: Lysidike and Astydameia (West l.c.).

123. For other examples of poets playing off myth and history at the court of Philip V, C. F. Edson, *HSCP* 45 (1934), 213-41 and F. W. Walbank, *CQ* 36 (1942), 134-45, 37 (1943), 1-13 and 38 (1944), 87-8.

124. *SH* 207; *FGrH* 143 F 15; S. Swain, "Arrian the epic poet," *JHS* 111 (1991), 211.

125. Swain 1991, 214; on Alexander, F. Millar, *A Study of Cassius Dio* (Oxford 1964), 151, 214-18. Nestor of Laranda wrote an *Alexandreias* under Severus (Suda s.v. and Steph. Byz. s.v. Ὑστάσπαι), Nestor's son Peisander a *Heroïcae Theogamiae* in no fewer than 60 books (Suda s.v.; Heitsch ii. S 6).

126. *FGrH* 163; *SH* 723.

Simonides of Magnesia-by-Sipylos, epic poet; flourished under Antiochus the Great, and wrote on the deeds of Antiochus and the battle against the Gauls, when he destroyed their cavalry with his elephants.

On the face of it, "Antiochus the Great" has to be Antiochus III (223-187). There is no problem in postulating an otherwise undocumented Galatian victory during his reign,[127] but a Galatian victory won with the aid of elephants looks like the victory of Antiochus I Soter in 268 or 269,[128] whence the general assumption that Simonides was a contemporary and panegyrist of Antiochus I (281-261).[129] But the ὅτε clause is awkwardly tacked on, and might be a later addition by someone familiar with the colorful account in Lucian (which some have supposed to derive its colour from Simonides's "epic").[130] There is no reason why a poet at the court of Antiochus III should not have produced a fresh version of his great-grandfather's greatest victory. It was not till the end of the fifth century that Timotheus and Choerilus of Samos wrote their poems on the Greek victory over the Persians, and West has argued that (the Cean) Simonides's elegy on Plataea was not written until a decade or so after the battle.[131] There is still some uncertainty whether the Pergamene triumphal monument over the Gauls was dedicated by Attalus I (who won the victory) or Attalus II half a century later.[132]

More important still, once again there are no titles. Indeed, while we should expect a bravura account of Seleucid victories from a court poet, it is hard to see one battle as material for an entire epic. The same applies to the supposed "epic" (ἔπος) on the battle of Philippi by Boethus tyrant of Tarsus mentioned by Strabo,[133] and perhaps too Callistus's account of the Emperor Julian's Persian expedition "in heroic metre."[134] Even Claudian made no more than one book out of the battle of Pollentia.[135] While we cannot exclude the possibility of a multi-book epic, there are no positive grounds for crediting Simonides with anything more than encomia on Antiochus.

127. So A. Momigliano, *Boll. Fil. Class.* 36 (1929/30), 151-55 = *Quinto Contributo* (Rome 1975), 591-96.

128. For the date, M. Wörrle, *Chiron* 5 (1975), 59-87.

129. B. Bar-Kochva, *PCPS* 199 (1973), 1-8; H. H. Scullard, *The Elephant in the Greek and Roman World* (London 1974), 120-23; *SH* 723; Fantuzzi 1988, lxxxiv.

130. *Zeuxis* 8-11; *Laps. sal.* 9; e.g. A. Reinach, *Monuments Piot* 21 (1913), 194-97; cf. P. Bienkowski, *Les Celtes dans les arts mineurs greco-romains* (Cracow 1928), 149-50.

131. West, *ZPE* 98 (1993), 9.

132. J. J. Pollitt, *Art in the Hellenistic Age* (Cambridge 1986), 91, 296.

133. *SH* 230; it is only in the plural that ἔπος denotes Epic.(*LSJ* s.v.; West 1974, 7).

134. Socrates, *Hist. Eccles.* iii. 21; *PLRE* I. 176. But since it is known to have described Julian's death, it may have been later (and longer), falling into a different category.

135. Rhianus's multi-book *Messeniaca* covered the revolt of Aristomenes as a whole, though in largely fictionalized form and centuries after the event (§ 6 below);

It is salutary to reflect how false an idea we would have of the poetry of Aratus, Callimachus, Nicander and Theocritus if we knew only that they wrote poems in honour of Philadelphus and Gonatas—or of Euphorion if we knew only that he wrote at the court of Antiochus the Great. All would have been dismissed as·epic panegyrists of royal victories. As it happens, we know more and so we know better. And yet we make precisely that assumption about Leschides, Musaeus and Simonides. Yet again, it must be emphasized that no ancient text[136] either states or implies that large-scale epic was the dominant genre at Hellenistic courts.

In addition to encomia on their respective kings, Leschides, Musaeus and Simonides will have written a variety of other poems on other themes. Like their predecessors in the archaic and their successors in the imperial age, Hellenistic court poets were more likely to be called on to celebrate weddings and funerals than wars. Literary historians have been so obsessed with epics that they have overlooked the more routine occasions of life at court. Callimachus's *Lock of Berenice* is paralleled by the contest Stratonice the wife of Seleukos set her poets on the subject of her hair.[137] Callimachus wrote on the death and deification of Arsinoë (F 228), and Theocritus's *Berenice* (F iii) may have celebrated the death of Soter's widow. Aratus wrote three epicedia, one for his brother (*SH* 103-5); Parthenius four (608-14, 615, 626, 629), one for his wife; Euphorion one for a friend (F 21 Powell); some are also ascribed to Theocritus.[138] Calvus wrote one for his wife;[139] and Catullus one for his brother (101). Hellenistic royalty and their ministers set great store by victories in the great athletic festivals. Callimachus wrote at least three epinicia on such victories, and the Milan roll has now revealed no fewer than nineteen epinician epigrams by Posidippus. A competent poet wrote the elaborate epigram on the monument for Attalus of Pergamum's Olympic chariot victory in 268 or 264.[140]

The evidence for wedding poetry was collected in Ch. III. 4 and VI. 3. Callimachus (F 392) and Posidippus (*SH* 961) both celebrated the wedding of Arsinoë II. Eratosthenes (F 28 Powell) and Parthenius (*SH* 649) wrote epithalamia, as did Catullus (61-2) and his friends Calvus and Ticidas (F 4-8; F 1). The fact that Philodemus belittles the genre as contributing no more to the occasion than the cook[141] merely illustrates how routine a feature of Hellenistic weddings epithalamia had become. None of these poems

---

136. Except (of course) for the *Aetia* prologue on its traditional interpretation.

137. Lucian, *De imag.* 5 (a different situation, since Stratonice's hair had been falling out following an illness).

138. Suda s.v. with Pfeiffer, *CQ* 37 (1943), 32 n. 50.

139. F 15-16 Morel, with E. Fraenkel, *Kleine Beiträge* (Rome 1964), 109-10.

140. J. Ebert, *Griechiche Epigramme auf Sieger* (Berlin 1972), 176-81.

141. Philodemus, *Über die Musik IV. Buch*, ed. A. J. Neubecher (Naples 1986), p. 43.

will have run to more than a couple of hundred lines. It is nothing less than absurd to suppose that short poems were considered an audacious aberration—and no less absurd to suppose that all these epithalamia and epicedia were written for reading rather than performance.[142]

For Ziegler, Musaeus and Simonides were but the tip of an iceberg:

> We cannot doubt for a moment that the innumerable other kings and dynasts of the Hellenistic world, around the Mediterranean, in Asia Minor and indeed deep into Inner Asia, each had many heralds to proclaim their glory in verse.

Ziegler went further. These poets won wide popular success ("ein breites Publikum," p. 21), more characteristic representatives of Hellenistic poetry than the school of Callimachus. This goes too far—beyond both evidence and probability. For although the major works of Callimachus and Euphorion have perished no less than those of the Pergamenes, abundant evidence of their popularity and influence is provided by the many hundreds of references and quotations in later writers. But apart from their Suda-entries, there is not one quotation from Leschides, Musaeus or Simonides in any of the grammarians, geographers and scholiasts. Nor have we found a single papyrus there is any reason to assign to their work, in contrast to the eighty odd Callimachus and Euphorion papyri.[143] In fact, there is nothing to challenge in the succinct verdict of Christ and Schmid that formed Ziegler's starting point: that these poems "found no popular favour and disappeared without trace."[144]

According to the editors of *SH*, of the 39 "epic" poets they included, all but five wrote on historical events.[145] An impressive statistic, but the truth is that of all the poems listed under this rubric, not a single one can be stated with any confidence to have been a historical epic, if by epic we mean a full-scale narrative in several books. The great majority were surely *encomia* on the various kings. Such poems will certainly have dealt with historical events, but that is a very different matter. They describe battles rather than wars, and even battles less for their own sake than for the glory they bring their honorand. In short, while the subject matter is historical rather than mythical, they are in no sense historical epics. And this means that they cannot after all be seen as forerunners of Naevius and Ennius.

In his old age (ca 200), Naevius told the story of the first Punic War (264-241), including in a prelude or digressions the foundation and early history of both Rome and Carthage.[146] Ennius told the entire story of

---

142. On the rôle of literature at weddings, D. A. Russell, *PCPS* 205 (1979), 104-17.
143. There are now almost 70 Callimachus papyri and at least 10 of Euphorion (Marcotte and Mertens 1990); Arrianus is quoted twice by Steph. Byz.: *SH* 208-09.
144. Christ-Schmid-Stähelin, *Gesch. d. griech. Literatur* II[6] (1920), 139; Ziegler 11.
145. *SH* xvii; Lloyd-Jones, *Acad. Pap.* II. 236-37; Zwierlein, *Rh. Mus.* 131 (1988), 78.
146. U. Hübner, *Philologus* 116 (1972), 261-76.

Rome's history from its mythical beginnings right down to his own day. There is no precedent for either enterprise in Hellenistic epic. Ennius at any rate certainly praises individuals, but the real hero of his narrative is Roman *virtus*:

> moribus antiquis stat res Romana virisque.

Given their more restricted focus, there may have been more panegyric in some of the later Roman epics, but their length alone guarantees a basically narrative rather than topical structure. A certain Hostius celebrated Tuditanus's victory of 129 in a *Bellum Histricum* of at least three books; Furius of Antium Catulus's Cimbric victory of 101; Furius Bibaculus and Varro Atax the Gallic campaigns of Caesar in works entitled respectively *Annales Belli Gallici* and *Bellum Sequanicum*—not to mention the *Annales* of Volusius immortalized by Catullus.[147] We have only a handful of fragments from these epics, but the evidence on their nature and scale is explicit and uniform in just those areas where our Hellenistic evidence is not.

The same difference of emphasis is conspicuous in Roman painting of the third and second centuries. At a time when Hellenistic painting was mainly devoted to mythical and allegorical scenes, we find "a monotonous predilection on the part of the Romans for representation of their achievements in battle," on tomb frescoes, temple walls and portable panels.[148] The openly propagandistic function of such paintings is well illustrated by the story that L. Hostilius Mancinus stood by a picture of the siege of Carthage explaining his rôle in person to spectators during his campaign for the consulate of 145. It is not surprising that the Roman nobility should expect the poetry they commissioned to fulfil the same function. In the case of Catulus and Furius the relationship between patron and poet was such that Catulus actually presented his memoirs to Furius.[149]

"Rhianus, the two Choerili, and their emulators pointed the way," claims J. B. Hainsworth. But none of them wrote anything remotely like Ennius or Naevius: the younger Choerilus recorded the deeds of a living ruler; the older a single war in the past; Rhianus the legendary past. R. Häußler simply assumed that Leschides played Ennius to Eumenes's Fulvius Nobilior.[150] But it is not even certain that Leschides wrote before Ennius—or Rhianus before Naevius for that matter. The first Greek Ennius

---

147. Courtney, *FLP* 52-55, 97-8, 237-38, 195-200; F. Leo, *Gesch. d. röm. Literatur* I (1913), 405; Häußler 1976, 276-78; P. White, *Promised Verse* (1993), 79 counts two dozen epic poets from the Republic and early empire.

148. C. M. Dawson, *Romano-Campanian Landscape Painting* (*YCS* 9; New Haven 1944), 50-54; Roger Ling, *Roman Painting* (Cambridge 1991), 8-11.

149. Pliny, *NH* 35. 23); Cicero, *Brutus* 132.

150. Hainsworth 1991, 77; Häußler 1976, 83.

on record is Cicero's client Archias. To judge from Cicero's no doubt tendentious description, Archias wrote a fairly comprehensive account of the Mithridatic war—naturally highlighting the achievements of Lucullus.[151] But then Archias was writing for Roman patrons, who rapidly acquired a taste for historical epic that cannot be documented in their Hellenistic predecessors.[152]

Misgeld saw Hellenistic historical epic as a "depravation" of the form, a "coarsening of the poetry" caused by the growing pressure to glorify the divine kings of the age.[153] That was a sweeping diagnosis for any physician to make in the absence of the patient. And we can now see that it was false. However deplorable the modern reader may find the flattery and hyperbole of panegyrical poetry, it did not come about through a gradual deterioration of genuine historical narrative. Panegyric was a different genre to start with: its only purpose was praise, and its subject matter was arranged topically. There was never any narrative to deteriorate.[154] There is no evidence that the court poets of Alexander and his successors ever wrote narrative epics rather than formal panegyrics on the monarchs they served.

5

Hellenistic poets praised their rulers more briefly and in a variety of metres. In elegy, for example, following a tradition that goes back to at any rate the fifth century. Critias's elegy in honour of Alcibiades has already been cited (Ch. VI. 3). Then there is the elegy glorifying Plato's brothers Glaucon and Adeimantus, of which Plato quotes the first line: "Sons of Ariston, godlike race of a famous sire." This elegy, he adds, was written by a lover of Glaucon (generally identified as Critias) soon after the brothers had distinguished themselves in the battle of Megara (probably in 409).[155] As Reitzenstein saw, this encomiastic elegy is related to funerary epigram.[156] Another link is the fourteen-line elegiac eulogy of the Athenian army that captured Eion from the Persians in 475, inscribed on

151. *Mithridaticum vero bellum magnum atque difficile et in multa varietate terra marique versatum totum ab hoc expressum est. qui libri...* (*pro Archia* 21; *SH* 195).

152. So briefly O. Murray, *JRS* 75 (1985), 42; cf. Hardie 1983, 87.

153. W. R. Misgeld, *Rhianos von Bene und das historische Epos im Hellenismus* (Diss. Köln 1969), 55.

154. Though the subdivision for "deeds in war" will often, as in Claudian's panegyrics on Honorius and Stilicho and as indeed Menander recommended (ἐν δὲ τούτοις ἅπασι διηγήματα θήσεις, p. 138. 28 R-W), have contained substantial stretches of narrative.

155. Adesp. 1 West = Pl. *Rep.* 368A, with Davies, *Athen. Prop. Familes* (1971), 332.

156. *RE* 6. 1 (1907), 88.

three separate herms in the Athenian Agora. Not the least interesting feature of this unusual piece is the way Cimon's troops are directly compared to the Athenians at Troy.[157]

A disciple of Isocrates called Philiscus wrote an elegiac tribute to Lysias from which Ps-Plutarch quotes eight lines, evidently no more than a fragment. Though it was clearly not written for inscription, Ps-Plutarch describes the poem as an epigram,[158] perhaps because of its funerary nature, perhaps because of its modest length. More complex (it seems) was Aristotle's so-called "altar-elegy" addressed to Eudemus, on the conventional view written in praise of Plato soon after his death (347), but on Gaiser's more speculative interpretation a consolatory address to Eudemus of Cyprus on the death of Dion of Syracuse (354).[159] On any hypothesis it certainly contained a eulogy of Plato.

Callimachus himself wrote three or perhaps even four elegies in honour of his patrons: an epithalamium on Arsinoë (Ch. VI. 3); epinicians for Berenice and Sosibius; and most famous of all, the Lock of Berenice. Modern scholars oddly tend to suppose that these were eccentric experiments without influence. We shall see in Ch. XVIII that this was not how Roman poets saw them. *SH* 978 seems to be another elegy on Arsinoë, by Posidippus. Then there is the fragmentary *SH* 958, which may commemorate Philadelphus's suppression of a revolt of Gallic mercenaries in 274/2, an event also referred to by Callimachus (*Hymn* iv. 171-85).[160] If *SH* 969, another third-century papyrus but in a different hand, is not part of this poem, we have another Ptolemaic elegy addressed to a military man (l. 3, θρασὺς ἐν πολέμοις). A certain Archimelus wrote an 18-line "epigram" (as it is described by Athenaeus) in praise of an enormous cargo ship built by Hiero II of Syracuse ca 240; Hiero sent him 1500 bushels of wheat in reward.[161] *SH* 979 is a short elegy/long epigram on Ptolemy Philopator, described as "mighty in war and letters." *SH* 982 is another such piece on Octavian as conqueror and liberator of Egypt. *AP* vii. 241 by Antipater of Sidon is yet another, on the death of a young Ptolemaic prince.[162] We might add two long epigrams by Posidippus, one on the building of the Pharos, the other on a shrine built by Arsinoë;[163] and the epigram on the victory monument of Attalus the father of King Attalus I at Pergamum (Ebert no. 59).

157. *FGE* 255-9, with Jacoby, *Hesperia* 14 (1945), 185-211.

158. ἐποίησε δὲ καὶ εἰς αὐτὸν ἐπίγραμμα, *Vitae X Orat.* 3, 836C = *IEG* ii² p. 95.

159. F 673 Rose/West; K. Gaiser, *Mus: Helv.* 23 (1966), 84-106.

160. Fraser II. 925-27; Nachtergael 1975, 184-7. *SH* 958 has also been referred to Antigonus Gonatas, Antiochus I or III and one or more Attalid monarchs.

161. *SH* 202; against Page's scathing scepticism (*FGE* 26-29), Duncan-Jones, *CQ* 27 (1977), 331-32.

162. *HE* II. 54, identifying the youth as Eupator son of Philometor.

163. *HE* 3100-19, with II. 489-92.

It is striking how much better documented these elegies and epigrams are than the long epics that have been held to dominate Hellenistic encomiastic poetry. Indeed, the recent discovery of (the Cean) Simonides's elegies on the great battles of the Persian wars suggests that, down to the fifth century, it was elegy rather than epic that had served as the normal medium for recent military narrative. · The real novelty of Choerilus of Samos may have consisted in transferring such subject matter to epic (it may be more than coincidence that he chose a theme already treated in a famous series of elegies).[164]

Nor should we underestimate the propaganda value of epigrams. When Plutarch mentions the poems that were written about the Macedonian defeat at Cynoscephalae in 197, the example he quotes as the most popular is an epigram by Alcaeus of Messene. It is a sharp attack on Philip V for leaving so many of his men to die on the battlefield, and Philip took the trouble to respond to it himself.[165] The much richer Roman evidence illustrates in detail how, in the course of the passage from Republic to Empire, poets and patrons alike "became increasingly aware that the appetite for praise could be gratified by simpler genres than epic."[166] Cultivated rulers like Philadelphus and Gonatas must have realized before Augustus that sophisticated occasional poetry more in touch with the taste of the times would find more readers of the right sort and confer its own sort of immortality.

There is in addition another entire category of poems on Hellenistic kings and heroes: short choral songs, normally described as paeans. Many paeans are formal hymns, addressed to various gods, principally Apollo. But they also appear in a number of less formal contexts; at symposia, weddings and (most frequently) as a victory cry.[167] There seem to be no regular defining characteristics. Rather it is the occasion or even the singer's state of mind that gives the poem its identity: it is addressed to the god either in a moment of need or in gratitude for help already rendered.[168] Since the god is appealed to as benefactor and saviour, often in an entreaty to avert plague or famine, it was no large step to address in similar terms a mortal who had rendered, or was known to be capable of rendering similar services. The one paean on a Hellenistic ruler we have more or less com-

164. The overlap between the new P. Oxy. 3965 and the previously known elegiac fragments of 2327 reveals at one stroke two II s. papyri of Simonides's elegies.

165. μάλιστα διὰ στόματος ἦν, V. Tit. 9; Ch. III. 7.

166. Peter White, *Promised Verse* (1993), 82.

167. The standard work is now L. Käppel, *Paian: Studien zur Geschichte einer Gattung* (Berlin 1992); see too A. Fairbanks, *A Study of the Greek Paean* (Cornell Studies in Class. Phil. 12), 1900; L. Deubner, "Paian," *NJb* 22 (1919), 385-406 = *Kl. Schr.* (1982), 204-25; von Blumenthal, *RE* 18. 2 (1942), 2340-62; West, *Ancient Greek Music* (Oxford 1992), 15-16. On the paean before battle, W. K. Pritchett, *The Greek State at War* (1971), 105-08.

168. So Käppel 1992, 43f., with M. W. Dickie, *BMCR* 4 (1993), 100-05.

plete (no. 6) pairs Demetrius Poliorcetes with Demeter, directly evoking the Eleusinian Mysteries, and then proceeds:

> Other gods are far away, or deaf, or do not exist,
> or pay us no heed; but you we see present among us.

No. 12 addresses Flamininus as saviour ($\sigma\hat{\omega}\tau\epsilon\rho$). And although we do not have the paeans addressed to Antigonus the One-eyed and Demetrius in 307, we know from the other honours voted them on their relief of Athens that both again were accorded the title of saviour.[169] According to a well-informed writer of the following century (Duris of Samos), Lysander was "the first of the Greeks to whom cities erected altars and sacrificed to as to a god, and to whom paeans were sung" (no. 1 below). The innovation was not to everyone's taste. Half a century later Aristotle was prosecuted for impiety on the ground that a poem he wrote in honour of his friend Hermias the tyrant of Atarneus, killed by the Persians in 345/4, was a paean.[170] Athenaeus points out (apparently from Hermippos) that the poem lacks the traditional refrain ($i\grave{\eta}$ $\Pi\alpha\iota\acute{\alpha}\nu$ or $i\grave{\eta}$ $\Pi\alpha\iota\hat{\eta}o\nu$)[171] and is best classified as a skolion.[172] He then goes on to cite five examples of paeans on living men equipped with a refrain, in many cases supplying valuable details about composer, occasion and even performers.[173]

It may be useful to list them here together with what can be added to Athenaeus's list from other sources.[174] Paeans (or something similar) are recorded for the following:

1) Lysander: performed on Samos in 404 (Duris, in Athen. 696 E; *FGrH* 76 F26, 71); fragment (*PMG* 867) quoted by Plutarch, *Lys*. 18. 4. from Duris: C. Habicht, *Gottmenschentum und griechische Städte*[2] (1970), 8; Käppel no. 35.

2) Agemon of Corinth: performed by "the Corinthians" (Polemo of Ilium in Athen. 696 F; *FHG* III 137).

---

169. For these honours, see C. Habicht, *Gottmenschentum und griechische Städte*[2] (1970), 44-48; R. A. Billows, *Antigonus the One-eyed* (1990), 149-50.

170. Athen. 696 B-7B; Diog. Laert. 5. 6; Did. *Comm. Dem.* col. 6. 18f.; *PMG* 842; E. Derenne, *Les procès d'impieté* (1930), 188f.; C. M. Bowra, *CQ* 32 (1938), 182-89; I. Düring, *Aristotle in the Ancient Biographical Tradition* (Göteborg 1957), 272-77; *FGE* 93-5; R. Renehan, *GRBS* 23 (1982), 251-74; for the date, M. Sordi, *Kokalos* 5 (1959), 107-18.

171. Callimachus gives a neat aetiology which explains his preference for the aspirated form: *Hymn to Apollo* 103, with Williams ad loc.

172. For a dispute between Callimachus and Aristarchus about whether an ode of Bacchylides was a paean or dithyramb, see P. Oxy. 2368 = *SH* 293, with W. Luppe, *Analecta Papyrologica* i (1989), 23-29.

173. As Wehrli points out, *Hermippos der Kallimacheer* (1974), 75, Hermippos cannot be Athenaeus's source for all the examples cited, since some (e.g. Polemon) outlived him.

174. What follows is a more comprehensive and detailed list than Käppel's (pp. 346-49), which is limited to texts that include the term paean.

3) Demetrius of Phalerum: dithyramb performed at the Dionysia in Athens, written by Siron (or Castorion) of Soli (*SH* 312; M. L. West, *Greek Metre* 143 n. 14).

4) Antigonus the One-eyed and Demetrius Poliorcetes: after their capture of Munichia in 307, performed by "the Athenians," written by Hermocles or Hermodotus of Cyzicus, who won a prize for the best paean (*SH* 492; Athen. 697A; Philochorus, *FGrH* 328 F 165: *Suppl.* I 541-2; II 437; Habicht, *Gottmenschentum* 47).

5) Ptolemy Soter; performed by the people of Rhodes, according to Gorgon, *On the Rhodian Festivals* (Athen. 696 F; *FGrH* 515 F19).

6) Demetrius Poliorcetes: performed at Athens in 291, in ithyphallics; entire text quoted from Duris by Athen. 253 A; *FGrH* 76 F13; *CA* pp. 173-5; O. Weinreich, *NJb* 2 (1926), 646-9 = *Kl. Schr.* II (1973), 190-4 (though confusing the circumstances with no. 4); C. Habicht, *Gottmenschentum* 232.

7) Craterus the Macedonian: performed at Delphi ca 280, written by Alexinus of Elis, according to Hermippos *On Aristotle* Bk i (*SH* 40; Athen. 696 E; *FGrH* 342 T3).

8) Seleucus I: written 281/80 and partially preserved in stone at Erythrae, in dactyloepitrites; *CA* p. 140; Käppel no. 38.

9) Ptolemy Philadelphus (or Philopator): by Theocles, in ithyphallics, performed at the Soteria in Alexandria (Athen. 497C; Fraser I. 232-3; II. 383).

10) According to Plutarch, Aratus of Sicyon himself, wearing a garland on his head, sung paeans to Antigonus Doson in 225/4 (*Cleom.* 16. 4-5).

11) During Marcellus's triumph of 222 in Rome, according to Plutarch (*Marcell.* 8. 2), his troops "sang specially composed songs (μέλη) together with epinician paeans in praise of the god and their general."

12) On Aratus's death in 213, the people of Sicyon brought his body into the city with paeans and dances (Plutarch, *V. Arat.* 53, with much detail about the clothing worn for the ceremony; μέλη were sung to the cithara by the artists of Dionysus).[175]

13) T. Flamininus: performed by the Chalcidians ca 195, in ithyphallics; Plut. *Tit.* 16; *CA* p. 173; Käppel no. 43.

14) A chorus of boys sung a παραβώμιον and a chorus of girls a hymn for Queen Apollonis the mother of Eumenes II at Teos early in the 2nd c. (*OGIS* 309. 7-10, with L. Robert, *Études anatoliennes* [Paris 1937], 2-20).

---

175. The singing of paeans in commemoration of a man's death should perhaps be classified differently, as an element of hero-cult rather than ruler-cult. Habicht points out (*Gottmenschentum* 8, with n. 5, correcting von Blumenthal in *RE* 18. 2 (1942), 2353-4) that this is the first example of a paean sung for a hero. This practice seems to have been an extension of the singing of paeans to living rulers rather than vice versa.

15) On the anniversary of Philopoemen's death in 182, annual sacrifices were held at Megalopolis and "the young sang encomia and hymns on his virtue" (Diodorus 29. 18; J. M. Bremer, *Faith, Hope and Worship* ed. H. J. Versnel [Leiden 1981], 201).

16) When Metellus Pius, cos. 80, won a minor victory over Sertorius in Spain, he was welcomed with altars and sacrifices in the cities, wore the *toga picta* at banquets, and used mechanical victories to place gold crowns on his head while choirs sang victory hymns (ἐπινικίους ὕμνους) to his glory (Plutarch, *Sert.* 22. 3). Whether or not the poems were in Latin, much of the ritual is Greek.[176]

17) After M. Antonius's arrival in 41, "all Asia," according to Plutarch, "was filled with incense, paeans and groans." Of course, he is quoting a famous line of Sophocles, but it is tempting to guess that he was prompted to quote this particular line by the mention of real paeans in his source.[177]

Every one of these poems is either expressly stated to have been performed publicly by choruses in the traditional style or is preserved on stone, which guarantees prior public performance.[178]

When the time came to praise real-life kings and heroes, it is not suprising that paeans rather than epics should have been the norm, especially in the early Hellenistic age. Their literary ambitions seem to have been modest,[179] and we know of none by any poets of the first rank, though the paeans on Antigonus and Demetrius (no. 4 above) are said to have won the prize in a contest between "all the writers of paeans." The choral performance of a relatively short and simple hymn, normally at a festival, inevitably reached a far wider audience than a long, stylized epic, and was then prominently inscribed in a public place. There was also the important advantage that such performances fitted within the traditional religious framework of the cities.

Horace's lyric epinicia tend to be studied in terms of Pindaric imitation vs Horatian originality.[180] Yet it is hardly possible to doubt that Horace

176. S. Weinstock, *Divus Julius* (Oxford 1971), 296 (citing the other texts, but oddly not Plutarch). According to Cicero, Pius was so eager to have his deeds immortalized that he even tried Cordoban (i.e. Latin) poets, despite their outlandish style (*pro Archia* 26). But Plutarch says he had Pergamene hangings on his walls even on campaign, and the mechanical victories are also Pergamene (Plutarch l.c. and *Sulla* 11. 1-2). He may have kept a Greek poet in his retinue.

177. *V. Anton.* 24: ἡ γὰρ ᾿Ασία πᾶσα...ὁμοῦ μὲν θυμιαμάτων ἔγεμεν, ὁμοῦ δὲ παιάνων τε καὶ στεναγμάτων (Soph. *OT* 4).

178. For another dozen Hellenistic paeans to gods preserved epigraphically, see Powell, *CA* pp.132-71, with Fairbank, *Study of the Greek Paean* 10-153; von Blumenthal, *RE* 18. 2 (1942), 2358; West, *Ancient Greek Music* (1992), 279-80, 288-301.

179. "nullo honore carmina haec habentur, vix meliora quae sollemni occasione oblata nova fiunt" (Wilamowitz, in Norden, *Agnostos Theos*[2] [1923], 392).

180. E. Fraenkel, *Horace* (1957), 426-40.

was also influenced by this modest but continuous Hellenistic tradition of choral lyric—even if only to reject it for more ancient models. It must surely have been on the Hellenistic model that Livius Andronicus composed a procession song in 207 B.C. (Livy xxvii. 37. 7), as Fraenkel had already argued (though without drawing the same conclusion for Horace). And we might add the paeans sung by Marcellus's soldiers in 222.

This is not to say that anyone would turn down an epic. But the legendary badness of the Alexander quintet cannot have encouraged the Diadochi to search for their personal Homers. Some of these kings were cultivated men, in tune with current literary fashions (Ch. I. 2): Philadelphus had none other than Philitas and Zenodotus as his personal tutors. According to Clausen, Callimachus's "famous refusal to write an epic surely implies a widely held view that poets ought to write epics and perhaps even some expectation on the part of those in high places."[181] But this is to read the Augustan *recusatio* back into the *Aetia* prologue (Ch. XVIII). Not only Callimachus himself but Aratus, Apollonius, Euphorion, Lycophron and Nicander, all those now patronizingly dismissed as scholar-poets and assumed to have written exclusively for fellow pedants and cognoscenti, found favour at the courts of one or more Hellenistic monarchs.[182] By contrast the only poet of the age who is known to have written voluminous epics, Rhianus, seems to have achieved no such worldly success. Indeed he may never have left his native Crete.[183] Callimachus, Nicander and Theocritus are the only panegyrists of Hellenistic royalty whose works have (at least in part) come down to us. It is merely perverse to claim that they were less popular than other poets of whom we know nothing whatever. The "epic" eulogies that survive —Theocritus 16, 17 and 24—are all decidedly short, ranging from 109 to 170 lines. There is simply no basis for the dominant assumption that the advent of the Hellenistic kings created an immediate demand for large-scale historical epics.

6

The case of mythological epic is rather different. It certainly existed, though once more there is little than can be firmly dated to the century between Antimachus and Callimachus.[184]

181. Clausen 1964, 181; Callimachus "was speaking for a minority; most poets were busy celebrating kings and battles" (*Virgil's Aeneid* [1987], 125 n. 4).

182. Aratus was with both Gonatas and Antiochus Soter; Alexander Aetolus and Lycophron with Gonatas and Philadelphus; Nicander I with Gonatas, Nicander II with Attalus I; Euphorion with Antiochus III.

183. Kent Rigsby, *REG* 99 (1986), 354-5; see too § 6 below.

184. Wilamowitz, *HD* I 104-05, has already remarked that to all intents and purpose Rhianus and Apollonius were the first epic poets of any note since Antimachus.

Diotimus and Phaedimus of Bisanthe in Thrace both wrote epics on Heracles. Phaedimus dates from the second half of the third century;[185] if Diotimus is the Diotimus of Adramyttium mocked by Aratus, he might be a contemporary of Callimachus, but the name is not uncommon.[186] The prolific and influential Euphorion of Chalcis was not born till 275,[187] and so not active till the last decade or so of Callimachus's life. In any case, Euphorion established himself at the court of Antiochus III in Antioch, and seems to have "had no direct connection with Alexandria and the Ptolemies."[188] Neoptolemus of Parium, author of a *Dionysias*, wrote at the end of the third century.[189] Cleo of Curium (possibly to be identified with the elegist Cleo quoted by a lexicographer)[190] wrote an *Argonautica* which is said by the scholia to have been used by Apollonius, but he could have been pre-Hellenistic. There is no evidence that another *Argonautica*, by Dionysius Scytobrachion, was earlier than Callimachus.[191] A tantalizing new papyrus that apparently compares Apollonius, Cleo and Dionysius has cast no new light on their relative dates and interrelationship.[192]

The date of the eleven-book *Thebaïs* of Menelaus of Aegae is likewise quite uncertain,[193] and Menelaus was praised by Longinus for his meticulous craftsmanship.[194] In fact only two poets come into serious consideration: Hermesianax and the witty gourmet Antagoras. Antagoras lived for a while at the court of Antigonus Gonatas and later at Athens, where he wrote epitaphs for two heads of the Academy, Polemo and Crates, and feuded with a third, Arcesilas.[195] Late sources also ascribe a *Thebaïs* to him, and though some have held it to be a doublet of Antimachus's *Thebaïs*, there seems no sufficient reason to doubt its existence.[196] It might

---

185. *HW* II. 453; Peek, *RE* 19. 2 (1938), 1537, no. 9; Fantuzzi 1988, lxxix.

186. *SH* 392-95; *HE* II. 271; Wilamowitz, *Eur. Herakles* I[1] 310 n.78 = II[4] 67 n.123.

187. *CA* pp. 28-58; *SH* 413-54; Fraser II. 792 n. 13; B. A. Van Groningen, *Euphorion* (Amsterdam 1977).

188. Pfeiffer 1968, 150; the soberest discussion of dates and places is that of Fraser, *Gnomon* 28 (1956), 578-582. See too Lloyd-Jones, *CR* 29 (1974), 14-17.

189. Mette, *RE* 16. 2 (1935), 2467; C. O. Brink, *Horace on Poetry* (1963), 43f.

190. J. S. Rusten, *Dionysius Scytobrachion* (1982), 57-61; *SH* 339-40; Weinberger, *RE* 11. 2 (1921), 719, no.9.

191. Rusten 1982, F 36; SH 390; D. P. Nelis inconclusively argues that he wrote before Apollonius (*CQ* 41 [1991], 104-05).

192. Ch. XII. 1; the lines from an *Argonautica* published by M. Haslam in P. Oxy. LIII (1986), no. 3698 (to which should be added 2513 in the same hand) are archaic rather than Hellenistic (Haslam, p. 10).

193. *SH* 551-57; Fiehn, *RE* 15. 1 (1931), 833, no. 10 (which of the many places called Aegae is unknown: *RE* 1 [1893], 944-5).

194. τὸ ἀκριβές τε καὶ ἄμωμον, Jo. Sic. *Rhet. gr.* VI. 93 Walz; a "Callimachean," according to Christ-Schmid-Stählin, *Gesch. Gr. Lit.* II. 1[6] (1920), 321; Fantuzzi 1988, lxxii.

195. F 2-3 Powell; Aelian, *VH* 14. 25.

196. F 4; T.B.L. Webster, *Hellenistic Poetry and Art* (1964), 30; Fantuzzi 1988, lxi; Matthews, *Eranos* 77 (1979), 43-50; Ch. II. 5.

be added that Callimachus neatly adapted the first line of Antagoras's *Hymn to Eros* in the proem to his own *Hymn to Zeus*, which does not suggest that he held him in contempt.[197]

Hermesianax is credited with a *Persica* by a scholion on Nicander viewed with (perhaps unjustified) scepticism by Rohde, Susemihl and Powell.[198] The form of the title suggests epic and a historical theme cannot be ruled out, but which Persian war is Hermesianax likely to have written about? All other citations of Hermesianax are for mythical themes, and one of them does concern Persia: the saga of Cyrus and Nanis, the daughter of Croesus, assigned by Powell to his elegy *Leontion*.[199] We shall see in the following chapter that, while Hermesianax may indeed have been one of Callimachus's targets, it will have been the *Leontion* rather than an epic he had in mind. The first post-Antimachean mythological epic on a large scale that can be securely dated relative to Callimachus is none other than Apollonius's *Argonautica*, and it was undoubtedly written after (and under the influence of) the *Aetia*.

Related to but (as Jacoby saw) nonetheless distinct from mythological epic is the somewhat more abundant category of ethnographical or regional epic, treating particular regions from mythological to historical times, though seldom to the writer's own day, or anywhere near it.[200] The principal exponent of this form seems to have been Rhianus of Lebena in Crete,[201] author of a *Messeniaca* in at least 6 books, and *Achaica, Eliaca* and *Thessalica*, the last in at least 16 books.[202] Thanks to Pausanias (who drew on it for his Bk iv) we know most about the *Messeniaca*, which dealt with the revolt of Aristomenes in the so-called second Messenian war of ca 600 B.C. Jacoby maintained that the *Messeniaca* was a genuinely historical rather than ethnographical epic,[203] but since it presents a largely fictional-

197. Antag. F I. 1 (with R. Renehan, *HSCP* 68 [1974], 379-81): ἐν δοιῇ μοι θυμός, ὅ τοι γένος ἀμφιβόητον ~ Call. *HZ* 5: ἐν δοιῇ μάλα θυμός, ἐπεὶ γένος ἀμφήριστον. For Call.'s priority, Wilamowitz, *Antig. v. Karystos* (1881), 69; Renehan, l.c.; McLennan's note ad 1.

198. See Powell's note on *CA* F 12, p. 106; see too Ch. VIII. 2.

199. Parthenius 22 = F 6 Powell; *FGrH* 691 T1, cf. F1. Mimnermus's elegy *Smyrneïs* also has an "epic" title.

200. See Jacoby's brief but important discussion in *FGrH* IIIa (1943), 87-89. The local epics of the archaic age—*Phoronis, Phocaïs, Thesprotis, Korinthiaca*, etc.—must have been entirely mythical. On the *Meropis* papyrus (*SH* 903A), see Lloyd-Jones, *Academic Papers* I (1990), 21-29.

201. For the fragments, *CA* pp. 9-21; *SH* 715-16, 923, 946; *HE* I. 174-76; *FGrH* 265 (with elaborate commentary, IIIa, pp. 87-200); Fantuzzi 1988, lxxxii.

202. 23 of the 26 quotations from the *Thessalica* come from Steph. Byz., 9 from Bk iv, and one each from v, vi, vi, vii, xiv, xv and xvi.

203. Jacoby, *FGrH* IIIA Komm. 87f.; but this was because (like G. L. Huxley, *Early Sparta* [London 1962], 89-93) he identified Rhianus's Leotychidas (Paus. iv. 15. 1 = F 43) with the second Spartan king of that name (ca 491-476) rather than the first (? ca 600), as (more probably) Beloch, *Hermes* 35 (1900), 254-9; Pearson, *Historia* 11 (1962), 417-23; H. T. Wade-Gery, *Ancient Society and Institutions: Studies...V. Ehrenberg* (London 1967), 289-302; V. Parker, *Chiron* 21 (1991), 25-47.

ized version of a 400-year-old war, it is not clear that the distinction is very helpful. As Pearson put it, the poem "is historical only in so far as its setting is historical, not mythological."[204] It is generally assumed that the four-book *Heracleia* was a straightforward mythological epic, but the quotations suggest a regional emphasis.

Misgeld stressed the links of regional to historical epic,[205] but we have seen that genuinely historical epic may have been rather short-lived, and regional poetry seems to have been more concerned with mythical origins than recent history. More significant are the links to city encomion. For the regional epic is surely a more systematic version of the prize poems that "made worthy mention" of the gods, myths, temples and ancestors of the cities hosting the great festivals. Whence the suggestion made above that Nicander's prize poem at Delphi may have been an excerpt from his *Aetolica*. They are also linked to the great outpouring of regional historical writing all over the early Hellenistic world (Ch. II. 4). The two most conspicuous surviving representatives of this movement among the poets are (of course) Callimachus (especially but not exclusively the *Aetia*) and Apollonius (his lost foundation poetry as well as the *Argonautica*). As already remarked, the richest single source for these lost local histories is the scholia to the *Argonautica*. Many of these poems will have told of kings and heroes, and some were no doubt pretty bad. Nonetheless, it is not obvious that these were the *sort* of poems Callimachus would have disapproved of; nor is it clear in any case whether any of them were written before the *Aetia*.

Following Wilamowitz, Jacoby rather perversely argued that Rhianus was an older contemporary of Callimachus, against the only ancient witness, the statement in his Suda-entry that he was a contemporary of Eratosthenes. But we saw in Ch. VIII that these synchronisms in the Lives of the third-century poets are more consistent and authoritative than generally supposed. The three poets never mentioned in the *Lives* of Aratus, Nicander and Theocritus are Apollonius, Euphorion and Rhianus. There are independent grounds for believing that the eight writers who are mentioned there did indeed flourish in the first half of the century. Nor is this just an argument from silence: Apollonius, Euphorion and Rhianus are all said to have been contemporaries of Eratosthenes, which puts them firmly in the second half of the century.[206]

204. Pearson 1962, 418.

205. Misgeld 1969, 116-21.

206. Eratosthenes lived till ca 200 (Fraser II. 489-90); a son of Rhianus may be attested by a Delphic inscription of the early II c. (Rigsby, *REG* 1986, 355).

Wilamowitz weakly argued that Callimachus got the story of Apollo's love for Admetus (*Hymn* ii. 49) from Rhianus F 10,[207] but the reverse is at least as likely.[208] Pfeiffer argued that F 20 imitated the *Hecale*,[209] and in his epigrams (surprisingly neglected in this matter) Rhianus is clearly revealed as an imitator of Callimachus. The fact that he wrote a series of elegant pederastic epigrams is proof enough in itself. The Hellenistic erotic epigram seems to have been virtually invented by Asclepiades and rapidly perfected by Callimachus, the first exponent of the pederastic epigram:[210] not a love story, but a single erotic motif developed in allusive and witty fashion. Rhianus IV, asking whether Cleonicus has met the Graces since he is such a Grace himself, is modelled on Callimachus XV, praising Queen Berenice II as the fourth Grace. It is obviously less natural to compare a boy to the female Graces. In Rhianus I the Hours and Graces pour oil on young Menecrates's buttocks. That the Hours and Graces should bestow beauty is natural and documented. But the Hours normally pour dew, rain or springwater,[211] and the only other text where the Graces are associated with oil is *Aetia* F 7. 13-14, where Callimachus begs them to wipe the oil that drips from their hair on his elegies. Rhianus has neatly adapted the Graces's hair-oil to the rubbing-oil that enhances the charms of his boy-friend's rear. It is unlikely that he would ever have thought of associating rubbing-oil with the Graces but for Callimachus.[212] Rhianus IX is surely modeled on Callimachus IV, the famous poem on the loss of half his soul.[213] Furthermore, it has long been noticed that Rhianus is also one of the first imitators of Leonidas, pioneer of the anathematic epigram and an approximate contemporary of Callimachus.[214] Since Callimachus XV on Berenice cannot have been written before 246, it looks as if Rhianus's floruit falls in the last third of the century.

Bing analysed a couple of brief fragments of epic narrative about Spartans conjecturally attributed to the *Messeniaca*, claiming that the poet "does not seek out the Homeric *hapax legomena* or disputed words that are

207. F. Williams 1978, 49-50, suspending judgment; in *Glaube der Hellenen* ii[2] (1956), 313-14 Wilamowitz dropped Rhianus to the second half of the century without comment.

208. So Susemihl 1891, 399 n. 141.

209. Pfeiffer on F 266; Hollis 1990, 27.

210. Reitzenstein, *Epigr. und Skolion* (1893), 159; Ludwig, *GRBS* 4 (1963), 60-62; Hutchinson 1988, 20-25, 73-76, 264-76; Giangrande, *L'Épigramme grecque* (1968), 93-177.

211. Gow on Theocritus i. 150.

212. Note that Callimachus XV describes Berenice as wet with incense, presumably meaning that her statue "is still moist with the perfume with which it has been anointed" (*HE* II. 172; for the practice of anointing statues, Pfeiffer on Call. F 7. 12). S. Tarán (1979, 40-45) argues that Rhianus I is also later than Dioscorides X; Dioscorides certainly imitates Callimachus (*HE* II. 240).

213. ἥμισύ μευ...ἥμισυ δ᾽οὐκ οἶδ᾽...πλήν (Call.) ~ ἥμισύ μεν...ἥμισυ δ᾽...οὐκ οἶδ᾽...πλήν (Rhian.); cf. G. Luck, *GGA* 219 (1967), 60.

214. Reitzenstein 1893, 157-8; Luck, *GGA* 219 (1967), 34-35.

so characteristic of the Hellenistic avant garde" and concluding that they "probably provide us with a fair example of those traits that characterized the bulk of the epic produced at this time."[215] That is to say, on the basis of these fragments Rhianus is treated as representative of pre-Alexandrian epic. But the attribution is quite uncertain;[216] the papyrus itself is of the third century A.D., and Lloyd-Jones and Parsons were inclined to believe the poem too of imperial date. Bing did not even mention the securely attributed 21 lines of F 1, which *do* exploit Homeric rarities.[217] Moreover epigram II gives a neat pederastic connotation to the Homeric formula ἀγαθὴ κουροτρόφος, used once of Ithaca in the *Odyssey*. More generally, the subtle and allusive way Rhianus plays with the motifs of Alexandrian love epigram does not make it very probable that his epic style could be compared to the braying of donkeys.

So Rhianus's floruit fell in the generation after Callimachus. But the origin of regional epic may be more complex if it is the elder Nicander who wrote *Aetolica, Oetaïca, Thebaïca* and (perhaps) *Boeotica*—not to mention the possibility that the elder Choerilus wrote a *Samiaca*.[218] This is presumably the same Nicander who wrote the *Transformations*, almost all linked to particular places, local landmarks or religious rites.[219] The elder Nicander was a contemporary of Aratus and Callimachus. But he drew on the *Hecale*,[220] and the date of his Delphic victory (254/3) suggests that much of his oeuvre may have been written later than *Aetia* I-II. Nor can Nicander be seen as a representative of traditional epic; indeed, he has always been treated as the quintessential Alexandrian.

A number of other works apparently of this nature are known by repute, none of them plausibly datable to or before the lifetime of Callimachus. The *Mopsopia* of Euphorion is certainly post-Callimachean.[221] The same applies to the ten-book *Bithyniaca* of Demosthenes of Bithynia, possibly as early as the third century B.C., but also assigned to the imperial age.[222] Lloyd-Jones has recently praised Demosthenes's "elegant style,

---

215. P. Oxy. 2883 = *SH* 946-47; cf. Bing 1988, 51-56.

216. Despite Livrea's overconfident "dubitare non licet," *Gnomon* 57 (1985), 600.

217. *CA* 9-10, analysed by Giangrande in *L'Ant. Class.* 39 (1978), 35-43 and 62-64.

218. Samos had an unusually strong and early local historiography: Jacoby, *Atthis* (1949), 182-85. The *Dardanica* of Hegemon is another unknown quantity; the *Sicelica* of the fourth century Polycritus of Mende seems to have been a different sort of work, paradoxographic rather than ethnographic (*SH* 696-97; *FGrH* 559 F 2, with Komm. 516-17).

219. P.M.C. Forbes Irving, *Metamorphosis in Greek Myth* (Oxford 1990), 27.

220. Hollis 1990, 30.

221. *CA* 37; Hollis, *ZPE* 93 (1992), 10-11.

222. Schwartz, *RE* 5. 1 (1903), 188-89, no. 9; *FGrH* 699; F. W. Walbank, *Comm. on Polybius* II (1967), 318-19; Fantuzzi 1988, lxvi. Apparently unaware of any controversy about his date, H. White (*L'Ant. Class.* 60 [1991], 216) takes it for granted that Demosthenes's *Bithyniaca* is the sort of poem attacked in the *Aetia* prologue!

correct poetic diction and Callimachean metre."[223] The *Cumaïca* of Hyperochus of Cumae and the *Messeniaca* of Aeschylus of Alexandria may both be of Roman date.[224] The *Rhodiaca* of Idaeus of Rhodes and *Macedonica* or *Lacedaemonica* of Phaestus seem entirely undatable.[225] It is among these "ethnic epics" that we should probably classify two second- or first-century Jewish epics of which Eusebius has preserved a few extracts: the "elder" Philo's *On Jerusalem*, and Theodotus's *On the Jews*.[226]

7

Ziegler wrote of the "hundreds of thousands of books, hundreds of thousands of verses of non-callimachean epic poetry" that the Telchines praised and Callimachus damned. But not only is there very little direct evidence for this alleged outpouring of traditional epic in the century or so before Callimachus. What would have been its social context? Festivals at which multi-book poems could be performed in full were many centuries in the past.[227] Only brief extracts could have been recited in the contests of Hellenistic festivals. Long epics must surely now have been written for private reading rather than public performance, in which case, given their archaizing language, they can hardly have been aimed at a wide audience. On the traditional interpretation of the *Aetia* prologue, we have hitherto been asked to believe that short poems were considered eccentric and provocative, a minority taste without influence till Roman times. The truth is that only short epics can be assigned any plausible social context. By Callimachus's day, the popular significance of the term ἐπῶν ποιητής was someone who wrote short hexameter poems on local cults and heroes or short hexameter encomia on important people. In this context it is difficult to see why there should have been a "debate" on the "validity" of epic.

There was no doubt as much bad poetry written in the third century as in any other age. But Callimachus cannot have been concerned with the always abundant work of the second rank. The object of his ire must surely have been poetry that *purported* to be of the first rank, poetry that was currently but (as he thought) unjustly admired by the pundits of the age, the

---

223. *Academic Papers* II (1990), 26.

224. *SH* 498 and *FGrH* 576 (Komm. p. 607); *SH* 13 and *FGrH* 488.

225. *SH* 502 and 670; Stoessl, *RE* 19. 2 (1938), 1608 no. 5; *FGrH* 593 F 1 (Komm. p. 629); Fantuzzi 1988, lxxix.

226. *SH* 681-86 and 757-64; E Schürer, *History of the Jewish People in the Age of Jesus Christ*, rev. G. Vermes, F. Millar and M. Goodman III. 1 (Edinburgh 1986), 559-62; Fantuzzi 1988, lxxx; Lloyd-Jones, *Academic Papers* II (1990), 239.

227. For what is known of archaic festivals, W. G. Thalman, *Conventions of Form and Thought in Early Greek Epic Poetry* (Baltimore 1984), 117f.

arbiters of contemporary taste. Transposed into modern terms, we might imagine an acrimonious debate about the Great American Novel. Serious critics would agree in ignoring such popular favourites as Jackie Collins or Stephen King, reserving their abuse for the serious contenders.

It is significant that the Florentine scholiast did not put the names of any epic poets on his list of Telchines. The only two on the list who are poets at all, Posidippus and Asclepiades, were best known for precisely the sort of sophisticated miniature work that was Callimachus's speciality. Indeed, Callimachus clearly admired and certainly imitated Asclepiades's epigrams.[228] In addition to his surviving epigrams, Asclepiades wrote short poems in a variety of metres, choliambics, and hymns.[229] Posidippus seems to have been the first known specialist in the epigram. On the face of it, *animae naturaliter Callimacheae*. It is difficult to see why either should have admired multi-book *Thebaids* or *Messeniaca*, much less wanted Callimachus to add to their number. On the other hand, we know from their epigrams that there was one poem on which Posidippus and Asclepiades *did* cross swords with Callimachus, not an epic but epic in style and dimensions: the subject of the following chapter, Antimachus's celebrated elegy the *Lyde*.

228. E.g. Gow and Page on Asclepiades IV, VI and XIII.
229. HE II. 115; *SH* 215-20.

Chapter XI

Fat Ladies

1

Asclepiades himself may have played a part in fostering the sudden notoriety of the *Lyde* in Ptolemaic Alexandria. The following epigram (*AP* ix. 63) has the appearance of being an introductory epigraph for a copy of the poem:

Λύδη καὶ γένος εἰμὶ καὶ οὔνομα· τῶν δ' ἀπὸ Κόδρου
  σεμνοτέρη πασῶν εἰμι δι' Ἀντίμαχον.
τίς γὰρ ἔμ' οὐκ ἤεισε; τίς οὐκ ἀνελέξατο Λύδην,
  τὸ ξυνὸν Μουσῶν γράμμα καὶ Ἀντιμάχου;

Lyde is my name and I am of Lydian stock; Antimachus has made me more exalted than any woman descended from Codros [i.e. Athenian]. Who has not sung of my fame? Who has not read of Lyde, the joint work of the Muses and Antimachus?

Two other poets associated with Asclepiades and like him active in Alexandria[1] help to fill out the picture. Posidippus wrote one epigram linking Antimachus and Mimnermus as love poets and another (according to the Apollonius scholia) on a theme drawn from the *Lyde*.[2] An unfortunately corrupt epigram by Hedylus appears to link the *Lyde* with Asclepiades.[3] Another contemporary poet, Hermesianax, mentions the *Lyde* prominently in his *Leontion*.[4] Nicander too is said to have been a keen imitator of Antimachus, though this may refer to his *Thebaid*.[5] Finally, there is a new Berlin papyrus of the second century B.C. that opens as follows:[6]

Λ]υδην εὔυμνον ἀείσας
ἀθ]ανάταισιν ἴσην.

1. On the links between Asclepiades, Posidippus and Hedylus, my *Greek Anth.* 369-76.
2. *AP* xii. 168; *SH* 703.
3. VI Gow-Page (Athenaeus 473AB) line 5, as emended in Appendix A.
4. F 7. 41f.
5. ζηλωτὴς Ἀντιμάχου, διόπερ πολλαῖς λέξεσιν αὐτοῦ κέχρηται· διὸ καὶ ἐν ἐνίοις δωρίζει, Σ Ther. 2.5.
6. P. Berol. 21340, published with useful notes by W. Brashear, *Proc. of the 20th Intern. Congress of Papyrologists*, ed. A. Bülow-Jacobsen (Copenhagen 1994), 286-88.

The person the poet is singing of is said to be equal to the immortals. Obviously then a mortal woman, much celebrated in song. The first word should be this person's name, and (as Parsons saw at once) Lyde fits to perfection, a woman sung of in a poem which was itself much praised. As we have seen (Ch. III. 4), perhaps from the *Writing Tablets* (Δέλτοι) of Antimachus himself,[7] a reference to his own more famous poem. But obviously a later poet is another possibility.

Callimachus resisted the vogue. In a lost prose work, perhaps the *Against Praxiphanes*, he criticized Plato as a poor judge of literature for liking Antimachus (F 589). He also wrote an epigram that mocked not only the *Lyde* but Asclepiades's epigram as well (F 398):

Λύδη καὶ παχὺ γράμμα καὶ οὐ τορόν.

The rhythm and articulation are identical to Asclepiades's first line, and γράμμα picks up the γράμμα in his last line. There can be little doubt that Callimachus was responding to Asclepiades's epigram. It is curious that so little attention has been paid to the one opportunity we have to study Callimachus's response to a surviving piece of literary criticism by an identifiable contemporary poet—a poet (moreover) who appears on the Florentine list of Telchines.

Is it just that they strongly disagreed in their estimate of a poem written more than a century before—or was the *Lyde* a cloak for some more personal issue? The fact that, on the evidence of their epigrams, the two poets seem to share common goals and techniques is not the objection it has sometimes been assumed to the hypothesis of rivalry. It is often precisely where differences seem smallest that disagreement is fiercest.

It is time to take a closer look at Asclepiades's epigram. The key phrase is τῶν δ' ἀπὸ Κόδρου / σεμνοτέρη πασῶν. There are two details here that have not been sufficiently explained by the commentators: the female descendants of Codros,[8] and the meaning of σεμνοτέρη. "Better born than Codros" (εὐγενέστερος Κόδρου) was a proverbial phrase,[9] and the point might just be that, though a simple barbarian maid, Lyde has through Antimachus become more famous than the noblest of the noble. But σεμνός does not really mean either "noble" or "famous." It is primarily "an attribute of deities, their sanctuaries and their rituals."[10] Applied to

---

7. So Parsons ap. Brashear; for the only fragment, B. Wyss, *Antimachi Colophonii Reliquiae* (Berlin 1936), F 74 with pp. xxiv-v.

8. The specificity of the reference excludes earlier Attic heroines such as the daughters of Erectheus and Cecrops, the pauper Hecale (Emily Kearns, *The Heroes of Attica* [London 1989], 139-207) and Aethra (Call. F 371, with Hollis, *ZPE* 93 [1992], 1-2).

9. Lucian *Dial. Mort.* 19. 4; *Timon* 23; Ach. Tat. 6. 12. 4; Them. *Or.* 21. 250B; Liban. *Epp.* 298. 3; Zenob. *Cent.* 4. 3 (= *Paroem. graeci* i. 84); Suda s.v. εὐγενέστερος Κόδρου; Schol. Plato *Symp.* 208d.

10. Dover on Ar. *Frogs* 178; Richardson on *H. Dem.* 478; Barrett on Eur. *Hipp.* 99.

humans it means "dignified," "worthy of respect," "important," often (especially in comedy) ironically, "pompous," "self-important."[11] In practice people of consequence will usually be both well known and well born, but σεμνός always emphasizes power and respect rather than fame or blueness of blood. I cite three examples applied to women: Aristophanes, *Eccles.* 617, where αἱ σεμναί are "grand ladies"; Xenophon, *Mem.* i.2.24, where because of his good looks Alcibiades is pursued by "many women of good family" (ὑπὸ πολλῶν καὶ σεμνῶν γυναικῶν);[12] and Isocrates, 3. 42, of a good marriage (σεμνοτέρα contrasted with ταπεινοτέρα).[13]

Yet Asclepiades's basic point must be the immortality that only poetry can confer. So far as we know, the *Lyde* had very little to say about Lyde herself; it was a collection of unhappy mythical love stories which the poet composed to console himself for the death of his own beloved.[14] Her name was thus made famous by the poem named after her. Superficially there is a neat contrast between barbarian maid and Athenian king, but the sort of fame poetry confers has nothing to do with royal descent. We might simply conclude that Asclepiades expressed himself rather loosely, but that is not the way of Alexandrian epigrammatists, who choose every word with care.

Rather we should ask which women descended from Codros were in fact made famous by poetry. On Codros's death his eldest sons Medon and Neleus quarrelled, and after consulting Delphi Neleus set sail to colonize Ionia.[15] According to a variety of local traditions there were almost twenty Codrids (some described as bastards), who between them founded (or refounded after driving out the Carians) most of the Greek cities of Ionia.[16] None of these sons or grandsons have developed stories; hardly a detail that goes beyond the founding of their respective cities.[17] It is not therefore surprising that we hear next to nothing of female Codrids. Indeed there are

11. *LSJ* s.v. II; Bauer-Arndt-Gingrich, *New Test. Lex.*[5] s.v. 1a; Dover on Ar. *Cl.* 48.

12. Cf. Xen. *Hell.* v.4.4, τὰς σεμνοτάτας καὶ καλλίστας in Thebes; Plato *Rep.* 475B.

13. Cf. Ar. *Poet.* 1448b25, σεμνότεροι opposed to εὐτελέστεροι, again = grand folk.

14. Plut. *Consol. Apoll.* 9 = 106BC.

15. A common pattern in colonization stories: C. Dougherty, *The Poetics of Colonization* (Oxford 1993), 17; J. Fontenrose, *The Delphic Oracle* (Berkeley 1978), 121, 380.

16. To the 14 names in Strabo (14.1.3) and Pausanias (vii. 3) listed by M. B. Sakellariou, *La Migration grecque en Ionie* (Athens 1958), 22-26, add Lampsos for Klazomenai (Ephorus, *FGrH* 70 F 25) and twin Kodrids called Phobos and Blepsos in Charon, *FGrH* 262 F 7. See Sakellariou's index for individual names and places, and Jacoby, *FGrH* IIIb (Suppl.) I. 32-34 and II. 35-39; the earliest detailed account must have been Panyasis's 7000 line epic περὶ Κόδρον καὶ Νηλέα καὶ τὰς Ἰωνικὰς ἀποικίας (Suda s.v.). Genuine Athenian influence is attested by Attic pottery types at sites like Miletus (V. R. Desborough, *The Greek Dark Ages* [1972], 179f.).

17. For example, the story about Neleus Callimachus alludes to in *H.Art.* 225-27, more fully in the scholia on *H. Zeus* 77, perhaps from the version in *Aetia* III (F 80); or the story of Knopos and Erythrai in Polyaenus 8. 43, discussed by W. Burkert, *Structure and History in Greek Mythology and Ritual* (Berkeley 1979), 59-62.

only two identifiable female descendants of Codros—both of them featured in elegies of Callimachus.

First, there is Leimonis, daughter of Hippomenes the last Codrid ruler of Athens. Hippomenes discovered that his daughter had been seduced and killed her by locking her up in a room with a ravenous horse.[18] Second, Cydippe of Naxos, unknown to poetry before Callimachus dug her out of an obscure local history. Of the two, Leimonis was known only for her cruel fate, and it was her father who achieved the fame of a proverb: "more impious than Hippomenes."[19] Cydippe was the heroine of one of Callimachus's most famous poems, styled Κοδρεΐδης at F 75. 32, daughter of Promethos at F 67. 7 (Promethos founded Colophon and then fled to Naxos after killing his brother).[20] We saw in Ch. IX. 3 that there are solid grounds for dating the *Cydippe* earlier than *Aetia* I-II, and so to the lifetime of Asclepiades. There can be little doubt that informed contemporaries would have identified Asclepiades's Codrid female as Cydippe.

The *Cydippe* was an elegy like the *Lyde*, and elegy (as we shall see) is the theme of the *Aetia* prologue. That explains Codros. As for σεμνοτέρη, given the literary context there can be little doubt that Asclepiades chose it for its stylistic connotations, found as early as Aristophanes and standard by Aristotle: "elevated," "dignified."[21] It was precisely the elevation, the dignity of Antimachus's style that critics singled out, some in admiration, others (notably Callimachus) in disparagement. Posidippus, another name on the Florentine list, describes him as sober (σώφρων).[22] The *Cydippe*, with its garrulous narrator constantly interrupting himself, was anything but dignified or sober. It may have been in response to the reproach of being undignified that he wrote in prologue 6 of "steering his song into a small compass *like a child*" (παῖς ἅτε).[23]

In calling Lyde more exalted than the granddaughters of Codros, Asclepiades ascribes to the heroines the qualities of the elegies named after them—as Callimachus was to do in the *Aetia* prologue. Cydippe may have been better born than Lyde, but *Lyde* had the dignity *Cydippe* lacked. So Asclepiades's epigram does more than merely praise Antimachus. Im-

---

18. F 94-95, with Pfeiffer's commentary.

19. ἀσεβέστερος Ἱππομένους, Diogen. iii. 1, with Schneidewin's note.

20. Paus. vii. 3. 3; there was a tribe named after Promethos in late 4th c. Colophon: L. Robert, *Rev. de Phil.* 62 (1936), 162-64 = *Op. Min. Sel.* II. 1241-43. Killing a brother is less a biographical detail than a device to motivate departure and link traditions.

21. Dover on *Frogs* 1004; Aristot. *Rhet.* 1404b10; 1408b35; *Poet.* 1449a21; for the rhetoricians, R. Volkmann, *Die Rhetorik der Griechen und Römer*[2] (1885), 557. The long section on σεμνότης in Hermogenes (§ 6, pp. 242-54 Rabe) describes how to achieve it.

22. *AP* xii. 168. 1-2.

23. For other possible explanations, Ch. VII. 1; B. Snell, *Discovery of the Mind* (1953), 271 ("joy in the naive and primitive"); J. C. Bramble, *Persius and the Programmatic Satire* (1974), 185 ("simplicity of style").

plicitly it extols the *Lyde* over Callimachus's *Cydippe*. Naturally Callimachus could not let the challenge pass unanswered. His initial response was an epigram, of which we have only F 398.[24]

There is an obvious link here with the *Aetia* prologue. For brief as it is, we have in Callimachus's response one of the key stylistic terms of the prologue, παχύ (F 1. 23). Furthermore, comparison with Asclepiades explains both the origin and the application of the term. The stylistic elevation that Asclepiades had approvingly called σεμνόν Callimachus dismisses as παχύ. Yet it was not (as modern scholars have assumed) epic they disagreed about, but the style of elegy. Nor was it (as common sense should have suggested) for refusing to write an epic that Callimachus was criticized, but for actually writing one particular elegy. As we shall see, traditionalists disapproved of the light touch and intrusive narrator of the *Cydippe*. Asclepiades reasserted the claims of the *Lyde*, with its traditional style and invisible epic narrator. Callimachus returned to the fray with a more ambitious elegy—*Aetia* I-II—which began with a polemical prologue.

2

It is time to turn to the *Aetia* prologue, unfortunately to its most controversial section (9-12).[25] The παχύ of F 398 reappears in the prologue as one half of a fat vs thin antithesis (θύος ὅττι πάχιστον). It is tempting to identify the "big lady" of line 12 as the *Lyde*, but there are problems:

[......]..ρεην ὀλιγόστιχος· ἀλλὰ καθέλκει
....πολὺ τὴν μακρὴν ὄμπνια Θεσμοφόρο[ς]·
τοῖν δὲ] δυοῖν Μίμνερμος ὅτι γλυκύς, αἱ κατὰ λεπτόν
......] ἡ μεγάλη δ' οὐκ ἐδίδαξε γυνή.

Thesmophoros (1. 10) is Demeter, and Philitas wrote a poem of that name; l. 11 seems to refer to two poems by Mimnermus. Small though they are, the gaps have proved surprisingly hard to fill. According to the well-informed Florentine scholiast, who at any rate had the complete text in front of him, Callimachus is praising the short poems of Mimnermus and Philitas over their long poems.

Since this is the first stage in Callimachus's reply to the Telchines, it must be related to their criticism that he has not written ἓν ἄεισμα διηνεκές. As we have seen, it is one of the firmest axioms of modern Callimachean scholarship that he is "rejecting epic." But neither Mimnermus

24. For the possibility that we do in fact have a bit more, see below, § 3 and 6.
25. For modern discussions, Lehnus 1989, 58-59; A. Allen, *The Fragments of Mimnermus* (Stuttgart 1993), 146-56.

nor Philitas can have had any relevance to a debate about *epic*.[26] Both were elegists. Indeed, according to Hermesianax, Mimnermus invented elegy. However we identify the mysterious "tall lady" (line 10) and "big lady" (line 12), there is no reason to doubt that both were elegies no less than the shorter poems Callimachus preferred. It follows that the debate between Callimachus and his critics concerned elegy, not epic.

If so, where is Antimachus? In order to obtain a direct reference to the *Lyde* we would have to assume that the short poems of Mimnermus and Philitas are being compared with the long poems of other poets. Attempts to extract such a sense have indeed often been made. For example, Matthews proposed to supplement the beginning of line 10 with θεῦν, construing this "long goddess" as a reference to Antimachus's *Artemis*.[27] He then supplemented the beginning of line 9 [Κῶος δὴ γ]ὰρ ἔην, and interpreted as follows: "Yes, the Coan did indeed write short poems, but his *Demeter* outweighs the big lady [Antimachus's *Artemis*]."

In itself this is not impossible, though the picture of two goddesses being weighed against each other is a trifle incongruous. More important, it is only the *Lyde* that was controversial; there is no reason to believe that the obscure (perhaps even non-existent) *Artemis*[28] aroused the same passions. Moreover if we introduce a second poet into this couplet, we have to do the same with 11-12.[29] Here we may begin with M. Puelma's influential suggestion[30] that the gap in line 12 should be supplemented Κῶϊαι, and the couplet translated as follows: "the slender Coan maidens [= the poetry of Philitas] taught that Mimnermus is sweet, not the big lady [= Antimachus's *Lyde*]." This is alleged to mean that Philitas's elegant poetry displays the sweetness of Mimnermus while Antimachus's *Lyde* does not. But this is hardly what the Greek says. Nor is it likely that an adverbial κατὰ λεπτόν could be applied to even metaphorical maidens,[31] in any case an improbable way of referring to any poem of Philitas.[32] Puelma saw the issue as which of the two, Antimachus or Philitas, could be given the title Mimnermus *redivivus*. But given his plural supplement, this would be a strained interpetation of τοῖν δὲ δυοῖν—and an improbable issue.

---

26. "Natürlich gilt sein Grundsatz für Epos und Elegie gleichermaßen," Herter 1973, 195, but few have paid any attention to his warning.

27. V. J. Matthews, *Mnemosyne* 32 (1979), 128-37.

28. Only attested by Stephanus Byz. p. 379. 11 Meineke = F 75 Wyss: see P. Carrara, *Prometheus* 9 (1983), 213-16. There seems to have been no general criticism of Antimachus's other works: § 7 below.

29. Though see Hollis, *CQ* 28 (1978), 406, for a way round this (which still involves convicting the Florentine scholiast of error).

30. *Philologus* 101 (1957), 96f.; cf. G. Lohse, *Antike und Abendland* 19 (1973) 22 ("mit einiger Sicherheit"); V. J. Matthews, *Mnem.* 32 (1980), 134f.

31. As pointed out by Wimmel, *Hermes* 86 (1958), 347 n. 4 (with other objections).

32. His best known works were a *Demeter*, a *Bittis* (see below) and a *Hermes*—none readily identifiable as "Coan maidens."

A. Barigazzi, accepting the traditional ῥήσιες for the missing word in line 12, interpreted somewhat differently: "the short elegies of the pair [the two books of Mimnermus] teach that Mimnermus is sweet, but the big lady does not [show that Antimachus is sweet]."[33] Once again, an improbable antithesis and hopelessly contorted Greek. If Mimnermus's poems are better, why not just leave it at that? If they are shorter, the exact opposite of Barigazzi's interpretation would at least make sense: one of Mimnermus's poems outclassing all of Antimachus's. But it makes no sense at all to prefer two poems by Mimnermus to one by Antimachus.

Not only do all such interpretations offer barely intelligible Greek and utterly incredible sense. We would also have to accept that the Florentine scholiast completely misunderstood the text in front of him. It is true that he does not tell us all we should like to know,[34] but it is another matter to claim that what he does tell us is downright wrong. So long as the Florentine scholia were thought to be a late and much reduced abridgment of a detailed commentary, it was not unreasonable to suppose that the abridgment might be careless and the details confused. But if (as argued in Ch. IV. 4) we identify them with the Diegeseis and recognize their sole purpose to be summarizing the text, so gross an error becomes less likely.

Furthermore, as Vitelli and Norsa pointed out long ago, anyone preferring a short poem by A to a long poem by B would be more likely to explain his preference in terms of the quality of the writer than the length of the poem. If Callimachus had wanted to say that Philitas and Mimnermus were better than Antimachus, why introduce the irrelevant complication of length?

On the most natural interpretation, lines 9-12 appear to compare long and short poems, and the Florentine scholiast confirms that Callimachus did indeed compare the long and short poems of Mimnermus and Philitas. Modern attempts to contradict this interpretation, though now best forgotten, were at any rate inspired by a feeling of unease at two features of the *Aetia* prologue that need to be addressed. First, a feeling that Antimachus *ought* to be mentioned; and second, a feeling that Mimnermus and Philitas ought *not* to be criticized at all. Fortunately, both points admit of different and more satisfactory explanations.

3

In line 9 almost all recent critics have accepted Pfeiffer's [ἦ μὲν δὴ] γὰρ ἔην [ὀλ]ιγόστιχος, taking ἔην as first person and pretending that it is pres-

---

33. *Hermes* 84 (1956), 167-68; cf. Matthews, *Mnemosyne* 1980, 134.
34. Matthews, *Mnem.* 1980, 137; cf. Hollis, *CQ* 1978, 405.

ent rather than imperfect:[35] "Indeed I do write short poems." This statement is then claimed as key evidence for Callimachus's literary views.[36] To
quote at random a few recent studies, G. Lohse, H. Reinsch-Werner, and
R. Pretagostini[37] all quote these words as a specific and clear affirmation
that Callimachus wrote only short poems. Yet although both verb and
predicate are clearly legible, the words that refer them to the poet are
restored—and surely wrongly restored.

This is supposed to be his reply to the criticism that he "rolls forth a
short tale." But how feeble to reply: "Yes, I do." Normally each phrase in
the prologue adds something new—the Persian chain, the fat victim, the
main road, the braying of the ass. And then what happens in the rest of the
couplet? The "bountiful Thesmophoros outweighs by far the long *." The
obvious guess is that the missing monosyllable at the beginning of 10 con-
ceals another title by Philitas. But whatever the second title, what is the
connection of thought in: "I write short poems. *But* Philitas's *Demeter* outweighs by far his tall lady?" What is the force of the adversative? However
well known Philitas's poems, it is intolerably abrupt to introduce them like
this. As Herter concluded in his last survey, recanting his earlier opinion,
"Philitas must have been named here."[38]

The only satisfactory supplement[39] is Wimmel's [Κώϊος οὐκ] ἄρ᾽ ἔην,
taking ἔην as third person and accepting the tense as imperfect: "the man
from Cos did not write short poems. No, but his *Demeter* far outweighs his
tall lady." Now there is a perfectly logical and satisfactory sequence of
thought. The first topic Callimachus turns to in his reply is the authorities
in the field. Since his point is that their short poems are better than their
long ones, we naturally infer that the Telchines had praised Philitas's long
ones, or at any rate praised his work indiscriminately. Callimachus concedes that Philitas was not a concise writer (οὐκ ἄρ᾽ ἔην ὀλιγόστιχος),[40]
but adds that his *Demeter* was better than some longer poem.

He then turns to Mimnermus: of his two works (τοῖν δὲ] δυοῖν), it is the
"minor poems" (κατὰ λεπτόν), not the "big lady" that show him at his best
("teach that he is sweet"). That there were "two books" of Mimnermus is

35. A variation on this is Torraca's ναὶ ναὶ δὴ] γάρ (1969, 31-32).

36. Notably by Pfeiffer himself (1968, 137).

37. Lohse, *Antike und Abendland* 19 (1973), 23; Reinsch-Werner 1976, 8; Pretagostini
1984, 123-24.

38. "ausdrücklich genannt gewesen sein muß," Herter 1973, 195 with 1937, 102, with
bibliography and analysis.

39. Perhaps one letter too long, but see n. 38 below. I cannot accept C. W. Müller's
Κώϊος—ἦ γὰ]ρ ἔην ("Der Koer—wahrlich er war doch geringzeilig," 1987, 90) any more
than the rest of his analysis (89-97).

40. ἄρα plus imperfect of sudden realization (Denniston, *Greek Particles* 36): "he was
not after all..."

attested by the Horatian commentator Porphyrio,[41] and the extant quotations are cited from only two poems, the *Nanno* and the *Smyrneïs*. Both have been claimed by different scholars as Callimachus's "big lady."

The *Smyrneïs* dealt with a battle between Smyrna and King Gyges of Lydia in the 660s. According to Plutarch,[42] it contained an elaborate proem invoking the Muses, and the one fragment specifically assigned to the poem runs as follows:[43]

ὡς οἱ πὰρ βασιλῆος ἐπεί ῥ' ἐνδέξατο μῦθον,
ἤϊξαν κοίλῃς ἀσπίσι φραξάμενοι.

Evidently the king has just delivered a rousing speech to his troops as they prepare for battle. The language is epic-sounding and formulaic (the last three words of line 2 reappear as Tyrtaeus F 19 .7 West). The very title is reminiscent of epic.[44]

The *Nanno* is more of a puzzle. Though supposedly inspired by a hetaira of that name, there is no sign of her in the seven fragments, two of which mention boys, the rest a variety of topics. It is suggestive to compare the sections Hermesianax devotes to Mimnermus and Antimachus, each of six lines. While linking Antimachus with Lyde alone, he devotes only half a line to Nanno, and the rest to his feuds and revels with three men. The implication is that the *Nanno* consisted of a series of separate poems. The very name suggests the word νᾶνος, "dwarf,"[45] whereas, if we accept A. Colonna's attractive suggestion that the *Smyrneïs* included the mythical foundation of the city by the Amazon Smyrna,[46] what better candidate for a "big lady" than an Amazon?

An epigram of Martial may lend some support to this interpretation. I have published too many books, he complains; Persius scores more with his one volume than "slender Marsus in his entire Amazon" (*quam levis in tota Marsus Amazonide*).[47] Another of Martial's epigrams is clearly modelled on the *Aetia* prologue (depreciation of grand themes, conversation with a Muse, a slender pipe),[48] and here we have a more precise allusion

---

41. *duos libros luculent<is vers>ibus scripsit*, on Horace, *Epp.* 2. 2. 101; cf. West 1974, 72-6; C. W. Müller, "Die antike Buchausgabe des Mimnermos," *Rhein. Mus.* 131 (1988), 197-211; A. Allen, *The Fragments of Mimnermus* (1993), 20-26; C. Dougherty, *JHS* 114 (1994), 38.

42. 9. 29. 4; cf. 4. 21. 5; West, F 13.

43. F 13a West = 21 Gentili-Prato (ignoring one or two dots and brackets).

44. For a list of such titles, see Ch. X. 4, n. 115.

45. As pointed out by E. L. Bowie, *JHS* 106 (1986), 28.

46. *Athenaeum* 30 (1952), 194; cf. S. Mazzarino, *Il pensiero storico classico* I (Bari 1966), 37-42; G. Serrao, *Storia e civiltà dei Greci* 9 (Milan 1977), 222 n. 93; Pretagostini 1984, 133-34; K. Töchterle, *Rhein. Mus.* 123 (1980), 225-34; A.W.H. Adkins, *Poetic Craft in the Early Greek Elegists* (Chicago 1985), 93-94.

47. iv. 29. 7-8.

48. E.g. viii. 3, with P. E. Knox, *AJP* 115 (1994), 141.

than has so far been appreciated. The reference is to Domitius Marsus, best known for his epigrams and elegies (whence *levis*/λεπτός) and elsewhere mentioned several times with approval by Martial as one of his predecessors.[49] Editors have rightly been surprised that Martial should pick Marsus "as a typical long-winded epicist."[50] The answer is that, like Callimachus, he picked an elegiac predecessor who for all his virtues was less than concise.[51] There was no epic *Amazonis*; Martial is simply describing Marsus's elegies on the "dusky Melaenis"[52] in Callimachean terms as a big lady—like the *Smyrneïs* an Amazon.

It is important to bear in mind that Antimachus was editor and critic as well as poet. There can be little doubt that it was he who established Colophon rather than the better attested Smyrna as Mimnermus's birthplace (as he certainly did for Homer).[53] The very idea of a long poem inspired by a woman is an anachronism in the seventh century. It is tempting to suppose that it was Antimachus himself who in effect created the *Nanno* by arranging Mimnermus's shorter elegies so as to give prominence to those featuring Nanno, to provide a precedent for his own elegiac miscellany, the *Lyde*.[54] This Antimachean connection explains Callimachus's qualified attitude to Mimnermus.

But there may have been a genuine distinction between *Nanno* and *Smyrneïs* nonetheless. In an important recent paper E. L. Bowie argued that archaic elegy fell into two quite distinct categories: short pieces written for the symposium, and longer narrative elegies written for public festivals. Whatever its original audience, Mimnermus's *Smyrneïs* seems a clear example of a narrative elegy. And Tyrtaeus wrote an elegy on the Spartan conquest of Messenia, whether or not this is to be identified with the so-called *Eunomia*.[55] In 1974 West had argued that the subject matter of these poems was "taken from recent history, and they cannot quite be regarded as containing narrative for its own sake as an epic does."

49. H. Bardon, *La littérature latine inconnue* ii (Paris 1956), 53-57; J. P. Sullivan, *Martial: the unexpected classic* (Cambridge 1991), 98-99; E. Courtney, *Fragmentary Latin Poets* (Oxford 1993), 300-05.

50. Shackleton Bailey's note in his new Loeb edition (1993).

51. *Marsi doctique Pedonis / saepe duplex unum pagina tractat opus*, ii. 77. 5-6.

52. Martial vii. 29. 8; pace Courtney 1993, 300, surely elegies rather than epigrams.

53. On the stronger claims of Smyrna, see Jacoby, *Hermes* 53 (1918), 268f.= *Kl. phil. Schriften* i (1961), 311f.; West. *Studies* 73. On Homer, see Wyss's edition, pp. xxx, 62.

54. "Nanno arrives at Alexandria...hand in hand with Lyde....Mimnermus arrives a Colophonian, bearing (alone of the early elegists) a book named after a woman," West, *Studies* 75-76.

55. "Early Greek Elegy, Symposium, and Public Festival," *JHS* 106 (1986), 27-35; C. Dougherty, *JHS* 114 (1994), 35-46. According to A. Ford (*CP* 83 [1988], 303), public performance of elegy would have been called ῥαψῳδία; but *AP* ix. 369 which he cites for "rhapsody in elegiacs" clearly implies nothing of the sort.

None of Bowie's counter-examples from more remote history were above suspicion or uncertainty: the *Archaeologia* of Samos attributed to Semonides of Amorgos; the *Ionica* (in 7000 pentameters) ascribed to Panyassis; the Ktisis of Colophon (in 2000 lines) attributed to Xenophanes. Jacoby considered the last two at least forgeries of the unscrupulous Lobon.[56] But the situation has now been transformed by Parsons's publication of P. Oxy. 3965. Whether or not archaic poets wrote elegiac ktiseis, we now know that Simonides wrote a series of elegies on the great victories of the Persian wars,[57] continuing a tradition of narrative elegy on military themes not otherwise documented since the age of Mimnermus and Tyrtaeus. We now have to take more seriously the texts that refer to an elegy on Marathon by Aeschylus (§ 5). West was right about the concentration on themes from recent history, but the best preserved of the new elegies, on Plataea, contains long stretches of straightforward narrative.

It begins (as we know Mimnermus's *Smyrneïs* did) with a long proem, on the death of Achilles, and since this has no direct connection with Plataea, it might be held to imply performance at one of Achilles's cult centres. Given the emphasis in what survives of the narrative on the land, king and heroes of Sparta (F 11. 25, 29, 31, 33-4), a shrine in Sparta itself is the obvious guess.[58] Then follows a brief invocation of the "many-named" Muse,[59] before narrative beginning *in medias res* (F 11. 29-34):

Leaving the Eurotas and the city of Sparta behind them, they set out together with the horse-taming sons of Tyndarus... Excellent Pausanias, son of the god-like Cleombrotus led them...

οἳ μὲν ἄρ᾽ Εὐ]ρώταν κα[ὶ Σπάρτη]ς ἄστυ λιπόντ[ες
  ὥρμησαν] Ζηνὸς παισὶ σὺν ἱπποδάμοις...
Τυνδαρίδα]ις ἥρωσι.../[...υἱὸς θείοιο Κλεο]μβ[ρ]ότου ἔξ[α]γ᾽ ἄριστος /...
Παυσανίης...

There are broken traces of another 80 lines or so, and though little connected sense can be made out, where it can we still seem to have narrative (e.g. F 13. 11, οἳ] δ᾽ ἐπεὶ ἐς πεδίον). The best evidence for the general character of this narrative comes from Plutarch's attack on Herodotus. After citing six lines praising the Corinthian contribution to the victory (an overlap with the new papyrus identifies them as part of this poem), he adds: "these lines are not by someone writing for a chorus in Corinth or an ode in praise of the city, but someone simply describing the events in an

---

56. West *Studies* 14; Jacoby, *FGrH* IIIb Komm. pp. 440, 450, 456; Bowie 1986, 31-32; Rösler in *Sympotica* (1990), 235.

57. Parsons, *P. Oxy.* LIX (1992), 4-50; West, *IEG* ii² F 1-18; ZPE 98 (1993), 1-14.

58. An annual festival in Achilles's honour was held at Brasiai in Laconia (Paus. 3. 24. 4); ib 20. 8 for another shrine near Sparta; ib. 6. 23. 3 for one at Elis; 2. 1. 8 at Corinth.

59. Π[ολυώνυμ]ε Μοῦσα (F 11. 21); cf. πολυω[νυμ- at F adesp. eleg. 61. 3.

elegy."[60] The implication is that Simonides's elegy was pure narrative, or at any rate very different from the style of epinicion.[61]

As Parsons has observed, the opening hymn to Achilles implies a comparison of the Persian and Trojan wars, setting the poet's theme on a heroic plane. The language is elevated: Corinth is ἐπικλέα ἔργα Κορίνθου (F 11. 35) or Ἐφύρη, and the Corinthians οἵ·τε πόλιν Γλαύκοιο Κορίνθιον ἄστυ νέμοντες (F 15); the Peloponnese is the island Τανταλίδεω Πέλοπος (F 11. 36). F 11. 1-3 has what may be an epic simile, and the proem closes with that standard sign-off formula of the epic proem, αὐτὰρ ἐγώ (F 11. 20). On the other hand, none of these elegies seems to have been on the epic scale—presumably no more than a few hundred lines in length. If the fragments published as P. Oxy. 2327 and 3965 come from single rolls, each of those rolls contained a plurality of both sympotic and narrative elegies.

Exiguous as they are, the fragments of Mimnermus and Tyrtaeus suggest that narrative elegy did not confine itself to the omniscient invisible narrator; both poets included themselves in their narrative. For example, Tyrtaeus writes in the first person, of how "we" arrived in the Peloponnese (εὐρεῖαν Πέλοπος νῆσον ἀφικόμεθα, F 2. 15) and took Messenia (Μεσσήνην εἵλομεν εὐρύχορον) (F 5. 2). This "we" does not imply the poet in person; rather it is projected into the remote past, establishing continuity between past and present for a Spartan audience.[62] This may be the explanation of Mimnermus F 9. 2 as well: "we came to lovely Asia in our ships...and took Aeolian Smyrna" (ἱμερτὴν Ἀσίην νηυσὶν ἀφικόμεθα...Σμύρνην εἵλομεν Αἰολίδα); though a speech by a character in the narrative (cf. F 13a, quoted above) is another possibility. More significant, in F 14 Mimnermus gives a source reference, a story he claims to have "heard of from my elders."[63] It seems fairly clear that both poems were written from a patriotic point of view, a perspective conspicuous by its absence from Homeric epic.[64] Unfortunately the new Simonides fragments do not reveal anything comparable. There is one apparent first person, [?προ]λέγω, in F 14. 3, which West with some plausibility assigns to a speech.[65] Nonetheless, since (in Edith Hall's phrase) "the story of the invention of the barbarian is the story of the Greeks' conflict with the Persians,"[66] we can hardly doubt that Simonides's elegy was any less partisan than his predecessors'.

60. ἁπλῶς [ἄλλως MSS] δὲ τὰς πράξεις ἐκείνας ἐν ἐλεγείᾳ γράφων (*Mor.* 872E).

61. He did in fact write an epinicion on at any rate Artemisium (*PMG* 533) as well as many other poems on Persian themes (Bowra, *Greek Lyric Poetry*[2] [Oxford 1961], 342f.).

62. W. Rösler, *Sympotica* (1990), 234-35.

63. F 9 is quoted from the *Nanno* (? wrongly: Bowie 1986, 29-30); F 14 is unassigned.

64. Edith Hall, *Inventing the Barbarian* (Oxford 1989), 14-15.

65. *ZPE* 98 (1993), 8, with a bolder restoration than in his edition.

66. Hall 1989, 56 and passim.

This gives a new dimension to the debate between Callimachus and his critics. According to Plutarch (*Mor.* 106B), Antimachus wrote his poem to console himself for Lyde's death. There was in fact a continuing tradition of consolatory elegy, from Archilochus to Simonides and Archelaus, a sub-division (so to speak) of sympotic elegy.[67] But the main subject matter of the *Lyde* was more suited to narrative elegy than sympotic elegy: a series of mythological tales, kicking off with a comprehensive treatment of the Argonauts.[68] There was no doubt a frame in which the poet told the story of his love for Lyde and her untimely fate. We may even have a line from this personal frame, if Pfeiffer was right to ascribe to Antimachus a line from the Lycophron scholia previously ascribed to Callimachus: "I sat down on the gold-bearing banks of the Pactolus."[69] For according to Hermesianax, it was to the Pactolus (a river in Lydia) that Antimachus went when struck with love for Lyde (F 7. 42). There may also have been a personal conclusion to the poem, and occasional apostrophes during its course, as there are to Hermesianax's mistress Leontion in his poem named after her (Ch. XIII. 3). Yet it is hard to see how there could have been a personal perspective behind the narrative of the many individual stories, nor do the (admittedly scanty) fragments suggest that there was.

On the basis of the personal frame, Francis Cairns made the *Lyde* a key precursor of "subjective" Latin love elegy.[70] Since no suitably "subjective" passages were forthcoming from the *Lyde* itself, he blandly assumed that we could get an idea what they were like by turning to Callimachus's *Aetia.* He was right to see the *Aetia* as basically the same sort of poem as the *Lyde*: both are catalogues of mythical narrative set in a personal frame. But the difference lies in the relationship of frame to narrative. Callimachus did everything he could to bridge the gap, to push the person of the narrator from the frame into the narrative itself, while Antimachus was apparently content with the invisible narrator as well as the elevated language of epic (Ch. XII. 2). Whence the attack on epic in the *Aetia* prologue; not epic itself, but the style and manner of epic. Given its subject matter and structure, the *Lyde* looked more like the hated Cyclic epic in elegiacs than a new *Nanno*. This is why Callimachus approved of the *Nanno* but condemned the *Smyrneïs*.

The Florentine scholiast was right after all: lines 9-12 praise the shorter poems of Mimnermus and Philitas over their long poems. But that is not the whole story. Scholars who tried to squeeze the *Lyde* into these lines

---

67. Archilochus F 9-13 W; Simonides F 91 W = Page *FGE* 295; Archelaus F 1 W; Bowie 1986, 23; Pfeiffer, *CQ* 37 (1943), 145-46.

68. Wyss 1936, xix-xxiv; Ch. XII. 2.

69. Πακτωλοῦ χρυσέοισιν ἐπ᾽ ἀνδήροισι θάασσον, F 814 = Antim. F *191 W = *SH* 79; Krevans 1993, 153-4.

70. F. Cairns *Tibullus* (1979), 218-23.

were right in their instincts if misguided in their methods. For Callimachus is not simply assessing the poems of Mimnermus and Philitas on their own merits. He is considering them as authorities and models.

Why these authorities? Mimnermus was inescapable, cited as exemplary by Posidippus, Alexander Aetolus (F 5. 4) and Hermesianax (F 7. 35-8) as well as by Callimachus. Above all (of course) he was Antimachus's model. But as the texts cited at the beginning of this chapter so eloquently illustrate, by Callimachus's day the other classic elegist was Antimachus. Nothing could be more pointed and tendentious than *not* to cite the *Lyde* in such a context. For all his virtues, to cite Philitas instead was provocative. Any contemporary reading about the tall lady of one elegist (1. 10) and the big lady of another (1. 12) could not help but think of the fat lady (παχὺ γράμμα) of the third who is not named.

Much ingenuity has been devoted to identifying the second poem of Philitas evoked in F. 1. 10. Ever since the publication of the papyrus, a stream of different monosyllabic supplements has been proposed for the beginning of line 10—δρῦν, γραῦν, ναῦν, Κῶν, ῥοῦν, and now θεῦν—none of which, when qualified by μακρήν, can be made to yield a plausible reference to any identifiable poem of Philitas.[71] The quest for the magic monosyllable has distracted attention from the fact (which can hardly be coincidence) that in both cases the long poem Callimachus depreciates is designated by a feminine adjective plus article. I suggest that this is all the description he gave, a "tall lady" to balance the "big lady" of the next couplet. If so, the obvious guess is the elegy on his mistress Bittis mentioned by Hermesianax:[72]

οἶσθα δὲ καὶ τὸν ἀοιδόν, ὃν Εὐρυπύλου πολιῆται
　　Κῷοι χάλκειον στῆσαν ὑπὸ πλατάνῳ
Βιττίδα μολπάζοντα θοήν, περὶ πάντα Φιλίταν
　　ῥήματα καὶ πᾶσαν τρυόμενον λαλιήν.

And you know the poet whom the Coan citizens of Eurypylus set up in bronze beneath the plane tree, singing of his volatile Bittis, Philitas worn out with his research on every word and utterance.

Unfortunately, we do not have a single fragment from this poem, though Athenaeus does cite from Philitas the words θρήσασθαι πλατάνῳ γραίη ὕπο (F 14). This is no doubt the plane tree under which Hermesianax pictures the poet singing of his flighty mistress.[73] Not even the title is actually

---

71. His best-known works were a *Demeter*, a *Bittis* (see below) and a *Hermes*—none readily identifiable as "Coan maidens."

72. F 7. 75-78, as translated by Cairns, *Tibullus* 220; see App. C.

73. L. Alfonsi interprets Βιττίδα μολπάζοντα θοήν "cantando Bittide in brevi, in corti canti" (*Aegyptus* 22 [1943], 164). Not only would this assign an unparalleled and implausible meaning to the Greek; it goes against the obvious rhetoric of the context in prol. 9-10. If it is the *Bittis* Callimachus has in mind, it must be Philitas's *long* poem. According to Giangrande (*SMA* II [1981], 403-4), θοήν means "tall," which he surprisingly asserts to be "apposite."

documented, though *Bittis* is both the obvious assumption and implied by Ovid's comparison with the *Lyde* (*Tristia* i. 6. 1-2):

> nec tantum Clario Lyde dilecta poetae
> nec tantum Coo Bittis amata suo est.

Though meaning "tall" when applied.to a person, in a literary context μακρή would obviously suggest first "long" and then "boring,"[74] just as μέγας too (at least in Callimachus's lexicon) takes on much less favorable connotations when applied to a book. This parallel double entendre is surely deliberate. Any noun at the beginning of 10 would spoil the balance. Though a little on the short side,[75] the missing monosyllable might be no more than an emphatic δή. δή is in fact found often with πολύς from Homer on, in earlier poets normally following the adjective, though δή in first position is a positive affectation of Callimachus.[76]

In view of Philitas's obvious importance for the poets and scholars of Alexandria's golden age, it is frustrating that we know so little about him and his *Bittis*.[77] But we do know that he had a disciple, Hermesianax of (again) Colophon, a somewhat older contemporary of Callimachus.[78]

---

74. T. D. Papanghelis sees echoes of Callimachus's attack on the μεγάλη γυνή in the tall Quintia of Catullus 86 (*Mnemos.* 44 [1991], 372-86). But Catullus's point is that, though he admits Quintia to be fair, tall and well proportioned (*candida, longa, recta*), he cannot consider her beautiful because she lacks *venustas*. That is to say, the quality he finds lacking is quite separate from her size, which is counted among her virtues (as generally in antiquity; Fordyce ad loc.). Papanghelis claims that in l. 4 (*nulla in tam magnost corpore mica salis*) Quintia's size "seems to be more of a liability than an asset," but the implication is surely rather that the larger the body, the more some charm might have been expected. It is difficult to see how any literary polemic can be extracted from this.

. 75. The "letters before πολύ occupied *approximately* the same space as παῖς in line 6," Hollis in *CQ* 28 (1978), 402 n. 1, reporting a consultation with Parsons. But Parsons warned "how dangerous it is to be dogmatic," remarking that "scribes are not regular in their letter-sizes and spacing." It might be added that, although some form of πολύ is assured by the London scholia, the "vestiges before την are extremely slight, and though not inconsistent with, cannot be said to confirm, πο]λύ" (A. S. Hunt, *Ox. Pap.* XVII [1927], 52). It is possible that the line began πουλύ and something else stood before the την.

76. Denniston, *Greek Particles* ² 205 (227-28 for position). For initial δή in Callimachus, Pfeiffer's ind. verb. s. v., esp. F 75. 51; *Hy.* III. 202; IV. 307; in second position, cf. *Hy.* V. 58 (πουλύ...δή); for μέγα δή, IV. 60 and 189; V. 122; *Ep.* 43. 5. Another example of emphatic δή would be created by Pfeiffer's supplement for 9, rejected above; cf. too *SH* 254. 25, ἦ μὲν δὴ πο[λύ. Note too δὴ πολύ in Hedylus VI Gow-Page (unless corrupt: see *HE* II 294 and Appendix I) and initial emphatic δή in Alexander Aetolus, F· 13. 18. My first thought was πάρ, a poeticization of the everyday expression παρὰ πολύ "by far" (LSJ s.v. πολύς IV. 5). But (though slightly longer) the note of the London scholiast—ἤτοι πολὺ καθέλκει ἢ πολὺ μακρ(ήν)—is against this, and δή is much more Callimachean.

77. For what little is known, see now P. E. Knox, *PLILS* 7 (1993), 61-83.

78. See Fraser II. 883 n. 61 on Pausanias's discussion of Hermesianax's date (i. 9. 7), based on his failure to record the destruction of Colophon by Lysimachus—itself not securely datable. Fraser places the *Leontion* ca 280-70. His relationship to Philitas is attested by Schol. Nic. *Ther.* 3 = Powell F 12, discussed in Ch. VIII. 2.

Hermesianax wrote an elegy in three books, the *Leontion*, once again called after a mistress. Indeed, in the course of the 98 line fragment from Bk III preserved by Athenaeus (F 7), he discusses all three of his predecessors, mentioning Lyde and Bittis by name. Though largely ignored in modern discussions, the *Leontion* should and (thanks to Athenaeus) fortunately can be considered in the context of the debate about the *Lyde*.

If there was room for disagreement about the *Lyde*, there can be none about the *Leontion*. It is surely the silliest surviving product of its age.[79] The thesis of the long fragment from Bk III is that none of the great writers and thinkers managed to avoid the yoke of love.[80] A recent paper by Peter Bing rightly sets it in the context of the widespread Hellenistic interest in the lives of poets and philosophers, Callimachus's *Pinakes* and the vogue for epigrams on writers.[81] But there is little genuine biographical material, and little attempt to characterize either the partners or the romance in any of these monotonously ill-starred couples.

Significantly enough, the most successful section is that on Orpheus (F 7. 1-14), whose love for his wife was part of the traditional story. In most other cases Hermesianax had to invent. It was an amusing enough notion to claim that Homer wrote out of love for Penelope and to infer from the constant repetition of the words ἢ οἵη in the *Catalogue of Women* that Hesiod was in love with a girl called Eoea. But it was neither clever nor witty to write of Socrates that, though solving many a puzzle, he could find no remedy for his love of Aspasia (91-4). No one who had ever opened Plato would have made Socrates either solve puzzles or fall for women. Nor was it either original or witty to present Alcaeus and Anacreon as rivals for the favours of Sappho (47-56). The comic poet Diphilus had recently written a play in which (with similar disregard of chronology) Archilochus and Hipponax were rivals for Sappho,[82] and the Peripatetic biographer Chamaeleon had Sappho reject Anacreon.[83] For Euripides he was able to exploit a genu-

79. For attempts at rehabilitation, O. Crusius, finding gentle irony and roguish humour (*RE* 5. 2 [1905], 2281-82), E. Degani (*Storia e civiltà dei Greci* 9^2 [1981], 305-06), G. Giangrande (*Scr. Min. Alex.* II [1981], 387-410), M. Huys 1991, 83; Bing (n. 80).

80. The text of these lines presents innumerable problems: in addition to Powell (*CA* 98-105), see J. Defradas, *Les élégiaques grecs* (Paris 1962), 92-102 and G. Giangrande (*Scr. Min. Alex.* II [1981], 387-410 (ultra-conservative); Couat 1882 (tr. J. Loeb 1931), 82-103 is also still worth consulting.

81. *Nomodeiktes: Greek Studies in Honor of M. Ostwald* (Ann Arbor 1993), 619-31; cf. Bing 1988, 58-64.

82. *CAF* F 69-79 = F 70-71, *PCG* V (1986), 94; Schol. Ov. Ibis p. 156 La Penna with M. Davies, *Prometheus* 7 (1981), 123-24 and *QUUC* 12 (1982), 15-16. At least six comedies entitled *Sappho* are known: Dover, *Greek Homosexuality* (1978), 174.

83. If F 7. 52 alludes to Sappho's Lesbianism (Giangrande, *Scr. Min. Alex.* II. 401), this too comes from Chamaeleon, who identified the girl from Lesbos in *PMG* 358 as Sappho: D. Giordano, *Chamaeleontis Fragmenta*^{2} (Bologna 1990), F 25, with pp. 151-3.

ine biographical tradition: the life-long misogynist finally caught in the toils of love (61-8).[84] Yet inconsequentially enough he goes on to have him killed by a pack of dogs when the alternative tradition of sparagmos by enraged women[85] would have made a more appropriate conclusion.

Structure and style are no more inventive. Poets succeed each other mechanically in pairs: epic (Hesiod and Homer), elegiac (Mimnermus and Antimachus), lyric (Alcaeus and Anacreon), tragic (Sophocles and Euripides); 4 lines each for Alcaeus, Sophocles, Philitas, Pythagoras and Aristippus; 6 for Hesiod, Mimnermus, Antimachus, Anacreon, Philoxenus and Socrates; 8 for Homer and Euripides. The writing is everywhere lazy and formulaic: having buried his beloved Lyde, Antimachus returns (45-6) ἄκρην ἐς Κολοφῶνα, γόων δ᾽ ἐνεπλήσατο βίβλους, exactly duplicating the articulation of line 25 (λόγων ἀνεγράψατο βίβλους), repeated again in line 47 (πόσους ἀνεδέξατο κώμους). The adjectives μέγας and πᾶς appear six and ten times respectively in 98 lines; ἀποπρολιπόντα in 21 is followed by ἀποπρολιπών in 44; Musaeus is Χαρίτων ἤρανος, Hesiod ἤρανον ἱστορίης (16, 22); μαλακοῦ πνεῦμα appears in the same *sedes* in lines 14 and 36. Lovers are all "much suffering": Orpheus (πόλλ᾽ ἔτλη, 7), Hesiod (πόλλ᾽ ἔπαθεν, 25), Homer (πολλὰ παθών, 31), Mimnermus (πολλὸν ἀνατλάς, 35). His fairly mechanical Homerizing is discussed in a wider context in Ch. XIII. 3.

In a Colophonian poet, the idea of a catalogue of suffering lovers addressed to the object of the poet's own affections was undoubtedly inspired by and modelled on the *Lyde* as much as on his own teacher's *Bittis* and (more remotely) the *Nanno*. Athenaeus mentions both *Nanno* and *Lyde* before quoting the long extract from the *Leontion*.

So (Callimachus suggests) just as the longer poems of Mimnermus spawned the *Lyde*, so did the longer poems of Philitas spawn the *Leontion*. Mimnermus and Philitas were excellent poets, but some of their poems were better than others. Since the main counts against the *Lyde* were its length and diffuseness (the *Leontion* too ran to three books), it comes as no surprise that it is the shorter poems of Mimnermus and Philitas that Callimachus prefers.

The lexicographers quote a fragment to which surprisingly little attention has been paid (F 532):

τῷ ἴκελον τὸ γράμμα τὸ Κῷον.

84. I am not persuaded by Giangrande (in the light of σκολιὰς...ἐκηβολίας in *AP* vii. 29. 6) that ὑπὸ σκολιοῖο τυπέντα τόξου (63-4) implies homosexual love (*SMA* II. 402-03).
85. Recorded in the Suda s. v. Προμέρου κύνες; see Powell on l. 68.

In a poem of Callimachus, a "Coan book" is surely a poem by Philitas. It is natural to compare the fragment on the *Lyde*,

Λύδη καὶ παχὺ γράμμα καὶ οὐ τορόν.

γράμμα Κῷον balances παχὺ γράμμα, and it is tempting (with Puelma) to infer that both are fragments of the same poem. Pfeiffer suggested that Philitas's poems are as delicate as the silk for which his native Cos was famous. Yet attractive as it might seem to read silk as a metaphor for refinement in style (= λεπτότης), it is not in fact found so used: silk connotes rather luxury and (because transparent) immorality, applied to style, effeminacy.[86] Moreover it begs the question to assume a metaphor that implies a favourable judgment on Philitas.

What or who is this γράμμα Κῷον being compared to? To the works of Mimnermus, it has usually been supposed, on the analogy of prol. 9-12.[87] According to Puelma the epigram thus reconstructed made the same far-fetched threefold comparison he had detected in the *Aetia* prologue: Philitas rather than Antimachus as the true heir of Mimnermus. But τῷ implies just one antecedent, and that was surely Antimachus, the subject of the first couplet.[88] In other words, Philitas is being criticized for the same vices as Antimachus.[89] For Puelma, it was axiomatic that Callimachus could not possibly be criticizing either Mimnermus or Philitas: he was simply praising his own elegiac predecessors.[90] But where else does Callimachus praise his predecessors so simply? When he praises Ion in *Iamb* 13, it is as a model for his own versatility, and the famous epigram on Aratus is not at all the straightforward praise of Hesiod most people assume (Ch. XIII. 2).

Here too the situation is more complex than Puelma allowed. Callimachus's attitude to Philitas is as qualified here as in the *Aetia* prologue. He is not dismissing all Philitas's poems any more than he dismissed all of Mimnermus's in the prologue—or for that matter all of Antimachus's (§ 7). Again it is just one poem that is at issue (τὸ γράμμα τὸ Κῷον), again surely the *Bittis*. If I am right about Asclepiades's epigram on the *Lyde*, it was in the παχὺ γράμμα epigram that Callimachus first broached the themes he was to develop more fully and colourfully in the *Aetia* prologue. So it would not be surprising to find the same link between *Lyde* and *Bittis*.

---

86. K. F. Smith on Tibullus ii. 3. 53; J. C. Bramble, *Persius and the Programmatic Satire* (1974), 39; *illa translucida et versicolor quorundam elocutio res ipsas effeminat*, Quint. viii pr. 20; when Plutarch applies λεπτός metaphorically to delicate (?silk) clothing at *Mor.* 42D, this is an ironic (negative) reference to the spare (artificial) Attic style.

87. E.g. G. Vitelli, *Bull. Soc. arch. d'Alexandrie* n. s. 8 (1933), 142; cf. Pfeiffer ad loc.

88. For a reconstruction, *exempli gratia*, of the whole first couplet, § 6.

89. So P. E. Knox, *PLILS* 7 (1993), 68.

90. *Mus. Helv.* 11 (1954), 102f.

4

That Callimachus was criticizing Mimnermus and Philitas with an eye on the current literary scene can be illustrated in another way. Why is it that the "minor poems" of Mimnermus are called αἱ κατὰ λεπτόν? It has (of course) been realized that κατὰ λεπτόν was the title of a collection of Aratus's minor poems (*SH* 108-9). And it was on the basis of Callimachus's welcome to Aratus's *Phaenomena*—χαίρετε, λεπταὶ ῥήσιες, "Hail, subtle discourses" (*Ep.* 27)—that ῥήσιες was conjectured as the missing word at the beginning of prol. 12. This is certainly wrong. Martin West quite rightly impugned it as "less appropriate here" and "a substandard self-quotation,"[91] but oddly enough did not think to query the supplement itself.

The word ῥῆσις normally refers to a speech, to speech as opposed to narrative (e.g. in epic, Plato, *Rep.* 393B), or (as often) to a speech in a drama (e.g. Εὐριπίδου ῥῆσιν, "a speech from Euripides," in Aristophanes, *Nub.* 1371).[92] The verb used is always λέγειν,[93] not ἀείδειν; ῥῆσις is not a song or a poem, but the spoken word.[94] Callimachus was naturally well aware of this. He uses the word on four other occasions, every time in this sense. Three times in his *Iambi*, referring to speeches made by interlocutors,[95] and once in another epigram (*AP* ix. 566):

μικρή τις, Διόνυσε, καλὰ πρήσσοντι ποιητῇ
ῥῆσις· ὁ μὲν "νικῶ" φησὶ τὸ μακρότατον.

The poet who fares well [in the contest] makes a short speech, Dionysus; "I've won" is the most he says.

It would therefore be a most inappropriate word to use of a poem being praised for its elegance.[96] So why did Callimachus use it? In 1960 J.-M.

91. *Studies* 74 n. 2.

92. "A ῥῆσις is a consecutive speech or declamation as opposed to brief dialogue in Drama or to the narrative in Epic," W. Headlam on Herodas 3. 30 (p . 136).

93. A. *Suppl.* 615, ῥῆσιν...λέγων; *Ag.* 1322, εἰπεῖν ῥῆσιν; Eur. F 149. 20-21 Austin, ῥήσεις...λέγει; Ar. *Ach.* 416, λέξαι...ῥῆσιν; *Vesp.* 580, ἐκ τῆς Νιόβης εἴπῃ ῥῆσιν; Ephippus F 16. 3 (*PCG* V. 145), ῥήσεις τε κατὰ δεῖπνον λέγοι; Theophr. *Char.* 27, ῥήσεις μανθάνειν καὶ ταύτας λέγειν.

94. Note the clear distinction made by (for example) Theophr. *Char.* 15. 14, οὔτε ᾆσαι οὔτε ῥῆσιν εἰπεῖν, and Aeschines, *In Tim.* 168, ὡς ἐν τῷ πότῳ ἡμῶν κιθαρίζοι καὶ λέγοι ῥήσεις τινάς. Dover rightly accepts Borthwick's emendation ᾖγ' for the MSS ᾖσε (vel. sim.) at Ar. *Nub.* 1371; to the parallel he cites for this use of ἄγειν, add Callim. F 191. 31-2.

95. F 194. 93, where one character τῇ ῥήσει ἤλγησε of the other; 203. 24, where one character responds to the ῥῆσις of another; and 191. 31, where Hipponax bids someone write down his ῥῆσις before he starts.

96. The obscure but perhaps Neronian (*GP* II 464) Pinytus's line on Sappho, αἱ δὲ σοφαὶ κείνης ῥήσιες ἀθάνατοι (*AP* 7. 16. 1), clearly derives from Callimachus.

322 Fat Ladies

Jacques pointed out an acrostich in Aratus's *Phaenomena*, to which W. Levitan in 1979 added another.[97] Building on the playfulness they reveal, Levitan went on to point out that in addition Aratus punningly alludes to his own name in the second line of the poem:[98]

ἐκ Διὸς ἀρχώμεσθα, τὸν οὐδέποτ' ἄνδρες ἐῶμεν
ἄρρητον.

There can be no doubt that contemporaries were alert to these little word-games. For both Callimachus and Leonidas praised the *Phaenomena*, and, against the normal prosody, both gave Aratus's name in the same curiously artificial form, with long initial alpha and "Ionic" eta for the second alpha, ῎Αρητος.[99] Leonidas also signalled his recognition of the pun in another way (*AP* ix. 25):

αἰνείσθω δὲ καμὼν ἔργον μέγα καὶ Διὸς εἶναι
δεύτερος ὅστις ἔθηκ' ἄστρα φαεινότερα.

Let him be praised who toiled at this great work, and let it be said that after Zeus he comes second, who made the stars shine more brightly.

In addition to the surface compliment (Zeus made the stars; Aratus made them brighter by writing about them), Leonidas is clearly alluding to the fact that Aratus himself, after "beginning with Zeus" in line 1, then introduced his own name into line 2, "second after Zeus." Callimachus signalled his recognition by a further pun of his own.[100] The neatest one he could think of rendered unavoidable a word he would otherwise not even have considered in such a context: ῥήσιες ᾿Αρήτου/ἀρρήτου, "utterances of Aratus/the unutterable."[101] Is it likely that he would have been so lazy as to use the same noun as well as the same adjective to describe the very different poetry of Mimnermus with no such compulsion? Surely not. No obvious alternative suggests itself for the gap in prol. 12,[102] but then why should Callimachus have used an obvious word?[103]

97. Jaccques, *RÉA* 62 (1960), 52-59; Levitan, *Glyph* 5 (1979), 55-68.

98. p. 68 n. 18, in an unobtrusive footnote. Curiously enough it was not long before two more scholars independently made the same observation: D. A. Kidd, *CQ* 31 [1981], 355; and N. Hopkinson, *A Hellenistic Anthology* (1988), 139. See now the comprehensive treatment by P. Bing, *HSCP* 93 (1990), 281-5.

99. Meleager 3974 Gow-Page shows that short initial alpha was the normal scansion. It is worth noting that Callimachus's η is preserved even in the Aratus scholia, where we might have expected the standard orthography to prevail (*Vita I* p. 9. 16 Martin).

100. Briefly noted (but not explained) by P. Bing, *HSCP* 93 (1990), 281-85.

101. Kidd aptly compares Antigonos Gonatas's compliment to the poet: εὐδοξότερον ποιεῖς τὸν Εὔδοξον (*Vita I* p. 8. 9 Martin = p. 77 Maass).

102. Milne solved the problem in another way with his ὧδε μέν from Schol. Lond. (recently adopted by C. W. Müller 1987, 89), but (as Pfeiffer saw) the Schol. must be referring to ὧδε in l. 16.

103. As Wilamowitz remarked once when refusing to fill gaps in the *Ektheosis Arsinoes*: "denn die Worte des Kallimachos finden zu wollen, hieße einen Dichter arg unterschätzen,

Fortunately, it seems to have been the adjective rather than the missing noun that carries the essence of Callimachus's literary judgment. The question is, why did Callimachus characterize Mimnermus's *Nanno* with the epithet he had applied to Aratus?

No word in the Hellenistic poetic lexicon has been more minutely investigated over the past half century than λεπτός.[104] It is a nice example of a word that entirely changed its connotation over the years. In Homer it means "weak" or "feeble"; used metaphorically in Aristophanes and other comic poets it is frankly contemptuous. Witness the numerous compounds it spawned: λεπτολόγος, ὑπολεπτολόγος, διαλεπτολογοῦμαι; overly subtle, sophistic, fancy-schmancy.[105] The earliest examples of λεπτός applied to the intellect come in Euripides's *Medea* (529 and 1082; also F inc. 924). The usage was evidently found controversial, since it is often turned against him and the philosophers in Attic comedy. In *Clouds* 359, for example, Socrates is addressed as λεπτοτάτων λήρων ἱερεῦ. But by Callimachus's day it implied the highest praise: refined, polished, elegant. It has always been assumed that it was Callimachus himself who brought about this change. There are serious reasons for doubting this.

As we shall see in more detail in Chapter XIII, it is the standard view that when Callimachus applied the word to Aratus's *Phaenomena*, he was setting his own seal of approval on the new poem, indicating that it came up to his own standards of refinement (λεπτότης). But he was not the only poet so to style the *Phaenomena*. This is how it was greeted by Leonidas of Tarentum (*AP* ix. 25):

γράμμα τόδ' Ἀρήτοιο δαήμονος, ὅς ποτε λεπτῇ
φροντίδι δηναίους ἀστέρας ἐφράσατο.

Then there is the last line of the epigram by "King Ptolemy" (presumably Philadelphus)[106] quoted in *Vita I* of Aratus (*SH* 712):

ἀλλ' ὅ γε λεπτολόγος σκῆπτρον Ἄρατος ἔχει.

Philadelphus and Leonidas may both have been influenced by Callimachus (though Leonidas's dates are uncertain and elsewhere he shows little trace

---

der immer etwas Apartes apart zu sagen weiß, gelehrt und erfindsam, auch wo er unsern Geschmack verletzt" (*SB Berlin* 1912, I, 531).

104. Reitzenstein 1931, 25-39; Puelma Piwonka, *Lucilius und Kallimachos* (1948), 160f.; Wimmel 1960, Stichwortindex s. v.; Jacques, *RÉA* 62 (1960), 52-59; Vogt, *AuA* 13 (1967), 84-87; Lohse, *AuA* 19 (1973), 21-34; Cairns, *Tibullus* (1979), 5.

105. For a good collection of examples, J. D. Denniston, *CQ* 21 (1927), 119; Dover on Ar. *Clouds* 153.

106. To Page's arguments in favour of Philadelphus (*FGE* 84), I would add that the poets to whom Aratus is judged superior are surely predecessors rather than successors. For other views, Fraser II. 1090 n. 459; cf. n. 443; and Gabathuler 1937, 94-95.

of Callimachean influence).[107] Indeed, Kaibel argued that Leonidas only knew Aratus from Callimachus's epigram.[108] But if so, why single out that particular word? Indeed, why write at all on a poem he had never seen? As Gow and Page more reasonably conclude, except for the epithet "the two epigrams have little in common."[109] The way Leonidas picks up the pun on Aratus's name proves that he knew at least the beginning of the poem at first hand. He may therefore have had independent knowledge of the significance of λεπτός to Aratus.

Two considerations suggest that it was Aratus who originated this particular use of the term. First, there is the fact that he gave a book of his own the title κατὰ λεπτόν.[110] Second, there is Jacques's acrostich, revealing λεπτή spelled out three times in *Phaenomena* 783-7:[111]

ΛΕΠΤΗ μὲν καθαρή τε περὶ τρίτον ἦμαρ ἐοῦσα
Εὔδιός κ᾽ εἴη, λεπτὴ δὲ καὶ εὖ μάλ᾽ ἐρευθὴς
Πνευματίη, παχίων δὲ καὶ ἀμβλείῃσι κεραίαις
Τέτρατον ἐκ τρίτατοιο φόως ἀμενηνὸν ἔχουσα
Ἠὲ νότου ἀμβλύνετ᾽ ἢ ὕδατος ἐγγὺς ἐόντος.

If she [the moon] is slender and clear about the third day, she heralds calm; if slender and very ruddy, wind; but if thick and with blunted horns she show but a feeble light on the third and fourth night, her beams are blunted by the South wind or imminent rain.

Since the same word appears twice in the text of the passage as well as in the acrostich, coincidence can be eliminated.[112] All doubt is removed by the similarly signposted acrostich πᾶσα detected by Levitan at 803-06, confirmed by πάντη at the beginning of 802, πάντα in 803, πᾶσιν and πάντα again in 805—and πᾶς in the first three lines of the acrostich itself:[113]

πάντη γὰρ καθαρῇ κε μάλ᾽ εὔδια τεκμήραιο·
Πάντα δ᾽ ἐρευθομένη δοκέειν ἀνέμοιο κελεύθους·
Αλλοθι δ᾽ ἄλλο μελαινομένη δοκέειν ὑετοῖο.
Σήματα δ᾽ οὐ μάλα πᾶσιν ἐπ᾽ ἤμασι πάντα τέτυκται·
Ἀλλ᾽ ὅσα μὲν τριτάτη τε τεταρταίῃ τε πέλονται...

107. Fraser I. 561-62; II. 802 n. 80-81.
108. *Hermes* 29 (1894), 122; L. mistakenly praises Aratus for treating the planets.
109. *HE* II. 396.
110. Documentation in *SH* 108-89; for καὶ κατὰ λεπτὸν ἄλλα in *Vita I* p. 9. 21, both Martin and Lloyd-Jones/Parsons seem to have overlooked Birt's surely certain supplement <καὶ> ἄλλα, as often at the end of lists of titles in Suda-entries (*Erklärung des Catalepton* [1910], 7 n. 1).
111. *RÉA* 62 (1960), 48-61; the translation quoted above is by G. R. Mair (Loeb 1921).
112. "Ein Zufall ist hier ausgeschlossen," E. Vogt, "Das Akrostichon in der griechischen Literatur" *AuA* 13 (1967), 84; see too E. Courtney, *Philologus* 134 (1990), 10-11.
113. *Glyph* 5 (1979), 55-68, with Bing, *HSCP* 93 (1990), 281 n. 1.

If the second acrostich reveals little more than the virtuosity of repeating the key word in a number of grammatical variants, there is clearly more significance to the repetitions in the first.[114] Not only three examples of λεπτή in five lines, but two other Callimachean buzz-words, καθαρή (*Hymn to Apollo* 111: *AP* 9. 565. 1) and παχίων (prol. 23; F 398) in 783 and 785. But are they Callimachean rather than Aratean? Jacques himself, Vogt, Lohse, Schwinge and now Bing had no doubt that Aratus was alluding to the *Aetia* prologue, making the Callimachean ideal of λεπτότης his own.[115] But it is with Aratus that Callimachus, Leonidas and King Ptolemy associate the word.

The only other occurrence in Callimachus is prol. 12, where the *Nanno* is called κατὰ λεπτόν. Now one thing we can be certain of is that this was not Mimnermus's title. Not only are such fanciful titles quite alien to archaic poetry.[116] It was not till the age of Callimachus and Aratus that λεπτός even acquired these favorable literary connotations. In the context, it is more likely that Callimachus alludes to Aratus's title than that Aratus took his title from Callimachus.[117] So one certainly and perhaps both of Callimachus's two examples of λεπτός refer to Aratus. As for the famous reference to the μοῦσα λεπταλέη a few lines later (using the slightly different epic form), it should be noted that this is not represented as Callimachus's own characterization of his verse, but advice from Apollo.

There are also other grounds for refusing to tie the word too closely to Callimachus. An elegant epigram by Hedylus of Samos opens as follows:

πίνωμεν, καὶ γάρ τι νέον, καὶ γάρ τι παρ᾽ οἶνον
εὕροιμεν λεπτὸν καί τι μελιχρὸν ἔπος (IV GP).

Let us drink; for in our cups we may discover some poem that is new, refined and sweet.

---

114. Levitan's third acrostich (808-812) is, as he admits, "incomplete or, if complete, mispelled" (p. 58): ΣΕΜΕΙΗ where we want ΣΗΜΕΙΑ. And while it might be argued that a mispelled acrostich is no acrostich at all, it is nonetheless perhaps close enough to look more than mere coincidence after the earlier acrostich—and after σήματα in 805 and σημαίνει in 808 (see too M. W. Haslam, *HSCP* 94 [1992], 201). There is also the contemporary parallel of the apparently mispelled Nicander acrostich in *Alex.* 266-274 (Lobel, *CQ* 22 [1928], 114; Gow and Scholfield p. 177). That can be corrected by emendation (Jacques, *RÉA* 57 [1955], 20), but doubts remain (Levitan, p. 60; Courtney, *Philol.* 134 [1990], 12-13, comparing the apparently mispelled Silius acrostich), and there is always the possibility of corruption in the text of Aratus.

115. Jacques 53f.; Vogt, *AuA* 1967, 87; Lohse *AuA* 1973, 33; E.-R. Schwinge, *Künstlichkeit von Kunst* (Zetemata 84, München 1986), 15-16; Bing 1990, 282.

116. As West remarks (*Studies* 75), all we usually find is ἐν ταῖς ἐλεγείαις or the like.

117. In *Philologus* 101 (1957), 95 n. 2 M. Puelma unjustifiably assumes that a collection of Philitas's "Kleinelegien" might have been called κατὰ λεπτόν, quoting Aratus as merely one example of the title. It should be noticed in this connection that Theocritus too gave one of his poems (16) a title borrowed from Aratus, Χάριτες (*SH* 117).

The combination of λεπτόν and μελιχρόν might seem to point directly and straightforwardly to Callimachus. But Hedylus was an admirer of Asclepiades (whom he names) and Posidippus; indeed, he may have edited a collection of their epigrams.[118] Whether or not we are justified in counting Posidippus and Asclepiades among the Telchines, both undoubtedly disagreed with Callimachus about Antimachus's *Lyde*. And if an emendation is accepted, Hedylus too refers to the *Lyde* with admiration (App. A). It does not look as if λεπτότης was in any straightforward way the hallmark of a style or type of poetry uniquely associated with Callimachus or rejected by his literary enemies.

It seems impossible to read any coherent literary message into Aratus's meteorological context. Once he had used λεπτή of the slender crescent moon, it was natural enough to use παχίων to denote the filling out of the moon's disc. λεπτός/παχύς were standard antonyms in a variety of connotations, like thick/thin.[119] καθαρή too is a perfectly natural word to use of a clear moon on a bright night. Nonetheless, the epigrams of Callimachus, Leonidas and King Ptolemy, all celebrating this very poem, put it beyond doubt that λεπτή had literary connotations for Aratus. Consequently its triple underlining cannot fail to highlight the juxtaposition of all three words within the same brief passage. The fact that Callimachus makes similar use of the same three terms certainly confirms their literary resonance in Aratus. But it does not prove that Callimachus originated this use and that Aratus is simply quoting him. The natural inference is surely that Aratus is the originator.[120]

One of the poems included in Aratus's κατὰ λεπτόν seems to have been a *Hymn to Apollo* (*SH* 109). In its two extant lines Delos addresses Leto, recalling Callimachus's *Hymn to Delos*, datable to ca 275. There seems to be some sort of connection between the two poems. If it was a book of hymns, it may also have contained Aratus's *Hymn to Pan*, which can perhaps be dated to 277/8.[121] The choice of title must have had something to do with Aratus's concern for λεπτότης.

Since we have a good deal of personal poetry by Callimachus, we naturally tend to see the literary issues of the age through his eyes—as, in later

118. For the evidence, my *Greek Anthology* 369-76.

119. E.g. of character, ἐς τὰς τέχνας παχέες καὶ οὐ λεπτοὶ οὐδὲ ὀξέες, Hippocrates, *Airs Waters Places* 24. 52 (I. 136 Loeb ed.); of physical types, *On Joints* 8. 65 (III. 218 Loeb); of sounds, φωνάς...ἢ λεπτὰς ἢ παχείας, Aristotle, *de audibilibus* 803b30; cf. 804a10-14. For a nice epigrammatic antithesis in a great admirer of Callimachus, Gregory Nazianzen, see his *carm.* I. 2. 10. 589 (*PG* 37. 723, line 2): παχεῖα γαστὴρ λεπτὸν οὐ τίκτει νόον. λεπτομερῶς and παχυμερῶς are regularly opposed, "in detail" and "broadly speaking" respectively (e.g. Jo. Sard., *In Aphth.* p. 217. 1 Rabe).

120. As hinted long ago by Dilthey: *nisi forte ad ipsum Aratum aliquo modo illud redit*, meaning *quod λεπτή dicitur Arati poesis* (1863, 13 n. 1).

121. *SH* 115; Tarn, *JHS* 40 (1920), 149, with W. Ludwig, *RE* Supp. X (1965), 29.

ages, with Cicero, the younger Pliny, Symmachus, Sidonius Apollinaris. But Aratus too was a prominent man of letters in his own right, author of a large number of other books, prose and verse, in addition to the *Phaenomena*.[122] In the eyes of posterity it was Callimachus who came to embody λεπτότης, especially (through Vergil) at Rome. Modern readers find it hard to imagine how he saw Aratus as a kindred spirit at all. After a century or two, even Aratus's own commentators missed the acrostichs in the *Phaenomena*.[123] But there can be no doubt that Callimachus saw something in Aratus that he found missing in most of his contemporaries. It was surely for this reason that he paid Aratus the compliment of borrowing his critical terminology.

The Aratus acrostich also has important chronological implications. It highlights no fewer than three of the terms Callimachus exploited in the controversy that led to his *Aetia*. So long as the *Aetia* prologue was seen as an addition of Callimachus's old age ca 245, these could be seen as war-cries he had raised throughout his life. But if the prologue is simply the introduction to a poem he published ca 270, concerned with the issues of the day, the probability is that *Phaenomena* and *Aetia* appeared within two or three years rather than two or three decades of each other. Everything we know about the date of Aratus suggests that he was born well before Callimachus, not least a plain statement in *Vita I* that Callimachus himself "refers to Aratus as an older man" (Ch. VIII. 5). The only evidence we have for the date of the *Phaenomena* is that it was written at the court of Gonatas, that is to say not earlier than ca 275. It is perfectly reasonable to suppose that it was published not long before the publication of *Aetia* I-II ca 270.

In Callimachus's eyes each poem enshrined the ideal of λεπτότης in its own way. He saw the same qualities in some of Mimnermus's elegies, and described them in the same terms. This is not a judgment on Mimnermus in

122. See the full list given in *SH* 83-120.

123. Passed over in the voluminous scholia. There is one case in Vergil similar enough to suggest imitation, the account in *Aen*. 7. 601-15 of the opening of the gates of war:

> Mos erat Hesperio in Latio, quem protinus urbes
> Albanae coluere sacrum, nunc maxima rerum
> Roma colit, cum prima movent in proelia **Martem**,
> Sive Getis inferre manu lacrimabile bellum...

So D. P. Fowler, *CQ* 33 (1983), 298. I am not convinced by the alleged partial reverse acrostich MA(ro) VE(rgilius) PU(blius) at *Georgics* i. 429, 431 and 433: E. L. Brown, *Numeri Vergiliani* (1963), 96-115, with D. O. Ross, *Backgrounds to Augustan Poetry* (1975), 29 and R. F. Thomas on *Geo*. 1. 427-37 (p. 139). The pun on Aratus's name in *Phaen*. 2 might be thought to lend some support, but as Thomas notes on *Geo*. 1. 433, Vergil's imitation of 783-7 does not employ "the equally well-established Latin equivalents *tenuis* and *pinguis*" (p. 140). Did Vergil "suppress" this touch (Thomas), or just not notice it? No comment in the Vergil scholia. Nor am I persuaded by H. Dettmer's "signature" in Prop. i. 22. 2 (*LCM* 13 [1988], 55-6). For the relative unimportance of acrostichs, above Ch. II. 2.

and for himself. Callimachus wrote with a view to Mimnermus's influence on contemporary poets, for both good and bad. Just as the negative side of his double-edged judgment evokes the despised Antimachus, so does the positive side evoke the admired Aratus.[124]

5

It is contemporary elegy that was the bone of contention between Callimachus and his critics. One of the features of the *Aetia* prologue that has misled scholars into thinking of epic is the big-and-crude side of the successive antitheses: fat victim vs slender Muse; main road vs narrow path; braying of donkey vs song of cicada. What then does the small-and-refined side refer to? Evidently to short poems, but how short—and was brevity all that mattered?

Much has been written in recent years on Callimachus's poetics. But some of the most basic questions remain to be asked. For example, what parallel is there in ancient literary criticism for the depreciation of one genre in favour of another? Callimachus was familiar (of course) with the Aristotelian approach to literature through the different genres, criticizing their different functions and representatives one at a time. And whereas someone who in his own poetry mixed up the genres might favour a different approach, it would be surprising if Callimachus had extolled minor genres unspecified in such extravagant terms over epic. Is it really credible that he dismissd *all* epic as fat, commonplace and noisy? Realizing the absurdity of so extreme a position, many scholars have insisted that "Callimachus did not condemn Homer...rather...those who imitated Homer, who copied the epic form, not realizing that it was by now empty and obsolete."[125] That would certainly be a more sensible point of view, but how can so subtle and qualified a position be got out of Callimachus's all too clear and unqualified language?

But for this obsession with epic, it would have been seen long ago that Callimachus is comparing styles, not genres. Once more, the key is supplied by his models. It has long been realized that it is the agon in

---

124. Another possible example of such contemporary allusion might be cited. At prol. 16 (if Housman's supplement is right) Callimachus referred to his own poetry as ἀηδονίδες. This term also appears in his famous epigram on the elegist Heraclitus (*AP* vi. 80. 5), where it is usually supposed to have been the title·of a book by Heraclitus (*HE* II 192; Gabathuler, *Hellenistische Epigramme auf Dichter* [1937], 59 n. 58).

125. E.g. Clausen 1964, 184. So too R.O.A.M. Lyne, *MD* 12 (1984), 18: "Callimachus, whose diction bespeaks obsessive love of and familiarity with Homer, has no grudge against the master... It is the epigones whose epics are uncouth and filthily written; it is the fading post-Homeric epic tradition that he eschews."

Aristophanes's *Frogs*, the comparison between Aeschylus and Euripides, that most influenced the imagery of the *Aetia* prologue.[126]

For example, with Callimachus's famous claim,

βρονταν οὐκ ἐμὸν, ἀλλὰ Διός (F 1. 20),

compare *Frogs* 814, where Aeschylus is described on his first appearance as ἐπιβρεμέτας, the thunderer, a word used by Homer of Zeus. Closer still is *Acharnians* 530-1 on Pericles's oratory:

ἐντεῦθεν ὀργῇ Περικλέης οὐλύμπιος
ἤστραπτ᾽, ἐβρόντα, ξυνεκύκα τὴν Ἑλλάδα.

With Apollo's instruction to Callimachus:

[......] ἀοιδέ, τὸ μὲν θύος ὅττι πάχιστον
[θρέψαι, τὴ]ν Μοῦσαν δ᾽, ὠγαθέ, λεπταλέην (F 1. 23-4),

compare Euripides's complaint that when he took tragedy over from Aeschylus, she was "swollen with high-falutin and weighty words," so that he had to "slim her down (ἴσχνανα) and reduce her weight by means of little verses and walks and laxatives" (940-42).

Where Aristophanes speaks of a κρίσις...τέχνης (785f.), Callimachus writes τέχνη [κρίνετε] (F 1. 17-18). Euripides claims to feed on the upper air (*Frogs* 892), while Callimachus wants to become a cicada so that he can feed on the divine air (F 1. 34). With μέγα ψοφέουσαν ἀοιδήν (F 1. 19), compare *Frogs* 492, τὸν ψόφον τῶν ῥημάτων, and (again of Aeschylus) *Clouds* 1367, ψόφου πλέων. Finally, Callimachus twice exploits the motif of the scales on which Dionysus weighs the poems of Aeschylus and Euripides (*Frogs* 1365f.). First at line 9, when Philitas's Demeter "outweighs" (καθέλκει, cf. καθέλξει at *Frogs* 1398) his "tall lady." And again at lines 17-18, judge poetry by its art, not the "Persian chain."

Those who have discussed these links have been mainly concerned with the sterile question whether the later rhetoricians who use such metaphors got them from Aristophanes and Callimachus, or whether Aristophanes and Callimachus got them from lost earlier rhetoricans,[127] "a strange but typical example of the modern quest for hidden sources. The natural assumption is that the Hellenistic poets derived their critical terminology directly from the poets of the fifth century, whom they knew so well."[128]

So Pfeiffer in 1968. But the underlying idea has reappeared in a recent study.[129] No one who has compared the two passages as a whole will be in

126. E.g. Snell, *The Discovery of the Mind* (1953), 117; Wimmel 1960, 115 n.1; Cairns, *Tibullus* (1979), 8-9.

127. M. Pohlenz, *NGG* 1920, 142-78 = *Kleine Schriften* II (1965), 436-72; E. Reitzenstein, *Festschrift R. Reitzenstein* (1931), 37f.; cf. D. L. Clayman, *WS* 90 (1977), 27-34.

128. Pfeiffer 1968, 137-38; see too his earlier formulation in *JHS* 75 (1955), 72.

129. The "literary criticism and terminology later associated with Hellenistic writers and surviving most prominently in Callimachus...is already found in a detailed if embryo form"

much doubt that Callimachus (who certainly knew *Frogs* well, cf. F 194. 78-80) had the agon as a whole directly in mind when he wrote his prologue. It is not just individual metaphors they share, but the basic concept of comparing the stylistic extremes to be found within the same genre, more specifically between the old-fashioned and the modern. The difference between the way the two poets developed the idea is (of course) that Aristophanes eventually decided for the old-fashioned (Aeschylus),[130] whereas Callimachus emphatically preferred the modern. And where Aristophanes had made good-natured fun of the old and grand, there is no mistaking the contemptuous tone in Callimachus.

It was different ways of writing tragedy that Aristophanes was debating. For Callimachus, it was different ways of writing elegy. We have already seen that the "fat" metaphor links the θύος πάχιστον of line 23 with three separate long elegies: the *Lyde* (παχὺ γράμμα) and the fat and tall ladies of lines 10-12, long elegies of Mimnermus and Philitas respectively. If it was really epic Callimachus had in mind, why are all the examples he cites elegies?

He uses terms that suggest epic simply because epic epitomizes the grand style, the real object of his polemic. Aristophanes characterizes Aeschylean style and themes in the same way. The contest, predict the chorus (in hexameters), will be λόγων κορυθαίολα νείκη, with Aeschylus φρίξας ...λασιαύχενα χαίταν while Euripides καταλεπτολογήσει, φθονεροὺς κινοῦσα χαλινούς, "shaking the reins of envy" (*Frogs* 822-9).[131] Aeschylus is often σεμνός (833, 1004, 1020), the word Asclepiades applied to Antimachus (and so naturally not used by Callimachus),[132] whereas Euripides is repeatedly characterized by λεπτός terms (828, 956, 1109, 1113). Aristophanes also parallels Callimachus's denunciation of epic subject matter (kings and heroes): where Aeschylus put on the stage heroes from the pages of Homer (1040-42), Euripides produced lustful women, adulterers and pimps (1043, 1079-81). The famous epigram on Aratus (*AP* ix. 507) also borrows a striking metaphor from the *Frogs*: ἀπομαξαμένη of Aeschylus's imitation of Homer (1040), applied to Aratus's imitation (ἀπεμάξατο) of Hesiod (Ch. XIII. 3).

The comparison between Callimachus and Aristophanes was made long ago by the unknown author of a life of the Hadrianic poet Dionysius Peri-

---

in the *Frogs* (Cairns, *Tibullus* 8).

130. In the end on moral and political, not stylistic grounds.

131. It is by no means clear just what the last phrase means (see Dover ad loc.), but it is clearly depreciatory.

132. As already noted, it is the favourable term for the sort of elevation Callimachus denounces as παχύ.

egetes. After characterizing Dionysius's style in all the usual hackneyed metaphors (lean but not feeble, flowery but not sweet), the writer adds:[133]

> Aristophanes really ridicules fatness in poems (τὴν δὲ παχύτητα τῶν ποιημάτων ἱκανῶς μὲν διασύρει) in his *Frogs*—and so does Callimachus too: "Lyde, a fat and unclear book."

The observation is no less significant or apt because Aristophanes does not happen to use the word παχύς itself. The ancient critic, familiar with the idiom, was in no doubt that it was style, not genre, that both poets were concerned with.

There is also one other late text that may have more to tell us of the age of Callimachus than the age it purports to describe. According to the (in its present form no doubt late antique) *Life of Aeschylus* (§ 8), the poet

> went to the court of Hieron, according to some because he was criticized by the Athenians and defeated by the young Sophocles, according to others because he was defeated by Simonides in a <contest for an> elegy/epigram (ἐλεγεῖον) for those who died at Marathon. An ἐλεγεῖον has to have the slender qualities (λεπτότητος μετέχειν θέλει) necessary to arouse emotion, and Aeschylus's (as remarked) was not suitable.

Wilamowitz assumed that an elegy was meant,[134] Jacoby (very emphatically) an epitaph.[135] In fact usage would seem to permit either,[136] and public competition is far more likely for an elegy than an epigram—and explicitly documented at the Panathenaea.[137] Of course, both suggestions are poor motives for going to Sicily and few would take the passage very seriously for the biography of either Simonides or Aeschylus.[138] But that need not mean that all the details are invented. As it happens Plutarch cites an elegy by Aeschylus for a detail in the battle of Marathon,[139] and if Simonides wrote elegies on Plataea and Artemisium, why not Marathon too? The idea that it was precisely in λεπτότης that Simonides's elegies excelled Aeschylus's, anachronistic as it is for the age of Marathon, might likewise have been inspired by a reading of the *Frogs* in the light of the *Aetia* prologue.[140]

---

133. *Geographi Graeci Minores* II, ed. C. Müller (Paris 1860), p. 427*b*. 6.

134. *Sappho und Simonides* (Berlin 1913), 143-44.

135. *Kl. phil. Schr.* i (Berlin 1961), 483 n. 91.

136. West 1974, 3-4; Bowie 1986, 25-26; G. Lambin, *Rev. de Phil.* 62 (1988), 71.

137. [Plut.] *De mus.* 1134A; Davison, *JHS* 78 (1958), 39-40; Bowie 1986, 27.

138. Jacoby 1961, 483-89; Lefkowitz 1981, 71-72; Page, *FGE* 223.

139. *Quaest. conv.* i. 10. 3 (628DE); cf. West *IEG* ii². 28-29; Jacoby, *Kl. phil. Schr.*i (1961), 486 n. 101.

140. This echoes Dionysius's assessment of Simonides's style compared to Pindar's (τὸ οἰκτίζεσθαι μὴ μεγαλοπρεπῶς ἀλλὰ παθητικῶς, de imitat. II. 205. 10 Usen.-Rad.), but the combination of Aeschylus, elegy and λεπτότης points to Callimachus via Aristophanes.

6

Another relevant text is Antipater of Sidon's rather ponderous epigram on Antimachus:[141]

ὄβριμον ἀκαμάτου στίχον αἴνεσον Ἀντιμάχοιο,
  ἄξιον ἀρχαίων ὀφρύος ἡμιθέων,
Πιερίδων χαλκευτὸν ἐπ' ἄκμοσιν, εἰ τορὸν οὖας
  ἔλλαχες, εἰ ζαλοῖς τὰν ἀγέλαστον ὄπα,
εἰ τὰν ἄτριπτον καὶ ἀνέμβατον ἀτραπὸν ἄλλοις
  μαίεαι. εἰ δ' ὕμνων σκᾶπτρον Ὅμηρος ἔχει,
καὶ Ζεύς τοι κρέσσων Ἐνοσίχθονος· ἀλλ' Ἐνοσίχθων
  τοῦ μὲν ἔφυ μείων, ἀθανάτων δ' ὕπατος·
καὶ ναετὴρ Κολοφῶνος ὑπέζευκται μὲν Ὁμήρῳ,
  ἀγεῖται δ' ἄλλων πλάθεος ὑμνοπόλων.

Praise the sturdy verse of tireless Antimachus, worthy of the majesty of the heroes of old, beaten on the anvil of the Muses, if you have a keen ear, if you aspire to gravity of diction, if you would aim for a path untrodden and unapproached by others. If Homer holds the sceptre of epic, just as Zeus is greater than Poseidon while Poseidon his inferior is still the chief of the < other > gods, so the Colophonian bows before Homer yet leads all the other poets.

Not only does the poet praise Antimachus as second only to Homer. It cannot be coincidence that he pointedly employs two of Callimachus's critical terms—both of which he turns to Antimachus's advantage. Where Callimachus had dismissed the *Lyde* as "unclear" (οὐ τορόν), Antipater claims that anyone with a τορὸν οὖας, a "keen ear" (that is for poetry), would *praise* Antimachus.[142] Where Callimachus had rejected epic bombast to take the "untrodden paths" (κελεύθους [ἀτρίπτο]υς),[143] Antipater proclaims that it is precisely those who wish to travel the untrodden path who should praise Antimachus. Finally, there is the rôle of the Muses.

---

141. *AP* vii. 109 = Ant. Sid. LXVI Gow-Page; translation adapted from Paton. The ascription in *AP* to Antipater of Thessalonica (unfortunately repeated in Wyss, T 27, p. lxix) is, as Gow rightly concludes, "plainly false." The poem stands in a solid Meleagrian sequence, and the style and Doric forms point clearly to the Sidonian. In addition to *HE* II. 87, see A. D. Skiadas, *Homer im griech. Epigramm* (Athens 1965), 118-24.

142. To be sure, τορός is being used in a slightly different sense (see Gow ad loc.; "if you are an acute critic," Lloyd-Jones, *JHS* 1963, 81-82), but it is the same word that Callimachus had used so contemptuously of the same poet (on its meaning in Callimachus, see below).

143. Pfeiffer's supplement is confirmed, not merely by Oppian, *Hal* 4. 68 (ἀτρίπτοισι κελεύθοις) and the various Latin imitations quoted in his note, but also by Antipater and (not least) Pindar, *Paean.* 7b. 11, where the poet apparently refuses to "drive along the well-trodden path" (τριπτὸν κατ' ἀμαξιτόν) of Homer."

Asclepiades had proclaimed the *Lyde* the joint product of Antimachus and the Muses. Not only did Callimachus implicitly deny this by arrogating to himself the favour of the Muses; he represented the *Aetia* as quite literally a joint product of the Muses and himself, the product of their *conversation*. While changing the metaphor, Antipater returns to Asclepiades's position: Antimachus's epic was indeed produced by the Muses, on their anvil.[144]

There may also be other levels of polemic in Antipater's poem. For example, it may be more than coincidence that he uses the phrase σκᾶπτρον Ὅμηρος ἔχει to close a pentameter in line 6. For Callimachus, condemnation of Antimachus went hand in hand with praise of Aratus. Nothing in Antipater seems to echo anything in Callimachus's epigram on Aratus, but compare the closing pentameter of King Ptolemy's (*SH* 712. 4):

ἀλλ' ὅ γε λεπτολόγος σκῆπτρον Ἄρατος ἔχει.

Could it be that Antipater was restoring the sceptre from Aratus to its rightful owner?

According to Gow, "Antipater's lines plainly refer only to his *Thebaid*, an epic...and not to the *Lyde*, an elegiac poem."[145] Yet the most interesting aspect of Antipater's polemic is the fact that he *combines* Callimachus's criticism of the *Lyde* (τορὸν οὖας) with the *Aetia* prologue (ἄτριπτον...ἀτραπόν). Even if it were to be objected that the word ἄτριπτος in F 1. 28 is a restoration (however probable), the basic point remains unaffected, since the metaphor of true poetry as the untrodden path is repeatedly restated by Callimachus in slightly different terms, twice in the same passage of the *Aetia* prologue and again in a famous epigram.[146] It looks as if Antipater understood Callimachus's criticism as taking in Antimachus's poetry as a whole rather than just the *Lyde*. This would be the more understandable if (as I have argued) the main thrust of Callimachus's criticism was precisely that there was too little difference between Antimachus's epic and elegiac style.

What Callimachus condemned as bombast (παχύ), Antipater admired as elevated and stately; as ὄβριμον, "mighty," a word applied by Homer to Ares, Achilles and Hector.[147] Antimachus himself is ἀκάματος, implying that he consistently maintains the high style that alone is "worthy of the dignity of the heroes of old" (ἄξιον ἀρχαίων ὀφρύος[148] ἡμιθέων). As for

144. This rather inappropriate image seems to derive from Pindar, *P*. 1. 87, ἀψευδεῖ δὲ πρὸς ἄκμονι χάλκευε γλῶσσαν, where however the reference is not to the writing of poetry, but to speaking the truth.

145. *HE* II. 87.

146. ἑτέρων ἴχνια μὴ καθ' ὁμά (l. 26); μηδ' οἷμον ἀνὰ πλατύν (28); *AP* 12. 43, οὐδὲ κελεύθῳ / χαίρω τίς πολλοὺς ὧδε καὶ ὧδε φέρει.

147. Ebeling, *Lexicon Homericum* II (1885), 21.

148. Another metaphor applied to Aeschylus by Aristophanes (*Frogs* 925).

his praise of Antimachus's ἀγέλαστον ὄπα, the allusion (I suggest) is to
the lightness and wit of the Callimachean style, *unworthy* (in Antipater's
judgment) of the many heroic themes he treated in the *Aetia* and *Hecale*.
Antimachus, by contrast, was always appropriately dignified.[149] It was
precisely this feature of Antimachus's style that Asclepiades had characterized as σεμνοτέρη.

These are not casual allusions to Callimachus's criticisms. Antipater's
entire poem (as Dilthey saw long ago) is a defense of Antimachus.
Antipater closes by insisting that, while Antimachus is naturally not as
good as Homer, he is still the best of the rest. This point too should be a
response to some criticism of Callimachus, no doubt made in the complete
epigram of which we have only F 398. In what way did Callimachus link
Antimachus and Homer? Most moderns, following Dilthey's lead, would
answer that he classified them *together*, condemning Antimachus for reviv-
ing the obsolete pomposity of the Homeric style.[150]

But if Callimachus had really taken this line, how do we explain his frequent and subtle Homeric imitations and his evident fascination with the
niceties of Homeric diction? There may in fact be a way to recover what he
said about Antimachus and Homer. The source is a text long known but
never exploited in connection with Callimachus, *Ep.* 54 of Gregory
Nazianzen:[151]

> τὸ λακωνίζειν οὐ τοῦτό ἐστι, ὅπερ οἴει, ὀλίγας συλλαβὰς γράφειν, ἀλλὰ
> περὶ πλείστων ὀλίγας. οὕτως ἐγὼ καὶ βραχυλογώτατον Ὅμηρον λέγω, καὶ
> πολὺν τὸν Ἀντίμαχον. πῶς; τοῖς πράγμασι κρίνων τὸ μῆκος, ἀλλ' οὐ τοῖς
> γράμμασι.

> Being laconic is not what you think, writing few syllables, but writing little
> about much. So in my judgment Homer is the most succinct of writers, while
> Antimachus is verbose. How can this be? I judge length by substance rather
> than words.

The letter is addressed to Gregory's literary friend Nicobulus, a poet himself,[152] who would have appreciated the allusions. To start with, this is the
complete letter, which is therefore itself a perfect illustration of "being
laconic." The comparison between Homer and Antimachus is neatly ex-

---

149. So already Dilthey, more eloquently if with several errors of detail: *sermonis enim
cultui delicato et quasi enervi austerum adeoque ferreum Antimachi genus oppositum est*
(1863, 20). We may compare an epigram by Antipater's homonym from Thessalonica, contrasting "masculine Homer" with the "waterdrinkers," chief among whom he means Callimachus (*AP* 11. 20; on the "waterdrinkers," Ch. XIII. 1).

150. *nosse sufficiat, Callimachi sensum ab Homericis carminibus abhorruisse, ut quae
destituta essent novarum rerum lenociniis atque exquisitiorum fabularum oblectamentis* (21).

151. *Epp.* 54 = T 36 in Wyss 1936, lxxi.

152. M.-M. Hauser-Meury, *Prosopographie zu den Schriften Gregors von Nazianz*
(Bonn 1960), 128-31.

pressed, but is it likely to be an independent judgment by Gregory, based simply and solely on his own reading? Ancient (like modern) commentators naturally drew attention to the rapidity[153] and brevity[154] of Homeric narration, but there seems to be no other example of an *unfavorable* comparison between Homer and Antimachus in this respect. Antimachus enjoyed a curiously contradictory reputation. In the rhetorical tradition (ordinarily the most likely source for a late antique orator like Gregory) the judgment was highly favorable: second epic poet after Homer, or at any rate in the top three or four. So Dionysius of Halicarnassus, Quintilian, Sopater, Proclus. The Emperor Hadrian actually preferred Antimachus to Homer.[155] It was in the poetic tradition that he was damned, by Callimachus and poets dependent on Callimachus (Catullus, for example)[156] or scholiasts citing Callimachus.[157]

Now Gregory was perhaps the most enthusiastic reader Callimachus had in the fourth century of our era. Any observant reader of Pfeiffer's edition will have noticed the frequent echoes and occasional verbatim quotations cited from Gregory's poems, letters and treatises,[158] and with the aid of the TLG the list can now be extended. In particular, there are perhaps as many as ten reminiscences from the forty lines of the *Aetia* prologue alone.[159] The final sentence of *Ep.* 54 is a less colourful version of F 1. 17-18 (τέχνη κρίνετε, μὴ σχοίνῳ Περσίδι τὴν σοφίην), a passage that he quotes

153. Erbse's index s.v. *brevitas, Scholia Graeca in Homeri Iliadem* vii (1988), p. 150*b*.; e.g. the note on Ο. 6-7 (Erbse IV. 4. 67f.), θαυμασίως δὲ ἐν τάχει πάντα παρέλαβε.

154. Philemon F 97K = 99K-A (*PCG* VII. 281): οὗτος γὰρ ἡμῖν μυριάδας ἐπῶν γράφει,/ ἀλλ' οὐδὲ εἰς Ὅμηρον εἴρηκεν μακρόν; for many more references, J. Baar, *Index zu den Ilias-Scholien* (Baden-Baden 1961) and Erbse, *Scholia Graeca in Homeri Iliadem* vi (1983), p. 495, s.v. σύντομος and συντομία; M. Van der Valk, *Eustathii Comm. in Iliadem* II (Leiden 1976), lvi-lvii; J. Rusten, *Dionysius Scytobrachion* (1982), 61-2.

155. T 24, 28, 31, 35 and 38 Wyss; for the various canons of epic poets, *PEG* i. 166, 173-74. Hadrian is also said to have preferred Ennius to Vergil.

156. *at populus tumido gaudeat Antimacho* (where *tumido* = παχεῖ), Catullus 95. 10.

157. T 19 = Call. F 398. Duris of Samos is also said to have criticized him (T 1). Proclus the Neoplatonist, obliged to defend Plato's well known praise of Antimachus, accuses Callimachus and Duris of "talking nonsense" (T 1).

158. A few are collected in Pfeiffer's index (II p. 132); see too Hollis 1990, 165, 321.

159. 4: *carm.* II. 2. 4. 184 (*PG* 37. 1519), διηνεκὲς εἰς ἓν ἀγείρω; 4/9: *carm.* I. 2. 14-15 (*PG* 37. 471), πολλαῖς χιλιάσιν ἐπέων...ὀλιγόστιχα ταῦτα χαράξω; 6: *carm.* II. 2. 1. 324 (*PG* 37. 1474), πολλὰς εἰς ἐτέων δεκάδας; 8: *carm.* II. 2. 1. 7-16, φθόνῳ...φθόνῳ...τήκοντι...τέμνων ὁδοὺς ἀτρίπτους; 18: see next note; 28: *carm.* I. 2. 2. 64 (*PG* 37. 583), στεινὸν δὲ διεξελάσῃς πυλεῶν; 37: *AP* 8. 152. 3, οὐ νέμεσις· κείνοις γάρ...; and though there are certainly other possible sources (Pfeiffer, *Hermes* 1928, 324), given Gregory's evident fascination with this passage, it may be from 33-4 that εἰ ὄντως δρόσῳ μόνη τρέφονται τέττιγες in *Epp.* 26 derives. Two of Gregory's epitaphs use the phrase ἐπὶ τυτθόν, but in the sense "for a short time": *AP* 8. 125. 1 and 124. 1 (where the MS and editors give ἔτι, but sense and context require ἐπί; just as in 125. 1 ἐπὶ τυτθόν is picked up by οὐ μακρόν in l. 2, so it is picked up in 124 by οὐκ ἐπὶ δήν in l. 4). For πολλάκι and ἐπιτρύζουσιν in l. 1 see the texts cited on pp. 339-40.

more or less verbatim in the related *Ep.* 51: τί...τῇ Περσικῇ σχοίνῳ μετρεῖσθαι δεῖ τὴν σοφίαν. "What evil Telchines, what spiteful demons," he exclaimed in his polemic against Julian, inspired the Apostate to forbid Christians to teach the Classics (τίνες Τελχῖνες πονηροὶ καὶ βάσκανοι δαίμονες)![160] We may·safely assume that Gregory was familiar with the main lines of Callimachean literary polemic.

In the circumstances, it is tempting to infer that it was from Callimachus (whether directly or indirectly) that Gregory drew his unfavourable comparison between Homer and Antimachus. It should be noted that the epithet with which he characterizes Antimachus is πολύν, which in the context must be equivalent to πολυλογώτατον ("verbose"), in opposition to βραχυλογώτατον. This is certainly no normal prose usage, but would be natural enough in a poet, unable or unwilling to use so cumbersome and prosaic a term in opposition to (say) σύντομος. This inference from Gregory is supported by two passages in Plutarch. First, his treatise on garrulity, which cites two poets in particular as exemplary: first Homer (504CD), who always entertains because of his constant novelty, while the garrulous man will drone on forever, "especially if he has read Antimachus of Colophon" (513B). Second, *Life of Timoleon* 26, which draws a slightly different contrast between Antimachus and Homer; Antimachus was powerful, but forced and laborious, while Homer had the charm of seeming to have been composed easily and without effort.

We may compare Callimachus's epitaph on Theris the Cretan (*AP* vii. 447):

σύντομος ἦν ὁ ξεῖνος, ὃ καὶ στίχος οὐ μακρὰ λέξων
  "Θῆρις Ἀρισταίου Κρής" ἐπ' ἐμοὶ δολιχός.

The stranger was a man of few words, and the verse on me, though brief—Theris the Cretan, son of Aristaeus—is long enough.

The details of this poem must remain uncertain,[161] but the general point is clear enough: the *relativity* of long and short. It would be an elegant paradox to represent the 48 books of Homer as "more succinct" than Antimachus. F 398 might be filled out (purely exempli gratia) on the following lines:[162]

---

160. *Or.* 4. 101 (*PG* 35. 636C); he also protests when a literary friend calls him a Telchis: *Ep.* 190 (*PG* 37. 309B).

161. Is the tomb the speaker, so that ἐπ' ἐμοὶ refers to the verse inscribed on itself? Or is it Theris who is speaking: "the verse is too long for me." Planudes's ὑπ' ἐμοί raises further possibilities, and some have suggested that Theris was short of stature rather than (or in addition to) speech: *HE* II. 192-3; Fraser II. 825 n. 212.

162. For the possibility that F 532 comes from later in the same epigram, p. 320 above; Callimachus presumably discussed Antimachus in more detail in his (prose) *Against Praxiphanes* as well, but this is not likely to have survived till Gregory's day.

Λύδη καὶ παχὺ γράμμα καὶ οὐ τορόν· < ἦ γὰρ Ὅμηρος
σύντομος αὐτὸς ἔην, Ἀντίμαχος δὲ πολύς. >

For Callimachus, repudiation of Antimachus did not imply repudiation of
Homer. Bombast and lack of clarity (παχὺ...καὶ οὐ τορόν) were *not* characteristic of Homeric style, nor were they to be found only in epic (as we saw
in the *Frogs*). In fact the Homeric commentators regularly praise Homer
for the absence of precisely these vices. As one scholiast put it, echoing the
standard doctrine of the schools: "a narrative should have three virtues,
clarity, conciseness and plausibility" (τρεῖς δὲ ἀρεταὶ διηγήσεως, σαφήνεια, συντομία, πιθανότης).[163] Despite its sheer length, Homeric narrative is conspicuously clear and concise.[164] Interestingly enough, Wilamowitz made exactly the same point about Aratus. After citing παχὺ ...καὶ
οὐ τορόν as the antithesis of Callimachus's stylistic ideal, he remarked that
"Aratus's aim was to be succinct and clear, σύντομος and σαφής."[165]
Obviously Callimachus set himself the same goals. It was in this sense that
Homer himself, epic style and 48 books notwithstanding, was "the most
concise of poets" (βραχυλογώτατον). It was not for attempting to write
like Homer that Antimachus was condemned. It was not the genre but the
poet who was at fault.

7

So there was no great dispute about different types of poetry; no battle
between traditional epic and modern poetry; between bad, boring long
poems and elegant, witty brief ones. Just a few contemporaries who disagreed about one particular poem. Epic had nothing to do with it. The
debate about Antimachus centered on his elegy the *Lyde*. There is no reason
to believe that even Callimachus disapproved of his epic *Thebaid*.[166] It
receives nothing but praise from all quarters; we now have fragments from
three or four copies dating from the Roman period, as well as substantial
fragments from a commentary of the same date.[167] As late as the second
century, the *Thebaid* was generally reckoned the second epic after Homer.

---

163. Schol. E. 9a; for the tradition, Volkmann, *Rhetorik²* (1885), 153.

164. For Homeric συντομία, above; for clarity, Erbse's index s.v. σαφήνεια and σαφής.

165. *HD* I. 203 ("Aratos will knapp und klar sein, σύντομος und σαφής").

166. It is not as obvious as D.W.T.W. Vessey thought that, if Callimachus "disliked the
Lyde, he is likely to have had an even lower opinion of the *Thebais*, which he must have
regarded as an example of that hated genre τὸ ποίημα τὸ κυκλικόν" (*Hermes* 99 [1971], 3).

167. See the fragments collected in *SH* 52-76 and 912 (*P. Oxy.* 2516, 2518-19), to
which we may now add the new scraps published by H. Maehler, *Atti del XVII Congresso
Internazionale di Papirologia* II (Naples 1984), 289-296. *SH* 62-75 (*P. Oxy.* 2516) comes
from the poem that was the object of the commentary published in Wyss pp. 76-89, which
cannot be identified with certainty as the *Thebaid*. On the fame of the *Thebaid*, see Vessey,
Hermes 99 (1971), 1-10; *Philologus* 114 (1970), 118-43 (probably not used by Statius); and

It was only the *Lyde* that was controversial. Not that it really deserved all Callimachus's abuse. It was not extravagantly bad nor even extravagantly long. Until Callimachus wrote it was universally considered a masterpiece. As for the assumption that Callimachus lost the battle, this too is no more than an inference from the polemical way he chose to present himself, a lone voice of sanity in a world of bad taste. There is nothing outside his own polemic to support the view that he was an unpopular minority taste until the age of Catullus. There is no real evidence that the *Aetia* itself was ever controversial at all. It seems to have been an instant success and the *Lyde* disappeared almost without trace; not a single papyrus and the merest handful of quotations in the grammarians.

Henrichs, *GRBS* 13 (1972), 77.

Chapter XII

One Continuous Poem

1

And yet scholars write of "Callimachus's famous refusal to write an epic,"[1] and reconstruct his epic likes and dislikes with extraordinary precision. Here is the relevant passage of the *Aetia* prologue. It will be noticed that both text and translation differ somewhat from current editions, foreshadowing the interpretation that follows:

πολλάκ]ι μοι Τελχῖνες ἐπιτρύζουσιν ἀοιδῆς
νήϊδες οἳ Μούσης οὐκ ἐγένοντο φίλοι,
εἵνεκεν οὐχ ἓν ἄεισμα διηνεκὲς ἢ βασιλ[ήων
πρήξι]ας ἐν πολλαῖς ἤνυσα χιλιάσιν
ἢ προτέ]ρους ἥρωας, ἔπος δ' ἐπὶ τυτθὸν ἐλ[αύνω
παῖς ἅτε, τῶν δ' ἐτέων ἡ δεκὰς οὐκ ὀλίγη.

Again and again the Telchines squeak away at me, ignorant of poetry as they are, no friends of the Muses, because (they claim) it is not one continuous poem I have written on the deeds of kings or heroes of old in many thousands of lines, but instead childlike steer my song into small compass, despite my decades not a few.

First, a few notes on the text. Line 1: A) πολλάκ]ι Lobel, followed by Torraca (1969, 22; see Pfeiffer for other suggestions). As E. Fraenkel pointed out ("Eine Anfangsformel Attischer Reden," *Glotta* 39 [1960], 1-5 = *Kl. Beitr.* II [1964], 505-10), many speeches in Attic drama, Thucydides and the orators begin with some such formula as πολλάκις μέν..., οἱ μὲν πολλοί..., πολλῶν μέν...(e.g. Aesch. *Pers.* 176; *Ag.* 1372; Soph. *Tr.* 49; Eur. *Alc.* 747; Thuc. 1. 80. 1, 2. 35. 1, 3. 37. 1; Ar. *Thesm.* 830; Lys. 3. 1; Dem. 9. 1). Ten epigrams in the Anthology begin with πολλάκι(ς), another dozen with πολλά, πολλοί or the like (Beckby's ed. IV² 741), to which we may add the early Ptolemaic elegy *SH* 969. 1 (cf. *SH* 391. 1). Gregory Nazianzen began at least four poems with πολλάκι(ς): *carm.* II. 1. 19. 1; II. i. 51. 1; *AP* 8. 37 and 210). It would strike a very natural note as the first word of a personal address by the poet. Many of the later poetic examples may be influenced by this much quoted poem.

1. E.g. W. Clausen, *GRBS* 5 (1964), 181.

Line 1: B) With Hunt (and Pfeiffer's first thoughts: 1928, 309), I read ἀοιδῆς, dependent on νήϊδες, rather than -ῇ (η the Florentine scholiast), for two reasons. First, νῆϊς used absolutely means "feeble" or "powerless" (note especially the one Homeric example, H. 198, and *h. Merc.* 487), not "ignorant" in the abusive sense required by the context. Elsewhere Callimachus uses the word with the genitive, and in the neutral sense "inexperienced in," "unacquainted with": F 75. 49, χαλεποῦ νήϊδές εἰσι θεοῦ (= Eros); F 178. 33, ναυτιλίης εἰ νῆϊν ἔχεις βίον. Compare Choerilus of Samos, F 2. 1-2, ἴδρις ἀοιδῆς / Μουσάων θεράπων (*PEG* 191); cf. too Pindar, F 198a, ἀδαήμονα Μοισᾶν, and νῆϊς ἔφυς Μουσέων in anon. *AP* ix. 191. 6 and 583. 2. There are also problems of construction and interpretation with the dative. Does the verb govern a double dative, or do we (with Pfeiffer) construe: μοι τρύζουσιν ἐπὶ ἀοιδῇ ("squeak at my poem")?

Line 1: C) τρύζουσιν is usually translated "mutter," "murmur" or "grumble," but is only elsewhere used of mice (Babrius 112. 8), cicadas (Paul Sil, *AP* vi. 54. 7), bats and birds (often in Gregory Nazianzen: bats, *Or.* 35. 2 (*PG* 35. 257D); birds, *carm.* II. 2. 3. 96 (*PG* 35. 1487. 4; cf. ib. 1506. 9); *PG* 35. 925. 20 and 1229. 35; and, metaphorically, *carm.* II. 1. 19. 72 (*PG* 35. 1277. 2), πολλοὶ μὲν τρύζεσκον ἐμοῖς παθέεσσιν ἄπιστοι. "Squeak" better suits the little gnome-like creatures the "real" Telchines are, and also better conveys Callimachus's contempt. Hunter 1992, 190 argues for "indistinct muttering," a "whispering campaign."

Line 1: D) I prefer Friedlaender's ἐλ[αύνω to Hunt's generally accepted ἐλ[ίσσω. ἐλίσσω normally means read (turn the roll) rather than write.[2] Compare rather "steer your own course" (τὴν κατὰ σαυτὸν ἔλα, *AP* vii. 89. 12 and 16) in the famous epigram on Pittacus. Moreover L. Lehnus has recently drawn attention to a likely echo in a riddle epigram of Metrodorus:[3]

> ὦ μάκαρ, ὃς δισσὰς ἤνυσα χιλιάδας
> πρὸς δ' ἔτι πέντ' ἐπὶ ταῖς ἑκατοντάδας ἔνθεν ἐλαύνω.

To be sure the units here are measurements of distance, and ἐλαύνω means simply "drive" or "travel." Nonetheless, it is hard to doubt that ἤνυσα χιλιάδας is an echo of so famous a passage, in which case Metrodorus's ἐλαύνω in the same metrical position suggests a further echo.

Line 2: Given the centrality of the entire chorus of Muses in the *Aetia* as a whole, with Wilamowitz I print Μούσης for the Μούσης of the papyrus.

Now for interpretation. First, it cannot be emphasized too strongly that lines 3-4 are not normative but descriptive. The critics are not (as usually

---

2. See, despite his note on F 1. 6, the texts cited by Pfeiffer on F 468 (esp. *SH* 705. 16).
3. *AP* xiv. 121. 10-11; *ZPE* 89 (1991), 24.

assumed) complaining because Callimachus has *refused* to write an epic—or any other sort of poem. Why should he? Why should anyone have wanted him to? By all means criticize a man for poems he *has* written. But who ever heard of anyone being criticized for *not* writing a poem, especially for not writing a very specific sort of poem?[4]

Still less is he laying down what other poets should or should not do. He is simply reporting what critics (allegedly) criticize *about his own poetry*. This criticism cannot be interpreted (as in practice it usually has been) in a vacuum. The *Aetia* prologue is not an independent poem. It is a prologue. On the traditional view it is the prologue to Callimachus's entire oeuvre, republished in Pfeiffer's collected edition of ca 245. On my view, it is simply the prologue to *Aetia* I-II published ca 270. On either hypothesis, Callimachus's words must apply to the poem or poems the prologue introduces.

The traditional interpretation in practice rests on the tacit assumption that the criticism Callimachus puts in the mouth of the Telchines accurately and fairly reflects real criticisms made of his work. For Lyne, "Callimachus *accepts* an accusation that he does not write poems on a grand scale."[5] Newman was concerned to discover just what inspired the "ferocity" and "venom" of these critics:[6] "Only a flouting of tradition to this degree [i.e. not writing an epic!] could account for the venomous reaction of conservatives, who had found their dearest prejudices challenged." But one usually caricatures criticisms one deigns to reply to. And in any case, the venom and ferocity is all on Callimachus's side.

Much of the *Aetia* prologue simply illustrates Callimachus's lexicon of critical abuse, as vivid and varied as any before Housman. But there is surely some descriptive content in ἓν ἄεισμα διηνεκές, "one continuous song." διηνεκές must imply something more specific than just length, adequately taken care of in the "many thousands of lines." It is not a standard rhetorical term, and seems not to have been applied elsewhere to a poem.[7] In a couple of texts we find the near-synonym συνεχής applied to the *Iliad*. μακράν τινα καὶ συνεχῆ ποίησιν, according to Dio Chrysostom (*Or.* 36. 12)—but he is contrasting it with the distichs of Phocylides! Eustathius too describes the *Iliad* as συνεχές,[8] but when making the point that it was the Alexandrians who divided it into 24 books. Neither is characterizing it as a particular sort of poem.

---

4. As we shall see in Ch. XVIII, the *recusatio* of the Roman poets is very different.

5. *MD* 12 (1984), 17.

6. *The Classical Epic Tradition* (1986), 26; cf. 31, "This was the challenge that outraged his critics. Nothing less explains their ferocity."

7. It is however found as a grammatical term, of words that influence the accent of the following word; H. Erbse, *Scholia Graeca in Homeri Iliadem* vi (1983), index, p. 311 (s.v.).

8. 5. 32 = I. 9. 1 van der Valk.

A recently found fragmentary discussion of poetic οἰκονομία seems to compare the *Argonautica* of Apollonius, Cleo of Curium and Dionysius Scytobrachion.[9] One of the three is described as "succinct" (σύντομός τις, line 11); then we have "more Homeric" (13); then, after an apparent reference to digressions (παρεκβάς), the words συνεχέσι καὶ πολυστίχοις (17). It might seem tempting to interpret it in terms of the traditional view of the *Aetia* prologue: a verbose, traditionalist Apollonius contrasted with poets who cultivated brevity and discontinuity. But with only the right-hand side of the column and no indication how long the lines are, there is no way of telling which of the three is being praised for brevity.[10] The editors of *SH* take it to be Apollonius. "More Homeric" must in any case imply praise rather than blame; comparisons with Homer are always positive (Ch. X. 3), and Homeric συντομία was proverbial (p. 335). More important, the writer is comparing three epic poets, not epic with something else. No support here for the traditional interpretation of the *Aetia* prologue—but a nice parallel for my interpretation (Ch. XI. 5), a comparison of different representatives of the same genre.

Amplified as it is with kings and heroes in many thousands of lines, ἓν ἄεισμα διηνεκές has often been read as a straightforward definition of epic. It is scarcely that. At least four very different interpretations have been proposed, and it may help to begin by distinguishing them.

1) Malcolm Heath has recently suggested (as a remote possibility) that "Callimachus is presenting the *Aetia* as themselves a refutation of his critics; in that case 'single and continuous' will be true of the *Aetia*, and must therefore have the sense 'formally connected' rather than 'possessing a unified subject-matter.'"[11] This is essentially a view I once held myself, but ἄεισμα διηνεκές can hardly be divorced from the undoubtedly pejorative "many thousands of lines": it must be what he has not written rather than what he has written.

2) Most have assumed that "continuous song" simply means "narrative" or "epic," giving διηνεκές no limiting force. So Wilamowitz (before the publication of the *Aetia* prologue):[12] "it is hard to believe that, after the publication of the *Aetia* or *Hecale*, Callimachus could have said of himself, εἵνεκεν οὐχ ἓν ἄεισμα διηνεκὲς ἤνυσα." That is to say, he took it for granted that *any* long poem would qualify as an ἄεισμα διηνεκές, continuous narrative. But not all epics do consist of *continuous* narrative—most conspicuously (as we shall see) the two longest and most famous of all, the *Iliad* and *Odyssey*.

---

9. J.S. Rusten, *Dionysius Scytobrachion* (Cologne 1982), 53-64 = *SH* 339A (II A.D.); M. Campbell, *CR* 33 (1983), 315; Hutchinson 1988, 86 n. 2.

10. In a comparison, a ὁ δέ would be enough to change the reference.

11. M. Heath, *Unity in Greek Poetics* (Oxford 1989), 56.

12. *HD* I. 184; so too M. Pohlenz, *Hermes* 68 (1933), 320 n.2.

3) For Brink, what Callimachus condemned was "the long, *uninter-rupted*, epic poem," leading him to the opposite conclusion. ἕν he identified as the unity for which Aristotle admired Homer, assuming that it was for this very quality that Callimachus rejected imitation of Homer.[13] This was also Pfeiffer's view: "The new poetical school of Callimachus and his followers was ostentatiously ·anti-Aristotelian. Rejecting unity, completeness, and magnitude, it consciously aimed at a discontinuous form."[14] So too more recently Lyne: "Callimachus is admitting...that he neglects what most ancient critics, certainly Aristotle, would deem a cardinal virtue: unity of plot, continuity· of narrative technique."[15] But what would unity have meant to Callimachus? For modern critics, unity is both a positive and a central quality in any work of literature; to accuse a work of lacking unity is automatically to disparage it.[16] To reject the concept would indeed be provocative. But Heath's recent book has questioned its centrality in ancient critical writing.[17] We do not need to accept his thesis in its strongest form; however much it may be in some sense presupposed, there is no single ancient term for the modern concept of unity and it is not often expressly and explicitly formulated. Not even Aristotle's "single plot" and "one action" are quite unity as modern critics use the term; his ἕν καὶ ὅλον is as much concerned with wholeness and proportion as unity.[18] Callimachus's ἕν need not and should not be read as anything so simple and drastic as a rejection of unity in the modern sense. ἕν (as we shall see) takes its colour and emphasis from διηνεκές.

4) The fourth interpretation goes back more than a century to L. Adam,[19] and in my judgment is the only one that does justice to the facts. He argued that the reference is to continuous, linear narrative, or to put it in Callimachean idiom, the "Cyclic" manner, in which the poet simply records one event after another without any structure or climax, as though writing a chronicle. Here is the famous passage of Aristotle on Homeric unity of action:[20]

---

13. *CQ* 40 (1946), 17-18.

14. Pfeiffer 1968, 137. It is hard to imagine what a work lacking all these qualities would look like, and it is significant that it is only conveniently lost works like the *Aetia* and *Hecale* for which such claims have been made.

15. R.O.A.M. Lyne, *MD* 12 (1984), 18.

16. The *Hymn to Artemis*, for example, has often been criticised for lack of unity: for a recent defense on traditional lines, P. Bing and V. Uhrmeister, *JHS* 114 (1994), 19-34.

17. Heath 1989; for various reservations, D. M. Schenkeveld, *Mnemos.* 45 (1992), 1-8; A. Ford, *Arion* n.s. 3 (1991), 125-54.

18. So Horace's *simplex dumtaxat et unum*: Brink, *Horace on Poetry* II (1971), 77-104.

19. *Die Aristotelische Theorie vom Epos nach ihrer Entwicklung bei Griechen und Römern* (Wiesbaden 1889), 74; so too S. Koster, *Antike Epostheorien* (Wiesbaden 1970), 117-19; Hunter 1993, 190-95.

20. *Poetics* 1451a16-35. The reference to the wound on Parnassus is a notorious puzzle, since it *is* in fact mentioned in the *Odyssey* (it is the source of the scar recognized by Eurycleia). The solution, as K. Gautar saw (*Ziva Antika* 11 [1962], 294; cf. G. E. Dimock,

So it seems clear that poets who composed *Heracleïds, Theseïds* and the like were making a mistake. They think that since Heracles was a single person it follows that the plot will be single too. But Homer, superior as he is in all other respects, appears to have grasped this point well also, thanks either to art or nature, for in composing an *Odyssey* he did not incorporate into it everything that happened to the hero (for example, how he was wounded on Mt. Parnassus or how he feigned madness at the muster, neither of which events, by happening, made it at all necessary or probable that the other should happen). Instead, he composed the *Odyssey* and the *Iliad* similarly around a unified action of the kind we have been talking about.

The action of both *Iliad* and *Odyssey* covered only a few weeks. Most of Odysseus's wanderings are related in flashbacks; and it was precisely the remarkable concentration of the *Iliad* on the single theme of Achilles's wrath that spawned Cyclic sequels to tell the rest of the story of the Trojan war.[21] There was no accepted ancient term to denote this "chronicle" style. Horace too, like Callimachus, expressed it through negatives: the good poet will *not* begin the story of Diomedes's return as far back as the death of Meleager, or the Trojan war with the twin egg:

> nec reditum Diomedis ab interitu Meleagri,
> nec gemino bellum Troianum orditur ab ovo.

Like Homer, he will begin *in medias res* and build up to a natural conclusion. On the Brink-Pfeiffer interpretation, neither *Aetia* nor *Hecale* could be considered an ἄεισμα διηνεκές because, though long, they were not unified or uninterrupted. But whereas the *Aetia* could fairly be described as lacking both unity and continuity as usually defined, the *Hecale* (as we shall see) could not.

The root meaning of διηνεκές[22] suggests "continuous" or "unbroken," and a number of usages (e.g. applied to time or laws or, in Aristotle, to the universe)[23] suggest temporal rather than thematic continuity. In poetry, perhaps the closest parallel is the Homeric formula διηνεκέως ἀγορεύειν,

---

The Unity of the Odyssey [1989], 3-4), lies in the μέν and δέ; Aristotle means that Homer included only the first of the two episodes, *deliberately* omitting the second because the two could not cohere in the same poem. The story of the boar hunt illustrates Odysseus's heroism, the pretence of cowardice the reverse. A poem that told both stories would have no unity. For other recent discussions, P. J. van der Eijk, *Mnemosyne* 40 (1987), 140-3; N. van der Ben, ib. 143-8; Heath 1989, 48.

21. According to Proclus, the Cycle survived "not so much for its quality as for the sequence of events it contains" (διὰ τὴν ἀκολουθίαν τῶν ἐν αὐτῷ πραγμάτων, p. 97. 10 Allen).

22. δια + ενεκ, related to ἐνεγκεῖν: H. Frisk, *Griech. Etym. Wörterbuch* I (1960), 391.

23. *LSJ* s.v. (p. 427).

"tell from beginning to end."[24] Newman has acutely observed that in Apollonius this same formula seems to carry a more negative connotation: the speaker is reluctant to provide what he sees as tedious detail.[25] Applied to the structure of a poem, such a word would suit *Heracleïds* and *Theseïds* rather than *Iliad* and · *Odyssey*. The one relevant detail in the new Scytobrachion papyrus is its association of συνεχέσι καὶ πολυστίχοις (*SH* 339A. 17), where συνεχέσι clearly has negative connotations, "continuous" in the sense "never-ending."

If διηνεκές has pejorative connotations, so too does ἕν. The reference is less to unity than to uniformity, what both ancient critics and the scholiasts on Homer and Vergil call μονοειδεία, τὸ μονοειδές, τὸ ὁμοειδές. They mention it as something to be avoided, and praise writers for the different ways they contrive to avoid it, for their *poikilia* or *variatio*.[26] An example where we find distinctly negative Latin equivalents for both ἕν and διηνεκές is Ti. Claudius Donatus's note on *Aen.* 6. 854, *ne una et continua narratio taediosa sit.*[27]

Even closer and more directly relevant is the second stanza of Horace *Odes* i. 7. Let others praise the great cities of Greece:

> sunt quibus *unum* opus est intactae Palladis urbem
> *carmine perpetuo* celebrare...

In a context where Horace is criticizing long Greek poems, few have doubted an echo of the *Aetia* prologue. Once again, we have Latin equivalents for both ἕν and διηνεκές, both again depreciatory. The *unum* functions differently in Horace ("there are some whose only object..."), but if it was inspired (as seems virtually certain) by Callimachus's ἕν, then Horace surely read it as implying monotony rather than unity.

2

Such an interpretation of ἓν ἄεισμα διηνεκές suits what else we know of Callimachus's poetics very well. Avoidance of μονοειδεία would be natural in one who prided himself on his πολυειδεία.[28] Now that we no longer

---

24. A. Heubeck, S. West, J. B. Hainsworth, *Comm. on Homer's Odyssey* i (1988), 244.

25. I. 649; II. 391; III. 401; Newman 1974, 355.

26. Arist. *Rhet.* 1414b29; Polyb. 9. 1. 2; Dion. Hal. *Lys.* 15; *Ant.* 1. 8. 3; the Homer scholia passim: H. Erbse, *Scholia Graeca in Homeri Iliadem* vi (Berlin 1983), index, pp. 411 (μονοειδεία), 420 (ὁμοειδές); Kroll, *Studien* 1924, 226; Heath 1989, 102-123, 159, 175.

27. For other examples, the index to Georgii's edition of Ti. Cl. Donatus II (1905), 671 s.v. *interruptio taedii evitandi causa*; cf. Servius on *Geo.* ii. 195, *varietatis causa, ne uniformis narratio sit*; Heath 1989, 159.

28. Dieg. to F 203.

have to explain Callimachus's work in terms of deliberate rejection of unity,[29] we may turn to examining what sort of unity (however defined) it actually possesses. As Naeke saw in a brilliantly intuitive study 150 years ago, long before the discovery of any of the papyri, the *Hecale* was *not* an ἄεισμα διηνεκές (in the bad sense); it was Homeric rather than Cyclic. There is a unified action which incorporates past and future events in skilfully integrated flashbacks and prophecies. Naeke emphasized[30]

> quam diversae a scriptoribus rerum Atticarum, quos Plutarchus sequitur, vel Theseidos alicuius, rationes fuerint Callimachi, qui ex tanto fabularum numero unam tantum more tractandam epico elegisset.

Not only did Callimachus not reject Aristotle's teaching. He even took one of Aristotle's own illustrations of an unsuitable subject for epic treatment—the Theseus saga—and showed how the job could be done by selecting a single exploit. Though no longer than two or three medium sized books of Homer, Callimachus clearly took great pains to endow his miniepic with a genuinely Homeric unity.

The same seems to have been true of the (at least) six-book *Messeniaca* of his younger contemporary Rhianus. It was an early nineteenth-century critic, A. Meineke, who drew this important conclusion[31] from the following passage of Pausanias:[32]

> The history of this war of the Messenians was composed by Rhianus of <Le>bena in epic verse, and by Myron of Priene in prose. Neither of these writers composed a complete history of the war from beginning to end: each of them chose a special part.... Rhianus did not touch on the first war at all: what he did write was the history of the Messenians revolt from the Lacedaemonians, and not the whole of it, but only the events subsequent to the battle of the Great Trench, as the place was called. The Messenian, for whose sake I have made all this mention of Rhianus and Myron, is Aristomenes, the first and greatest glory of the Messenian name.

Pausanias goes on to compare Rhianus's technique directly with Homer: "in Rhianus's epic Aristomenes shines out like Achilles in Homer's *Iliad*" (4. 6. 3). Of course, this cannot in itself have made it a good poem. But it does show that some poets did take Aristotle's criticisms to heart. Newman writes contemptuously of "pseudo-Homeric" poets producing "imitations

---

29. So, rightly, Newman 1986, 44.

30. *Opusc. Acad.* II (1845), 205; cf. Adam, *Aristotelische Theorie* 86. For Naeke's work on the *Hecale*, G. Benedetto, *Il sogno e l'invettiva* (Florence 1993), passim.

31. "So sind wir zur der Annahme berechtigt, dass das Gedicht des Rhianos ein wohlgeschlossenes Ganze gebildet habe, welches in der Verherrlichung des Aristomenes seinen poetischen Mittelpunkt hatte und den Namen eines Epos im höheren Sinne verdiente," *Abhandlungen der Königl. Akademie der Wissenschaften* 1832, 99f.; cf. Adam, *Aristotelische Theorie* (1889), 87-89; Koster, *Antike Epostheorien* (1970), 122-23.

32. IV. 6. 1-2 (tr. J. G. Frazer) = *FGrH* 265 F 42, with Jacoby's very full notes.

of Homer's mannerisms which miss his essence," but admires Apollonius's *Argonautica* as a "revivification of the epic style" under "the influence and example of Callimachus."[33] Rhianus he does not even mention. Callimachus's criticisms of the μεγὰ ψοφέουσαν ἀοιδήν and the main road certainly allude to the traditional high style of epic, what might be called "Homer's mannerisms." But, as Aristotle saw, the structure of the *Iliad* is something closer to its essence. And it is Rhianus who imitated the structure of the *Iliad*, while the *Argonautica* has no such clear-cut focus or structure.[34]

It was clearly literary rather than personal motives that prompted Rhianus to focus his epic on the figure of Aristomenes, a semi-legendary foreigner dead for half a millennium. We saw in Ch. X. 6 that Rhianus was heavily influenced by Callimachus's epigrams, and a fragment of his *Eliaca* imitates a passage in the *Hecale*.[35] The question about narrative poetry (elegy as well as epic) being debated in the third century was not whether it should be written at all, but rather *how* it should be written. The point was not that Homer was inimitable, but precisely that the source of his greatest strength *could* be imitated. Two hundred years later the lesson was not lost on Vergil; for all its originality and individuality, in structure the *Aeneid* is the most Homeric of all epics.

The same cannot be said of the *Aetia*, with a dozen or so separate episodes to each book. However ingenious the links between these episodes within the books, the general effect must have been variety rather than continuity. This was Callimachus's way of avoiding the monotony he attacks in the prologue. Nonetheless, it is a travesty of the facts to describe the *Aetia* (with Pfeiffer) as a "more or less loose series of pieces of a few lines." What after all would be so remarkable—or unusual—about a series of short poems? This would describe the greater part of Greek poetry outside epic and drama. Reinsch-Werner compared the *Aetia* to a book of Propertian elegies: "the four books consisted of completely separate, brief, loosely linked or quite unconnected stories, in some cases (e.g. the Lock of Berenice) already published on their own before being incorporated in the framework of the *Aetia*."[36]

We now know that the case of the Lock is irrelevant to *Aetia* I-II.[37] We also know that I-II were quite different in structure from III-IV; III-IV

---

33. *The Classical Epic Tradition* (1986), 45, 53, 523, 531; 101 (on Apollonius).

34. Notoriously, modern criticism has tended to focus on its lack of hero and structure; in defense, see now Heath 1989, 65-67; Hunter 1992 passim.

35. Rhian. F 20 ~ Call. F 84 Hollis, with p. 27.

36. *Callimachus Hesiodicus* (1976), 8.

37. In any case, *Aetia* III-IV must have appeared soon after the two Berenice poems were written (Callimachus was in his seventies). Both were no doubt publicly performed on some suitable occasion, and may have circulated separately as well (though the 7c. P.Oxy. 2258 is hardly evidence that the Lock circulated *before* publication in the *Aetia*). But that does not make *Aetia* III-IV a volume of *Kleine Schriften*.

must indeed have consisted of a sequence of separate poems, like the *Iambi* or a book of Propertius. But in form at any rate, I-II were structured as a continuous narrative extending over both books. Individual aetia were embedded in an unbroken dialogue between the poet and the Muses. This has to be seen as a centripetal device counteracting the centrifugal effect of the constantly changing subject matter. Another factor contributing to a degree of thematic coherence is the shared aetiological mode of the stories.

In a sentence that would have cut Callimachus to the heart, B. Wyss once remarked that "large parts of the *Aetia* were no doubt barely distinguishable from Antimachus's *Lyde*."[38] Certainly there were more similarities between these two scholar-poets than Callimachus might have cared to acknowledge. Scanty though the remains of Antimachus, it is clear that Callimachus drew heavily on the work of his predecessor.[39] Nonetheless, as already suggested in the preceding chapter, there were surely important respects in which *Aetia* I-II did differ from and even possess a unity (of a sort) lacking to the *Lyde*.

Antimachus "sat down in his empty house"[40] and put together in the form of a catalogue all the mythical love stories he could find to console himself for Lyde's death. There were many ways such a collection might have been organized, but Antimachus seems to have settled for a chronological rather than thematic principle. A series of references in the Apollonius scholia[41] suggest that he devoted at least one book to the saga of the Argonauts. He began at the beginning, with a catalogue of the Argonauts (F 56), the building of the Argo (F 57), and accounts of various heroes and stops on the way before finally reaching Medea (F 63-4)—and then taking the heroes home again (F 5). In some details he may even have been fuller than Apollonius. He also told of Bellerophon and Oedipus (F 68-70), and presumably many other stories with a more obvious love interest. Not just glancing allusions "but a detailed narrative in the epic manner."[42] In short,

---

38. *magnae partes Aetiorum...a Lyda vix distare viderentur* (p. xxiv).

39. As emphasized by Krevans 1993, 151-53.

40. E.F.M. Benecke, *Antimachus of Colophon and the Position of Women in Greek Poetry* (London 1896), 110. According to Benecke, since the *Lyde* was addressed to Antimachus's wife, it "initiat[ed] the greatest artistic revolution that the world has ever seen," because of its "respect for women and, above all, for marriage...the fundamental principle of the romantic feeling throughout the later Greek poetry" (ib. 108-110). Unfortunately, the passage on which he bases his argument—τήν τε 'Αντιμάχου Λύδην, προσέτι δὲ καὶ τὴν ὁμώνυμον ταύτης ἑταίραν ἣν ἠγάπα Λαμύνθιος ὁ Μιλήσιος, Athen. 596F—does *not* make the explicit distinction Benecke claims between Antimachus's *wife* and Lamynthius's *mistress*. On the contrary, since the entire passage is devoted to courtesans and mistresses, the presumption must be that Lyde was *not* Antimachus's wife.

41. F 58-65 Wyss = West, *Iambi et Elegi Graeci* II 38-40.

42. Wyss, xx-xxiv; Serrao, "La struttura della *Lide* di A.," *QUUC* 32 (1979), 91-98.

what purported to be a consolatory elegy was in fact an ἄεισμα διηνεκές in many thousands of lines telling the stories of kings and heroes.

It is hard to believe it coincidence that the second story in Bk I of the *Aetia* is an episode from the return of the Argonauts. Of course, since so little of the *Lyde* survives, we can only guess. But in the circumstances it is tempting to guess that Callimachus was trying to show how an unwieldy epic saga like the Argonauts could best be treated within the compass of an elegy—as a ·picturesque aetiology. A fragmentary second-century commentary on an unidentifiable poem of Antimachus (p. 81 Wyss) has revealed to us a clear case of an extant passage of the *Aetia* (F 65-6) correcting Antimachus on a point of information, from the *Argive History* of Agias and Derkylos.[43]

Antimachus was notorious for walking closely in Homer's footsteps, as noted by that learned Homerist Porphyry:[44]

> When Antimachus plagiarized Homer, he also corrected him. For example, when Homer says Ἰδεώ θ' ὃς κάρτιστος ἐπιχθονίων γένετ' ἄνδρων, Antimachus says Ἰδεώ θ' ὃς κάρτιστος ἐπιχθονίων ἦν ἄνδρων [F 77]. Lycophron approved this alteration, claiming that it strengthened the line. I say nothing about τὸν δ' ἀπομειβόμενος προσέφη κρείων Διομήδης [F 79], since Homer was satirized by Cratinus for his constant repetition of τὸν δ' ἀπομειβόμενος. Antimachus did not hesitate to use even this hackneyed formula. As for the Homeric lines λαῶν οἷσιν ἄνασσε, πατὴρ δ' ὡς ἤπιος ἦεν and οἱ δ' ἐκεῖ ἀμφοτέρωθεν ἐκαρτύναντο φάλαγγες, Antimachus put together half a line from each: λαῶν οἷσιν ἄνασσε, ἐκαρτύναντο φάλαγγες [F 42].

The "correction" approved by Lycophron is a far cry from the learned Homeric wordgames of the Alexandrians. Antimachus simply turned the line into a spondeiazon, a metrical pattern of which he was inordinately fond.[45] It seems clear from these examples that he continued in the age of the sophists to write as if there had been no break in the epic tradition, as if he were still a rhapsode composing in formulas.[46] Nor does there appear to have been any significant difference between his epic and elegiac style, if we may judge from the longest single fragment of the *Lyde* (F 57), rightly described by Wilamowitz as "virtually a cento of Homeric phrases":[47]

> ἐν δ' ἱστὸν θῆκεν, λαίφεσι δὲ λινέοις
> σοῦσ' ἐτίθει παντοῖα θεά, πόδας ἠδὲ κάλωας,

43. *FGrH* 305 F4.
44. As quoted by Eusebius, *Praep. Evang.* 10. 12, 467AC, given in full as Wyss F 42.
45. Wyss 1936, xxxiv-v; 2 in 3 lines in F 21, 2/2 in F 22, 2/5 in F 32, 1/4 in F 53. Krevans 1993, 158-9 suggests that Callimachus's criticism may 'include metrical roughness.
46. This is not to say that he was a purist; he uses a number of post-Homeric forms (Wyss xxxiii).
47. *HD* I 101; see too his publication of the ostracon (a Homeric glossary) that carries the fragment: *SB Berlin* 1918, 740-42 and Wyss ad. loc.

ἐν δ' ὑπέρας στρεπτὰς, ὅπλα τε πάντα νεώς.

With line 1 compare ε. 254, ἐν δ' ἱστὸν ποιεῖ; with line 2, ε. 260, ἐν δ' ὑπέρας τε κάλους τε πόδας τε; with line 3, μ. 410, κ. 404, 424, ὅπλα τε πάντα. Save for the Attic form κάλωας, these lines read like a typical scene from the *Odyssey* written in elegiacs instead of hexameters. And while εἶπε δὲ φωνήσας (F 70) is a variation on actual Homeric formulas, it nonetheless implies a standard epic speech. Similarly, though the epithet in ἀγακλυμένη Ἐρύθεια (F 66. 2) is not Homeric, it clearly recalls ornamental formulas like ἀγακλειτὴ Γαλάτεια (Σ. 45); in line 1 note the Homeric χρυσέῳ ἐν δέπαϊ (Χ. 285).[48] Lastly there is F 71, where ἠΰτε τις καύηξ δύπτη...ἁλμυρὸν ἐς πέλαγος has every appearance of being a full-blown epic simile, something Callimachus avoided in his elegies.[49] σοῦσον is a Homeric gloss, a variant attested in a fragmentary Ptolemaic glossary for φ. 390 and alleged to mean "gear" or "tackle."[50]

Since fewer than ten complete lines of the *Lyde* survive, the degree of straightforward, non-allusive epic colouring must be held striking. As Wilamowitz put it,[51]

> Antimachus wanted to renew epic and elegy, but not, like Empedocles, by infusing a new spirit and a new style, but by living in the old world and its language, by erudition, glossography (as the grammarians put it) and by outdoing Homer with his own techniques.

If well done, this was an acceptable style for heroic quests and battles. Antimachus's *Thebaïd* continued to find readers for centuries; they noted what Roman critics called its *gravitas* and Greeks its "austere style,"[52] but they liked it. The very fact that Plato liked him so much suggests that he was felt to embody what was thought best in old-fashioned virtue. The continuous repetition of the same line (for all its internal variety) was itself suited to large-scale narrative.

But was this the right style for an elegy? The one extant fragment of Mimnermus's *Smyrneïs* and the new Simonides fragments suggest that narrative elegy was written in something closer to the formulaic style of epic than the style of sympotic elegy.[53] But the *Lyde* was meant to be a recrea-

---

48. Accepting Casaubon's correction: see Wyss ad loc.

49. But not in his epic *Hecale*: Hollis 1990, 14-15; Ch. XVII. 1.

50. For the respective merits of σοῦσον and the vulgate ὅπλον, M. van der Valk, *Textual Criticism of the Odyssey* (Leiden 1949), 82; S. West, *The Ptolemaic Papyri of Homer* (Pap. Col. 3), Cologne 1967, 260-62.

51. *HD* I. 101 (discussing the *Thebais*, not the *Lyde* fragments).

52. Quintilian 10. 1. 53; Dion. Hal., *de comp. verb.* 22, test. 24 and 28 Wyss.

53. 13a West. But Nagy goes too far in claiming that archaic elegy as a whole is "oral" (*Theognis of Megara: Poetry and the Polis*, ed. T. J. Figueira and G. Nagy [Baltimore 1985], 48-50). P. Giannini (*QUUC* 16 [1973], 3-78) usefully illustrates the recurrence of certain word groups in the pentameter, many of them naturally determined by metrical considerations, but N. Greenberg emphasized in the same volume (*Theognis* 246f.; cf. A.W.H.

tion of the *Nanno* rather than the *Smyrneïs*. Even Antimachus's admirers noted the difference between the *Lyde* and its model. Posidippus contrasted Mimnermus and Antimachus as "sexy" (φιλέραστος) and "sobersides" (σώφρων).[54] And if a correction in Hedylus is accepted (Appendix A), a friend of the poet is said when drunk to have sung more sweetly than Asclepiades and more fiercely than the *Lyde*. Callimachus felt strongly that elegy called for lighter themes and a different narrative voice. It is not epic itself he is attacking, but the influence of the impersonal and prolix style of Cyclic epic on the fashionable genre of elegy. This was the "braying of donkeys."

It was suggested in the preceding chapter that Callimachus wrote the *Cydippe* as a deliberate anti-Antimachean experiment. We have two substantial fragments from the poem, one (F 75) at 77 lines the longest unbroken stretch of narrative to survive from the *Aetia*.[55] We have already considered the remarkable way the poet interrupts his narrative at 75. 4-9 (Ch. I. 3). It is important to be clear that this is not (as often implied) a case of the learned poet unable to resist the temptation of unloading an aetiology. The garrulity for which he affects to reproach himself is illustrated by the digression itself rather than its purported subject. Its purpose was twofold: to heighten the dramatic tension, and (more important) draw attention to the narrator behind the narrative, a pious but fussy fellow, not to be trusted with a secret.

At line 40, instead of simply relating how happy Acontius was on his wedding night, the poet speculates about what prizes he would have turned down to be with Cydippe, appealing to the experience of all who have been in love. The offspring of this marriage is described as "your clan the Acontiadae"; it is the story of "this love of yours" that the poet heard from old Xenomedes. Once again, these apostrophes draw our attention to the narrator rather than the mythological subject he purports to be addressing. We return to Acontius with another apostrophe (line 74) before yet another reference to the narrator himself: "the old man told of your passionate

---

Adkins, *Poetic Craft in the Early Greek Elegists* [Chicago 1985], 99f.) that archaic elegy "is not formulaic in the way the verse of Homer is," in particular that there is no trace of Parry's principle of formulaic economy. Nagy argues that doublets in the *Theognidea* and verses elsewhere transmitted under the names of Solon and Mimnermus "are a reflex of the workings of oral poetry...recomposed with every performance" (p. 49). But such "recomposition" is not at all the same thing as entire poems with double ascriptions. West's commonsense explanation is clearly preferable (*Studies* 1974, 40). There is a regrettable tendency in much modern writing on archaic poetry to confuse "oral culture" (meaning poetry composed for performance, whether at symposium or festival) with Parry-style oral composition. The former does not in the least imply the latter.

54. *AP* xii. 168. 1-2.

55. Usefully discussed by Harder 1990, 287-309; forthcoming study by Jennifer Lynn.

love, whence the maiden's story came to my Muse." That is to say, the Muse is represented as reading the story in Xenomedes![56] As Heinze put it, "Callimachus narrates in such a way that the reader never forgets the person of the narrator for the story he is telling."[57]

For all its many allusive digressions, the *Cydippe* cannot have been more than a couple of hundred lines long.[58] The *Aetia* posed very different problems of structure and narrative voice. To write a poem of the length of *Aetia* I-II (not less than ca 2000 lines) without compromising his artistic principles was an undertaking of a different order. As we shall see in the next chapter, the problem with catalogue-poetry was how to link individual stories. Antimachus's link (unhappy love) was thematic in a very general way. There was nothing in the *Lyde* comparable to Callimachus's framework of a dialogue with the Muses. But Callimachus's Muses were more than just a structural device. They allowed the poet to inject the unifying personality of a narrator (not necessarily his own of course) into what otherwise might indeed have been no more than a succession of unconnected stories. It is an amusing irony that Asclepiades himself may have given Callimachus the idea of using the Muses in this way. For in the last line of his epigram on the *Lyde* he had claimed it as

τὸ ξυνὸν Μουσῶν γράμμα καὶ Ἀντιμάχου.

the common composition of Antimachus and the Muses.

Not so, thought Callimachus, and produced a poem of his own in which the Muses were quite literally presented as co-authors.

The highly personal prologue requires no further comment at this stage. But the Somnium is more than the Hesiodic initiation that has so obsessed recent Callimachean scholarship (Ch. XIII. 1). To treat the Muses as sources of knowledge was as much Homeric as Hesiodic.[59] The main purpose of the episode was to set the scene for the dialogue between the poet and the Muses that was to continue throughout the poem. Callimachus presented his alter ego as a bookish young man eager for knowledge. His persistent, not to say importunate quizzing of the Muses contributes far more to the poem than a framework (Ch. IV. 5). Bk II opened with the narrator at a symposium in contemporary Alexandria, not just to honour Pollis, but to bring that narrator before the reader almost as conspicuously as at the beginning of Bk I. F 43. 84—"So [Clio] spoke, but I wanted to know this

---

56. This passage is surely final proof of the general assumption that Bks III-IV were no longer constructed as a dialogue between the poet and the Muses.

57. "Ovids elegische Erzählung," in *Vom Geist des Römertums*[3] (Darmstadt 1960), 375. See too J. F. Miller, "Callimachus and the Augustan Aetiological Essay," *ANRW* II. 30. 1 (1982), 374-76.

58. It was later incorporated into *Aetia* III as just one of its ten or so aetia.

59. See (for example) Penelope Murray, *JHS* 101 (1981), 87-100.

too, for my secret wonder grew"—once again draws attention to the narrator. When the Ician guest calls him "thrice blessed...if you lead a life ignorant of sea-faring" (F 178. 32-3), we have one figure in the frame characterizing another from his appearance and conversation. Nor is it only the Muses and the Ician with whom the narrator converses. In F 7 there is that remarkable request that the Graces wipe the oil from their hands on his elegies "that they may live for many a year." In Bks III-IV Callimachus dropped the framework of dialogue with the Muses, and uses other devices instead, notably extended apostrophe: e.g. F 102, "You were archon of Ephesus, Pasicles..."; Euthycles the Locrian seems to have been apostrophized throughout his sad story (F 84-5). F 114 is an extended dialogue between the poet and a statue of Delian Apollo. In F 56 = *SH* 264 the narrator draws his listeners/readers into the actual process of his narration by suggesting that they may anticipate him and cut his poem short—though he will go ahead and report what Heracles said anyway.

The claim that he "sings nothing unattested" (ἀμάρτυρον οὐδὲν ἀείδω, F 612) has usually been taken literally as the pedant's credo, the triumph of erudition over imagination. More probably it was made defensively (or defiantly) when he was saying something incredible, or something invented rather than attested (note the specificity of *nota cano* in Ovid after a list of bizarre love stories).[60] The detailed account of Xenomedes's *History of Ceos* in the *Cydippe* (F 75. 53-77) is regularly cited as the classic example of the pedant versifying his footnotes. But it is important to attend to the form of these "bibliographical" asides. If Callimachus had simply felt obliged to indicate his source, why not a straightforward parenthesis, "as Xenomedes relates." Instead he chose to interpose himself between the reader and his source. That is art, not pedantry. It is one of a variety of carefully planned devices through which the poet insistently projects himself into his own narrative. As Joseph Solodow has written of a poem where a similar problem was solved in much the same way:[61]

> the world of the [*Metamorphoses*] does not altogether lack a point of focus. One thing does stand out, dominating and informing the whole: the narrator himself, the poet Ovid. His distinctive voice we learn to recognize as we read the poem, we feel him present everywhere mediating the transmission of the stories....He alone unifies the poem.

We might quibble with the unqualified identification of the narrator of the *Metamorphoses* with Ovid himself,[62] but that narrator's distinctive voice does indeed dominate the *Metamorphoses*. Like Callimachus, though in a

60. *AA* i. 297, with Hollis's note on the passage.

61. Joseph B. Solodow, *The World of Ovid's Metamorphoses* (Chapel Hill 1988), 37.

62. For the different voices in Ovid's different poems, Carole Newlands, *Arethusa* 25 (1992), 33-35.

somewhat different way, Ovid too constantly dwells on the source and credibility of his narrative.[63] In both cases the reader is constantly aware of a narrator behind the narrative.

3

So the opening of the *Aetia* prologue is more complex than hitherto supposed. Callimachus begins by stating that his current poem (the one the prologue introduces) is not one of those never-ending narratives the critics enjoy. Their attitude is (of course) caricatured. No one in third-century Alexandria really preferred the braying of donkeys to the chirping of the cicada—least of all the refined Asclepiades and his circle. That just meant anyone who admitted enjoying the *Lyde*.

That it is his own poem he is talking about is confirmed by a section of the prologue that, in comparison with the rest, has attracted little attention, lines 13-16:

μακρ]ὸν ἐπὶ Θρήϊκας ἀπ' Αἰγύπτοιο [πέτοιτο
    αἵματ]ι Πυγμαίων ἡδομένη [γ]έρα[νος,
Μασσαγέται καὶ μακρὸν ὀϊστεύοιεν ἐπ' ἄνδρα
    Μῆδον,] ἀ[ηδονίδες] δ' ὧδε μελιχρ[ό]τεραι.

Much scholarly ingenuity has been devoted to tracing Callimachus's source here, on the assumption that he must be making fun of some unlucky epic in particular, one that treated of battles between Scythians and Persians and cranes and pygmies. Since Choerilus of Samos wrote a *Persica*, he has long been the favorite candidate for at any rate the Persians. According to Wimmel, Scythians/Persians imply historical epic while cranes/pygmies imply mythical epic. More recently, A. Bernabé has transformed a puzzling reference to a *Germania* by Choerilus into a *Gerania*, an epic on cranes![64] Choerilus could then be seen as a source for every detail in these lines.

The problem is that the emphasis of the lines is not on Scythians and Persians and cranes as inappropriate poetic subject matter, but simply on the *distance* that cranes fly[65] and Scythians shoot.[66] These long distances

---

63. "[Ovid] never makes himself more evident than when he turns on his own narrative and criticizes it. Not only does he remind us again and again that *he* is telling the story; he also frequently hints that it is not altogether reliable, but instead is *merely* a story that *he* is telling" (Solodow 64). See too A. M. Keith, *The Play of Fictions* (Ann Arbor 1992), 3f., and, for the *Fasti*, Newlands 1992, 48-52.

64. *Schol. Bern.* on *Geo.* 1. 482; Bernabé, *Emerita* 52 (1984), 319-23; *PEG* I (1987), p. 193, F 4; for earlier discussions, Barigazzi, *Hermes* 84 (1956), 162-82; Wimmel 1960, 99-100; Bornmann, *Maia* 19 (1967), 44-50; Huxley, *GRBS* 10 (1969), 16-17.

65. The distance cranes covered in their migrations is often mentioned in literature: D'Arcy W. Thompson, *Glossary of Greek Birds*[2] (1936), 71-2.

66. So Bornmann 1967, 48: "se i due esempi sono unificati dall' idea della lunghezza, come possono nello stesso tempo alludere al contenuto di due episodi trattati da Cherilo?"

are then contrasted with Callimachus's own short poem. They are just colourful ways of evoking length:[67] the crane may fly all the way from Egypt to Thrace, and the Massagetae (famed archers) may shoot down Medes from afar, but poems are sweeter "like this." What does "like this" (ὧδε) refer to? Clearly not ·to the distance or length suggested by the two immediately preceding illustrations. In the context of the prologue as a whole, it must mean (as the London scholiast explains)[68] the exact opposite, namely short. This much is not in doubt, though there is a problem in referring ὧδε all the way back to the preference expressed in lines 9-12 for the short poems of Mimnermus and Philitas, especially since the note on which that discussion ended was their long poems (μεγάλη...γυνή). L. Torraca has already made the sensible observation that Callimachus is alluding "to his own poems."[69] Surely so, but which ones? Hardly just the prologue, which is far too short for comparison with the elegies mentioned—and too abusive to be described without perversity as "sweet." On the other hand the reference can hardly be to the entire corpus of Callimachus's poetic works, republished in Pfeiffer's collected edition. Other objections to that edition aside, Callimachus can hardly have referred to his collected works in ten rolls (including the *Hecale* and *Aetia* I-IV) as *all* being short and sweet. The answer is surely that just one poem is in question, a work of middling length, not in "many thousands of lines," but not really ἐπὶ τυτθόν either. In the context, the one poem that is "sweeter this way" can only be the *Aetia* itself. Callimachus did not need to be more explicit, because anyone reading the prologue was holding the first roll of *Aetia* I-II in his hands as he read. He could not fail to see that "like this" meant "like an elegy in two books."

In the hyperbolic world of Callimachean prefaces, it should come as no surprise that his "tiny song" should turn out to be his most ambitious poem so far. According to Otis,[70] "By the 'short epic' (ἔπος τυτθὸν) he meant a self-contained single poem of about 200-500 hexameters." That is to say, Otis directly traced to Callimachus the so-called "epyllion." No matter that Callimachus himself never wrote such a 200-500 line epic (the *Hecale* was

---

67. Bornmann attempts an interpretation in terms of Lucretius's antithesis between the honking of cranes and the delicate song of the swan (4. 180-03), based on the similar point in Antip. Sid. *AP* 7. 713. 7-8. This would indeed be a nice Callimachean point, but (a) Callimachus makes it later in the prologue with the even more vivid contrast between cicada and donkey; (b) there is simply no room in the papyrus to squeeze in a reference to sound (μακρ]όν in 13 balances μακρόν in 15); and (c) any such reference to sound would work against the emphasis on length that links Scythians/Persians and cranes/pygmies.

68. ὧδε, οὕτω(ς) ἡδύ(τεραι?) ἐν το(ῖς) μικ(ροῖς), p. 7 Pfeiffer = p. 14 Torraca.

69. *Il prologo dei Telchini e l'inizio degli Aitia di Callimacho* (Napoli 1960), 47.

70. *Ovid as an Epic Poet*[2] (1970), 5; so too in his *Virgil* (1964), 10 ('little epic'), 19.

two or three times that length). This interpretation rests on a double mis-construction of the text. In the first place, however we supplement the end of line 5, τυτθόν is governed by ἐπί; it does not qualify ἔπος.[71] There is no possible justification for this use of τυτθὸν ἔπος as a quasi-technical term.[72] In the second, ἔπος is not in any case being used here to designate epic specifically, merely "poem" in general,[73] in fact (of course) the poem the prologue is introducing, Callimachus's own *Aetia*.

Aetia I-II; some 2000 lines, will no doubt seem on the long side to those who see Callimachus as the uncompromising champion of brevity. But length is a relative concept. It is essential to consider Callimachus's polemic in context—and in perspective.

The widespread belief that the prologue is a defiant defence of the short poem largely rests on a conjectural restoration of line 9:

[ἦ μὲν δὴ] γὰρ ἔην [ὀλ]ιγόστιχος.

Yes indeed, I do [rather *did*] write short poems.

We have already seen that this text is impossible on many counts—not least the imperfect tense, which would imply that Callimachus *used* to write short poems. With Wimmel, we must restore [Κῷος οὐκ] ἄρ' ἔην and refer the line to Philitas. For Callimachus that leaves only the Telchines' claim that he "spins his song in small compass" (ἐπὶ τυτθόν). This is *not* an affirmation by the poet, but an accusation put in the mouth of his critics.[74] Not only, therefore, is it automatically suspect. At best it can only refer to his past poems, not the current work. Our suspicions should only deepen when we reflect that to take it literally and seriously saddles Callimachus with a doctrine not only absurd in itself, but plainly contradicted by his own *Aetia* and *Hecale*.

According to C. O. Brink,[75]

> "Short poem" and "long poem" were after all the battle-cries of the two oppos-ing factions in the tussles of the côteries. Callimachus' own position as the leader of a school advocating the highly-wrought short poem is too well known to require documentation.

71. So already Pfeiffer, *Hermes* 1928, 310-11.

72. In his *Virgil* (1964), 10 Otis even uses it in the plural: "Callimachus...insisted on writing little poems (ἔπη τυτθά)." The habit is spreading: J. C. Bramble, *Persius and the Programmatic Satire* (Cambridge 1974), 181 ("the ἔπος τυτθόν"); W. W. Briggs, *ANRW* 31. 2 (1981), 950 ("short poem"); Griffiths 1979, 56 ("the purveyors of the ἔπος τυτθόν"); Gutzwiller 1981, 4: "short tale (ἔπος τυτθόν)"; J. F. Miller, *Ovid's Elegiac Festivals* (Frankfurt 1991), 17 (citing *exiguum...opus* at *Fasti* ii. 4 as Ovid's translation of the phrase).

73. "Epos gilt hier allgemein als 'Dichterwort' und umfaßt alle Gattungen, vorausgesetzt eben, daß sie kurz sind," S. Koster, *Antike Epostheorien* (1970), 118.

74. Contrast Lyne 1984, 17, claiming that Call. "accepts" the accusation, "admitt-ing—and not overtly defending himself...."

75. *Horace on Poetry: Prolegomena to the Literary Epistles* (Cambridge 1963), 71.

Such "documentation" as there is crumbles to the touch. For while

αὖθι δὲ τέχνῃ
κρίνετε, μὴ σχοίνῳ Περσίδι τὴν σοφίην

makes clear that length should not be valued above art, it does not imply that *brevity* should be valued above art. The main preoccupation of the *Aetia* prologue is not length in and for itself, but art and quality.

If the *Aetia* was intended, as I believe, to challenge the *Lyde* as a model narrative elegy, it could not be *truly* short, no longer than (say) a Theocritean *Idyll*. Bks I-II must have amounted to at least 2000 lines.[76] It was poems in *many* thousands of lines he was holding up to ridicule when he wrote of cranes flying from Egypt to Thrace. The length of the *Lyde* is unfortunately unknown; most quotations are just "from the *Lyde*." There is one from "Bk II" and perhaps one from "Bk III," if an uncertain emendation by Voss is accepted in F 67.[77] The appearance of Agatharchides's epitome suggests a work of considerable compass,[78] though it is important to bear in mind that length is only one of the vices Callimachus pillories.

The *Hecale* too was short compared to the *Iliad* or Antimachus's *Thebaid*. But at an estimated 1000/1500 lines,[79] it is far longer than any surviving example of the rather dubious genre of "epyllion" to which it has usually been assigned (Ch. XVII). Perhaps the most interesting aspect of the well-known scholion to the end of the second *Hymn*,

in these lines he is attacking those who mocked him for not being able to write a long poem (μέγα ποίημα), which is why he was forced (ἠναγκάσθη) to write the *Hecale*,

lies in the acknowledgment that the *Hecale* was considered a long poem. It is also worth adding that the one contemporary poem Callimachus is known to have admired[80] ran to 1154 lines, Aratus's *Phaenomena*. It simply will not do to classify the *Aetia* with the epigrams and hymns and define it (with Pfeiffer) as a "loose series of pieces of a few lines." In both subject matter and technique the *Aetia* undoubtedly has more in common with the *Argonautica*. Both *Aetia* and *Hecale* exhibit a complex structure and sophisticated narrative technique that are the deliberate result of an attempt to write narrative poetry on an altogether different scale from what was either necessary or possible in (say) the hymn or the Theocritean *Idyll*.

76. And the final four book edition to 4-5000 lines, almost as long as the four books of Apollonius's *Argonautica* and the optimum length laid down by Aristotle for an *epic* (*Poetics* 1459.21). But the prologue refers only to I-II.

77. See West's note to his T 19 (*Iambi et Elegi Graeci* II [1972], 38).

78. Photius, *Bibl.* 213, p. 171a19 Bekker.

79. For the various ways of estimating its length, see Hollis 1990, 337-340.

80. Not counting the *Nightingales* of Heraclitus (*AP* vi. 80), about which we know nothing (presumably a collection of short poems).

But brevity alone was not enough. It is flabbiness and bombast Callimachus dwells on rather than length in and for itself, the lack of artistry
that makes a poem *seem* never-ending. The achievements of what has
rightly been called the Alexandrian poetic revolution were first realized in
the smallest genres: the epigram, the hymn, the bucolic idyll. But what of
the larger genres? Did Callimachus really take the defeatist position that it
was no longer possible to write a good poem of more than 200 lines?[81] Did
he really find even Homer wanting?

So it has often been claimed. According to Brink:[82] "Theoretically Callimachus and others endorsed the primacy of the long epic of Homer, but
in practice eschewed it because it did not seem amenable to artistic
harmony as they understood it." Where is there even a hint of any such
extravagant doctrine in Callimachus? All he says in the *Aetia* prologue is
(in effect) that since his new poem is *not* an unbroken narrative many thousands of lines long, it will not please the critics. He certainly does not say
that it would be *impossible* to write a good long poem. He is only concerned with *bad* long poems—one specific long poem: the *Lyde.*

So the *Aetia* prologue is a reply, not to Callimachus's critics in general,
but to criticisms real or imagined that (he suggests) they are likely to make
of the *Aetia*. There is an exact parallel in a work that Callimachus himself
both saw and intended as in some sense a pendant to the *Aetia*, his *Iambi.*
The *Aetia* begins with a reply to critics; the *Iambi* include (indeed on the
majority view close with) a reply to critics (*Iamb* 13). According to the
Diegeseis, Callimachus is answering those who criticized his "polyeideia,"
writing in many different genres. To some extent this might apply to Callimachus's varied oeuvre as a whole. Yet as Dawson and Clayman have
emphasized, in what we have of the actual text of the poem, Callimachus is
clearly concerned with criticisms of his *Iambi* (for example, that he mixed
up his dialects).

Just as *Iamb* 13 replies to criticisms of the *Iambi*, so too, (I suggest)
does the *Aetia* prologue reply to criticisms of the *Aetia*. This raises the
question whether either or both reply to actual criticisms levelled at either
work by specific critics. Or is Callimachus (in the manner of the orators)
simply setting up in advance caricatures of criticisms that he can easily
demolish?

The two cases have usually been studied separately, and there has been
a tendency to opt for the former alternative. This would allow for individual *Aetia* and *Iambi* to circulate for years before Caliimachus finally col-

81. It is tempting to compare Neoptolemus's remark that the perfect poet "will bestow
harmony...also on long poems" (cf. Brink, *Horace on Poetry* I. 55-57), but C. Mangoni's
new edition (Philodemus, *On poems* col. xvi. 5) has removed both "harmony" and "long."

82. *Horace on Poetry* I. 57; compare too p. 74: "the forms which Callimachus and his
colleagues had declared untenable for a modern poet."

lected them into books, in both cases adding a reply to the criticisms they had accumulated over the years. For a variety of reasons (both literary and chronological) adduced in various parts of this study, this now seems the less likely hypothesis. If we assume early publication in book form of both *Aetia* I-II and *Iambi*, both replies are best read as dramatized presentations of the critical principles underlying the two works rather than serious defences of embattled positions.

The parallelism between the two replies is striking—and hardly accidental. Both open with a summary (or rather caricature) of the critics' objections, in both cases what purport to be direct quotations of their very words. We have seen from the *Aetia* epilogue (F 112) that Callimachus was already planning the *Iambi* when he published *Aetia* I-II, though there is also another factor that may have prompted the different arrangement of the two poems. *Iamb* 13 deals with specific features of the preceding poems with which the reader of a prologue would not yet be familiar. The *Aetia* prologue is much more general, not presupposing knowledge of any specific features of the *Aetia*.

4

In the light of this interpretation of the *Aetia* prologue we may now take a fresh look at the proem to Ovid's *Metamorphoses*:[83]

> In nova fert animus mutatas dicere formas
> corpora: di, coeptis (nam vos mutastis et illa)
> adspirate meis primaque ab origine mundi
> ad mea perpetuum deducite tempora carmen.

carmen perpetuum is a more or less literal rendering of Callimachus's term into Latin. But what did it mean? According to Otis,[84] "its presence here, at the very beginning of Ovid's poem, is an assertion that Ovid is about to do precisely what Callimachus with great deliberation avoided." But what could be the purpose of so crude and direct a confutation? For most readers, the *Metamorphoses* makes a thoroughly Callimachean impression. What did Ovid think Callimachus meant by διηνεκές? His own *perpetuum* clearly implies temporal continuity:

> primaque ab origine mundi

---

83. Accepting Lejay's *illa* for the MSS *illas* in line 2 (E. J. Kenney, *Proc. Camb. Phil. Soc.* 22 [1976], 46-53; D. Kovacs, *CQ* 37 [1987], 458-65); the gods have changed Ovid's *coepta* (i.e. from elegy to epic, from elegiac to hexameter) as well as the humans whose stories he tells.

84. *Ovid as an Epic Poet*[2] (1970), 46.

ad mea perpetuum deducite tempora carmen.

Indeed, he restates the point more emphatically still when addressing Augustus in *Tristia* ii. 557-60:[85]

> atque utinam revoces animum paulisper ab ira,
>   et vacuo iubeas hinc tibi pauca legi,.
> pauca, quibus prima surgens ab origine mundi
>   in tua deduxi tempora, Caesar, opus.

> Relent for a moment from your anger, and bid a few lines [of my *Metamorphoses*] be read to you, the few lines in which, after beginning with the origin of the world, I brought the work right down to your times, Caesar.

Curiously enough, Ovidian commentators seem to assume that this chronological dimension was added by Ovid: "Ovid's *perpetuum...carmen* refers to temporal rather than thematic continuity."[86] But so does Callimachus's ἄεισμα διηνεκές. Why resist the obvious conclusion that this is how he read Callimachus?

Recent papers by Gilbert and Kenney simultaneously drew attention to an elegant double entendre in Ovid's *deducite* (line 4): not merely "bring down" to the present day, but (as often of refined poetry) "polish."[87] That is to say, Ovid is alluding to Vergil's version of Callimachus's μοῦσα λεπταλέη. The *Metamorphoses* will be a *deductum* as well as a *perpetuum carmen*, as if "to assure Ovid's readers that there would be no betrayal of Callimachus" (Gilbert). In fact this does not pose quite the "contradiction in terms" Kenney sees. Ovid is using *perpetuum* in a subtly different, more positive way than Callimachus. What Callimachus had in mind was poetasters who did not know where to begin or end their catalogues of adventures: in the context, διηνεκές implies that they meandered on without purpose or climax. Ovid has done something quite different: he has woven all his tales of transformation together into an unbroken supertale going all the way from the Creation to Augustus. It is in addition both witty and highly personal, a Callimachean combination of qualities Ovid had long since made his own. Of course, it may be doubted whether even Ovid took his own chronological framework seriously, undermined as it is by the frivolity of his own transitions. It adds little or nothing to our enjoy-

---

85. The reference of 560 is to *Met.* xv. 745-870; Shackleton Bailey, *CQ* 32 (1982), 393.

86. C. D. Gilbert, *CQ* n.s. 26 (1986), 112 n.3; so too A. S. Hollis, *Ovid Metamorphoses, Bk VIII* (1970), xi-xii; Kenney 1976, 51.

87. *tenui deducta poemata filo*, Horace, *Epp.* 2. 1. 225; *deducta mihi voce garrienti*, Cornificius, F 1; *deductum dicere carmen*, Vergil, *Ecl.* 6. 5; *novo deduxi carmina versu*, Propertius I. 16. 41; Gilbert, *CQ* 26 (1976), 111-2; Kenney 1976, 51; S. Hinds, *The Metamorphosis of Persephone* (Cambridge 1987), 18-20; D. Kovacs, *CQ* 37 (1987), 458-65. The point had in fact already been briefly stated by Newman, *Augustus and the New Poets* (1967), 404.

ment of individual tales.[88] But it was an ingenious tour de force, and sophisticated readers would at once have recognized that Ovid's poem was not really going to be what Callimachus meant by ἄεισμα διηνεκές.[89]

88. "whatever thematic architecture Ovid's ingenuity might devise or the percipience of modern critics detect, the poem is bound to appeal to most readers as a collection of stories" (E. J. Kenney, in J. W. Binns [ed.], *Ovid* [1973], 116).

89. This is not to say (with R. Coleman, *CQ* 65 [1971], 471) that Callimachus would have approved of the *Metamorphoses*; I feel sure that he would have found it much too self-indulgent (cf. Newman 1967, 407, 411). The fact that Ennius too began a long narrative poem with a highly personal dream revelation has led some to deny that Ennius even knew Callimachus. Others found other solutions: e.g. O. Skutsch's argument that Ennius's claim to be the reincarnation of Homer was an ingenious way of evading the Callimachean ban (*Annals of Quintus Ennius* [Oxford 1985], 148): the ban on imitating Homer could not apply to Homer himself! Once it is realized that Callimachus did not ban either epic or imitation of Homer, the dilemma disappears. Of course Ennius knew the *Aetia*, and of course he was imitating its famous opening scene—which is not to say that it was the happiest poetic conception (in Callimachean terms the *Annales* was the worst sort of ἄεισμα διηνεκές, a chronological narrative with no unity of action).

Chapter XIII

Hesiodic Elegy

1

Hesiod was popular in Hellenistic times, studied by scholars, imitated by poets and a source of inspiration even for sculptors.[1] But was Callimachus in the forefront of these admirers, as widely supposed? There are good reasons for scepticism. It seems to have been E. Reitzenstein who gave currency to the influential notion of the *Aetia* as a "Hesiodic epic." On his view, Callimachus distinguished two different styles in epic, a *genus grande* and a *genus tenue*. Homer was naturally the founder and best exponent of the first, but his excellence was inimitable. Fortunately, there was also Hesiod, who "stood beside Homer as the founder of the epic γένος λεπτόν,"[2] chosen as the model for Callimachus's elegiac epic, the *Aetia*.

This hypothesis has come to be treated as fact over the past half century. According to a recent study of the classical epic tradition,[3] Callimachus regarded Hesiod "as the patron of the new Alexandrian epic" and "rejoiced to find in Aratus an experiment in writing a relatively large-scale poem in a way that was not pseudo-Homeric." Furthermore, according to a new study of Vergil's *Georgics*, "the ideals that Callimachus upheld and took Hesiod to exemplify were later adopted by a group of influential Roman poets."[4] Thus we are asked to believe that "references to Hesiod in Virgil and Propertius are really references to Callimachus or his conception of Hesiod";[5] Linus giving Gallus the reeds *Ascraeo quos ante seni* (*Buc.* vi. 70) means that Gallus wrote "Hesiodic-Callimachean poetry."[6]

Some may be surprised, others relieved to discover that there is not a scrap of ancient evidence for this bizarre doctrine. Its shaky foundations are

---

1. Scholars, M. L. West, *Hesiod: Works and Days* (1978), 63-68; poets, below § 3; for the influence of the *Theogony* on the gigantomachy frieze at Pergamum, E. Simon, *Pergamon und Hesiod* (Mainz 1975).

2. "Zur Stiltheorie des Kallimachos," *Festschrift R. Reitzenstein* (1931), 41f.

3. J. K. Newman, *The Classical Epic Tradition* (1986), 523 and 45.

4. J. Farrell, *Vergil's Georgics and the Traditions of Ancient Epic* (Oxford 1991), 31.

5. W. Clausen, *GRBS* 5 (1964), 196, quoted and endorsed by J.R.G. Wright, *Proc. Camb. Phil. Soc.* n. s. 29 (1983), 114.

6. D. O. Ross Jr., *Backgrounds to Augustan Poetry* (Cambridge 1975), 119-20.

(1) the alleged Hesiodic inspiration of the *Aetia*, and (2) a long discredited misinterpretation of Callimachus's famous epigram on Aratus. Nothing else. The truth, as we shall see, is that it was pseudo-Hesiodic rather than pseudo-Homeric writing that aroused Callimachus's ire.

For Reinsch-Werner, the "Hesiodic" initiation of the Somnium was the culmination of Callimachus's reply to his critics.[7] Reitzenstein inferred from three later epigrammatists that Callimachus described himself drinking from the same spring on Helicon as Hesiod, to demonstrate his allegiance to the Master.[8] To underline his rejection of Homer, he deliberately changed the Hesiodic symbol of "Dichterweihe," the laurel branch, because it was too similar to the staff (ῥάβδος) of the Homeric rhapsode.

Ancient critics did indeed so interpret Hesiod's branch.[9] Pausanias describes a picture of Hesiod which showed him with a lyre on his knees, "not at all appropriate for Hesiod; it is clear from his verses that he sang with a laurel staff in his hand."[10] One tradition made him the first rhapsode.[11] But there is not the slightest evidence that Callimachus nurtured such hostility to rhapsodes.[12] In an interesting passage of the *Aetia* he works in an etymology of the word:[13]

> καὶ τὸν ἐπὶ ῥάβδῳ μῦθον ὑφαινόμενον...
> ἠνεκὲς ἀείδω δειδεγμένος.

I < heard > the story woven with the aid of a staff
and tell it from beginning to end.

This is one of the two poetic texts the scholiasts quote to illustrate the etymology—together with Hesiod, F 357 M-W, where Hesiod and Homer together are described as "stitching a song" (ῥάψαντες ἀοιδήν).[14] In the context of his poem, Callimachus presumably means that he has read this

7. *Callimachus Hesiodicus* (1976), 6.
8. Reitzenstein 1931, 52-69 (developing an unhappy guess of Wilamowitz, *HD* I 95-6). So too, at greater length, A. Kambylis, *Die Dichterweihe und ihre Symbolik* (1965), 98-102.
9. See the various texts and modern references quoted by M. L. West, *Hesiod: Theogony* (1966), 163-64.
10. Pausanias 9. 30. 2.
11. A certain Nicocles or Nicocrates, *FGrH* 376 F8. The passage is best read in its context, a learned discussion of rhapsodes and the etymology of the term in the *Scholia Vetera* to Pindar (*Nem* ii. 1 = III, pp. 29-31 Drachmann). This is also the source of the passage from Callimachus quoted above.
12. According to A. Ford, ῥαψῳδία need not imply epic: *CP* 83 (1988), 300-307.
13. F 26. 5-8. The text is so fragmentary that someone other than the poet (though not a Muse, in view of the masculine participle) could be the speaker, but even so there is no hint of disapproval.
14. Schol. Pind. *Nem*. ii.1 (III. 30 Drachman). It is interesting that Callimachus should use the metaphor of weaving rather than stitching in a context that nonetheless suggests the popular ancient derivation of ῥαψῳδία from ῥάβδος (on which, Ford, *CP* 83 [1988], 300).

story in an epic poem. The analogy of his other conversations with the Muses suggests that he is telling them the version he has heard to see whether they will confirm it.

It will be worth taking a closer look at the epigrams that refer to Hesiod drinking holy water. First, *AP* vii. 55, by Alcaeus of Messene:

Λοκρίδος ἐν νέμεϊ σκιερῷ νέκυν Ἡσιόδοιο
　　Νύμφαι κρηνίδων λοῦσαν ἀπὸ σφετέρων,
καὶ τάφον ὑψώσαντο· γάλακτι δὲ ποιμένες αἰγῶν
　　ἔρραναν, ξανθῷ μιξάμενοι μέλιτι·
τοίην γὰρ καὶ γῆρυν ἀπέπνεεν ἐννέα Μουσέων
　　ὁ πρέσβυς καθαρῶν γευσάμενος λιβάδων.

In a shady grove of Locris the Nymphs washed the body of Hesiod with water from their springs and raised a tomb. The goat-herds drenched it with their milk, mixing in golden honey. For such was the song the old man breathed, having tasted the pure water of the nine Muses.

Reitzenstein quoted only the last couplet. The poem as a whole is concerned not with Hesiod's initiation, but with his death,[15] naturally not mentioned by Callimachus. The motifs of the breath of song and honey both come from the *Theogony* itself.[16] Why should we assume that the one detail of the drink comes from Callimachus? The second epigram (by Antipater of Sidon) celebrates a cup-bearer called Helicon who pours out Italian wine; it begins by comparing him to Boeotian Helicon, which once "gushed forth from its springs the water of sweet speech for Hesiod" (*AP* xi. 24.). Quite apart from the frivolity of the comparison, there is no drinking here. From the last, *AP* ix. 64 by (probably) Archias, Reitzenstein again quoted only one couplet mentioning a drink of "holy water from the Heliconian spring," but not the preceding couplet, in which the Muses also give him the "holy branch of laurel." And he does even mention a first-century text that represents both Homer and the bucolic poet Bion drinking from holy springs, Bion from Arethusa and Homer from Hippocrene.[17] Instead he concludes that "these epigrams *can only* derive from Callimachus's account of the poetic initiation of Hesiod, *which is therefore known to us more or less completely.*"[18] There is not the slightest reason to suppose that a single one of them has any connection with the *Aetia*.

In fact there may be no particular significance in the drinking. It is the water that is important.[19] In Hesiod the Muses dance around Hippocrene

15. On the strange traditions about Hesiod's death, R. Scodel, *GRBS* 21 (1980), 301-20.
16. lines 31, 40, 83-84, with West p. 183 for honey.
17. *Epit. Bion.* 76 (Arethusa = Sicily = Theocritus); also Ovid, *Amores* 3. 9. 25-6.
18. "die uns damit ziemlich lückenlos bekannt ist," p. 55 (my italics). After Hesiod's initiation, he goes on, "Die eigene Weihung des Kallimachos muß in der gleichen Weise erfolgt sein" (p. 56)!
19. Wimmel, *Kallimachos in Rom* (Wiesbaden 1960), 222-37.

and wash in its waters. In Nicander Hesiod sings "beside the waters of Permessus" (*Ther.* 12).[20] Gallus too walked beside the Permessus, and Propertius talks of bathing in it.[21] But when Lucretius pictures himself on Helicon, his plan is "integros accedere fontis *atque haurire*" (i. 927-8).[22] Drinking was an obvious way of tapping this power, and we hardly need to derive it from one particular source. Callimachus's memorable description of his own sort of poetry as "a narrow trickle from a sacred spring" (πίδακος ἐξ ἱερῆς ὀλίγη λιβάς) may have played some part in the development of the concept, but even so he does not say that he drank this trickle.

Some texts seem to draw a distinction between different sources of water. For example, at the close of 2. 10 Propertius claims that his poetry does not yet know the "Ascraean springs"; "Love [i.e. his elegies] has only bathed in the Permessus." This derives from *Eclogue* vi. 64f., where one of the Muses finds Gallus wandering by the Permessus and takes him up the mountain, where Linus gives him Hesiod's pipes. Presumably this has some basis in one of Gallus's own poems, which in turn, according to Servius, derives from Euphorion. Gallus's interest in Euphorion is borne out by Vergil himself at *Ecl* x. 50-51, not to mention various other sources.[23] The notion that Hippocrene represented a higher sort of poetry may have been a refinement devised by Gallus or Euphorion, but there is nothing to connect it with Callimachus.[24] Nor is there any hint of a choice between styles or genres. Far from it; the *Aetia* prologue simply rejects the high style. The germs of such a distinction might perhaps be seen in the epilogue, with the *Iambi* representing the lower slopes of Helicon. But this would be the opposite direction from Gallus and Propertius; they were reaching for the higher slopes.

It seems fairly clear that the symbolism of poetic initiation was greatly elaborated in the century or so after Callimachus. The rôle played therein by water was but one aspect of this elaboration. For example, in Propertius 3. 3 it is Apollo who gives the poet a drink from the Castalian fountain; in Callimachus the god just speaks to him. Another, more puzzling development is the theme of Callimachus as a drinker of water rather than wine.[25]

---

20. As the scholia to Nicander point out, there is no discussion of bites and poisons such as the text describes in any known Hesiodic poem: *poeta videtur auctores confudisse*, comment Merkelbach and West (*Fragmenta Hesiodea* [1967], F 367).

21. Vergil, *Ecl.* 6. 64f.; Prop. 2. 10. 25-6.

22. For other examples, Wimmel 226; N. B. Crowther, *Mnemosyne* 32 (1979), 1-11.

23. D. O. Ross, Jr., *Backgrounds to Augustan Poetry* (Cambridge 1975), 31, 40-43, with J. E. G. Zetzel, *CP* 72 (1977), 250-1.

24. It is true that Callimachus does mention Linus later on in the *Aetia* (F 26-28), but in a completely different connection: Ross, *Backgrounds* 22-23.

25. Wimmel 1960, 225; N. B. Crowther, "Water and wine as symbols of inspiration," *Mnemosyne* 32 (1979), 1-11; P. E. Knox, "Wine, Water and Callimachean Polemics," *HSCP* 89 (1985), 107-19.

The most explicit of these poems is *AP* xi. 20 by the Augustan Antipater of Thessalonica:

φεύγεθ᾽ ὅσοι λόκκας ἢ λοφνίδας ἢ καμασῆνας
    ᾄδετε, ποιητῶν φῦλον ἀκανθολόγων,
οἵ τ᾽ ἐπέων κόσμον λελυγισμένον ἀσκήσαντες,
    κρήνης ἐξ ἱερῆς πίνετε λιτὸν ὕδωρ.
σήμερον Ἀρχιλόχοιο καὶ ἄρσενος ἦμαρ Ὁμήρου
    σπένδομεν· ὁ κρητὴρ οὐ δέχεθ᾽ ὑδροπότας.

Off with you, singers of cloaks and torches and fish,[26] you brood of thorn-gathering poets, you who practice your fancy-pansy verses, drinking simple water from a holy spring. Today we pour the wine in honour of Archilochus and manly Homer. No water-bibbers at our bowl!

Line 4 gives the game away. The "simple water from the holy spring" clearly comes from the end of the *Hymn to Apollo*, kein Trinkwasser. A joke about Callimachus and water is likely to have been inspired by some unusual reference, such as prol. 33-4, the wish that he might turn into a cicada and live on dew. Why should anyone have been amused by anything so conventional as a reference to drinking from Hippocrene? We might compare jokes about Pindar and water, inspired by the beginning of the first *Olympian*.[27] There is certainly no serious contrast here between water-drinking Callimachus and wine-drinking Homer—itself no more than a joke.[28]

When Reitzenstein wrote, we had not a single certain fragment from the *Somnium*. Only an anonymous elegiac couplet quoted by Fronto which described the Muses meeting Hesiod while he was grazing his flocks by Hippocrene. But in 1948 Lobel published a scrap of papyrus containing miserable remnants from 8 lines. By great good fortune the first two could be identified with Fronto's couplet and the fifth with another known fragment:[29]

ποιμ]ένι μῆλα νέμ[οντι παρ᾽ ἴχνιον ὀξέος ἵππου
    Ἡσιόδ]ῳ Μουσέων ἐσμὸ[ς ὅτ᾽ ἠντίασεν
    ]έν οἱ Χάεος γενεσ[
    ]ἐπὶ πτέρῃης ὑδα[
τεύχω]ν ὡς ἑτέρῳ τις ἑῷ[κακὸν ἥπατι τεύχει
    ]ῶ ζώειν ἄξιον α[

---

26. Obviously obscure words for these items; the fact that they begin with a kappa and two lambdas suggests that Antipater consulted an alphabetically arranged glossary.

27. A characteristic chapter of Athenaeus gives a long list of water-drinkers (but no Callimachus): ii, 43F-45C.

28. *laudibus arguitur vini vinosus Homerus*, Horace, *Epp*. 1. 19. 6f. (Mayer ad loc.). It is hardly necessary to add that Callimachus was not a teetotaller. In both the *Aetia* (F 178) and his own epitaph (*Ep*. 35) he makes it clear that he enjoyed a glass of wine with friends.

29. P. Oxy. 2208. 1 (XIX [1948], 1-2, with pl. I) = Pfeiffer F 2.

].εν πάντες σε· τὸ γα[
].δε πρήσσειν εὐμα[
]..ιπα.[..].[

Little enough, but enough to put out of court once for all some of the wilder Hesiodic speculations. The traces of line 3 are clear enough to show that the Muses told "him about the origin of Chaos." Evidently the allusion is to *Theogony* 116,

ἦ τοι μὲν πρώτιστα Χάος γένετ᾽, αὐτὰρ ἔπειτα...

This is the beginning of the *Theogony* proper; the story of Chaos is the first thing the Muses tell Hesiod in response to his prayer that they "tell him what came first." It follows that Callimachus's narrative ran as follows:

When a band of Muses met Hesiod while he was grazing his flocks by the print of the swift horse, <they told him about> the origin of Chaos...

No drinking from springs. If this is all Callimachus had to say, it does not look as if there was any initiation at all. To judge from the precise description of where he met the Muses, this is the first time he has mentioned Hesiod. Nor is there any indication in the traces of what follows that he returns to Hesiod. It is true that line 5 seems to echo line 265 of the *Works and Days*:

οἵ τ᾽ αὐτῷ κακὰ τεύχει ἀνὴρ ἄλλῳ κακὰ τεύχων.

The man who does harm to another does harm to his own heart.

Lobel assumed that the point of the allusion was to suggest that the Muses had revealed to Hesiod the contents of *Works and Days* as well as *Theogony*.[30] For Reinsch-Werner, it was simply one more illustration of overwhelming Hesiodic influence on Callimachus. But it is not a line that is highly characteristic of the *Works and Days*.[31] It is more relevant to note that line 5 picks up line 8 of the prologue (Ch. IV. 5):

[μοῦνον ἐὸν] τήκ[ειν] ἧπαρ ἐπιστάμενον.

who only know how to waste away their own hearts.

It is hard to see why the young Callimachus should have been inspired to say this to the Muses. Presumably it is the first thing they say to him. So far from giving the *Aetia* a Hesiodic flavour, it injects into the Hesiodic context an echo of the Callimachean controversies of the prologue. The

---

30. P. Oxy. XIX, p. 1; I find it hard to accept his further suggestion (p. 2) that ζώειν ἄξιον in line 6 is an echo of *Works* 112, ὥστε θεοὶ δ᾽ ἔζωον, supplementing ἀ[θανάτων and suggesting a reference to the golden age in Hesiod. I cannot see how ἄξιον fits here. More probably the words develop somehow the proverb in the preceding line.

31. Rather a "pre-existing proverb, not especially appropriate" in the context (West).

Muses tell him (in effect) that the malice of the Telchines will harm only themselves.

I suggest that the sequence of thought here was roughly on the following lines (italics indicating guesswork):

I decided to take the opportunity of asking some questions, remembering that when the Muses met Hesiod they told him about the origin of Chaos...

That would explain both the temporal conjunction that introduces lines 1-2 and the return to Callimachus's affairs by line 5.

The moment he mentioned seeing Muses on Helicon, it was clear to any educated reader that Callimachus had the beginning of the *Theogony* in mind. But readers who knew him would not expect anything so trite as a laborious re-enactment of Hesiod's investiture. That was implied in the mere fact of the imitation. The Muses would only have appeared to a true poet. In any case, young Callimachus had already experienced a much more striking and idiosyncratic divine epiphany, when Apollo himself appeared to him. No laurel branches, no drinks from holy springs. The god evidently recognizes that this youth has the gift already: he just gives him some advice on style. This is what we expect from Callimachus.

It is not Hesiod who is the issue here, nor Hesiodic poetry. It was not initiation by the Muses that caught his fancy, but *conversation* with the Muses. Indeed Callimachus uses this very word himself. Almost immediately after the note in the Oxyrhynchus scholia explaining the tenth Muse, we find a lemma λέσχης (glossed ὁμιλίας), precisely "conversation," followed by "alternating" (ἀμοιβ[, no legible gloss). His two retrospective allusions to the encounter are no less instructive. At prol. 37-8 he says only that the Muses "looked on him with favour when he was a child." In the epilogue he refers to the Muses "conversing with him by the footprint of the fiery horse as he tended his tawny sheep" (F 112. 5-6, cited below). It is not for inspiration that he looks to the Muses, but information.

What may have been a genuine mystical experience for Hesiod[32] Callimachus characteristically treats as a poetic device. He had a lot of separate aetiological stories to fit together. One option open to him, the obvious one, was to set them in a chronological framework, in other words to write an ἄεισμα διηνεκές. This was what Hesiod himself had done. The *Theogony* and its successor the *Catalogue of Women* were archetypal examples of the ἄεισμα διηνεκές. The last thing Callimachus wanted was to write a whole poem like the *Theogony*. But its proem gave him the idea of using the framework of conversation with the Muses as the structure for the whole of his own poem.

32. Kambylis, *Die Dichterweihe und ihre Symbolik* (1965), 52-61; West 1966, 158-161.

What is both original and important about the *Aetia* is not the influence of any one model, but its structure, above all its intrusive narrator. To be sure, this at least is Hesiodic rather than Homeric. In contrast to the invisible Homeric narrator, Hesiod "goes out of his way to be informative about himself and his family," notably (in the *Works and Days*) his brother Perses. Modern readers have been preoccupied with the unreal question "whether he is a figure of flesh and blood."[33] Callimachus may have been more struck by the way the dynamic between narrator and addressee (however inconsistently handled) holds the various themes of the poem together, though he developed it in a quite different way that owes more to the wilful and witty Pindaric narrator than to Hesiod.

This might have been inferred long ago from the Florentine scholiast:

ὡς κατ' ὄναρ συμμείξας ταῖς Μούσαις ἐν Ἑλικῶνι εἰλήφοι παρ' αὐτῶν τὴν τῶν αἰτίων ἐξήγησιν ἀρτιγένειος ὤν...

In the context συμμείξας clearly bears one of its commonest meanings, "meet for conversation," "talk or converse with" (LSJ II. 1). Compare too the late but well-informed anonymous epigram that apostrophizes Callimachus's famous dream (*AP* vii. 42. 5-8):

εὖτε μιν ἐκ Λιβύης ἀναείρας εἰς Ἑλικῶνα
ἤγαγες ἐν μέσσαις Πιερίδεσσι φέρων·
αἱ δέ οἱ εἰρομένῳ ἀμφ' ὠγυγίων ἡρώων
Αἴτια καὶ μακάρων εἶρον ἀμειβόμεναι.

...when you snatched him up and bore him from Libya to Helicon, setting him down in the midst of the Muses. Replying to his questions, they told him the Origins of the heroes of old and the blessed gods.

Here there is no mention of Hesiod at all. The dream whisks Callimachus into the company of the Muses on Helicon and they immediately start trading αἴτια. Of course, these are very abbreviated accounts. Nonetheless, they are the only witnesses we have who at least purport to be describing what Callimachus actually said. To these may be added a third testimonium which appears to have been overlooked, from a Cyrenean poet and man of letters from late antiquity. In the introduction to a book on divination from dreams, Synesius cites the following illustration:[34]

> Nor would it be in the least surprising if a man untouched by the Muses fell asleep, met the Muses in a dream, and, after exchanging question and answer with them, became a skilful poet, a product of my native land.

---

33. West, *Hesiod: Works and Days* (1978), 33-40.

34. *de insomniis* 4 (134D Petau = *Synesii Opuscula*, ed. N. Terzaghi, Rome 1944, p. 150. 20f.). Not noticing the allusion, A. Fitzgerald translated ἄμουσος "quite uncultured" (*Essays and Hymns of Synesius of Cyrene* II [Oxford 1930], 331). A. Garzya's recent Italian version translates correctly ("ignaro di poesia," *Opere di Sinesio di Cirene*, Turin 1989, 563), but, like Terzaghi, supposes an allusion to Hesiod.

εἴ τις καταδαρθὼν ἄμουσος, ἔπειτα ἐντυχὼν ὄναρ ταῖς Μούσαις, καὶ τὰ μὲν
εἰπὼν τὰ δὲ ἀκούσας ποιητής ἐστι δεξιός, ὥσπερ ὁ καθ᾽ ἡμᾶς χῶρος[35]
ἤνεγκεν, οὐδὲ τοῦτο τῶν λίαν ἐστὶ παραδόξων.

Editors of Synesius have identified this as an allusion to the *Theogony*
proem, but in Hesiod there is neither dream[36] nor cross-questioning of the
Muses. Since Synesius twice elsewhere alludes to the *Somnium* and once to
the epilogue,[37] there can be no question about his familiarity with the
Aetia. Synesius confirms the dream encounter, a welcome addition to our
otherwise anonymous testimony. And as in the epigram and the scholia, the
cross-questioning of the Muses directly follows the encounter.

Finally there is the fictitious epitaph that apostrophizes the poet ὦ
μάκαρ, ἀμβροσίῃσι συνέστιε φίλτατε Μούσαις.[38] It is a trifling enough
piece, not unfairly dismissed by Page as "undistinguished." But it is worth
pointing out that, apart from a line of Theognis (1013), the only other surviving poem that opens ἆ μάκαρ is F 2 (= *SH* 317) of Choerilus of Samos,
ἆ μάκαρ, ὅστις ἔην κεῖνον χρόνον...μουσάων θεράπων. From Hesiod
(*Theog*. 100) to Choerilus, the poet had regularly been the servant of the
Muses,[39] but Callimachus was their "boon companion." The parallelism
between συνέστιος and the συμμείξας of the Florentine scholiast suggests
conversation between equals rather than the dependence of an initiation.
Both texts imply that Callimachus's dreaming alter ego enjoyed a new and
altogether unhesiodic relationship with his Muses.

35. My correction of the manuscript χρόνος, which would mean, as Garzya translates,
"quali il nostro tempo produce." But how could Synesius give a series of clues that in combination identify a well-known poet who died 650 years ago—and then say "such as our own
age has produced." When citing the example of Callimachus of Cyrene, the natural point for
a later Cyrenean poet to make is that they shared a common birthplace. In this context it is
worth noting that both Callimachus and Synesius referred to Cyrene as their "mother"
(μητέρα, Syn. *Ep.* 5 [4], p. 12. 2 Garzya; Call. F 602. 3). κατά plus acc. is used here as an
"Umschreibung" for the genitive, a common late usage: for other examples in Synesius see
W. Fritz, *Die Briefe des Bischofs Synesius von Kyrene* (Leipzig 1898), 150. If this was corrupted into the more common formula, twice elsewhere used by Synesius (τοῖς καθ᾽ ἡμᾶς
χρόνοις, *Ep.* 110. 4; τοῦ καθ᾽ ἡμᾶς χρόνου, *De insomniis* 12. 46), οὐδὲ τοῦτο τῶν λίαν ἐστὶ
παραδόξων.

36. To be sure some later sources did interpret the *Theogony* proem as a dream
encounter, but this is certainly not a natural reading of the extant text: *Hesiodo pastori
vigilanti Musae obviam venerant*, as Pfeiffer put it (ad F 2). The Emperor Marcus quoted
Callimachus F 2. 1-2 to Fronto to prove to him that the Muses encountered Hesiod *ambulanti*
(*Ep*. 1. 4. 6, p. 8 van den Hout). The later scholia were doubtless misled by Callimachus: for
more detail, see Kambylis, *Dichterweihe* 55-59.

37. Syn. *hy*. 1. 45 = *Aet*. F 1. 34; Syn. *Ep*. 154 (p. 274. 17 Garzya) = F 1. 1; Syn. *hy*.
8. 31 = F 112. 8.

38. *AP* vii. 41 = *FGE* 350. 3, with Lloyd-Jones, *Acad. Papers* II (1990), 227.

39. Already by Aristophanes's day (*Birds* 909, 913) it had become a "humorous cliché"
(West on Hes. *Theog*. 100).

We have only a few lines of Callimachus's own account. But they are the crucial few lines, and it is the scholiast, the epigrams and Synesius they support, not Reitzenstein. Reitzenstein and his followers relied on sources we have no reason to believe had Callimachus in mind at all: entirely general accounts of the sources of poetic inspiration, just the sort of stuff we should expect an idiosyncratic, ironic writer like Callimachus to avoid. To be sure, he did mention Hippocrene, and Aganippe as well. But the source from which we have learnt this, the Oxyrhynchus scholiast,[40] has also revealed that his interest in mentioning these springs was (as we might have expected) to explain how they got their names.

It is generally assumed that Callimachus returned to Hesiod in the so-called epilogue. Here is the relevant passage once more (F 112. 4-7):

> ...τῷ Μοῦσαι πελλὰ νέμοντι βοτά
> σὺν μύθους ἐβάλοντο παρ' ἴχν[ι]ον ὀξέος ἵππου·
> χαῖρε, σὺν εὐεστοῖ δ' ἔρχεο λωϊτέρῃ.

Certainly lines 5-6 repeat the essence of F 2. 1-2, where Hesiod is referred to by name:

> ποιμένι μῆλα νέμοντι παρ' ἴχνιον ὀξέος ἵππου
> Ἡσιόδῳ Μουσέων ἑσμὸς ὅτ' ἠντίασεν.

But it is not Hesiod who is grazing his flock in the epilogue. The Muses told him no stories. The person to whom the Muses have been telling stories for the last 2000 lines is the young Callimachus. In lines 1-2 Callimachus appears to be addressing Arsinoë (Ch. VI. 6). Lines 5-6 surely refer to the two books of his poem just concluded, the stories the Muses told him in his dream on Helicon. Line 7 greets Arsinoë (or perhaps some deity; line 8 is a similar greeting to Zeus and the "entire royal house"). If the shepherd had been Hesiod, how could Callimachus have switched so abruptly from past to present and back again? But it would be perfectly natural for him to have referred back to the subject matter of his own poem in this way. It would also give some edge to the otherwise unparalleled repetition of almost a whole line if the subject at least were someone else.[41]

There is no question that the *Somnium* is inspired by a famous passage of Hesiod. And there are undoubtedly other passages where the influence of Hesiod can be detected—if not so many or so significant as Reinsch-Werner claimed. But nothing suggests that Hesiod was uniquely important for Callimachus. At a linguistic level the influence of Homer is un-

---

40. Pfeiffer II. 102-03: Aganippe was apparently called Περμησσοῦ παρθένος 'Αονίου.

41. The examples quoted in Pfeiffer's index under the rubric "C. sua ipse verba repetit" are otherwise only brief phrases, and then normally with some variation—and never within the same poem. Like Pfeiffer, I am not counting the distich from F 1. 37-8 repeated in error at the end of *Ep.* 21 (= *AP* vii. 525).

questionably more pronounced. And the memorable sequence of stylistic metaphors in Apollo's speech comes straight from the agon in Aristophanes's *Frogs* (Ch. XI. 5). This speech serves as the vehicle for some of Callimachus's most deeply held views on the nature of poetry. Should we be claiming an Aristophanic "programme" instead? Is Hesiod really more important than Aristophanes for the opening of the *Aetia*?

In order to understand Callimachus's literary aims we must begin by acknowledging that he wrote in more *different* styles and genres than almost any previous poet: elegy, epic, drama, iambics and epigram. No one as versatile as that can possibly have had any one literary guru. An inevitable consequence of such versatility is that the individual genres were not likely to come out pure. Each would undergo some influence from the others. This is exactly the accusation to which *Iamb* 13 responds.

It is tantalizing that we have lost some of the most important parts of this important poem, but what we have opens with the charge that he had not "gone to Ephesus and mixed with Ionians," as anyone who wanted to write "proper scazons" should have done. On the contrary, his verses "talk Ionic and Doric and a mixture of the two." How preposterous (τεῦ μέχρι τολμᾶς;)! In reply, Callimachus asks: " < Who laid down such laws? > 'You write pentameters; you hexameters. To you the gods have allotted tragedy.' Nobody, of course..."

According to the Diegetes, in response to the criticism of writing in too many genres (πολυειδεία, F 203. 1), Callimachus claimed to be "imitating" Ion of Chios.[42] The Diegetes is simplifying, of course. Not surprisingly, since we may be sure that Callimachus also simplified the situation, as he did in the *Aetia* prologue. The basis of the criticism cannot have been his versatility in itself, but rather the consequent distortion of individual genres. Scazons should be in pure ionic, but Callimachus's are a hybrid.

The criticism that he has not been to Ephesus means that he should have made an exclusive study of Hipponax. It is instructive here to turn to the opening of the first *Iambus*:

Ἀκούσαθ' Ἱππώνακτος· οὐ γὰρ ἀλλ' ἥκω
ἐκ τῶν ὅκου βοῦν κολλύβου πιπρήσκουσιν.

Harken to Hipponax. Yes, I've come from where they sell a side of beef for a penny.

What could appear more programmatic? If we knew less about the rest of the *Iambi* than we do, we might have been tempted to see Hipponax as Callimachus's guru, another model he was setting up for modern poetry in place of Homer. As it happens, we know that he was criticized precisely

---

42. Ἴωνα μιμεῖται τὸν τραγικόν, Pfeiffer I, p. 205.

for *not* following Hipponax closely enough. Not through incompetence, of course, but from design. Into the Hipponactean framework he deliberately filtered in all sorts of other influences, not only in details like dialect, but in subject matter too (e.g. the epinician). His purpose was evidently to enrich individual genres by cross-fertilization from whatever other influences caught his fancy.

In the case of the *Iambi* he did at any rate retain the metre and something of the style of Hipponax. But the *Aetia* was not even written in the same metre as Hesiod. And while, as we shall shortly see, it can be categorized as a catalogue poem of sorts, in structure as well as content and above all in metrical practice it is totally un-Hesiodic. To be sure, there are one or two stylistic devices Callimachus shares with Hesiod: picturesque vignettes, fables and proverbs. As K. von Fritz put it[43]

> We might perhaps (at least partly) explain Callimachus's admiration for Hesiod by supposing that, as a self-conscious and refined poet, he had a marked taste for the naive, which he both imitated and treated ironically in his own poetry.

This is true enough. But we find this fondness for proverbs and fables in the *Iambi* and *Hymns* no less than the *Aetia*—and not least in the epigrams. It will be enough to quote one example that has been generally misunderstood: the long epigram on the marital advice of Pittacus the sage (*AP* vii. 89). There is more to it than the "flatness" seen by Gow and Page. In two papers on the form of fables, E. Fraenkel pointed out with many examples, first that the "So you too (οὕτω καὶ σύ)" of the last line is the standard way in which such homely texts draw their lesson; and second, that the simple paratactic structure of the poem as a whole (ὁ δὲ...οἱ δὲ...χὠ μὲν...οἱ δ') captures perfectly the artless style of the fable.[44] Clearly it would be absurd to see Hesiod as the sole or even major source of this notable feature of the Callimachean manner. When he quoted Ion as his model in *Iamb* 13, he meant, not that he was imitating some particular poem of Ion, but that he was imitating Ion's *versatility*. Though best known as a tragedian, Ion also wrote dithyrambs, paeans, encomia, hymns, elegies, skolia, epigrams and perhaps comedies too, not to mention some interesting and perhaps influential prose works.[45]

43. "Das hesiodische in den Werken Hesiods," in *Hésiode et son influence* (Entretiens sur l'Antiquité Classique VII, Fondation Hardt) Geneva 1960, 47.

44. "Zur Form der αἶνοι," *Rh. Mus.* 73 (1920), 366 with *Eranos* 49 (1951), 53 = *Kl. Beitr.* i. 236 and ii. 55; for the first formula, note too *Iamb* 14 (F 226, Dieg.).

45. Jacoby, *CQ* 41 (1947), 1f.; K. J. Dover, *Chios: A Conference at the Homereion on Chios* (Oxford 1986), 27-37.

2

Thus armed, we may now turn to the epigram on Aratus (*Ep.* 27 = *AP* ix. 507):[46]

Ἡσιόδου τό τ' ἄεισμα καὶ ὁ τρόπος· οὐ τὸν ἀοιδόν
ἔσχατον ἀλλ' ὀκνέω μὴ τὸ μελιχρότατον
τῶν ἐπέων ὁ Σολεὺς ἀπεμάξατο. χαίρετε λεπταί
ῥήσιες, Ἀρήτου σύντονος ἀγρυπνίη.

For reasons that will soon become clear, discussion of details must precede translation. The poem is regularly quoted as though it were entirely unproblematic, a straightforward eulogy of Aratus for imitating Hesiod. According to Farrell, Vergil "learned from Callimachus to revere Aratus as a kind of neo-Hesiod."[47] Von Fritz wondered whether his suggestion (just quoted) accounted for what he described as the "entirely genuine and not in the least condescending admiration" of the epigram for Hesiod. Reitzenstein and his followers went much further than this. But *is* it so straightforward, so unambiguous? All that seems beyond dispute is (a) that the poem as a whole must be favourable to Aratus; and (b) that lines 2-3 praise him through some sort of antithesis, not A but B.

Reitzenstein followed Wilamowitz in printing Scaliger's ἀοιδῶν in line 1, identifying ἀοιδῶν ἔσχατος as Homer[48] and assuming that Aratus is being praised for *not* imitating Homer[49]—a hit at Apollonius, according to Wilamowitz.[50] There are a number of objections to this view—and a number of alternative interpretations.

1) While no one would quarrel with the description "highest" or "best" of poets for Homer, ἔσχατος is simply not found in this sense without some support in the context, here absent.[51] On the contrary, applied to a person without qualification, it seems always to bear a pejorative sense, "last" or "worst." Anyone who (quite naturally) so read the word here

46. The issues are clearly stated by Gow and Page, *HE* II 208-09; for earlier references, M. Gabathuler, *Hellenistische Epigramme auf Dichter* (Diss. Basel 1937), 12, 59-61; for later bibliography, Herter, *RE* Supp. XIII (1973), 226; most recently, E.-R. Schwinge, *Künstlichkeit von Kunst* (1986), 11-16.

47. Farrell 1991, 164.

48. So, to quote a recent example at random, Farrell 1991, 44 and 164, twice quoting the text of the epigram in full without any indication that ἀοιδῶν is not the transmitted text, and without offering either translation or interpretation.

49. This idea seems to go back to Dilthey (1863, 12f.); more recently, Lyne 1984, 18.

50. *HD* I 206.

51. As B. A. van Groningen, (*La poésie verbale grecque* [Amsterdam 1953], 81-82) and W. Ludwig (*Hermes* 91 [1963], 427-28) rightly emphasised; so too G. Lohse, *AuA* 19 (1973), 31. Even so, H. Herter reaffirmed his earlier support (1937, 188) "so schwer auch die lobende Bedeutung von ἔσχατον zu belegen sein mag" (*Gnomon* 27 [1955], 256 n. 1).

would miss the (alleged) point entirely. Until an unqualified example of ἔσχατος = best can be found, this interpretation can hardly be taken seriously.

2) Even if it could mean "best," there would still be problems. For it would be paradoxical to reject "best" in any circumstances, least of all for "sweetest." It would be another matter to contrast sweet with (say) majestic or grandiloquent. There are times when grandiloquence is out of place and sweet might be just right, but best is always best. No one wanting to claim that Hesiod was better than Homer would call Homer "best of poets" while doing so.

Elsewhere Callimachus does apply "sweet" to the refined style: to the elegies of Mimnermus at F 1. 11; to his own ib. 16. But that does not in itself imply the exclusion or rejection of epic. For example, another elegist of the age, Hermesianax, calls Homer "sweetest of all poets" (F 7. 28), no doubt echoing the description of Homer himself in the *Hymn to Apollo*.[52]

3) We should be reluctant to attribute to Callimachus the false and absurd claim that Aratus rejected Homer for Hesiod. Though he chose a Hesiodic rather than Homeric theme, and occasionally imitated specific passages of Hesiod, his debt to Homer is unquestionably greater.[53] He had, after all, edited both *Iliad* and *Odyssey*.[54] It is not enough to reply (with Reinsch-Werner) that no one writing hexameters could avoid using Homeric language. Aratus deliberately imitated a number of specific Homeric passages.[55] Furthermore, and more remarkable still, it seems clear that the acrostich λεπτή at lines 783-7 was modelled on the (no doubt quite accidental) acrostich λευκή with which book 24 of the *Iliad* opens.[56] Both acrostichs are adjectives, with the same case, same gender, same accent, same metrical value, same number of letters, beginning and ending with the same letters. Here is particularly striking proof of deliberate Homeric emulation. It is relevant to compare the case of Nicander, author of various didactic poems and so (it might be thought) another imitator of Hesiod (whom he cites by name at the beginning of his *Theriaca*) rather than Homer. Yet over and above the fact that he is a particularly keen Homeric "glosshunter,"[57] Nicander actually describes himself as "Homeric" (Ὁμ-

52. ἥδιστον πάντων δαίμονα μουσοπόλων (F 7. 28) ~ ἀνὴρ ἥδιστος ἀοιδῶν (*HAp.* 169).

53. "In dieser Hinsicht sind die Homerischen Epen aber wohl noch wichtiger," Ludwig, *Hermes* 91 (1963), 442-45, quoting a number of specific illustrations.

54. Pfeiffer 1968, 121-22; Martin, *Histoire* 174.

55. A. Ronconi, "Arato interprete di Omero," *Stud. ital.* 14 (1937), 167f.; 237f.; A. Traina, "Variazioni omeriche in Arato," *Maia* 8 (1956), 39f.; Ludwig, *Hermes* 91 (1963), 442-5.

56. On which see J.-M. Jacques, *RÉA* 62 (1960), 48-50; E. Vogt, *AuA* 13 (1967), 85.

57. W. Kroll's phrase, *RE* 17. 1 (1936), 259. Note too that Nicander worked his own name into an acrostich at *Ther.* 345-53, and tried to do so again at *Alex.* 266-74: E. Lobel, *CQ* 22 (1928), 114.

ἤρειος) in his sphragis (line 957).[58]

4) Some time ago, a neglected article by H. N. Porter pointed out that in his metrical practice Aratus did owe more to Hesiod than to Homer.[59] Porter dealt with sense pauses and restrictions on the placing of words ending with a long syllable in the arsis of the third, fourth and fifth feet. His four yardsticks were the practice of Homer, Hesiod, Callimachus and Apollonius. Callimachus, as is well known, refined the Homeric hexameter by rejecting some Homeric patterns and using others exclusively. Aratus, by contrast, followed Hesiod in affecting some of the less common Homeric lines, those rejected completely by Callimachus.[60] That is to say, wherever Aratus is closer to Hesiod than to Homer, Callimachus is closer to Homer. As Porter himself concluded:

> Callimachus, a nice critic, gave high praise to the *Phaenomena* though his own practice in composition was so different. He could not, for example, have written lines 2 and 3 of the text from which we took our start [*Phaen.* 1-4].

There can be little doubt that this is part at least of what Callimachus had in mind when he praised Aratus for catching Hesiod's "manner" (τρόπος). But it was one thing to praise the Hesiodic colouring that was natural and appropriate in a didactic poem written in hexameters. There is nothing here to suggest that this was an ideal at which he aimed himself.

5) According to *Vita I*, Callimachus mentioned Aratus "not only in his Epigrams[61] but also in his πρὸς Πραξιφάνην, praising him highly as an excellent poet and learned man."[62] Rohde thought the second title designated no more than a book dedicated to Praxiphanes.[63] Since the appearance of his name among the Telchines in the Florentine scholia, it has been identified rather as a polemic *against* Praxiphanes. This is no doubt correct,[64] but there is no evidence whatever that the "subject of the work, or at least the chief subject, was the Long Epic (Schol. Flor.), a problem in which...Callimachus fundamentally differed from the Peripatos."[65] The Florentine scholia say nothing about Long Epic; there is no evidence that Callimachus differed from the Peripatos about epic; there is no evidence that Aratus played any part in any such controversy (if there was one); and the reference in the *Vita* does not in itself imply that Callimachus was

58. It was perhaps understandable that Colophonian poets should claim such a title.

59. "Hesiod and Aratus," *TAPA* 77 (1946), 158-170; Ludwig, *RE* Supp. X (1965), 34-6.

60. Hollis's account of Callimachean metric (1990, 15-23) illustrates a number of other respects in which Callimachus differs sharply from Aratus.

61. Which need not imply more than one epigram; it is a title, his Epigram Book.

62. *Scholia vetera in Aratum* p. 9. 8 Martin = F 460 Pf.

63. *Der griechische Roman*³ (1914), 106 n. 3; cf. Brink, *CQ* 1946, 12-14.

64. πρός in titles is common in both senses: for discussion, Brink, *CQ* 40 (1946), 14.

65. Brink, *CQ* 1946, 25, followed by Wehrli, *Schule des Aristoteles* IX² (1969), 111.

defending Aratus against Praxiphanes, on this or any other count. In short, there is nothing here either to support Reitzenstein's case.

6) A marginally better way of interpreting the epigram (with W. Ludwig)[66] is to give ἔσχατον its pejorative sense and read it as a litotes referring to Hesiod. That is more natural Greek, but the antithesis is poor: "The song and style is Hesiod's; it is not the worst of poets Aratus has imitated, but the sweetest of his verses." To this view van Groningen rightly objected that οὐ τὸν ἀοιδῶν ἔσχατον "is merely the negative and imprecise expression of the positive and precise idea that follows."[67] With Callimachus, we expect a sharper point than this.

7) According to van Groningen, the epigram is a response to the criticism that Aratus had picked a bad model. "No (Callimachus replies), he did *not* imitate the worst of poets, but in fact the very sweetest of poems." Yet a good epigram should not depend for its point on something the average reader could not be expected to know.[68] Nor is it likely that Aratus's poem was ever controversial. Hesiodic poetry was all the rage in the early third century (§ 3), nor was it even the first Hellenistic didactic poem.[69] Aratus's Hesiodic colouring was so mild (as Callimachus goes on to point out) that such a strong reaction is incredible.

All these interpretations presuppose Scaliger's ἀοιδῶν for the ἀοιδόν of both *AP* and *Vita I* of Aratus. Most critics have wasted no time on the unanimous transmitted text. But as Kaibel saw a century ago, it can be construed to yield both a satisfactory sense and an excellent antithesis: "imitated the poet not to the uttermost, not down to the last detail (οὐ τὸν ἀοιδὸν ἔσχατον), but, it must be admitted (ὀκνέω μή), only the sweetest part of his verses."[70] That is to say, Callimachus's praise is qualified. Aratus did not imitate the more extreme Hesiodic features, only the sweetest bits.

Reitzenstein's most recent and enthusiastic disciple, Hannelore Reinsch-Werner, denounced this interpretation precisely because of its qualified attitude towards Hesiod, arguing that "nowhere else in Callimachus is there any indication that Hesiod is anything but wholly exemplary."[71] The truth is that there is no indication anywhere in Callimachus that Hesiod is "ex-

66. *Hermes* 91 (1963), 427-28.

67. "ne serait que l'expression négative et indécise de l'idée positive et précise qui suit" (*La poésie verbale grecque* [1953], 82-83).

68. It could be objected that this is precisely the case with the *Aetia* prologue. But there it is at least obvious that Callimachus *is* replying to his critics, and however much he caricatures it, he does at least purport to quote their criticism.

69. It is a pity that we have nothing from the didactic poems of Menecrates of Ephesus, said to have been Aratus's teacher. He wrote an *Erga* and a work on astronomy (*SH* 542-50). It would be interesting to know if he too had followed Hesiodic metrical patterns.

70. *Hermes* 29 (1894), 120; see too A. W. Mair (Loeb 1921), 156.

71. Reinsch-Werner 1976, 12.

emplary" at all. It is disturbing to report that her polemic against Kaibel betrays no awareness that he was interpreting a different text—the transmitted text.[72]

She also argued that, after a beginning proclaiming "here is pure Hesiod," it would have been a contradiction to praise Aratus for not imitating him to the limit. But Ἡσιόδου τό τ᾽ ἄεισμα καὶ ὁ τρόπος does *not* mean "here is pure Hesiod." Callimachus begins by enumerating two Hesiodic features that (he concedes) Aratus has captured, his "song" (meaning subject matter) and his "manner" (style and metrical technique); and goes on to claim that he ἀπεμάξατο only the sweetest part of Hesiod, a word most commentators have been content to render "imitate" without further comment. But the root meaning is "wipe off" or "skim off," extended to the "levelling" of grain by drawing a strickle across the container. Even in the metaphorical sense "take an impression," "imitate" (as in Callimachus's model, *Frogs* 1040),[73] there is often more than a hint still of the root meaning. For example, Nonnus, *Dion.* 46. 18,

ἤθεα σῆς δολίης ἀπεμάξαο καὶ σὺ τεκούσης,

where (as so often) Rouse catches the nuance nicely:

You also have a touch of your deceitful mother.

Callimachus uses the word once elsewhere metaphorically, at *Hymn to Delos* 14, where the sea rolling round the island

Ἰκαρίου πολλὴν ἀπομάσσεται ὕδατος ἄχνην.

Here the picture is quite clearly of foam being "skimmed off" the surface of the sea.

The root meaning is surely uppermost in the Aratus epigram too: he is being praised for "skimming off" the sweetest part of Hesiod's poetry. The implication is that there was a substantial residue left behind that was not sweet, or at any rate not as sweet. This squares perfectly with the interpretation of ἔσχατον as "to the limit," "in every respect."

Both Reinsch-Werner and Ludwig assumed that τὸ μελιχρότατον τῶν ἐπέων designated a specific poem of Hesiod, namely the *Works and Days*, described as "the sweetest *of epics*."[74] It was no doubt primarily the *Works and Days* that Callimachus had in mind,[75] but he is not referring to any particular poem. Not (surely) "the sweetest [sc. epic] of epics," but "the

---

72. She prints Scaliger's ἀοιδῶν without even indicating that it is an emendation.

73. LSJ, s.v. III; Dover on *Frogs* 1040.

74. Ludwig, p. 428; Reinsch-Werner, p. 326 (twice); Reitzenstein is a little vague.

75. Hardly the pseudo-Hesiodic *Astronomia*, as Merkelbach and West assumed (quoting *Ep.* 27 under the testimonia to that poem in their *Fragmenta Hesiodea* [1967], 148). See Ludwig, *Hermes* 91 (1963), 428-9.

sweetest part, feature or element *of his verses.*" I would suggest the following translation of the first two and a half lines:

> It is Hesiod's song and style. The man from Soloi has not captured the poet entire, but skimmed off the sweetest part of his verses.

This interpretation has the added advantage of helping out the inconcinnity of the antithesis between οὐ τὸν ἀοιδόν (m.) and ἀλλὰ τό μελιχρότατον (n.). If it is felt that this inconcinnity still leaves the balance of the antithesis less than perfect, I venture to put forward a suggestion of my own that would restore a perhaps needed neuter article with ἔσχατον: οὐ τό γ᾽ ἀοιδοῦ, "not the most extreme feature of the poet."[76]

Every line in the poem tells the same story, even the closing apostrophe, which has given rise to much misunderstanding and unnecessary emendation.[77] I take it that the point turns on an elaborate word play. On one level, ἀγρυπνίη represents unremitting (i.e. sleepless) labour,[78] at another it suggests that the astronomical poet works at night. In musical jargon, σύντονος, "severe," is the opposite of ἀνειμένη, "relaxed." Most people relax at night, but of course Aratus is looking at the stars, and does not. The root meaning of λεπτός is "husked," "peeled," here "refined," "subtle," in the context picking up the root meaning of ἀπεμάξατο. Aratus has first skimmed off and then refined the best of the raw material in Hesiod. So what the compliment of the last line and a half adds up to is: refinement (λεπταὶ ῥήσιες) that is the result of painstaking labour.

We saw in an earlier chapter that it was from Aratus that Callimachus borrowed his famous concept of λεπτότης. Since he clearly adopted the ideal for himself, for most purposes it does not greatly matter who originated it. But for the interpretation of *Ep.* 27 it does make a difference. It was not for writing a "Hesiodic epic" that Callimachus admired Aratus, but for his *refinement*, his linguistic polish, his avoidance of the commonplace. For all his merits, Hesiod was by any criteria one of the most *un*refined of all the major Greek poets. This (of course) is the point of Callimachus's epigram. In the ordinary way, Hesiod might have seemed an unpromising model for a modern poet. But Aratus pulled it off, by skilful selection of detail. He contrived to catch something of the Hesiodic manner and *still* write a modern poem.

---

76. G. Luck, *Gnomon* 33 (1961), 368 n.1, suggested οὐ τό γ᾽ ἀοιδῶν, which I confess I cannot understand. Page, *Epigr. Graeca* 1402, suggested οὗτοι ἀοιδῶν ἐσχάτου, which offers no clear gain in sense in return for such extensive rewriting—and a double correption.

77. G. Lohse, *Hermes* 95 (1967), 379-81; Cameron, *CR* 86 (1972), 169-70; L. Lehnus, *Riv. di Fil.* 118 (1990), 31.

78. For a study of metaphorical ἀγρυπνία, R. F. Thomas, *HSCP* 83 (1979), 195-205.

3

The ancient Lives of Aratus record a debate as to whether the poet owed more to Hesiod or Homer. Reitzenstein saw this as a debate that went back to the age of Callimachus, one aspect of the larger Hellenistic debate on the imitation of Homer as a generic model.[79] It must be said that the Lives themselves lend no support whatever to such a view.

According to *Vita II*, at the verbal level (κατὰ τὴν τῶν ἐπῶν σύνθεσιν) Aratus was an imitator of Homer, "but some say he was rather an imitator of Hesiod." The latter claim is substantiated by comparing Aratus's first line with the beginning of the *Works and Days* to establish that both begin with Zeus, and then quoting his use of the story of the golden age "and other myths like Hesiod." This adds up to no more than saying that his style was Homeric but his subject matter Hesiodic. The ancient scholia on Aratus quote Homer twice as often as Hesiod.[80] According to *Vita III* a certain Dionysius[81] wrote a work *On the comparison of Aratus and Homer*. *Vita II* quotes an extract from the commentary by Boethus of Sidon, who wrote no more than a century after Callimachus:[82]

> In Bk I of his work on Aratus he says that the poet is not an imitator of Hesiod, but rather of Homer. For the invention (πλάσμα) of his poem is more elevated than Hesiod...because he has the power of the physical philosophers [namely the cosmological poets].

There is no suggestion here of any debate about which was the more suitable model. Simply traditional scholarly study trying to establish which was in fact the more influential model. Those who argued for Homer rather than Hesiod were no doubt reacting to Callimachus's (already very qualified) praise of his Hesiodic qualities. Reinsch-Werner thought Reitzenstein's interpretation the only one that set Callimachus's epigram in its literary-historical context. But this was a context Reitzenstein had invented himself. The true, documented literary-historical context he simply ignored.

It was neither Callimachus nor Aratus who began the Hellenistic vogue for Hesiodic poetry, not did it first appear or attain its greatest popularity in epic. It was not so much a hackneyed epic vogue Callimachus was combatting as a hackneyed elegiac vogue. This (of course) is why the *Aetia* prologue is concerned not with epic but with elegy, explicitly alluding to

---

79. Swallowed (e.g.) by Farrell 1991, 45, 217.

80. See Martin's index: pp. 574 (Hesiod), 575-6 (Homer); or E. Maass, *Commentariorum in Aratum Reliquiae* (1898), 636 and 637-8.

81. Perhaps Dionysius of Phaselis: Ch. VIII. 2.

82. Martin, *Histoire du Texte* 18-22 (on Boethus) and 188-9.

individual works by the most celebrated ancient and modern elegists respectively—Mimnermus and Philitas.

Inasmuch as it was a catalogue of unhappy love stories, Antimachus's *Lyde* may be considered the first Hesiodic elegy. Nor did the poets of the early third century restrict themselves to praising the *Lyde*. They produced elegiac catalogues of their own, one after another.[83]

It is unfortunate that we know so little of what may have been the first, the evidently substantial elegy of Philitas that Callimachus disparaged as his "big lady," though it is an old and reasonable guess that it was named after the Bittis he is represented as singing about by his disciple Hermesianax (F 7. 77). Another big lady was the *Leontion* (again named after a mistress) of Hermesianax. The one surviving fragment, from Bk III, is much the most crudely Hesiodic poem to have survived from the golden age of Hellenistic literature.[84] In less than 100 lines Hermesianax introduces no fewer than five of the lovers in what Athenaeus bluntly calls his "catalogue" with a Hesiodic οἷος formula (F 7. 1; 57; 71; 85; 89).

From the same period we are fortunate to have a substantial fragment from another such elegiac catalogue, the *Loves*, or *Beautiful Boys* of Phanocles.[85] The first line of this fragment is unmistakably alluded to by Apollonius (iv. 903), which makes him a predecessor or contemporary of Callimachus. Here we find the same mechanical linking of successive stories as in Hermesianax: two of the three extant fragments begin ἢ ὡς (F 1. 1; 3. 1).[86] It is no doubt only coincidence (though an interesting coincidence) that the longest story to survive from each concerns Orpheus, Hermesianax telling of his love for Argiope (F 7. 1f.), Phanocles for Calaïs (F 1). Several shorter fragments and testimonia add the names of many other hetero- and homosexual pairs celebrated by the two poets. They evidently cast their net as widely as Antimachus, who included even the love story of Oedipus (F 70 Wyss)! It is difficult to believe that Philitas's *Bittis* was significantly different in kind from its predecessor and successors, especially in the light of the sweeping criticism in the *Aetia* prologue, which appears to take in all earlier elegists.

Next comes another of Callimachus's older contemporaries, Alexander Aetolus.[87] The long fragment from his *Apollo* quoted by Parthenius may

83. For a brief characterization, see the chapter "Kataloggedichte" in F. Skutsch, *Aus Vergils Frühzeit* (Leipzig 1901), 50-60 (mainly on the later period); Hopkinson 1988, 117-18; L. Watson, *Arae: The Curse Poetry of Antiquity* (Leeds 1991), 96-100.

84. *CA*, pp. 98-105; also useful are Gulick's translation and notes in the Loeb Athenaeus (VI [1937], 218-229) and J. Defradas, *Les élégiaques grecs* (Paris 1962), 91-102.

85. *CA*, pp. 106-09; von Blumenthal, *RE* 19. 2 (1938), 1781-3; on his date, Leutsch, *Philol.* 12 (1857), 66; Wilamowitz, *HD* I. 198; Marcovich, *AJP* 100 (1979), 360-66.

86. εἰδὼς MSS; ἢ ὡς Powell, though so already Crusius, *RE* 5. 2. (1905), 2282 n.**.

87. Alexander was at the court of Antigonus with Aratus: Fraser I. 555.

have been a catalogue of clients at the oracle of Didymaean Apollo (Ch. VI. 7). There is less to be said about Alexander's other identifiable elegy, called *Muses*. The only fragment cited from it by name (*CA* 124) gives an account of Timotheus's *Hymn to Artemis* (*PMG* 778); F 5 (conjecturally assigned to the *Muses*) describes the popularity of the parodists Boeotus and Euboeus at Syracuse. Given the controversial role played by Mimnermus in the literary polemics of the age, it is curious to find Boeotus praised here for reaching the "heights" of Mimnermus (F 5. 4, unfortunately a very corrupt passage). It is an attractive but unverifiable conjecture that the poem was a catalogue of the literary genres, or at least of earlier poets.

The γυναικῶν κατάλογος of Nicaenetus of Samos, a younger contemporary of Callimachus, is unfortunately no more than a title. He is called ἐποποιός and wrote one hexameter poem, but also a number of elegiac epigrams. Given the evident popularity of the elegiac catalogue at this period, it ought not to be taken for granted that the κατάλογος was an epic.[88] Even less is known of the *Or such men as* of Sosicrates (or Sostratus) of Phanagoreia, though the title (᾽Hoῖoι) marks it out as a complement to Nicaenetus's *Catalogue*, perhaps on male lovers of the gods.[89] If Sostratus is the correct form, then we may assign to this work the account of the seven different lives and loves (alternately as man and woman) of Teiresias summarized by Eustathius (*SH* 733). This would nicely fit the title, as would another story Eustathius reports from Sostratus, about Paris as the lover of Apollo.[90] If so, we would have proof that the poem was an elegy, since Eustathius says so. In addition, the sands of Egypt have recently presented us with an elegiac curse poem, discussed further below.

Last comes Callimachus himself. Though seldom explicitly so categorized, the *Aetia* clearly belongs to the same family. It is an elegiac catalogue poem in several books, differing only in theme (aetiological stories), arrangement and treatment. Looking at the poem in this context, no one would have seen the reference to Hesiod in the *Somnium* as programmatic or polemical. It was certainly not intended to indicate that Callimachus was proposing to write in a genre or manner that was new. Both would have been obvious enough to any contemporary from the metre and title alone.

We have no information on how Antimachus linked his stories. The likelihood that the whole of Bk I was devoted to the Argonauts (including a

---

88. *CA*, p.2, F 2; Diehl, *RE* 17. 1 (1936), 245.

89. *SH* 731-5; the title is quoted (together with that of Nicaenetus) by Athen. 590B. It does not seem necessary, with Gulick (Loeb ad loc.) or Hopkinson (1988, 178) to see it as a "parody" of Hesiod.

90. He says Alexandros, but evidently meant Helenos: *SH* 734, with notes.

non-erotic version of the split with Heracles) suggests that individual stories were merged into a continuous, more or less chronological narrative (Ch. XII. 2). With Hermesianax the structure was monotonous and the mechanisms all too obvious. For example, two epic poets (Hesiod and Homer) followed by two elegiac (Mimnermus and Antimachus), two lyric (Alcaeus and Anacreon) and two tragic (Sophocles and Euripides); 4 lines each allotted to Alcaeus, Sophocles, Philitas, Pythagoras and Aristippus; 6 to Hesiod, Mimnermus, Antimachus, Anacreon, Philoxenus and Socrates; 8 to Homer and Euripides. The crudely Hesiodic οἷος is repeated five times in 15 stories.[91] Then second-person apostrophes, presumably (as Rohde saw) to Leontion. There was personal potential here, but Hermesianax handles them all in the same mechanical way, merely as variations on the οἷος formula. E.g. the story of Philitas's love is introduced οἶσθα δὲ καὶ τὸν ἀοιδόν...(F 7. 75); at line 49 γιγνώσκεις the story of Alcaeus, and then even this formula is repeated within 25 lines, γιγνώσκεις ἀΐουσα (73, of Philoxenus). Hermesianax's third device was to use the first person, though in no less impersonal and mechanical a way. At lines 21 and 61 he introduces new stories with the formula φημὶ δὲ καὶ. It may be more than coincidence that this seems to have been the formula with which Callimachus replied to the Telchines at prol. 7: [φημὶ δὲ] καὶ Τε[λ]χῖσιν ἐγὼ τόδε. In his vocabulary, too, Hermesianax drew heavily and mechanically on Homer and Hesiod.[92]

In Phanocles there are no first or second persons, only two ἢ ὡς formulas in three fragments. The 28-line fragment "contains very few words not found in Homer, the Homeric hymns, or early elegy," and many of the epithets are conventional.[93] For example: 6 θαλερόν, 7 κακομήχανοι ἀμφιχυθεῖσαι, 10 θηλυτέρων, 14 γλαυκοῖς, 15 πολιή, 24 δεινόν, 26 στυγεροῦ.

There is rather more to be said about Alexander Aetolus. The basic technique of his "prophecy" is future tenses. In itself this is natural and reasonable enough. Callimachus uses the same technique for Athena's prophetic speech in his fifth hymn (107-130), though with more subtlety than Alexander, who has 16 futures in 34 lines. Even the god's asides are in the future; e.g. the reference at F 3. 9-10 to Actaeon who "will be a joy to Corinth and a bane to the harsh Bacchiads." Clearly the dramatic date of the prophecies is before the age of the Bacchiads. Who is it then who is consulting the oracle? Perhaps Branchus (subject of the partly extant poem by Callimachus, F 229). At all events, certainly not the poet himself, the fruitful device used by Callimachus throughout *Aetia* I-II. If the *Apollo*

---

91. And yet Giangrande can claim (*Scr. Alex. Min.* II 391) that H. "introduces each poet in a new manner."

92. H. Lloyd-Jones, *Acad. Papers* II (1990), 209; further below.

93. Lloyd-Jones, *Acad. Papers* II 212-3; Hopkinson 1988, 179; Stern, *QUUC* 32 (1979), 135-43.

(like Lycophron's *Alexandra*) was couched in the future tense throughout, the monotony would soon have become intolerable.

The one long fragment does not begin with any specific introductory formula, but the pomp of formulaic epic proclaims the beginning nonetheless:

παῖς Ἱπποκλῆος Φόβιος Νειληιάδαο
ἔσται ἰθαιγενέων γνήσιος ἐκ πατέρων (F 3. 1-2).

Here we may compare the opening lines of the Orpheus story in Hermesianax and Phanocles respectively:

οἵην μὲν φίλος υἱὸς ἀνήγαγεν Οἰάγροιο (F 7.1).

ἢ ὡς Οἰάγροιο πάϊς Θρηίκιος Ὀρφεύς (F 1.1).

Whichever came second simply repeated his predecessor's colourless patronymic Οἰάγροιο. In fact, what was said earlier about banal or inappropriate epic influence on Antimachus's elegiac style applies equally to Alexander. The most conspicuous single example is when the queen kills the young man who has rejected her advances. How should a lady do the deed: poison, or a dainty dagger? Without a hint of wit or irony Alexander describes how, like some Ajax or Diomede, she

ἀμφοτέραις χείρεσσι μυλακρίδα λᾶαν ἐνήσει (F 3. 31),

will drop a millstone on him with both hands.

It is surely this sort of thing Callimachus had in mind when he wrote of the braying of donkeys. The climax of the story, when the queen is turned down and plots her beloved's doom, is all told in one breathless couplet. So far from the one speech making us feel something of the murderess's passion, she devotes six routine lines to asking him to fetch a cup she has dropped down the well.[94] Since the characters were never alive, we feel no sorrow when Alexander does them to death in the same mechanical way.

A popular subdivision of catalogue poetry was curse poetry.[95] Until recently, Callimachus's *Ibis* was generally held to have been the model (if not the first) Hellenistic curse poem,[96] but we now have almost fifty lines of what seems to be an earlier example, a poem in which, bizarrely enough, the writer threatens to tattoo his enemy with representations of punishments suffered by mythical sinners.[97] Or so at any rate Lloyd-Jones

94. There is a good appreciation of Alexander's versification, vocabulary and style in Couat 1931 (1882), 111-14; "tadeln kann man weder die Sprache noch den Versbau, aber das Ganze zu loben wird nicht leicht einer geneigt sein," Wilamowitz, *HD* I. 198.

95. Studied in detail by L. Watson, *Arae: The Curse Poetry of Antiquity* (Leeds 1991).

96. Wilamowitz, *BKT* v. 1 (1907), 64; Watson 1991, 167. The earliest is the Ἀραί of Moiro.

97. Obviously the poet is exploiting the motif of "penal tattooing" for criminals, widely documented among the Greeks and Romans, especially (but not exclusively) for slaves: for

interpreted the fragment from a second-century B.C. papyrus roll published by Papathomopoulos in 1962.[98] In 1987 Giangrande vehemently rejected this interpretation, vigorously supported (as usual) by loyal disciples,[99] but his timing was bad. For in 1991 another fragment of the same papyrus identified and published by M. Huys proved Lloyd-Jones right.[100] We now know that three successive sections of the poem began with the word στίξω,[101] "I shall tattoo" (I. 5, II. 4, III. 18), in each case introducing a new myth.[102] This is certainly more original than ἢ οἷος, but even so was bound to become monotonous in a poem of any length. Lloyd-Jones emphasized the conventional diction, more straightforwardly close to Homer and earlier poets than Callimachus and his followers.[103] Huys's detailed commentary has confirmed this conclusion. He skilfully illustrates the way the poet adapts and varies Homeric models,[104] but the overall effect is overwhelmingly Homeric nonetheless.

While not insisting on an identification, Lloyd-Jones pointed to stylistic similarities with Phanocles and was fairly sure that "the new poem belongs to that very obscure period in Greek literary history, the first part of the third century." Huys accepted the general point, but argued instead for Hermesianax. The poet is certainly repetitious in much the same way as Hermesianax,[105] and the new column tells the story of Heracles's battle with the Centaur Eurytion (I. 5f.), a battle for which Pausanias cites Hermesianax.[106] But the story is not so very rare,[107] nor does the new version fit Pausanias's citation (for the smallness of the city of Olenos). We have

---

details, C. P. Jones, *JRS* 77 (1987), 147f.

98. *Rech. de Pap.* 2 (1962), 99-111; H. Lloyd-Jones and J.W.B. Barns, *SIFC* 35 (1963), 205-27 = Lloyd-Jones, *Acad. Papers* II (1990), 195-215; *SH* 970.

99. *Mus. Phil. Lond.* 8 (1987), 111-18; M. A. Rossi, *L'Ant. class.* 57 (1988), 311; K. Alexander, *A Stylistic Commentary on Phanocles* (Amsterdam 1988), 123-162.

100. *Le Poème élégiaque hellénistique P. Brux. Inv. E. 8934 et P. Sorbonn. Inv. 2254* (Pap. Brux. Graec. II. 22, Bruxelles 1991); also Bremer and Huys in *ZPE* 92 (1992), 118-20.

101. The universal Greek term for tattooing: Jones 1987, 139-55.

102. Although all that remains of III. 18 is στίξ[ω, a paragraphos immediately above indicates a new section: see Huys p. 15 for the placing of paragraphoi in the papyrus.

103. "Callimachus would not have used ἀναιδέα λᾶαν ((l. 4) or σὺν ἀργιόδοντα (l. 14), nor would he have written τὸ γὰρ φίλον ἔπλετο κούρῃ (l. 16), which so closely resembles the Homeric τὸ γὰρ φίλον ἔπλετο θυμῷ" (Lloyd-Jones 1990, 209).

104. E.g. (omitting a few dots and brackets) Τριτωνὶς Ἀθήνη for the Homeric γλαυκῶπις Ἀθήνη, καὶ ἀπειθέα χῶρον for καὶ ἀτερπέα χῶρον: for a full collection of examples, Huys pp. 82-86; Bremer and Huýs 1992, 119-20.

105. καὶ εἰν Ἀίδεω in successive pentameters (I. 5, 7); ἀξυνέτου γλώσσης χάριν in I. 6 followed by γλώσσης δοὺς χάριν ἀξυνέτως five lines later (described as "variation élégante" by Huys); for other examples, Huys pp. 91-2; for Hermesianax's repetions, Ch. XI. 3.

106. *CA* 106 F 9, with Huys pp. 77-79.

107. For the various versions, Huys p. 40.

too little of either the new poem or Hermesianax to justify a confident conclusion,[108] and it is perhaps worth briefly stating the claims of a third possibility: the poetess Moiro of Byzantium. Not only did she write elegies (as
well as hexameters and lyrics) around 300, but alone of the three she is
known to have written a curse poem, entitled Ἀραί, *Curses*, cited more
than two centuries later by Parthenius.[109] Her admiration for Homer was
such that she so named her son—surely something of an embarrassment for
the young man when he too in due course turned to poetry.[110]

Whoever the author, it is particularly valuable in the present context to
find yet another catalogue elegy from the generation before Callimachus
which, despite its ultimate Hesiodic inspiration,[111] is so heavily under the
influence of Homer.[112] Here again we see the artificiality and irrelevance
of the supposed antithesis between Homer and Hesiod. If I am right, what
Callimachus objected to was elegies that pushed mechanical imitation of
either Homer or Hesiod too far. Against this context, the qualified attitude
to Hesiodic imitation displayed in the Aratus epigram assumes a new and
highly pointed relevance. For in Hermesianax we have a poet who *did*
imitate the ἔσχατον rather than the μελιχρότατον of Hesiod. So far from
commending imitation of Hesiod rather than Homer in his epigram, Callimachus was praising Aratus for *not* going all the way in his Hesiodic
imitation, for selecting (like Callimachus himself) the "sweetest" elements.
The evidence suggests that at the time Callimachus was writing his *Aetia*,
Hesiodic elegy was more in vogue than Cyclic epic. And Apollo had
warned him (prol. 25-6), τὰ μὴ πατέουσιν ἅμαξαι, τὰ στείβειν.

---

108. S. R. Slings argues that the prosody is looser than Hermesianax's (*ZPE* 98 [1993],
29-37), and suggests a "clumsy amateur" instead; against, Lloyd-Jones, ib. 101 (1994), 4-7.

109. *CA* 21-3; Susemihl I. 381; *HE* II. 413-5.

110. Homer the younger, one of the tragic Pleiad: Susemihl I. 271-72.

111. In addition to Huys passim, see Watson 1991, 261-64.

112. When Callimachus pictures poets tattooing other poets in *Iamb* 13, it may be more
than the tattooing of runaway slaves he has in mind.

Chapter XIV

The Cyclic Poem

1

No text has been more widely cited as evidence of Callimachus's alleged distaste for epic than *AP* xii. 43:[1]

ἐχθαίρω τὸ ποίημα τὸ κυκλικὸν, οὐδὲ κελεύθῳ
　χαίρω τὶς πολλοὺς ὧδε καὶ ὧδε φέρει·
μισέω καὶ περίφοιτον ἐρώμενον, οὐδ᾽ ἀπὸ κρήνης
　πίνω· σικχαίνω πάντα τὰ δημόσια.
Λυσανίη, σὺ δὲ ναίχι καλὸς καλός· ἀλλὰ πρὶν εἰπεῖν
　τοῦτο σαφῶς, ἠχώ φησί τις "ἄλλος ἔχει."

I loath the Cyclic poem, nor do I take any pleasure in the road that carries many this way and that. I also loath a gadabout lover, nor do I drink from the public fountain. In fact, I detest everything vulgar. Lysanies, you are so, so handsome—but before I get the words out clearly Echo says "he's someone else's."

Scholars more interested in Callimachus's views on literature than love simply quote the first five words, which, taken by themselves, look unequivocal enough: "I hate the Cyclic poem." Yet in context this is not at all the *ex cathedra* judgment that Pfeifer's "angry pronunciamento"[2] or Conte's "manifesto of the new poetry" would suggest.[3] Most then go on to assume that Cyclic poetry stands for all post-Homeric epic, including (in fact especially) Antimachus and Apollonius.[4] Some would even include Homer himself in the indictment; for example, the recent translation by W. R. Johnson:[5]

I detest the grandeur of oral saga...

There are major objections to this sort of interpretation.

1. II GP = 28 Pf.; my translation makes no attempt to render the final "echo."
2. Pfeiffer 1968, 230.
3. *YCS* 29 (1992), 149; he also calls it a "literary profession of faith."
4. For example, V. J. Matthews cites the poem as evidence that Callimachus "completely rejected imitation of Homeric poetry" (*Eranos* 77 [1979], 47).
5. *The Idea of Lyric* (Berkeley 1982), 100. Unsatisfactory in a different way is Paton's "I detest poems all about the same trite stories..."

2

To start with the poem must be studied as a whole. For it is much more
than a statement of Callimachus's poetic creed.[6] It is a subtle erotic
poem—too subtle indeed for most critics and commentators, who (when
they do not ignore) make heavy weather of the last couplet, some actually
deleting it as an interpolation.[7]

As Henrichs has observed, the first four lines are a reverse priamel,
four things the poet does not like.[8] The last couplet states what he does
like. The originality and appeal of the whole lies in the final twist. Callimachus cannot after all have what he likes—because it turns out to be just
another example of what he does not like.

It is reading the poem back to front to state (with Zetzel) that Callimachus "expressed his scorn for common or public themes in no
uncertain terms, comparing epic poetry to a common whore."[9] For the successive images of the first four lines—the main road, the "gadabout lover"
and the public fountain—are not intended to refer *back* to the Cyclic poem,
but *forward* to the erotic last couplet. The Cyclic poem is merely the first
(and most paradoxical) of these images. In fact, like some of the best of
Callimachus's other epigrams, this one too begins by misdirecting us. We
might compare *AP* vii. 521 ("If you go to Cyzicus, it is easy to find Hip-
pakos and Didyme..."), which eventually turns out to be a funerary poem,
with all the ingredients of a regular epitaph (name of deceased, parents, and
native city), but arranged in an unexpected way.

Just so xii. 43, which begins as though a poem about literature. To his
dislike of the Cyclic poem, Callimachus adds main roads. In the light of
the metaphorical main roads of F 1. 25-8, we are tempted to look for
literary undertones here too. On the face of it the "gadabout lover"
(περίφοιτον ἐρώμενον) in line 3 represents a change of tack. But Richard
Thomas has suggested an interpretation in terms of the use of περιπατεῖν
in New Comedy for "the young lover's vigil before the house of his
beloved."[10] For Thomas the περίφοιτον ἐρώμενον "is the frustrated lover
who wanders about in New Comedy."[11] He offers as a free translation: "I
also hate (along with bad epic) comedy and all its stereotypes."

6. Koster 1970, 119 cites the first couplet for Callimachus's literary views without giving
any hint that the poem as a whole dealt with another subject.

7. For modern studies up to 1988, Lehnus 1989, 295-97; the main issues are well set out
in Gow and Page (*HE* II. 155-7), more polemically in the various papers of Giangrande.

8. Henrichs 1979, 207-12.

9. *Ancient Writers: Greece and Rome* ii, ed. T. J. Luce (New York 1982), 648.

10. Even in New Comedy περιπατεῖν is used in a variety of other senses, as Thomas
concedes.

11. *HSCP* 83 (1979), 182-84, a "sure conclusion."

It is axiomatic for Thomas that the poem as a whole is "patently a major statement of literary theory"[12]—the tedious fallacy of assuming that Callimachus was more interested in poetical theory than poetry. It is sufficient refutation by itself that ἐρώμενος means not (active) "lover," but (passive) "beloved."[13] After all, ·Callimachus wrote a number of epigrams about the inaccessibility of the ideal ἐρώμενος, of which this very poem (not that Thomas mentions it) is perhaps the most striking and elaborate example. He agrees (in a footnote) that Callimachus almost certainly had in mind Theognis 579-82:

> ἐχθαίρω κακὸν ἄνδρα, καλυψαμένη δὲ πάρειμι
>   σμικρῆς ὄρνιθος κοῦφον ἔχοντα νόον·
> ἐχθαίρω δὲ γυναῖκα περίδρομον, ἄνδρά τε μάργον,
>   ὃς τὴν ἀλλοτρίην βούλετ' ἄρουραν ἀροῦν.

But (he argues) "verbal reminiscence does not imply the same poetic purpose." Maybe it does not *guarantee*, but it surely implies it, as does the other example of περίφοιτος in an epigram of Callimachus: τὰ δῶρα τἀφροδίτῃ / Σῖμον ἡ περίφοιτος, εἰκόν' αὐτῆς / ἔθηκε τήν τε μίτρην / ἢ μαστοὺς ἐφίλησε... (*AP* xiii. 24 = XX GP). The goddess to whom the dedication is being made and the objects dedicated confirm the usual assumption that the dedicator is a hetaira and that περίφοιτος = "promiscuous." Thomas dismisses even this parallel from Callimachus himself in a footnote, with the claim that it "in no way works against" his interpretation. But when combined with Theognis it surely establishes beyond reasonable doubt that περίφοιτον ἐρώμενον in *AP* xii. 43 means "promiscuous (male) beloved." While a case might be made for an alternative sense for *either* περίφοιτον *or* ἐρώμενον if the context required it,[14] to reject the natural interpretation of the two combined in an erotic epigram is simply out of the question. There is no relevant reference here to literary theory.

Last comes drinking from the fountain, evidently a public fountain. Once more it is Theognis (959-62) who seems to be Callimachus's main inspiration:

12. *HSCP* 83 (1979), 182.

13. To this overwhelmingly well-documented objection from usage Thomas feebly replies that the "possible objection to allowing ἐρώμενον to have middle force can be answered first with the point that there is no reason *prima facie* why it should not," yet he cannot in fact find a single example of the form ἐρώμενος in the sense required, and finally pleads "Callimachean *variatio*."

14. For example, in the only (dubious) cases Thomas was able to cite from an Alexandrian poet of ἐράομαι middle for active (Theocr. i. 78; ii. 149; Gow saw both as "eccentric forms of ἔραμαι") the context requires the active meaning. In such cases, the implications of the context and the possibility of ambiguity are always key factors.

ἔστε μὲν αὐτὸς ἔπινον ἀπὸ κρήνης μελανύδρου,
    ἡδύ τί μοι ἐδόκει καὶ καλὸν ἦμεν ὕδωρ·
νῦν δ᾿ ἤδη τεθόλωται, ὕδωρ δ᾿ ἀναμίσγεται ὕδει·
    ἄλλης δὴ κρήνης πίομαι ἢ ποταμοῦ.

In Theognis the imagery is sexual throughout. Drinking alone (αὐτός) is loving without a rival; the muddying of the water signifies infidelity; and drinking from another source seeking another love. In view of the metaphorical river and spring in the *Hymn to Apollo* (Ch. XV), Callimachus's fountain *might* have a literary reference. But sandwiched between the preceding gadabout lover and the overtly erotic following couplet, and in view of Theognis's erotic fountain, it seems natural to see the erotic metaphor as predominating in Callimachus too.

The turning point is the main road. While appearing to maintain the literary misdirection of the Cyclic poem, leading us to expect a literary climax, in fact it inaugurates the very different motif of distaste for things public that will dominate the rest of the poem and lead to an erotic climax.

Some critics, mistakenly thinking that the gadabout lover was (or should be) the climax of Callimachus's list, have faulted him for placing it third instead of last. But he has deliberately mixed up very disparate objects of his distaste. Thus to pass from a promiscuous lover (whom all would despise) to a public fountain (which most of us drink from without a thought) serves to underline Callimachus's altogether exceptional fastidiousness.

In the last couplet he turns to what he likes, the boy Lysanies (a predominantly Cyrenean name,[15] not that this makes the poem autobiographical or places its composition in Cyrene). But no sooner has he uttered aloud the usual exclamation of the lover, ναίχι καλὸς καλός,[16] than a distorting echo repeats part of his words in such a way that he seems to hear (according to the text of *AP*), ἄλλος ἔχει, "another has him." In real life, of course, Echo reverberates indistinctly any sound that is loud and clear enough. But in literature, a favourite motif is the distinct repetition of just part of an utterance, usually the last word or two, in such a way that its sense is reversed or it becomes an omen.[17] For example, the six

15. *LGPN* 1 (1987), 292 (also common on Rhodes).

16. For a list of the 283 καλός-graffiti (including literary texts) known when they wrote, D. M. Robinson and E. J. Fluck, *A Study of the Greek Love-Names* (Baltimore 1937); J. D. Beazley, *Attic Black-figure Vase-painters* (Oxford 1956), 664-78, *Attic Red-figure Vase-painters* ii² (1963), 1559-1616 and *Paralipomena* (1971), 505f. listed almost 300 kalos names from vases alone, some attested by 30 different vases, one by more than 50. For a series of rock-inscriptions from Thasos with καλός-acclamatioris, Y. Garlan and O. Masson, *BCH* 106 (1982), 3-21.

17. What the Greeks called a κληδών, an "omen, presage contained in a chance utterance" (LSJ s.v. I).

lines of *APl* 152 each close with a one-word echo of this sort: for example, ἁ δέ μ᾽ οὐ φιλεῖ in line 2 is echoed φιλεῖ, "she loves me" instead of "she doesn't love me."[18] But Callimachus adds a characteristically ingenious touch: it is Echo's vulgar pronunciation that is responsible for the distortion. For the distortion turns on the phonetic equivalence of ἔχει = (ν)αίχι.

The spelling of Ptolemaic papyri confirms the equivalence of αι = ε and ει = ι in popular pronunciation.[19] Nor is this the only example in Callimachus. In the long Acontius fragment the Etesian winds are derived from the "entreaties" of the priests of Ceos (ἐτησίαι from αἰτεῖσθαι).[20] And in *Hymn to Apollo* 103 the ritual address ἰὴ ἰὴ παιῆον is derived from people telling the young Apollo ἵει, ἵει, παῖ, ἰόν, "shoot, shoot your arrow, boy."[21] Some scholars have treated all three cases as evidence for pronunciation.[22] But fanciful etymologies in a context that encourages the reader to look for them are hardly parallel to a simple mishearing.

The general point has never been in doubt, but the details of the distortion are nonetheless problematic. In the first place, Echo seems to reverse the order of the poet's words (ναίχι καλός / ἄλλος ἔχει); in the second, Echo seems to repeat not the second half of the utterance as a whole, but the second half of both the individual words, dropping both the κ of καλός and the ν of ναίχι. Wilkinson feebly argued that the echo of just the syllables ((κ)αλός, (ν)αίχι) "was enough to make the point."[23] But who can believe that so consummate a craftsman as Callimachus was satisfied with so irregular and approximate an echo? According to Koenen there are two echoes, each truncated.[24] This is not only implausibly complicated; why do the successive echoes truncate the exclamation so differently?

It is not uncommon to find an intensifying ναί or ναίχι before or (more commonly after) the καλός on vase graffiti.[25] Elsewhere Callimachus intensifies the καλός in a different way, καλὸς ὁ παῖς...λίην καλός (*AP* xii. 51); Strato refers to a boy as ἄγαν καλός (xi. 22); Meleager as καλὸς γὰρ, ναὶ Κύπριν, ὅλος καλός (xii. 154); and there are other examples in Hellenistic epigrams of repeated καλός.[26] ναίχι is a vulgarism, found only

18. See too *AP* ix. 177; Ovid, *Met.* iii. 359f.; Giangrande, *Eranos* 1969, 5 n. 11.

19. E. Mayser and H. Schmoll, *Grammatik der griechischen Papyri aus der Ptolemäerzeit* I. 1² (Berlin 1970), 85 (αι = ε) and 60-70 (ει = ι), neither spelling found in Attic inscriptions before the Roman period (L. Threatte, *The Grammar of Attic Inscriptions* I (Berlin 1980), 294-9 and 199-202), but then inscriptions are inevitably more conservative.

20. F 75. 36, with K. Strunk, *Glotta* 38 (1960), 86.

21. Strunk 1960, 79-80; Williams's note ad loc.

22. Strunk 1960 (also quoting earlier examples); Koenen 1994, 88.

23. *CR* 17 (1967), 5-6.

24. Koenen 1993, 87-88.

25. E.g. Robinson and Fluck nos. 187-88, 190, 214.

26. Anon. *AP* xii. 62. 1; 130. 1; [Theoc.] 8. 73.

once even in comedy,[27] and so undoubtedly chosen with some care by Callimachus. It is an important element in the phrase, and must be given full weight in Echo's distortion.

According to Giangrande, ναίχι καλὸς καλός is not just praise of Lysanias's beauty, but "a declaration of love by the ἐρῶν to the ἐρώμενος."[28] This cannot possibly be true of the vast majority of καλός graffiti, inscribed as they were on vases, walls, stelai or tree-trunks;[29] in most cases there is no reason to believe admirer and admired even acquainted. The author of [Theocritus] 8. 73-5 describes how a girl cried καλὸς καλός at him as he passed by with his herd, to which he made no reply, but looked down and went on his way. She may have loved him from afar, but her advances were not welcome and she could not reasonably have complained of betrayal if she learned that he was already in love with the "fair Nais" (8. 43). On the evidence of the epigram, there is no reason to believe that Callimachus had ever even spoken to Lysanies.

Giangrande emended to κάλλος ἔχει, "another has him as well," arguing (repeatedly) that the point of the poem is the poet's discovery that Lysanies is a gadabout lover.[30] But there is nothing to suggest that Lysanies is his lover at all, let alone that he has betrayed him. The implication is rather (a) that matters have progressed no further than the poet expressing his appreciation of Lysanies's good looks in the usual way; and (b) that Lysanies has a lover already.

ἔχειν is standard Greek for "have as wife" (normally without γυναῖκα),[31] and, by natural extension, "have as a lover," that is to say a regular or steady lover, whether male or female.[32] So far from Echo telling the poet that his own lover is cheating on him, she tells him that he is someone else's lover. There is no hint that Lysanies is promiscuous; simply that he has a boyfriend already.

27. Due seminari romani di Eduard Fraenkel [Rome 1977], 52; K. J. Dover, Greek and the Greeks i (Oxford 1987), 23.

28. Most emphatically at Giangrande 1975, 16-17; cf. 1967, 8 n. 17.

29. K. J. Dover, Greek Homosexuality (London 1978), 111-12.

30. "Callimachus, Poetry and Love," Eranos 67 (1969), 33-42; restated (ever more polemically and abusively, but with no new arguments or evidence) in Eranos 70 (1972), 87-90; Maia 26 (1972), 228-30; Maia 26 (1974), 228f.; Quad. Urbin. 19 (1975), 111f.; Mus. Phil. Lond. 4 (1981), 32; Quad. Urbin. 34 (1990), 159-61. It is sobering to reflect that this chapter will inevitably provoke yet another outburst.

31. LSJ s.v. A. 4; for Herodotus (e.g.), Powell's Lexicon (1938), s.v. 2a and b; there is one case in Callimachus, where Cydippe swears νυμφίον ἐξέμεναι Acontius (F 75. 27).

32. For example, Thuc. 6. 54. 2 of Aristogeiton and Harmodius, ἐραστὴς ὢν εἶχεν αὐτόν; anon. skolion PMG 904. 2, κἀγὼ παῖδα καλὴν τὴν μὲν ἔχω, τὴν δ' ἔραμαι λαβεῖν; Asclepiades, AP, v. 158. 4, μὴ λυπηθῇς ἤν τις ἔχῃ μ' ἕτερος; Aristippus in Diog. Laertius 2. 75, ἔχω Λαΐδα, ἀλλ' οὐχ ἔχομαι; Theocr. ii. 158; Philodemus, AP vi. 46. 2 and 308. 3. See too Giangrande 1969, 8 n. 17 for other cases where ἔχειν simply = "have intercourse with."

Anyone would be distressed if his lover betrayed him. What we expect after lines 1-4 is a dénouement that arises out of Callimachus's exceptional fastidiousness. For someone with Callimachus's almost pathological distaste for sharing anything with anybody, even so insubstantial a hint of a rival as an echo is enough to discourage. Here we may compare *AP* xii. 102, another misdirected erotic poem: After devoting four lines to the hunter who pursues beasts in the hills and snow, but refuses to touch a wounded animal, he concludes:

> χοὐμὸς ἔρως τοιόσδε· τὰ μὲν φεύγοντα διώκειν
> οἶδε, τὰ δ᾽ ἐν μέσσῳ κείμενα παρπέταται.

A lover does not have to be promiscuous or unfaithful for Callimachus to "pass him by," merely available. This is in essence the same unattainable counsel of perfection as xii. 43.

Since Echo so often picks up the end of an utterance, it is not in itself impossible (as Giangrande argued) that she clips off the first letter of (ν)αίχι, which the poet hears as ἔχει. But problems remain. While the reader with κάλλος rather than καλός on the page in front of him will get the point easily enough, how is the speaker himself supposed to reinterpret his καλός as κάλλος just because of Echo's (as he hears it) ἔχει?

The simplest solution is to read ἄλλον...ἔχει.[33] If the relationship is mutual, there is no difference between "another has him" and "he has another." The accusative could easily have been attracted into the nominative by the preceding τις. Now we only have to follow Callimachus's own explanation to the letter. Echo interrupts him before he has quite finished his exclamation (πρὶν εἰπεῖν τοῦτο σαφῶς). The first word Echo says has to be ναίχι. The poet has not yet sounded the final consonant of the second καλός when Echo's ναίχι (which he hears as νεχει) interrupts him, with the syllables αλο still on his lips: αλο...νεχει = ἄλλον ἔχει.

So what does the epigram tell us about Callimachus's attitude to Cyclic poetry? Certainly that he did not like it; that he was as fastidious about literature as he was about love. But why Cyclic poetry? Rather than assume (as many have, from Welcker on) that "Cyclic poem" is here an oblique reference to Antimachus or Apollonius, let us consider what the term actually meant to Callimachus and his contemporaries, and what it was they disliked about it.[34]

33. Schneider long ago suggested ἄλλον...ἔχειν, side-stepping the problem of Echo's actual words by turning the phrase into *oratio obliqua*. But I am not aware that anyone has proposed ἄλλον...ἔχει.

34. The evidence is collected in T. W. Allen, *Homeri opera* v (1912), 93f.; M. Davies, *Epicorum Graecorum Fragmenta* (1988) and (more generous in both content and annotation) A. Bernabé, *PEG* i (1987); see too A. Lesky, *History of Greek Literature*[2] (1966), 79-88 and M. Davies, *The Epic Cycle* (Bristol 1989).

There is no evidence that any poem later than the sixth century was ever counted as part of the Epic Cycle.[35] A scholion on Clement of Alexandria limits it to the *Cypria, Aethiopis, Ilias parva, Iliu persis, Nostoi* and *Telegoneia*, the six poems that fill in the gaps before, between and after the *Iliad* and *Odyssey*, poems old enough to be ascribed to Homer and so worth distinguishing from the genuine article. The grammarian Proclus prefixed a *Titanomachia* and a Theban sequence (*Oedipodea, Thebais, Epigonoi*).[36] It was the *Cypria* and *Ilias parva* that Aristotle singled out for disunity of plot compared with the *Iliad* and *Odyssey* (*Poetics* 1459c1). Modern scholars have found other ways of demonstrating their inferiority.[37]

The few surviving references to the Cycle in the Homer scholia derive from Aristarchus and identify linguistic usages which are post- or un-Homeric.[38] Another much commoner term used the same way in the Scholia is οἱ νεώτεροι, again designating later writers cited for post-Homeric usages. But in contrast to κυκλικός, οἱ νεώτεροι is employed with much wider reference, taking in Callimachus and Apollonius and even the tragedians.[39] There is no evidence that "Cyclic" was ever used as a catchall designation of early epic, much less epic poetry in general. Even on the more comprehensive definition, there remains a large body of early epic never classified as Cyclic: for example, the various anonymous poems cited under the titles *Alcmeonis, Phocaïs, Minyas, Danaïs, Phoronis, Naupactia,* and *Amphiari exelasis*; not to mention the other ranking poets of the epic canon, Hesiod, Creophylus, Asius, Peisander, Eumelus, Panyassis and Antimachus.[40] Interestingly enough, however (perhaps not surprisingly after the last chapter) at least one source, Philo of Byblus, did count Hesiod as Cyclic: "Hesiod and the notorious Cyclic poets who write *Theogonies* and *Gigantomachies* and *Titanomachies*."[41]

---

35. "Quamquam cyclicos poetas parvi aestimant Scholiastae, apud eos κυκλικῶς non 'vulgariter, inepte' vel sim., sed 'cyclicorum poetarum modo' tantum significat," Bernabé, *PEG* i. 8 (with bibliography). This is not to say that all Cyclic poems were written as early as the seventh century; some—e.g. the *Cypria*—may be as late as the second half of the sixth: J. Wackernagel, *Sprachliche Untersuchungen zu Homer* (1916), 178f.; Davies, *The Epic Cycle* 3-4.

36. These are the works included as Cyclic by Davies and discussed in his *The Epic Cycle*.

37. J. Griffin, "The Epic Cycle and the Uniqueness of Homer," *JHS* 97 (1977), 39-53.

38. Preserved in the A Scholia by the Augustan Aristonicus, as first recognized by K. Lehrs, *De Aristarchi studiis Homericis* (1833), 1-15; Pfeiffer, 1968, 214; 213; cf. Bernabé, *PEG* i. 7-8.

39. A. Severyns, *Le cycle épique dans l'école d' Aristarque* (Paris 1928), 31-61; Cameron, *HSCP* 84 (1980), 135-39 (quoting also examples of *neoterici* in the Latin Scholia, referring to the poets of the Silver Age).

40. Some 40 names are included by Bernabé and Davies, who both go down to the fifth century. For a general attempt to characterize these writers, G. L. Huxley, *Greek Epic Poetry from Eumelus to Panyassis* (London 1969), with M. L. West, *CR* 21 (1971), 67-9.

41. *FGrH* 790 F 2 (40); Davies, *EGF* 16; Bernabé, *PEG* i. 8.

There is no reason to believe that Callimachus' words were either intended or understood to apply to all or any of these works—even Antimachus. It is true that one set of late scholiasts calls Antimachus a Cyclic poet, the commentaries on Horace ascribed to Porphyrio and Ps-Acro: *Antimachus fuit cyclicus poeta* and *cyclicus...significat Antimachum poetam.* The passage of Horace that is the object of these comments (*AP* 136-7) runs as follows:

> nec sic incipies ut scriptor cyclicus olim:
> "fortunam Priami cantabo et nobile bellum."

Horace is offering his own translation of what is clearly a Cyclic poem in the strict sense, a poem about the Trojan war. Antimachus did not write on the Trojan war. His only epic was a *Thebaid.* The scholiasts are not quoting genuine information about Antimachus; they are *guessing* the identity of Horace's "scriptor cyclicus." For some reason Antimachus's name had got into the Horatian scholiastic tradition, perhaps a distant echo of Callimachean polemic mediated through Latin poets like Catullus and taken to refer to the epic poem that was still read rather than his now forgotten elegy. According to the same Porphyrio scholia, Antimachus "filled 24 books before bringing the seven leaders to Thebes." Though repeated as fact by modern critics who should know better,[42] this cannot possibly be true.[43] Indeed on the basis of the surviving fragments, B. Wyss argued that the seven were all at Thebes as early as Bk i, and that the next few books were devoted to flashbacks describing their respective exiles in the best Homeric manner.[44] The only genuine information on show here is that Antimachus wrote 24 books. The rest is guesswork using this information to explain Horace.

According to Henrichs, "Thematically, all four items in his catalogue participate in the same defect, to wit lack of exclusiveness. Poetry in the tradition of the epic cycle touches on too many subjects, just as a busy road, a promiscuous lover, and the parish pump serve too many needs." That is to say, Henrichs assumes that Callimachus is criticizing the Cycle on Aristotelian grounds, for lacking any unifying focus. It is likely enough that Callimachus would have agreed with Aristotle's position: his depreciatory use of the term Cycle is in itself disproof enough of Pfeiffer's improbable assertion that Callimachus's views on epic were anti-Aristotelian.[45] But how can this be got from what Callimachus actually says? For the Cyclic poem does not "lack exclusiveness" in the same way

---

42. E.g. Headlam, *Herodas* (1922), xi; Newman 1986, 101.
43. Versions of both notes also appear in other late Horatian scholia (Wyss, p. lxvi).
44. Wyss 1936, ix-x.
45. Pfeiffer 1968, 137: "The new poetical school of Callimachus and his followers was ostentatiously anti-Aristotelian. Rejecting unity, completeness, and magnitude..."

as the main road, the gadabout lover, the public fountain and above all the beautiful Lysanies. It was having to share them with others that Callimachus disliked. This cannot have been what he disliked about Cyclic poetry.

In view of his well-documented preoccupation with Homeric language and style, we may assume that it was mainly in un-Homeric features of language and style that Callimachus, like Aristarchus, recognized the cloven hoof of the Cyclic poet. The sort of things Aristarchus stigmatized as κυκλικόν were: pointless and insensitive repetition (κυκλικῶς ταυτολογεῖται);[46] misuse of words (e.g. νείκεσσε where there was no connotation of reproach: κυκλικῶς κατακέχρηται· οὐδὲν γὰρ λέγεται ἐπιπληκτικόν);[47] and indiscriminate use of epithets (e.g. the description of the trees in Alcinous's orchard *Od.* vii. 115: οὐ κυκλικῶς τὰ ἐπίθετα προσέρριπται, ἀλλ᾽ ἑκάστου δένδρου τὸ ἰδίωμα διὰ τοῦ ἐπιθέτου προστετήρηται).[48] Aristarchus provided the detailed linguistic proof of Aristotle's intuition that the Cyclic poems could not have been written by Homer.

κυκλικῶς in such comments clearly means "in the manner of the Cyclic poets,"[49] though, given its uniformly depreciatory connotation in Aristarchus, it is easy to believe (as LSJ allege, though without producing any convincing examples)[50] that the adjective might eventually have come to bear the secondary meaning "commonplace" or "conventional." Commentators often allege that this is its meaning (or at any rate connotation) in Callimachus's epigram. But such a secondary meaning, if it existed at all, must surely have been a post-Aristarchan development.

Whatever general depreciatory undertones he intended, there seems no reason to doubt that it was the sub-Homeric Cycle poetry Callimachus was attacking. We may compare the following poem by the first- or second-century A.D. epigrammatist Pollianus (*AP* xi. 130):

τοὺς κυκλικοὺς τούτους, τοὺς "αὐτὰρ ἔπειτα" λέγοντας
    μισῶ, λωποδύτας ἀλλοτρίων ἐπέων.
καὶ διὰ τοῦτ᾽ ἐλέγοις προσέχω πλέον· οὐδὲν ἔχω γὰρ
    Παρθενίου κλέπτειν ἢ πάλι Καλλιμάχου.
"θηρὶ μὲν οὐατόεντι" γενοίμην, εἴ ποτε γράψω
    "εἴκελος," "ἐκ ποταμῶν χλωρὰ χελιδόνια."
οἱ δ᾽ οὕτως τὸν Ὅμηρον ἀναιδῶς λωποδυτοῦσιν,
    ὥστε γράφειν ἤδη "μῆνιν ἄειδε, θεά."

46. Σ to Ο. 610-4*a* (IV. 127. 33 Erbse).
47. Σ to Ζ.325*a* (II. 188. 88 Erbse); cf: I. 222*a* (II.447. 25 Erbse).
48. Σ BEP to η. 115; Pfeiffer, *HCS* 230, n.3.
49. So rightly H. J. Blumenthal, *CQ* n.s. 28 (1978), 125-26.
50. In fact the only reasonably secure example appears to be a passage of the second century A.D. philosopher Numenius, quoted by Eusebius, *PE* 11. 22. 9: Blumenthal 1978, 126-27.

Before we proceed, there is a textual point to be cleared up. Both *AP* and *APl* offer κυκλίους in line 1, which is held to be equivalent, here alone in Greek literature, to κυκλικός and to denote epic. Pollianus's poem has a rubric all to itself in *LSJ*,[51] and Brink (for example) goes out of his way to state that "Pollianus' use of κύκλιος...for the writers of the epic cycle seems to be exceptional and late."[52] But applied to a literary genre, κύκλιος is elsewhere invariably linked to χορός, normally in the plural, and refers to dithyrambic poetry. The origin of the term is supposed to have been the circular formation of dithyrambic choruses, contrasted to the rectangular arrangement of dramatic choruses.[53] The dithyrambic poet was regularly styled ὁ τῶν κυκλίων χορῶν ποιητής, and a dithyrambic contest was an ἀγὼν τῶν κυκλίων χορῶν.[54] In the fifth century, a pipe-player (αὐλητής) accompanied the chorus. As time passed and the musical element came to dominate, it was the pipe-player who became the star and the chorus who accompanied him.[55] In later times agonistic inscriptions record the αὐλητὴς μετὰ χόρου or χοραύλης or κύκλιος αὐλητής, but we still find frequent mention of the ἀγὼν τῶν κυκλίων χορῶν. That is to say, κύκλιος continued to bear the same technical reference in Pollianus's day, at the turn of the first and second centuries A.D. Such contests continued to be a standard event at early imperial festivals,[56] and must have been familiar to him. Is it credible that he should have so misused so standard and familiar a term? Since only one letter distinguishes κύκλιος from κυκλικός, the obvious solution is that it is not Pollianus but some later copyist who confused the words.

There is in fact one further, less well known apparent example of κύκλιος = Cyclic, in an epigram from a copy of the *Bibliotheca* attributed to Apollodorus. It does not survive in any extant manuscript, but is quoted in Photius's brief summary in his own *Bibliotheca*. In line 5, both Photius manuscripts and all editors offer κυκλίων where I would correct to κυκλικῶν:[57]

51. So LSJ s.v. κύκλιος 3 (which does not cite the Apollodorus epigram discussed below).

52. *Horace on Poetry* II (Cambridge 1971), 213.

53. Athen. 181C; A. W. Pickard-Cambridge, *Dithyramb, Tragedy and Comedy*[2] (Oxford 1962), 32.

54. Pickard-Cambridge, *Dith. Trag. and Comedy*[2] l.c.; *Dramatic Festivals of Athens*[2] (Oxford 1968), 74, 239; L. Robert, *Études épigr. et philol.* (Paris 1938), 34-35.

55. E. Reisch, χορικοὶ ἀγῶνες, *RE* 3. 2 (1899), 2434-8; L. Robert, l.c.; B. Gentili, *Poetry and its Public in Ancient Greece* (Baltimore 1988), 27-30.

56. O. Crusius, *RE* 5. 1 (1903), 1226-29; Robert, l.c.; Pickard-Cambridge, *Dramatic Festivals*[2] 74; M. Wörrle, *Stadt und Fest im kaiserzeitlichen Kleinasien* (Vestigia 39), Munich 1988, 230, 250; West, *Ancient Greek Music* 93 n. 63.

57. Cod. 186 (p. 142b Bekker = III. 40 Henry); R. Wagner, *Mythographi Graeci* i (1904), 3.

αἰῶνος <σ>πειρήμα<τ'> ἀφυσσάμενος ἀπ' ἐμεῖο
παιδείης, μύθους γνῶθι παλαιγενέας,
μηδ' ἐς Ὁμηρείην σελίδ' ἔμβλεπε μηδ' ἐλεγείην,
μὴ τραγικὴν Μοῦσαν μηδὲ μελογραφίην,
μὴ κυκλικῶν ζήτει πολύθρουν στίχον· εἰς ἐμὲ δ' ἀθρῶν
εὑρήσεις ἐν ἐμοὶ πάνθ' ὅσα κόσμος ἔχει.

Drawing the coils of time from my erudition, learn the myths of old. Do not
look into the book of Homer, nor elegy, nor the tragic Muse, nor lyric poetry,
nor look for the clamorous verse of the Cyclic poets. Look at me; in me you
will find every story in the world.

What the writer means is that, thanks to the material collected in the
Bibliotheca, readers no longer need search for the relevant information in
the poems listed. In the ordinary way, epigrams on books seldom derive
from the author himself; many are much later compositions, some even
Byzantine.[58] But there are indications that this poem is early, perhaps even
by Ps-Apollodorus himself.[59] First, book-epigrams of the Byzantine period
are never in elegiacs. Second, the conception of time as a snake with coils
is a familiar ancient (especially Orphic) motif,[60] surely suggested to the
author by the sort of poems he was reading. Third, it is now generally
agreed that the *Bibliotheca* is not (as used to be thought) based entirely on
earlier mythological manuals, but directly derived from the original poetic
sources: for the Trojan cycle, as the epigram says, Homer, tragedy, and the
Epic Cycle.[61] This is surely the proud boast of the author: his book really
did save people the trouble of reading the archaic and classical poets—some
of them actually lost by late antiquity. So there can be no question that the
reference in line 5 is to the poems of the Epic Cycle proper (several of
them cited by name in the course of the book), not dithyrambs. There is
also surely a depreciatory note in the "clamorous" (πολύθρουν), suggesting

58. See my *Greek Anthology* 333, where I now regret having classified the Apollodorus
epigram as Byzantine, mainly on the basis of the hiatus entailed by the transmitted reading
<σ>πείρημα in l. 1 (printed in all editions). But σπειρήματα in the plural (Salmasius) are
more likely on grounds of sense as well as metre: see F. Jacobs, *Animadv. in Anth. Graec.*
III. 2 (1801), 184. Salmasius's παρ' for ἀπ' would further improve the metre. Most of those
transmitted in the Anthology are directly ascribed to later poets: see the 96 collected in M.
Gabathuler, *Hellenistische Epigramme auf Dichter* (Leipzig 1937).
59. There seems little doubt that the book cannot be earlier than the 1st c. A.D., and so
not by the mid 2c. Apollodorus of Athens: M. van der Valk, *RÉG* 71 (1958), 167.
60. A. D. Nock, *Essays on Religion and the Ancient World* i (Oxford 1972), 386;
Cameron, *Claudian* (1970), 206; West, *The Orphic Poems* (Oxford 1983), 190-91, 200, 231.
61. See in particular van der Valk, *RÉG* 71 (1958), 100-68; The "elegy" cited is perhaps less archaic than the mass of mythological lore in Antimachus, Hermesianax, Callimachus and co. It is perhaps odd that Hesiod is not mentioned, given the importance of the
catalogue for the *Bibl.* (West, *The Hesiodic Catalogue of Women* [Oxford 1985], 45); according to van der Valk, he is "obviously...included in Homer" (p. 168 n. 251).

personal familiarity with these generally despised works, another pointer to
a relatively early date.

The μισῶ in line 2 of Pollianus and the direct quotation from F 1. 31 in
line 5 put it beyond doubt that he was directly inspired by Callimachus.
His point is that Cyclic poets shamelessly steal their stale phrases from
Homer, whereas no one would get away with stealing the highly individual
phrases of elegists like Callimachus or Parthenius.

Despite its Callimachean inspiration, we must beware of imputing to
Callimachus the emphasis of Pollianus's invective. Pollianus attacks the
Cyclics for simply *copying* Homer, for lack of originality. Callimachus
would certainly have condemned them on this count, but he would also
have agreed with Aristarchus in condemning the *un*-Homeric features of
their style and language. Nonetheless it seems clear that, like Callimachus,
Pollianus was attacking Cyclic rather than later epic poets. For the
indiscriminate repetition of formulas like αὐτὰρ ἔπειτα which he cites as
characterictic of their style is not at all characteristic of (say) Apollonius,
whereas there are no fewer than three examples of αὐτὰρ (ἔπειτα) in five
lines of F 11 of the Cyclic *Thebaid*. For Pollianus as for Horace, as earlier
for Callimachus and Aristarchus, Cyclic poetry meant Cyclic poetry, not
epic poetry in general.

The appreciation of Callimachus's epigram does not require that its
opening words be provocative or controversial, in Pfeiffer's phrase an
"angry pronunciamento." There is no reason to believe that anyone in
third-century Alexandria, much less such as Asclepiades or Posidippus,
admired the Epic Cycle. Without further indication, depreciation of Cyclic
poetry does not imply criticism of either Homer on the one hand, or
Antimachus or Apollonius on the other. It must be significant that he mentions a type of poetry generally held in low esteem when he could easily
have been more explicit and provocative if he had chosen (ἐχθαίρω
Λύδην..., Ἀντίμαχον μισῶ..., τὸν Ῥόδιον μισῶ...). Despite the opening
misdirection, the primary purpose of the poem is surely erotic rather than
literary, the point being the disparity of the successive objects of his dislike
rather than any particular sort of poetry.

3

Callimachus's most substantial philological enterprise was his *Pinakes*, a
biographical and bibliographical catalogue of the library of Alexandria.
There was (of course) a section on epic (F 452-3), and Callimachus will
therefore have been faced with the question of the authorship of the Cyclic
poems. There is no way of telling how far he went beyond Aristotelian

intuition in the direction of the detailed philological analysis of Aristarchus.[62] *AP* xii. 43 suggests that he found most of them very inferior
stuff—bad enough to stand as the paradigm of bad poetry.

Yet there is not a scrap of evidence that he condemned all post-Homeric
epic. Here we do actually have some evidence, the epigram he wrote
(Strabo 14. 638 = 55 GP) on Creophylus's *Oechalias Halosis*, a very early
epic that does not seem to have been reckoned a part of the Cycle proper:

τοῦ Σαμίου πόνος εἰμὶ δόμῳ ποτὲ θεῖον ἀοιδόν
δεξαμένου, κλείω δ' Εὔρυτον ὅσσ' ἔπαθεν,
καὶ ξανθὴν Ἰόλειαν· Ὁμήρειον δὲ καλεῦμαι
γράμμα. Κρεωφύλῳ, Ζεῦ φίλε, τοῦτο μέγα.

I am the work of the Samian who once entertained the divine bard in his house.
I tell of the sufferings of Eurytus and fair-haired Iole. I am called Homer's
book. Dear god, that is quite a compliment for Creophylus.

Creophylus's poem (of which only one line survives) formed part of the
Heracles saga, telling the story of Heracles's capture of Oechalia and the
sufferings of its king Eurytus and his daughter Iole. He is in addition the
only rhapsode personally associated with Homer; the founder or eponym of
a school of Creophyleioi on Samos like the Homeridae of Chios; and as
Burkert has pointed out, his poem was also Homeric rather than Cyclic (in
the Aristotelian sense) in that it was no *Heracleia*, listing all the hero's
labours and adventures, but apparently focused on the sufferings of the
house of Eurytus, who had played Heracles false.[63]

Creophylus is said to have been the pupil, friend or even son-in-law of
Homer, and to have received the dedication of the *Oechalias Halosis* in
return for entertaining Homer. Obviously Callimachus rejected the tradition
that Homer wrote the poem. But Gabathuler went much further, detecting
"biting scorn" and "clear irony," concluding that the point of the epigram
was to brand "pseudo-Homeric as worthless."[64] So most recent critics.[65]
Indeed, according to Giangrande, Callimachus "explicitly says...that "the
Homer-like" (Ὁμήρειον γράμμα), that is to say, poetry which imitates
Homer in so unoriginal, mirror-like fashion as to be capable of being mistaken for Homer's, is worth nothing."[66] If the poem says this at all, it
certainly does not say it explicitly.

62. It is tantalizing that we do not have the epigram that apparently accepted the
authenticity of the ps-Homeric *Margites* (F 397); for the other testimonia and some new fragments, West, *IEG* ii² 69-78.
63. "Die Leistung eines Kreophylos: Kreophyleer, Homeriden und die archaische Hera-
klesepik," *Museum Helveticum* 29 (1972), 74-85; Bernabé, *PEG* i. 157-64.
64. *Hellenistische Epigramme auf Dichter* (1937), 61.
65. E.g. Clausen 1964, 184; Giangrande, *CR* 19 (1969), 160; *Quad. Urbin.* 19 (1975),
111-2.
66. *PLLS* 2 (1976), 272 = *Scr. Min. Alex.* i (1980), 290.

Let us try approaching it with minds free of modern dogma. The first two and a half lines identify Creophylus's native city (thus deciding against the rival claim of Chios) and give a neutral summary of his poem. Indeed, the simplicity of the reference to the sufferings of Eurytus and Iole might be thought to suggest that these sufferings were told with dignity and effect. According to Gabathuler, the epic-sounding ξανθὴν Ἰόλειαν was intended by its very triteness to condemn Creophylus's style. But this phrase (also in Hesiod F 26. 31 M-W), though formulaic, is hardly bombastic; more likely it is simply a quotation from Creophylus, if anything a poignant evocation of the woman for whose sake Oechalia was sacked. Nor is there any twist or shift of tone at the end. Certainly Callimachus thought Creophylus inferior to Homer, but all poets were inferior to Homer; it would be a compliment for *any* poet to have a poem mistaken for Homer. I cannot detect any suggestion that Callimachus thought the attribution preposterous. On the contrary, his point is surely that, to have been attributed (even in error) to Homer, the *Oechalias Halosis* was at any rate far superior to the general run of post-Homeric epics. The irony is gentle rather than biting. As Eichgrün rightly observes, the poem incidentally reveals unqualified admiration for Homer.[67]

τοῦ Σαμίου πόνος εἰμί. The book itself is speaking; this is the inscription to a copy of Creophylus's epic. We need not believe that Callimachus "edited" the poem; his scholarly interests lay in other directions. But he did take the trouble to write an introductory epigram for his own or a library copy of Creophylus (perhaps while writing the relevant entry in his *Pinakes*). It does not look as if it aroused in him the scorn and venom he is popularly supposed to have reserved for non-Homeric epic. If it had, he would have left us in no doubt. A neutral epigraph from Callimachus was something of a critical *nihil obstat*.

4

A new Oxyrhynchus papyrus reveals the first four words of an epigram, probably by Philodemus, that begins:[68] οὐ μισῶ τὸ ποίημα. Epigrams beginning with an emphatic μισῶ, ἐχθαίρω or *odi* are not uncommon right down into the Byzantine age, with the nun Kassia.[69] But the similarity to Callimachus's poem is so close that it is hard to believe that Philodemus

---

67. "No criticism of the poem is intended, though the quatrain as a whole may be slightly disparaging" (Gow, *HE* II. 207); cf. Eichgrün 1961, 69.

68. P. Oxy. 3724, col. iv. 8; on the ascription of most of these incipits to Philodemus, see (in addition to Parsons's introduction and notes) my *Greek Anthology*, Appendix VIII.

69. O. Weinreich, *Die Distichen des Catull* (1926), 32-83; for Kassia, K. Krumbacher, *SB München* 1897, 363f.

did not consciously have it in mind. But how did the poem continue, and what was the purpose of the allusion?

It is naturally tempting to guess that the next words were τὸ κυκλικόν, and that Philodemus's poem was an answer to Callimachus, that is to say a repudiation of his views. Yet merely to say that one did *not* hate the Cyclic poem[70] would be a very lame reply; nor is it likely that Philodemus admired the Epic Cycle. More probably, after opening "I don't hate A," the poem continued "or B, or C, or D, but I really do hate E," again a negative priamel. That is to say, while alluding to Callimachus's epigram, the poet's purpose was not to repudiate Callimachus's views on literature but simply to make use of the formal structure of a famous epigram to make a quite different point of his own.

70. I also suspect that Philodemus used some other epithet, surprising readers with a reference to something other than the Cyclic poem his opening words had led them to expect.

Chapter XV

The *Hymn to Apollo*

1

There remains *Hymn to Apollo* 105-112, a passage that has for so long been thought to recapitulate Callimachus's "rejection of epic" that it requires detailed discussion:

ὁ Φθόνος Ἀπόλλωνος ἐπ' οὔατα λάθριος εἶπεν·
"οὐκ ἄγαμαι τὸν ἀοιδὸν ὃς οὐδ' ὅσα πόντος ἀείδει."
τὸν Φθόνον ὡπόλλων ποδί τ' ἤλασεν ὧδέ τ' ἔειπεν·
"'Ασσυρίου ποταμοῖο μέγας ῥόος, ἀλλὰ τὰ πολλά
λύματα γῆς καὶ πολλὸν ἐφ' ὕδατι συρφετὸν ἕλκει.
Δηοῖ δ' οὐκ ἀπὸ παντὸς ὕδωρ φορέουσι μέλισσαι,
ἀλλ' ἥτις καθαρή τε καὶ ἀχράαντος ἀνέρπει
πίδακος ἐξ ἱερῆς ὀλίγη λιβὰς ἄκρον ἄωτον."

Envy spoke privately into Apollo's ear: "I do not admire the poet who does not sing like the sea." Apollo gave Envy a kick and said: "Great is the stream of the Assyrian river, but it carries much filth and refuse in its waters. And the Bees do not bring water from everywhere to Demeter, but only the pure and undefiled stream that trickles from a holy fountain, the best of the best." Hail, lord; but let Blame go where Envy dwells.

This is not the place to settle all the problems of this controversial passage. All I am concerned with here is F. Williams's recent suggestion that πόντος in line 106 represents Homer.[1] I quote first from his analysis of the problem:

> the dispute here, as in the *Aetia* prologue, is at least in part between long poems and short poems.... However, the terms in which Callimachus presents the dispute here are more complex than those of the *Aetia*, and admit of a more precise interpretation. Phthonos condemns the poet whose song is not *even* as great (οὐδ' ὅσα) as the sea. The words carry two important implications: first that the sea represents, at least for Phthonos, a positive standard of what is good in poetry; secondly, that as well as the quantitative judgment he has made, it would also be possible to compare the poet...with the sea in terms of

1. *Callimachus Hymn to Apollo: A Commentary* (Oxford 1978), 85-89, with full bibliography; Lehnus 1989, 233-41. In *Corolla Londiniensis* 2 (1982), 57-67, Giangrande claims to have "demolished" all objections to Williams's theory. Readers may judge.

quality.... In other words, οὐδ' ὅσα implies an unspoken οἷα.... Apollo in his reply does not challenge Phthonos' respect for the sea....

Now his solution:

> Once πόντος in 106 is seen as indicating Homer, the whole passage comes into sharp focus. Phthonos' complaint is that Callimachus does not emulate even the length of Homer's poems.... Apollo, *expressing of course Callimachus' own views*, rejects the suggestion that poems which are merely lengthy are by that token "Homeric".... Callimachus' own goal is to emulate and recreate Homer in a more meaningful and original way than merely to reproduce slavishly the external dimensions of his epics [emphasis added].

Both analysis and solution are misconceived. I concentrate on the objections most relevant to the thesis of this study. 1) Any utterance by a character designated Φθόνος must of necessity be φθονερόν, hostile or unfair. Compare the absurdly exaggerated and unfair criticisms bandied to and fro by Callimachus and his critics, designated βασκανίης...γένος, in the *Aetia* prologue. According to Williams, Φθόνος is making a balanced criticism that allows for considerations of quality as well as quantity. Yet to introduce Phthonos at all automatically leads the reader to expect *unbalanced* criticism, in the context purely quantitative.

2) As for the claim that "Apollo...does not challenge Phthonos's respect for the sea," Apollo's immediate reaction is to kick Phthonos! Is it possible to conceive of a more pointed rejection?

3) Williams quoted numerous texts where Homer is *compared* to the sea, the source from which all later poets derive.[2] Most are Roman, but even if we concede (as Brink also argued) that the conceit was already current in Hellenistic times, even so his thesis fails. For in none of these texts does πόντος or ὠκεανός by itself directly denote Homer, without some other help or indication in the context. Giangrande insists that it is "a commonly accepted metaphor in antiquity," but assertion (however often repeated) is no substitute for evidence.[3]

4) The antithesis between the huge river and the tiny spring is (taken by itself) sharp and clear, like the series of similar sharp antitheses in the *Aetia* prologue. But if πόντος is Homer and so the ultimate source of all other bodies of water, springs no less than rivers (Williams, pp. 87-8), then the contrast is muddied. Both river and spring derive from the same source. Williams acknowledges and even tries to make a virtue of this, but his explanation is hopelessly complicated and unconvincing[4] ("Thus three analogies are being used, and two standards of comparison, size and purity:

---

2. See too the similar list of passages assembled by C. O. Brink, *AJP* 93 (1972), 553-55; for Homer as the source of all subsequent literature, Ch. X. 3.

3. At one point three times on the same page (*Cor. Lond.* 1982, 60), but not one text.

4. So too Hutchinson 1988, 68 n. 85 ("impossibly devious").

πόντος is large, and pure; the ποταμός is large, and impure; the spray from the πῖδαξ is small, and pure. Phthonos approves of πόντος, as does Apollo by implication; but Apollo condemns the ποταμός and approves of the water from the πῖδαξ...").

5) Williams insists that οὐδ᾽ ὅσα πόντος ἀείδει must mean "not *even as much as* the sea," implying the unstated· *qualitative* judgment that is so central to his interpretation. But as Köhnken has pointed out, if we construe οὐδέ "not even," the meaning implied would be "even less than the sea," which makes no sense at all. In *Argonautica* iii.932-3,[5]

ἀκλεὴς ὅδε μάντις, ὃς οὐδ᾽ ὅσα παῖδες ἴσασιν
οἶδε νόῳ φράσσασθαι,

"not even as much as children" clearly means "even less than children" (children being used as a yardstick because they know little). There is no qualitative implication. Earlier editors resorted to conjecture: οὐχ ὅσα (Scaliger and Reiske), οὐ τόσα (Meineke). Unnecessarily. οὐδέ is simply being used in its well documented sense as an "emphatic negative":[6] "I do not admire the poet who positively refuses to sing as much as the sea."

6) Following Erbse,[7] Williams argues that the relevant fact about the sea here is its purity. Yet in a Callimachean literary context, purity is always associated with smallness (i.e. the spring rather than the river), whereas the sea is the largest single entity with which man comes into contact, ἀπείρονα πόντον. The sea does the one thing a poem should not do (at least for Callimachus): it rolls on for ever. It is surely inconceivable that Callimachus of all poets could have expected readers who knew his tastes to identify πόντος, without any preparation, as a symbol of purity rather than of size. It follows that πόντος alone cannot designate Homer.

7) Last and most relevant to the present discussion, as the extracts quoted above abundantly illustrate, Williams's interpretation rests entirely on the unquestioned assumption that Callimachus was debating the issue of Homeric imitation, that famous debate about which modern critics have so much to say and ancient sources not a single word.[8] In fact there seems no

5. Which Vian, following many earlier scholars, claims (*Apollonios de Rhodes* II [1980], 139) to be a "Transposition sans intention polémique" of Callimachus's line. See however Williams ad loc. (p. 90) and Bundy, *CSCA* 5 (1972), 40.

6. Denniston, *Greek Particles*[2] (1950), 197-98 (mainly from Herodotus); cf. A. Köhnken, *AJP* 102 (1981), 416. To quote only one example, Plato, *Symp.* 202C: πῶς ἂν ...ὁμολογοῖτο μέγας θεὸς εἶναι παρὰ πάντων, οἳ φασιν αὐτὸν οὐδὲ θεὸν εἶναι; ("who deny that he is a god at all").

7. *Hermes* 83 (1955), 411-28.

8. Giangrande characteristically goes further than even Williams: "In Hellenistic times, epic poets...tried to outdo Homer by writing gigantic works, even longer than the Homeric poems: this has been too well demonstrated by Ziegler..."—again repeated several times, again without documentation.

reason to doubt that Callimachus is making essentially the same point here as in the *Aetia* prologue: small-and-refined is better than large-and-crude, whatever sort of poetry is concerned.

With the lone exception of E. L. Bundy, it has always been felt that these lines are pure literary polemic, entirely irrelevant to their hymnic context.[9] It is by no means self-evident that this is so. Having at lines 30-31 announced that his hymn will last for several days, so inexhaustible a theme is Apollo,[10] Callimachus then cuts it short after barely 100 lines. At 546 lines, the Homeric hymn to Apollo is five times as long. It is natural that Callimachus should make some comment on this conspicuous failure to fulfil not only traditional expectations but his own promise. This is why he introduces Phthonos, who predictably complains that it should have been longer—the longer the better. Phthonos's complaint is clearly based on considerations of quantity alone. It is Apollo who introduces the idea of quality when he rejects this advice, contrasting the pure spray from a holy fountain with the muddy Euphrates. That is to say, there is no essential difference between sea and river; both are large bodies of water that roll on forever. Apollo switches from sea to river simply because, thanks to its sediment, the river lends itself better to his qualitative argument.

It is instructive here to compare Horace's imitation, his well-known criticism of the "muddy" style of Lucilius (*Serm.* i. 4. 11): *cum flueret lutulentus, erat quod tollere velles*. When the two passages are read together, it should be clear that the point of the image is not so much the size or the length of the river in itself, as the mud and refuse that is carried along in its torrent (λύματα γῆς καὶ πολλὸν ἐφ᾽ ὕδατι συρφετὸν ἕλκει). It is meant to suggest diffuse and careless writing rather than any specific sort of poem. After all, the "pure spray" of which Apollo approves is clearly the brief hymn Callimachus is bringing to its close, and the work with which it is implicitly contrasted is no epic, but simply the much longer and less carefully polished hymn that a lesser artist might have produced. To be sure, it is a description that would fit much of Cyclic epic well enough, but for Callimachus (as we have seen) it also fitted the elegiac style of Antimachus (*lutulentus* ~ οὐ τορόν).

For Horace, it fitted the satirist Lucilius. Elsewhere Horace restates his criticism of Lucilius in more positive terms (*Serm.* i. x. 9-10):

> est brevitate opus, ut currat sententia neu se
> impediat verbis lassas onerantibus aures.

Mutatis mutandis, this reflects, in more concrete terms, the essence of Callimachus's criticism in both hymn and prologue. The redundant and for-

---

9. For example: "The poet turns aside from his subject to offer an attack on his poetic detractors" (Zetzel, *Critical Inquiry* 10 [1983], 93).

10. See Williams ad loc. (p. 38) and Bundy, *CSCA* 5 (1972), 59f.

mulaic epic style that modern critics have identified and explained as a survival from an age of oral composition was inappropriate to the poetry of a more sophisticated age. This applied to the heavy-handed Hesiodizing of Hermesianax no less than the hackneyed Homerizing of Antimachus. The so-called debate about· "Homeric imitation" has been too crudely formulated.[11] It was not a question of how to write epic; the problem was how to de-epicize elegy.

2

The close parallelism between the end of the *Hymn to Apollo* and the *Aetia* prologue—by which I mean not merely the denunciation of large-and-crude but also its association with φθόνος/βασκανίη—suggests that the *Hymn to Apollo* might be more or less contemporary with *Aetia* I-II. This is not an original suggestion, of course. But since hitherto the *Aetia* prologue has been considered one of Callimachus's latest works, so too has the *Hymn to Apollo*. For example, when Williams states that "there are good grounds for seeing the hymn as a comparatively late product of the poet's maturer style," the only real argument he cites is "the close similarity between the final section and the prologue to the *Aetia*."

It is true that the account of the founding of Cyrene would suit very well the reconciliation of Egypt and Cyrene symbolized in the wedding of Euergetes and Berenice in 246. But if so, it is remarkable indeed that there should be no mention of either Berenice or the wedding. It would suit some earlier occasion before the estrangement just as well. And as Williams himself conceded, as a loyal Cyrenean Callimachus could have written the passage at any time, without intending any contemporary reference.[12] It is also true that the scholia identify the king of line 26 as Euergetes, who did not come to the throne until 246. The scholia on Callimachus's hymns are rather sparse compared with those on Theocritus, Apollonius and Nicander,

---

11. Certainly what Williams calls "constant interplay between imitation and variation of Homer" is a feature of Callimachus's style. But it is far too narrow an approach to suppose that Callimachus was attempting "to answer both in practical and theoretical terms the question of how a learned modern poet could appropriately draw on the riches of Homeric poetry in order to create a new idiom" (Williams, p. 4). According to Giangrande (*L' Antiquité Classique* 39 [1970], 48), "Rhianus was, like all Alexandrians, *poeta...Homerici dicendi generis peritissimus*, fully acquainted with the 'exceptions' and 'rarities' in Homeric morphology and syntax." The key words are "like all Alexandrians." A critical tool that cannot distinguish between Callimachus and Rhianus is hardly sharp enough to cut to the heart of so elusive a problem as style. Homeric wordgames are merely the bread and butter of Callimachus's style; they are not what lifts him above the herd. To discover this requires more than the apparatus criticus and the *Lexicon Homericum*.

12. See Williams's note on line 68.

but they do preserve some genuine information not known from other sources,[13] and we should not lightly dismiss this particular note. On the other hand (as Wilamowitz saw), it gives a reason for the identification which would suit Philadelphus better: "he honours him as a god because he was a lover of literature (φιλόλογον)."[14] The form of the note suggests inference rather than information. Williams misses the point here. To be sure, if he was writing in or after 246, Callimachus *might* have called Euergetes "a lover of literature." But he did not do so here: there is no mention of literature in the context. It was the scholiast who picked on love of literature as a defining characteristic of Euergetes. Wrongly, of course; however cultivated Euergetes may have been, love of literature was a *defining* characteristic of Philadelphus. Indeed, that very term is applied to Philadelphus in the account of the Alexandrian library preserved by Tzetzes.[15] Not that any Ptolemy would have been "honoured as a god" because of his literary interests. The man who wrote that clearly had no understanding of Ptolemaic ruler cult. Given Callimachus's known dates, both Philadelphus and Euergetes are possibilities, but there are no positive reasons in favour of either.

Is the unnamed king a Ptolemy at all? If the poem does not celebrate the reconciliation of Egypt and Cyrene in 246, why is so much space devoted to Cyrene? Such a long account of Cyrene in so short a hymn to Apollo suggests that it was written for performance there.[16] Since ἐμὴν πόλιν in line 65 certainly refers to Cyrene, there is no reason why anyone should identify ἡμετέροις βασιλεῦσιν in 68 as Philadelphus and his heir the future Euergetes. They must be the Battiad kings of Cyrene.[17] Who then is ἐμῷ βασιλῆι in 26? There is nothing to point to an Egyptian ruler, and in view of line 68, a king of Cyrene is surely more likely. If so, the hymn would have to have been written before 250: the king would then be Berenice's father Magas, who died in that year.

Indeed a positive argument in favour of Magas has recently been adduced by Laronde. The context of the reference is as follows:

κακὸν μακάρεσσιν ἐρίζειν.
ὃς μάχεται μακάρεσσιν, ἐμῷ βασιλῆι μάχοιτο.
ὅστις ἐμῷ βασιλῆι, καὶ Ἀπόλλωνι μάχοιτο (25-7).

13. Pfeiffer I. lxxviii-ix.
14. Williams cites *SH* 979. 6-7, which praises even Philopator for his "excellence in warfare and the Muses," but it is one thing to pay a routine compliment, and another (in effect) to choose Euergetes over Philadelphus (the only other candidate) on this basis.
15. φιλολογώτατος ὤν...τὰς βίβλους εἰς Ἀλεξάνδρειαν συνήθροισεν, *De Com.* p. 43 Koster.
16. See Mair 1921, 21-24; Laronde 1987, 362-65; Ch. II. 8.
17. So Laronde 1987, 362.

It is wrong to strive with the gods. He who strives with the gods would fight with my king. He who fights with my king would fight with Apollo himself.

Why is the king so closely identified with Apollo? Apollo was not especially prominent in the religious life of Egypt. But he was the principal deity of Cyrene.[18] Furthermore, Magas himself was the eponymous priest of Apollo.[19]

Magas is in fact named elsewhere in Callimachus, together with Berenice, in an unidentifiable elegiac fragment (F 388. 7, 11). This could be another poem on Berenice II dating from 246 or later. But the reference might be to Berenice I, the mother of Magas and Philadelphus, in which case it could be an early work instead. The scholion on *Hymn* ii. 26 might then be a pure guess after all (Euergetes is mentioned twice in the Suda life), or perhaps the sole remaining detail from an originally more detailed note reviewing various possible identifications.

In the absence of any other pointers to date, we can hardly exclude the possibility that the *Hymn to Apollo* is actually an early work. If (as here argued) *Aetia* I-II complete with prologue date from ca 270 rather than ca 245, so too perhaps does the *Hymn to Apollo*. Even with the more precise chronology offered in earlier chapters of this book, it will not be easy to pin down Callimachus's "maturer style." The biological metaphor itself is of questionable value. Technique may improve (or at least develop) with experience, but many a creative writer begins rather than finishes with his most striking and idiosyncratic work. We have already seen that *Acontius and Cydippe* may be early.

18. Fraser I. 788-89; Laronde 1987, 169-71.
19. *SEG* xviii. 743; J. and L. Robert, *BE* 1961, 836; Laronde 1987, 362.

Chapter XVI

Theocritus

This chapter makes no attempt to analyse the relationship between Theocritus and Callimachus, an important yet intangible theme that has yet to find definitive treatment. But most attempts so far have been predicated on the assumption that poets and critics of the age were sharply divided about the "viability" of epic, with Theocritus taking Callimachus's side, whether or not Apollonius is seen as their opponent. What follows seeks to remove the foundations on which this simplistic assumption rests: four different ways in which Theocritus has been brought into this supposed debate about epic.

1

The main text is a brief passage in the seventh *Idyll* (7. 37-48) that needs to be studied at some length in context. The poem opens with the young poet Simichidas meeting the mysterious Lycidas. It used to be fashionable to interpret this enigmatic work as a "bucolic masquerade," with Simichidas representing Theocritus and Lycidas some older poet (variously identified) who allegedly "initiated" Theocritus into bucolic poetry.[1] Recent criticism has in general been moving away from this position in the direction indicated by Archibald Cameron (no relation), who argued that the actual description of Simichidas's encounter with Lycidas is modelled on encounters with disguised deities in epic.[2] F. Williams went one step further:[3] not just

1. See Gow ad loc.; G. Giangrande, *L' Antiquité Classique* 37 (1968), 491-533; K. J. Dover, *Theocritus: Select Poems* (1971), 148-50; E. L. Bowie, *CQ* 35 (1985), 67-91, arguing (implausibly, to my mind) that Simichidas = Theocritus while Lycidas is a character in a bucolic poem by Philitas. The most recent discussions (with extensive bibliographies) are Hutchinson 1988, 201-12, Goldhill, *The Poet's Voice* (1991), 225-40 and Gutzwiller, *Theocritus' Pastoral Analogies* (1992), 158-171; S. Hatzicosta, *Stylistic Commentary on Theocritus' Idyll VII* (Amsterdam 1982) quotes many parallels, but is valueless for interpretation. Where interpretations differ so widely and so often depend on gauging tone, I have only documented points central to my thesis.
2. *Miscellanea di studi alessandri in memoria di A. Rostagni* (Turin 1963), 291-307; reinforced with many more parallels by T.E.V. Pearce, *Rhein. Mus.* 131 (1988), 276-304; for further epic parallels, A. Kurz, *Le Corpus Theocriteum et Homère* (Berne 1982), 130-33.
3. "A Theophany in Theocritus," *CQ* 21 (1971), 137-45.

any god, but Apollo. Was it not as Apollo *Lycios* that the god of poetry appeared to another young poet in the *Aetia* prologue? Theocritus is careful not to be explicit, to leave a pleasing aura of mysterious ambiguity. If this attractive suggestion is accepted, we have the key to some of the most puzzling features of the encounter. Simichidas does not realize that it is Apollo himself he has rashly challenged to a contest—whence that persistent mocking smile of Lycidas (20, 42, 128).

Simichidas and Lycidas do not greet each other with the open mutual compliments of Thyrsis and the goatherd in *Idyll* I. Only Lycidas looks and smells like a genuine rustic (Simichidas comments disdainfully on his outlandish rustic outfit, 14-19), while Simichidas seems to be a town-dweller (line 2). Lycidas suggests, not without a touch of malice, that since Simichidas is in such a hurry, he must be planning to gatecrash a party (ἦ μετὰ δαῖτ᾽ ἄκλητος ἐπείγεαι, 24)[4] or visit some *town-dweller's* winepress. That is to say, he knows that Simichidas has not come out at noontide in his fine boots (26) to watch sheep. Simichidas gives as good as he gets in reply, observing: "all men say that you are by far the best piper *among the herdsmen and rustics* (28-29)." It is difficult not to detect a patronizing note in this compliment: it is only fellow rustics that Lycidas could defeat. Furthermore, Simichidas goes on to announce his own conviction that he is Lycidas's equal (ἰσοφαρίζειν ἔλπομαι).

Only ten lines later Simichidas alleges that "all men reckon me too (κἠμέ) the best of poets," though he adds, with affected modesty, that he is not quick to believe it (ἐγὼ δέ τις οὐ ταχυπειθής). No indeed. He does not reckon that he is yet a match for Asclepiades or Philitas; compared to them he is like a frog vying with crickets (39-41):

οὐ Δᾶν· οὐ γάρ πω κατ᾽ ἐμὸν νόον οὔτε τὸν ἐσθλόν
Σικελίδαν νίκημι τὸν ἐκ Σάμω οὔτε Φιλίταν
ἀείδων, βάτραχος δὲ ποτ᾽ ἀκρίδας ὥς τις ἐρίσδω.

Even after Lycidas has sung (52-89), Simichidas prefaces his own song with the claim that the fame of his poems may have reached the throne of Zeus,[5] immodestly adding: "but this is the best by far with which I shall begin to *do you honour* (γεραίρειν)." Thus Simichidas's attitude to Lycidas is characterized by a boastful and patronizing tone throughout.[6]

---

4. δαῖτα κλητός cannot formally be excluded, but would be very flat.

5. Usually taken as implying an interest by Ptolemy Philadelphus in Theocritus (e.g. Gow on vii. 93; E. L. Bowie, *CQ* 35 [1985], 68). But of course this depends in turn on the identification Simichidas = Theocritus.

6. This consistent portrayal of Simichidas seems to me hard to make sense of on Bowie's thesis that Lycidas is a Philitan character, and it is significant that in effect he denies it ("Simichidas opens with straight praise of Lycidas, which can be read as commendation and admiration of Philitas by Theocritus...," p. 78); see too Gutzwiller 1991, 161-7.

After lines 39-41 (quoted above), Simichidas continues, ὡς ἐφάμαν ἐπίταδες, where ἐπίταδες, "deliberately," implies that his words were designed to provoke Lycidas. "He seems to mean that his modesty was calculated to induce Lycidas to take part in the friendly exchange of songs suggested at 36" (βουκολιασδώμεσθα), comments Gow. But the "modesty" of 39-41 is seriously undercut by the οὐ...πω of 39: he is "not *yet*" a match for Asclepiades and Philitas, implying that it is only a matter of time before he will be.[7] He is trying to provoke Lycidas, but by boastfulness rather than modesty. That is to say, the boastfulness is more a tactic than a character trait. In itself the tactic is shrewd enough; it is not by modesty that challengers get to compete with champions. But it is not a prudent line to take with a god.

Here now is the crucial passage (42-48):

> ὡς ἐφάμαν ἐπίταδες· ὁ δ' αἰπόλος ἁδὺ γελάσσας,
> "τάν τοι," ἔφα, "κορύναν δωρύττομαι, οὕνεκεν ἐσσί
> πᾶν ἐπ' ἀλαθείᾳ πεπλασμένον ἐκ Διὸς ἔρνος.
> ὥς μοι καὶ τέκτων μέγ' ἀπέχθεται ὅστις ἐρευνῇ
> ἶσον ὄρευς κορυφᾷ τελέσαι δόμον Ὠρομέδοντος,
> καὶ Μοισᾶν ὄρνιχες ὅσοι ποτὶ Χῖον ἀοιδόν
> ἀντία κοκκύζοντες ἐτώσια μοχθίζοντι."

After another of those smiles (ἁδὺ γελάσσας) Lycidas promises to give Simichidas a staff.[8]

Hesiodic staffs followed by cockerels of the Muses vying with Homer have naturally been claimed as proof of rivalry between Homeric and Hesiodic styles. According to Otis, "Lycidas's estimate of Simichidas...is...obviously the view which Theocritus accepts as an accurate description of his own poetic aim and achievement"; the "truth" (ἀλαθεία) of line 44 is the "refusal to "rival" or imitate Homer." Van Sickle agreed: "the experience in bucolic is thus characterized as more Hesiodic than Homeric...expressing hate for those who emulate Homer with long poems."[9] This is heady stuff. Before we can feel any confidence in so extravagant a reading of Lycidas's words, we must begin with his smiles.

ἁδὺ γελάσσας is not at all the "pleasant" laugh of Gow's translation. In the Ionic form ἡδὺ γελάσσας, this is a common Homeric formula, (usually, as here, at the line-end), never (as might be expected from the usual connotations of ἡδύς) of pleasant, sweet or gentle laughter, but almost invariably of laughter at someone's misfortune. For example, *Iliad* ii. 270 (the Greeks at Thersites's beating); xi. 378 (Paris, when he wounds Diomede); xxiii.784 (at Ajax's misfortune in the funeral games); *Odyssey*

---

7. So C. Segal, *AJP* 95 (1974), 130-31.
8. Though not otherwise attested, δωρύττομαι is generally agreed to be a future form.
9. Otis 1964, 402; Van Sickle, *Quad. Urb.* 19 (1975), 45-72.

xvi. 358; xviii. 35, 111; xxi. 376 (all of the mockery of the suitors); and not least *Hom. Hy.* v. 49 (of a boastful laugh by Aphrodite). A less obvious case is *Iliad* xxi. 508, where Zeus smiles at Artemis when she complains to him about being ill-treated by Hera. But while it is true enough that Zeus is treating Artemis "the way any indulgent father would treat a small child" and *Schadenfreude* would indeed be "utterly out of place in this scene,"[10] he is still surely laughing *at* her.

The most relevant parallel to Lycidas's smile is the end of Theocritus 1, when Aphrodite arrives as Daphnis is on the point of death (1. 95-6):

> ἦνθέ γε μὰν ἀδεῖα καὶ ἁ Κύπρις γελάοισα,
> λάθρη μὲν γελάοισα, βαρὺν δ' ἀνὰ θυμὸν ἔχοισα.

This is a long-standing puzzle. Assuming that ἀδεῖα is neuter plural (and so equivalent to ἀδύ), does the last phrase imply distress or anger? Is Aphrodite concealing her anger with a sweet smile, or inwardly delighted while pretending grief? A careful recent study by Gregory Crane concludes that Aphrodite is in fact grieving to see Daphnis so close to death, but is concealing this grief "behind her gently mocking laughter."[11] This seems to make the best sense of the poem as a whole and is probably right. Nonetheless, Crane's analysis of the examples he assembled (using the *TLG*) of the phrase ἡδὺ γελᾶν leaves much to be desired.

To start with, he claims that the "most relevant parallels for Theocritus" come not from Homer, but from later sources. We should of course expect that, in ordinary speech, ἡδύ would not retain these sinister Homeric overtones—and the less so the more remote the work concerned from epic. So it is hardly surprising that the novelist Longus "uses γελάσας...ἡδύ in an unambiguously positive manner."[12] No reader would expect Homeric resonances in such a text. But Theocritus was himself writing in epic hexameters, for an audience steeped in Homer, and both here and again at line 128 he uses the exact Homeric formula in a common Homeric position at the line-end. Readers who knew their Homer would at once be alerted.

In addition, Crane misinterprets at least three of the examples he quotes from the humbler genre of epigram. First, a poem about a small boy who begs his mother not to beat him for losing his nuts (*AP* xiv. 116), stolen from him by some girls, described as teases (φιλοπαίγμονες). When one of

---

10. G. Crane (next note) p. 164 n. 11.

11. "The Laughter of Aphrodite," *HSCP* 91 (1987), 161-84, with full discussion of the earlier literature, especially Gow ad loc. and G. Zuntz, *CQ* n. s. 10 (1960), 37-40 = *Opuscula Selecta* (1972), 83-6. Hutchinson 1988, 149 n. 13 believes 95-6 corrupt. On any interpretation, λάθρη is a problem (though see the scholia ad loc, with Crane 1987, 163).

12. *Daphnis and Chloe* iii. 22. 4; iv. 18. 1. It is scarcely relevant that Longus "knew Theocritus's poetry well" (Crane 1987, 165).

these thieves ἡδὺ γελᾷ, we can hardly construe it as innocent delight. Then there is Meleager's poem on the cockerel whose crow wakens lovers too soon. This is a particularly clear example, because the bird has already been described as δυσέρωτι, κακάγγελε, τρισάλαστε and γαῦρος before the lover protests at the way it makes "sweet mockery over my distress," ἐπ' ἐμαῖς ἁδὺ γελᾷς ὀδύναις (AP xii. 137. 4). In this case the irony of ἁδὺ infects the following phrase as well: "is this the loving thanks (φίλη χάρις) you have for the one who reared you?" Last there is the mouse in a gem by Nicarchus (AP xi. 391. 3-4) who reassures the miser Asclepiades that he has not come for food, merely lodging:

ἡδὺ δ' ὁ μῦς γελάσας, "μηδέν, φίλε," φησί, "φοβηθῇς,
    οὐχὶ τροφῆς παρὰ σοὶ χρῄζομεν, ἀλλὰ μονῆς."

The reader who was led by the mock-epic opening of line 3 to look for a touch of sarcasm would surely not feel he had been misled.[13]

The least satisfactory part of Crane's discussion is his treatment of the two references in 7. For not only is Lycidas described as ἁδὺ γελάσσας when he promises Simichidas the staff at line 42. Exactly the same phrase is applied to him again at line 128 when he actually hands it over. On the first passage, Crane comments that "Lycidas immediately follows his laugh by handing over his staff, an unequivocal gesture of approval." On the second, "Lycidas approves of and supports the younger poet, and there is no way to escape the friendliness of this laugh." But given the hints in the context that Lycidas's attitude to the younger poet is something less than straightforwardly friendly, the repetition is itself significant. No sensitive ancient reader would have missed the reiterated Homeric resonance. He would surely have concluded that Lycidas was laughing at Simichidas—though of course it is essential to the dramatic context that Simichidas himself, the narrator, should not realize this. The device is also found in the miniature narrative of an epigram by Asclepiades (X = AP v. 150), where the speaker complains that his girlfriend has stood him up despite having sworn to come by the holy Thesmophoros. The informed reader is meant to interpret this oath in the light of his knowledge that men were excluded from the Thesmophoria. Yet the point of the poem is clearly that the trusting speaker himself failed to realize this, or he would not have anxiously waited till past midnight. At 128-9 Simichidas pointedly remarks that Lycidas's second "sweet smile" was just like his first (ἁδὺ γελάσσας / ὡς πάρος), reminding readers—though again not himself—of the more systematically ironic context of the first laugh. It is paradoxical that we

13. To be sure, there is "nothing vicious in the girl's delight," but that does not exclude mischievous taunting. Nor does the fact that the mouse speaks "with amusement and good humour" (both Crane 1987, 164) exclude gentle sarcasm.

cannot help but hear Homeric resonances in the very passage where we are asked to believe Theocritus is rejecting Homeric pretensions.

If Lycidas is laughing at his cocky young competitor, his presentation of the staff can hardly be construed straightforwardly as a compliment. It cannot in any case be a judgment on his poetry, since Lycidas has not heard any yet. Moreover, if there is some uncertainty about the tone of Lycidas's offer, there can be none about its timing. Instead of waiting for Simichidas to recite his poem and then judging it, Lycidas promises the staff at once, as though taking Simichidas, untried, at his own inflated valuation.

When Lycidas finally hands over the promised staff, it is described as ἐκ Μοισᾶν ξεινήϊον (129). Moderns with Hesiodic initiations on the brain think at once of the *Theogony* proem and Callimachus's *Somnium*,[14] ignoring the fact that Theocritus himself explains the staff quite otherwise—and in some detail. In the first place, it is the wrong sort of staff. Lines 13-19 give a townsman's amused description of Lycidas's rustic outfit, specifying his "*curved* stick of wild olive" (ῥοικὰν...κορύναν). At 128 it is characterized outright as a λαγωβόλον, the shepherd's or goatherd's crook, otherwise known as καλαῦροψ. The hook was essential for its function, to catch the animal by its leg or neck or to throw after it. Homer refers to "as far as a rustic can throw his crook," and the scholia duly emphasize its curvature.[15] According to the scholarly Antimachus, they had handles at one end by which rustics carried them (καλαύροπας οὐατοέσσας, F 91 Wyss). Theocritus elsewhere makes a cowherd wish for a "curved crook" (ῥοικόν τι λαγωβόλον) so that he could keep his calves out of the olive grove (4. 49), and they are often mentioned in the rustic dedications that were so fashionable in the early Hellenistic age.[16] Rustics in comedy were always shown with the λαγωβόλον.[17]

Despite the fact that Hesiod represents himself as a shepherd, by common consent ancient critics identified the staff the Muses gave him *not* as the shepherd's crook but as the staff of the rhapsode, properly of laurel wood. Hesiod's word (*Theog.* 30) is σκῆπτρον, elsewhere used for "the staff carried by kings, priests and prophets...also by heralds and, temporarily, by anyone who stands up to speak in the assembly of leaders."[18] As we have seen (Ch. XIII. 1), on the basis of this passage Hesiod was identified as the first rhapsode.[19] The rhapsode's staff was long and

---

14. According to M. Puelma, for example, both are "selbstbiographische Initiationsgedichte hesiodischer Tradition," *Mus. Helv.* 17 (1960), 163.

15. ὅσσον τίς τ' ἔρριψε καλαύροπα βουκόλος ἀνήρ, Ψ. 845; Ebeling, *Lex. Hom.* s.v.

16. In general, see Gow's note on Theoc. 4. 49

17. Pollux 4. 120 (i. 236. 17 Bethe).

18. West on *Theog.* 30 (pp. 163-64); cf. Kirk on *Iliad* ii. 109 (pp. 128-29); H. M. and N. K. Chadwick, *The Growth of Literature* i (Cambridge 1932), 653-56; R. B. Onians, *The Origins of European Thought*[2] (Cambridge 1954), 456 n.2.

19. Nicocles or Nicocrates, *FGrH* 376 F8; Pausan. 9. 30. 2; West on *Theog.* 30.

straight.[20] There can be no question that Theocritus's readers would have known the difference and instantly identified the staff Lycidas gives Simichidas as the curved crook of the herdsman.

We have already seen reason to doubt Callimachus's "Dichterweihe," and in Theocritus 7 the concept is downright inappropriate. In his own judgment at least Simichidas is already· a well-known poet when he meets Lycidas (37-8), and 50 lines later (91-2) he specifies that it was the Nymphs, not the Muses, who "taught" him his craft (δίδαξαν, as in *Theogony* 22). ξεινήϊον should make us think rather of the *Odyssey*, for it is the token of epic guest-friendship.[21] The staff is not a gift from the Muses; it is simply a rustic gift such as bucolic poets regularly give each other after singing contests. For example, in 1 and 6 and (above all) the post-Theocritean 9, where one of the gifts is (as here) a staff, grown on the poet's own father's land. One of Vergil's rustics likewise gives another a crook (*pedum*), described by Servius (on *Buc.* v. 88) as "the curved staff herdsmen use to catch sheep and goats." Even in Theocritus staffs are essential tools of the herdsman's trade (e.g. 4. 49), not mere symbols of poetry.[22] What Lycidas gives Simichidas is just a memento of the relationship struck up between the two men through their contest in song (ἐκ Μοισᾶν).[23]

This is not to say that there may not be a hint of Hesiod's staff. But how significant a hint? Given the pervading irony and the references to Asclepiades, Philitas and Homer, this is hardly the place to identify a "Hesiodic moment of truth."[24] Lycidas's mocking smile robs the occasion of the solemnity often read into it, and (as Goldhill has underlined) "the very offer is constituted as a pun."[25]

"τάν τοι," ἔφα, "κορύναν δωρύττομαι, οὔνεκεν ἐσσί
πᾶν ἐπ' ἀλαθείᾳ πεπλασμένον ἐκ Διὸς ἔρνος.

20. A famous vase by the Kleophrades painter (ca 500 B.C.) has long been identified as a rhapsode with his staff, but J. Herington has recently argued that it is "nothing but a walking stick...of an Athenian gentleman...performing in a private context" (*Poetry into Drama* [Berkeley 1985], 14). If so, we have no certain representation of an archaic rhapsode (Herington 226 n. 23).

21. Ebeling, *Lex. Hom.* s.v. (p. 1176); Finley, *The World of Odysseus*[2] (1965), 99f.

22. ῥόπαλον ἐκ θατέρου τῶν ἄκρων ἐπικάμπιον, οἶα φέρουσι βουκόλοι καὶ νομεῖς, οἳ μὲν καλαύροπας οἳ δὲ λαγωβόλα καλοῦντες, Dion. Hal. 14. 2: and see other material collected by Gow on Theoc. 4. 49.

23. "as a result of this exchange of songs, [Lycidas and Simichidas] are ξένοι ἐκ Μουσῶν as Telemachus and Peisistratus are ξεῖνοι...ἐκ πατέρων φιλότητος (*Od.* 15. 196)," Gow II. 163.

24. So rightly Goldhill 1991, 231-32. On the other hand Giangrande's claim that it is a mock investiture, a "parody of Hesiod's initiation by the Muses" seems to go too far.

25. Goldhill 1991, 231-2; cf. Hatzikosta 1982, 87.

"I'll give you my *staff* because you are a *twig*." While it is possible to read this as a compliment, implying a new poetic generation (sapling taking over from the parent tree), it might as easily be an insult: "I'll give you my staff because you're a chip off the old block"—namely as wooden as the staff, stupid! ἐπ' ἀλαθείᾳ might just be an intensifying phrase, "really and truly," but more probably the "truth"·Lycidas praises is something Simichidas has just said; he is picking up the one true statement among Simichidas's boasts, his mock concession that he is no match for Asclepiades and Philitas. Quite right, retorts Lycidas with an ironic smile, you are not their equal.[26]

He then underlines the folly of excessive ambition with two colourful analogies, the builder who tries to build his house too high, and the cockerels of the Muses who cackle in vain against Homer. For no good reason these two analogies have traditionally been construed as a "polemic against contemporary poetry in epic style" (G. Lohse). Even the usually cautious Dover claimed that the "view of poetry" expressed here "was pungently defended by Kallimachos."[27] According to Zanker, Simichidas and Lycidas "express their *common* abhorrence of *contemporary* poets who persist in emulating Homer" (emphasis added). According to Halperin, "By proclaiming his dislike of *contemporary* efforts to emulate Homer and by opposing them to the example of his *own* poetry, Theocritus places himself within the same faction of aesthetic politics as Callimachus....Both Theocritus and Callimachus define the character and limits of their poetry by contrast with the Homeric epic."[28]

Gow claims that the lines "are not very relevantly placed in the mouth of Lycidas." On the contrary, what would be irrelevant and unmotivated in Lycidas's mouth is an attack on epic poetry. The postulated sequence of thought is apparently as follows: hearing the names Asclepiades and Philitas, he nods approvingly at the implied praise of such models of small-scale poetry, and says (in effect): "I agree, Homerizing epics are such a bore." But the fact that Simichidas hopes to surpass Asclepiades and Philitas need not mean that it was their style or themes he admired, still less that he disapproved of epic. It was their *reputation* he hopes to surpass. Asclepiades and Philitas happened to be the most celebrated poets of the early third century; it was natural that any ambitious poet should see himself as their rival. In any case, if Asclepiades is correctly identified as one of the Telchines, Callimachus represented him as *approving* of epicising poetry!

The link between Simichidas's speech and Lycidas's reply is surely ambition. Simichidas boasts of his ambition to surpass (νίκημι) Asclepiades

26. So C. P. Segal, *AJP* 95 (1974), 131.

27. G. Lohse, *Hermes* 94 (1966), 413-25; Dover, *Theocritus* (London 1971), 147.

28. Zanker 1987, 119; Halperin 1983, 244 (emphasis added).

and Philitas; Lycidas disapproves of excessive ambition. Homer is mentioned simply and solely because he is by any standard the one poet whom *no one* could rival. This is simply the motif treated in an earlier chapter, Homer the supreme poet, the yardstick for all subsequent literature (Ch. X. 3). For the impudent young "Salonhirt" Simichidas to claim rivalry with such as Asclepiades and Philitas was like trying to rival Homer—or build a house as high as a mountain.

The polemic of the *Aetia* prologue has an entirely different focus. Callimachus (as we have seen) was not concerned with anything so specific as epic, but with the *quality* of poetry. He denounces any and all poems that are long, rambling or commonplace, always contrasting the positive qualities they ought to have—brevity, elegance, originality. That is to say, the basis of Callimachus's criticism is purely *literary*. Theocritus's Homeric analogy does not make a literary point at all. The function of both his analogies is simply to underline the *futility* of Simichidas's claim to be spoken of in the same breath as Asclepiades and Philitas. If you try to build a house as high as a mountain, it will just fall down. In the same way the "cockerels of the Muses" are any poets who strive to rival their betters. In the context it has to be Homer's *reputation* as the best of poets that is their (unattainable) goal, not the fact that he happened to be the author of multi-book narrative. It is not just other epic poets but *all* other poets who are inferior to Homer.

If Homeric rivalry was Theocritus's concern, why confuse the issue by introducing rivalry with two other poets, neither of whom wrote either epic or bucolic? Asclepiades's reputation rests on his sophisticated and witty epigrams; the Theocritean scholia correctly describe him as an epigrammatist. But it has become fashionable lately to assign Philitas a rôle in the development of bucolic, mainly on the insubstantial basis of a character in Longus's *Daphnis and Chloe* called Philitas said in his youth to have sung and piped while herding his flocks.[29] Yet since the poet was a contemporary of Asclepiades and Theocritus himself, we might have expected a reference in the often informative Theocritus scholia if he had written bucolic. It is true that Hermesianax refers to a statue of Philitas singing beneath a plane-tree (F 7. 76), but while the posture suits the bucolic singer,[30] in extant bucolic the tree is always the oak, elm or beech, never the plane; and Philitas's song is of Bittis.

---

29. ii. 32. 3; 5. 3; 32. 3; 35. 3-4: F. Cairns, *Tibullus* (1979), 25-27; I. M. LeM. DuQuesnay, in D. West and A. Woodman, *Creative Imitation and Latin Literature* (Cambridge 1979), 60; and (more prudent) R. L. Hunter, *A Study of Daphnis and Chloe* (1983), 76-78; Bowie 1985 passim.

30. Clausen on *Buc.* iii. 55; it is (of course) unlikely that this was the posture of the statue itself (poets were normally shown seated holding a scroll: p. 68).

The only extant poem that could be cited is a quatrain celebrating a staff made of alder-wood, from which it has been inferred that Philitas was "first among the Alexandrians to allude to the *Theogony* in formulating a statement of poetic principles."[31] We should perhaps take a closer look at a potentially symbolic staff in a poet Theocritus actually mentions:

οὔ μέ τις ἐξ ὀρέων ἀποφώλιος ἀγροιώτης
  αἱρήσει κλήθρην, αἱρόμενος μακέλην·
ἀλλ' ἐπέων εἰδὼς κόσμον καὶ πολλὰ μογήσας
  μύθων παντοίων οἶμον ἐπιστάμενος.

I am an alder: no empty-headed, mattock-wielding rustic from the mountains will pick me up, but some hard-working man who understands the ornaments of poetry and knows the way of stories of every kind.

In that it draws so sharp and contemptuous a distinction between poets and rustics, this does not suggest a poet who wrote anything like Theocritean bucolic, especially since it is a poet who knows "every kind of story" that the staff wants as owner. The staff is not in itself a symbol of poetry; it is not a gift from the Muses or Apollo. It is an ordinary piece of alder-wood that happens to be a snob; it would rather be used by a poet than a rustic.

It is in fact a riddle: what is made of wood and could be used by either a rustic or a poet? Peter Bing has recently suggested a writing-tablet, observing that, while "tablets have a long history of speech, the staff has none."[32] He was even able to point to the numerous alder-wood writing-tablets of the Roman period found at Vindolanda. That would eliminate Philitas entirely from the present discussion. But doubts remain.

Certainly an artefact made from alder-wood rather than the tree itself. For while there are countless uses to which a rustic might put an entire tree, a poet could not himself transform a tree into writing-tablets. That would require a carpenter—not to mention the despised rustic to cut the tree down first. It must also be an artefact that could be used by either rustic or poet *as it is*. But why would a rustic ever think of picking up a writing tablet? Whether empty-headed or not, a rustic must surely be presumed illiterate.

Not a shepherd's crook, useless to the poet. All that is really left is a staff, which both could use. We have already seen that, despite the modern conviction that he hated everything to do with epic, Callimachus himself etymologized the rhapsode in Bk I of the *Aetia* (F 26. 5). We now find that Philitas regarded it as an honourable profession. He cannot (of course) have been familiar with genuine rhapsodes, already objects of fun by

31. Philitas F 10, with Powell's note ad loc. (*CA* pp. 92-3); J. Van Sickle, *Quad. Urb.* 19 (1975), 59 n. 61; E. L. Bowie, *CQ* 35 (1985), 75; P. Bing, *Rh. Mus.* 129 (1986), 222-25.
32. "The Alder and the Poet," *Rhein. Mus.* 129 (1986), 222-25, with a full account of earlier solutions.

Plato's day, though competitors in the category of rhapsode at the Hellenistic musical contests may have performed with the traditional staff.[33] But insofar as he sees a wooden staff as a symbol of the poetic vocation, it has to be epic poetry he has in mind. This is after all what we should expect from the author of a work on Homeric glosses.[34] The alder poem is full of Homeric vocabulary and formulas; line 4 (μύθων παντοίων οἶμον) in particular suggests epic (compare *Odyssey* 22. 347, θεὸς δέ μοι ἐν φρεσὶν οἴμας παντοίας ἐνέφυσεν).[35] It is perverse (with Van Sickle) to interpret in terms of the "slight style," a formula (πολλὰ μογήσας) that occurs 23 times in Homer. Insofar as Philitas had Hesiod's staff in mind, he must have shared the usual view that it was his rhapsode's staff.

Not only does the alder poem cast no light on Lycidas's staff or bucolic poetry. It lends no support to the notion of rivalry with Homer either. Another text hard to square with any such notion is a striking passage in an anonymous *Lament* for the late second- or early first-century Bion of Smyrna, latest in the bucolic canon. Just as Ionia once mourned Homer, now she mourns another son, Bion (δεύτερον ἄλγος); both drank from springs, Homer from Hippocrene, Bion from Arethusa;[36] Homer sang of Helen, Achilles and Menelaus, Bion of Pan, kisses and love (70-84). The comparison is remarkably restrained: no polemic, no suggestion that Pan and kisses are better than the Trojan saga. Bion is not said to surpass Homer, nor even in so many words to be his equal, much less his rival; merely to draw the comparison was compliment enough.

We may return to Callimachus and Theocritus. There are certainly interesting similarities between the *Aetia* prologue and the encounter between Lycidas and Simichidas. *If* Lycidas is Apollo, then in both passages Apollo appears to the budding young poet—an Apollo in both cases identified by the same cult title (Lyc-) not elsewhere associated with his rôle as god of poetry. More precisely, both poets refer or allude to the same two poets, Asclepiades and Philitas. Theocritus directly by name; Callimachus to a poem of Philitas in the *Aetia* prologue and to Asclepiades by implication on the *Lyde* in F 398, not to mention his presence on the Florentine list of Telchines.

But even if all these parallels are found cogent (and the identification of Lycidas as Apollo must remain speculative), their significance should not be exaggerated. Callimachus's praise of Philitas is qualified (Ch. XI. 2) and his attitude to Asclepiades (at any rate on the subject of Antimachus)

33. H. T. Wade-Gery, *The Poet of the Iliad* (Cambridge 1952), 29-31; Herington 1985, 167-76; for Hellenistic rhapsodes, G. M. Sifakis, *Studies in the History of Hellenistic Drama* (London 1967), index s.v.

34. Collected by G. Kuchenmüller, *Philetae Coi Reliquiae* (Berlin 1928), 91-113.

35. On οἴμη in Homer, A. Ford, *Homer: the poetry of the past* (Ithaca 1992), 42-43.

36. Arethusa stands for Theocritean bucolic, because of its Sicilian setting.

hostile, while Theocritus appears to be praising both as models of their kind. But then this praise is put in the mouth of the foolish young Simichidas, in a context heavy with irony. It is significant that, in contrast to Simichidas's appeal to two recent, perhaps still living poets, Lycidas appeals to figures of the remote, mythical past, Daphnis and Comatas (83f.).

Since Callimachus and Theocritus lived and wrote in Alexandria at the same time, some relationship, both personal and literary, is likely enough. Yet for all their apparent common concerns, and for all the effort devoted to discerning precise links and parallels between them,[37] there is little enough that could be called an agreed result.[38] Theocritus's datable poems all seem to fall in the 270s, and it is certainly possible that he wrote 7 at about the time Callimachus published *Aetia* I-II. Yet if he really "ranged himself...quite firmly on the same side" as Callimachus,[39] why not hold up Callimachus rather than his fellow-elegist Philitas or his rival Asclepiades as a model poet?

According to Williams, in both Theocritus 7 and *Aetia* prologue "the god of poetry manifests himself to a would-be poet, and issues authoritative edicts on how poetry should and should not be written; in both instances he vigorously condemns the fault of over-ambition in poets."[40] Yet the fact is that only Callimachus "issues edicts" about the writing of poetry. The "over-ambition" he condemns is purely stylistic, bombast, the μέγα ψοφέουσαν ἀοιδήν. What Theocritus condemns is, not imitation of the style of Asclepiades, Philitas or Homer, but the presumption of inexperienced poets who claim equality with such masters. Not only is there no clear evidence that Theocritus is defending Callimachean ideals. It is by no means clear that he is defending his own poetry either. As Hutchinson (who reached a similar conclusion from a different direction) has emphasized, Theocritus's lines are spoken by a character as part of a dramatic situation, not (as in Callimachus) by a narrator who purports to be the author *in propria persona*. Given the continuing uncertainty about the interpretation of this situation, it must remain uncertain how far Simichidas's speech reflects real Theocritean views.

Homer and Hesiod are but two of the wide range of poets alluded to in Theocritus 7, and to focus on them to the exclusion of the rest is to miss much of the richly allusive texture of the poem as a whole. As Nita Krevans sensibly put it, "by including all of them in *Idyll* 7, Theocritus

---

37. Gercke, *Rhein. Mus.* 42 (1887), 595; G. Schlatter, *Theokrit und Kallimachos* (Diss. Zürich 1941); G. Giangrande, *L' Antiquité Classique* 39 (1970), 65-72.

38. See the useful if fairly negative survey in Hutchinson 1988, 197-203.

39. Gow I. xxii; cf. II. 144.

40. *CQ* 21 (1971), 144.

deliberately emphasizes the diversity of his sources, as opposed to designating one figure as the model for his poetry."[41]

2

In one of those moments of aberration to which we are all vulnerable, Wilamowitz lent his authority to a strange misinterpretation of ps.-Theocritus *Ep.* 27:[42]

ἄλλος ὁ Χῖος, ἐγὼ δὲ Θεόκριτος ὃς τάδ᾽ ἔγραψα
εἷς ἀπὸ τῶν πολλῶν εἰμὶ Συρακοσίων,
υἱὸς Πραξαγόραο περικλειτᾶς τε Φιλίννας·
Μοῦσαν δ᾽ ὀθνείαν οὔτιν᾽ ἐφελκυσάμην.

The Chian is another, but the Theocritus who wrote this is I, one of the many in Syracuse, son of Praxagoras and Philinna of wide renown, and it is no alien Muse I have assumed.

Wilamowitz took "the Chian" to be Homer, and paraphrased the poem as follows: "I am an epic poet, but not in the Homeric style; I have my own Muse."[43] And he has been enthusiastically supported in more recent times by D. M. Halperin[44] and Joseph Farrell.[45]

Halperin argued that this was "the opinion of ancient critics," on the basis of a *Life of Homer* in which "Theocritus in his epigrams" is cited in support of the claims of Chios to Homer's birthplace. What he did not (apparently) notice is that the phrase "in his epigrams" is missing from one of the only two manuscripts that carry the *Life*. The Theocritean reference must (of course) be to 7. 47 (quoted above) or 22. 218 (quoted below), the two passages in which the poet cites Homer directly as "the Chian bard"—not to a epigram *on* Theocritus.[46] There cannot be the slightest real doubt that the author of the epigram is distinguishing between two different writers of the same name, Theocritus of Chios and Theocritus of Syracuse.

Since Vergil's day, the name Theocritus has been synonymous with the Syracusan, the founder of bucolic poetry. But in the early Hellenistic world

41. *TAPA* 113 (1983), 203.
42. *AP* ix. 434; also in the Theocritus scholia and now P. Oxy. 3726.
43. *Textgesch. gr. Bukoliker* (1906), 125-26; *Sappho und Simonides* (1913), 300 n. 3.
44. *Before Pastoral* (Yale 1983), 250-53, not even mentioning Theocritus of Chios.
45. *Virgil's Georgics and the Traditions of Ancient Epic* (Oxford 1991), 43-45.
46. *Vita Hom.* VI. 8 (p. 250 Allen); this is the best informed of the Lives, the original of which, by a process similar to that applied to the Lives of Aratus in Ch. VIII, can be assigned to the first century B.C. (T. W. Allen, *Homer: The Origins and Transmission* [Oxford 1924], 28-34). ἐν τοῖς ἐπιγράμμασιν must be an interpolation by someone who knew only the epigram from the scholiastic tradition.

Theocritus of Chios (mentioned more than once in this book) was far better known. Apart from his own works (of which only a number of his witticisms and an abusive epigram on Aristotle survive),[47] he was the subject of a book by an otherwise unknown Bryon, *Concerning Theocritus*, quoted by both Didymus and Diogenes Laertius.[48] Their composite Suda-entry gives the Chian first:

> Theocritus of Chios, rhetor, pupil of Metrodorus the Isocratean; wrote chreiai; political rival of Theopompus the historian. A history of Libya and remarkable letters are attributed to him. There is also another (καὶ ἕτερος) Theocritus, son of Praxagoras and Philinna; [some say of Simmichos]; a Syracusan; [some say a Coan who moved to Syracuse]. He wrote the so-called Bucolics in the Doric dialect. Some ascribe to him the following: *Proitides, Hopes, Hymns, Heroines,* funerary lyrics, elegies, iambics, epigrams. There were three bucolic poets: this Theocritus, Moschus of Sicily and Bion of Smyrna, from a village called Flossa.

The format of this double Suda notice suggests derivation from the *On Poets and Writers of the Same Name* by the mid first-century B.C. Demetrius of Magnesia, a friend of Cicero and Atticus.[49] Two passages of Diogenes Laertius show that it was the format of Demetrius's book to deal with the most famous bearer of the name first, and then enumerate the others. For example, after discussing Thales, Diogenes adds: "there are five other (καὶ ἄλλοι) Thaleses, as Demetrius of Magnesia says" (i. 38); then, on Pittacus: "there is another (καὶ ἕτερος) Pittacus...as Demetrius says" (i. 79).

Demetrius clearly had reliable information about the Chian. We may compare the Augustan Strabo: "Famous natives of Chios are...Theopompus the historian and Theocritus the sophist, the latter being political rivals" (14, 645). But he seems to have had no genuine biographical information at all about the Syracusan. Simmichos and Cos (both perhaps later interpolations) were inferred from a biographical reading of *Idyll* 7,[50] and the rest comes from the epigram. The implication is that as late as the first century the Chian was still the first person the name Theocritus called to mind.

According to Wilamowitz and Halperin "taking on a foreign Muse" means following in the path of Homer rather than developing a voice of

---

47. Page, *FGE* 93-95; Gow, *Theocritus* II. 549-50; Billows, *Antigonus* (1990), 437; above, Ch. I. 2 and II. 5.

48. Did. *Comm. Dem.* col. vi. 1. 44 (Βρύων), whence we may correct the parallel citation (giving Ἀμβρύων) in D.L. 5. 11; cf. P. Foucart, *Étude sur Didymos* (Mém. de l'Acad. des Inscr. et Belles-Lettres 38. 1) Paris 1906, 126-7. Presumably less a biography than a collection and elucidation of his witty sayings, in the tradition of περί-literature; on Bryon, a Chian and no doubt disciple of Theocritus, R. Laqueur, *RE* no. 2.

49. See J. Mejer's collection and analysis of the fragments in *Hermes* 109 (1981), 447-72.

50. Gow, *Theocritus* I. xvi.

one's own. In Farrell's paraphrase, "I am not, like most, a mere epigone of Homer." But what an absurdly inadequate characterization of bucolic! We surely expect something more positive than "not Homer." According to Halperin, the epigram "if not actually by Theocritus, was composed by someone familiar with his poetry."[51] On the contrary, once Χῖος is identified as the better-known Theocritus of Chios, there is nothing to suggest any familiarity whatever; not a hint (for example) that this was the inventor of bucolic. Indeed the writer seems to have no very high opinion of his subject, styling him merely "one of the many Theocrituses of Syracuse" (εἷς ἀπὸ τῶν πολλῶν εἰμὶ Συρακοσίων).[52]

Such an epigram is not in any case a likely vehicle for a literary judgment. It is clearly neither an autobiographical poem by Theocritus himself (like *AP* vii. 415 and 525 by Callimachus) nor an appreciation by a fellow poet. For example, we naturally expect and find something of Callimachus's own literary principles in his epigrams on contemporary poets like Aratus, Heracleitus and Theaetetus.[53] What purports to be a laudatory epitaph on Euphorion by Theodoridas is in fact shot through with obscene double entendres.[54] But most of the 96 Hellenistic epigrams on poets studied by M. Gabathuler (to which we may add the many anonyma he omitted) celebrate poets long dead.[55] Those that supply biographical information were no doubt intended as epigraphs for copies of their work.[56] On the face of it, the Theocritus epigram falls into this last category. To be sure Asclepiades's polemical poem on the *Lyde* opening Λύδη καὶ γένος εἰμὶ καὶ οὔνομα (*AP* ix. 63) is skilfully disguised as such an epigraph. But it would be intolerably abrupt for a quatrain whose first three lines were entirely devoted to biography to close with a polemical literary judgment.

Gow was on the right lines in his reluctant suggestion that the epigram is the work of an editor anxious to include only genuine Theocritus: "I have appropriated no Muse [= poem] by others." Theocritean manuscripts do include work by other bucolic poets, as (it seems) did the first-century edition by Artemidorus.[57] But such anxiety about authenticity sits awkwardly with that dismissal of the poet as "one of the many Syracusans." The closest linguistic parallel is Plato, *Gorgias* 465B, where ἀλλότριον

51. Farrell 1991, 44; Halperin 1983, 251.
52. Misconstrued by Farrell as "from the masses of Syracuse" (p. 43), which would be even more dismissive.
53. *AP* ix. 507; vii. 80; ix. 565.
54. *AP* vii. 406, with *HE* II. 545-6; W. Seelbach, *Die Epigr. des Mnasalkes und Theodoridas* (1964), 83-88.
55. *Hellenistische Epigramme auf Dichter* (Diss. Basel 1937).
56. E.g. *AP* vii. 21 by Simias: τόν σε χοροῖς μέλψαντα Σοφοκλέα, παῖδα Σοφίλλου, / τὸν τραγικῆς Μούσης ἀστέρα Κεκρόπιον...
57. *AP* ix. 434; Wilamowitz 1906, 124-25; Gow I. lx.

κάλλος ἐφελκομένους means "those who assume a borrowed beauty" (with the aid of make-up and depilatories).[58] We do not need to look beyond line 1 to see in what sense Theocritus claims "not to have assumed a borrowed Muse." We have already been told that he is not the Chian Theocritus; the Muse he has not assumed is (of course) that of the Chian Theocritus. This may seem a disappointingly lame conclusion, but then most anonymous book epigrams are disappointingly lame. I would agree that it is early, and therein lies such interest as it has; it dates from a period when the Chian was still the better-known poet of the name—and the Syracusan was not yet identified with bucolic.[59]

Behind the strange notion that Theocritus is proclaiming his independence from Homer is his use of the hexameter metre. On the basis of lists of hexameter poets in texts of the Roman period, Halperin concluded that "the bucolic poems of Theocritus belonged in antiquity to the genre of *epos* and that our poet is likely to have regarded his own compositions as a kind of 'epic' poetry." He then goes on to inquire: "How did Theocritus define his place within the epic tradition?" He assumes (like many others) that *epos* (left in transliterated Greek as though a technical term) is the Greek for what we capitalize as Epic. It is certainly not that. When modern critics use that term, they normally have some sort of heroic saga in mind, anything from the *Iliad* to *Ben Hur*. No ancient writer uses ἔπος in the singular for Epic in this sense, though ἔπη in the plural is sometimes (certainly not invariably) so used (whence the term ἐπῶν ποιητής). We have already seen that, though often applied to writers of Epic in the modern sense, ἐποποιός and ἐπῶν ποιητής in themselves imply no more than poets who wrote in hexameters (Ch. X. 2).

The fullest ancient definition of epic we possess is that of Aristotle (whose term is ἐποποιΐα). Since among other things it implies substantial length (μῆκος) and concern with superior people (σπουδαῖοι),[60] it is unlikely that Aristotle (or most other ancient reader) would have counted bucolic as Epic in Halperin's sense. By the third century hexameters had been used for many sorts of poetry other than heroic narrative; many "Homeric" forms and formulas simply became characteristic of hexameter (and elegiac) poetry. People cannot possibly have approached all hexameter verse with a view to defining its place in an all-embracing "Epic tradition." Over and above the difference in dialect, the metrical idiosyncracies and the obvious debt to drama and mime that distinguish Theocritean from

58. Since (a) the words cited constitute an all but perfect pentameter, and (b) this is the only other passage cited in LSJ (s.v. III. 5) for this meaning, I wonder whether Plato might in fact be citing from an earlier elegist, who was imitated by our epigrammatist.

59. For the latter point, see a forthcoming paper by Kathryn Gutzwiller.

60. *Poetics* 48a11; 59b18; with (e.g.) D. W. Lucas's notes.

Homeric hexameters, the most characteristically Theocritean poems, the so-called bucolic idylls, lack that most essential feature of Epic, narrative.

We might compare the very different kinds of poetry written in the iambic metre. By the fifth century archaic iambus had evolved into two very different forms, tragedy and comedy: tragedy dealt with passion and death among mythical kings and heroes; Old Comedy with political fantasy; New Comedy with the romances and deceptions of bourgeois young Athenians. But Callimachus's neo-archaic *Iambi* create neither tragic nor comic expectations. The strict tragic trimeter was able to attain a dignity far exceeding the looser trimeters of Attic comedy.[61] Whenever they wished, comic poets could instantly evoke the dignity of tragedy for parodic purposes by using a tragic turn of phrase or a stricter line. In the same way Theocritus could create momentary epic overtones in an otherwise quite unepic poem by the use of a Homeric formula (for example, ἡδὺ γελάσσας). But otherwise no reader of the bucolic idylls was in any danger of being distracted by heroic expectations.

3

Another topic that has much exercised critics is Theocritus's relationship to Apollonius. There are obvious verbal and thematic parallels between the *Hylas* and *Dioscuri* (13 and 22) on the one hand and Apollonius's account of these two stories in *Argon.* i. 1187-ii. 97. No one doubts that one poet had the text of the other before him when he wrote.[62] But which?

Such evidence as we have on their respective dates leaves little doubt that Theocritus was the older of the two men. This does not in itself (of course) prove that he wrote first. A senior poet might easily have been provoked by the challenge of a younger contemporary, and we have seen that the third century was a golden age of literary polemic.

Wilamowitz and more recently Gow and Dover argued for the priority of Apollonius.[63] Not only that. Wilamowitz and Gow further argued that Theocritus, like a true disciple of Callimachus, was correcting Apollonius, showing the misguided epic poet how to rewrite the stories of Hylas and

61. On the links between Attic comedy and iambus, R. M. Rosen, *Old Comedy and the Iambographic Tradition* (Atlanta 1988).

62. The links between the two versions of the Dioscuri story are less close, but if they are judged to prove knowledge (whichever way) in the one case, it seems natural to presume knowledge in the other too.

63. Dover 1971, 179-81; see too G. Serrao, *Problemi di poesia alessandrina* (Rome 1971), 111-50; M. Campbell, *Hermes* 102 (1974), 39-41; H. Fuchs, *Die Hylasgeschichte bei Apollonios Rhodios und Theokrit* (Diss. Würzburg 1979); most recently, A. Sens, *CQ* 44 (1994), 69-74.

Pollux in a smaller genre and slighter style. Köhnken and Vian took the opposite view, that Theocritus wrote first.[64]

The issue (as usual) was stated in its sharpest terms by Otis: these texts are "the only two instances in which we can actually see the difference between the continuous poem (ἓν ἄεισμα διηνεκές) and the short epos (ἔπος τυτθόν) of Callimachus's definition."[65] That is to say (according to Otis), Apollonius tells the story of Heracles and Hylas as just one detail in the saga of the Argonauts, while Theocritus abstracts it from its Argonautic background and turns it into a love story, playing down the traditional heroic side of Heracles. Passing over his pseudo-Callimachean terminology, Otis's description of the differences between Apollonius's epic hero and Theocritus's love-lorn pederast is just and perceptive. It is his explanation that is at fault.

Taking for granted the hypothesis of a debate about the "viability" of epic, Otis also took it for granted that Theocritus was criticizing Apollonius's anachronistic epic treatment. If published first, Apollonius's account of the Hylas story may or may not have given Theocritus the idea for his own very different treatment. But there seems no reason to regard that treatment as a polemic against anything so specific yet abstract as epic.[66]

The situation is in any case rather more complicated than has generally been allowed. It has generally been assumed that everything turns on settling just the one question of priority, a straightforward contrast between old-fashioned epic and modern erotic vignette. Yet what of all the other versions of the Hylas story (to concentrate on 13)?

The scholia to *Argon.* i. 1289 list no fewer than nine versions in which Heracles leaves the Argonauts for some other reason than love of Hylas. Of these nine, the most widely read at the time of both Theocritus and Apollonius was surely the one in Antimachus's *Lyde.* According to Antimachus, Heracles was thrown out by the other heroes because he was weighing down the Argo (F 58 Wyss)! Since Antimachus's purpose was to collect unhappy love stories, it seems a reasonable inference that he did not know the story of Heracles's love for Hylas. According to Gow, "Hylas belongs to the local mythology of the Ciani, a people living on the southern shore of the Propontis, and there is little evidence for the story in earlier Greek" (II. 231). As late as Callimachus's day we find Posidippus simply repeating the Antimachean version in an epigram (*SH* 703).

---

64. A. Köhnken, *Apollonios Rhodios und Theokrit* (Hypomnemata 12), Göttingen 1965; F. Vian, *Apollonios de Rhodes: Argonautiques* i (Paris 1974), 39-49.

65. Otis 1964, 398-405.

66. A. Sens, arguing for the priority of Apollonius but sensibly dropping the supposed debate about epic, explains Theocritus's variations as an attempt to "endow the Amycus episode with a refinement and wit appropriate to his chosen form" (*CQ* 1994, 74).

It may in fact have been none other than Callimachus who unearthed the Hylas story. According to i. 1207 Hylas left on his fateful errand for water carrying a bronze kalpis (κάλπις), which is said to be a Thessalian word for hydria, the sort of pot a woman would normally use. A first-century B.C. spell in hexameters has the word in precisely this sense.[67] The scholiast comments that it would be "unseemly" for a young man to have carried a hydria, and that Callimachus "more plausibly" said amphora (F 596). The implication is that this was the word Callimachus applied to the vessel carried by Hylas in a version of his own. On the other hand it might be argued that Callimachus wrote after Apollonius and was correcting his usage. A post-Apollonian version by Callimachus would obviously have major repercussions on the question of the relationship between Theocritus and Apollonius. Yet Theocritus seems to have no interest in correcting Apollonius on this point. His χάλκεον ἄγγος at 13. 39 picks up Apollonius's epithet, but uses a less rather than a more precise noun. And at line 46 he uses the rare word κρωσσός, which is regularly glossed ὑδρία. If anything, Theocritus is laying himself open to the same objection as Apollonius. Not that Apollonius's κάλπις has to designate a vessel that only women might carry, since Callimachus himself uses the word of bronze vessels given to men as prizes in athletic contests.[68] Lastly Pfeiffer suggests (on F 596) that the scholiast may not be referring to a Callimachean version of the Hylas story at all, but to *Iamb* 8, the description of the Aeginetan race in which men had to run the final leg carrying amphoras of water.

But if the Callimachean version must remain in doubt, it is nonetheless probable that Apollonius was at any rate the first to incorporate Hylas into the Argonautic saga. And while the Apollonian version is not overtly pederastic, there are erotic undercurrents. Heracles's frenzy at Hylas's disappearance (i. 1261-72) is not ascribed to love, but no alternative explanation is offered, and the "gadfly" (μύωπι, 1265) that drives him surely implies erotic passion rather than parental anxiety.[69] All we have been told about their relationship is that Heracles "took him away" (ἀπούρας) from his home after killing his father (i. 1212). In Homer this word always implies force and is in addition the standard term for the taking of Briseïs from Achilles (A. 356 = 507 = B. 240; A. 430; I. 107, 131, 273; T. 89). Apollonius's vocabulary thus suggests the possibility that Hylas was taken as erotic booty. It is too simple to brand Apollonius's handling of the story as typical of "Antimachean" epic. It was not because he was writing epic

---

67. παρθενικαὶ κυανώπιδες ἤρυσαν ὕδωρ / κάλπισι κυανέαις, *SH* 900. 12.

68. F 384. 36; the word is also commonly used later for a funerary urn: Gow and Page on *HE* 3365.

69. So rightly Hunter 1993, 38-39; for μύωψ (and οἶστρος) of love, *Arg.* iii. 275-77, with Hunter's note; Headlam's note on Herodas i. 57.; Nonn. i. 48; Lucian *Am.* 2.

that Apollonius failed to develop the erotic motivation latent in his version, but because his focus, quite properly in a narrative of the Argonauts, was on Heracles's departure from the expedition. Just as he borrowed Callimachus's account of the killing of Hylas's father without repeating the details,[70] so (I suggest) he simply took over the outline of Theocritus's account of Heracles's departure, thus avoiding rivalry with a source he could count on being familiar to his readers.

In 1968 D. J. Mastronarde published a reading of 13 as "an important exploration of the relevance of the epic hero in a post-heroic era."[71] But in what sense is the age of the Ptolemies "post-heroic" in a way that (say) fifth-century Athens was not (in its own way the era of Antigonus the One-eyed and Demetrius the Besieger was very much an age of heroes)? Already in fifth- and fourth-century comedy and satyr-drama we find a remarkably, not to say extravagantly unheroic Heracles, with "constant emphasis on the hero's voracity for food, wine and women—in that order."[72] The heroic Heracles we find in no more than 14 tragedies with 8 corresponding vase illustrations; the comic Heracles in more than 70 comedies and satyr-plays, with more than 100 vase illustrations.[73] Already in the Hesiodic *Wedding of Ceyx* Heracles gatecrashes the wedding banquet and after eating the company under the table regales them with a succession of riddles.[74] More typically Alexandrian is the cultivated Heracles of the *Heracliscus*;[75] and we have already noted the serious treatment of the divine Heracles as ancestor of the Ptolemies in both Callimachus and Theocritus (Ch. IX. 2). There is certainly no straightforward contrast between a "traditionally" heroic Heracles in the *Argonautica* and the "modern" Heracles of Theocritus's *Hylas*. Recent work has revealed Apollonius's Heracles to be a highly complex and sophisticated figure.[76]

We might also compare Theocritus's Cyclops, another epic figure given a comic, bucolic treatment. But when unprovoked by intruders, already in the *Odyssey* (ix. 105-35) the Cyclopes are shown as vegetarians and teetotallers, living in a sort of bucolic utopia. Theocritus is simply developing a side of their life Homer only hints at, giving a more positive significance to their rustic existence. This is a characteristically Alexandrian way of handling Homer, but it does not imply a rejection of "traditional

70. F 24-25 (p. 250); obviously there might have been some erotic reference here.

71. "Theocritus' Idyll 13: Love and the Hero," *TAPA* 99 (1968), 273-90 at p. 275.

72. For a succinct survey of the literary evidence, G. K. Galinsky, *The Herakles Theme* (Oxford 1972), 81-100; for the no less abundant artistic evidence (going down to 300 B.C.), R. Vollkommer, *Herakles in the Art of Classical Greece* (Oxford 1988).

73. Vollkommer 1988, 61-65 (tragedies); 67 (satyr-plays); 74 (comedies).

74. F 263-69 M-W; Merkelbach and West, *Rhein. Mus.* 108 (1965), 300-17.

75. Galinsky 1972, 101-25 on his "intellectualization"; for the *Heracliscus*, Ch. II. 3.

76. D. C. Feeney, *The Gods in Epic* (Oxford 1991), 93-98; R. L. Hunter, *The Argonautica of Apollonius* (Cambridge 1993), 25-41.

heroism," much less epic. In this case, moreover, Theocritus is more directly influenced by a famous dithyramb of Philoxenus of Syracuse, which showed a parodic Cyclops serenading Galatea. Galatea and her Cyclops also appeared in a series of fourth-century comedies.[77] Whatever the origin and significance of bucolic, it is far too simplistic to see it as a "questioning of the relative value of epic as opposed to realism, homely rusticism, and pastoral idealism."[78]

I have no intention of burdening readers with yet another detailed comparison of the two episodes in the two poets. Many attempts have been made to establish priority this way, some reaching one conclusion, some the other.[79] If it were possible to prove so limited a point to everyone's satisfaction, it would surely have been done by now. But there is a curious feature about the distribution of the episodes in the work of the two poets which has not so far been adequately accounted for.

In Apollonius, the Hylas episode closes Bk i and the Amycus episode opens Bk ii. That is to say, the two episodes are *consecutive*. In Theocritus's oeuvre there is no connection between the two versions of the two stories. Hylas is treated in 13, a poem all to himself, while Amycus is allotted just one section in a hymn to the Dioscuri (22). For those who see Theocritus as teaching Apollonius a lesson, Theocritus picked the stories he did because he found them together in Apollonius. But even if we concede for the sake of argument that the Apollonian versions are in both cases inferior, neither is conspicuously bad in itself—worse (that is) than a dozen other episodes in Apollonius Theocritus might have picked instead if that had been his intention.

If we assume the priority of Apollonius, it is surely a very odd coincidence that the two episodes that best suited Theocritus's purpose should occur consecutively. On the other hand, if we assume the priority of Theocritus, Apollonius would naturally have worked right through Theocritus as he did Callimachus, looking for adventures and aetiologies for his own poem. We have already seen that the pederastic version of the Hylas story was unknown to earlier versions of the Argonautic saga. If Theocritus wrote first, Apollonius would certainly have wanted to include a version so congenial to contemporary taste. As for the fight between Pollux and Amycus, Theocritus's version (as distinct from his presentation) does not significantly differ from the numerous more or less comic versions known from earlier literature and art.[80] It is Apollonius who innovates, by

---

77. For all the documentation, Gutzwiller 1991, 63-65.

78. Mastronarde 1968, 281.

79. The most systematic is A. Köhnken 1965, deciding for the priority of Theocritus; against, see the reviews by J. Griffin, *CR* 16 (1966), 300-02; H. Tränkle, *Gnomon* 39 (1967), 831-33; Campbell, *Hermes* 102 (1974), 39-41.

80. Vian, i. 134-41; G. Beckel, *LIMC* i (1981), 738-42.

making Amycus (in keeping with the perils the Argonauts encounter on their journey) a more serious threat and so deserving death rather than the good beating he gets in the earlier versions.[81]

We have already seen (Ch. IX. 3) that Apollonius drew two of his episodes from Callimachus, the Anaphe story from *Aetia* I and the Hydrophoria story from the *Iambi:* Those two episodes close the *Argonautica*, appearing consecutively together at the end of Bk iv. The obvious interpretation of their juxtaposition (as we saw) is that Apollonius was thus underlining his debt to the older poet, his teacher. Surely the same explanation applies to the juxtaposition of the two stories from Theocritus. It was Theocritus who wrote first.

4

As for 22, the Theocritean version of the Amycus story is not without problems of its own.[82] The poem opens in traditional manner as a variation on the thirty-third Homeric Hymn, an address to the Dioscuri. The poet concludes his invocation by promising to celebrate the twins separately: lines 27-134 treat the boxing match between Pollux and Amycus, and 136-211 the duel between Castor and Lynceus.

If it was Theocritus's purpose to teach Apollonius a lesson, why complicate the issue by making the lesson one half of sharply contrasting panels in a two-part treatment of twins? The reader is naturally encouraged to compare and contrast the panels with each other rather than one panel with some other work. Carroll Moulton and F. T. Griffiths have attempted interpretations in terms of the contrast between the panels, but neither really works.

According to Moulton, there is a stylistic contrast between the two parts (the first Callimachean/modern, the second Homeric/traditional), accompanied by a moral contrast:

> Pollux is the vehicle for civilizing values, Castor the representative of the old heroic mores, a code of force which Theocritus, no doubt, found quite as objectionable as the old-fashioned poetry which embodied it.

Theocritus "is showing that he can write not only in the elegant new style associated with Callimachus and his adherents but also in the more conventional Homeric fashion which Apollonius retained." Thus the poem as a whole "can be interpreted as commenting on both the style and subject mat-

---

81. In art he is regularly shown bound to a tree after the encounter; Beckel, l.c.

82. For an up-to-date account of the problems and literature, S. Laursen, "Theocritus' Hymn to the Dioscuri: Unity and Intention," *Class. et Med.* 43 (1992), 71-95; Hutchinson 1988, 162-7.

ter of traditional epic."[83] Castor's battle is certainly described in heavily Homeric language, but there is nothing modern about the "civilizing values" of Pollux. For what he does is teach Amycus a lesson in the heroic code of hospitality. Pollux politely offers Amycus gifts in the best epic manner, but Amycus offensively rejects them and refuses to allow the heroes so much as a drink of water from the spring he guards. There can be little doubt (as A. Kurz has illustrated in detail),

that Theocritus had in mind two specific passages of Homer that make the same point: Odysseus and the Cyclops (9. 105-565) and Odysseus and the insolent beggar Irus (18. 1-107). Just as Odysseus tells Irus never to be bossy to strangers again (106), so Pollux makes Amycus swear never to be unpleasant to strangers again (22. 134).[84]

As Simon Laursen has put it, "the contrast between the two fighting scenes cannot be a contrast between archaizing and modernistic ways to narrate myth" (p. 81). The first part of the poem is no less "Homeric" than the second, if in a different way (thematic rather than verbal). But there is a contrast of a different sort. In heroic terms, there can be no question that Amycus is in the wrong and Pollux justified in teaching him a lesson. The second duel is very different. Here the Dioscuri carry off the two daughters of Leucippus when they were on the point of marrying their long-time fiancés Lynceus and Idas, the sons of Aphareus. Castor kills Lynceus, and when his brother Idas tries to intervene, Zeus strikes him dead in front of his own father's tomb.

The kidnapping of the Leucippides is not linked to the battle with Lynceus and Idas in the earliest versions of the myth, but it is certainly pre-Theocritean.[85] The question is whether Theocritus is intensifying for some purpose of his own or merely dramatizing the injustice of the Dioscuri. The situation is set out in an eloquent and indignant speech by Lynceus, which (on the transmitted text) remains unanswered. Wilamowitz was so troubled by Castor's failure to respond to the charges that he posited a lacuna after line 170 for a speech by Castor, and he has been widely followed (notably by Gow and Dover). There are one or two textual problems at this point, but nothing to warrant such drastic intervention. As Griffiths justly observes, "What defense can Castor make in any case?"[86]

Griffiths's own solution links Castor's silence to the fact that the actual battle is described in a pastiche of Homeric battle vocabulary.[87] For Griffiths, Theocritus "is clearly amusing himself with the pitfalls of the Hom-

---

83. "Theocritus and the Dioscuri," *GRBS* 14 (1973), 41-47; against, Hutchinson 167.

84. *Le Corpus Theocriteum et Homère* (Berne 1982), 79-109; Laursen 1992, 75-82.

85. An Apulian vase of 350/40 and a Lycian relief of ca 370: *LIMC* iii (1986), nos. 203 and 208, with A. Hermary's analysis of the sources on p. 590.

86. Griffiths 1976, 356.

87. The Homeric parallels are quoted in Gow's notes to 181-204.

ericizing style, as hardly surprises us from a consummate parodist who nowhere takes the traditional heroism seriously"; he "clearly is doing so to mock the pretensions of the latter-day Homeridae." That is to say, he is deliberately writing badly so as to make fun of bad heroic poetry. "Can the reference be to anyone ·but Apollonius?," he asks.[88] But even if we accept for the sake of argument that Apollonius wrote "traditional" epic,[89] he certainly did not write Homeric pastiche. Nor could even the most malicious critic have thought that Homeric battle vocabulary was an appropriate way to make fun of Apollonius or even catch the essence of his style. For the *Argonautica* is that oddity among heroic poems, an epic in which the heroes never fight a battle!

For Griffiths, Castor represents "the brutality of the old heroism," supposedly the essence of "traditional" epic. But while the *Iliad* may be, in a phrase of Simone Weil, a "poem of force," it is by no means a glorification of brutality. In the *Odyssey*, by and large wickedness and presumption are punished; in the *Iliad*, though heroes win glory by prowess in battle, the emphasis falls overwhelmingly on their mortality, with constant evocation of the pathos of early death and grieving loved ones.[90] It was for representing heroes like Achilles indulging in unheroic lamentation that Plato wanted to ban Homer from his ideal city (*Rep.* 387D-388B). As for Apollonius, no surviving epic features less brutal heroes than the *Argonautica*.

Dubious parallels have been alleged for this supposed "subversive" attitude to heroic values. For example, following an influential article by J. C. Bramble, it has become fashionable so to interpret Catullus's *Peleus and Thetis*, allegedly derived from some Hellenistic model.[91] To be sure, the description of the desertion of Ariadne on the bedspread and the praise of their future son Achilles as a killing machine cast a shadow over the wedding of Peleus and Thetis. But it is not clear that this amounts to anything more than the dramatic irony we find in much earlier mythological wedding poems: Sappho F 44 on Hector and Andromache or the song about Peleus and Thetis that precedes Iphigeneia's "wedding" in Euripides.[92]

Perhaps the explanation for these puzzling features in Theocritus 22 is to be sought in another direction, in life rather than literature. Theocritus was writing in Alexandria, where the cult of the Dioscuri was important to the royal house. Both Philadelphus and Euergetes are known from con-

88. Griffiths 1976, 359; *GRBS* 17 (1976), 362.

89. The *Argonautica* is at any rate more traditional in form than (say) the *Aetia*.

90. See particularly J. Griffin, *Homer on Life and Death* (Oxford 1980), 81-143.

91. *PCPS* 16 (1970), 22-41; for more radical doubts and fuller bibliography, J. H. Dee, *ICS* 7 (1982), 98-109; Heath 1989, 60-62. I am unconvinced by the claim (D. Konstan, *Catullus's Indictment of Rome*, Amsterdam 1977) that it was the decline of Roman morality Catullus was attacking.

92. *IA* 1036-79; for other examples, J. Stern, *RBPh* 56 (1978), 29-37.

temporary dedications to have shared a temple with the Dioscuri, and there are reasons for believing that Arsinoë played a part in establishing their cult in Alexandria.[93] The great Pharos of Alexandria was dedicated to "the Saviour Gods" (Θεοῖς Σωτῆρσι), whether the Dioscuri or the royal couple is uncertain.[94] Already by the late fourth century we find the iconography of the Dioscuri assimilated to that of Alexander, and a coin of Seleucus I shows the same phenomenon.[95]

It is the Dioscuri Callimachus represents as carrying the dead Arsinoë off to heaven, just as they had carried off their sister Helen (F 228).[96] Another poem of Callimachus invokes Helen together with the Dioscuri (F 228). Theocritus had compared Arsinoë to Helen at *Adoniazusai* 110, and linked Helen together with the Dioscuri as patrons of poetry in 22. 216, a compliment better suited to Arsinoë than the wife of Menelaus. Having named Helen, it is perhaps understandable that he should go on to name Menelaus in the following line (22. 217). But there is surely a deeper reason as well.

Another poem that may conceal several layers of meaning is 18, on the wedding of Helen and Menelaus. The theme suggests Theocritus's Alexandrian period. Helen and Menelaus are Egypt's only link to the Trojan saga;[97] but for Helen and Menelaus neither *Iliad* nor *Odyssey* would ever have been written. This is not to say that Helen represents Arsinoë in any simple or consistent way,[98] still less that the poem is an epithalamium for her marriage to Philadelphus. For if the comparison is pressed, no wedding in mythology was more ill-omened than that of Helen and Menelaus. Indeed Jacob Stern has argued that the poet cannot have expected his readers to suspend this knowledge. This is a point that arises often in modern discussions of mythical allusions: how much of the rest of the saga is an allusion to one detail intended to trigger?

A recent paper by Tonio Hölscher has drawn attention to an extreme example, the representation in art of Octavian as Orestes.[99] To be sure both avenged their fathers—but no artist can have wanted to call to mind the rest of the saga of the House of Atreus![100] Stern cited other cases of ironic

---

93. Fraser I. 207; D. B. Thompson, *Ptolemaic Oinochoai and Portraits in Faience* (Oxford 1973), 66-7; for Ptolemaic festivals to the Dioscuri, F. Perpillou-Thomas, *Fêtes d'Égypte ptolemaïque et romaine* (Louvain 1993), 83-7.

94. Fraser I. 18-19.

95. A. Hermary, *LIMC* iii (1986), 592-93.

96. As more than once described in Euripides: see Pfeiffer's note on F 228. 6.

97. So Griffiths 1979, 86-91.

98. Any more than Aeneas does Augustus in the *Aeneid*.

99. "Augustus and Orestes," *Études et Travaux (Travaux du centre d'archéologie méditerranéenne de l'académie polonaise des sciences* 30, 1992), 164-68.

100. Hölscher himself went too far in drawing the parallel between Clytemnestra and Cleopatra "who had lived with Caesar in marriage-like relations." It was for marrying Antony that Cleopatra became Octavian's enemy, nor did he kill her. It is of course easier for the artist to confine his reference to the one detail he chooses to represent.

epithalamia (some already mentioned), from Euripides to Catullus.[101] But there is nothing in Theocritus 18 itself to evoke the Paris episode, and Alexandrian audiences must have been accustomed to push it to the back of their minds. After all, according to the local version (which was at least as old as Herodotus), it was not the real Helen but a facsimile Paris took to Troy; she remained in Egypt all the ·time, to be happily reunited with Menelaus there on his return.[102] In rebuttal of what he sees as Herodotus's hostile account of Menelaus's behaviour in Egypt, Plutarch remarks that "numerous honours are still paid to both Helen and Menelaus in Egypt" (*Mor.* 857B). Theocritus underlines that Menelaus will have Zeus himself as his father-in-law, and speculates about what sort of child Helen will present to her new husband.[103]

Menelaus might also have another reference in early third-century Alexandria. One of Soter's most important lieutenants throughout his long reign was a brother called Menelaus, one time ruler of Cyprus and "still prominent in Alexandria as the eponymous priest of Alexander in 284."[104] This man is likely to have had a family. The dynastic potential for Theocritus's epithalamium was considerable. How far it was actualized depends on the exact date and circumstances of composition and performance, which of course we do not and cannot know.

Like the Attic dramatists, Hellenistic poets could surely count on readers tuning out inappropriate or inconvenient alternative versions. Perhaps it was so with the darker stories about the Dioscuri, especially in Alexandria.[105]

That the Dioscuri of 22 do indeed in some sense represent the Ptolemaic saviour-gods is strongly suggested by the poet's insistence on their patronage of poets, together with Helen (215-7)—hardly their usual rôle (in 18 too Helen is praised for her skill with the lyre, hardly a traditional detail).[106] If so, this might explain a detail that has greatly puzzled critics.

101. J. Stern, "Theocritus' *Epithalamium for Helen," RBPh* 56 (1978), 29-37.

102. N. Austin, *Helen of Troy and her Shameless Phantom* (Ithaca 1994). Theocritus may have had in mind the picture of the couple reunited in domestic postwar bliss already in *Odyssey* 4 (so M. C. Pantelia, *Hermes* 123 [1995], 76-81).

103. According to [Hesiod], a daughter Hermione and a son Nicostratos: West, *The Hesiodic Catalogue of Women* (Oxford 1985), 118-19; according to the *Cypria*, a son Pleisthenes (F 12B).

104. Bagnall, *Ptolemaic Possessions* (1976), 41; *Pros. Ptol.* vi (1968), 14, no. 14537.

105. Griffiths thought that allusion to the royal cults could not extend beyond the prelude of 22 because "the twins descend to barbarity in the second episode," concluding that "the poem is probably best explained as a purely literary exercise" (1979, 52 n. 5). But perhaps after all Dover was right to suggest that Theocritus simply "accept[ed] the lawless brutality of the Dioskouroi as a datum."

106. Griffiths 1979, 88, "the poet's need to compliment a patron of poetry."

Why did Theocritus change the usual version, that Lynceus kills Castor, the occasion for his alternating immortality with Pollux? If his Dioscuri are the Ptolemaic saviour-gods, then it becomes problematic for one of them to die, nor could the dynastic cult cope with alternating immortality. Better quietly to drop this detail.

The claim that it is "hard to resist the Tyndarids, for mighty are they and sons of a mighty sire" (212-13)[107] might then be a statement of the futility of resistance to the Ptolemies. The Dioscuri appear on Seleucid coins as symbols of military victory.[108] We may recall the remarkable line in Callimachus's *Hymn to Apollo*: ὃς μάχεται μακάρεσσιν, ἐμῷ βασιλῆι μάχοιτο (26). The Homeric battle vocabulary need not be parodic;[109] perhaps it was simply intended to create an atmosphere of military might.

The poem closes with the claim that it was "to bring glory to you, princes" that Homer "hymned the town of Priam and the ships of the Achaeans." On the face of it, he is addressing the Dioscuri[110] and means the *Iliad*. Yet their only mention in the *Iliad* is where Helen remarks that they are nowhere to be seen (3. 236f.). Indeed it is precisely because of their encounter with Lynceus and Idas that the Dioscuri miss the Trojan war. Perhaps Theocritus's point is that on his version, in which they both "survive the episode in which they were normally killed,"[111] they should in fact have been present! It may also be that he had the *Cypria* in mind as well as the *Iliad*. For it is the kidnapping of the brides of Lynceus and Idas in the *Cypria* that is said to have given Paris the idea of kidnapping Helen:[112] that is to say, the kidnapping was (at least indirectly) the cause of the Trojan war. Gow objected that Theocritus elsewhere "seems not to have ascribed [the *Cypria*] to Homer"). But whatever he may really have thought about its authorship, for the purposes of his compliment to the living Dioscuri who were his patrons it was natural that he should accept the traditional ascription. In any event, if any part of his poem had been intended to depreciate heroic poetry, it was singularly perverse to close with so pointed a claim to be following in Homer's footsteps.

107. Essentially the conclusion to Pindar's version: χαλεπὰ δ'ἔρις ἀνθρώποις ὁμιλεῖν κρεσσόνων, *N*. 10. 72.

108. Hermary, *LIMC* iii (1986), 592-93 with nos. 10-11.

109. So rightly Hutchinson 1988, 166.

110. Dover implausibly identifies the ἄνακτες as "the gods and heroes of legend as a whole," but how can the epilogue to a hymn to the Dioscuri not be addressed to them?

111. A. Sens, *TAPA* 122 (1992), 348. I quote without comment the two possibilities canvassed by Laursen 1992, 92: "Either Theocritus wants us to understand that the Dioscuri are such a cruel pair that it was a benefit for their reputation not to be exposed in such a well-known poem as the *Iliad*, or he thinks that the *Iliad* contains so much meaningless bloodshed that it was a benefit for the reputation of the Dioscuri that they did not partake in it."

112. F 11 Bernabé, with M. Davies, *The Epic Cycle* (Bristol 1989), 40; 33-52 on the *Cypria* in general.

Chapter XVII

Hecale and Epyllion

1

Elegy was the great preoccupation of the age of Callimachus, and it was naturally the style appropriate for elegy rather than epic that Callimachus addressed in the prologue to his own original and polemical new elegy. But we cannot leave it there. For Callimachus did write an epic, albeit a one-book epic, the *Hecale*.[1] It is often assumed that the date of the *Hecale* relative to the *Aetia* can be fixed from the opening of the *Aetia* prologue. He cannot (so it is argued) have claimed never to have written "one continuous song" if he had already published the *Hecale*. But if that phrase had the pejorative connotations suggested in Ch. XII, then he never wrote such a work.

On the other hand, there are grounds for dating the *Hecale* before the *Aetia*. There are a number of close verbal parallels between the *Hecale* and the *Argonautica*, and Hollis argues that Apollonius is the borrower. Furthermore, there are three separate parallels between the *Hecale* and Callimachus's own fourth *Iambus*, and Hollis again argues for the priority of the *Hecale*.[2] Given the lack of an extended context in all the Callimachean passages, the argument cannot be pressed in either case. But if it holds, then it might be better to place *Hecale* before *Aetia*. For otherwise, on the chronology suggested in Ch. IX, we should have to squash *Aetia*, *Hecale* and *Iambi* between ca 270 and 268. The epilogue (F 112) suggests that *Iambi* directly followed *Aetia*.

Why did Callimachus write this second long poem? Naturally we need not take seriously the scholiast who tells us that it was a response to "those who mocked him for his inability to write a long poem."[3] The "mocked" (σκώπτοντας) allows us to identify this as no more than an inference from the *Aetia* prologue. Nonetheless, there may be a sense in which the two poems were intended to be, respectively, a model epic and model elegy. Hitherto surprisingly little attention has been paid to the fact that they are

---

1. Now to be read in the admirable edition by A. S. Hollis, *Callimachus Hecale* (Oxford 1990); see too E. Livrea, ΚΡΕΣΣΟΝΑ ΒΑΣΚΑΝΙΗΣ: *Quindici studi di poesia ellenistica* (Messina-Firenze 1993), 1-63.
2. Hollis 1990, 27; 4.
3. Schol. *H. Apoll.* 106.

in different metres. This is in part at least because of the traditional assumption that the *Aetia* prologue was itself concerned with epic. Thus both *Aetia* and *Hecale* could be seen as squibs in the same battle against epic.

It is an interesting coincidence that the most Callimachean Roman elegist also finally turned to epic. In Ovid's case the reason was perhaps less the greater elevation of theme he had in mind than the problem of writing genuine narrative on a large scale in the self-contained post-Propertian elegiac couplet. But Callimachus's flexible couplets, if inevitably somewhat lighter than his hexameters, were nonetheless a perfectly adequate narrative instrument.

Since Heinze's famous essay of 1919 there has been much discussion of the difference between Ovid's elegiac and hexameter narrative style.[4] Is there any difference between Callimachus's hexameter and elegiac style? There seems to have been little serious study of the question—as may be seen from the characteristically wrongheaded assessment of Brooks Otis:

> the fact is that Callimachus's elegiac and hexameter narratives are much the same, though undoubtedly his *Aetia* accentuated the familiar and light manner while his *Hecale* aspired more to objectivity and epic elevation. But there is little or no difference of narrative style between his hexameter hymns and his elegiac *Baths of Pallas*.[5]

Although his qualifications redress the balance somewhat, Otis made the error of confusing metre and genre. Hymns are hymns, whatever the metre (or dialect). And if there is one thing we can be certain of about Callimachus's varied works, it is that they were classified by genre rather than metre. As we saw in Ch. VI, his epigrams included a number of short poems in metres other than the elegiac couplet and his *Iambi* poems in a number of metres other than choliambs. And although we do not have the confirmation of a preface, the sequence of the hymns, the same in both manuscripts and papyri, is almost certainly to be attributed to the poet himself. The case is succinctly stated by N. Hopkinson:[6]

> the arrangement is symmetrical: two short, two long, two short poems...; the first pair 'masculine,' the second 'mixed' (twins), the third 'feminine'; the flanking pairs broadly 'mimetic,' the middle pair more traditionally 'epic.' The last pair, however, are distinguished by their Doric dialect from the epic/Ionic *hh*. 1-4.

4. Otis, *Ovid as an Epic Poet*[2] (Cambridge 1970), 4-44; D. A. Little in E. Zinn (ed.), *Ovids Ars Amatoria und Remedia Amoris: Untersuchungen zum Aufbau* (Stuttgart 1970), 64-105; S. Hinds, *The Metamorphosis of Persephone* (Cambridge 1987), 99-133.

5. Otis 1970, 24.

6. Hopkinson 1984, 13-17.

The difference of metre between 5 (elegiacs) and 6 (hexameters) is only one of a long series of similarities and differences between the two hymns that it took Hopkinson four pages to list.

In an earlier chapter, we saw that one of the most conspicuous and original features of the *Aetia* was the injection of the personality of the narrator into the narrative.[7] The narrator of the *Hecale*, by contrast, is invisible. Of an originally ca 4000 lines of the *Aetia* we possess ca 550 of which enough remains to form any impression, less than a seventh of the whole. Of the *Hecale* we have ca 200 lines of which enough remains out of a total of 1000 or so,[8] perhaps a fifth of the whole. That is to say, proportionately we have more of the *Hecale* than the *Aetia*. So the disproportion between the two poems in this matter can hardly be ascribed to the vicissitudes of preservation.

This observation cuts both ways, underlining the prominence of the personal element in the *Aetia* as much as its absence in the *Hecale*. The cause is surely the difference of genre: personal elegy as against impersonal epic. We saw that Otis was wrong to expect any general stylistic difference between Callimachus's elegiac and hexameter hymns. But even here there is one exception. The first person in the hymns normally refers to the poet only insofar as he counts himself one of the worshippers addressing the god in question. Even in the *Hymn to Apollo*, "my king," "my city" and "our kings" in 26, 65 and 68 identify the speaker as a Cyrenean addressing fellow Cyreneans rather than as the poet Callimachus. The only unmistakable exception is from the elegiac hymn to Athena (5. 55-6):

πότνι' Ἀθαναία, σὺ μὲν ἔξιθι· μέσφα δ' ἐγώ τι
ταῖσδ' ἐρέω· μῦθος δ' οὐκ ἐμός, ἀλλ' ἑτέρων.

By way of digression, lines 56-136 tell the tale of the blinding of Tiresias. After repeating for the third time (after 33 and 43) the ritual appeal to Athena to come forth from her shrine, the poet abruptly changes mood: "meantime, while we are waiting, I shall speak to these ladies; the story is not mine, but told by others...." As with the narratorial interludes in the *Aetia*, this is not (of course) a glimpse of the poet's real world; it is not his purpose to communicate information about sources (not even named),[9] or even to disavow responsibility, *more Herodoteo*, for a dubious story. Rather, as in certain passages in the *Aetia*, by playing with traditional disclaimers these lines direct our attention less to the poet's sources than to his own personal and original use of them. That is conspicuously so here, for

7. Not necessarily (of course) the real personality of Callimachus of Cyrene.

8. For the various estimates, Hollis 1990, 337-40, suspecting that it may have been even longer.

9. Perhaps Pherecydes, perhaps Agias and Dercyllos: Bulloch 1985, 17-19; L. R. Lacy, *JHS* 110 (1990), 30.

the blinding of Tiresias is by common consent one of the finest narratives in all Callimachus. By suggesting that there is just enough time for the story before the arrival of the goddess, they actually heighten the dramatic tension they purport to be breaking.[10] While there is certainly no general stylistic difference between the hexameter and elegiac hymns, it may be more than coincidence that the closest approximation to the narrative mode of the *Aetia* comes in his one elegiac hymn.

This is not to say that there are no personal passages in the hexameter hymns. The epilogue to the *Hymn to Apollo* is an obvious example. But the personal message is there mediated obliquely and enigmatically. No one who was not already familiar with the specialized polemical connotations of "spring" and "envy" in the Callimachean lexicon could have made head or tail of it. There is no use of the first person. That is the hallmark of Callimachus's elegiac style, as revealed throughout the *Aetia*—and in this one passage of the *Hymn to Athena*.

Both first person and narrator are entirely absent from the *Hecale*, as too is that allied feature of Callimachus's elegiac style, the dramatic apostrophe. The subject matter of the *Hecale* is indeed much the same as that of the *Aetia*: aetiological explanations of myth and cult practices. But the presentation is quite different: the "objective" epic manner.

The *Aetia* begins with a highly personal and polemical prologue, and (perhaps) ends with a programmatic epilogue. The *Iambi* too begin with a programmatic introductory poem and include (even if they do not end with) a polemical epilogue. We are fortunate enough to possess what we know from the *Diegeseis* to be the opening line of the *Hecale* (F 230),

Ἀκταίη τις ἔναιεν Ἐρεχθέος ἔν ποτε γουνῷ,

the beginning of a characterization of Hecale herself. No personal prologue. The poem began, as an epic should, *in medias res*, without even invoking the Muse.

Next, structure. The *Aetia* is a series of separate aetiological tales, just as Ovid's *Metamorphoses* is a series of separate tales of metamorphosis. As we have seen, Callimachus used a variety of devices to impose some sort of personal (if not Aristotelian) unity on at any rate *Aetia* I-II. The *Hecale*, though likewise touching on a variety of different themes, is nonetheless characterized by a genuine (if complex) structural unity.

The basic plot is simple. Theseus takes refuge from a storm in Hecale's humble cottage, and goes off next morning to kill the Marathonian bull. On his return he discovers that Hecale has died, whereupon he establishes heroic honours for her. Thus the action itself covers a period of barely 24 hours, though by skilful use of flashback (in the form of speeches) digres-

10. Bulloch's note well illustrates literary models but has little on dramatic function.

sion and foreshadowing (in the form of aetiology), he contrives to take in much of the early lives of both Theseus and Hecale—and their posthumous influence as well.

Callimachus deploys in miniature just those unifying techniques that set the *Iliad* and *Odyssey* apart from Cyclic epic—and Apollonius. To those who see Callimachus as pursuing a deliberate aim of unhomeric disunity, evidence of a sort can certainly be found in the *Aetia*—but hardly in the *Hecale*.

In addition to the regular Homeric word-games (imitations with some elegant variation), we also find many more straightforward Homeric echoes in the *Hecale* than in the *Aetia*. F 260 (= 69 H) lines 2-4, the scene where the Athenians welcome the victorious Theseus, provides a good example:

ὡς ἴδον, ὡ[ς] ἅμα πάντες ὑπέτρεσαν, οὐδέ τις ἔτλη
ἄνδρα μέγαν καὶ θῆρα πελώριον ἄντα ἰδέσθαι,
μέσφ' ὅτε δὴ Θησεύς φιν ἀπόπροθι μακρὸν ἄϋσε.

The opening of line 2 is modelled on *Il.* 14. 294: ὡς δ'ἴδεν, ὥς μιν...; with the central phrase, compare *Il.* 15. 636: αἱ δέ τε πᾶσαι ὑπέτρεσαν; if the line really ended οὐδέ τις ἔτλη, so do nine lines in Homer; μακρὸν ἄϋσε is also a Homeric formula, though not at this place in the line. More unusual still, line 22 of the long fragment preserved on the Vienna tablet reproduces unchanged the first four feet of one Homeric line and the last two of another:[11]

καδδραθέτην δ' οὐ πολλὸν ἐπὶ χρόνον, αἶψα γὰρ ἦλθεν

The Homeric models are *Od.* 15. 493f. καδδραθέτην δ' οὐ πολλὸν ἐπὶ χρόνον, ἀλλὰ μίνυνθα; and *Od.* 12. 407, οὐ μάλα πολλὸν ἐπὶ χρόνον· αἶψα γὰρ ἦλθε. Also noteworthy is the painstaking sequence of time indicators in F 238. 15-21 (ὄφρα μέν...τόφρα δ'...ὁππ[ότε]...τῆμος) "very much in the Homeric manner, though not exactly paralleled by any passage of Homer."[12]

It is (of course) an axiom of the Giangrande school that Homeric imitation by the Alexandrian poets is *always* accompanied by variation.[13] So why not here? Given his normal practice we can hardly accuse Callimachus of formulaic writing. These occasional pure Homeric echoes and mannerisms were surely intended to create a more straightforwardly epic atmosphere. Not that the overall effect of the passage is in the least Homeric:

11. F 351. 22 = 74. 22 H (omitting a couple of dots and brackets).
12. Hollis 1990, 156, citing *Il.* 11. 84f. (ὄφρα μέν...τόφρα...ἦμος δὲ...τῆμος), 8. 66f., 16. 777f., *Od.* 9. 56f.
13. Most explicitly stated in *PLLS* 2 (1976), 273 ("the cardinal principle") = *SMA* 1 (1980), 291f., together with other papers reprinted in the same volume, esp. 11-23 and 33-64.

They slept for no long time, for soon frosty dawn came when no longer are the hands of thieves on the hunt, for already the lights of dawn shine out and the man who draws water is singing the well-song. The axle shrieking under the wagon wakes the man whose house is beside the highway and crowds of blacksmith slaves, themselves deaf, torment his hearing.

"The pattern of this description is Homeric," as Gordon Williams has well observed, "but Callimachus has developed it in quite a different way by a series of impressionistic sketches, which are separated from one another by changes of syntactical structure and point of view...surprising the reader...by unexpected and carefully random detail."[14]

In addition there are many allusions to specific Homeric passages. Hecale's humble cottage recalls Eumaeus's cottage (Pfeiffer on F 239); Hecale washing Theseus's feet recalls Eurycleia washing Odysseus's feet (F 246). πρηεῖα γυναικῶν in F 263 is a pseudo-Homeric formula coined on the analogy of δῖα γυναικῶν to suit Hecale. Hollis also draws attention to a number of minor and (taken individually), inconspicuous linguistic indications, such as pleonastic δέ τε *metri gratia*, which reveal the *Hecale* closer to Homer than Callimachus's other works.[15] For example, according to the statistics compiled by Ruijgh, there are only eleven exampes of epic τε in Callimachus's *Hymns*, giving a percentage of 1 every 98 lines, close to Theocritus's 1:85 and a long way from Apollonius's 1:36 (which is close to Homer's 1:32).[16] But it is misleading to cite such figures as "a reflection of the different attitude of the two Alexandrian poets to traditional epic."[17] Apollonius (as we shall see) was not writing "traditional" epic, while Theocritus and (in his *Hymns*) Callimachus were not writing epic (in the sense of extended narrative) at all. Yet there are perhaps eight or nine examples in the *Hecale* alone, a much higher proportion than in the rest of his works.[18]

This is not to say that the overall effect of the *Hecale* is straightforwardly Homeric. Far from it. In a variety of ways Homeric expectations are subtly deflected. For example, the conventionally Homeric passage from F 260 quoted above closes in typically Callimachean fashion with an aetiology: the jubilant Athenians shower Theseus with leaves (φύλλα), thus establishing the custom of showering victors in the games with leaves (φυλλοβολία). F 304 describes, in sonorous phrases appropriate to a Homeric war-helmet, a modest felt cap. Gutzwiller drew attention to the fact that virtually every detail in the account of Hecale's entertainment of

14. *Trad. and Originality in Roman poetry* (Oxford 1968), 656 (whence the translation).
15. Hollis 1990, 12 n. 6; 304; 299.
16. C. J. Ruijgh, *Autour de 'te épique'* (Amsterdam 1971), 967-70.
17. G. R. McLennan, *Callimachus: Hymn to Zeus* (Rome 1977), 85.
18. See Hollis's cautious conclusion, 1990, 304.

Theseus has its Homeric antecedent.[19] "Despite this evident similarity in outline," she concluded, "there is an important difference... Lacking the expensive equipage of the aristocratic household, Hecale must make do with common implements, rough furniture, and coarse food. This is the incongruity of the section: the contrast between the elegance of the Homeric precedent and the rusticity of Hecale's hospitality."

In fact throughout the poem Callimachus is subtly undermining the basic classical axiom that epic, like tragedy, deals with great deeds of great men, in Aristotelian terminology *spoudaia* by *spoudaioi*. Most obviously, instead of calling his poem after the brave young hero Theseus, he calls it after an obscure old pauper. The scene we might have expected to be the high point of the poem, the battle with the Marathonian bull, was apparently despatched in a few lines, while whole pages were devoted to the reminiscences of a 500-year-old crow (unlike the poet, it might be added, a self-conscious and intrusive internal narrator).

It would have been mere archaism to reproduce a counterfeit Homeric style—and quite unlike Callimachus. Elsewhere he tells us that one of the things critics did not like about his *Iambi* was the mixture of dialects, Doric along with the Ionic proper to iambi (F 203. 18). Of course, we do not need to believe that anyone really criticized this; what we can be sure of is that Callimachus wanted to make sure readers knew that the mixture was deliberate, not the result of ignorance or carelessness. If he had wished, he could easily have produced a complete book in perfect Hipponactean metres and dialect. So little survives of the poems in Doric (6, 7, 9, 11) and so little is known of their models that we cannot even guess what prompted his choice of Doric rather than Ionic. We do not really know why he used Doric for the fifth and sixth hymns.[20]

A more surprising idiosyncracy of the *Hecale* (as Hollis has pointed out) is the traces of "Attic colour and vocabulary" derived from Attic comedy.[21] What Hollis did not explicitly note is that in many cases these are not just items of vocabulary but *objects*: ἀσκάντης, a sort of stool, σιπύη, a bread-bin, and μετάκερας, warm water. Hecale and Theseus were Attic heroes. How better to underline this than to show them using down-to-earth Attic terms for everyday objects like stools and bread-bins? For all anyone knew such terms might already have been in use in heroic Attica anyway.

F 297 (91 H) calls Salamis by its archaic name Kolouris, presumably found in one of the Atthidographers.[22] Another Attic expression Callim-

---

19. F 239-52 = 27-39 H; Gutzwiller 1981, 55.

20. See Hopkinson 1984, 44.

21. Hollis 1990, 9; *ZPE* 93 (1992), 4-6.

22. The dates allow use of Philochorus (Hollis 1990, 6-7); the earlier Androtion, Phanodemus and Demon also treated the legendary period (*FGrH* 324-25, 327-28).

achus lovingly uses is ἀμπρεύειν, "used of animals conveying loads with a tow-rope (ἀμπρόν) attached to a cart" (F 272 = 52 H). *SH* 288. 25 (= 74 H) refers to a water-drawer singing a "rope-song" (ἱμαῖον), no doubt derived from Aristophanes's *Frogs* 1297. In F 288. 10-11 (= 74H) the crow swears a multiple·oath, again a feature "characteristic of the dialogue of comedy."[23]

It is important to be clear that this is not simply a case of "mixing of genres." It was surely not at all Callimachus's purpose to mix epic with comedy. Hecale was a figure of Attic legend, and the poem an aetiology of an Attic festival evoking many details of Attic cult, locale and antiquities. How better to give his poem an authentically Attic colouring than by a subtle use of vocabulary from that quintessentially Attic poetic form, Old Comedy. Work on the vocabulary of the Attic comic poets seems to have begun with Lycophron's *On Comedy* and continued by Euphronius and Eratosthenes.[24] There is no direct evidence that Callimachus himself did any specialized work on the subject, but he is frequently quoted in the Aristophanes scholia.[25]

G. Zanker has recently argued that the *Hecale* "may be seen as a break with the whole of the Greek epic tradition," with Hecale herself as "a new kind of epic hero."[26] This seems to me to go too far. It is true that Hellenistic poets liked themes from everyday life, the bourgeois housewives of Theocritus's *Adoniazusae* and the low-life characters of Herodas's *Mimiambi*. But Herodas and Theocritus were confessedly writing in different genres, the mime or an elevated version of the mime. It is natural too to compare Apollonius's memorable portrait of Aphrodite and Eros as a suburban mother unable to control her spoilt son. Apollonius was writing an epic, but the humanization of divine behaviour was a conspicuous (even scandalous) feature of Homer. Much modern writing on Apollonius has been devoted to the fact that his heroes (especially Jason) are often portrayed as less than heroic. It depends what is meant by heroic (see further below). But he certainly did not make them bourgeois or proletarian.

The *Hecale* is no proletarian epic. Like Eumaeus in the Odyssey no less than Electra's farmer husband in Euripides's play of that name, Hecale was well born and had once been rich (F 254 = 41 H). The quality for which she was famous, her hospitality (φιλοξενία, F 231 = 2 H. 2; F 263 = 80 H. 4) is an archetypally epic virtue. The moment Theseus arrives, she offers him the run of her home like any epic king or queen, though in

23. Hollis 1990, 247-48; add Dover, *CQ* 35 (1985), 328 (whence the quotation).

24. C. Strecker, *De Lycophrone, Euphronio, Eratosthene comicorum interpretibus* (Diss. Greifswald 1884); Pfeiffer 1968, 121-22; Hollis, *ZPE* 93 (1992), 5-6.

25. J. W. White, *The Scholia on the Aves of Aristophanes* (Boston 1914), xvii.

26. "Callimachus's *Hecale*: A New Kind of Epic Hero?" *Antichthon* 11 (1979), 73; 77.

details more reminiscent of more lowly epic forbears, Eumaeus and Eurycleia.

Nor is the subject matter wholly "mean" (φαυλόν, to use Aristotle's term). Hecale is undoubtedly the focus of the poem, but that does not make her a "new kind of epic hero." She *becomes* a hero in the technical sense when Theseus institutes her cult, but she does not actually do anything herself except provide hospitality—certainly nothing out of keeping with her sex and status. The main action (however circumscribed) is after all the bona fide hero Theseus killing a monster.

The originality and fascination of the poem lies in the way Callimachus uses every artifice to shift the balance from the heroic to the unheroic, while still producing a recognizably epic poem. But he does not do this in any straightforward way, simply by pouring new wine into old bottles; in Bulloch's words, "although the forms and material are provided by the old world their manner is that of the new."[27] Still less by parody: there is no sign that his purpose was to discredit the epic forms by filling them with unworthy or comical acts and agents. To quote Bulloch again, Callimachus's concentration on the ordinary "was not a *diminution* of the grand themes of tradition, but rather an essential reworking of convention, and the establishing of a new realism." There is no suggestion that the heavy Homeric colouring of the lines quoted above is ironic. The long account of Hecale's entertainment is certainly not a parody of epic entertainments; some of the traditional formulas were already adapted to Eumaeus's humble entertainment of Odysseus in the *Odyssey*. Beyond question Callimachus was trying to write a new sort of epic, antiquarian rather than heroic, concise and unified rather than rambling and episodic. But by no means a burlesque.

It is easy to make too much of the so-called "mixing of the genres"—or at any rate the motives behind it. An earlier chapter mentioned a variety of modern claims that the aim of Hellenistic poets was to "flout" or "violate" the traditional generic boundaries (Ch. VI. 3). This was certainly not Callimachus's attitude to epic and elegy. So far from treating them as indistinguishable (this was in effect his criticism of the *Lyde*), he seems to have done his best to preserve their individualities. While anxious to increase and enhance the rôle of the narrator in elegiac narrative, he was no less anxious to keep it invisible in epic narrative.

In Apollonius's epic narrative, by contrast, we find "a far greater prominence for the poet's person, the narrating *ego*, than is found in Homer"; some first person verbs in the catalogue of ships in Bk i imply consultation of sources almost in the Callimachean manner.[28] Since on the provisional

27. Bulloch 1985, 564.
28. Hunter 1993, 106, 127.

chronology here followed the *Hecale* may be earlier than the *Argonautica*, probably no criticism is intended. But it is nonetheless striking to find Callimachus's epic technique in some respects more conservative than Apollonius's.

Writing of the entire class of so-called epyllia, Gutzwiller claims that "the tone of high seriousness which was considered essential to epic is gone."[29] There are two issues here. First, the other poems she discusses are indeed by and large fairly lighthearted in tone (§ 2). Yet while the *Hecale* is scarcely a work of high seriousness, neither is it a witty jeu d'esprit like Moschus's *Europa*. At bottom it is the story of the last day in the life of an old woman who had once enjoyed wealth and happiness, now reduced to grief and poverty. In a speech of which we have only sadly tattered fragments (*SH* 286-7 = F 47-9 H), she recalls with pride her two promising sons, who "sprang up like aspens." This fine phrase (ἀναδραμέτην ἄτε κερκίδες) undoubtedly echoes Thetis's remark that Achilles "sprang up like a sapling" (ἀνέδραμεν ἔρνεϊ ἶσος), another mother speaking of a son destined to die young—a powerful and obviously non-ironic Homeric reminiscence. The successive disasters that took away her wealth and family are missing but it has generally been inferred from her bitter curse of the robber Cercyon that he killed one of her sons. There must have been another emotional scene when she learned that Theseus had recently slain Cercyon, thus taking on her behalf the revenge she had long been hoping for. The poem concluded with her death and the honours established in her memory. Though no doubt as witty and allusive as the rest of Callimachus's work, the overall tone of the poem must have been basically serious.

We now know that the *Victoria Berenices* was not just one among many aetiological stories, but the opening poem of the second half of the *Aetia*, and an encomion of the new Queen Berenice. It therefore becomes correspondingly more surprising that Callimachus should have used so similar a story for his *Hecale*: in both poems a monster-slaying hero (Heracles/Theseus) spends the night before one of his most celebrated exploits in the cottage of a pauper (Molorchus/Hecale). The pauper entertains the hero as royally as his/her slender resources allow, in each case providing the aetiology of a festival.[30] Such striking thematic and structural similarities between the two poems must surely have highlighted differences no less striking, differences in tone and treatment called for by the difference in genre. The basic seriousness of tone here claimed for the *Hecale* will have been less prominent in the *VB*. For example, there was

29. *Studies in the Hellenistic Epyllion* (Königstein 1981), 2-3.
30. Fuhrer 1992 argues that the *VB* did not in fact provide an aetiology for the Nemean games.

probably nothing in the *Hecale* to compare with the aetiology of the mousetrap in the *VB*.[31] It was not by chance that Heracles rather than Theseus is the hero of the *VB*; there was no rich comic tradition for Theseus as there was for Heracles.

2

The *Hecale* has always been seen as the prime example, perhaps the first example, of the subgenre "epyllion" or miniature epic[32] that was to enjoy such a vogue in late Republican Rome. Half a century ago a valuable article by W. Allen Jr cast doubt on both term and genre.[33] It is not just that the term is modern. What is in question rather is the claim that there exist sufficient short poems united by sufficient shared features to justify the assumption of a fully fledged subgenre, whether ancient or modern.

The most recent attempt to define and describe the genre in detail is that of Kathryn Gutzwiller.[34] She lists seven epyllia: three poems of Theocritus: the *Heracliscus, Hylas* and *Heracles the lionslayer*; two by Callimachus, the *Hymn to Demeter* and the *Hecale*; and two later works, Moschus's *Europa* and the fragmentary *Epithalamium of Achilles and Deidamia*. Most of what she has to say about the individual poems is sensible and perceptive. It is the selection itself that prompts questions. In what respects does the *Hymn to Demeter* resemble the *Hecale* more than the rest of Callimachus's hymns? Do these three poems of Theocritus have more in common with the two poems of Callimachus than the rest of Theocritus's oeuvre? Is it of no consequence that the *Hecale* is 10 or 15 times as long as the *Hylas*, only 75 lines including a preface? A new papyrus has revealed that the hexameter *Hermes* of Callimachus's disciple Eratosthenes was more than 20 times as long, perhaps almost 1700 lines.[35] Is it really metre alone rather than narrative that is the key component in the definition of epyllion? For on narrative grounds the *Hymn to Athena* surely deserves a place. The inclusion of hymns cuts across what might otherwise have seemed an important potential difference: namely that hymns deal with gods while most other epyllia with mortals.

According to Gutzwiller, the poems she selected "display a consistency of technique which makes them a logical grouping"; they are "epic, but

---

31. F 177 = *SH* 259.

32. The term preferred by P. Toohey, *Reading Epic: an introduction to the ancient narratives* (London 1992), 100.

33. "The Epyllion: A Chapter in the History of Lit. Criticism," *TAPA* 71 (1940), 1-26.

34. Gutzwiller 1981; see too M. M. Crump, *The Epyllion from Theocritus to Ovid* (Oxford 1931); the brief but important remarks in Hollis 1990, 23-6; and the useful, well-informed overview in Toohey 1992, 100-120.

35. Between 1540 and 1670 lines; see Parsons's notes to P. Oxy. 3000; *SH* 397.

epic written in the manner of the slender Muse of Callimachean poetics."
The key feature they share is "the subversion of the archaic ideal."[36] This
is often true of her selection, though it does not follow that it is the result
of a conscious rejection of epic, much less a reaction to the popularity of
epic. And it is going too far to claim that "the story is told in such a way as
to...mock the conventional heroic interpretation." The sample is small and
heterogeneous. If we had more examples, we might find considerably more
variety of tone and subject matter.

It is often maintained that one of the defining features of epyllion is a
long digression, often in the form of an ecphrasis.[37] Certainly it is a characteristic feature of the Roman examples—Catullus 64, *Culex*, and (to a
lesser extent) *Ciris*.[38] It is often assumed that the practice derives from, or
was at any rate popularized by the *Hecale*. There are indeed several digressions of various sorts in the *Hecale* (notably the long speech of the
crow),[39] but no formal digression and certainly no ecphrasis. Nor is there
anything of the sort in any of the three Theocritean poems. Thus the earliest preserved example in Moschus's *Europa* owes nothing to the *Hecale*.
It is indeed a feature borrowed from archaic poetry, the clearest example
being the Hesiodic *Shield of Heracles*, a narrative of Heracles's battle with
Cycnus interrupted by a description of his shield. Though hardly by
Hesiod, it is an authentically archaic poem which we know to have been
much studied by the Alexandrians;[40] Apollonius pronounced it genuine,
while Aristophanes disagreed.[41] It was (of course) modelled on the description of the shield of Achilles in the *Iliad*. Whether it was Moschus himself
or some earlier Hellenistic poet who revived the ecphrasis-digression, it
was certainly not Callimachus.

Problems also arise when we try to pin down the "archaic ideals" that
epyllia are supposed to be subverting. For example, Apollonius's
Argonautica, though certainly written on the scale of traditional epic, does
not in any straightforward way embody "old epic values." Nor does much
of old epic for that matter.[42] As an important paper by Jasper Griffin has
underlined, Cyclic epic is distinguished by "monsters, miracles, metamorphoses, and an untragic attitude towards mortality, all seasoned with

36. Gutzwiller 1981, 2 and 5.

37. Crump 1931, 23, 100-01; more cautiously Hollis 1990, 25; Toohey 1992, 101.

38. R.O.A.M. Lyne, *Ciris: A Poem Attributed to Virgil* (Cambridge 1978), 34-35, will
not allow that the Britomartis section (294-309) is a "formal digression," which, in order to
maintain the integrity of the genre, he claims to be no more than an "optional" feature.

39. On the speech of the crow (and its imitation by Ovid) see now A. M. Keith, *The
Play of Fictions* (Ann Arbor 1992), 9-20, 43-45.

40. Robert Lamberton, *Hesiod* (New Haven 1988), 138-44.

41. Pfeiffer 1968, 144. 177.

42. J. Griffin, "Heroic and unheroic attitudes in Homer," *Chios: A Conference at the
Homereion in Chios 1984* (Oxford 1986), 3-13.

exoticism and romance."[43] Length aside, these are pretty much the qualities critics have identified as characteristic of epyllion. The later epyllia, notably those by the Latin poets, are full of the exotic and romantic. Yet there is nothing of the sort in the *Hecale*.

Wilamowitz pointed out that there was no obvious difference in either tone or subject matter between the short hexameter poems and the elegies of the age.[44] For example, when Parthenius made his collection of plots for Cornelius Gallus, plots identified by modern scholars as ideal for epyllia, he states in his preface that they are for Gallus "to turn into your own epic or elegiac poetry."

Inevitably Theocritus's hexameter *Hylas* (13) is counted as an epyllion, but its form (a letter to a friend), brevity (75 lines including the frame) and erotic subject matter align it with elegy rather than epic. Like 11 (*Cyclops*) it is addressed to his friend Nicias: we thought we had invented love, but long before us it happened to Heracles himself. When the nymphs take Hylas Heracles loses control, oblivious of his obligation to the other Argonauts, and they sail without him, branding him a deserter. Within the epistolary frame, the implication is clearly that Nicias should treat the story of Heracles as a warning: immoderate love can bring disgrace. It is no accident that Propertius saw the poem as a suitable model for one of his elegies, neatly adapting it into a different sort of cautionary tale: Gallus should take good care of his beloved; look what happened to Heracles when he let Hylas wander off on his own. When we add that there are no digressions, flashbacks, prophecies or even aetiologies[45] in Theocritus's narrative of only 70 lines,[46] it seems unhelpful to bracket the *Hylas* with the *Hecale*—or even the *Europa*.

Hollis remarks that "several epyllia are named after a female character,"[47] but what of *Lyde, Leontion, Bittis* and *Cydippe*? Elegies named after (or about) a woman are certainly no less common. One poem that might have modified the picture if it had survived is the *Erigone* of Eratosthenes, described by Longinus as a perfect piece of work. It told the story of Dionysus's discovery of wine and among other things provided an aetiology of Attic tragedy. Yet it was an elegy.[48]

It has often been remarked that epyllia tend to tell obscure stories. Yet again this does not distinguish them from the aetiological elegies of the age, nor could a large theme like the saga of Troy or Thebes or the adven-

---

43. "The Epic Cycle and the Uniqueness of Homer," *JHS* 97 (1977), 53.

44. *HD* I. 184.

45. Except for the half-line explanation of the stabilizing of the Symplegades in line 24.

46. There is however one characteristically epic simile at 49-52.

47. Hollis 1990, 25; Toohey 1992, 101.

48. F. Solmsen, *TAPA* 78 (1947), 252-75; R. Merkelbach, *Miscellanea...A. Rostagni* (Turin 1963), 471-526.

tures of Heracles or the Argonauts be handled in a few hundred lines. Inevitably, anyone wishing to write a short poem would pick a less well-known story, or a less familiar adventure of a well-known hero. Moreover, the very scale of such poems is almost bound in itself to result in a less than epic tone and treatment. For example, if a chapter in Parthenius had ascribed to Callimachus a short hexameter poem on the wedding of Ceyx in which much space was devoted to the amount of food Heracles consumed and the riddles with which he regaled the wedding guests, it would have been classified as a typical Hellenistic epyllion. In fact it was Hesiod who wrote such a poem.[49] If the *Wedding of Ceyx* had survived along with the *Shield of Heracles* (not to mention the Homeric *Hymn to Hermes*), the history of the epyllion might have worn a rather different perspective.

On the traditional view the dominant form of poetry in the third century was long epic. On this assumption, it was short epic that needed explaining. Actually short epic was the dominant form. The problems of the epyllion dissolve when reconsidered in the light of the results obtained in Ch. II, VI and X. In Ch. VI we noted the great metrical simplification of the Hellenistic age: many subjects previously treated in lyric or choral form were handled in hexameters or elegiacs. In Ch. II and X we saw that hexameters were widely used (a) for short poems on local cults and myths in the musical agones; (b) for encomia of local gentry and rulers, as well as (c) for epithalamia, epicedia and many other sorts of occasional poetry. Indeed, innumerable short hexameter poems must have been written all over the Hellenistic world, by poets of every sort and ability. Some of the prize poems of Demoteles of Andros, Amphiclos of Chios and their fellows must have been cast in the form of hymns, if only because a hymn to (say) Delian or Delphian Apollo was such a convenient form for "making worthy mention" of the cults and temples of Delos and Delphi. Others will have been simple narratives; some will have had digressions, some not. Only the tiniest fraction of this immense body of work has come down to us. But what has is assumed to be sophisticated and experimental and included in the modern canon of epyllion; for example Theocritus's *Heracliscus*, usually treated as a classic example of purely literary composition for the book, but (as we saw in Ch. II. 5) in fact written for a poetic contest.

If the *Hecale* is to be set in a contemporary literary context, the most helpful as well as the best documented is the category of hexameter poems that "make worthy mention of the ancestors and myths of the city"—in this case Athens. It may be significant that Eratosthenes and Euphorion, who both lived for some while in Athens, also wrote elaborate poems on Athenian antiquities: Eratosthenes an *Erigone*, Euphorion a *Mopsopia*.[50]

---

49. F 263-9 M-W, with *Rhein. Mus.* 108 (1965), 300-17.
50. A. S. Hollis, "Attica in Hellenistic Poetry," *ZPE* 93 (1992), 1-15.

This would nicely explain the immense pains he devoted to giving the poem an authentically Attic colour. At more than 1000 lines, certainly not a prize piece routinely entered for a contest, but a more sophisticated and literary version of that sort of poem nonetheless, perhaps specially written for a visit to Athens.[51] Maybe the inscription rewarding the poet in the usual way with proxeny and citizenship for the honour done the city will turn up some day.

Epyllion is a handy term for a short hexameter poem, but does it really identify a significant Hellenistic poetic form? The evidence of the festivals suggests that short hexameter poems in the epic mode were ten a penny. To judge from the debate about the *Lyde*, it was elegy that preoccupied the more reflective poets and critics of the age. In whatever terms contemporaries formulated it, a key element in their disagreement seems to have been the rôle of the narrator in narrative.[52] It was naturally elegy that offered more opportunities for experimentation and innovation in this area, and there can be little doubt that Callimachus himself was more interested in elegy. Even if, as suggested in this chapter, he wrote the *Hecale* as a model epic, *poetarum in usum*, to highlight what he saw as the differences as well as the similarities between epic and elegy, it did not exercise the same influence.[53] Certainly it was as an elegist that he entered the canon of Greek literary history. It was to Callimachus rather than Mimnermus or Antimachus that the Roman elegists looked as their model.

The Hellenistic poems classified as epyllia do not really have that much in common—a good deal less than their Latin counterparts. The only Hellenistic poem that resembles the Latin epyllia in any significant way, down to its long ecphrasis, is the *Europa* of Moschus, a disciple of Aristarchus who cannot have written much before the second half of the second century. The *Europa* is a work of great charm, often cited as the high-watermark of Hellenistic rococo: "small-scale, Homeric in diction, un-homeric in treatment, ecphrastic, pictorial, pseudo-naive."[54] At 166 lines it is not on the same scale as the *Hecale*, nor does it have its basic serious-ness. But in one respect at least it follows the Callimachean model: it "lacks the intrusive presence of the poet-narrator."[55] Despite its small

51. It is not necessary to suppose that Callimachus visited and performed in person; like Pindar, he may have sent a text for performance by a friend or disciple.

52. It is this (I suspect) that lay behind Callimachus's reservations about the "tall lady" of Philitas; in diction and allusiveness the *Bittis* no doubt passed muster, but the hostility that greeted Callimachus's *Aetia* suggests that Philitas's narrative voice was traditional.

53. It is tantalizing that we are deprived of the opportunity of comparing the elegiac technique of his disciple Eratosthenes.

54. Hopkinson, *A Hellenistic Anthology* (1988), 202; E. Fraenkel, *Horace* (1957), 195-96; Toohey 1992, 105-06.

55. R. L. Hunter, *Apollonius of Rhodes* (1993), 115.

scale, it perhaps deserves to be described as a genuine "miniature epic" in a way that (for example) none of the Theocritean poems do.

The Theocritean examples are not really much like either the *Europa* or the *Hecale*. Nor are there any "programmatic" allusions to the *Hecale* in any of the Latin epyllia in the way there are to Callimachean elegy in the Latin elegists (Ch. XVIII). It is not clear that the *Hecale* did in fact "spawn a subgenre"[56] at all; with the possible exception of the *Hermes* of his known disciple Eratosthenes (lost beyond conjecture), it has no identifiable descendants. A famous passage in Cicero's *Tusculans* (iii. 45) associates modern poets who despise Ennius with Euphorion. Whether or not Euphorion wrote epyllia, the evidence suggests that the epyllion as we find it in Moschus and Catullus is a post-Callimachean development.

3

So Callimachus's famous literary theories do not really amount to much—as theories. His colourful polemic is essentially negative, not what he liked but what he did not like. The perfect poem would be not long, not flabby, not noisy. These negatives do not add up to any particular genre or type of poem. Certainly not epic, since he wrote his own. Nor was he simply pushing elegy as an alternative, since his harshest words were reserved for an elegy. But if the *Lyde* epitomized badness, there are no precise indications just how goodness might be attained. It was hackneyed *narrative* he was attacking, in whatever metre.

Callimachus's own narrative, whether in epic or (especially) elegy, was indeed very different from his more traditional predecessors. But the nature of these differences could not have been inferred from his polemic.[57] While repudiating epic bombast, when he came to write epic himself, Callimachus carefully affected many epic trimmings he had avoided in his elegies.

To be sure he was careful to avoid the bombast he so brilliantly pil-loried, but bombast was not an inescapable feature of epic. Antimachus's elegy was bombastic in a way Homer's epic was not. Apollonius on the whole avoided bombast, and the *Argonautica* was not significantly longer than the *Aetia*. But would that have been enough to win Callimachus's approval? In the past, it was taken for granted that he was bound to have hated Apollonius simply and solely because he wrote "traditional epic." More recently it has become fashionable to see the *Argonautica* as the

---

56. Toohey 1992, 101. Contrast Clausen's strange verdict that the epyllion was "a form that Callimachus invented but did not exploit," *Cambr. Hist. Latin Literature* (Cambridge 1982), 186.

57. So already Hutchinson 1988, 83.

epitome of Callimacheanism.[58] Yet it can hardly escape the criticism of being an ἄεισμα διηνεκές. Would this have earned his wrath? We simply do not know. The polemic has too little descriptive content to tell us. If his judgments on Aratus and Antimachus had not survived, who would have guessed that he admired·the epic poet and despised the elegist?

In effect his polemic was a plea for ·originality and quality. Better than any theory, some would say. The trick is bringing it off. And who is to be the judge?

58. Notably Newman 1986, Ch. III; J. J. Clauss, *The Best of the Argonauts* (Berkeley 1993).

Chapter XVIII

Vergil and the Augustan *Recusatio*

This concluding chapter makes no attempt to provide a general survey of the influence of Callimachus at Rome.[1] Its limited purpose is (1) to reexamine the rôle of the *Aetia* prologue in the development of the Augustan *recusatio*; (2) to argue that the way Augustan poets allude to the prologue supports the reading advanced in this book rather than the traditional reading; and (3) to draw attention to a neglected aspect of Callimachus's influence on the Augustan poets—as a model for panegyric.

1

The most important source of the modern misinterpretation of Callimachus's "kings and heroes" has undoubtedly been Vergil's famous imitation, *Buc.* vi. 3-8:

> cum canerem reges et proelia, Cynthius aurem
> vellit et admonuit: "pastorem, Tityre, pinguis
> pascere oportet ovis, deductum dicere carmen."
> nunc ego (namque super tibi erunt qui dicere laudes,
> Vare, tuas cupiant et tristia condere bella)
> agrestem tenui meditabor harundine Musam.

No one can be in any doubt that Vergil had the *Aetia* prologue in mind (4-5 are virtually a translation). Nonetheless there are a number of important differences between imitation and model.

First of all, in Vergil Apollo addresses the poet when he had already begun to write about *reges et proelia*, recommending something less ambitious instead. In Callimachus, the poet is just sitting there with an empty tablet on his knees:

> καὶ γὰρ ὅτε πρώτιστον ἐμοῖς ἐπὶ δέλτον ἔθηκα
> γούνασιν, Ἀ[πό]λλων εἶπεν ἐμοὶ Λύκιος (21-2).

---

1. See the full bibliography up to 1988 in Lehnus 1989, 358-87; Hutchinson 1988, 277-354 (sensibly sceptical); and R. F. Thomas in Harder 1993, 197-213. It will become obvious that I disagree with much of this fable convenue, though I have deliberately kept documentation to source references and a few important or characteristic secondary works.

There is no suggestion that he had already begun one sort of poem, much less an epic, when Apollo told him to write another.

Second, where Callimachus wrote "kings and heroes," Vergil has "kings and wars," recurring to the more specifically epic theme of war even more emphatically with the *tristia bella* of line 7. The *Aetia*, like the *Metamorphoses*, is full of kings and heroes, but not war. As we have already seen (Ch. X-XII), there is no reason to believe that Callimachus had military epic in mind at all.

Third, here as in a number of Horatian and Propertian *recusationes*, the poet directly addresses, as Callimachus does not, the author of the deeds he is refusing to celebrate, thus complicating his refusal and creating a need for delicacy and tact rather than polemic.[2] Which brings us to the fourth and perhaps most striking difference: contrary to the general assumption, there is no more than a hint in Vergil of Callimachus's polemic. While declining to write a particular epic, he does not denounce epic in and for itself, nor does he extol the virtues of his own alternative. The *recusationes* of the other Augustans go further still, often implying or even proclaiming the superiority of epic to their own humble efforts.

Why then adapt so much of the *Aetia* prologue and yet drop what no reader can fail to identify as its central feature? It is often supposed that the *recusatio* was typically a "vehicle for literary manifestos" and that the polemic of the *Aetia* prologue is characteristic of the form.[3] The truth is that, though undoubtedly the principal source of the first Augustan *recusatio*, in its original form the *Aetia* prologue is not itself a *recusatio* at all.

In its simplest form the *recusatio* is an apology by an author of erotic, sympotic or bucolic poetry for not writing in a higher style, in effect a variation on the affected modesty topos.[4] And just as that topos could involve the dedicatee in the poet's apology,[5] so too could the *recusatio* be turned into an encomiastic device, with the bucolic poet regretting his inability to do justice to the deeds of his patron. The term *recusatio* is in fact a misnomer, since in most cases the poet does not so much reject epic as simply name it to exemplify the high style supposedly beyond his powers. Of course, in many cases, as with that other linked device the *praeteritio*, the act of refusal is itself the compliment.[6]

---

2. P. White, *Promised Verse* (1993), 297 n. 29.

3. W. H. Race, *Classical Genres and English Poetry* [London 1988], 3. He also claims that *recusationes* "provide one of the most important means for redirecting a poetic tradition." No doubt they have this potential, but his only illustration presupposes that "rejection of epic" represented a real and significant "redirection" for both Callimachus and the Augustans.

4. E. R. Curtius, *European Literature and the Latin Middle Ages* (Princeton 1953), 83f.

5. For example, Vergil himself at *Geo.* iii. 41-2, *tua, Maecenas, haud mollia iussa: / te sine nil altum mens incohat*.

6. Gregson Davis (*Polyhymnia: The Rhetoric of Horatian Lyric Discourse* [Berkeley 1991], 28-30) suggests the ponderous but less misleading term "generic disavowal" instead

Vergil did not (of course) find this device in the supremely self-confident Callimachus. But he did not invent it either. There is a clear example of the simple form in a poem he must have known, some lines by the bucolic poet Bion of Smyrna:[7]

ἢν μὲν γὰρ βροτὸν ἄλλον ἢ ἀθανάτων τινὰ μέλπω,
βαμβαίνει μοι γλῶσσα καὶ ὡς πάρος οὐκέτ' ἀείδει·
ἢν δ' αὖτ' ἐς τὸν Ἔρωτα καὶ ἐς Λυκίδαν τι μελίσδω,
καὶ τόκα μοι χαίροισα διὰ στόματος ῥέει αὐδά (F 9 [6]. 8-11).

Every time I sing of another mortal or some god, my tongue stammers and does not sing as before; but if I sing of love and Lycidas, then my voice flows from my lips rejoicing.

Singing "of another mortal or some god" must mean attempting encomiastic or mythological poetry. Like the Roman poets but unlike Callimachus, Bion does not reject epic themes; they are simply beyond his powers. Like Propertius and Ovid, all he can do is sing of love. There is no depreciation of epic, any more than in the *Lament for Bion*, which respectfully compares him to Homer (Ch. XVI. 1).

Precisely this combination of motifs is also common in the so-called *Anacreontea*, where they are classified by Race as a form of the priamel.[8] The *Anacreontea* were much influenced by the bucolic poets,[9] and since *An.* 19 begins with a motto drawn from this very poem of Bion, it may well be (as Fantuzzi has suggested) that it was from Bion that the Anacreontic poet drew both motifs.[10] The clearest example is *An.* 23:

θέλω λέγειν 'Ατρείδας,
θέλω δὲ Κάδμον ᾄδειν,
ὁ βάρβιτος δὲ χορδαῖς
ἔρωτα μοῦνον ἠχεῖ...
χαίροιτε λοιπὸν ἡμῖν,
ἥρωες· ἡ λύρη γάρ
μόνους ἔρωτας ᾄδει.

I wish to tell of the sons of Atreus, I wish to sing of Cadmus; but my lyre-strings sing only of love....Farewell, heroes: my lyre sings only of the Loves.

---

of *recusatio*, rightly comparing the *praeteritio* as a "device of parsimonious inclusion." As a consequence he is less preoccupied with epic and the *Aetia* prologue and includes a larger and more varied selection of poems under his more comprehensive rubric.

7. For his date, M. Fantuzzi, *Bionis Smyrnaei Adonidis Epitaphium* (Liverpool 1985), 7.

8. W. H. Race, *The Classical Priamel from Homer to Boethius* (Leiden 1982), 108-9.

9. P. A. Rosenmeyer, *The Poetics of Imitation* (Cambridge 1992), 170-78.

10. M. Fantuzzi, *CQ* 44 (1994), 541-2; for the Anacreontic *recusationes*, Rosenmeyer 1992, 96f.

The repeated θέλω makes clear the original intention to treat epic themes. This is a particularly suggestive example, because it also provides by far the closest parallel to the conclusion of an Ovidian *recusatio*: *heroum clara valete / nomina* (*Am.* ii. 1. 35-6). Both poets end by wishing their abandoned heroes a cheerful goodbye.[11] In another Ovidian *recusatio* (*Am.* i. 1) Cupid steals a foot from the second of the poet's hexameters, supposedly destined for some epic, turning them into an elegiac couplet, fit only for love-poetry. It is generally assumed that Ovid boldly adapted "the Callimachean scenario,"[12] but the combination of mischievous Cupid (ubiquitous in Bion and the *Anacreontea*) and uncallimachean change of plan suggest that Ovid had something more like Bion or the *Anacreontea* in mind.[13] Unfortunately it is impossible to date individual *Anacreontea*. Some are certainly Hellenistic, some no less certainly Byzantine.[14] But 19 and 23 look early rather than late, and the fact that they share these motifs with Bion confirms that the motifs at any rate are pre-Augustan.

The basic form of the *recusatio* is therefore Hellenistic, but post-Callimachean. The fact that it is first found in bucolic suggests a reconsideration of a widely held view of Vergil's poetic development. In an influential article, W. Clausen emphasized the "programmatic" significance of the Callimachean allusion:[15]

> that the same poet who wrote *cum canerem reges et proelia* wrote, a few years later, *arma virumque cano* is one of the surprises of Latin literary history... The sixth *Bucolic*...is an uncompromising, if oblique statement of the Callimachean esthetic; a reader at the time of publication could not have anticipated that its author would one day write an epic.

That is to say, we are asked to believe that Vergil expected cultivated readers to infer from the Callimachean allusion alone that at the time of writing he had rejected forever the possibility of writing epic. More recently Richard Thomas has gone even further: in *Buc.* vi Vergil's "adherence to the poetics of Callimachus had been stated without qualification."[16] But there is no mention of epic in the *Aetia* prologue. The rejection of epic is entirely Vergil's own addition to Callimachus.

According to the scholia, he was alluding to an abortive start on the *Aeneid*—or to an abandoned epic on the kings of Alba Longa. Clausen

---

11. χαίροιτε...Ἔρωτες P, though in recent times everyone but Giangrande (*Quad. Urb.* 19 [1975], 189) has accepted Stephanus's ἥρωες.

12. See J. Mckeown's commentary (ii [1989], p. 8).

13. No mention of either Bion or the Anacreontic *recusationes* in Wimmel 1960.

14. West, *Carmina Anacreontea* (1984), xvi-xviii; D. A. Campbell, *Greek Lyric* ii (1988), 10-18; Rosenmeyer 1992, 115-25.

15. "Callimachus and Latin Poetry," *GRBS* 5 (1964), 195, still presupposed in his recently published commentary (Oxford 1994).

16. *Virgil Georgics* i (Cambridge 1988), 1; in *PLLS* 5 (1985), 62 he writes of the "depth of Vergil's commitment to Callimacheanism."

rightly rejected such explanations, but on the mistaken assumption that recognition of the Callimachean allusion was explanation enough. A more relevant objection is that Vergil himself makes it clear that it is, precisely, a poem on the deeds of Varus (Alfenus Varus, cos. suff. 39 B.C.) that he cannot write; Varus will have to be content with a pastoral poem (*te nostras, Vare, myricae...*). There seems no reason to doubt that Varus had achieved some recent military success, perhaps as proconsul in 38 B.C.[17] Naturally we do not need to believe that Vergil either began or even contemplated an epic on these achievements. Merely to mention them was compliment enough.

But this need not mean that Vergil had no deeper poetic purpose than praising a friend. A passage that is written with a precise contemporary reference does not have to be so restricted in its implications. Lines 1-12 are not simply a detachable proem despatching personal obligations. Vergil creates a backdrop of war against which he sets up varying images of love. Hence the qualification of the *bella* in line 7 as *tristia*. It is not so much the genre epic the bucolic poet rejects as its traditional themes, war and death.[18]

The sixth *Bucolic* is evidently a reflection on the nature and themes of poetry. An old view recently revived is that it is, more specifically, a meditation on the art of Cornelius Gallus.[19] We are on firmer ground in observing that none of the themes Vergil lists can be identified in any known poem of Callimachus. It is often claimed that the sensational and erotic tales to which Vergil alludes were popular in "Callimachean" poetry. Popular they may have been in Euphorion and Parthenius, Cinna and Gallus, but this was not a taste they had acquired from Callimachus. The only other direct Callimachean echo is in line 73, but to evaluate its significance we need to have 72-3 in front of us:

> his tibi Grynei nemoris dicatur origo
> ne qui sit lucus quo se plus iactet Apollo.

73 clearly alludes to *Hymn to Delos* 269-70 (οὐδέ τις ἄλλη / γαιάων τοσσόνδε θεῷ πεφιλήσεται ἄλλῳ, referring to Apollo). But 72 no less clearly alludes to Parthenius's poem *Delos*, which is known to have told of the Grynean grove of Apollo (*SH* 620, and note *Gryneus Apollo* in *Aen*. iv.

---

17. The apparent information about this campaign presented by Servius is unfortunately worthless, the result of confusing Alfenus Varus, Qinctilius Varus and L. Varius Rufus: M. Pavan and F. Della Corte, *Enciclopedia Virgiliana* I (Rome 1984), 92-93; R. J. Starr, *Historia* 43 (1994), 249-52.

18. The *tristia* should not be construed as part of the "rejection" of epic; *bella* are always *tristia* for Vergil (*Aen*. vii. 325; cf. Hor. *AP* 73).

19. D. O. Ross Jr, *Backgrounds to Augustan Poetry* (1975); R. Rutherford, *Greece and Rome* 36 (1989), 42f.; E. Courtney, *Quad. Urb*. 34 (1990), 99-112; Clausen 1994.

345). The primary reference here is surely to Parthenius; indeed it may be, as Courtney has suggested, that Parthenius "had a reminiscence of the passage of Callimachus in the context in which he mentioned Grynean Apollo."[20] The Callimachean echo is secondary at best. In fact the influence of Callimachus on *Buc.* vi cannot be proved to extend beyond the lines adapted from the *Aetia* prologue.[21]

It has long been realized that Silenus's speech (*Buc.* vi. 31-40) is closely based on Orpheus's speech in Apollonius (*namque canebat uti*... ~ ἤειδεν δ' ὡς..., *Arg.* i. 496-502). Indeed the correspondence extends to the speech as a whole rather than just one sentence, and yet for the Clausen-Thomas school it is axiomatic that the Apollonian allusion is incidental while the borrowing of the Callimachean phrase is programmatic for the *Bucolics* as a whole.

On the usual view Vergil made what has hitherto been considered Callimachus's polemical rejection of epic his own because he found himself in the same literary position as Callimachus: a refined poet who was heir to a stifling tradition of bad epic. We have now seen that this was not at all Callimachus's position; his bugbear was a vogue for bad elegiac poetry. But Vergil was indeed faced with a vogue for epic, dating from Ennius and still very much alive.[22] It may be that this is why he added the mention of epic to his Callimachean borrowing. It would not be surprising if he had a low opinion of some of these poems. But he certainly did not despise them all. Not to mention his obvious respect for Ennius, he did not disdain even recent historical epics. For example, we owe most of our knowledge of two on Caesar's Gallic wars, by Varro of Atax and Furius (the latter in at least eleven books), to the fact that Vergil did a number of lines the honour of careful imitation.[23]

I would like to suggest a somewhat different approach and emphasis. Having decided to pay Varus a compliment in the form of a *recusatio* (a device already established in bucolic poetry), Vergil was reminded by its apologetic antithesis between high and low style of the similar though polemical antithesis of the *Aetia* prologue. It was this antithesis that drew him to the prologue rather than its polemic, which was in fact ill suited to his own apologetic context; too sharp a depreciation of epic would risk depreciating Varus's achievements as well.

For the Clausen school, it is axiomatic that the original Callimachean polemic shines through sharp and clear in Vergil's contrast between *pingues oves* and *deductum carmen*. But neither term is polemical in itself.

---

20. Courtney 1990, 105.
21. Contrast Thomas's "pure Callimacheanism of the *Eclogues*," *PLLS* 5 (1985), 71.
22. For a good brief account, White 1993, 78-82.
23. *FLP* 195-200 and 235-45; most fragments are preserved in the Vergil scholia.

Compared with epic, bucolic is indeed *deductum*, and in Vergil's own usage *pingues* is not in the least "contemptuous" (Coleman). It is applied more than 20 times in the *Georgics* to animals, soil and plants, always in the thoroughly positive sense "plump" or "rich."[24] Horace 's adaptation—*pingue pecus domino facias et cetera praeter / ingenium*—represents the first half of Callimachus's antithesis more closely even than Vergil,[25] but turns the second into a joke, entirely dropping the polemical contrast. Happy on his modest estate, the poet wishes for everything to grow fat—except his wits. To be sure, the fact that only two lines later he calls his *Satires* a "pedestrian Muse" suggests that we are meant to see them in Callimachean terms as "a product of his *ingenium tenue*,"[26] but there is no polemic here either—or for that matter in Callimachus's πεζός (F 112). His θύος πάχιστον takes its depreciatory connotations from the pervasive polemic of the rest of the prologue, not to mention the παχὺ γράμμα of F 398. If Horace could imitate this famous passage without embracing its polemic, so surely could Vergil.

Some commentators have detected a certain tension between the supposed polemic and the compliment to Varus, but they have nonetheless always privileged the polemic, insisting on the importance of "rejection of epic" in a poem intended to "exemplify a contrasting idea of poetry."[27] But though relatively common, epics must always have been vastly outnumbered by all the poems in other genres, and it would be eccentric to suppose that, after the generation of Catullus and Cinna, it was necessary to "exemplify" an alternative. And if we cannot know what Vergil had in mind when he wrote the lines, we can form a fair idea of how they were interpreted by other Augustan poets. As we shall see, for all their Callimachean colour there is little sign in their own *recusationes* that Horace and Propertius read Vergil as attacking epic.

Indeed, there is less evidence than often supposed for a doctrinaire rejection of epic by the so-called "Callimachean" poets of the 50s-20s B.C. as a whole. Of course, everyone knows Catullus's mockery of the "shitty sheets" (*cacata carta*) of Volusius's *Annales* (*c.* 36). But there is no reason to believe that it was for being an epic that Catullus mocked them rather than for being a bad poem. For his own poem ends by describing them as

> pleni ruris et inficetiarum,
> Annales Volusi, cacata carta.

This characterization echoes his criticism of the poetaster Suffenus:

24. See Thomas's notes on i. 8 and 192.
25. *Serm.* ii. 6. 14-15 ~ τὸ μὲν θύος ὅττι πάχιστον / θρέψαι (F 1. 23-4).
26. N. Rudd, *The Satires of Horace* (Cambridge 1966), 244.
27. Clausen, *A Commentary on Vergil's Eclogues* (Oxford 1994), 177.

idem inficetost inficetior rure (*c.* 22.4).

To be sure Suffenus is said to have tossed off his verses by the thousand:

> puto esse ego illi milia aut decem aut plura...

But it is not so much the quantity, still less the genre (which is not specified), but solely the quality of Suffenus's poetry that Catullus finds fault with.

In *c.* 95 he contrasts the long epic of Volusius (who came from Hatria in the Po Delta) with the short epic of his friend Cinna:

> Smyrna mei Cinnae, nonam post denique messem,
>   quam coeptast nonamque edita post hiemem,
> milia cum interea quingenta Hatrianus[28] <in> uno...

> The Smyrna of my dear Cinna, finally published nine harvests and nine winters after it was begun, while the Hatrian...half a million verses in a single....

Unfortunately the next line is missing, but its general sense was clearly something like "spewed out...in a single year." That is to say, Cinna's poem is good because he polished and refined it for nine years, while Volusius's is bad because he churned the stuff out by the bucketful without giving it a second glance. It was no doubt with this passage in mind that Horace advised budding poets to keep their work back for nine years (*nonumque prematur in annum, AP* 388). It was for writing badly, for not revising and polishing, that Catullus damns Volusius, not for writing in the wrong genre. Of course a badly written epic was likely to be worse than a badly written ode simply because there was more of it to be bad. But this was not a danger to which epics alone were prone. Here we may again refer to Horace's criticism of Lucilius, who (*Serm.* i. 4. 9-10)

>   in hora saepe ducentos
> ut magnum, versus dictabat stans pede in uno.

If Lucilius had lived today, Horace goes on,

> demeteret sibi multa, recideret omne quod ultra
> perfectum traheretur...(ib.69f.).

> He would erase much that he had written and prune off all that dragged beyond the proper limit.

It was in their preoccupation with what Callimachus called ἀγρυπνία and Horace *limae labor et mora* rather than in their devotion to specific genres that the neoterics and Augustans showed themselves most truly Callimachean. It was natural that in the main they should confine themselves to the minor genres—but not inevitable. We have already seen how Callim-

---

28. *Hortensius* MSS; *Hatrianus* Munro, J. Solodow, *CP* 1987, 141; Courtney, *FLP* 231.

achus himself extended his method to a four-book narrative elegy and a miniature epic. It was Vergil himself who took the final step, a full-scale Callimachean epic.

Neither in Catullus nor elsewhere do we find any blanket condemnation of epic as epic. Horace mocks a poet called Furius "stuffed with rich tripe" (*pingui tentus omaso*) for "spitting hoary snow over the wintry Alps" (quoting one of Furius's own lines).[29] But as was only to be expected from one who stressed the importance of matching vocabulary to genre and context (*AP* 46-72, 86-119), it was not the genre but the unseemly word "spit" to which he took exception. His other attack on Furius (*Serm.* i. 10. 36-7) is likewise for verbal infelicities: *turgidus Alpinus iugulat dum Memnona dumque / defingit Rheni luteum caput.* The mocking sobriquet "Alpinus" must come from the evidently notorious line about the Alps, and if the impropriety of giving the Rhine a "muddy head" is unclear without the original context, there can be no doubt what Horace faulted in the killing of Memnon: *iugulare* is the word for slaughtering sacrificial animals (the only sense found in Vergil) or defeated gladiators or for committing murder,[30] and so inappropriate for the honourable death of an epic duel.

Despite his Callimachean vocabulary (*pingui* = παχύ),[31] Horace is not really making a Callimachean point: it is not the grand style he objects to, but incompetent attempts to realize it. The literary epistles do not suggest any general hostility to epic, and a few lines after attacking "Alpinus" he praises the "virile epic" of Varius.[32] To judge from the other fragments Furius was often more successful, whence the number of lines imitated by Vergil. Indeed he may be Furius Bibaculus, usually included in the canon of the neoterics. Some exclude him because of the epic; others deny him the epic so as to include him—both begging the question.[33] There is a similar controversy about Varro of Atax, likewise sometimes counted as a neoteric converted after an early epic phase ("later he seems to have come under the new Greek influence...").[34] Of course, no one can agree on a definition of "neotericism," itself an entirely bogus and inappropriate modern term.[35] Most of those agreed to be neoterics wrote those short epics nowadays known as epyllia. But an interest in short epics does not in itself imply active contempt for long epics, and if there is little evidence for Roman epic theory, there is plenty about practice, both before and after the

---

29. *Serm.* ii. 5. 40-41 ~ Furius F 15 with Courtney's valuable note, *FLP* 197-98.

30. The word is not thus unpoetical in itself (B. Axelson, *Unpoetische Wörter* [Lund 1945], 67); see A. Barchiesi, *Ovidii Epp. Heroidum 1-3* (Florence 1992), 74.

31. Though it is obviously the tripe that gives the phrase its contemptuous edge.

32. *forte epos acer, ut nemo, Varius ducit, Serm.* i. 10. 43-4.

33. Rudd 1966, 289 n. 52; Lyne, *CQ* 28 (1978), 171 n. 13; Courtney, *FLP* 199-200.

34. C. J. Fordyce, *OCD*[2] (1970), 1108; Rudd, l.c.; for the facts, Courtney *FLP* 236-37.

35. See my "Poetae Novelli," *HSCP* 84 (1980), 127-41, and Courtney, *FLP* 189-91.

publication of the *Aeneid*. In one of his last elegies (*ex Ponto* iv. 16) Ovid gives a long list of the poets of his own day. It is epic poets who both head and dominate the list, no fewer than seventeen of them, all of whom Ovid praises. Three years earlier he had written to his friend the epic poet Macer, who sang "whatever immortal Homer left unsung."[36]

Furthermore, while many of these poems were at any rate authentically epic in form, that is to say large-scale narrative sagas, others were closer to panegyric. In the first category comes Furius's *Annales*, complete with descriptions of dawn, Homeric battle-scenes, speeches and the like. But what of all those Greek "epics" Archias wrote on the deeds of Catulus, the Luculli and the Metelli? When Cicero claims that Archias's *libri* on the Mithradatic war "did honour not only to L. Lucullus but also to the Roman people" (*pro Archia* 21), we sense a shift of emphasis. The poem he began (but did not finish) on Cicero's consulship must have been closer to panegyric than epic, and the same is surely true of many of the poems produced to honour Roman magnates by both Greek and Roman poets of the age. Antipater of Thessalonica wrote a poem on a Thracian campaign by his patron Piso cos. 15 B.C. An epic, so it has been argued, perhaps explaining the attention paid to epic in Horace's *Ars Poetica*, dedicated to Piso.[37] In view of his encomiastic epigrams, more likely a panegyric.

The panegyrical literature of the empire has been exhaustively studied in recent years,[38] but the less abundant survivals from the last days of the Republic have been virtually ignored. What was the status of panegyric in the age of Vergil? It seems to be a tacit assumption of modern criticism that bucolic and didactic, elegy and epyllion stand on one side of the Callimachean divide; poems on *reges et proelia*, whether epics or panegyrics, squarely and irretrievably on the other. This is a serious oversimplification, for the age of Callimachus no less than for the age of Vergil. Not to mention the obscure poets of the Attalid court, both Theocritus and Callimachus wrote many encomia on rulers. Callimachus also wrote a number of epinicians on private citizens. Aratus, another poet we know Callimachus to have admired, wrote one encomion on Antigonus Gonatas, another on his wife Phila (daughter of Seleucus), and perhaps a third on their marriage.[39]

From the triumviral age we are lucky enough to possess two formal panegyrics, because of their scant literary merits more often disparaged

---

36. *tu canis aeterno quicquid restabat Homero, Ex Ponto* ii. 10. 13 (to be distinguished from the didactic poet Aemilius Macer, now in Courtney, *FLP* 292-99).

37. *AP* ix. 428 = GP I; *PIR*[2] C. 279; Syme, *The Augustan Aristocracy* (Oxford 1986), 346; E. Sacks, *BMCR* 3 (1992), 113.

38. L. Pernot, *La rhétorique de l'éloge dans le monde greco-romain* i-ii (Paris 1993); S. MacCormack, *Art and Ceremony in Late Antiquity* (Berkeley 1981).

39. *SH* 85, 99, 115, 116.

than read: the pseudo-Tibullan *Panegyricus Messalae* in 211 hexameters; and the pseudo-Vergilian *Catalepton* ix in 64 elegiac lines, both in all probability written in 27-26 B.C. Of these more below. No contemporary specimen of the mixed category survives (unless we count certain passages in the *Georgics* and *Aeneid*). But Varius's lost "panegyric" of Augustus was perhaps an example. Horace quotes a couple of lines which Porphyrio identifies as coming "notissimo ex panegyrico Augusti":[40]

> tene magis salvum populus velit an populum tu,
> servet in ambiguo qui consulit et tibi et urbi
> Iuppiter.

They are quite unepic in both rhythm and diction, and there can be little doubt that Horace made them up himself.[41] Yet the "famous panegyric on Augustus" may well have existed nonetheless. It was as an epic poet that Varius was best known to his contemporaries, as may be seen from Horace, *Serm.* i. 10. 43 and (above all) *Odes* i. 6, addressed to Agrippa:

> Scriberis Vario fortis et hostium
> victor Maeonii carminis alite,
> quam rem cumque ferox navibus aut equis
>   miles te duce gesserit.
>
> nos, Agrippa, neque haec dicere nec gravem
> Pelidae stomachum cedere nescii
> nec cursus duplicis per mare Ulixei
>   nec saevam Pelopis domum
>
> conamur, tenues grandia, dum pudor
> imbellisque lyrae Musa potens vetat
> laudes egregii Caesaris...

When Horace proceeds to ask in lines 13-16 *quis Martem...digne scripserit*, the answer to his question (despite the doubts of most commentators) is certainly Homer.[42] Clearly we are meant to think epic, but since the poet Horace suggests in his stead was known for his panegyrics, hardly traditional epic narrative. The forbidding Muse derives from Vergil's chiding Apollo, not Callimachus. And while it might seem obvious to interpret *tenues grandia* in line 9 as another "programmatic" allusion to the λεπτόν and the παχύ, once again there is no suggestion of polemic; in a literary context *grandis* normally has very positive associations.[43] Polemic would

40. *Epp.* i. 16. 27-9; "haec enim Var<i>us de Augusto scripserat," Ps.-Acro.

41. So Courtney, *FLP* 275 (arguing that the actual title was *Laudes* rather than *Panegyricus*) and the recent commentary by R. Mayer (Cambridge 1994).

42. So G. Davis, *Phoenix* 41 (1987), 292-95, though without sketching the wider context.

43. E.g. Ovid, *Amor.* 3. 1. 70, *a tergo grandius urget opus*, of his forthcoming tragedy; C. O. Brink on Horace, *AP* 27.

in any case have been entirely out of place, unless Horace was prepared to risk insulting Varius as well as Agrippa.

There is no need to see more than a glancing, subsidiary Callimachean allusion.[44] *tenues grandia* fits into a quite different category of *recusatio* commonplace (of which there is no hint in Callimachus), the *inability* of the writer to command the high style necessary for panegyric. As we saw in Ch. X. 4, Menander emphasizes the grandeur of style required, recommending the panegyrist to say in his proem that "only the grandiloquence (μεγαλοφωνία) of Homer would do justice to the theme." Centuries earlier Ennius is said to have made precisely this claim about the deeds of Scipio.[45] Homer is held up less as the supreme epic poet than simply as the master of the high style, above all genres. Nor is Homer the panegyrist a tasteless new creation of the late empire. Whether or not such handbooks existed by the age of Augustus, we find Ovid following Menander's advice to the letter (*Fasti* ii. 119-126):[46]

> nunc mihi mille sonos, quoque est memoratus Achilles,
>> vellem, Maeonide, pectus inesse tuum...
> quid volui demens elegis imponere tantum
>> ponderis? heroi res erat ista pedis.

The task of celebrating Augustus adequately would need Homer's gifts and "heroic" verse rather than elegy. Compare too *Pan. Mess.* 177-80:

> non ego sum satis ad tantae praeconia laudis,
> ipse mihi non si praescribat carmina Phoebus.
> est tibi, qui possit magnis se accingere rebus,
> Valgius: aeterno propior non alter Homero.

As in *Odes* i. 6, the poet proclaims his own inadequacy for the theme and suggests his friend Valgius instead (best known to us as an elegist),[47] one "closer to Homer than any man." In this case we know for certain that the writer, author himself of a 211 line panegyric of Messala, has a panegyric rather than true epic in mind.

As in Menander, Homer stands for the encomiastic style. That is why Horace throws in the tragic allusion as well (*nec saevam Pelopis domum*, line 8). A tragedian as well as an epic poet, Varius was ideally qualified in every department of the high style. Here we may compare Martial viii. 3, a less familiar example, preserving something of the polemic of the *Aetia* prologue: a Muse bids the poet sing with slender pipe, rejecting tragic bus-

---

44. Contrast J. V. Cody, *Horace and Callimachean Aesthetics* (Brussels 1976), 10.

45. Menander 369. 9; μόνον ἂν Ὅμηρον ἐπαξίους ἐπαίνους εἰπεῖν Σκιπίωνος (Suda s.v. Ἔννιος); Val. Max. 8. 14. 1: *vir Homerico quam rudi atque impolito praeconio dignior.*

46. Cf. *Pont.* iii. 3, 31-2: *nec me Maeonio consurgere carmine nec me / dicere magnorum passus es acta ducum*; ib. iii. 4. 83 (*elegi* inadequate to tell of Tiberius's triumphs).

47. For the little that survives, Courtney *FLP* 287-90.

kins and fierce wars in "equal measures" (namely hexameters). The latter represent epic, but the former evidently tragedy. It is the grand style rather than simply epic that Martial opposes to his own slender Muse. Just so Horace's recommendation of Varius. It was not the *length* of epic poetry to which he proclaims himself unequal, but the grand style of which Varius was master.

It was surely an encomion rather than a multi-book narrative that Varius's other friend Vergil refused to write an Varus's victories. After all, it is Varus's *laudes* that (according to Vergil) other poets will celebrate:

> nunc ego—namque super tibi erunt qui dicere *laudes,*
> Vare, tuas cupiant et tristia condere bella (6-7).

Poems that combine *laudes* with *bella* are hardly "pure" epics. Compare too the delayed proem to *Buc.* viii (addressed to Pollio in 39 or 38 B.C.):

> tu mihi seu magni superas iam saxa Timavi
> sive oram Illyrici legis aequoris, en erit umquam
> ille dies mihi cum liceat tua dicere facta?
> en erit ut liceat totum mihi ferre per orbem
> sola Sophocleo tua carmina digna coturno?

Here Vergil professes himself not reluctant but eager to sing of his patron's deeds. When will the longed for day come? In this case no one has been misled; no one doubts that this is merely another artful way of dodging the issue, an alternative strategy to the *recusatio*. But what sort of poem is it that Vergil affects to be so keen to write—if only the time were ripe? Coleman improbably suggests that Pollio had "commissioned" two poems. But even imaginary poems *non sunt multiplicanda praeter necessitatem*. Since Vergil mentions both the deeds and the poetry of his patron, the obvious presumption is that what he had in mind was one poem, the one sort of poem in which a man's military and literary achievements could be treated together—a panegyric. Not to mention countless examples from the age of the empire, the two almost contemporary extant panegyrics on Messala praise both his deeds and his poems, at more or less equal length. Indeed if it was as much panegyric as epic that Vergil had in mind, this would explain why he devotes so much space to Pollio's "Sophoclean buskin." The proem reflects in miniature the different themes of a full-scale panegyric. And if Vergil never wrote a full-scale panegyric, *Georgic* i. 24-42 shows how brilliantly he could write one in miniature.

An important study by Ian Duquesnay has shown how deeply *Buc.* iv is influenced by the pattern and topoi of the basilikos logos, in particular by Theocritus's encomion on Philadelphus.[48] But there is one detail that even

---

48. "Vergil's Fourth Eclogue," *PLLS* 1 (1976), 25-99.

Duquesnay missed. My own attention was first drawn to this feature by a cluster of texts in late fourth-century historians who all justify their decision to stop their narrative where they do on the grounds that "what follows needs to be told in the higher style." What they mean (of course) is that it is not possible to write *history* of current affairs; that required panegyric, and it was panegyric that had to be written in the "higher style." First Eutropius, breaking off with the death of Julian (361): *interim operi modum dabimus; nam reliqua stilo maiore dicenda sunt*. Then Ammianus Marcellinus, stopping with the death of Valens (378): those who continue the story *procudere linguas ad maiores moneo stilos* (31. 16. 9). Jerome's *Chronicle* stops at the same point, with the explanation that he "has reserved the remaining period of Gratian and Theodosius for the style of a more generous history" (*latioris historiae stilo reservavi*). Of uncertain but approximately the same date is one of the Lives in the so-called *Scriptores Historiae Augustae*: *Diocletianus et qui sequuntur stilo maiore dicendi sunt*. A minor variation on the motif (a rhetorical question, *quam magno* for *maiore*) is provided by the apostrophe to Valens that closes Festus's *Breviarium*: *quam magno deinceps ore tua, princeps invicte, facta sunt personanda*.[49]

Given their near contemporaneity, it is likely that at least one of these texts was inspired by one or more of the others. But it would be rash to be specific; there can be little doubt that the basic motif is a commonplace. For example, from a century earlier there is the *Cynegetica* of the African poet Nemesianus, written in 283. The poet promises that "soon" he will tell of the triumphs (at the time of writing not yet won) of the sons of the Emperor Carus: *mox vestros meliore lyra memorare triumphos / accingar* (*Cyn.* 63-4).[50] Once again, a promise of a subsequent poem in a style that will do justice to the theme. All these texts are in effect *recusationes*; the writers excuse themselves by pleading inability to rise to the eloquence required, the *stilus maior* of panegyric.

This nexus of texts enables us (I suggest) better to appreciate a series of closely parallel Augustan examples where the panegyrical dimension has often been missed. First, in *AA* 1. 205f. Ovid predicts the success of young Gaius Caesar's Eastern expedition:

> auguror en, vinces, votivaque carmina reddam
>   et *magno* nobis *ore sonandus* eris...

He then briefly sketches the sort of things he will tell of in this promised poem (*tergaque Parthorum Romanaque pectora dicam...*). "Ovid proposes

---

49. Eutr. *Brev.* 10. 18. 3; Jerome, *Chron. pr.* p. 7 Helm; *SHA Quadr. Tyr.* 15. 10.

50. A pointed reminiscence of *Geo.* iii. 46-7, *mox tamen ardentes accingar dicere pugnas / Caesaris*.

to write an epic poem...a *Bellum Parthicum*, describing the glorious campaign," according to Adrian Hollis.[51] To be sure, there was a tradition of multi-book epics on Roman wars (Ch. X. 4), and in this case the question is academic (not to say unreal), since Ovid certainly had no intention of writing the poem he sketches out. But his emphasis falls on the *style* rather than the genre or length of ·the promised poem (*magno ore ...sonandus eris*), employing exactly the same formula as Festus (*quam magno...ore tua...facta sunt personanda*). It is not a *narrative* of Gaius's war that he is promising, but a panegyric. We find the same formula again in Propertius ii. 10. 12, professing to long for the day when the poet will be able to devote himself to Caesar's wars: *magni nunc erit oris opus.*

It is understandable that modern readers should be misled. As we saw in Ch. X. 4, from the Hellenistic to the Byzantine age, high-flown epic hexameters were the preferred medium for encomion. Thus when Ovid refers, in (for example) the passage from *Fasti* ii. 119-126 quoted above, to a burden too great for his elegies, the need for heroic metre, and Homer's praise of Achilles, clearly we are meant to think of epic. Contemporaries, however, seeing that the theme proposed was the deeds of Augustus, would at once realize that in the context these terms identified the epic grandeur of encomion rather than large-scale narrative. In the rhetorical tradition Achilles was a man blessed in his panegyrist: witness Alexander's remark over Achilles's tomb at Sigeum: "fortunate youth, to have Homer for the herald of your glory."[52] This suggests another point. Propertius and (especially) Ovid have often been accused of insincerity and even absurdity when they profess to be contemplating poems on the wars of Augustus. Certainly neither poet ever seriously contemplated multi-book military narrative, but both may in all seriousness have sketched out encomia of one sort or another.[53] Indeed, in their own way both in the end actually wrote such poems: Propertius an aetiological elegy on the battle of Actium; Ovid elegies on an expected German triumph of Tiberius in 11 A.D. (*Tristia* iv. 2), his Danubian triumph in 12 (*Ex Ponto* iv. 2)[54] and an encomiastic propempticon for Gaius Caesar (§ 4 below). Critics solemnly debate whether Ovid really wrote that poem in Getic he describes in *Ex Ponto* iv. 13, yet ignore its purported theme: the apotheosis of Augustus, Tiberius's acceptance of power often refused, Livia the Vestal, Germanicus and Drusus—clearly a panegyric of the imperial house.

51. *Ovid Ars Amatoria* 1 (1977), 79.

52. Cicero, *pro Archia* 24; according to Menander, he should be compared to the emperor not only because of his military prowess (374. 2, p. 86) but also in the section on nurture, because of Chiron the centaur (371. 24, p. 82).

53. For a good example outside the framework of a regular *recusatio*, cf. *Ex Ponto* ii. 5. 27f., *nuper, ut huc magni pervenit fama triumphi, / ausus sum tantae sumere molis opus...*

54. R. Syme, *History in Ovid* (Oxford 1978), 38-42; G. D. Williams, *Banished Voices: Readings in Ovid's Exile Poetry* (Cambridge 1994), 97-8.

Next Horace, *Odes* iv. 2 (*Pindarum quisquis*), celebrating Augustus's German victories of 16 B.C. The poet suggests that Iullus Antonius might produce something better than his own laboured trifles:

> ...operosa parvus
> carmina fingo.
> concines *maiore* poeta *plectro*
> Caesarem... (iv. 2. 31-4).

As Fraenkel remarked, there is nothing in the context to suggest that Antonius is expected to write an epic rather than another lyric epinicion.[55] In this department Pindar was second only to Homer. It was not a question of genre, nor is Horace paying this young poetaster quite so unqualified a compliment as usually supposed. The solution, hinted at in the formula *maiore plectro*, is surely that Antonius specialized in panegyric (in whatever literary form).

Next *Tristia* ii. 63-5, again addressed to Augustus:

> inspice *maius opus*, quod adhuc sine fine tenetur...
> invenies vestri praeconia nominis illic.

Here the *maius opus* is the *Metamorphoses*, as the close of 63 confirms. The reason the poem is "unfinished" is that the final and greatest metamorphosis, the transformation of Augustus into a god (xv. 861-70), cannot take place until he is dead! It is not because it was in the epic metre or on an epic scale that he refers the princeps to his most ambitious poem, but (as the lines that follow make clear), simply and solely because of its (in fact rather spasmodic) praise of Augustus. Once again it is the *maius* that alerts us to the panegyrical dimension he is trying to ascribe to his poem.

When contemporary, forgeries can be as valuable as the genuine article. For example, the preface to the pseudo-Vergilian *Culex* (line 8), purporting to address the future Augustus,[56] closes with the promise

> posterius *graviore sono* tibi Musa loquetur.

Since the writer is only pretending to be the young Vergil, for once he does have a real poem in mind, namely the *Aeneid*—but again, clearly the *Aeneid* as praise of Augustus rather than long mythical narrative. Two slightly different but linked cases are *Metam.* x. 150, where Orpheus makes the claim *cecini plectro graviore Gigantas*; and *Agam.* 334, where

---

55. *Horace* (1957), 437 n. 2; so too M.C.J. Putnam, *Artifices of Eternity: Horace's Fourth Book of Odes* (1986), 57; contrast Kießling-Heinze ad loc. This remains true, even if we accept Ps.-Acro's claim that Iullus *heroico metro Diomedias XX libros scripsit egregios*.

56. In keeping with the fiction of being a youthful poem by Vergil, it purports to be addressed to Octavius while still a boy, before the death of Caesar—the most decisive of the many proofs of forgery: E. Fraenkel, *Kl. Beiträge* II (1964), 192.

Seneca's Apollo likewise sings of the battle with the Giants *chorda graviore*. Not panegyrics, but the Gigantomachy typifies the sublime theme that demands the sublimest of styles. For this very reason, from Pindar on the defeat of the Giants was a standard image for the victories of patrons and rulers, especially common in Augustan *recusationes*.[57]

The key feature all these passages share with the late imperial texts is the promise of a *future* poem (or history) in a "higher style" that will do justice to the achievements of the princeps.[58] Another variation is cases where the reference to greater things is internal, to the current poem itself. For example, *Fasti* ii. 3-4, again addressed to Augustus:

nunc primum velis, elegi, *maioribus* itis:
exiguum, memini, nuper eratis opus.

In what respect are the *Fasti* more elevated? Having already written the *Metamorphoses*, it cannot be a higher genre Ovid has in mind. Though the subject matter is more serious than his love elegies, he was still writing elegy, elegy in the Callimachean tradition, down to the framework of a dialogue with Muses and other deities. Lines 9-14 even repeat the motif of incapacity for war. The explanation comes at 15-16:

at tua prosequimur studioso pectore, Caesar,
nomina, per titulos ingredimurque tuos.

Even so I rehearse your titles and honours with all my heart and energy.

The key respect in which the *Fasti* outstrip Ovid's earlier work (or so he disingenuously protests) is in their treatment of the honours of Augustus.

This brings us back to Vergil. *Buc.* iv opens as follows:

Sicelides Musae, paulo *maiora* canamus.

In the light of the passages collected above, I suspect that *maiora* would have suggested a good deal more than "something above his present subject"[59] to contemporary readers. According to a much earlier commentator, "the *paulo* is well put; for although this eclogue differs from a bucolic poem, even so the poet inserts some details suited to the theme."[60] Writing

57. D. C. Innes, "Gigantomachy and Natural Philosophy," *CQ* 29 (1979), 165-68; P. Hardie, *Virgil's Aeneid: Cosmos and Imperium* (Oxford 1986), 85-90. It is perhaps more than coincidence that the most successful Latin panegyrist of late antiquity, the Alexandrian Claudian, also tried his hand at *Gigantomachies* in both Greek and Latin.

58. It is no objection that we sometimes find similar formulas where there are no panegyrical implications. For example, the *maius opus* of *Amor.* iii. 1. 24 is Ovid's projected tragedy, *Medea*; the *area maior* of *Fasti* iv. 10 is the *Fasti* itself; *quid maiora sequar?* in *Georg.* ii. 434 refers to different sorts of trees; *maius opus moveo* in *Aen.* vii. 45 to the Iliadic second half of the poem.

59. John Martyn, in his commentary of 1820.

60. *bene paulo; nam licet haec ecloga discedat a bucolico carmine, tamen inserit ei aliqua apta operi*, Servius, *In Buc.* p. 44 Thilo.

as he was in the generation after Eutropius, Festus and Ammianus, the *maiora* naturally led Servius to expect not just "something above" bucolic themes, but something radically different, panegyric. This is why he was moved to emphasize the (to him, though not to the modern reader surprising) fact that the poem is still nonetheless recognizably a bucolic.

Buc. iv is (of course) far more than a panegyric,[61] and the poems promised and rejected in the proems to *Buc.* viii and vi respectively were after all never written. But we can still ask what sort of expectations these proems would have created for the contemporary reader. Clausen believed that the Callimachean associations of vi guaranteed the expectation of epic, by which he obviously meant traditional, multi-book Homeric (or Ennian) narrative. But without those Callimachean associations, there is no reason why anyone should have expected epic in this sense rather than the briefer and by now fairly routine encomiastic epic. Are we really justified in investing Vergil's refusal to celebrate Varus's *proelia* with so much more significance than his eagerness to celebrate Pollio's? How can we be sure that the one was so much more seriously meant than the other? Are we really entitled to dismiss the one as elegant flattery and treat the other as nothing less than the key to Vergil's poetical evolution?

2

The standard treatment of the Augustan *recusatio* is a παχὺ γράμμα καὶ οὐ τορόν by W. Wimmel significantly entitled *Kallimachos in Rom*. But it is Bion or Vergil rather than Callimachus who is the principal inspiration for most of the dozen or so *recusationes* scattered through the oeuvre of Horace and Propertius. None of them reject epic in principle, and many are not concerned with epic at all.

We have already seen that *Odes* i. 6 owes little to Callimachus. In Odes ii. 12 (*nolis longa ferae bella Numantiae/..aptari citharae modis*) there is again no hint of Callimachus—and no specific reference to epic. Indeed Horace goes on to suggest that Maecenas himself might do more justice to *proelia Caesaris* in a prose history. *Odes* iv. 15 (*Phoebus volentem proelia me loqui / victas et urbes increpuit lyra*) seems to derive entirely from Vergil. It was Vergil's Apollo, not Callimachus's, who rebukes the poet and tells him to change his plans. The same applies to *Serm.* i. 10. 31-5, where Quirinus tells Horace in a dream to write in Latin rather than Greek. The situation is different, but the god ordering a change of plan comes from Vergil rather than Callimachus, even though Horace signals his recognition of the Callimachean original by adding (transposed from the

---

61. See now Clausen 1992, 119-50.

next section in the *Aetia*) a detail not in Vergil, the dream. In *Odes* iv. 2 it is Pindar, not Callimachus who is the model, and it is a panegyric (in whatever metre) that Horace is suggesting to Iullus Antonius. The *carmine perpetuo* of i. 7 is certainly Callimachean (p. 345), the only Roman imitation to imply a criticism of length. But as its opening words make clear—"*Laudabunt* alii claram Rhodon aut Mytilenen..."—it is encomion, not mythical or historical narrative that Horace has in mind.

The five Propertian *recusationes* are full of Callimachean allusions and have much to say about the respective merits of epic and love poetry. Nonetheless, Propertius never rejects epic in principle. Indeed he invariably represents it as a loftier genre to which he, the lowly poet of love, can never aspire. They may be summarized as follows:

II. 1: If I could write epic, I would sing of Caesar rather than myth or earlier history. But I cannot, so I will continue to sing of love.

III. 1: Many write of war; I write what can be read in peace. The poet's fame lives after him; but for Homer who would have heard of Troy?

III. 9: Each of us must do what he can. I cannot sing of Thebes or Troy. Enough for me to give pleasure alongside Callimachus and Philitas.

II. 10: I have outgrown love poetry, and will sing of Caesar's wars—when I am ready.

III. 3: Propertius dreams that he is on Helicon composing an epic when (who but?) Apollo chides him, and Calliope tells him to be content with love poetry.

We might also add I. 7 and (cf. II. 34B)

You write your epic on Thebes while I sing of love. But if you too fall in love you will not find epic much use.

Propertius's representation of epic as something to which his modest gifts will not rise is consistent—if not the whole story. We are not (of course) obliged to believe that he really held it in high esteem, and there is often more than a hint of irony, well brought out by Steele Commager. But Commager goes too far when he claims that "If II. 10 is virtually a parody of the heroic mode, the opening poem of the third book is an explicit rejection of it."[62]

To be sure, II. 10 makes it clear both by its tone and by the inappropriate selection of topics for the proposed epic, that Propertius has no serious intention of actually writing it. And there is certainly similar irony in III. 1, especially when Propertius compares himself as lover to a victor in war. Nonetheless it remains an implicit rather than explicit rejection of the heroic mode. To achieve its effect, the irony presupposes (however

62. *A Prolegomenon to Propertius* (Cincinnati 1974), 62.

much it undermines) traditional assumptions about the literary and moral superiority of epic and war to elegy and love.

Why was it that the "Roman Callimachus" (IV. 1. 64) paid even lip service to the heroic ideal that (on the traditional view) Callimachus himself had so contemptuously denounced? True the humble poet of love was a convenient pose, allowing him to reject· conventional Roman values as well as to parry requests for epic. But even that could hardly explain why he misrepresented the poet who (on the traditional view) had disparaged and defiantly *refused* to write epic as merely another feeble elegist like himself *unable* to do so. For example, III. 9. 43-4, rather than write epic,

> inter Callimachi sat erit placuisse libellos
> et cecinisse modis, Coe poeta, tuis.

Or II. 34B. 31-2, addressed to a poet of epic and tragedy who has fallen in love and will now have to give up serious themes for love poetry:

> tu satius memorem Musis imitere Philitan
> et non inflati somnia Callimachi.

Or again II.1.39-40:

> sed neque Phlegraeos Iovis Enceladique tumultus
> intonet angusto pectore Callimachus.

This couplet is full of confused Callimachean allusions. Where the real Callimachus had *refused* to thunder like Zeus (F 1. 20), Propertius's Callimachus is (again) *unable* to do so, because of his *angustum pectus*, where *angustum* means "slender" with the connotation "weak," not "slender" as (on the traditional view) a defiant alternative to the "fat" of epic.

It is also significant that, in what appears to be the most explicitly Callimachean passage in Propertius, when Apollo addresses the poet on the subject of epic in III. 3, it is in fact Roman models he follows throughout. The chiding Apollo and change of plan both come from Vergil, and the displacement of the dream either from Horace (*Serm.* i. 10. 31f.) or else from the proem to Ennius's *Annales*, directly quoted in line 6. And although a couple of lines in Apollo's speech do reflect genuine Callimachean principles and terminology,

> quid tibi cum tali demens, est flumine?...(15)
> mollia sunt parvis prata terenda rotis (18),

there is no polemical defence of the slender style against the grand style. In Propertius, the altogether uncallimachean purpose of Apollo's speech is to persuade the poet to stick with the slender style he is master of because it is appropriate for love poetry. E.g. line 21:

> cur tua praescriptos evecta est pagina gyros?

why has your page strayed outside its prescribed course?

In fact, here as in the three couplets quoted above, Callimachus is treated solely as a poet of love, a poet who (like Propertius) harmonized style to theme. In fact (of course) his elegies (as distinct from his epigrams) were by no means devoted to love. He is also repeatedly associated with Philitas, a poet whose style the real Callimachus had disparaged. But Propertius was not interested in the authentic distinction between λεπτόν and παχύ which (in Callimachus's eyes) set him apart from Philitas as an elegist. Propertius's distinction was between *molle* and *durum*, where both terms reflected style and content alike. All elegists were automatically *molles*. It is on these rather than genuinely Callimachean criteria that he looked to Philitas and Callimachus as his literary models.

The literary historian may be alarmed to reflect how confidently and yet how incorrectly we should have restored Apollo's speech in the *Aetia* prologue on the basis of the unanimous Latin tradition if prol. 20-30 (say) had been illegible in P. Oxy. 2079. But Propertius was not writing literary history or literary criticism. He was under no obligation to do justice to the views of earlier poets. All he needed was a model elegist to set against the obvious epic models.

The Callimachus described in this book, the poet who worked so hard to raise the standards of elegy, that Callimachus fitted Propertius's bill well enough. But not so the Callimachus of modern scholarship, who owes his fame to uncompromising rejection of epic. If (as argued in Ch. XI-XII) the polemic of the *Aetia* prologue was aimed at other elegists, Propertius did not need to bother about the details of an internal controversy long settled. He could adapt whatever suited his own purposes—in fact the concept of the slender style. This he proclaimed to be the style appropriate for love poetry, strengthening his case at a verbal level by rendering λεπτός by Latin *mollis* or *tenuis*, both words suitable and common epithets for *amor*. Thus Callimachus was invoked to provide what amounts to a theoretical justification for the restriction of elegy to erotic themes. This is not at all what the real Callimachus was saying to his contemporaries, but it is a simplification rather than a travesty. Propertius's own rejection of epic would surely have been formulated quite differently if he had read the *Aetia* prologue as a denunciation of epic.

There is a strange idea fashionable among many modern critics of Roman poetry that allusions to Callimachus are always or normally "programmatic." This is a surprising claim, made with little attempt at justification. Obviously some poetic allusions are more significant than others, intended to recall the context and associations of the original rather than just a verbal detail. But certain sorts of allusion to Callimachus are held to constitute a proclamation of allegiance, adherence to a "Callimachean aesthetic" or even a "Callimachean programme."[63]

It is not at all my purpose to minimize Callimachus's importance. Beyond question he influenced Roman poets in many ways: style, theme, structure, vocabulary, tone, metre, narrative technique. As the sands of Egypt restore more and more of the *Aetia* to us, fresh prospects for fruitful research keep opening up. But much modern criticism shows little interest in these wider prospects. The criterion required for adherence to the "Callimachean programme" is simply a reference to the *Aetia* prologue, often no more than use of a word like *tenuis* or *pinguis*. The acid test is rejection of epic—ironically enough the one doctrine we can now be reasonably sure Callimachus never held.

It is normal and respectable for a philosopher to call himself a Platonist or Epicurean and expound or refine the doctrines of his master. But it is not in general the way of poets to adopt as a whole the "programme" of an earlier poet. It should be obvious that poets like Horace and Propertius who wrote several *recusationes* each were more concerned to produce elegant variations of their own than reproduce the "doctrines" of Callimachus. Why should they need to keep proving their "allegiance" anyway? No one was likely to take them for epic poets.

Some of the more conspicuous aspects of Callimachus's "aesthetic" —notably his fondness for obscure and recherché vocabulary—were to be generally deplored. In fact it is obscurantism and pedantry that the term "Callimachean" evokes in writers of the early empire. For example, among the insults hurled at pedantic grammarians by the poets of the age are "Callimachus's dog-pack" (Antiphanes, *AP* xi. 322. 4), "Callimachus's irregulars" (Philip of Thessalonica, *AP* xi. 321. 3) and "Supercallimachuses" (Philip again, *AP* xi. 347. 6). When Propertius proclaimed himself the "Roman Callimachus" (iv. 1. 64), this was not a claim to be a Callimachean in the modern aesthetic sense, but a boast on a level with Vergil's claim to be the Roman Theocritus and Hesiod, or Horace's to be the Roman Archilochus and Alcaeus: it was simply a claim to be the classic Roman elegist. Propertius is often identified as a classic Callimachean in the modern sense too. It is true that he draws from the *Aetia* prologue a series of vivid images which he weaves, together with many other elements, into a powerful and complex evocation of the sources of poetic inspiration. But the overall effect is thoroughly uncallimachean. There is nothing surprising in this, of course. Imitation by a creative poet normally transforms rather than reproduces.

---

63. Among recent critics only Hutchinson is really sceptical about the influence of Callimachus's "doctrines" on the practice of the Augustans.

3

What is the relationship of the Callimachean allusion in *Buc.* vi to the obvious Theocritean inspiration of the *Bucolics* as a whole? Since the rediscovery of the *Aetia* prologue in 1927, lines 3-6 have seemed to leap out of their context. But Vergil took pains to dovetail them into his bucolic context. Callimachus's θύος, any sort of sacrificial victim, Vergil particularized into a sheep, so that its nurturer could be that indispensable Theocritean character, a shepherd. And then, by refusing to write of kings and wars, he transformed Callimachus's λεπτόν and παχύ from terms of style into identifications of genre, where (in the context) λεπτόν has to denote bucolic and παχύ epic (or panegyric). This is a fascinating transformation, the sort of thing we expect of a Vergil. But is it helpful or even accurate to call it a "Callimachean programme"?

We have already seen that there is nothing at all Callimachean in the cosmogonical and erotic themes of the song of Silenus. And although the Muses giving Gallus Hesiod's pipes is often claimed as an allusion to Callimachus ("we may add a further poetic generation present in the scene *by implication*),[64] we saw in Ch. XIII how little foundation there is for the modern belief that Hesiod stands for Callimachus in Augustan poetry.

Readers who knew their Callimachus would recognize at once that it was Vergil, not Callimachus, who had refused to write on kings and wars. For although Callimachus usually managed to steer clear of wars, he had written a number of poems on the doings and victories of royalty. Indeed in Roman eyes he must have seemed the second encomiast after Pindar—and, since most of his epinicia were in elegiacs, more accessible and imitable than his great predecessor.

Callimachus had shown that it was possible to write of kings and wars without simply uniting flattery and battles—and without all the trite epic trimmings. Not for Callimachus the crudity of a *recusatio*. He would go through the motions of taking on the job and still evade the issue. Catullus 66 has preserved for us a perfect example of Callimachus's craft, in both senses of the word. Faced with the task of celebrating Euergetes's Syrian war of 246, he focused instead on the lock of hair vowed by the new queen Berenice for her husband's safe return. On Euergetes's return the lock miraculously disappeared and a new constellation was sighted. This happy collaboration between astronomer royal and poet laureate produced a more lasting memorial of Euergetes's campaign than a dozen mini-Iliads.

As we saw in Ch. X, under the Republic Roman notables developed a taste for historical epic. It would not be surprising if more sophisticated

---

64. *Ascraeo quos ante seni, Buc.* vi. 70; Ross 1975, 33f.

poets faced with the task of commemorating the deeds of more cultivated grandees had turned to Callimachean encomion as a model. Though seldom identified as such, a number of examples do in fact survive from the decades after Catullus translated one of the most famous into Latin (*c.* 66).

Perhaps the clearest is Tibullus i. 7, an elegiac epinicion on Messala's Aquitanian triumph of 27 B.C. It is a complex poem that defies easy categorization.[65] The elegy begins (and ends) as a birthday poem, the day in question allegedly being the very day on which Messala won his triumph, to which it therefore provides a neat transition. Tibullus then refers to the part he himself had played in Messala's victories, first in Gaul and then in many other places, culminating with the Nile. The Nile is then identified with Osiris, and the core of the poem (lines 28-54) is a hymn to Osiris, identified with Dionysus and characterized as the bringer of deliverance to weary mortals. The transition back to Messala is skilfully effected by inviting Osiris to attend Messala's birthday celebration.

No other poem of Tibullus contains so many and such significant echoes of Callimachus.[66] Lines 27-28 address the Nile:

te canit atque suum pubes miratur Osirim
    barbara, Memphitem plangere docta bovem.

The foreign crowd that has been brought up to lament the bull of Memphis, sings of you and worships you as its Osiris.

There can be little doubt that Tibullus is directly echoing here a line of Callimachus quoted by scholiasts and lexicographers (F 383. 16 Pf.):

εἰδυῖαι φαλιὸν ταῦρον ἰηλεμίσαι,

knowing how to lament the white bull.

The "white bull" is Apis, the bull of Memphis. In addition to his subject matter, Tibullus also adapted from Callimachus his unusual infinitive after *docta*, as well as his choice of word for lament, *plangere*, like Callimachus's ἰηλεμίσαι properly applied to female lamentation. The lexicographers gave no context, but in 1941 the line turned up on *P. Oxy.* 2173, and has now been identified as part of the proem to the *Victoria Berenices* (*SH* 254. 16). That is to say, Tibullus's one elegiac epinicion incorporates a precise and pointed allusion to one of Callimachus's elegiac epinicia.

There are in addition two close parallels with F 384 Pf., the elegiac epinicion on Sosibius. First, with Tibullus's reference to the mystery of why or where the Nile hides its source (23-4), compare F 384. 31-2:

---

65. Cairns, *Generic Composition* (1972), 167-69; R. J. Ball, *Tibullus the Elegist* (Göttingen 1983), 71-89.
66. For Tibullus's debt to the Alexandrian poets, Bulloch, *PCPS* 19 (1973), 71-89; Cairns 1979, passim.

ὃν οὐδ᾽ ὅθεν οἶδεν ὁδεύω / θνητὸς ἀνήρ.

no mortal man knows whence I flow.

Then at 21-2 Tibullus asks whether he would describe

> qualis et arentes cum findit Sirius agros,
> fertilis aestiva Nilus abundet aqua. ˙

How fertile Nile floods in summer when Sirius cracks the thirsty fields.

Compare F 384. 27:

θηλύτατον καὶ Νεῖλος ἄγων ἐνιαύσιον ὕδωρ.

And the Nile, carrying every year its fertilizing water.

Of course, both these observations about the Nile are commonplace enough taken by themselves. What is not commonplace is that two elegiac epinicia should independently share this emphasis on the Nile. Given the certainty of the allusion to the *Victoria Berenices*, there seems no good reason to doubt that Tibullus knew the *Victoria Sosibii* as well. So he read or reread two Callimachean epinicia while composing his own.

No less clear an example is Propertius IV. 6, the Actium elegy.[67] A. Rostagni long ago pointed out the debt to Callimachus's *Hymn to Apollo*, conspicuous in the poet's priestly pose and call for silence (1-10).[68] The allusion to the once floating island of Delos (27-8) comes (of course) from Callimachus's *Hymn to Delos*. The more recent study by H. E. Pillinger[69] seeks to limit Callimachean influence to the hymns, concluding that "though we may recognize elements of etiology in the poem, the artistic conception as a whole is more hymnic than etiological" and that Propertius's poem is "as much a hymn to Apollo as a glorification of Augustus."[70] Yet the point of the opening allusions to sacrifice (*sacra facit vates*) turns on the "equation of poetic and ritual terminology"; the "sacrifice" is in fact the poem.[71] The emphasis falls not on Augustus's glory in general, but exclusively on victory in war; lines 15-68 deal with Actium, 77-84 with victories over the Sygambri, Ethiopians and Parthians. The tone of the poem as a whole is as much epinician as hymnic. After invoking Callimachus (*Cyreneas...aquas*) in line 4 and asking the Muse to help him tell an aetiology (line 11),

> Musa, Palatini referemus Apollinis aedem,

---

67. For an excellent account with full bibliography, Cairns 1988, 129-68 and 229-36.
68. *Poeti Alessandrini* (1916), 375-82.
69. "Some Callimachean Influences on Propertius, Book 4," *HSCP* 73 (1969), 188-99.
70. Cairns 1984, 137-43 also stresses the hymnic characteristics of the poem.
71. Pillinger 1969, 191; Williams, *Tradition and Originality* (1968), 52-53; 129-131.

it is obviously the *Aetia* Propertius has in mind, more particularly the *Coma Berenices*. Given the difference in subject matter, it is Callimachus's technique rather than any specific passage that he draws on. For what he does is to tell the story of Actium without describing either the battle or its preliminaries. After evoking the geographical setting "in allusive and barely intelligible language,"[72] the account of the battle itself consists of a mere four lines, in which the only combatants named are Apollo and Cleopatra. That is to say, Actium is completely fictionalized. This is the method Callimachus had so brilliantly exploited in the *Coma*, in which Euergetes's entire campaign is reduced to one and a half out of 84 lines.[73] By such a treatment the poet not only avoids the distasteful topics of war and politics, but even the need to be serious. The *Coma* had demonstrated (as F. Sweet put it), that "panegyric need not be written in a style of high seriousness to be successful."[74] It is the fanciful, allusive, asymmetrical style of Callimachean epinician that lies behind this curious Propertian experiment. All that is lacking is Callimachus's saving irony and wit.[75]

We may now pass to the first of the two anonymous panegyrics on Messala: *Catalepton* ix. The poem begins (after a brief appeal to the Muses) by invoking Messala as *triumphator* (and so again alluding to his Aquitanian triumph of 27 B.C.):

> victor adest, magni magnum decus ecce triumphi,
> > victor qua terrae, quaque patent maria,
> horrida barbaricae portans insignia pugnae,
> > magnus ut Oenides, utque superbus Eryx...

There is a section on Messala's poetry (bucolic in Greek), a learned eulogy of the (unnamed) woman he celebrated, and a final section on his wars, with much learned mythological colouring throughout (no one has so far explained just why Messala is compared to Diomedes and Eryx). The most interesting lines are the first two and the last four:

> pauca mihi niveo sed non incognita Phoebo,
> > pauca mihi doctae dicite Pierides (1-2).

Fairclough rendered *pauca* "some few *thoughts*," but the reference is surely to the brevity of his poem. The repetition of *pauca* and the request to learned Muses named after Hippocrene evoke the opening of the *Aetia*, especially when juxtaposed with the unmistakably Callimachean colouring of the closing quatrain:[76]

---

72. Williams 1968, 53.

73. Catullus 66. 35-36 (assuming that 79-88 were added by Catullus; Ch. IV. 1).

74. "Propertius and Political Panegyric," *Arethusa* 5 (1972), 169.

75. Whence the generally unfavourable verdict of modern readers: "one of the most ridiculous poems in the Latin language," according to G. Williams, *JRS* 52 (1962), 43.

76. In 61 I combine Sabbadini's *laudi* with Baehrens's *humiles* and punctuation.

si laudi aspirare, humiles si adire Cyrenas,
    si patrio Graios carmine adire sales
possumus, optatis plus iam procedimus ipsis.
    hos satis est; pingui nil mihi cum populo (61-4).

If I can succeed in praising you, if I can approach lowly Cyrene, if I can approach the wit of Greece with a Roman song, I am succeeding beyond my hopes. This is enough. Naught have I to do with the coarse mob.

pingui...populo does not mean "the stupid rabble" (Fairclough, Westendorp-Boerma). The snobbery is Callimachean, a fusion of Vergil's *pingues oves* with Catullus 95. 10 (praising his friend Cinna's epyllion *Smyrna*),

parva mei mihi sint cordi monumenta < sodalis > ,
    at populus tumido gaudeat Antimacho.

But the *Cyrenas* reveals the poet well aware of the Callimachean original behind his more immediate Latin sources. He contrasts the lowly "Cyrenean" style at which he is aiming with the *pinguis populus*. Surprisingly enough, the poem preserves more of the original Callimachean polemic than any of the Augustan *recusationes*, Vergil included. The writer skilfully formulated his affected modesty topos (*non nostrum est tantas, non, inquam, attingere laudes*, 55) so as not to mention the high style, thus avoiding the risk of his praise of the slender style casting doubt on Messala's deeds. On the contrary, since Messala himself wrote bucolic and love poetry, polemic actually contributes to panegyric. Though a poem of very modest quality, a fascinating illustration nonetheless of the possibilities of marrying Callimachean manifesto and encomion.

The pseudo-Tibullan poem is a more routine panegyric (and so in hexameters), with successive sections on the nobility of Messala's family, his oratorical ability and (especially) his military achievements. In a proem bemoaning (accurately enough) his lack of talent, the poet asks Messala not to reject his offering, quoting a series of learned mythical examples of humble mortals who rendered great services to mighty gods:

        etiam Phoebo gratissima dona
Cres tulit, et cunctis Baccho iucundior hospes
Icarus, ut puro testantur sidera caelo
Erigoneque Canisque, neget ne longior aetas.
quin etiam Alcides, deus ascensurus Olympum,
laeta Molorcheis posuit vestigia tectis (8-13).

Even to Phoebus did the Cretan bring a gift most welcome; and to Bacchus was Icarus a host more pleasing than any other, as the constellation of Erigone and her dog bear witness in the clear sky; nay, even Alcides, fated to ascend Olympus as a god, happily set foot in the hut of Molorchus.

The second and third allusions are straightforward enough: Icar(i)us entertained Dionysus in Attica and was later transformed into a constellation together with his daughter Erigone; and Heracles lodged with the poor man Molorchus on his way to kill the Nemean lion. But no commentator has been able to identify the mysterious Cretan who helped Apollo, in fact (as J. Solodow pointed out to me) Karmanor of Tarrha, who purified Apollo and Artemis after the slaying of Pytho at Delphi (Paus. ii. 7. 7).

The story of Erigone points to Eratosthenes's aetiological elegy of that name, and Karmanor turns up in a number of Cretan stories preserved by Pausanias (ii. 30. 3; x. 7. 2; x. 16. 3). In the present context the most important of these allusions is the one to Molorchus. For the only known source for Molorchus is the *Victoria Berenices*, the epinician elegy that opened *Aetia* III. Was the pseudo-Tibullan panegyrist aware of the epinician associations of his allusion? A similarly placed allusion in the almost exactly contemporary *Georgic* iii suggests that he was.

Georgic iii proper begins with line 49. Lines 1-48 are a combined epinicion to Octavian and outline of Vergil's own future poetic plans, envisaged as a temple full of statues which commemorate Octavian's triumphs. Lines 19-22 represent Vergil himself as a victor in the games:

cuncta mihi, Alpheum linquens lucosque Molorchi,
cursibus et crudo decernet Graecia caestu.
ipse caput tonsae foliis ornatus olivae
dona feram.

In the context, the groves of Molorchus denote the Nemean games, where Berenice won her victory. Not only did Vergil clearly have in mind the epinician associations of Molorchus. As Richard Thomas has pointed out, Vergil's allusion occurs at the beginning of *Georgic* iii, just as Callimachus tells the story of Molorchus at the beginning of *Aetia* III—both four-book works. Thomas also points to another Callimachean allusion at the beginning of *Georgic* iii, the grammatically peculiar reference to Apollo as *pastor ab Amphryso* at line 2 evidently taken from Νόμιον...ἐπ' Ἀμφρυσσῷ in *Hymn to Apollo* 47-8.

So when we find Molorchus's hut at the beginning of the pseudo-Tibullan panegyric, we are surely entitled to conclude that its author knew what he was doing. It seems more likely that the panegyrist borrowed from Vergil than vice versa, but given the similar context and purpose of the two writers, it is not impossible that both were inspired by the *Victoria Berenices* independently.

That makes no fewer than five cases of triumviral writers including conspicuous Callimachean allusions in panegyrical or epinician poems. The sixth is so familiar that it is easy to overlook. Addressing Octavian in the brief panegyric embodied in the proem to *Georgic* i, and so significantly positioned yet again, Vergil asks (line 32);

> anne novum tardis sidus te mensibus addas?

The only uncertainty here is whether he is echoing the Callimachean original (F 110. 64), where Aphrodite takes Berenice's lock and places it among the stars

> [Κύπρι]ς ἐν ἀρχαίοις ἄστρον [ἔθηκε νέον].

Or the Catullan translation (66. 64),

> sidus in antiquis diva nouum posuit.

Here Vergil has reversed the Callimachean location, transferring his allusion from the end of Callimachus's Bk IV to the beginning of his own Bk i. It may or may not have been Vergil Ovid had in mind a few years later when he wrote of Caesar (*Metam.* xv. 749) that his achievements and his son *in sidus vertere nouum*, but he will certainly have known the origination of the motif (hardly a routine feature of Hellenistic ruler cult) in Callimachus's best-known royal encomion.

Ovid himself adds another three, elegies on successive triumphs of Tiberius[77] and Gaius's Eastern expedition of 1 B.C. in *AA* 1. 117-218. Some have maintained that this passage was added in a second edition, a theory rejected in an earlier chapter (Ch. IV. 3). It is nonetheless a disproportionately long digression that "patently interrupts the sequence of operations in the chase for women."[78] Another possible explanation (I suggest) is that Ovid originally wrote the passage as an independent propempticon for Gaius's actual departure,[79] and subsequently inserted it in the larger poem he was writing at the time.[80] That would account for its length and encomiastic tone. But whether or not the lines ever existed separately from the *AA*, it was to Callimachus and Theocritus that Ovid turned when seeking appropriate comparisons for the youthful future princeps. Lines 187-88,

> parvus erat, manibusque duos Tirynthius angues
>   pressit, et in cunis iam Iove dignus erat,

---

77. *Tristia* iv. 2; *Ex Ponto* iv. 2.

78. R. Syme, *History in Ovid* (1978), 14; but see too Hollis 1977, xiii.

79. Ovid wrote other occasional poems that were apparently not published (an epithalamium for the wedding of his friend Paullus Fabius Maximus ca 17/15: *Ex Ponto* i. 2. 131-2); R. Syme, *History in Ovid* (1978), 144-5; *The Augustan Aristocracy* (1986), 403f.

80. On the neatness of the transition back into the main narrative (and against the once fashionable idea that the passage is ironical), G. Williams, *Change and Decline* (Berkeley 1978), 78-79.

reminded Hollis of Callimachus's *Hymn to Zeus* 55-7, where the precosity of the young Zeus implies the precosity of the young Philadelphus. I am reminded even more of Theocritus's *Heracliscus*, where we have the very same mythical comparison, young Heracles throttling snakes in his cradle, again implying the precosity of the young Philadelphus.

No fewer than six of these nine "Callimachean" encomia are, like their model, in elegiacs. There is no need to exaggerate the significance of Callimachean epinicion as a model for Roman panegyric. No doubt the average Roman general preferred more stirring stuff than elegant trifles on a lock of his wife's hair. It is significant that Messala and Octavian were both men of culture, poets themselves. Nevertheless, it is at least clear that panegyrists felt themselves as entitled as the love poets of the age to parade "programmatic" allusions to Callimachus.

Informed contemporary readers of *Buc.* vi would be well aware that it had been no part of Callimachus's own aesthetic programme to repudiate in principle the possibility of sophisticated poetry about *reges et proelia*. Callimachus was not trying to encourage his contemporaries to do anything so easy and obvious as write short poems. This is what most of them were doing anyway—not least the Telchines themselves, if Asclepiades and Posidippus were among them. Only a small minority of poets in any age since the rhapsodes had attempted large-scale epic. Callimachus was not concerned with genre as such, but with style and technique. Any competent craftsman (even a Posidippus) could write a subtle and polished short poem. The problem was how to write a subtle and polished long poem, something that was not just a catalogue or epic pastiche (exemplified for Callimachus by Antimachus's *Lyde*). This was the problem that Callimachus grappled with in different ways in both *Aetia* and *Hecale*, and it was the same problem that faced Vergil 200 years later. In coming to grips with it, he undoubtedly studied the Callimachean solutions very carefully. To give an example that contributes to the unique character of the *Aeneid*, it was a refinement of Callimachus's aetiological mode that allowed Vergil to foreshadow events at a variety of later stages in Roman history while restricting his primary narrative to a few years in the life of Aeneas.[81]

So rather than see the passage from *Bucolics* to *Aeneid* as a period in which Vergil gathered up the courage to transcend a non-existent Callimachean ban, we should be conducting a more open-minded investigation of Vergil's use of Callimachean techniques throughout his career. There have been some encouraging signs in the last year or two.[82]

---

81. E. V. George, *Aeneid VIII and the Aetia of Callimachus* (Leiden 1973).

82. Garth Tissol, "An Allusion to Callimachus' *Aetia* 3 in Vergil's *Aeneid* 11," *HSCP* 94 (1992), 263-68; A. S. Hollis, "Hellenistic Colouring in Virgil's *Aeneid*," ib. 269-85; M. Geymonat, "Callimachus at the End of Aeneas' Narration," ib. 95 (1993), 323-31; surprisingly little in Clausen, *Virgil's Aeneid and the Tradition of Hellenistic Poetry* (1987), who (p. 14) writes of the *Aeneid* as "not an abandonment but an extension of Callimachean poetics by Virgil, greatly daring, into an area of poetry precluded by Callimachus."

Appendix A

Hedylus and *Lyde*

ἐξ ἠοῦς εἰς νύκτα καὶ ἐκ νυκτὸς πάλι Σωκλῆς
εἰς ἠοῦν πίνει τετραχόοισι κάδοις,
εἶτ᾽ ἐξαίφνης που τυχὸν οἴχεται· ἀλλὰ παρ᾽ οἶνον
Σικελίδεω παίζει πουλὺ μελιχρότερον,
ἔστι δὲ †δὴ πολὺ† στιβαρώτερος· ὡς δ᾽ ἐπιλάμπει
ἡ χάρις ὥστε, φίλος, καὶ γράφε καὶ μέθυε.

In its general outline, the poem (Hedylus VI in Gow-Page) is straightforward enough. Socles drinks heavily, but when he is drinking (παρ᾽ οἶνον) he writes poems (παίζει) sweeter than Asclepiades. The idea that wine provides inspiration is found in another of his epigrams (V, cited together with VI in Ch. I above), where we find the same use of παίζειν for writing playful verse. Though not explicitly stated, the implication is clearly that Socles writes *better* drunk than sober.

But how do the first halves of lines 3 and 5 fit in? In what sense is he more "weighty" (στιβαρώτερος), and who is he more weighty than? Asclepiades still? What is the sense of οἴχεται in line 3? Where is it that he goes "all of a sudden"? And what is the text in line 5?

Most critics have assumed that στιβαρώτερος is a term of style, balancing μελιχρότερον. But Giangrande suggested an entirely different sense: "physically robust, able to carry his liquor well." He then ingeniously linked this with Socles's departure in line 3: instead of just collapsing into a drunken stupor like most people who have been drinking all night, Socles gets up and goes out to party and make love to his girlfriend.[1]

It may well be "an established sympotic motif" that, after a good carouse, young men, whether in company or on their own, go out on a κῶμος in search of love.[2] But can this motif really be accommodated so allusively in a poem that seems otherwise to have an altogether different point? To be sure, masters of the genre such as Callimachus and Asclepiades delight in misdirection, in suggesting one sort of poem and then surprising us with another. But this is not such a case. Giangrande's suggestion does not arise out of an unexpected twist in the final couplet. There is no surprise ending. The closing exhortation that Socles should

---

1. *L'Épigramme grecque* (1968), 160-63.
2. For the basic texts, F. O. Copley, *Exclusus Amator* (1956), and F. Cairns, *Generic Composition in Greek and Roman Poetry* (1972), index s.v. komos.

continue to drink and write recapitulates the motif (developed throughout the centre of the poem, from lines 3-5) that he writes best when drunk. It is in any case hard to believe that οἴχεται alone, without any other pointer in the context, could suggest "go out into the streets in search of female companionship." The normal meaning of the word is "go away" or "depart," with the common euphemistic extension "die," "be dead."

There is in fact a further extension or rather weakening of this sense, "be undone, ruined" (*LSJ* II. b), that might fit this poem well enough (e.g. Asclepiades, *AP* v. 162. 3, οἴχομ', Ἔρωτες, ὄλωλα, διοίχομαι). Every language has a wide selection of terms for destruction that, in the right context, imply drunkenness. In English (for example) we can so use wrecked, ruined, wasted, smashed, bombed, destroyed, shattered, annihilated, trashed, devastated, slaughtered, demolished, stoned, and no doubt many other such terms. We have only to allow that οἴχομαι, "I'm ruined," could be so used in Greek, and the first half of line 3 could then mean something like: "in no time he is a wreck." That is to say, the drink has reduced him to physical incapacity. This would explain perfectly the ἀλλά that introduces the next clause. Socles may be *physically* incapable when drunk, *but* this is also the condition in which he writes more sweetly than Asclepiades. This ἀλλά is not the only problem with Giangrande's interpretation. Why is Socles's departure in search of a girlfriend described *before* his ability to write excellent poetry when drunk? When does he write this poetry? Before he leaves the party or after he comes back?

There remains the first half of line 5. It is difficult to see why this alleged ability to take his liquor would make Socles a better man than Asclepiades. Giangrande refers to *AP* xii. 50 by Asclepiades, but this says no more than that wine assuages the pangs of love, meaning unhappy love. There is no suggestion that Asclepiades *prefers* wine to love. Nor is there any evidence that στιβαρός is elsewhere used in connection with either holding one's liquor or erotic prowess. There is no call to doubt the usual assumption that, in the context, στιβαρός is (as often elsewhere) a term of style, "austere, virile, robust." See Gow and Page's note on *AP* vii. 39 by Antipater of Thessalonica (II. 31), where it is applied to the style of Aeschylus.

And yet, as Gow and Page remark, "τὸ στιβαρόν is not a quality very naturally associated with τὸ μελιχρόν." But perhaps the two qualities are being contrasted rather than associated. Did Hedylus really use the epic form πουλύ twice in two lines? Not according to the only MS, which offers πολύ in both places. In line 4 the correction seems certain, but various other suggestions have been made for 5. ἔστι δὲ καὶ πολὺ δὴ Wilamowitz, ἔστι δὲ δὴ πολὺ δὴ Kaibel, but such exaggerated qualification of the adjective seems unlikely. I suggest ἔστι δέ που Λύδης, an almost perfect anagram of the transmitted text. Any scribe who failed to recognize the proper name was likely to see instead the more familiar words πο(υ)λύ δή, especially with πο(υ)λύ in the preceding line. The final sigma of Λύδης disappeared before the initial sigma of στιβαρώτερος.

Socles writes more sweetly than Asclepiades, but he is also more robust or sturdy than the *Lyde*. The austere, epic quality of the *Lyde* (Ch. XI passim) is mentioned more than once by our sources. When drinking a toast to the *Nanno* and *Lyde*, Posidippus describes their authors respectively as φιλεράστου Μιμνέρμου and σώφρονος Ἀντιμάχου, sexy Mimnermus and sobersides Antimachus. Then there is Antipater's epigram on Antimachus, discussed in detail in Ch. XI. 6, where it was pointed out that the *Lyde* as well as the *Thebaid* is meant:

> ὄβριμον ἀκαμάτου στίχον αἴνεσον Ἀντιμάχοιο,
> ἄξιον ἀρχαίων ὀφρύος ἡμιθέων.

Dionysius of Halicarnassus refers to his αὐστηρὰ ἁρμονία (*de comp. verb.* 22, p. 98. 6, cf. p. 96. 10 Usener-Radermacher), Quintilian to his *vis et gravitas* (10. 1. 53). So Socles is being praised for combining the characteristic features of two different poets—just as Simichidas in Theocritus 7 compares himself to two different poets, Asclepiades again and Philitas.

Appendix B

Thin Gentlemen

The poet Philitas was so thin, they say, that he had to wear lead weights on his shoes to avoid being blown away by a gust of wind.[1] We have two versions of the anecdote. First Aelian, *Varia Historia* 9. 14:

> Φιλίταν λέγουσι τὸν Κῶον λεπτότατον γενέσθαι τὸ σῶμα· ἐπεὶ τοίνυν ἀνατραπῆναι ῥᾴδιος ἦν ἐκ πάσης προφάσεως, μολύβδου φασὶ πεποιημένα εἶχεν ἐν τοῖς ὑποδήμασι πέλματα, ἵνα μὴ ἀνατρέπηται ὑπὸ τῶν ἀνέμων, εἰ ποτε σκληροὶ κατέπνεον.

They say that Philitas of Cos had an extremely thin body; since he could easily be knocked over by the slightest cause, they say he had lead soles on his shoes so as not to be knocked over by any fierce gusts of wind.

Second, Athenaeus 552B:

> λεπτότερος δ' ἦν καὶ Φιλίτας ὁ Κῷος ποιητής, ὃς καὶ διὰ τὴν τοῦ σώματος ἰσχνότητα σφαίρας ἐκ μολύβου πεποιημένας εἶχε περὶ τὼ πόδε ὡς μὴ ὑπὸ ἀνέμου ἀνατραπείη.

Philitas of Cos the poet was rather thin; because of the skinniness of his body he wore lead weights on his feet so as not to be knocked over by the wind.

The two versions are sufficiently similar in expression as well as content that we may reasonably infer that they derive from the same source. But what was that source, and why such a silly story?

Or is it so silly? In view of the importance of the concept of λεπτότης to Aratus and Callimachus, it is natural to wonder whether the word might in fact bear literary connotations for Philitas. It seems to have been Euripides who first used λεπτός in a positive sense, but it was evidently a controversial usage, since it is often turned against him and the philosophers in comedy (Ch. XI. 4). Could it have been Philitas who first applied it to literary refinement? Some such idea has long been lurking half-formulated at the back of scholarly minds,[2] and has now been stated firmly and openly by E. Calderón Dorda.[3] Without excluding the possibility that Philitas was indeed a man of notably slender physique,

---

1. A revised version of a paper first published in *CQ* 41 (1991), 534-38.
2. P. E. Easterling, *CHCL* i (1985), 30; Hopkinson 1988, 9, 90; Gutzwiller 1991, 204.
3. "Ateneo y la λεπτότης de Filetas," *Emerita* 58 (1990), 125-29.

Calderón Dorda is sure that the primary reference is "al carácter sutil de su poesía" (p. 129).

Aetia F 1. 10-12 suggests that Callimachus praised Philitas's short poems, but inasmuch as he seems to criticize some longer poem or poems, the passage cannot be held to imply unqualified admiration. It would certainly be interesting if we could take this Callimachean notion of poetic refinement back a generation. Unfortunately the anecdote about Philitas's λεπτότης can be shown to have nothing whatever to do with poetry.

Calderón Dorda has only quoted one of the two relevant passages of Aelian. The second reveals clearly the source of the tradition (*Varia Historia* 10. 6):

ἐκωμῳδοῦντο ἐς λεπτότητα Σαννυρίων ὁ κωμῳδίας ποιητὴς καὶ Μέλητος ὁ τραγῳδίας ποιητὴς καὶ Κινησίας <ὁ> κυκλίων χορῶν καὶ Φιλίτας <ὁ> ποιητὴς ἐξαμέτρων.

Sannyrion the comic poet, Meletus the tragedian, Cinesias the poet of the circular choruses[4] and Philitas the hexameter poet were all made fun of in comedy.

All these people were the butt of jokes in Attic comedy. The ultimate source for this passage can be identified with certainty. It is a list of thin people in Aristophanes's *Gerytades*:[5]

πρῶτα μὲν Σαννυρίων
ἀπὸ τῶν τρυγῳδῶν, ἀπὸ δὲ τῶν τραγικῶν χορῶν
Μέλητος, ἀπὸ δὲ τῶν κυκλίων Κινησίας.

First Sannyrion from among the comedians, then Meletus from the tragic and Cinesias from the circular choruses.

There is even a trace in Aelian of Aristophanes's periphrasis for the sort of poetry Cinesias wrote. This passage is quoted in a long section in Athenaeus entirely devoted to people mocked in Attic comedy for their thinness (551A-552F).[6] Athenaeus goes on at once to quote a passage of Strattis on Sannyrion's thinness (περὶ δὲ τοῦ Σαννυρίωνος καὶ Στράττις ἐν Ψυχασταῖς φησιν), and then quotes Sannyrion himself on Meletus (περὶ δὲ τοῦ Μελήτου αὐτὸς ὁ Σαννυρίων) and a series of passages on Cinesias. A page later no fewer than five texts are quoted on the thinness of a certain Philippides: the orator Hyperides and the comedians Alexis, Aristophon, Menander and Alexis again. The second passage of Aelian quoted above continues (like Athenaeus) with the cases of Panaretos and Hipponax and

4. I.e. dithyrambic poet: for this term, Ch. XIV. 2.

5. F 156. 8-10 K.-A. (*PCG* III. 2 [1984], 102).

6. It seems wasteful to consume half a page with references to successive volumes of Kassel-Austin when every passage can be found in context here; the references to Kock in Kaibel and Gulick will lead the curious to Kassel-Austin.

ends by quoting the example of Philippides, mentioning (without quoting) the passages of Hyperides and Alexis, though (like Athenaeus) quoting the verb πεφιλιππιῶσθαι = "to be very thin" from Alexis. It is clear that Aelian drew on the same source here as Athenaeus, a collection of passages from comedy. The only detail he adds that is not in our extant text of Athenaeus is the explicit statement that it was in comedy that Philitas too was mocked for his thinness.

In general there are far fewer allusions to contemporaries in Middle and New Comedy, but (in addition to politicians) two types that continue to be the butt of jokes are thin people—and philosophers, "pale ascetics...unpractical...out for private gain."[7] Another passage of Athenaeus shows that the popular image of Philitas was similar to that of the philosopher. He was after all one of the very first examples of a figure with a rich future on the comic stage: the professor.[8] At 401D one of the interlocutors addresses Ulpian, the host of Athenaeus's banquet, as follows:

> It is always your custom, Ulpian, to decline your share of any dish until you have learned whether the use of the word is ancient. Like Philitas of Cos, therefore, who pondered what he called "the lying word," you run the risk of some day being quite dried up (ἀφαυανθῆναι). For he became very much emaciated in body through these studies (ἰσχνὸς γὰρ πάνυ τὸ σῶμα διὰ τὰς ζητήσεις γενόμενος)[9] and died, as the epitaph on his tomb shows:

> ξεῖνε, Φιλίτας εἰμί. λόγων ὁ ψευδόμενός με
> ὤλεσε καὶ νυκτῶν φροντίδες ἑσπέριοι.

> Stranger, I am Philitas. The lying word caused
> my death, and night's evening thoughts.

The fullest discussion of this epigram is that of Denys Page, who concluded that "Philitas worried himself into his grave in the search for verbal errors (presumably in his own writings)."[10] But his assumption that ὁ ψευδόμενος "refers especially to literary usage which is not sanctioned by ancient authority" must be mistaken. The reference (as Lloyd-Jones has seen) is to the so-called liar's paradox, said to have been propounded by Eubulides of Miletus and normally referred to as ὁ ψευδόμενος.[11] There is

---

7. T.B.L. Webster, *Studies in Later Greek Comedy* (Manchester 1953), 111; Ch. II. 2.

8. On Philitas's position in the history of scholarship, see Pfeiffer 1968, 88-89.

9. Cf. Suda s.v. Φιλήτας·...ἰσχνωθεὶς ἐκ τοῦ ζητεῖν τὸν καλούμενον ψευδόμενον λόγον ἀπέθανεν.

10. *FGE* 442; "nights' evening-thoughts" is certainly a "very odd expression" (Page), but for a parallel see Lloyd-Jones, *CR* 32 (1982), 142 (= *Academic Papers* II. 228), explaining it as "night-worries that begin as early as the evening of the day before." καὶ νυκτῶν, Kaibel, ingeniously enough, but what a strange way to refer to anxious evenings devoted to riddles.

11. Diog. Laert. ii. 108; W. and M. Kneale, *The Development of Logic* (Oxford 1962), pp. 113-15; for many (often depreciatory) references to the paradox in both Greek and Latin literature, see A. S. Pease's note on Cicero, *de div.* ii. 11 (pp. 364-6). On Eubulides, E. G.

no other evidence that Philitas concerned himself with logic, and we should no doubt conclude that the writer picked on the paradox simply as a classic example of the sort of futile quibble on which an unworldly pedant might waste his time. Significantly enough, Eubulides and his "falsely pretentious arguments" (ψευδαλαζόσιν λόγοις) were mocked in an anonymous comic fragment.[12]

A passage of Plutarch helps to fill out the picture. When making the point that sickly people should not engage in public affairs he instances Prodicus the sophist and Philitas the poet, "men who though young were thin and sickly and usually bedridden" (νέους μὲν, ἰσχνοὺς δὲ καὶ νοσώδεις καὶ τὰ πολλὰ κλινοπετεῖς).[13] The famous description of Prodicus holding court while "still in bed, wrapped up in fleeces and rugs" in Plato's *Protagoras* (315D) corroborates the poor health of Prodicus, and there is no reason to doubt that Philitas suffered and in due course died from some wasting disease, which contemporaries jokingly attributed to the consuming passion of his pedantry.[14]

His pedantry too was a subject of jokes in the comedies of the day. Still another passage of Athenaeus quotes a long fragment from Strato's *Phoenicides* in which the speaker complains that his cook keeps using archaic words he does not understand, "so that he had to get some of Philitas's books and look up the meaning of every word":[15]

μίστυλλα, μοίρας, δίπτυχ᾽, ὀβελούς, ὥστ᾽ ἔδει
τὰ τοῦ Φιλίτα λαμβάνοντα βιβλία
σκοπεῖν ἕκαστον τί δύναται τῶν ῥημάτων.

Strato wrote at the turn of the fourth and third centuries. If a didascalia fragment is correctly restored, he may have won fourth prize in the Dionysia of 302 B.C.[16] If one passage of comedy can joke about Philitas's thinness and another about his pedantry, it is reasonable to assume that the idea of linking the two might also derive from a joke in comedy. The joke can be better appreciated if it is borne in mind that a high proportion of the surviving examples of Philitas's scholarship concern rare words for various types of cakes and drinking-cups.[17] Food was a favourite theme of Attic

12. Adesp. 294 = *CAF* iii. 461-2 Kock.

13. *An seni sit respublica gerenda* 791E.

14. Pfeiffer 1968, 41 (cf. 91), cites the text of Plutarch, but did not link its ἰσχνούς with the other texts on Philitas's thinness, nor his thinness with his pedantry.

15. Athen. 382B-383B, corrected from P. Cair. 65445; Strato F 1. 42-4 (*PCG* VII [1989], 620).

16. Kassel and Austin, *PCG* VII (1989), 617.

17. G. Kuchenmüller, *Philetae Coi Reliquiae* (Diss. Berlin 1927), 29-59.

comedy.[18] He could be portrayed as quite literally so obsessive about checking the linguistic pedigree of every dish and cup at table that the food was all gone by the time he was ready to eat.

Another early allusion to the supposedly debilitating effect of Philitas's linguistic researches comes in so early and well informed a source as his own disciple Hermesianax, who describes him as

Βιττίδα μολπάζοντα θοήν, περὶ πάντα Φιλίταν
ῥήματα καὶ πᾶσαν <τ>ρυόμενον λαλίην (F 7. 77-8).

According to Gulick's Loeb the sense is: "sang his love for the nimble Bittis, versed as he was in all the terms of love and in all its speech." But <τ>ρυόμενον, assuming (with Gulick and Defradas) Hermann's minimal correction of the only MS, should mean "worried," "worn out." The reference is to lexicographical rather than erotic anxieties: "weak with all the glosses, all the forms of speech" in the recent translation of Peter Bing and Rip Cohen.[19]

According to Bulloch,[20]

near contemporaries speak of [Philitas] wearing himself out with intellectual effort (a theme which later biographers developed into an account of his extraordinary physical slightness which necessitated his wearing weights on his feet in strong winds).

Not quite. The element of hyperbole was there from the first. It was Philitas's real physical slightness—a favourite comic theme—that contemporaries humorously explained as a consequence of his pedantry.

The word used for thin in almost every one of the passages assembled by Athenaeus as well as in both passages of Aelian is λεπτός.[21] It is also the word used in twelve out of fourteen sceptic epigrams of the Neronian age by Lucillius and Nicarchus.[22] It will be enough to quote a characteristic example by Lucillius, *AP* xi. 93:

τῶν Ἐπικουρείων ἀτόμων ποτὲ Μάρκος ὁ λεπτός,
τῇ κεφαλῇ τρήσας, εἰς τὸ μέσον διέβη.

Thin Marcus once made a hole in one of Epicurus's atoms
with his head, and went right through the middle of it.

18. H. Dohm, *Die Rolle des Kochs in der griech.-röm. Komödie* (Munich 1965).

19. *Games of Venus* (New York 1991), 129. λαλίη might (as elsewhere) refer to dialect (so Cairns, *Tibullus* 220): e.g. Matt. 26. 73; Bauer, *Lex.* s.v. 2a; LSJ s.v. II.

20. *CHCL* i (1985), 545.

21. Compare too Dionysius ὁ λεπτός who commented on a poem of Theodoridas (Athen. 475F), presumably the teacher of Fronto described as Dionysius *tenuis* or *tenuior* (Fronto, ed. van den Hout[2] p. 152. 2); *PIR*[2] D. 106; and Demetrius λεπτός the son of Demetrius Poliorcetes (Plut. *Dem.* 53. 4).

22. *AP* xi. 91-94, 99-103, 106-7, 110-11, 308; F. J. Brecht, *Motiv- und Typengeschichte des griechischen Spottepigramms* (Philologus Suppbd. xxii. 2), Leipzig 1930, pp. 91-3.

Nicarchus writes of three men competing to see who was the thinnest (xi. 110. 1-2):

τρεῖς λεπτοὶ πρῴην περὶ λεπτοσύνης ἐμάχοντο,
τίς προκριθεὶς εἴη λεπτεπιλεπτότερος...

The other day three thin men competed about thinness to see
who would be judged the very thinnest of them all...

Their respective claims are worthy of Henny Youngman.

Closest to the anecdote about Philitas is the story of Gaius, who (according to Lucillius, xi. 100) was so thin that he used to dive (ἐκολύμβα) with a stone or lead weight attached to his foot (τοῦ ποδὸς ἐκκρεμάσας ἢ λίθον ἢ μόλιβον). Brecht suggested that the story about Philitas derived from an epigram of this nature, but the scoptic epigram as we find it fully developed in Lucillius and Nicarchus seems to be an original creation of the early empire.[23] The epigram "on his tomb" quoted by Athenaeus fits into an entirely different and abundantly documented Hellenistic tradition, the pretended funerary epigram. It too was surely written by a contemporary, almost certainly while Philitas was still alive,[24] no doubt for an Alexandrian symposium.

It seems natural to suppose some link between comedy and epigram,[25] but it would be implausible to postulate direct derivation.[26] Jokes have a way of travelling through time and space independently of written sources, and the examples in comedy normally lack the element of paradox that is the essence of the scoptic epigram. Like voguish joke-sequences today (knock-knock jokes and lightbulb jokes), the idea itself is enough to spawn innumerable ingenious variations. The only coincidence in detail here between comedy and epigram—the lead weights on the feet—is also the most obvious. The original source of all these anecdotes about Philitas was surely Attic comedy. The story of his λεπτότης is just another of those evergreen thin jokes.

23. See my *Greek Anthology*, Ch. I; L. Robert, *L'Épigramme grecque* (1968), 181-291.

24. "Epigramma irrisorium," T. Preger, *Inscr. graec. metr. ex scriptoribus* (Leipzig 1891), no. 266.

25. It is curious that we do not find corresponding jokes in either comedy or epigram about fat people, a much richer source of humour in modern times. For example, Martial devotes both more space and more ingenuity to the thin half of his not-too-fat-not-too-thin poem xi. 100.

26. So Brecht, p. 3: "soll damit dem Dichter nicht eine direkte Herübernahme zugesprochen sein; es handelt sich nicht um subjektives Herübernehmen, sondern um objektiv begründete Motivwanderung."

Appendix C

Asclepiades's Girlfriends

1

The social, moral and marital status of the ladies of the Roman love elegists has long been solemnly debated—if to no agreed result.[1] By contrast, no attention at all has been paid to the women of a genre that is known to have exerted considerable influence on the elegists, Hellenistic love epigram.[2] It is easy to see why. Of its three most distinguished and prolific exponents, Meleager's fantastic arsenal of Cupids, arrows and torches is directed with no discernible difference of tone or circumstance against boys and girls alike. Callimachus writes only of boys. And as for Asclepiades, though he writes mainly of women,[3] in many different moods, it has always been taken for granted that they are "hetairas."

Critics prefer the word "hetaira" because it suggests something more glamorous and less sordid than "prostitute." Now some of the hetairas of fifth- and fourth-century Athens do seem to have been women of education and culture who could supply Athenian males with the sort of sexual companionship they did not get from their wives.[4] However, we must beware of swallowing uncritically the romanticized picture of the Intellectual Whore, more poet and philosopher than sexual gymnast. There can be little

1. A revised and expanded version of an article originally published in H. P. Foley (ed.), *Reflections of Women in Antiquity* (London 1981), 275-302.

2. A. A. Day, *Origins of Latin Love Elegy* (Oxford 1938), 102-37; E. Schulz-Vanheyden, *Properz und das griechische Epigramm* (Munster 1970).

3. Gow and Page argued that XXI-XXIV all celebrated children rather than handsome boys (II. 130-1), but Ludwig rightly doubts whether this is true of XXI (*L'Épigramme grecque* [1968], 320) and there can be little doubt that XII is pederastic, especially now that P. Oxy. 3724 (while supporting the transmitted word order in the final line) has revealed that line 5 ends (as Schneidewin had conjectured) ἐκείνου: M. Gigante, in M. Capasso (ed.), *Papiri letterari greci e latini* (Lecce 1992), 9-10.

4. There is no comprehensive critical study: see K. Schneider's article "Hetairai" in *RE* 8. 1331-72; H. Herter "Dirne," in *RAC* iii. 1149-1213 and "Die Soziologie der antiken Prostitution" in *JbAC* 3 (1960), 70-111; Eva C. Keuls, *The Reign of the Phallus* (New York 1985), 153-203. A major problem is our inability to identify hetairai on Attic vases with certainty (cf. D. Williams, in Averil Cameron and Amélie Kuhrt [edd.], *Images of Women in Antiquity* [London 1983], 97-105).

doubt that many hetairas acquired and used their culture in order to ensnare and fleece more cultivated and therefore wealthier clients, like the courtesans of Renaissance Rome and Venice[5] and the "pretty Horse-breakers," of nineteenth-century London and Paris,[6] to name two other brief moments in history when a small number of high-class prostitutes acquired not only great wealth but also a surprising degree of social acceptance. But at all times and places, and certainly in their golden age at Athens, even the most accomplished courtesans were best known for their rapacity.

Did this Athenian "Hetärenwesen" (to use the nice German term) survive in all its glory into the Hellenistic age? So most scholars have presumed. Yet the abundant (if suspect) information on hetairas in Book xiii of Athenaeus's *Deipnosophists* was collected almost entirely from Attic comedy and the Attic orators. It was originally put together by Hellenistic scholars evidently fascinated by the flamboyant femmes fatales they had read about in their classics. Athenaeus supplies an illuminating bibliography: "Aristophanes [of Byzantium], Apollodorus, Ammonius, Antiphanes, and Gorgias of Athens, all of whom have written on the hetairas of Athens" (567A). Aristophanes was apparently first in the field, but the later writers were able to add substantially to his total of 135 hetairas (583E). Another earlier writer laid under heavy contribution by Athenaeus is Machon, a contemporary of Asclepiades and Callimachus.[7] The obvious implication is that the radiant charmers of Athenian society were *not* still to be found at every Hellenistic symposium. Prostitution itself will naturally have continued to flourish, especially in a great seaport such as Alexandria.[8] But what was the social standing of even the most expensive? Did the jeunesse dorée still fight over the honor of squandering fortunes on them, as they did in fourth-century Athens and were to again in nineteenth-century London?[9] In most ages not even poets (who seldom have the money) are prepared to admit that they patronize prostitutes and even to

5. Georgina Masson, *Courtesans of the Italian Renaissance* (London 1975), and Paul Larivaille, *La vie quotidienne des courtisanes en Italie au temps de la Renaissance* (Rome 1975), the latter with a concluding chapter on "Le mythe de la courtisane" stressing the darker side.

6. Joanne Richardson, *The Courtesans: the demi-monde in nineteenth century France* (Cleveland and London 1967); Henry Blyth, *Skittles: the last Victorian Courtesan* (London 1970); Michael Harrison, *Fanfare of Strumpets* (London 1971); Charles Carlton, *Royal Mistresses* (London 1990), all with useful bibliographies.

7. See A.S.F. Gow's edition, *Machon: the fragments* (Cambridge 1965), with useful (if austere) commentary.

8. On prostitution in Ptolemaic Egypt see Lea Bringman, *Die Frau im ptolemäisch-kaiserlichen Aegypten* (Bonn 1939), 120-21.

9. E.g. Antiphanes, in Athenaeus XIII, 555 A; Harrison, *Fanfare of Strumpets* 121-2 (a fist-fight between two aristocrats over Lily Langtry in Hyde Park); cf. Masson, *Courtesans* 95.

boast of being their slaves. It may be significant that almost all the hetairas known by name after the fourth century were mistresses of Hellenistic kings, whom we should not lightly presume to have kept open salon.[10]

Nonetheless his commentators have taken it for granted that Asclepiades moved in the same erotic world as the feckless young heroes of New Comedy. Conspicuously so the authoritative edition of Gow and Page,[11] though no one has put it so bluntly as P. M. Fraser:[12]

> this world of venal love, in which the young of both sexes refuse and grant their favours with equanimity and impartiality, on a cash basis.

Is this really the world Asclepiades wrote of? Even as a fictive world, is it credible in any age?

The underlying assumption is presumably that no woman mentioned in an erotic poem can be respectable;[13] that even without specific pointers contemporary readers would automatically and instinctively have identified Asclepiades's girlfriends as prostitutes. The traditional view that in fifth- and fourth-century Athens "unmarried men had no opportunities for heterosexual activity except with prostitutes and slaves"[14] can hardly have been true in any strict sense, even in the upper classes.[15] But Athenian males liked to believe that respectable women never left the house, whence the stock motif that it was only at religious festivals that the respectable girls of New Comedy got pregnant.[16]

Whatever the truth of the supposed "oriental seclusion" of Athenian women, by the third century elsewhere in the Greek world the status of

10. The eye of the moralist may detect little difference between the mistress and the whore, but from the viewpoint of the woman, the element of choice and the possibility of fidelity, affection and permanence certainly raise the mistress above the level of the whore. Joanna Richardson deliberately omitted from her account of Parisian courtesans such colourful "non-professionals" as Mme de Staël, George Sand and Sarah Bernhardt.

11. I cite poems by their number in *HE* (though I often differ from their text). I have not given separate page references every time I quote their commentary on Asclepiades (II. 114-151), which is the work of Gow.

12. I. 564. D. H. Garrison, *Mild Frenzy: A Reading of the Hellenistic Love Epigram* (Wiesbaden 1978) 60, finds in Asclepiades a "distrust of women" that he traces to "the unsatisfactory nature of liaisons with hetairae."

13. With some reluctance I use the conventional term "respectable" to mean merely "not a prostitute": see further below.

14. A. W. Gomme and F. H. Sandbach, *Menander: a Commentary* (Oxford,1973), 32-34.

15. D. Cohen, *Law, Sexuality and Society: The enforcement of morals in classical Athens* (Cambridge 1991), 148-155.

16. So stock a feature of Menandrean comedy did this become that the youth who rapes the girl usually even bears the same name, Moschion: W. T. MacCary, *TAPA* 101 (1970), 286-89; see too Elaine Fantham, "Sex, Status, and Survival in Hellenistic Athens: a Study of Women in New Comedy," *Phoenix* 29 (1975), 44-74.

women was improving and pederasty in decline.[17] The romances of New Comedy are heterosexual, and the naked statues of Aphrodite that became so popular in the Hellenistic Age document the growth of a feminine erotic ideal.[18] The amours of the kings were almost exclusively heterosexual; anecdotes about royal mistresses became an established subgenre. And whether or not it is appropriate (as sometimes suggested) to apply the modern concept of "rôle-model" to their queens, the fact remains that a small number of women did acquire considerable power and visibility in the Hellenistic world. More specifically, there is evidence for a growth in education of women outside the home,[19] giving respectable women one of the advantages till then enjoyed by hetairas alone. Thus we need not automatically assume that any woman present at a symposium was a hetaira. For example, there is nothing in the poem itself to suggest that the girl Cynisca who participates in the rustic symposium of Theocritus 14 is a hetaira.[20] Aeschinas is distressed to have lost her, but there is no question of the depth and sincerity of her passion for Lykos. Gorgo and Praxinoa in Theocritus 15 are bourgeois housewives who move freely about Alexandria on foot, bumping into and talking with strange men whom they meet on the way.[21] Simaetha in Theocritus 2 is a poor but respectable girl who lives alone with a maid, a virgin until she gave herself to the faithless Delphis.[22] The so-called *Fragmentum Grenfellianum* is a lament sung by a girl who has walked through the streets at night (naturally with an attendant, line 25) to the house of the beloved who has left her to sleep alone.[23]

The pages that follow have the limited aim of suggesting (1) that there is seldom the slightest indication in the poems that Asclepiades's girlfriends expect money in return for their favours; and (2) that on the contrary,

17. Sarah B. Pomeroy, *Women in Hellenistic Egypt* (New York 1984); C. Vatin, *Recherches sur le mariage et la condition de la femme mariée à l'époque hellénistique* (Paris 1970).

18. R.R.R. Smith, *Hellenistic Sculpture* (London 1991), 82-83.

19. Pomeroy, *AJAH* 2 (1977), 51-68. This pattern was to repeat itself at Rome. In the course of the second century B.C. aristocratic society was invaded by Greek courtesans, women possessed of a glamour and culture unknown to the respectable materfamilias (see the excellent account in R.O.A.M. Lyne, *The Latin Love Poets* [Oxford 1980], 8-18). But this Greek "demi-monde" did not survive the emancipation of Roman women in the first century unchallenged: Catullus's Lesbia was the wife of a Roman aristocrat.

20. As for example Gow supposed (*Theocritus* II. 252), on the analogy of the fourth-century texts, rightly criticized by K. Latte, *Gnomon* 23 (1951), 25. Even if the name is meant to be significant (Bitchy), that need not be a pointer to "her profession" (Gow, and see now J. Stern, *GRBS* 16 [1975], 55); merely an indication that she has played Aeschinas false.

21. I think it is a mistake of emphasis to interpret this poem as merely a typical example of women attending a festival (as, for example, W. Headlam on Herodas I. 56; or Vatin, *Recherches* 263-7). Even in classical Athens many texts show women moving about freely outside their homes: Cohen, *Law, Sexuality and Society* 150-53.

22. On Simaetha's status see the careful discussion in K. J. Dover, *Theocritus: Select Poems* (London 1971), 94-96.

23. Powell, *CA*.177-80.

many of his poems make much better sense if we assume that they do not. The girls may not all be chaste, but with one or two exceptions that prove the rule, they are certainly not prostitutes.

2

We may begin with a simple case, Asclepiades III (*AP* v.153):

Νικαρέτης τὸ πόθοις βεβλημένον ἡδὺ πρόσωπον
πυκνὰ δι' ὑψηλῶν φαινόμενον θυρίδων.
αἱ χαροπαὶ Κλεοφῶντος ἐπὶ προθύροισι μάραναν,
Κύπρι φίλη, γλυκεροῦ βλέμματος ἀστεροπαί.

The bright lightning of the sweet eye of Cleophon blasted Nicarete's sweet face, smitten by the Desires, appearing often through the high windows, as he stood at the threshold, dear Cypris.

"The fact that Nicarete is often to be seen at her window probably indicates that she is a hetaira, or at least not unduly modest," remarks Gow primly. It is true that a prostitute might be pictured beckoning to potential customers through an open window, but that can hardly be the case here. In line 1, P (the only manuscript) offers πόθοισι. All editors since Wilamowitz have objected both to the prosody βεβλημένον and to the description of Nicarete as "smitten with desire." Hence Wilamowitz's widely accepted conjecture βεβαμμένον, "bathed *in* desire"—more appropriate to the presumed beckonings of the whore. Yet a simpler and more satisfactory way to correct the prosody (if correction is needed) is Pfeiffer's πόθοις.[24] And far from the announcement that Nicarete is "smitten with desire" anticipating line 3 "unsuitably" (Gow), on the contrary it alerts us for the eventual revelation of the source of her passion. For the point of the poem is surely that it is a one-way passion. It is Cleophon's flashing eyes that "wither" her from the porch. No doubt he is staring up at her flirtatiously, but there is no hint in the poem that he reciprocates her passion—or indeed that he has ever actually spoken to her. The fact that her face is *often* at an upstairs (ὑψηλῶν) window suggests that this is the only way she can get to see him. In fact, it is surely a story of (?first) love at a distance. Far from being a hetaira luring clients in off the streets, Nicarete is an innocent young girl kept in seclusion by her parents who is devastated by the sight of a handsome youth on the doorstep (perhaps a delivery boy), and forced to spend her days looking out of her bedroom window for his visits.

24. Published by W. Ludwig, *Gnomon* 38 (1966), 22f.; so too A. Zumbo, *Studi A. Ardizzoni* ii [1978], 1046-54. βληθείς in Meleager's imitation, *AP* xii. 72.3-4, lends some support to βεβλημένον.

The fact that Cleophon is standing on a threshold could be argued to suggest a paraclausithuron (so Kathryn Gutzwiller). But if so, one of a most unusual sort. For there is no suggestion that Nicarete has locked him out or that he is in any distress. We might hypothesize a husband, doorkeeper or parents, but there is no hint of them in the text.

Before passing on we ought perhaps to consider Praxilla F 8 (*PMG* 754), which is often held to have been Asclepiades's model:

ὦ διὰ τῶν θυρίδων καλὸν ἐμβλέποισα
παρθένε τὰν κεφαλὰν τὰ δ' ἔνερθε νύμφα.

You who look prettily in through windows, maiden in your head, bride below.

Most commentators have inferred from line 2 that the girl is a whore with the face of a virgin. Obviously, if Praxilla's poem is about a whore, this will have a bearing on the interpretation of Asclepiades's poem. But why is the girl looking *in* rather than out of the windows? Perhaps ἐκβλέποισα,[25] "looking out," remarks Page in his note, unless (he adds) the girl is so shameless that she is wandering down the street looking in windows to lure prospective clients out of their very front doors. Such aggressive salesmanship might astonish even in Times Square. W. Aly came up with an ingenious and attractive alternative:[26] no mortal girl at all, but Selene, the Moon, who gazes in through peoples' windows (explaining the plural) as she sweeps across the night sky "in maidenly inaccessiblity"; and when she is below the horizon during the day—τὰ δ' ἔνερθε—is Endymion's wife. This may be thought a shade too fanciful; it explains the "below" to perfection, but "maiden as to your head" rather less well. Yet the traditional explanation is no more satisfactory. While one can say in most languages that a girl has the face of a virgin but the heart or body of a whore, it is surely very odd to say that she has the head of a virgin but is a *bride* (or married woman) *beneath*. Marriage marks the end of virginity, to be sure, but most people consider it respectable enough. If we had the rest of Praxilla's poem these two lines might take on a meaning we could never have guessed. At all events, whether or not Asclepiades knew the poem, the interpretation of these two lines is far too uncertain to warrant importing the notion of an unchaste woman into Asclepiades.

Depending on the interpretation, Asclepiades may have nothing in common with Praxilla beyond a reference to windows. More relevant, in fact, is the scene in Aristophanes's *Ecclesiazusae* (884 f.) in which a young girl peeps out of an upper storey window. To be sure this girl is behaving more provocatively than Nicarete; she is hoping—unsuccessfully in the

25. So too presumably M. L. West (*Greek Lyric Poetry* [Oxford 1994], 189): "O Miss, from out your window blowing kisses—A Miss by your face, but lower down a Mrs."
26. *RE* xxii (1954), 1765.

event—that her boyfriend will pop up while mother is out. Yet it would be ruinous to the plot of the play if she were a prostitute.[27]

That some at least of the girls Asclepiades wrote of were not merely respectable but actually virgins is proved by II (v. 85), opening φείδῃ παρθενίης;

> Pretty maiden, what's the good
> of hoarding up your maidenhood?

in Phillimore's translation,[28] concluding with the reflection that was to be urged so often in future centuries on reluctant virgins,

> Once in Acheron we must,
> maiden, come to bones and dust.

Compare too the charming description of a young girl called Eirenion in XXXIV (v. 194, ascribed to "Asclepiades or Posidippus"), with whom all the boys are in love.[29] The attentions of the young men are inspired by the arrows of the Erotes, not her own coquettishness, and especially in view of the reference at line 4 to her "maidenly charms" there seems no reason to see her as a hetaira. Then there is *AP* v. 199 by Asclepiades's disciple Hedylus, about a girl (ironically called Aglaonice, "Splendid Victory") who has lost her virginity after a party, undone by wine and the love of Nicagoras.[30] "On the hetaira Aglaonice," sternly remarked the corrector of the Palatine manuscript; for once even Gow was moved to concede that this was "not necessarily" so. Young girls who go to riotous parties may not be as modest as their parents might wish, but they do not have to be prostitutes.

3

Next IV (v. 158):

> Ἑρμιόνη πιθανῇ ποτ' ἐγὼ συνέπαιζον ἐχούσῃ
>   ζώνιον ἐξ ἀνθέων ποικίλον, ὦ Παφίη,
> χρύσεα γράμματ' ἔχον· διόλου δ'ἐγέγραπτο "φίλει με,
>   καὶ μὴ λυπηθῇς ἤν τις ἔχῃ μ' ἕτερος."

---

27. See K. J. Dover, *Aristophanic Comedy* (Berkeley 1972), 192, 197.

28. An interesting selection of translations is included in W. and M. Wallace, *Asklepiades of Samos* (Oxford 1941).

29. According to Garrison, *Mild Frenzy*, p.50, "We have only the conventions of the genre to tell us that [Eirenion] is either a hetaera or a young music-girl destined to become a hetaera."

30. See the discussion by G.Giangrande, *L'Épigramme grecque* (1968), 150-52.

I played once with obliging Hermione, and she wore a girdle of variegated flowers, Paphian queen, with golden letters. All around it was written: "love me—and don't be upset if another has me."

"On a hetaira whose girdle warns the lover against jealousy" (Gow). "The adjective is somewhat surprising," he remarks on πιθανῇ. It is in fact a good example of a characteristic device of Asclepiades, a word or phrase in the first line that (for the alert reader) anticipates or foreshadows the conclusion of the poem.[31] Hermione is obliging, pliant, suggestible, accommodating. That is to say she gives in too easily. The point is caught in Phillimore's version,

> Once as I toyed with that Hermione
> whose tender heart no suitor could not melt,

but his explicitness destroys Asclepiades's subtlety. The reader cannot be sure which of the possible meanings of πιθανῇ to choose until he has got to the end of the poem. In the same way, it is not till he has got to the end of the Nicarete poem that the reader appreciates why she is smitten with desire. Further examples will be quoted below.

The point of the poem is that Hermione is *not* a whore. Indeed the poet takes her for a respectable woman. Although he has already noted her complaisance while they "play together," he is apparently surprised by the announcement of her promiscuity. If she had been a whore, obviously he would have expected both as a matter of course. συνέπαιζον certainly implies "amorous dalliance" (as Gow archly puts it), but clearly not (in the context) actual intercourse.[32] The girdle is of course an undergarment; it is not till he has partially undressed the girl that he comes across the gold letters.[33] We are hardly intended to think him too naive till then to see her true nature (that is the theme of poem VII). It is by her promiscuity and avarice that a hetaira reveals her nature, not by discreet advance warnings.

Like several others of Asclepiades's poems, this one is about a specific type of girl. Nothing so general as a hetaira, who is mercenary as well as promiscuous. She is simply a flirt, the girl who "can't say no." The poet should have guessed that a girl who gave away so easily to him would give away as easily to others. Provided he can accept this, he is free to love her with all his heart—scarcely the advice of a hetaira.

---

31. See the useful paper by W.G.Arnott in *CR* 19 (1969), 6-8.

32. It is regularly so used of playful erotic behaviour: see J. Henderson, *The Maculate Muse* (New Haven 1975), 157.

33. Gow has a characteristic note on whether the letters are "embroidered in gold thread" or "in metal appliqué."

4

Perhaps the most puzzling of Asclepiades's poems is IX (v. 7):

Λύχνε, σὲ γὰρ παρεοῦσα τρὶς ὤμοσεν Ἡράκλεια
    ἥξειν κοὐχ ἥκει· λύχνε σὺ δ᾽ εἰ θεὸς εἶ
τὴν δολίην ἐπάμυνον· ὅταν φίλον ἔνδον ἔχουσα
    παίζῃ ἀποσβεσθεὶς μηκέτι φῶς πάρεχε.

Lamp, three times Heracleia swore in your presence to come, and comes not.
Lamp, if you are a god, assist her trickery. When she has a friend at home and
is sporting with him, go out and provide no more light.

Commentators have made extraordinarily heavy weather of this poem, "une
des épigrammes les plus controversées de l'Anthologie" according to
Giangrande.[34] Is the lamp by which Heracleia perjures herself in her room
or the poet's? Or are there two different lamps; do lamps "make common
cause, [so] that the poet's lamp can control the behaviour of Heracleia's"
(Gow, with a variation, capitalizing Λύχνος, by M. Marcovich)?[35] Or is
the poet "waiting neither in his house nor in hers but in a room which she
uses for assignations" (Gow, developed by Giangrande)?

These explanations all share one fatal flaw. The one thing they do not
explain is the climax of the poem: in what way does the extinction of the
lamp pay Heracleia back for her trickery? "Lovers keep the lamp alight,"
comments Page, on a rather different poem by Meleager.[36] It is true that
Greek and Roman poets frequently refer to lamps as witnesses of lovemaking,[37] but that is because people normally make love in private at night. So
the bedroom lamp witnesses what others do not. The lamp may be called
the "guardian" of the poet's beloved; sometimes the poet will guess from
the light in her window that his girl is with another man; and, like every-
body else, lovers extinguish the lamp when they are ready for sleep. But
none of these variations on the motif is quite the same as saying that lovers
prefer actually to make love with the light on. That was no more than a

34. *RÉG* 86 (1973), 319-22. I agree with Gow and Page (II. 122-3) that Platnauer's
παρέοντα would mean much the same as P's παρεοῦσα, which I have therefore kept.

35. *Rh. Mus.* 114 (1971), 333-39.

36. In his note on Meleager LI.5 (II. 635). Both the similarities and still more the differences between this poem and Asclepiades IX are instructive. The poet appeals not to the
lamp but to Night, and all that he prays for is that, having made love and put out the lamp in
the usual way, his rival will fall asleep and never wake up again. He is not so unrealistic as
to imagine that there is any way of preventing them actually making love.

37. It will be enough to refer to the full collection of references and bibliography on the
lamp as both god and witness of lovemaking in K. Kost, *Musaios: Hero und Leander* (Bonn
1971), 126-132.

matter of taste—and of no great moment. As one poet admitted, while he liked *ludere teste lucerna*, his modest wife preferred the light off (Martial, xi. 104. 5-6). After all, the lamp will usually have "witnessed" quite enough to compromise the lovers even if they extinguish it before actually getting into bed.

To return to Asclepiades IX, whether Heracleia and the poet's rival are already making love or only about to, they are not likely to stop or abandon the idea just because the lamp goes out. The climax of the poem cannot rest on such an improbable assumption.[38] Most relevantly, on the univeral assumption that Heracleia is a prostitute, are we to believe that the client will ask for his money back if the light goes out? For that is the only way a prostitute could be punished effectively.

I suggest that Heracleia is not a prostitute, but another female type: this time the tease. Neither the poet nor the rival are "clients" (note that the latter is described merely as a "friend"), but admirers whom she has so far kept at arm's length. It was during a visit by the poet to her apartment to pay court to her that Heracleia (falsely) swore by the lamp to spend the night with him. To get his own back he envisages an occasion when she is "playing her game" with a rival: that is to say making him too promises she has no intention of keeping. παίζη again of flirting or petting rather than intercourse itself. It is at this moment that the poet wants the lamp to extinguish itself. How will the rival take it?

Naturally he will assume that Heracleia has turned it out. Now people do not normally turn their lamp out until they are ready for bed. The rival will hardly take it as a hint to leave or sleep in the spare room. He will assume that the "play" of line 3 was meant in earnest—and pounce.

On this interpretation it is a far more subtle poem: Heracleia's teasing really will be her undoing. And in support consider more closely the first verb in line 3: P offers ἀπάμυνον, which editors all interpret in the otherwise unparalleled sense "punish"; elsewhere it always means "keep off," "ward off," "repel," meanings wholly unsuitable here. But Planudes has ἐπάμυνον, which "should mean *assist* and is therefore improbable" (Gow). Not on my interpretation.[39] The lamp does in fact "assist" Heracleia's "trickery," in the sense that it furthers the course of action Heracleia had been *pretending* to follow. She is giving the rival her usual deceitful encouragement; the lamp makes him think it is genuine.

38. Unless the climax of the poem is meant to be an *anti*-climax, a futile, impotent gesture (so Gutzwiller).

39. It is a mistake on principle to prefer the Palatine to the Planudean text: see my *Greek Anthology* passim; Planudes drew on two separate redactions of Cephalas's anthology, and the numerous variants in the margins of *AP* (also dependent on Cephalas) suggest that Cephalas's was a variorum text.

Poem X (v. 150) ought perhaps to be considered together with this poem:

> Ὡμολόγησ᾽ ἥξειν εἰς νύκτα μοι ἡ ᾽πιβόητος
>   Νικὼ καὶ σεμνὴν ὤμοσε Θεσμοφόρον,
> κοὐχ ἥκει, φυλακὴ δὲ παροίχεται. ἆρ᾽ ἐπιορκεῖν
>   ἤθελε; τὸν λύχνον, παῖδες, ἀποβέσατε.

That Niko that people talk about[40] agreed to call on me at night, and swore by holy Demeter the lawgiver. She comes not and the watch is passing. Did she deliberately perjure herself? Boys, put out the lamp.

This lady looks somewhat shadier, but Gow was wrong to proclaim her a hetaira on the strength of the name, which was common among respectable women, most relevantly in his own Boy Meets Girl idyll XXXVI (v. 209). There are two details in the poem that need clarification. First, the lover reacts very differently to his disappointment this time. Instead of getting angry or giving way to despair or plotting revenge, he coolly gets ready for bed. If Niko was playing hard to get, it was a play that failed. Second, the oath. As Gow remarked, Aphrodite, who notoriously laughs at lovers' perjuries, might have been expected, but an oath by Demeter (whose Thesmophoria excluded men) makes much the same point.[41] At the time the lover evidently missed this, but on reflection he realizes that he should have guessed from the oath and takes his deception philosophically.

Connected with this poem is XIII (v. 164):[42]

> Νύξ, σὲ γάρ, οὐκ ἄλλην, μαρτύρομαι, οἷα μ᾽ ὑβρίζει
>   Πυθιὰς ἡ Νικοῦς οὖσα φιλεξαπάτις.
> κληθείς, οὐκ ἄκλητος, ἐλήλυθα· ταὐτὰ παθοῦσα
>   σοὶ μέμψαιτ᾽ ἐπ᾽ ἐμοι στᾶσα παρὰ προθύροις.

Night, it is you I call upon, no other, to witness what wrongs Pythias, Niko's girl, has done me, lover of deceit that she is. I came not uninvited, but at her invitation. May she suffer the same as she stands outside my door and complains to you about me.

"Niko's girl" is surely not the bawd whose house Pythias works from (so Gow). It may be that there is an allusion to the preceding poem, in which

---

40. ᾽πιβόητος is another of those ambiguous anticipatory epithets, but there is a complication. *AP* vii. 345, by the (?) contemporary Aeschrion opens ἐγὼ Φιλαινίς ἡ ᾽πίβωτος ἀνθρώποις, "I am Philaenis whom men talk about"—in fact the notorious whore /pornographer referred to below (n. 67). Now given their shared application of the same adjective, with prodelision (very rare in epigrams), to a dubious female, one of the two poems is presumably influenced by the other. Yet Aeschrion's purpose is to *defend* Philaenis against what he describes as slander: so his ἐπίβωτος is not straightforwardly derogatory.

41. Myrrhine in Ar. *Lys.* 940 makes a similarly deceitful oath to her husband by Artemis.

42. I venture to think that Salmasius's ταὐτά and Hecker's ἐμοί improve the flat text printed by Gow-Page.

case the reader might be meant to recall the faithless Niko and reflect "like mother like daughter." To invite a lover and then bar the door would be a calculated slight, incredible (or at any rate imprudent) in a professional. There is nothing in the poem to suggest that the poet cannot pay her price or that she was already entertaining another. On this interpretation, either Pythias does not reciprocate his passion; or she is playing hard to get; or she has chosen the most public and hurtful way of letting him know that the affair is over.

But more probably (as Hugh Lloyd-Jones suggested to me) Pythias is Niko's maid, that indispensable figure in New Comedy and Latin love elegy, the go-between. There is a maid called Pythias in Terence's *Eunuchus*, as presumably in its Menandrean source.[43] A memorable section in Ovid's *Ars Amatoria* gives sound practical advice on the subject.[44] *AP* v. 213 by Posidippus (discussed below) is a poem in which the speaker addresses the maid rather than the lady he has actually come to see.[45] If that is the case here, the poem takes on an entirely different meaning. Indeed, it ceases to be a poem about sexual fidelity at all: not a faithless hetaira, nor even a woman deceiving her lover, but a maid misleading her mistress's lover from some quite different motive. The section in the *Ars Amatoria* begins by emphasizing the importance of the maid in fixing the best time for assignations (*accessus molliet illa tuos...illa leget tempus...*). It follows that she was also well placed to spoil a suitor's chances, whether because he did not tip her enough or because she was promoting someone else's prospects instead.

5

XXV and XXVI (v. 181 and 185) both present us with hosts going over their shopping lists for a party. The text of 181 is often uncertain, but the general sense of the first eight lines is clear and it will suffice for our purpose to give the Wallaces' translation, which conveys something of the detail and vividness of the original. The host, Bacchon, is discussing the prices with his slave:

> Three quarts of nuts—when will he come?—
> and five rose wreaths—what now? Be dumb!
> You've got no money, I suppose.

43. On the Greek original, J.C.B. Lowe, *CQ* 33 (1983), 428-44; Lloyd-Jones, *Acad. Papers* II (1990), 93. On the other hand, Pythias is also the name of the wife and daughter of Aristotle.
44. *AA* i. 351-98, with Hollis's commentary.
45. Here Posidippus uses Pythias for the name of the lady instead of the maid.

> O God! I'm ruined! Will none dispose
> of this great brute? A thief, it's plain
> I have, no servant. You complain
> you haven't robbed me? No, not you!
> Bring me your cash-book to go through.
> Phryne, go get it... Oh, the cheat!
> For wine, five drachmas...two for meat;
> oysters and honey, cakes and trout...
> tomorrow we'll get it straightened out.

It is the last four lines that cause problems:

> αὔριον αὐτὰ καλῶς λογιούμεθα, νῦν δὲ πρὸς Αἴσχραν
>   τὴν μυρόπωλιν ἰὼν πέντε λάβ᾽ ἀργυρέας·
> εἰπὲ δὲ σημεῖον Βάκχων ὅτι πέντ᾽ ἐφίλησεν
>   ἑξῆς, ὧν κλίνη μάρτυς ἐπεγράφετο.

Now go to the perfume-seller Aeschra and get five silver flasks. And for identification tell her that I am the Bacchon who made love to her five times in a
row: the bed is a certified witness.

First the motif of the σημεῖον. In 1970 H. C. Youtie drew attention to an
interesting usage in private letters: the writer introduces with the formula
σημεῖον a proof of his identity that could only be known to his correspondent and himself.[46] R. Merkelbach at once recognized the relevance of this
usage both to this poem and to *AP* v. 213,[47] though in my opinion his discussion did not quite hit the nail on the head.

The σημεῖον is clearly the number of times Bacchon and Aeschra had
made love, a figure known only to them—and to the bed. But what of the
ἀργυρέας which has so exercised commentators? The Wallaces saw a
reference to "five pieces of silver which are either to be paid to or borrowed from Aeschra," translating "Bacchon will pay for his kisses yet." It
will be noticed that behind any such interpretation there lurks the assumption that Aeschra trades her favours for cash. As Meineke saw, the obvious
solution is to understand ληκύθους, "silver phials." Gow thought it "most
unlikely that perfume would be bought in silver λήκυθοι and that a host
purchasing perfume for his guests would buy it in separate receptacles."
Uncommon, perhaps, but not unprecedented. A Macedonian called Hippolochus describes a symposium he attended at this very period where twin
perfume flasks (λήκυθοι) of gold and silver were twice presented to each of
twenty guests.[48] The point and climax of Asclepiades's poem is precisely
that, after all the itemizing and penny-pinching of the first eight lines, the
poet sends out a slave, who has already stated that he has no money left,

46. *ZPE* 6 (1970), 105-16.
47. *ZPE* 6 (1970), 245-46.
48. Quoted Athen. 129A-C; for the context, Tarn, *Antigonus Gonatas* (1913), 248 n.94.

for a ridiculous extravagance, an individual silver perfume flask for each guest. And the reason, of course, is that this is the only shop where he can get *credit*—because of the hold he has over the girl who works there. This is why he humorously adds, as though she might try to deny it, that there was a witness of their lovemaking—the bed (ἐπιγράφεσθαι "is technical of the endorsement of witnesses on a deposition," Gow). Aeschra is not chaste —but not a prostitute either. She is a working woman, and in a luxury trade too.[49] It is the poet who is the sponger, trying to exploit *his* favours for gain.

Before considering Asclepiades's other shopping list poem, a word on the evidently related poem *AP* v. 213 by Posidippus. Though it is Pythias he has come to see, the speaker is apparently addressing the maid, whom he asks to intercede on his behalf:

Πυθιὰς εἰ μὲν ἔχει τιν' ἀπέρχομαι· εἰ δὲ καθεύδει
    ὧδε μόνη μικρὸν πρὸς Διὸς εἰσκαλέσαι.
εἰπὲ δὲ σημεῖον, μεθύων ὅτι καὶ διὰ κλωπῶν
    ἦλθον Ἔρωτι θρασεῖ χρώμενος ἡγεμόνι.

If Pythias is with someone, I'm off. If she's sleeping alone, let me in for a moment, for God's sake. Tell her in identification that I'm the one who came drunk, through footpads, with the boldness of Love as my guide.

In the light of the σημεῖον motif, it should be clear that we must restore P's ἦλθεν (universally rejected by editors) to the text in line 4, in place of the early modern conjecture ἦλθον.[50] The poet is not speaking of his present visit, but of the earlier occasion from which he hopes that Pythias will remember him.

Gow remarks that μεθύων, drunk, is "unexpected, since that is the usual condition of comasts." That (of course) is precisely the point. The poem fits into that well-known category, the paraclausithuron. To judge by the dozens of examples studied by F. A. Copley in his useful monograph,[51] the streets of Hellenistic cities were packed with young men driven by liquor and lecherousness to brave footpads in laying siege to the doors of any presentable female, respectable or not (Pythias clearly not, to judge from the equanimity with which the poet contemplates the possibility of a rival in her bed). Posidippus's description would have fitted 75 percent of

49. P. Herfst, *Le travail de la femme dans la Grèce ancienne* (Utrecht 1922), 45, wonders whether perfume-sellers may not also have made the perfumes they sold. On the perfume trade in Alexandria, see Fraser I. 141.

50. Merkelbach's διακλωπῶν, "furtively," is based on a misunderstanding of the poem: see Tarán (next note) 88 n.100, and my interpretation given above.

51. *Exclusus Amator* (Baltimore 1956), and for a detailed analysis of the epigrams, see now Sonya Tarán, *The Art of Variation in the Hellenistic Epigram* (Leiden 1979), 52-114. On the social context, above Ch. III n. 62.

Pythias's clients. It is as though a young man today, in a similar situation, had told the maid: she'll remember me, the football fan who called once a bit drunk on a Saturday night.

Posidippus was much influenced by the work of Aslcepiades,[52] and there can be no doubt that it was from this very poem of Asclepiades that he took the σημεῖον motif. But he has adapted it more cleverly than has been appreciated. Whereas the reader of Asclepiades's poem feels that Bacchon may well get his silver perfume pots, Posidippus's young man is surely going to have Pythias's door slammed in his face.

Now to the second of Asclepiades's shopping lists, XXVI (v. 185):

Εἰς ἀγορὰν βαδίσας, Δημήτριε, τρεῖς παρ' Ἀμύντου
  γλαυκίσκους αἴτει καὶ δέκα φυκίδια
καὶ κυφὰς καρῖδας—ἀριθμῆσαί σε δεῖ αὐτόν—
  εἴκοσι καὶ τέτορας. δεῦρο λαβὼν ἄπιθι,
καὶ παρὰ Θαυβαρίου ῥοδίνους ἓξ πρόσλαβε...
  καὶ Τρυφέραν ταχέως ἐν παρόδῳ κάλεσον.

Go to the market, Demetrius, and get from Amyntas three small herrings, ten wrasses and two dozen prawns (be sure to count them yourself). Then come straight back. Pick up six rose garlands at Thaubarius's stall and, since it's on your way, invite Tryphera.

This time the slave is given very precise instructions about which shops to go to as well as how many of each item to get. But what of the last item on the list? "A hetaira to entertain the party" runs the predictable note of Gow, again reflecting the general opinion of commentators and translators.

But is Tryphera really just a cynical afterthought on a level with the garlands? Surely the point of the poem is precisely that, in Giangrande's words, "the most important ingredient, as it were, is left with apparent nonchalance to the very end."[53] But not just because no good party was complete without a hetaira. Another dimension is added to the poem if we suppose that Tryphera is not a hetaira but the poet's latest flame; that he is only throwing the party so that he can invite her. But the bashful youth does not wish to seem to be attaching too much importance to the occasion, even in the eyes of his own slave. Hence the affectation of casualness. But we should not be misled. By telling the slave exactly which shops he should go to he has made sure that Tryphera's house will indeed be "on the way."

52. See my *Greek Anthology*, Appendix VII.
53. *L'Épigramme grecque* (1968), 142.

6

XX (xii. 161):

Δόρκιον ἡ φιλέφηβος ἐπίσταται ὡς ἁπαλὸς παῖς
ἕσθαι πανδήμου Κύπριδος ὠκὺ βέλος
ἵμερον ἀστράπτουσα κατ᾿ ὄμματος, ἠδ᾿ ὑπὲρ ὤμων
σὺν πετάσῳ γυμνὸν μηρὸν ἔφαινε χλαμύς.

Dorkion, who loves ephebes, knows, like a young boy, how to launch the swift dart of Aphrodite who welcomes all, flashing desire down from her eye; with her (ephebe's) hat over her shoulder her cloak revealed a bare thigh.

This poem has caused many problems. First, it should be noticed that we have yet another ambiguous anticipatory phrase in line 1: "like a young boy." For it is not till the last line that the poet discloses that Dorkion not only behaves like a boy (nothing so outrageous or even perhaps unusual) but actually *dresses* like one. Anyone familiar with the hundreds of representations of chlamys-draped youths (less often wearing or carrying around their necks the petasos, the characteristic hat of the ephebe) on Attic vases[54] will appreciate the revelation contained in the final word of the poem. The last line and the third have been much vexed and misunderstood. The expression is abrupt, but with ἡ for P's ἠ yields perfectly acceptable sense. Gow supposed that Dorkion "wore that provocative costume in such a manner that it did not conceal her charms." Giangrande was more explicit, arguing that her chlamys was worn so high that it betrayed her sex (adding the grotesque extra suggestion that πέτασος was an obscene allusion to the vulva).[55] Yet it is clear from the vases that the chlamys was a short cloak worn across the back; the petasos too was worn across the back if not on the head. There is no conceivable way that this costume, not in the least "provocative" in itself, could have concealed either the breast or the genital area of a girl. It goes without saying that, unlike the idealized youths on the vases, Dorkion will have been wearing the customary short chiton underneath, naturally (given her imposture) the short boy's chiton. The combined reference of cloak, hat and shoulders makes it clear that it is the back rather than the front of Dorkion the poet has in mind. Now even if she had hoisted chiton as well as chlamys, this is the last viewpoint from which a slim girl was likely to betray her sex.

54. There are a number of examples in the plates of K. J. Dover's *Greek Homosexuality* (Cambridge, Mass. 1978): e.g., R 336; 373; 406; 458; 462; 494; 498.

55. *Eranos* 65 (1967) 39-41, referring for support to the venerable but no less preposterous similar interpretation of εὐρώτας in *AP* v. 60. 6, on which see my paper in *GRBS* 22 (1981), 179-183.

Especially since her object was to conceal her sex and attract lovers who would take her for a boy. This, surely, is why the poet focuses on the view from the rear: the best way she can achieve her object is by deflecting the eyes of potential admirers *away* from her front. By wearing the chlamys and the short boy's chiton with its split sides she will display an attractive amount of thigh as she walks, and Greek pederastic writings wax warm on the attractions of the thigh.[56] The scene is caught to perfection in the following lines (surely known to Asclepiades) of the tragic poet Chaeremon (incidentally perhaps explaining the imperfect ἔφαινε which has puzzled commentators in Asclepiades):[57]

ἡ δὲ ῥαγέντων χλανιδίων ὑπὸ πτύχας / ἔφαινε μηρόν.

Her robes all torn, she *showed her thigh* from beneath its folds.

Ibycus called Spartan girls φαινομηρίδας (*PMG* 339) for showing more thigh than was proper.

So the poem describes the success, not the failure[58] of Dorkion's ruse. According to W. Ludwig, the name Dorkion "war bei Hetären verbreitet."[59] Connoisseurs of Greek names such as A. Wilhelm[60] and L. Robert[61] have insisted time and again that there are no names "common to" or (if unattested) "suitable for" hetairas, and the truth in this case is that the name Dorkion (diminutive of Dorkas, "little gazelle") is found once elsewhere, in a fragment of a Roman comedy, not obviously of a hetaira. Dorkas is common, always (it seems) of respectable women.[62] Since the gazelle won his name because of his large, bright eyes, and is proverbially one of the slenderest of creatures, the diminutive Dorkion is doubly appropriate for the boyish girl with the fetching eyes of our poem. Neither her name or her come-hither looks prove Dorkion a hetaira. After all, a

---

56. Dover, *Greek Homosexuality*, p. 70. For some illustrations (mythological) of women shown in the short chiton, see M., Bieber, *Ancient Copies* (New York 1977), pl. I-III. It is presumably the short chiton that is meant when we read of women who attended Plato's lectures "wearing male clothing" (Diogenes Laertius, III. 46).

57. *TGF*[2] 786 = Athenaeus XIII, 608 BC.

58. Contrast Aristophanes, *Eccles*. 95-97 (with R. G. Ussher's commentary, p. 89), a warning to the women disguised as men not to hitch their chitons too high and betray themselves when clambering over others already seated in the assembly.

59. *L'Épigramme grecque* 328.

60. "Die sogennante Hetäreninschrift aus Paros," *Athen. Mitt.* 1899, 409-40; cf. *JOAI* 26 (1929), 59-65.

61. *L'Épigramme grecque* 340-41; cf. *Bull. Epigr.* (1970) n. 200. The name "Tryphera," for instance, borne by the alleged hetaira of poem XXVI, "n'évoque pas une orgie sardanapalesque; il est porté comme nom de reine en Cappadoce." K. Schneider's useful list of 300 hetairas in *RE* 8. 1362-71 showed a bare 10 percent with what he considered "sprechender Hetärennamen"; the rest were all borne equally by respectable women.

62. See the examples collected in K. Mras's useful article "Die Personennamen in Lucians Hetärengesprächen," *Wien. Studien* 38 (1916), 28.

hetaira depended for her livelihood on fees or presents from her clients. Dorkion could hardly have counted on gifts from her indignant ephebes when they discovered (as sooner or later they were bound to) that she was not what she seemed.

7

Next some poems not in the first person. In XIX (xii. 153) a girl laments that Archeades, whom she used to tease, now does not look at her even in play; the course of honeyed Love does not run always sweet; the god often seems sweeter to those he has hurt. Clearly a respectable girl. The statement that Archeades is not interested in her οὐδ᾽ ὅσον παίζων suggests that, while no longer sweethearts, the couple still meet socially.

Next I (v. 160):

Ἡδὺ θέρους διψῶντι χίων ποτόν, ἡδὺ δὲ ναύταις
   ἐκ χειμῶνος ἰδεῖν εἰαρινὸν Στέφανον·
ἥδιον δ᾽ ὁπόταν κρύψῃ μία τοὺς φιλέοντας
   χλαῖνα, καὶ αἰνῆται Κύπρις ὑπ᾽ ἀμφοτέρων.

Sweet is a cool drink in summer for the thirsty; sweet for sailors the (rising of the Northern) Crown after winter; but sweeter still when one blanket covers two lovers and the Cyprian is honoured by both.

This fine priamel (which inspired a famous passage in Catullus) stands in no need of comment. Its conclusion is echoed in the conclusion to XXVI (v. 209), the story of how Cleander caught sight of Niko swimming off the "Paphian shore" and was consumed by passion for her. The goddess heard his prayer and "now their love for each other is equal" (line 7, νῦν δ᾽ ἴσος ἀμφοτέροις φιλίης πόθος). Compare too the opening of the girl's lament in the *Frag. Grenfellianum*: ἐξ ἀμφοτέρων γέγονεν αἵρεσις. ἐζευγίσμεθα ("from both of us came the choice; we are yoked together"). This is a far cry from the cynical commercialism perceived by Fraser.

8

Interesting in a quite different way is VII (*AP* v. 161):

αἱ Σάμιαι Βιττὼ καὶ Νάννιον εἰς ᾿Αφροδίτης
   φοιτᾶν τοῖς αὐτῆς οὐκ ἐθέλουσι νόμοις,
εἰς δ᾽ ἕτερ᾽ αὐτομολοῦσιν ἃ μὴ καλά. δεσπότι Κύπρι,
   μίσει τὰς κοίτης τῆς παρὰ σοὶ φυγάδας.

Here is the recent translation by Peter Bing and Rip Cohen:[63]

> Bitto and Nannion, the Samian girls, don't like
> to rendezvous with Aphrodite by her rules.
> They stray to other, unlovely things. Kypris, queen,
> hate those renegadès from your bed.

According to Dover, "this hostility on the part of a poet who elsewhere declares the strength of his own homosexual desire, is striking; that he treats a woman who rejects male lovers as a "deserter" and "fugitive" and as disobedient to the rules of Aphrodite suggests the possibility that the complete silence of comedy on the subject of female homosexuality is a reflex of male anxiety."[64] This seems rather a sweeping conclusion to draw from one text and a silence—the more so since Asclepiades does not in fact "declare...homosexual desire." Only one of his many erotic poems is certainly addressed to a boy lover (note 3), nor is there any obvious reason why a pederastic urge should have any bearing on a Greek male's attitude to lesbians.[65]

It may be that, like many men today, Asclepiades felt threatened by the thought of female homosexuality. But given his fondness for those apparently casual anticipatory epithets in the first line, it is tempting to look more closely at Σάμιαι. Gow and Page cite Plutarch *Greek Questions* 54 (*Mor.* 303C) "for the reputation of Samian women," but all Plutarch actually reports is a speculation that a puzzling Samian cult title of Aphrodite might reflect a *former* reputation for licentiousness dispelled by a sorcerer. More relevant is a fragment from Diphilus's *Theseus* (F 50) in which three Samian women celebrate the Adonia with sexy riddles. A fragment from another play (F 42. 39-40) has hetairas celebrate the Adonia, and the Geneva fragment of Menander's *Samia* has revealed another Samian hetaira (*Sam.* 21, 35-6). But that does not make Diphilus's three Samian women hetairas (as Detienne assumed). Athenaeus's summary describes them simply as "girls" (κόραι), and the *Samia* and *Lysistrata* (387-98) prove that, however licentious their behaviour, respectable women might also celebrate the Adonia.[66]

Nothing suggests that Asclepiades's two Samians were hetairas, nor would that explain their lesbianism in any case. The obvious factor here is surely that Asclepiades was a Samian himself. Since he would hardly have troubled to style them Samians on Samos, all three were presumably else-

63. *Games of Venus* (New York 1991), 132.

64. *Greek Homosexuality* (1978), 172-73.

65. The modern association of gay and lesbian is based on an ideology of oppression—and not always welcomed by lesbians.

66. M. Detienne, *The Gardens of Adonis* (1977), 64-66, 79-80, 99, with J. J. Winkler, *The Constraints of Desire* (New York 1990), 188-209; Cameron, *ZPE* 1996, forthcoming.

where. Perhaps the ethnic is meant to suggest the possibility of some connection between the Samian girls and their famous fellow countryman. The point might be that, when they appeared to be more interested in their own company than his, he was offended and took refuge in the age-old face-saving male assumption that they "must be lesbians." This would give added point to his venom. The obvious parallel is the poem in which Anacreon accuses a woman from Lesbos who spurns his advances of "gaping after" another woman. The neatest interpretation of this much discussed piece is (with Mace) to see it as a face-saving slur.[67]

9

Now for the exceptions that prove the rule. First VIII (v. 162):

Ἡ λαμυρή μ' ἔτρωσε Φιλαίνιον, εἰ δὲ τὸ τραῦμα
    μὴ σαφές, ἀλλ' ὁ πόνος δύεται εἰς ὄνυχα.
οἴχομ', Ἔρωτες, ὄλωλα, διοίχομαι, εἰς γὰρ ἑταίραν
    νυστάζων ἐπέβην, οἶδ', ἔθιγον τ' ἀίδαι.

Cruel Philaenion has bitten me. Though the bite does not show, the pain reaches to my fingertips. I am gone, Loves, finished, past hope. For half-asleep I trod on a whore, I know it, and her touch was death.

Here the girl bears a name formed from that of a particularly notorious hetaira, Philaenis, author of the first extant sex manual.[68] She is described as λαμυρή, which has been defined as "wantonly and insatiably gluttonous," whether for food or sex.[69] In this case both name and epithet prepare the educated reader for the worst. A fascinating paper by E. K. Borthwick has illustrated the comparison between the harlot and the viper that runs right through the poem:[70] the invisible but poisonous bite (1-2) got by treading inadvertently (4). P. Waltz, however, thought that still greater explicitness was desirable and conjectured ἔχιδναν, "viper," for ἑταίραν at the end of line 3, and he has been generally followed, notably by Gow and Page. Their argument is revealing: "a stylist does not say 'I have inadvertently encountered a harlot' when the harlot in question is the

---

67. F 13; Sarah T. Mace, "Amour encore!" *GRBS* 34 (1993) [1995], at 347-49.

68. P. Oxy. 2891. It seems to have been traditional to ascribe erotic manuals to female authors (M. L. West, *ZPE* 25 [1977], 118), and Philaenis's morals were defended by Aeschrion (Gow-Page II. 4-5). See K. Tsantsanoglou, *ZPE* 12 (1973), 183-195; D. W. Vessey, *Rev. Belg. Phil.* 54 (1976), 78-83.

69. By imperial times the word came to mean "charming," and according to Arnott (*Mus. Phil. Lond.* 7 [1986], 1-3), it bears this neutral meaning here, another of those ambiguous anticipatory phrases. But this seems unlikely, especially in view of the proper name, nor does his emendation at the end of the poem convince.

70. *CR* 17 (1967), 250-54.

subject of his epigram." So too Arnott: "Of course Philaenium was a hetaira."[71] That is to say, taking it for granted that all Asclepiades's girlfriends were hetairas, they found "hetaira" a very lame climax after three lines of preparation. Yet this is to pay too little attention to the metaphor in νυστάζων, literally "dozing." Just as someone walking in a field without due caution might tread on a snake, so the poet blundered into this unfortunate relationship unawares. Philaenion did not just turn out to be more mercenary or promiscuous than he had counted on; he was naive enough not to have realized that she was a hetaira at all. That is to say, he did not merely fail to recognize her for the viper she was; he failed to recognize that she was a *professional*. That recognition was indeed a climax.

Ovid *Amores* i. 10 makes a suggestive comparison. The poet describes how all his romantic ideals (skilfully built up by a series of mythical exempla) collapsed the moment his girl started asking for presents. Here the interesting point is his complaint that, unlike the common prostitute, she does not need the money in order to live. By analogy we might guess that Philaenion was not perhaps a regular professional (who would surely have asked for her money in advance) but a schemer who similarly won the poet's love before asking for presents. Hence his bitterness when he realizes the truth. Compare too the long fragment from Anaxilas's comedy *Neottis*, "The Chick":[72]

> ὅστις ἀνθρώπων ἑταίραν ἠγάπησε πώποτε,
> οὗτος οὐ γένος δύναιτ᾽ ἂν παρανομώτερον φράσαι.
> τίς γὰρ ἢ δράκαιν᾽ ἄμικτος ἢ χίμαιρα πυρπνόος
> ἢ χάρυβδις ἤ...λέαιν᾽, ἔχιδνα...

Anyone who has ever been in love with a hetaira would be unable to name a more lawless creature. For what savage dragon, what fire-breathing Chimaira, or Charybdis...lioness, viper...

Here as well (cf. too line 29, οἱ δ᾽ ἐρᾶσθαι προσδοκῶντες εὐθὺς εἰσιν ἠρμένοι) the emphasis falls on the folly of falling in love with one who only pretends to love for gain.

Then there is XLI (vii. 217):

> Ἀρχεάνασσαν ἔχω τὰν ἐκ Κολοφῶνος ἑταίραν,
>   ἇς καὶ ἐπὶ ῥυτίδων ὁ γλυκὺς ἕζετ᾽ Ἔρως.
> ἇς νέον ἥβης ἄνθος ἀποδρέψαντες ἐρασταὶ
>   πρωτόβολοι, δι᾽ ὅσης ἤλθετε πυρκαϊῆς.

Archeanassa have I, the hetaira of Colophon on whose very wrinkles sweet Love still sits. You lovers who plucked the fresh flower of her youth, you who were first struck, through what a furnace you passed!

---

71. *Mus. Phil. Lond.* 7 (1986), 3.
72. F 22, *CAF* ii. 270 = *PCG* II. 288-90 (Athen. 558A).

It is strange that Fraser should have revived[73] (after the refutations of Ludwig and Gow) the old view that this is an erotic poem commemorating a night Asclepiades spent with the elderly Archeanassa. There can be no doubt (as all the ancient anthologists thought) that this is an *epitaph*, and that the speaker (as so often) is the tomb. All that concerns us here is the way Asclepiades describes her bluntly as a hetaira and emphasizes the large number of lovers she has had.[74]

By Asclepiades's day there was beginning to develop the literature on hetairas to which reference has already been made. As may easily be seen from the liberal excerpts from it preserved in Athenaeus xiii, it focussed not on their intellectual accomplishments but on the number and variety of their lovers, their prices (a subject on which we are singularly well informed),[75] their witticisms (invariably obscene double entendres) and the sexual positions in which they specialized. Asclepiades VI (v. 203) is an early example of this genre:

Λυσιδίκη σοί, Κύπρι, τὸν ἱππαστῆρα μύωπα
χρύσεον εὐκνήμου κέντρον ἔθηκε ποδός,
ᾧ πολὺν ὕπτιον ἵππον ἐγύμνασεν, οὐδέ ποτ᾽ αὐτῆς
μηρὸς ἐφοινίχθη κοῦφα τινασσομένης.
ἦν γὰρ ἀκέντητος τελεοδρόμος, οὕνεκεν ὅπλον
σοὶ κατὰ μεσσοπύλης χρύσεον ἐκρέμασεν.

It is to you, Cypris, that Lysidice has dedicated the golden spur of her shapely foot, with which she has exercised many a stallion on his back while her own thigh was never reddened, so lightly did she bounce; for she would finish the course without applying the spur. So she hung this her weapon of gold on your central gate.

Evidently Lysidice is a κελητίζουσα, an "equestrienne";[76] that is to say she specializes in the superior position during intercourse.[77] But Gow (following Knauer and followed by Fraser)[78] found the poem "puzzling in detail,"

---

73. II. 805. I follow Ludwig *GRBS* 4 (1963), 63 n.9-10, in reading πρωτόβολοι (with the first hand in P and Plaudes) and ἇς (first hand in P).

74. An adapted and more erotic version was later ascribed to Plato to blacken his name: cf. Ludwig, *GRBS* 4 (1963), 63-68; McKay, *Hermes* (1974), 369-71.

75. Schneider, *RE* 8. 1344; Gow, *Machon* 120; A. W. Gomme and F. H. Sandbach, *Menander: A Commentary* (Oxford 1973), 298, 430, 587.

76. The nineteenth-century euphemism "horsewoman" or "horsebreaker," though in origin an "innocent" continuation of the word "whore," also alludes to the fact that the most celebrated made sure that they were expert riders of real horses as well: "The rigid Victorian mind could not accept that women demonstrating so aristocratic a talent could be anything but half acceptable" (Michael Harrison, *Fanfare of Strumpets*, p. 13).

77. For a number of texts, J. Henderson, *The Maculate Muse* (New Haven 1975), 164.

78. *HE* II. 120-21; Fraser, II. 805 n. 98; O. Knauer, *Die Epigramme des Asclepiades* (Würzburg 1935), 25.

arguing that in the last couplet "the rider is the man and the spur seems to have been transferred to him."

In a regular dedication (as can be seen from the many examples in *AP* vi, not to mention innumerable inscriptions) the dedicator presents to the deity some object for which he or she has no further use: married women their cut hair or discarded toys, retired warriors their weapons or craftsmen their tools.[79] Asclepiades's poem is a wicked parody of such dedications. It is beside the point to inquire whether there was "a real spur" (Knauer). Few dedications consisted of the actual discarded tools. Normally they were models or representations in wood, clay or bronze, occasionally in silver or (as here) gold, evidently from the most successful and grateful dedicators.[80] Knauer mistakenly thought the χρύσεον proof of mere literary fantasy rather than a clever circumstantial touch suggesting a woman at the top of her profession.

Like Knauer, Gow took ἀκέντητος to mean "not needing the spur," like the racehorse in Pindar, *O.* 1. 32, requiring Lysidice as horse rather than rider. But it can also mean "not using the spur." Many examples of similar variation between active and passive in adjectives of this form could be cited: e.g. ἀνόνητος, both "unprofitable" and "taking no profit from"; ἀδέητος, "not wanting" and "inexorable."[81] As for μηρὸς ἐφοινίχθη, not "her thighs did not bleed," i.e. from the blows of the spur; rather she rides her mount so lightly that her thighs do not chafe from the friction. Lysidice remains the rider throughout.[82]

---

79. W.H.D. Rouse, *Greek Votive Offerings* (Cambridge 1902), 70f., 113f., 242f., 268f.

80. Many gold objects are recorded in the long list of dedications from the temple of Apollo on Delos in the early II s. B.C. (Th. Homolle, *BCH* vi [1882], 111, 127-8); cf. Philos., *V. Apoll.* ii. 8; F.T. van Straten, in *Faith, Hope and Worship* ed. H.J. Versnel (Leiden 1981), 80; Rouse 1902, 78, 343-5.

81. The list could easily be extended by selection from the list of -ητος adjectives in C. D. Buck and W. Peterson, *Reverse Index of Greek Nouns and Adjectives* (Chicago 1949), 480-490. According to Fraser, τελεοδρόμος too implies that Lysidice "has become the ἵππος." But compare Dioscorides's imitation, where it is the girl who ἤνυσεν...τὸν Κύπριδος δόλιχον, "completed the race of Love" (*AP* v. 55. 4). Note δόλιχος, the long distance race, where στάδιον, "sprint," would have fitted the metre just as well, suggesting that she skilfully prolonged the session. Gow (ad. loc.) has a meticulous note on the different lengths of race but fails to see the point.

82. In Dioscorides's imitation (v. 55), a wonderfully sensuous piece of erotic writing, the couple do change positions, but there the poet makes the point explicitly. The lover begins by stretching Doris out on the bed (ὑπὲρ λεχέων διατείνας, l. 1) and then she straddles him (μέσον διαβᾶσα, l. 3). Gow found "difficulties" here (II. 239; see now O. J. Schrier, "Love with Doris," *Mnemosyne* 32 [1979], 307-26; B. Baldwin, ib. 33 [1980], 357-9; Amy Richlin, *The Garden of Priapus* [Yale 1983], 50, 235). But who would pay good money to a courtesan so gauche as to stay in one position all the time? πορφύρεα in l. 6 are (of course) the girl's breasts (Gow, 240; Fraser, I. 597, translates "limbs"). Did hetairas perhaps rouge their nipples?

Asclepiades skilfully misleads us in more than one way. At first, the spur leads us to expect a real horsewoman, with the spur (as usual) a symbol of her skill. As we read on we discover that she is a different sort of horsewoman, so skilful (and here metaphor merges with reality) that she does not need a spur; it is being discarded as superfluous, not retired after honourable service! On rereading, we realize we should have guessed from the start; a real horse(wo)man would dedicate to Poseidon (e.g. *AP* vi. 233 and 246) rather than Aphrodite. It is precisely the fact that the poem is a perversion of a conventional dedication that eliminates the possibility that Lysidice might just be a gifted amateur. For it is *professional* tools that are dedicated.

10

So it is an oversimplification to say that Asclepiades describes "the antics, professional and otherwise, of the hetaerae."[83] When he does write of hetairas he is content to focus on their traditional characteristics: rapacity, promiscuity, and sexual proficiency. But for the most part he is doing something more interesting: he is presenting us with a gallery of portraits of female *types*: the maiden who loves from afar; the reluctant virgin; the tease; the soft touch; the girl who can't say no; the mischievous maid; the transvestite with a taste for teenagers.

Just because they describe types, the relationship of the poems to life is problematic. A new papyrus or inscription may one day cast new light on the identification of Clodia or Cynthia. But we cannot even in principle hope for new evidence in the case of (say) Nikarete or Dorkion. Whatever they owe to real women of Asclepiades's acquaintance, as described they are creations of his imagination. All we can ask is how contemporaries would have interpreted the poems. And here we may compare a poem by another writer of the age, the first mimiamb of Herodas.

The bawd (or perhaps just matchmaker) Gyllis tries to persuade a young woman called Metriche to be nice to a certain Gryllos who is desperately in love with her, on the grounds that Metriche's man Mandris has been away from Alexandria for five months and has probably forgotten all about her. Most commentators have assumed that Metriche is the wife of Mandris, but Cunningham suggests that she is a hetaira.[84] It is true that in real life hetairas may have lived for long periods with one man—though hardly for five months without pay. But Metriche is indignant at Gyllis's proposition, cutting her off abruptly when she raises it again. Now an attractive girl

83. Fraser, I. 564.
84. *Herodas: Mimiambi* (Oxford 1973), 57.

who, in the face of strong temptation (Gryllos is wealthy and a double Olympic champion), is unswervingly loyal to a man who has been away overseas for five months does *not* fit the stereotype of the hetaira. On the contrary, she is being represented as the stereotype of the faithful wife. For example, it was at a festival, like some closeted New Comedy heroine, that she unwittingly inspired Gryllos's passion. We should also note that Gryllos did not just knock on her door wallet in hand; he approaches her discreetly through an intermediary. In so far as it matters for his appreciation of the poem, the contemporary reader was surely more likely to take her for Mandris's wife.[85]

Very few of the women described by Asclepiades fit the stereotype of the hetaira, an impression only heightened by his own occasional vivid use of this very stereotype. By contrast, the love epigrams of Callimachus, which are exclusively homosexual, lament with feeling the tricks of mercenary boys.[86] Even Fraser was struck by the fact that the theme of buying—or failing to buy—love was much more prominent in Callimachus than Asclepiades.[87] This is the more striking in that Callimachus was in some ways so clearly influenced by Asclepiades, who seems virtually to have invented the erotic epigram as we know it. Not only does this difference between their love poems surely reflect a real difference between the two men. More interesting still, we see a reversal of the old Athenian attitudes: homosexual love has become more mercenary, heterosexual love less so.

With nothing in most of Asclepiades's poems to suggest the financial transactions assumed by modern commentators, why should ancient readers have assumed them? The truth is (as their tone reveals) that the commentators are often applying their own standards of respectability as much as the standards of fifth-century Athens. Any woman who sleeps with or merely associates unchaperoned with a man to whom she is not married automatically excludes herself from the ranks of the respectable. Whether or not she actually charges hardly matters—especially if she is from the lower classes, "women who sell bread and willing prostitutes" in the revealing phrase of Anacreon.[88] Yet obviously it makes a profound difference to the attitudes of both parties if it is a commercial arrangement rather than a love affair in which they are engaged. Prostitution may pro-

---

85. In the real world she might also be considered a concubine (see Fantham, *Phoenix* 29 [1975], 64f.), but that would be to introduce an unnecessary complication here. All the poet needs is for her to be loyal and refuse so that Gyllis may continue her monologue.

86. Fraser, I. 790-92.

87. I. 791.

88. F 43, *PMG* 388. Beth Cohen, Sarah Pomeroy and Sonya Tarán commented on the original version, and this one has benefited from a forthcoming study of Hellenistic epigram by Kathryn Gutzwiller.

vide a temporary sexual outlet, but only in the most unusual circumstances can it provide a basis for love.

It is in the nature of things that young men in search of love rather than marriage are not going to find it among the truly respectable. But there have been few times and places where the only alternative was the whore, and Ptolemaic Alexandria, with its growing, fluid and often transitory population was surely not one. If perfume sellers and even neglected wives like Metriche are not allowed to have love affairs without being called hetairas, then the word has ceased to have a precise enough meaning to be useful. Some people prefer the old-fashioned term "demi-monde"; but though less straightforwardly mercenary in its connotations, it nonetheless reflects the moralizing viewpoint of a respectable "haut-monde." The real strength and interest of Asclepiades's love poems is that he reaches beyond these polarities and stereotypes and draws his memorable because recognizable characters from life.

BIBLIOGRAPHY

There seems little point in duplicating Luigi Lehnus's comprehensive *Bibliografia Callimachea 1489-1988* (Genova 1989), soon to appear in a revised and expanded second edition. There is also a useful bibliography in G. Weber, *Dichtung und höfische Gesellschaft* (Stuttgart 1993). What follows are a few recent, important or characteristic items together with a selection of works relating to the wider themes of this book. When citing a number of different works by the same scholar I sometimes use a short title (e.g. West, *Greek Metre*; my own *Greek Anthology*) rather than the year of publication. On the other hand, after citing in full a work not included in the bibliography, I often cite it again over the next page or two by name and year (e.g. Rosenmeyer 1992 on p. 456).

Bing, Peter *The Well-Read Muse: Present and Past in Callimachus and the Hellenistic Poets* (Hypomnemata 90), Göttingen 1988.

Bowie, E.L. "Early Greek Elegy, Symposium and Public Festival," *JHS* 106 (1986), 13-35.

Bulloch, A.W. *Callimachus: the Fifth Hymn* (Cambridge 1985).

———. "Hellenistic Poetry," *Cambridge History of Classical Literature* I (Cambridge 1985), 541-621.

———, E. S. Gruen, A.A. Long and A. F. Stewart (edd.) *Images and Ideologies: Self-definition in the Hellenistic World* (Berkeley 1994). [Bulloch 1993]

Cahen, Émile *Callimaque et son oeuvre poétique* (Paris 1929).

Cairns, Francis *Generic Composition in Greek and Latin Poetry* (Edinburgh 1972).

———. "Propertius and the Battle of Actium (4. 6)," *Poetry and Politics in the Age of Augustus*, edd. David West and Tony Woodman (Cambridge 1984), 129-169.

———. "Theocritus, *Idyll* 26," *Proceedings of the Cambridge Philological Society* 38 (1992), 2-38.

Cameron, Alan "Wandering Poets: a Literary Movement in Byzantine Egypt," *Historia* 14 (1965), 470-509.

———. *Claudian: Poetry and Propaganda at the Court of Honorius* (Oxford 1970).

———. "*Pap. Ant.* iii.115 and the Iambic Prologue in Late Greek Poetry," *Classical Quarterly* 20 (1970), 119-29.

———. "The Empress and the Poet: Paganism and Politics at the Court of Theodosius II," *Yale Classical Studies* 27 (1982), 217-89.

———. "Two Mistresses of Ptolemy Philadelphus," *GRBS* 31 (1990), 287-311.

———. "Genre and Style in Callimachus," *TAPA* 122 (1992), 305-12.

———. "Callimachus and his Critics," *Apodosis: Essays presented to Dr W.W. Cruickshank to mark his eightieth birthday* (London 1992), 1-9.

————. *The Greek Anthology: from Meleager to Planudes* (Oxford 1993).

————. "Ancient Anagrams," *AJP* 116 (1995).

————. "Callimachus, Delian Apollo and the Cabeiroi," to appear in *ZPE* 1996.

————. "Two New Poems of Posidippus," to appear in *ZPE* 1996.

Clausen, W. "Callimachus and Latin Poetry," *GRBS* 5 (1964), 181-196.

Clayman, Dee L. *Callimachus' Iambi* (Mnemosyne Suppl. 59), Leiden 1980.

————. "Callimachus' *Iambi* and *Aetia*," *ZPE* 74 (1988), 277-86.

Couat, Auguste *La Poésie alexandrine* (Paris 1882) = *Alexandrian Poetry under the first three Ptolemies*, with a supplementary chapter by E. Cahen, translated by James Loeb (London 1931).

Dawson, C. M. "The *Iambi* of Callimachus: a Hellenistic poet's experimental laboratory," *Yale Classical Studies* 11 (1950), 1-168.

Depew, Mary "Mimesis and Aetiology in Callimachus' Hymns" in Harder 1993, 57-77.

Dilthey, Carolus (Karl) *De Callimachi Cydippa* (Leipzig 1863).

Dover, K.J. *Theocritus: Select Poems* (London 1971)

Ebert, Joachim *Griechische Epigramme auf Sieger an gymnischen und hippischen Agonen* (Abhandl. d. sächs. Akad. Leipzig 63. 2, Berlin 1972).

Eichgrün, Egon *Kallimachos und Apollonios Rhodios* (Diss. Berlin 1961).

Fantuzzi, Marco "Il sistema letterario della poesia Alessandrina nel III sec. A.C.," *Lo spazio letterario della Grecia antica: I: la produzione e la circolazione del testo: II: l'Ellenismo* edd. G. Cambiano, L. Canfora, D. Lanza (Roma 1993), 31-73.

————. "Teocrito e la poesia bucolica," *ib.* 145-195.

Fraser, P.M. *Ptolemaic Alexandria* I-II (Oxford 1972).

Fuhrer, Therese "A Pindaric feature in the Poetry of Callimachus," *AJP* 109 (1988), 53-68.

————. *Die Auseinandersetzung mit den Chorlyrikern in den Epinikien des Kallimachos* (Schweizerische Beiträge zur Altertumswissenschaft 23, Basel 1992).

————. "Callimachus's Epinician Poems," in Harder 1993, 79-97.

Gallavotti, C. "Il libro dei Giambi di Callimaco," *Antiquitas* i (1946), 11-22.

Giangrande, G. "Sympotic Literature and Epigram," *L'Épigramme grecque* (Fondation Hardt: Entretiens sur l'antiquité classique 14) Geneva 1968, 93-177.

————. "Callimachus, Poetry and Love," *Eranos* 67 (1975), 33-42.

Goldhill, Simon *The Poet's Voice: Essays on Poetics and Greek Literature* (Cambridge 1991).

Griffiths, Frederick T. *Theocritus at Court* (Mnemosyne Suppl. 55), Leiden 1979.

Gutzwiller, Kathryn J. *Studies in the Hellenistic Epyllion* (Beiträge zur Klassischen Philologie 114) Königstein 1981.

————. "Callimachus's Lock of Berenice," *AJP* 113 (1992), 359-385.

Halperin, David *Before Pastoral: Theocritus and the Ancient Tradition of Bucolic Poetry* (New Haven 1983).

Harder, M.A., Regtuit, R.F., Wakker G.C. *Callimachus* (Hellenistica Groningana 1) Groningen 1993. [Harder 1993]

————. "Untrodden Paths: Where do they lead?" *HSCP* 93 (1990), 287-309.

————. "Aspects of the Structure of Callimachus' *Aetia*," in Harder 1993, 99-110.

Hardie, Alex *Statius and the Silvae: Poets, Patrons and Epideixis in the Graeco-Roman World* (Liverpool 1983).

Heath, Malcolm *Unity in Greek Poetics* (Oxford 1989).

Heitsch, E. *Griechischen Dichterfragmente der römischen Kaiserzeit* i² (1963) and ii (1964).

Herter, Hans "Kallimachos aus Kyrene," *RE Suppl.* 5 (1931), 184-226.

————. "Litteratur zur hellenistischen Dichtung…1921 bis 1935," *Bursians Jahresbericht* 255 (1937), 82-218 and 285 (1944/1955), 213-410.

————. "Kallimachos aus Kyrene," *RE Suppl.* 13 (1973 (184-226.

Hollis, A. S. *Callimachus: Hecale* (Oxford 1990).

Hopkinson, Neil *Callimachus: Hymn to Demeter* (Cambridge 1984)

————. *A Hellenistic Anthology* (Cambridge 1988)

Hunter, R. L. *Apollonius of Rhodes: Argonautica Book III* (Cambridge 1989).

————. *The Argonautica of Apollonius: Literary Studies* (Cambridge 1993).

Hutchinson, G. O. *Hellenistic Poetry* (Oxford 1988).

Kambylis, Athanasios *Die Dichterweihe und ihre Symbolik: Untersuchungen zu Hesiodos, Kallimachos, Properz und Ennius* (Heidelberg 1965).

Koenen, Ludwig "The Ptolemaic King as a Religious Figure," in Bulloch 1993, 25-115.

Köhnken, Adolf *Apollonios Rhodios und Theokrit* (Hypomnemata 12), Göttingen 1965.

————. "Apollo's Retort to Envy's Criticism," *AJP* 102 (1981), 411-422.

Knox, Peter E. "The Epilogue to the *Aetia*," *GRBS* 26 (1985), 59-65.

————. "The Epilogue to the *Aetia*: An Epilogue," *ZPE* 96 (1993), 175-8.

————. "Philetas and Roman Poetry," *PLILS* 7 (1993), 61-83.

Koster, Severin *Antike Epostheorien* (Palingenesia 5), Wiesbaden 1970.

Laronde, A. *Libykai Historiai: Recherches sur l'histoire de Cyrène* (Paris 1987).

Lefkowitz, Mary *The Lives of the Greek Poets* (London 1981).

Legrand, Ph.-E. "Problèmes alexandrins. I: Pourquoi furent composés les *Hymnes* de Callimaque?" *RÉA* 3 (1901), 281-312.

Lehnus, L. "Callimaco tra la polis e il regno," *Lo spazio letterario* I. 2 (Rome 1993), 75-105.

Livrea, E. "P. Oxy. 2463: Lycophron and Callimachus," *CQ* 39 (1989), 141-147.

————. KPECCONA BACKANIHC: *Quindici studi di poesia ellenistica* (Florence 1993).

Lloyd-Jones, Hugh "The Seal of Posidippus," *JHS* 83 (1963), 75-99.

————. "A Hellenistic Miscellany," *SIFC* 3 ser. 2 (1984), 52-71.

Maas, P. "Διηγήσεις di poemi di Callimaco: Exkurs I-III," *Papiri della R. Università di Milano* I (Milan 1937), 155-171.

Marcotte, Didier and Paul Mertens "Les papyrus de Callimaque," in *Miscellanea papyrologica in occasione del bicentenario dell'edizione della Charta Borgiana*, ed. M. Capasso, G.M. Savorelli, R. Pintaudi (Florence 1990), 409-427.

Mastronarde, Donald J. "Theocritus' Idyll 13: Love and the Hero," *TAPA* 99 (1968), 273-90.

Meillier, C. *Callimaque et son Temps* (Lille 1979).

Mejer, J. *Diogenes Laertius and his Hellenistic Background* (Hermes Einzelschriften 40), Wiesbaden 1978.

Otis, Brooks *Virgil: A Study in Civilized Poetry* (Oxford 1964).

Parsons, P.J. "Callimachus: Victoria Berenices," *ZPE* 25 (1977), 1-50.

Peremans, W. and Van 't Dack, E. *Prosopographia Ptolemaica VI: La Cour, Les relations internationales et les possessions extérieures, la vie culturelle* (Studia Hellenistica 17, Louvain 1968).

Pfeiffer, Rudolf "Ein neues Altersgedicht des Kallimachos," *Hermes* 63 (1928), 302-341.

――――. *A History of Classical Scholarship* (Oxford 1968).

Reitzenstein, Erich "Zur Stiltheorie des Kallimachos," *Festschrift R. Reitzenstein* (Lepizig/Berlin 1931), 23-69.

Reitzenstein, Richard *Epigramm und Skolion: ein Beitrag zur Geschichte der Alexandrinischen Dichtung* (Giessen 1893).

Rossi, L.E. "I generi letterari e le loro leggi scritte e non scritte nelle letterature classiche," *BICS* 18 (1971), 69-94.

Susemihl, Franz *Geschichte der griechischen Litteratur in der Alexandrinerzeit* I-II (Leipzig 1891-2).

Thomas, R.F. "New Comedy, Callimachus and Roman Poetry," *HSCP* 83 (1979), 179-206.

Torraca, L. *Il prologo dei Telchini e l'inizio degli Aitia di Callimaco* (Naples 1969; 1973²).

Viljamaa, T. *Studies in Greek Encomiastic Poetry of the Early Byzantine Period* (Helsinki 1968).

Watson, Lindsay *Arae: The Curse Poetry of Antiquity* (Leeds 1991).

Weber, Gregor *Dichtung und Höfische Gesellschaft: die Rezeption von Zeitgeschichte am Hof der ersten drei Ptolemäer* (Hermes Einzelschrift 62), Stuttgart 1993.

Wendel, C. *Die Überlieferung der Scholien zu Apollonios von Rhodos* (Abh. Göttingen 1932).

West, Martin L. *Studies in Greek Elegy and Iambus* (Berlin 1974).

――――. *Greek Metre* (Oxford 1982).

――――. *Ancient Greek Music* (Oxford 1992).

White, Peter *Promised Verse: Poets in the Society of Augustan Rome* (Cambridge Mass. 1993).

Wilamowitz-Moellendorff, U. von *Antigonos von Karystos* (Berlin 1881).

――――. *Hellenistische Dichtung in der Zeit des Kallimachos* (Berlin 1924).[HD]

Will, Édouard *Histoire politique du Monde Hellénistique* I² (Nancy 1979).

Wyss, Bernhardus *Antimachi Colophonii Reliquiae* (Berlin 1936).

Zanker, Graham *Realism in Alexandrian Poetry: A Literature and its Audience* (London 1987).

Zetzel, J.E.G. "Recreating the Canon: Augustan Poetry and the Alexandrian Past," *Critical Inquiry* 10 (1983), 83-105.

Ziegler, Konrat *Das hellenistische Epos: ein vergessenes Kapitel griechischer Dichtung*² (Leipzig 1966); = *L'epos ellenistico* trans. F. De Martino with an introduction by M. Fantuzzi (Bari 1988).

INDEX

Abuse, ritual at symposium, 97-8, 243.
Acontius and Cydippe, 19-22, 255-61, 351-52.
acrostichs, 37-8, 322, 324-25.
Adonis, 30, 55-6; festivals of, 512.
adultery, punishment for, 101-02.
Aeschylus, elegies, 313; style of, 329-31; *Life* of, 331.
Aeschylus of Alexandria, 301.
Aetia, difference in structure between I-II and III-IV, 107-8.
aetiological poetry, 42-4.
Agamestor of Pharsalus, 152.
Aganippe, 371.
Agatharchides of Cnidos, 123.
Agathon, 196.
Agias and Dercylus, 224.
Agis of Argos, 270.
Agrionia, 59.
Ainos, in Thrace, 212.
ἀκούειν = read, 46.
Alcaeus of Messene, 100-02, 291, 364.
Alcibiades, 147, 149, 305.
Alcman, 181.
Alexander Aetolus, 25, 52, 62, 171, 189, 316, 381-5.
Alexander the Great, 17, 73.
Alexander poets, 278-79, 289.
Alexandrian library, 4, 215-19.
Alexandrianism, 25; Roman, 28.
ambassadors, of Hellenistic kings, 11.
Ammianus Marcellinus, 466.
Amphicles of Delos, 47-48.
Amphiclos of Chios, 47, 66.
Amycus, versions of story, 430.
Anacreon, 85.
Anacreontea, 456-57.
ἀναγιγνώσκειν = read aloud, 46.
Anaxarchus, 74.
Anaximenes of Lampsacus, 51, 278.
Androkles, son of Callimachus, 7.
Annikeris, 8.
Antagoras of Rhodes, 17, 51, 189, 223, 296-97.
Antigonus of Alexandria, 192.
Antigonus of Carystus, 81, 89, 189-90, 208.
Antigonus Gonatas, king, 11, 25, 73, 189, 281.
Antigonus the One-eyed, 14, 16.
Antilochus, poet, 278.
Antimachus of Colophon, 48, 83, 87-8,

232, 265, 270, 395, Ch. XI passim; and catalogue poetry, 381-82; and Homer, 334-36, 349-50; Thebaid, 395; and women, 348 n. 40; editor and critic, 312.
Antiochus, I and III, kings, 285.
Antipater of Sidon, 290, 332-34.
Antipater of Thessalonica, 366, 462.
antiquarianism, 42.
Antoninus Liberalis, 43, 124.
Antonius, Iullus, 225, 468.
Antyllus, medical writer, 44.
Anyte, poetess, 77.
Apollo, oracles of, 12; and Muses, 169.
Apollodorus, 397-98.
Apollonius of Alabanda, 214-5.
Apollonius of Perga, 114-15.
Apollonius of Rhodes, 26, 43, 51, 172; *Lives* of, 194, 213, 214-19; and papyri, 218; and Ibis, 225-8; alleged lampoon on Callimachus, 227-8; not named in Schol. Flor., 231; links with Callimachus, 247-57; links with Theocritus, 253, 426-30.
Apollonius, son of Sotades, 188.
Aratus of Sicyon, 99, 291.
Aratus of Soloi, 6-7, 25, 28, 69, 77, 82; life and *Lives* of, 189-214, 269, 380; and λεπτότης, 321-28; and acrostichs, 324-25; date of, 327; epigram on, 374-79; and Homer, 375, 380; metrical practice, 376.
Arcesilas of Pitane, 201.
archaic epigram, 7.
Archelaus of Macedon, 196, 245.
Archelaus of Priene, 273-77.
Archestratus of Gela, 269.
Archias, 48, 180, 288-89, 364, 462.
Archimedes, 18.
Archimelus, 290.
Argentarius, 92.
Argonauts, 349.
Aristarchus, 96, 395-6.
Aristeas, Letter of, 5, 81.
Aristodama of Smyrna, 47.
Aristomenes, 347-48.
Ariston of Phocaea, 48.
Aristonoos, 47.
Aristophanes, 39, 61, 87, 329-31, 372, 378, 444, 488-90, 499.
Aristophanes of Byzantium, 50, 111, 122.
Aristotheus of Troizen, 49.

INDEX LOCORUM